Everyman's

Dictionary of Abbreviations

JOHN PAXTON

Everyman's
Dictionary
of
Abbreviations

LONDON
J. M. DENT & SONS LTD

First published 1974

© J. M. Dent & Sons Ltd 1974

Made in Great Britain
at the
Aldine Press · Letchworth · Herts
for
J. M. DENT & SONS LTD
Aldine House · Albemarle Street · London

ISBN: 0 460 07894 1

To Nchls and Jnthy

This work could not have been accomplished without the active co-operation of organizations everywhere. I am much indebted to them, as well as to Roberto Crnjar, Jane Fernandes, Regina Fugmann and Allen Varley, who prepared specialized lists of abbreviations.

I give my thanks also to Donald Ross of Dent's who helped in the planning of the book and who has been a wonderful mentor and friend; to my long-suffering family who have lived with about 45,000 pieces of paper for three years; to Swan Lennard-Payne, who was in at the beginning and dealt with correspondence to and from all parts of the world, and came to my rescue in the 'typing marathon' at the end; to Virginia Walker whose meticulous typing has helped me tremendously; and to Evelyn Beadle who has carried the burden of sorting the order, of the months of typing and superb sub-editing. But errors and inconsistencies remain entirely my own.

J. P.

Preface

The manufacture of abbreviations is one of the largest and fastest growing industries in the world today. Wartime is generally a great period o growth, but the tremendous extension in the development of technology has caused the last two decades to be boom years. The rate of growth is so high that it is possible that hundreds of abbreviations of all kinds in the fields of science, economics and administration alone have been created daily in the Western world. Many of them may never be known outside their own circles; many may be discarded and many may soon be forgotten. My principal task in this new compilation, therefore, has been to provide a representative selection of the old and the new (omitting the potentially ephemeral) to serve the purposes of the student and scholar, the administrator, the business man, the exporter and the community of the general reader at home and at work.

To produce this dictionary of abbreviations it has been necessary to communicate with a large number of organizations throughout the world; and I have recorded the abbreviations substantially in the style in which I have received or otherwise collected them.

This has demonstrated that the modern practice of omitting from abbreviations the full point (period) continues to grow, and it is particularly true in military and data processing terms. The unpointed style, too, may be used for advertising or for bold headings while the pointed is kept for more formal use; but on the whole the inconsistency of usage is noticeable, particularly in the names of institutions and organizations, even when a pronounceable style of abbreviation is accepted. The North Atlantic Treaty Organization, for example, can be found variously in official publications as NATO, NATO, N.A.T.O. Pointed and unpointed styles of all categories, not necessarily organizations, are grouped separately in this dictionary. Correspondingly, single letter abbreviations or symbols which may occur in small letters or capitals, pointed or unpointed, are placed in separate groups. The reader who does not find an entry in one group should look in another, in most cases adjoining.

Some organizations including the professions and government departments specify an official abbreviation for a particular word, yet a variant of the official may be found in general or common use. Where this happens and space permits I have shown both styles, and identified the official one.

I have not, however, attempted to dictate a single correct style when several styles can be used by the same organization. I have sought to incorporate abbreviations (contractions, shortened forms, initials and their variants), and symbols (the conventional signs of the arts and the sciences) from as many fields of global activity as is possible within the practical limits of a book of some 200,000 words. Everyday abbreviations in common currency have their places here, but special emphasis has been placed on economic and commercial matters including particularly employers' associations and trade union organizations. The proliferation of the acronym, a pronounceable name of convenience formed of initial letters of organizations, etc. e.g. *Oxfam, Ensa* or of parts of words, e.g. *radar, ra*dio *d*etection *a*nd *r*anging, has been a marked feature of twentieth-century abbreviation and many examples are given here. The acronymous title is indeed so highly valued that the title of an organization may well be formulated from the several letters of an apposite word describing its interest or function.

The Dictionary contains around 25,000 entries with a total of over 37,000 definitions, many extended by explanations.

A dictionary that has to deal with any aspect of the technical terms and speech of an innovating society must necessarily be a growing concern, and I will be grateful to readers for suggestions for the improvement and extension of the present work.

John Paxton

1973

Entries and Definitions

This dictionary contains abbreviations of different kinds and alphabetical signs and symbols. The term abbreviations includes contracted and shortened forms of words and phrases, and acronyms and initials.

All entry headings are printed in bold type and are arranged in strict alphabetical order. Those with lower-case (small) letters in roman (ordinary) type come before those with roman capital or small letters. Headings without full points (periods) come before those with full points. The following order of 'C' is an example:

ca, cA, Ca, CA, ca., Ca., c.a, c.a., c.A., C.a., C.A, CA., C.A.

Subordinate modifications include accents, hyphens and obliques such as că, ca′, cᵃ, c-a, c/a, c and a, c & a, and are followed by entries containing numbers, as ca³, ca₃, ca-3 and ca/3. Signs based on letters of the alphabet or numerals e.g. @, £, % and foreign type characters come after the modifications. Entries prefixed by a numeral appear in the alphabetical sequence of the first letter following the numeral.

Headings which require the use of italic type for words and phrases not naturalized in English follow the corresponding roman type entry.

The common practice of omitting the full point after the last letter of a contracted form, if it is the last letter of the word, is not followed in the dictionary. It is to be understood therefore that unpointed contractions are here advisedly so printed. Signs and symbols do not necessarily carry the initial letters of the words they stand for, and are unpointed.

In definitions small letters are used for common nouns in preference to capital letters if either form is admissible. Capitals are used for 'proper names', all words written with a capital initial letter. Plurals formed by the addition of 's' have not usually been regarded, but abnormal formations may be given. A single tense only of verb abbreviations is defined.

The heading is followed by a simple definition, preceded in the case of languages other than English by the name of the language involved, the definition in that language in italics, and translation into English unless it is unnecessary. To save repetition of the word 'or', an oblique sign is used to indicate alternative definitions. The definition may be supplemented by a phrase or sentence of explanation or (in brackets) a subject reference such as chem., mus., or naut., the country of origin or use, or a cross-reference to a related entry.

Abbreviations

in the Dictionary in definitions and explanatory phrases

abbrev. abbreviation
abol. abolish; abolition
accy. accountancy
A.D. Anno Domini
admin. administrative
Admin. Administration
advert. advertising
aero. aeronautics
agric. Agric. agriculture
alt. alternative
amal. amalgamated
ann. annual
approx. approximately
arch. architecture
Argen. Argentina
assn. Assn. association
astr. astronomy
ath. athletics
Atl. Atlantic
attrib. attributed
Aust. Australia

B.C. before Christ
Belg. Belgian; Belgium
B.F.P. British Fishing Port Registration
bibliog. bibliography
biol. biology
bk. book
bot. botany
Bp. Bishop
Braz. Brazil
Brit. Britain; British
B.V.R. British Vehicle Registration

c circa
Can. Canada
cap. capital
cartog. cartography
cent. century
Ch. Church
chem. chemistry
co. Co. company
C. of E. Church of England
Col. Columbia
Coll. College
colloq. colloquial
com. commerce
Confed. Confederation
Czech. Czechoslovakia

Dan. Danish
Den. Denmark
dent. dentistry
dip. diplomacy
Dom. Rep. Dominican Republic
dyn. dynamics

E. East
Ecu. Ecuador
educ. education
E.E.C. European Economic Community
E. Ger. East Germany (G.D.R.)
elec. electrical; electricity
Eng. England; English
engn. engineering
E.S.S.A. Environmental Science Services Administration
estab. established

xi

F.A.O. Food and Agriculture Organization
Fed. Federation
fem. feminine
fin. finance; financial
F.P. Fishing Ports Registration
Fr. French
freem. freemasonry

G.B. Great Britain
G.D.R. German Democratic Republic (E. Ger.)
geog. geography
Ger. German; Germany
Gib. Gibraltar
Gk. Greek
govt(s). government(s)

h.m. head master
H.M.S.O. Her/His Majesty's Stationery Office
Hond. Honduras
hort. horticulture
H.Q. Headquarters

I.C.A.M. International Civil Aircraft Markings
ichth. ichthyology
i.e. *id est* that is
inhab. inhabitants
insce. insurance
Intern. International
Is. Island
It. Italian
I.V.R. International Vehicle Registration

Jap. Japan
jnl. journal
jnt. joint

knit. knitting

L. Latin
leg. legal
Lond. London
Ltd. Limited
Lux. Luxembourg

Madag. Madagascar
magnet. magnetics
math. mathematics
mech. mechanics
med. medical; medicine
met. meteorology
Mex. Mexico
mil. military
M.O.D. Ministry of Defence
mon. monetary
mus. music

N. North
N.A.S.A. National Aeronautics and Space Administration
Nat. National
N.A.T.O. North Atlantic Treaty Organization
naut. nautical
nav. navigation
Neth. Netherlands
N.I. Northern Ireland
Nor. Norway
N.S.W. New South Wales
numis. numismatics
N.Z. New Zealand

organ. organization

Pak. Pakistan
Pan. Panama
Para. Paraguay
phar. pharmacy
photo. photography
phys. physics
pol. political
Pol. Poland; Polish
Port. Portugal; Portuguese
Presby. Presbyterian
psy. psychology
pub. publication; publishing

R.A.F. Royal Air Force
rail. railroad; railway
R.C. Roman Catholic
R.C.A.F. Royal Canadian Air Force
Rep. Republic
RoSPA Royal Society for the Prevention of Accidents
Russ. Russia; Russian

s sign; symbol
S. South
S. Afr. South Africa
sci. science
Scot. Scotland; Scottish
Shake. Shakespeare
ship. shipping
Soc. Society
Sp. Spanish
Swed. Sweden; Swedish
Switz. Switzerland

Tanz. Tanzania
tax. taxation
tech. technical
tex. textiles
transp. transport
T.U. Trade Union
T.U.C. Trades Union Congress
Turk. Turkey; Turkish
typ. typography

U.K. United Kingdom
UKAEA United Kingdom Atomic
  Energy Authority

UNESCO United Nations Educa-
  tional, Scientific and Cultural
  Organization
Univ. University
U.N.O. United Nations Organiza-
  tion
Uru. Uruguay
U.S. United States
U.S.A. United States of America
USAF United States Air Force
USN United States Navy
U.S.S.R. Union of Soviet Socialist
  Republics

Ven. Venezuela
Vic. Victoria (Aust.)

W. West
W. Ger. West Germany
WW1 1914–1918 war
WW2 1939–1945 war

Zamb. Zambia

A

a about; acre; acreage; acting; active; adjective; advance; advanced; afternoon; alcohol; anonymous; answer; atto-, 10^{-18}

a L. *ante*, before

@ at (com.)

A *s* Aberdeen (B.F.P.); adult, designating films suitable for adult audiences; Ampère, unit of elec. current; *s* Argon (also Ar); atomic weight; Australia; Australian; Austria (I.V.R.); *s* London (B.V.R.)

A̅ Alto (mus.)

Å Ångström, unit of measurement, named after Ångström

A² It. *A due*, for, or divided between, two voices or instruments (mus.)

a. Fr. *accepté*, on bills of exchange; accepted; Ger. *acceptiert*, on bills of exchange; acid; actual; address; age; amateur; area; arrive; arriving

ā., āā., Ā., ĀĀ. *s* in med. prescriptions, of each a like quantity, or equal parts

a. L. *anno*, in the year; L. *annus*, year; L. *ante*, before; L. *aqua*, water

A. absolute; academician; academy; Fr. *avancer*, to accelerate a clock; ace; acting (rank); adjutant; admiral; air; Alfred; Fr. *Altesse*, Highness; America; American; Amos (Bible); anna (coin); anode (elec.); anterior; annual (hort.); armoured; art; article; artillery; assistant; associate; athletic; August

Ā. *s* in med. prescriptions, of each a like quantity

A. It. *alto* (mus.)

A.1. *s* 'first-class' ships in Lloyd's Register

aa absolute alcohol; acting appointment; approximate absolute; arithmetic average; author's alteration

AA *s* Alloa (B.F.P.); anti-Aircraft, also Ack Ack; *Aerolineas Argentinas*, Argentine Airlines; American Airlines; *s* Hampshire (B.V.R.)

āā. *s* in med. prescriptions, of each a like quantity

a.a. always afloat; *s* take one of each (photo.)

AA. *s* Certificate issued by Mercantile Marine Office which states that all crew matters pertaining to vessel are in order

ĀĀ. *s* in med. prescriptions, of each a like quantity

A.A. advertising agency; Advertising Association; age allowance (tax.); Air Attaché; Alcoholics Anonymous; all along; Anglers' Association; Architectural Association; Army Act; Associate in Accounting; Associate in Agriculture; Associate in Arts; Association of Agriculture; audio-animatronics; Augustinians of the Assumption; Automobile Association

A.A. L. *Archaeologia Aeliana*; *Astronautica Acta*, jnl. of the Intern. Astronautical Fed.

A. & A. additions and amendments

A-A-A amino-acid lysine

A.A.A. Agricultural Adjustment Act (U.S.A.); Agricultural Adjustment Administration (U.S.A.); Allied Artists of America; Amateur Athletic Association, founded in 1880; American Airship Association; American Anthropological Association; American Automobile Associa-

1

tion; Army Audit Agency (U.S.A.); Association of Attenders and Alumni (of the Hague Academy of International Law); Association of Average Adjusters; Australian Automobile Association

A.A.A.A. American Association for the Advancement of Atheism; American Association of Advertising Agencies; American Aviation Association of America; Australian Association of Advertising Agencies

A.A.A.E. American Association of Airport Executives

A.A.A.L. American Academy of Arts and Letters

A.A.A.M. American Association of Aircraft Manufacturers

AAAN American Academy of Applied Nutrition

A.A.A.S. American Academy of Arts and Sciences; American Academy of Asian Studies; American Association for the Advancement of Science; Associate of the American Antiquarian Society

AAB aircraft accident board; Association of Applied Biologists

AABB American Association of Blood Banks

AA BB split shot standards (angling)

AABC American Amateur Baseball Congress; Association for the Advancement of Blind Children (U.S.A.)

A.A.B.L. Associated Australian Banks in London

A.A.B.M. Association of American Battery Manufacturers; Australian Association of British Manufacturers

AAC Aeronautical Advisory Council; Agricultural Advisory Council; Alaskan Air Command (USAF); American Alpine Club; American Cement Corporation

A.A.C. Amateur Athletic Club; Army Air Corps; *Associação Academica de Coimbra*, Coimbra Academic Assn. (Port.); Austrian Alpine Club; automatic amplitude control

A.A.C. L. *anno ante Christum*, in the year before Christ

AACB Aeronautics and Astronautics Coordinating Board (U.S.A.)

AACC American Association of Contamination Control; American Association of Clinical Chemists; area approach control centre

A.A.C.C.A. Associate of the Association of Certified and Corporate Accountants

A.A.C.E. Aberdeen Association of Civil Engineers; American Association of Cost Engineers

A.A.C.O.B.S. Australian Advisory Council on Bibliographical Services

A.A.C.P. American Association for Child Psychiatry; Anglo-American Council on Productivity

A.A.C.R. Association for the Advancement of Civil Rights (Gib.)

A.A.C.S. Aberdeen-Angus Cattle Society; Airways and Air Communications Service (U.S.A.)

aad alloxazine adenine dinucleotide

A.A.D.C. air *aide-de-camp*; army air defense command (U.S.A.)

AADE American Association of Dental Editors/Examiners

AADS army air defense system (U.S.A.)

AAE American Association of Engineers; Association for Adult Education

A.A.E.C. Australian Atomic Energy Commission

A.Ae.E. Associate of Aeronautical Engineering

A.A.E.E. Aircraft and Armament Experimental Establishment

AAES Association of Agricultural Education Staffs; Australian Army Education Service

AAEW Atlantic airborne early warning

AAF., A.A.F. Army Air Force (U.S.A.)

A.A.F. Auxiliary Air Force, *now* R.Aux.A.F.

aafc anti-aircraft fire control

AAFCE Allied Air Forces Central Europe

A.A.F.I.S. Army and Air Force Intelligence Staff

A.A.F.N.E. Allied Air Forces Northern Europe

A.A.F.S.E. Allied Air Forces Southern Europe

A.A.G. Air Adjutant-General; Assistant Adjutant-General; Association of American Geographers

A.A.G.O. Associate of American Guild of Organists

A.A.G.S. Association of African Geological Surveys

AAHPER American Association for Health, Physical Education and Recreation

A.A.I. Associate of the Chartered Auctioneers' and Estate Agents' Institute; Association of Art Institutions

AAIA Association of American Indian Affairs

A.A.I.A. Associate of the Association of International Accountants; Associate of the Australian Institute of Advertising

AAID American Association of Industrial Dentists

2

AAIE American Association of Industrial Editors/Engineers

A.A.I.I. Associate of the Australian Insurance Institute

AAIN American Association of Industrial Nurses

A.A.L. Academy of Art and Literature; Arctic Aeromedical Laboratory (U.S.A.); Association of Assistant Librarians

A.A.L.D. Australian Army Legal Department

A.A.L.L. American Association of Law Libraries

A.A.L.P.A. Incorporated Society of Auctioneers and Landed Property Agents

A.A.L.S. Association of American Library Schools

A.A.L.T. American Association of Library Trustees

AAM air-to-air missile; American Association of Microbiology; American Association of Museums; Australian Air Mission

A.A.M. Anti-Apartheid Movement; Association of Assistant Mistresses in Secondary Schools

A.A.M.C. Australian Army Medical Corps

AAMS American Air Mail Society

AAMW Association of Advertising Men and Women (U.S.A.)

A.A.M.W.S. Australian Army Medical Women's Service

A.A.N.A. Australian Association of National Advertisers

A.A.N.S. Australian Army Nursing Service

A.A.N.S.W. Archives Authority of New South Wales

AAO American Association of Orthodontists

a.a.O. Ger. *am angeführten Orte*, at the place quoted

AAOA Ambulance Association of America

A.A.O.C. Australian Army Ordnance Corps

AAOM American Academy of Occupational Medicine

AAP *Apollo* Applications Programme (U.S.A.); Australian Associated Press

AAPA American Association of Port Authorities

A.A.P.C. All African People's Conference

AAPE American Academy of Physical Education

A.A.P.G. American Association of Petroleum Geologists

A.A.P.H.I. Associate of the Association of Public Health Inspectors

AAPOR American Association of Public Opinion Research

A.A.P.P. Association of Amusement Park Proprietors

A.A.P.S. American Association for the Promotion of Science

AAPSO Afro-Asian People's Solidarity Organisation

A.A.P.S.S. American Academy of Political and Social Science

A.A.P.S.W. Associate of the Association of Psychiatric Social Workers

AAPT American Association of Physics Teachers; Associate of the Association of Photographic Technicians; Association of Asphalt Paving Technologists (U.S.A.)

AAPTS & R Australian Association for Predetermined Time Standards and Research

A.A.Q.M.G. acting/assistant quartermaster-general

a.a.r. after action report; against all risks; aircraft accident record/report; average annual rainfall

A.A.R. Association of American Railroads

AARP American Association of Retired People

A.A.S. Aberdeen Art Society; American Antiquarian Society; American Astronautical/Astronomical Society; Army Air Service; Associate in Applied Science; Association for Archery in Schools; Association of Asian Studies; Association of Architects and Surveyors; Australian Academy of Science; Auxiliary Ambulance Service

A.A.S. L. *Academiae Americanae Socius*, (Fellow of the) American Academy of Arts and Sciences; L. *Acta Apostolicae Sedis*, Acts of the Apostolic See, official publication of the Holy See

A.A.S.A. Associate of the Australian Society of Accountants

AASB American Association of Small Businesses

A.A.S.C. Allied Air Support Command; Australian Army Service Corps

A.A.S.F. Advanced Air Striking Force

AASG Association of American State Geologists

AASHO American Association of State Highway Officials

AASL American Association of School/State Librarians

AASM Associated African States and Madagascar, agreement signed Yaoundé, 1963

AASR Airport and Airways Surveillance Radar (Raytheon)

A.A.S.S. American Association for Social Security

A.A.S.S. L. *Americanae Antiquarianae Societatis Socius*, Associate of the American Antiquarian Soc.

A.A.S.T.C. Associate in Architecture Sydney Technical College

AAT achievement anxiety test (psy.); Anglo-Australian Telescope, in N.S.W., Australia

A.A.T.A. Anglo-American Tourist Association

AATC Army Aviation Test Command (U.S.A.)

AATCC American Association of Textile Colour Chemists

A.A.T.N.U. Fr. *Administration de l'assistance technique des Nations Unies*, United Nations Technical Assistance Admin.

AATRI Army Air Traffic Regulation and Identification (U.S.A.)

AATT American Association of Textile Technology

A.A.T.T.A. Arab Association of Tourism and Travel Agents

A.A.T.U.F. All-African Trade Union Federation

A.A.U. Agricultural Adjustment Unit, Newcastle Univ.; Amateur Athletic Union (U.S.A.); Association of American Universities

A.A.U.N. American/Australian Association for United Nations

AAUP American Association of University Presses/Professors

A.A.U.Q. Associate in Accountancy University of Queensland (Aust.)

A.A.U.W. American Association of University Women

A.A.V.C. Australian Army Veterinary Corps

AAVS American Anti-Vivisection Society

AAWC Australian Advisory War Council

AAZPA American Association of Zoological Parks and Aquariums

ab air break; anchor bolt

Ab alabamine (chem.)

AB *s* a human blood type of the ABO group; automated bibliography; *s* Aberystwyth (B.F.P.); *s* Worcestershire (B.V.R.)

ab. It. *abitanti*, population; about

a/b. airborne

a.B. Ger. *auf Bestellung*, on order

A/B. *Aktiebolaget*, limited company (Swed.)

A.B. able-bodied seaman; advisory board; air board; Fr. *Alliance balkanique*, Balkan Alliance; L. *Artium Baccalaureus*, Bachelor of Arts; asthmatic bronchitis

ABA *AB Aerotransport* (Swedish division of SAS); Amateur Boxing Association

A.B.A. American Bankers' Association; American Bar Association; American/Australian Booksellers' Association; Associate of the British Archaeological Association; Association of British Archaeologists

A.B.A.A. Antiquarian Booksellers' Association of America; Associate of British Association of Accountants and Auditors

A.B.A.C. Association of British Aero Clubs and Centres

A.B.A.I. Amateur Basketball Association of Ireland

A.B.A.S. Amateur Basketball Association of Scotland

abb. abbess; abbey; It. *abbonamento*, subscription; abbot; It. *abbuono*, allowance or discount (com.)

Abb., Abbild. Ger. *Abbildung*, illustration

A.B.B.A. Amateur Basket Ball Association; American Board of Bio-Analysis

abbr., abbrev. abbreviate; abbreviated; abbreviation; It. *abbreviazione*, abbreviation

Abby Abigail

ABC advanced biomedical capsule; alphabet; already been converted; American Broadcasting Company; Audit Bureau of Circulations, alt. forms OJD (Fr.), IVW (Ger.), IAD (It.) (advert.); automatic brake control

A.B.C. Aerated Bread Company; air bridge to Canada; America-Britain-Canada; American Book-prices Current; animal birth control; alum, blood, clay and charcoal, employed as precipitants in process of sewage treatment; Argentina-Brazil-Chile; Associated British Cinemas; Australian Bankruptcy Cases; Australian Broadcasting Commission; automatic binary computer

ABCA Army Bureau of Current Affairs

A.B.C.B. Association of Birmingham Clearing Banks

A.B.C.C. Association of British Chambers of Commerce; Association of British Correspondence Colleges

A.B.C.D. American, British, Chinese, Dutch powers in Pacific, WW2; Atomic Biological and Chemical Protection and Damage Control

A.B.C.F.M. American Board of Commissioners for Foreign Missions

ABC Islands Aruba, Bonaire, Curaçao (Neth. Antilles)

ABCM Associate of Bandsmen's College of Music; Association of British Chemical Manufacturers, *now* CIA

ABD advanced base depot (USN); American Board of Dermatology

abd. abdias; abdicate; average body dose (radiation)

A.B.D.A. American, British, Dutch, Australian Command in Pacific, WW2

abdom. abdomen; abdominal

Abe Abraham; Abram

Aber. Aberdeen; Aberdonian

Aberc. Abercrombian; Abercrombie

Abf. Ger. *Abfahrt*, departure

A.B.F. Actors' Benevolent Fund; Associated British Foods

A.B.F.M. American Board of Foreign Missions

A.B.G.B. Ger. *Allgemeines Bürgerliches Gesetzbuch*, Austrian Civil Code

abgk. Ger. *abgekürzt*, abbreviated

Abh. Ger. *Abhandlungen*, transactions, treatises

A.B.I. Associate of the Institute of Book-keepers; It. *Associazione Bibliotecari Italiani*, Assn. of It. Librarians

A.B.I.A. Associate of the Bankers' Institute of Australasia

A.B.I.M. American Board of International Missions; Association of British Insecticide Manufacturers

ab init. L. *ab initio*, from the beginning

abk. Ger. *abgekürzt*, abbreviated

abl, ablat. ablative

Abl. Sp. *Abril*, April

ABLA American Business Law Association

A.B.L.C. Association of British Launderers & Cleaners

ABLE activity balance line evaluation

A.B.L.S. Association of British Library Schools; Bachelor of Arts in Library Science

A.B.M. anti-ballistic missile; assistant beach master; Associate in Business Management; Australian Board of Missions; automatic batch mix

ABMA American Brush Manufacturers' Association; army ballistic missile agency

A.B.M.A.C. Association of British Manufacturers of Agricultural Chemicals

ABMEWS Anti-ballistic missile early warning system

A.B.M.P.M. Association of British Manufacturers of Printers' Machinery

A.B.M.S. American Bureau of Metal Statistics

A.B.M.U. American Baptist Missionary Union

abn airborne

Abn. Aberdeen

A.B.N. Anti-bolshevik Bloc of Nations

ABNE Association for the Benefit of Non-contract Employees

ABO *s* a classification of human blood; American Board of Ophthalmology /Opticianry/Orthodontics/Otolaryngology

abo. aboriginal

A.B.O.F. Association of British Organic Fertilisers

ABOG American Board of Obstetrics and Gynecology

A-bomb atomic bomb, first detonated experimentally 16 July 1945, first used operationally at Hiroshima 6 Aug. 1945 and at Nagasaki 9 Aug. 1945

ABOS American Board of Oral/Orthopedic Surgery

ABP American Board of Pathology/Pediatrics / Pedodontics / Peridontology / Prosthodontics

Abp. Archbishop

A.B.P. arterial blood pressure; Associated Book Publishers

A.B.P.A. Australian Book Publishers' Association

A.B.P.C. American Book Publishers' Council; Associated British Picture Corporation

ABPD American Board of Pediatric Dermatology

A.B.P.I. Association of the British Pharmaceutical Industry

ABPN American Board of Psychiatry and Neurology; Association of British Paediatric Nurses

ABPO advanced base personnel officer

ABPS American Board of Plastic Surgery

A.B.Ps.S. Associate of the British Psychological Society

A.B.P.V.M. Association of British Plywood and Veneer Manufacturers

ABR American Board of Radiology; *s Real Aerovias Brasil*, Brazilian airline

abr. abridge; abridgement

Abr. Abraham

ABRACADABRA *Ab*breviations and Related *A*cronyms *A*ssociated with *De*fense, *A*stronautics, *B*usiness and *R*adioelectronics, title of publication of Raytheon Co. of Lexington, Mass.

ABRES advanced ballistics re-entry system

A.B.R.F.M. Association of British Roofing Felt Manufacturers

A.B.R.O. Animal Breeding Research Organization, Edinburgh; Army in Burma Reserve of Officers

A.B.R.R.M. Association of British Reclaimed Rubber Manufacturers

A.B.R.S. Association of British Riding Schools

A.B.R.S.M. Associated Board of the Royal Schools of Music

ABS acrylonitrile-butadiene-styrene copolymer (plastic); sodium alkyl benzene sulphonate

abs. absence; absent; absolute; absorbent; abstract; Fr. *aux bon soins de*, in care of

Abs. Ger. *Absatz*, paragraph; Ger. *Absender*, sender

A.B.S. American Bible Society; American Board of Surgery; American Bureau of Shipping; Architects' Benevolent Society; Associate of the Building Societies Institute; Association of Broadcasting Staff

Abschn. Ger. *Abschnitt*, paragraph or chapter

abse.re. L. *absente reo*, the defendant being absent

abs.feb. L. *absent febre*, when there is no fever (med.)

A.B.S.I. Associate of the Boot and Shoe Institution

ABSIE American Broadcasting Station in Europe, WW2

A.B.S.M. Associate of Birmingham & Midland Institute School of Music; — (T.T.D.) Teacher's Training Diploma

A.B.S.M.G.P. Associate Member of the British Society of Master Glass-Painters

absol. absolute

abs.re. L. *absente reo*, the defendant being absent

abstr. abstract

abs.visc. viscosity, absolute

A.B.S.W. Association of British Science Writers

abt. about

Abt. Ger. *Abteilung*, division or part

A.B.T. Association of Building Technicians

A.B.T.A. Allied Brewery Traders' Association; Association of British Travel Agents; Australian British Trade Association

ABTAC Australian Book Trade Advisory Committee

ABTICS Abstract and Book Title Index Card Service of the Iron and Steel Institute

ABTUC All-Burma Trade Union Congress

A.B.U. Asian Broadcasting Union, H.Q. Tokyo; Assembly of the Baptist Union

A.-B.U. Anglo-Belgian Union

abv. above

Aby Abraham; Abram

A.B.Y.A. Association of British Yacht Agents

a/c account; Port. *ao cuidado de*, care of

Ac *s* actinium (chem.)

AC alternating current; *s* Warwickshire (B.V.R.)

A/C account; aircraft; aircraftman

ac. acre; activity

a.c. It. *a capo*, new line; Fr. *à compte*, on account; advisory committee; Fr. *année courante*, this year; It. *assegno circolare*, banker's draft or cashier's check; author's correction

a.c. L. *anno corrente*, this year; L. *ante cibum*, before meals (med.)

a.C. Port. *antes de Cristo*, before Christ (BC); It. *avanti Cristo*, before Christ (BC)

A.C. aero club; air command; air commodore; air control; air corps; air council; aircraftman; Alpine Club; alternating current (elec.); ambulance corps; analogue computer; analytical chemist; annual conference; appeal case/court; army corps/council; artillery college; arts council; assistant commissioner; athletic club; Atlantic Charter; L. *Auditor Camerae*, Auditor of the Papal Treasury; It. *Azione Cattolica*, Catholic Action, non-political organization aiming to educate the social and moral conscience of Italy

A. & C. addenda and corrigenda; Antony and Cleopatra (Shake.)

A.c. L. *ante Christum*, before Christ

A.C.A. adjacent-channel attenuation; advanced combat aircraft; Agricultural Co-operative Association; American Composers' Alliance; Amusement Caterers' Association; Anglers' Co-operative Association; Arts Council of America; Associate (of the Institute of) Chartered Accountants in England and Wales, or Ireland; Australian Council for Aeronautics

A.C.A.A. Associate of the Australasian Institute of Cost Accountants

ACAB Army Contract Adjustment Board (U.S.A.)

Acad. academic; academical; academy

Acad. b.a. Fr. *Académie des beaux-arts*, Academy of Fine Arts

Acad. fran. Fr. *Académie française*, French Academy

ACADI *Association des Cadres Dirigeants de l'Industrie*, Assn. of Industrial Executives (France)

Acad. med./mus./sci. Academy of medicine/music/science

Acad.St.Cec. It. *Academia di Santa Cecilia*, Rome

A.C. & A.E. Association of Chemical and Allied Employers

A.C.A.O. Assistant County Advisory Officer

Acap. Acapulco

A.C.A.S. Assistant Chief of Air Staff

ACB Fr. *Association Canadienne des Bibliothèques*, Canadian Library Assn.

ACBI Associate of the Institute of Book-keepers

ACBS Accrediting Commission for Business Schools

ACBWS automatic chemical biological warning system

acc. acceleration; accent; acceptance, bill of exchange; accompanied; according; account; accusative

A.C.C. administrative co-ordination committee; advanced communications course; Agricultural Credit Corporation; air co-ordinating committee (U.S.A.); army cadet college; Army Catering Corps; Assistant County Commissioner, Scouting; Associated Chemical Companies

A.C.C.A. Aeronautical Chamber of Commerce of America; Agricultural Central Co-operative Association; Association of Certified and Corporate Accountants

acce. acceptance

accel. It. *accelerando*, quicker (mus.)

accep^{on} Fr. *acceptation*, acceptance

access. accessory

ACCHAN *A*llied *C*ommand *Chan*nel (NATO)

A.C.C.M. Advisory Council for the Church's Ministry (C. of E.)

A.C.C.O. Associate of the Canadian College of Organists; Association of Child Care Officers

accom. accommodation

accomp. accompanied; accompaniment; accompany

A.C.C.P. American College of Chest Physicians

accred. accredited

A.C.C.S. Associate of the Corporation of Certified Secretaries

acct. account; accountant; accounting

acctd. accented

accus. accusative

accy. accountancy

acd. accord

ACDA Arms Control and Disarmament Agency (U.S.A.); Aviation Combat Development Agency

A.C.D.C.M. Archbishop of Canterbury's Diploma in Church Music

A.Cdre. air commodore

acdt. accident

ACE Advisory Centre for Education; alcohol-chloroform-ether, anaesthetic (med.)

A.C.E. Allied Command Europe; American Council on Education; Association of Circulation Executives; Association of Consulting Engineers; Association of Cultural Exchange; Australian College of Education; Automatic Computing Engine

ACEA Action Committee for European Aerospace

A.C.Ed. Associate in Commercial Education

A.C.E.N. Assembly of Captive European Nations

A.C.E.R. Australian Council for Education Research

Acet. acetone; — **a.** acetone-acid

A.C.E.T. Advisory Committee on Electronics and Telecommunications

A.C.F. Fr. *Académie Canadienne Française*, French Canadian Academy; Active Citizen Force (S.Afr.); Army Cadet Force; army council form; Australian Comforts Fund; *Automobile Club de France*

A.C.F.A. Army Cadet Force Association

A.C.F.A.S. *Association Canadienne-Française pour l'avancement des sciences*, French Canadian Assn. for the Advancement of Science

ac. ft. acre foot

Acft. aircraft; — **c.** — carrier

ACG *An Comunn Gaidhealach*, the Gaelic Society, known as the Highland Association, founded Scot., 1891, to encourage teaching of the language and support Highland culture, traditions, social and economic welfare

A.C.G. Assistant Chaplain-General; automatic control gear

A.C.G.B. Arts Council of Great Britain, estab. 1946 to develop and improve knowledge, understanding and practice of the arts, to increase accessibility of the arts to the public and to advise and co-operate with government departments, local authorities and other organizations

A.C.G.B.I. Automobile Club of Great Britain and Ireland

A.C.G.F.C. Associate of the City and Guilds Finsbury College, London

A.C.G.I. Associate of the City and Guilds of London Institute

ACGIH American Conference of Governmental Industrial Hygienists

A Ch. acetylcholine

ACHR American Society of Human Rights

A.Ch.S. Associate of the Society of Chiropodists

A.C.I. Fr. *Alliance Coopérative Internationale*, Intern. Co-operative Alliance; Alloy Castings Institute; army council instruction; Associate of the Clothing Institute; Associate of the Institute of Commerce; Fr. *assuré contre l'incendie*, insured against fire; It. *Automobile Club d'Italia*, Italian Automobile Club

A.C.I.A. Associate of the Corporation of Insurance Agents

A.C.I.A.A. Australian Commercial and Industrial Artists' Association

A.C.I.B. Associate of the Corporation of Insurance Brokers

ACIC Aeronautical Charting and Information Center (U.S.A.)

ACICAFE Fr. *Association du commerce et de l'industrie du café dans la C.E.E.*, Assn. for the Coffee Trade and Industry in the EEC

acid. acidulated drop

A.C.I.G.S. Assistant Chief of the Imperial General Staff

A.C.I.I. Associate (Member) of the Chartered Insurance Institute

A.C.I.O.P.J.F. Fr. *Association catholique internationale des œuvres de protection de la jeune fille*, Intern. Catholic Girls' Soc.

A.C.I.S. American Committee for Irish Studies; Associate of the Chartered Institute of Secretaries

A.C.I.V. Associate of the Commonwealth Institute of Valuers

A.C.J.P. airways corporations joint pensions

ack. acknowledge

Ack Ack, AA anti-aircraft

ackt. acknowledgment

A.C.L. action centred leadership, leadership training devised by the Industrial Society; Atlas Computer Laboratory

ACLA Anti-Communist League of America

ACLANT Allied Command Atlantic

ACLC Air Cadet League of Canada

A.C.L.P. Association of Contact Lens Practitioners

ACLS American Council of Learned Societies; automatic carrier landing system

A.Cl.S Additional Clergy Society

ACM Association for Computing Machinery (U.S.A.); authorized controlled material

A.C.M. Air Chief Marshal; American Campaign Medal

A.C.M.A. Agricultural Co-operative Managers' Association; Asbestos Cement Manufacturers' Association; Associate of the Institute of Cost and Management Accountants, *formerly* **A.C.W.A**; Athletic Clothing Manufacturers' Association

ACMC Association of Canadian Medical Colleges

ACME advanced computer for medical research; Advisory Council on Medical Education (U.S.A.); Association of Consulting Management Engineers (U.S.A.)

A.C.M.E.T. Advisory Council on Middle East Trade

A.C.M.F. Air Corps Medical Forces (U.S.A.); Allied Central Mediterranean Forces; Australian Commonwealth Military Forces

A.C.M.M. Associate of the Conservatorium of Music, Melbourne (Aust.)

acmp. accompany

A.C.M.P. Assistant Commissioner of the Metropolitan Police

A.C.M.R.R. Advisory Committee on Marine Resources Research (F.A.O.)

ACMT American College of Medical Technologists

acn all concerned notified

ACN American College of Neuropsychiatrists

A.c.n. L. *ante Christum natum*, before the birth of Christ

ACNA Advisory Council on Naval Affairs (U.S.A.); Arctic Institute of North America

A.C.N.S. Assistant Chief of Naval Staff; Associated Correspondents News Service

ACNY Advertising Club of New York

a.co. Sp. *a cargo*, against

A.C.O. Admiralty Compass Observatory; Association of Children's Officers

A C of S Assistant Chief of Staff

acog aircraft on ground

ACom, A.Comm. Associate in Commerce

A.Comm.A. Associate of the Society of Commercial Accountants

A.C.O.P. Association of Chief Officers of Police

A.C.O.R.D. Advisory Council on Research and Development

ACORN associative content retrieval network; automatic check-out and recording network

A.C.O.S. American College of Osteopathic Surgeons; assistant chief of staff

A.C.P. American College of Pharmacists/Physicians; Associate of the College of Preceptors; Association of Circus Proprietors of Great Britain; Association of Clinical Pathologists; Association of Correctors of the Press; *Automóvel Clube de Portugal*, Portuguese Automobile Club

A.C.P.A. American Concrete Paving Association (U.S.A.); Associate of the Institution of Certified Public Accountants

ACPM American Congress of Physical Medicine and Rehabilitation

acpt. acceptance

8

acq. acquire; acquittal

ACR advanced capabilities radar; aircraft control room; American College in Rome; Association of College Registrars

A.C.R. Admiral Commanding Reserves

A.C.R.B. Fr. *Aero-Club Royal de Belgique*, Royal Belgian Aero Club

acrd. accrued

ACRE advanced cryogenic rocket engineering; automatic checkout and readiness equipment

acrg. acreage

ACRI Air-Conditioning and Refrigeration Institute (U.S.A.)

ACRL Association of College and Research Libraries (U.S.A.)

acron. acronym, a pronounceable name formed of initial letters of organizations, etc., e.g. NATO

A.C.R.R. American Council on Race Relations

A.C.R.S. Advisory Committee on Reactor Safeguards (U.S.A.)

ACS airport catering services; American Ceramic Society; American Chemical Society; assembly control system; Australian Computer Society

a/c.s. aircraft security vessel

a.c.s. anodal closing sound

A.C.S. Additional Curates Society; Admiral Commanding Submarines; admiralty computing service; American College of Surgeons; Associate in Commercial Science

ACSA Allied Communications Security Agency

A.C.S.E. Association of Consulting Structural Engineers (Aust.)

A.C.S.E.A. Allied Command South East Asia

A.C.S.I.L. Admiralty Centre for Scientific Information and Liaison, *now* NSTIC

A.C.S.L. Assistant Cub Scout Leader

A.C.S.M. American Congress on Surveying and Mapping; Associate of the Camborne School of Metalliferous Mining

A.C.S.N. Association of Collegiate Schools of Nursing

ACSOC Acoustical Society of America

A.C.S.P.A. Australian Council of Salaried and Professional Associations

ACSS automated colour separation system

ACT Advisory Council on Technology; anological circuit technique; Associated Container Transportation

act. acting; active; activities; actuary

A.C.T. Agricultural Central Trading Ltd; Air Council for Training; Australian Capital Territory; Australian College of Theology

a cta. Sp. *a cuenta*, on account

A.C.T.C. Art Class Teacher's Certificate

actg. acting

acth *a*drenocorticotropic*h*ormone, an anti-rheumatic drug

A.C.T.O. Advisory Council on the Treatment of Offenders

Acts Acts of the Apostles (Bible)

A.C.T.S. Acoustic Control and Telemetry System (U.S.A.); Associate of the Society of Certificated Teachers of Shorthand; Australian Catholic Truth Society

ACTT Association of Cinematograph, Television and Allied Technicians

ACTU Australian Council of Trade Unions

A.C.U. Actors' Church Union; American Congregational Union; Association of Commonwealth Universities; Auto-Cycle Union, formed 1903 as branch of Royal Automobile Club with over 800 member clubs, 'to look after the needs of motor cyclists and foster improvement of their machines'

A.C.U.A. Association of Cambridge University Assistants

ACUE American Committee of United Europe

ACUS Atlantic Council of the United States

acv actual cash value; air cushion vehicle, pop. name 'hovercraft'

A.C.V. Associate of the College of Violinists; Associated Commercial Vehicles

a.c.w. air control and warning; aircraftwoman; alternating continuous waves; automatic car wash

A.C.W.A. Associate of the Institute of Cost and Works Accountants, *now* **A.C.M.A.**

ACWS aircraft control and warning system

A.C.W.W. Associated Country Women of the World

acy average crop yield

ad advantage (tennis); average deviation

ad, adv., advert., advt advertisement

Ad Adam

A/d, a.d. after date

AD *Acción Democrática*, Democratic Action Party, founded 1937, forced underground by Perez Jimenez dictatorship, regained legality in 1958 (Ven.); air dried; *s* Ardrossan (B.F.P.); *s* Gloucestershire (B.V.R.)

A-D Albrecht Dürer (1471–1528), Ger. painter and engraver

A/D aerodrome; after date; analog to digital, data conversion

ad. adapt; adaptation; adapter; adverb

ad. L. *addatur*, let there be added (med.); L. *adde*, up to (med.)

a.d. L. *ante diem*, before the day

a. D. Ger. *ausser Dienst*, retired, on half pay

A.D. accidental damage (insce.); active duty; administrative department; air defence; armament depot; autograph document; average deviation

A.D. L. *anno Domini*, in the year of our Lord (always placed before figures)

Ada Adelaide

ADA acetone-dicarboxylic acid; Agricultural Development Association; Air Defense Agency (U.S.A.); Association of Drainage Authorities; Atomic Development Authority

A.D.A. action data automation; Aluminium Development Association; American Dental Association; Americans for Democratic Action; Australian Dental Association

ADAA American Dental Assistants Association; Art Dealers Association of America

adag, adago, adgo, ado° It. *Adagio*, slowly (mus.)

A.D.A.G.P. Fr. *Association pour la diffusion des arts graphiques et plastiques*

adaml advise by airmail

adap. adapted

ADAPSO Association of Data Processing Organizations (U.S.A.)

ADAPTS air-deliverable anti-pollution transfer system (US Coast Guard)

ADAS auxiliary data annotation set

A.D.A.W.S. action data automation and weapons systems; assistant director of army welfare services

A-day assault day

ADB African/Asian Development Bank; Atlantic Development Board (Can.)

A.D.B. accidental death benefit; Bachelor of Domestic Arts

A.D.B.M. Association of Dry Battery Manufacturers

ADC Air Defense Command (USAF)

A.D.C. aerodrome control; Agricultural Development Corporation (Jamaica); *aide-de-camp*; Aid to Dependent Children; amateur dramatic club; Army Dental Corps, *now* R.A.D.C.; Art Directors' Club; assistant district commissioner (Scouting); automatic digital calculator

A.D. and C., A.D.C. advise duration and charge

ADCC Air Defense Control Center (U.S.A.)

ADCI American Die Casting Institute

ADCONSEN with *ad*vice and *con*sent of the *Sen*ate (U.S.A.)

A.D.C.T. Art Directors' Club, Toronto

add., adds. address

add. L. *addenda*, to be added, additions

A.D.D.C. Air Defense Direction Center (U.S.A.)

A.D.D.F. Abu Dhabi Defence Force

Addie, Addy Adelina

addit., addl., addnl. additional; **addn.** addition

A.D.D.S. assistant director of dental services

ad effect. L. *ad effectum*, until effective (med.)

Adel Adelaide

ADELA, Adela Adela Investment Company, South America, is an international privately financed company giving financial, technical and promotional help to productive private enterprise in developing nations in Western Hemisphere

ADEPT A distinctly empirical prover of theorems

a des. It. *a destra*, to the right

ad eund. L. *ad eundem gradum*, to the same degree

adf after deducting freight; air/automatic direction finder

Adf. Adolph

A.D.F. Alexandra Day Fund; automatic direction finder

A.D.F.A. Australian Dried Fruits Association

ad fin. L. *ad finem*, near the end

A.D.F.W. assistant director of fortifications and works

A.D.G. assistant director-general

A.D.G.B. air defence of Great Britain

A.D.G.M.S. assistant director-general of medical services

ad gr. acid. L. *ad gratam aciditatem*, to an agreeable acidity (med.)

ad gr. gust. L. *ad gratum gustum*, to an agreeable taste (med.)

A.D.H. assistant director of hygiene; Association of Dental Hospitals, of G.B. and N.I.

ad h.l. L. *ad hunc locum*, at this place

A.D.I. American Documentation Institute, *now* ASIS; approved driving instructor

ad inf, ad inf. L. *ad infinitum*, to infinity

ad init. L. *ad initium*, at the beginning

ad int. L. *ad interim*, in the meantime

ADIZ air defense identification zone (U.S.A.)

adj. adjacent; adjective; adjourned; adjustment

Adj., Adjt. adjutant

A.D.J.A.G. assistant deputy judge advocate general

Adjt.-Gen. adjutant-general

a.d.l. activities of daily living

A.D.L. assistant director of labour

ad lib. L. *ad libitum*, at pleasure

ad loc. L. *ad locum*, at the place

A.D.L.P. Australian Democratic Labour Party, founded 1955 as a right-wing splinter party

adm. admission; admitted; average daily membership

Adm. administration; admiral (*also* Adml.); admiralty

A.D.M. annual delegate meeting

ADMA American Drug Manufacturers' Association; Aviation Distributors' and Manufacturers' Association (U.S.A.)

Ad. Man. advertisement manager

admin. administration; administrator

Admin. Apost. Administrator Apostolic

admix. administratrix

Adml. admiral

A.D.M.M. Association of Dandy Roll and Mould Makers

A.D.M.O.(C.A.) Assistant Director of Meteorological Office (Civil Aviation)

admov. L. *admoveatur*, let it apply

Adm. Rev. L. *Admodum Reverendus*, Very Reverend

A.D.M.S. assistant director of medical services

A.D.M.T. Association of Dental Manufacturers and Traders of the United Kingdom

admx. administratrix

ADN Ger. *Allgemeiner Deutscher Nachrichtendienst*, news agency owned by GDR; *s* Peoples' Dem. Rep. of Yemen, *formerly* Southern Yemen, *formerly* Aden (I.V.R.)

A.D.N.A. assistant director of naval accounts

A.D.N.C. assistant director of naval construction

ad neut. L. *ad neutralizandum*, until neutral (med.)

A.D.N.I. assistant director of naval intelligence

ADO advanced development objective (USAF)

A.D.O. air defence officer; assistant district officer; Association of Dispensing Opticians

A.D.O.F. assistant director of ordnance factories

Adolph. Adolphus

A.D.O.S. assistant director of ordnance service

ADP Adenosine disphosphate; air defence position; automatic data processing

A.D.P. Association of Dental Prosthesis

ADPLAN advanced planning

A.D.P.R. assistant director of public relations

ADPSO Association of Data Processing Service Organizations

ADR accident data recorder; *Association pour le Développement de la Recherche*, Assn. for the Development of Research (France)

A.D.R.A. Animal Diseases Research Association, Edinburgh

ADS accurately defined systems (computer); advanced dressing station; air defense sector (U.S.A.)

ad s. L. *ad sectam*, at the suit of

a.d.s. autograph document signed

Ad.S. Fr. *Académie des Sciences*

ad saec. L. *ad saeculum*, to the century

ad sat. L. *ad saturandum*, to saturation (med.)

A.D.S.C.A.T. Association of Distributors to the Self-Service and Coin-op Laundry and Allied Trades

ADSOC Administrative Support Operations Center (U.S.A.)

ADSS Australian Defence Scientific Service

adst.feb. L. *adstante febre*, when fever is present (med.)

A.D.T. American District Telegraph; Ger. *an demselben Tage*, the same day; assistant director of transport; average daily traffic

ADTECH advanced decoy technology

ad us. L. *ad usum*, according to custom

ad us. ext. L. *ad usum externum*, for external use (med.)

adv advance; adverb; advertisement; advice; advise; advisory; advocate

adv. L. *adversus*, against

Adv. Advent

ad val. L. *ad valorem*, according to value

advb. adverb

Adv. Bse. advanced base

adven. adventure

adv. pmt. advance payment

A.D.V.S. assistant director of veterinary services

advv. adverbs

A.D.W. air defence warning; assistant director of works

A.D.W.E. & M. assistant director of works, electrical and mechanical

11

ADX automatic data/digital exchange

AE *s* Bristol (B.V.R.); *s* third-class ships in Lloyd's Register

ae. L. *aetatis*, of, or at, the age of

A.E. adult education; aeronautical engineer/engineering; age exemption (tax.); agricultural engineer/engineering; *Aktie bolaget Atomenergi*, Swedish Atomic Energy Corporation; All England; army education; atomic energy; pen-name of George Russell (1867–1935), Brit. politician and essayist

A.E.A. Actors' Equity Association (U.S.A.); Agricultural Education Association, Staff. Coll. of Agric.; Agricultural Engineers Association; air efficiency award; air entraining agent (concrete); American Economic Association; Atomic Energy Authority, estab. 1954 to control research and development

A.E.A.A. Sp. *Asociación de Escritores y Artistas Americanos*, Assn. of [S.] American Writers and Artists

A.E.A.F. Allied Expeditionary Air Force

AEAUSA Adult Education Association of the United States of America

A.E.B. area electricity board; Associated Examining Board

A.E.C. Agricultural Executive Committee; American Express Company; Army Education Corps, *now* R.A.E.C.; Army Electronics Command; Associated Equipment Company; Fr. *Association européenne de céramique*, European Ceramic Assn.; Association of Education Committees; Atomic Energy Commission (U.S.A.)

A.E.C.B. Atomic Energy Control Board (Can.)

A.E.C.I. African Explosives and Chemical Industries

A.E.C.L. Atomic Energy of Canada Limited

A. Ed. Associate of Education

A.E.D. Association of Engineering Distributors; automated engineering design

A.E.D. L. *Artium Elegantium Doctor*, Doctor of Fine Arts

AEDC Arnold Engineering Development Center (USAF)

A.E.D.E. Fr. *Association européenne des enseignants*, European Teachers' Assn.

AEDS Association for Educational Data Systems (U.S.A.); Atomic Energy Detection Systems

A.E.D.T. Fr. *Association européenne des organisations nationales des commerçants-détaillants en textiles*, European

Assn. of Nat. Organizations of Textile Retailers

A.E.D.U. Admiralty Experimental Diving Unit

A.E.E. airborne evaluation equipment; Atomic Energy Establishment

A.E.E.C. Airlines Electronic Engineering Committee (U.S.A.); Army Equipment Engineering Establishment (Can.)

A.E.E.F. Fr. *Association européenne des exploitations frigorifiques*, European Refrigeration Development Assn.

A.E.E.N. Fr. *Agence Européenne pour l'Energie Nucléaire*, European Agency for Atomic Energy

A.E.E.W. Atomic Energy Establishment Winfrith

A.E.F. *Afrique Equatoriale Française*, French Equatorial Africa; Allied/American/Australian Expeditionary Force; Amalgamated Union of Engineering and Foundry Workers; Fr. *Centre d'action européenne fédéraliste*, European Centre for Federalist Action

A.E.F.M. Fr. *Association européenne des festivals de musique*, European Association of Music Festivals

AEG active element group; Ger. *Allgemeine Elektrizitäts-Gesellschaft*, General Electric Co.

a.e.g. all edges gilt

AEGIS Aid for the Elderly in Government Institutions; An existing general information system

A.E.G.M. Anglican Evangelical Group Movement

A.E.H. A. E. Housman (1859–1936), Eng. poet and scholar

A.E.H.A. Association of Electrical Housecraft Advisers

A.E.I. American Express International; Associated Electrical Industries; Fr. *Association des écoles internationales*, Intern. Schools Assn.; *Associazione Ellettrotecnica Italiana*, Italian Electronics Assn.

A.E.I.O.U. L. *Austria Erit In Orbe Ultima*, Austria will be the world's last survivor; *Austriae Est Imperare Orbi Universi*, It is given to Austria to rule the whole world. Variants on a Hapsburg acrostic

A.E.J.I. Association for Education in Journalism; Association of European Jute Industries

A.E.L. Admiralty Engineering Laboratory; aeronautical/aircraft engine laboratory; Associated Engineering, Limited; automation engineering laboratory

A.E.L.E. Fr. *Association européenne de libre-échange*, European Free Trade Assn.

A.E.L.T.C. All England Lawn Tennis Club

A.E. & M.P. Ambassador Extraordinary and Minister Plenipotentiary

A.E.M.T. Association of Electrical Machinery Trades

aen., ae., AE. L. *aeneus*, made of copper (numis.)

Aen. L. *The Aeneid*, Virgil's epic

A. En. Associate in English

A.E.N.A. All England Netball Association, founded 1926

A. Eng. Associate in Engineering

Aen. Nas. L. *Aenei Nasi*, of the Brazen Nose i.e. Brasenose College, Oxford, founded 1509

A.E.O. assistant education officer; assistant experimental officer

aeop amend existing orders pertaining to

A.E.O.S. Ancient Egyptian Order of Sciots

A.E.P. Fr. *Agence Européenne de Productivité*, European Production Agency; Association of Embroiderers and Pleaters; average evoked potential

A.E. & P. Ambassador Extraordinary and Plenipotentiary

AEPI American Educational Publishers Institute

aeq. L. *aequales*, equal, equals

aer. aeronautics; aeroplane

A.E.R. army emergency reserve

aera. aeration

A.E.R.A. American Educational Research Association; Associate Engraver, Royal Academy; Associate of the British Electrical & Allied Industries Research Association

Aer. E. aeronautical engineer

A.E.R.E. Atomic Energy Research Establishment

A.E.R.I. Agricultural Economics Research Institute, Univ. of Oxford

AERNO aeronautical equipment reference number

aero. aeronautic; aeronautical

Aeroflot Soviet Air Lines

Aero O/Y Finnair, Finnish Air Lines

aerosp. aerospace

A.E.R.T.E.L. Fr. *Association européenne rubans, tresses, tissus élastiques*, European Ribbon, Braid and Elastic Material Assn.

AES Aerospace Electrical Society (U.S.A.); Airways Engineering Society (U.S.A.); Audio Engineering Society

Aes. Aesop, Gk. composer of animal fables

A.E.S. Agricultural Economics Society, Univ. of Reading

AESE Association of Earth Science Editors (U.S.A.)

aesth. aesthetics

aet. L. *aetatis*, of, or at, the age of

A.E.T. Associate in Electrical/Electronic Technology

A.E.T.F.A.T. Fr. *Association pour l'étude taxonomique de la flore d'Afrique tropicale*, Assn. for the Taxonomic Study of Tropical African Flora

A. et M. Fr. *Arts et Métiers*, Arts and Crafts

AETR advanced engineering test reactor

A.E.U. Amalgamated Engineering Union; American Ethical Union

AEV aerothermodynamic elastic vehicle; air evacuation

A.E.W. Admiralty Experimental Works; airborne early warning

A.E.W. & C. airborne early warning and control

A.E.W.H.A. All England Women's Hockey Association

A.E.W.L.A. All England Women's Lacrosse Association, founded as the Ladies Lacrosse Assn. in 1912. In 1705 a French historian when visiting Quebec saw lacrosse being played and was interested in the stick they used, a crook, across which thongs had been drawn to form a pocket. It reminded him of a bishop's crozier and he called the game he saw 'the game of the crozier—la crosse'

AEWS advanced earth satellite weapons system; aircraft early warning system

2ªf. Port. *segunda-feira*, Monday

3ªf. Port. *terça-feira*, Tuesday

4ªf. Port. *quarta-feira*, Wednesday

5ªf. Port. *quinta-feira*, Thursday

6ªf. Port. *sexta-feira*, Friday

Af afgháni, currency unit of Afghanistan

AF 'across the flats', type of nut; air force; Air Foundation (U.S.A.); Air France, national airline of France; audio frequency; *s* Cornwall (B.V.R.)

Af. Africa; African; Afrikaans

a.f. Sp. *a favor*, in favour

a.f. L. *anno futuro*, next year

A/F. anti-flooding

A.F. *Académie Française*, French Academy; *Action Française*, former Fr. jnl., and political party; admiral of the fleet; advanced freight; *Armée Française*, French Army; army form; Associate Fellow; Associated Fisheries; automatic (smoke) filter

A.-F. Anglo-French

AFA Air Force Association (U.S.A.); American Foundrymen's Association

A.F.A. Air Force Act; Amateur Fenc-

13

ing Association, national governing body (U.K.); African/Amateur Football Association; Associate in Fine Arts; Associate of the Faculty of Actuaries (in Scot.); Associate of the Faculty of Auditors

AFAC American Fisheries Advisory Committee

AFAFC Air Force Accounting and Finance Center (U.S.A.)

A.F.A.I.M. Associate Fellow of the Australian Institute of Management

AFAITC Armed Forces Air Intelligence Training Center (U.S.A.)

A.F.A.M., AF & AM Ancient Free and Accepted Masons

AFAP Fr. *Association française pour l'Accroissement de la Productivité*, French Assn. for Increased Productivity

A.F.A.S. Associate of the Faculty of Architects and Surveyors; *Association française pour l'avancement des sciences*, French Assn. for the Advancement of the Sciences

A.F.A.S.I.C. Association for all Speech Impaired Children

A.F.B. air force base; American Foundation for the Blind

A.F.B.F. American Farm Bureau Federation

A.F.B.M.D. Air Force Ballistic Missile Division (U.S.A.)

A.F.B.S. American and Foreign Bible Society

a.f.c. automatic frequency control

A.F.C. Air Force Cross; Amateur Football Club; Association Football Club; Australian Flying Corps

A.F.C.A.I. Associate Fellow of the Canadian Aeronautical Institute

AFCE automatic flight control equipment

A.F.C.E. Associate in Fuel Technology and Chemical Engineering

AFCEA Armed Forces Communications and Electronics Association (U.S.A.)

AFCENT, AFCent Allied Forces in Central Europe (NATO)

AFCET *Association française pour la Cybernetique Économique et Technique*, French Assn. for Economic and Technical Cybernetics

afco automatic fuel cut-off

A.F.C.O. Admiralty Fleet Confidential Order

AFCRL Air Force Cambridge Research Laboratories, *formerly* AFCRC (U.S.A.)

AFCS adaptive/automatic flight control system; Air Force Communications Service

a.f.c.s. adaptive/automatic flight control system

A.F.C.U. American and Foreign Christian Union

A.F.C.W. Association of Family Case Workers

A.F.D. accelerated freeze dried/drying; air force depot; Doctor of Fine Arts

A.F.D.S. Air Fighting Development Squadron

AFEA American Farm Economics Association; American Film Export Association

A.F.E.E. airborne forces experimental establishment

A.F.E.R.O. Asia and the Far East Regional Office (FAO)

A.F.E.S. Admiralty Fuel Experimental Station

AFEX Air Forces Europe Exchange (U.S.A.); Armed Forces Exchange (U.S.A.)

aff. affairs; affectionate; affiliate; affirmative

AFFL Agricultural Finance Federation, Ltd.

afft. affidavit

AFFTC Air Force Flight Test Center (U.S.A.)

Afg. Dan. *afgang*, departure

Afg., Afgh., Afghan. Afghanistan

AFH American Foundation for Homeopathy

AFHC Air Force Headquarters Command

A.F.H.Q. Air Force/Allied Forces/Armed Forces Headquarters

A.F.I. American Film Institute; Associate of the Faculty of Insurance

A.F.I.A. American Foreign Insurance Association; Apparel and Fashion Industry's Association; Associate of the Federal Institute of Accountants (Aust.)

A.F.I.A.S. Associate Fellow of the Institute of the Aerospace Sciences (U.S.A.)

AFII American Federation of International Institutes

A.F.I.I.M. Associate Fellow of the Institute of Industrial Managers

Afi-Ran Africa, India Ocean Region Air Navigation

AFITAE *Association française d'Ingénieurs et Techniciens de l'Aéronautique et de l'Espace*, French Assn. of Aeronautical and Space Engineers and Technicians

AFL *Aeroflot*, Soviet Air Lines; American Federation of Labor, *now* AFL-CIO

A.F.L. Air Force List; Port. *Associação de Futebol de Lisboa*, Lisbon Football Assn.

A.F.L.A. Amateur Fencers' League

14

of America; American Foreign Law Association; Asian Federation of Library Associations; Associate of the Association of Fire Loss Adjusters

AFLC Air Force Logistics Command

AFL-CIO American Federation of Labor-Congress of Industrial Organizations

aflt. afloat

AFM American Federation of Musicians; assistant field manager; Associated Feed Manufacturers

A.F.M. Air Force Medal

AFMA Armed Forces Management Association; Artificial Flower Manufacturers' Association of Great Britain

AFMDC Air Force Missile Development Center (U.S.A.)

AFMEC African Methodist Episcopal Church

AFMED, AFMed Allied Forces Mediterranean

afmo. Sp. *afectísimo*, very affectionately

AFMTC Air Force Missile Test Center (U.S.A.)

A.F.N. American/Armed Forces Network

A.F.N.E. Allied Forces Northern Europe

AFNIL *Agence Francophone pour la Numérotation Internationale du Livre*, French Standard Book Numbering Agency

AFNOR *Association française de Normalisation*, French Standards Assn.

AFNORTH Allied Forces Northern Europe

A.F.O. Admiralty Fleet Order; army forwarding officer

AFOAR Air Force Office of Aerospace Research (U.S.A.)

AFOAS Air Force Office of Aerospace Sciences (U.S.A.)

AFOSR Air Force Office of Scientific Research (U.S.A.)

A.F.P. *Agence France Press*, French independent news agency

A.Fr. Algerian franc; Anglo-French

Afr. Africa; Africaan; African

A.F.R. air-fuel ratio

AFRA American Farm Research Association; American Federation of Television and Radio Artists

A.F.R.Ae.S. Associate Fellow of Royal Aeronautical Society

AFRASEC Afro-Asian Organisation for Economic Co-operation

Afrik. Afrikaans

AFRO Africa Regional Office of FAO

A.F.R.T.S. Armed Forces Radio and Television Service (U.S.A.)

A.F.S. Advanced Flying School; air force station; Alaska Ferry Service; American Field Service; American Fisheries Society; Army Fire Service; Associate Surveyor Member of the Faculty of Architects and Surveyors; Atlantic Ferry Service; Auxiliary Fire Service

AFSA American Foreign Service Association; Armed Forces Security Agency (U.S.A.)

AFSBO American Federation of Small Business Organizations

AFSC Air Force Systems Command; American Federation of Soroptimist Clubs; Armed Forces Staff College

afsd. aforesaid

A.F.S.I.L. Accommodation for Students in London

AFSOUTH, AFSouth Allied Forces Southern Europe

aft. after; afternoon

A.F.T. American Federation of Teachers

AFTE American Federation of Technical Engineers

AFTM American Foundation of Tropical Medicine

aftn. afternoon

A.F.T.N. aeronautical fixed telecommunications network

AFTR American Federal Tax Reports

A.F.U. advanced flying unit; Fr. *Association Foncière Urbaine*, Urban Land Association

A.F.U.L.E. Australian Federated Union of Locomotive Enginemen

A.F.V. armoured fighting/force vehicle

AFVG Anglo-French variable geometry (aero.)

A.F.W. army field workshop

Ag *s* L. *argentum*, silver (chem.)

AG Ger. *Aktiengesellschaft*, joint stock company; Attorney General; *s* Ayrshire (B.V.R.)

a/g airgraph

Ag. agent; agreement; agriculture; August

a.-g. anti-gas

A.G. accountant-general; Action Group Party, Nigeria; adjutant-general; Agent-General, of colonies; air gunner; It. *Alberghi per la Gioventù*, Youth Hostels; Argovia; art gallery

a-g-a air-to-ground-to-air

Aga Aga cooker, name derived from title of Swed. co. which produced the cooker, Aktiebolaget Gas Accumulator

AGA American Gas Association

A.G.A. Amateur Gymnastics Association; American Genetic Association; Australian Garrison Artillery

AGACS Automatic Ground-to-Air Communications System

AGARD Advisory Group for Aeronautical Research and Development (NATO)

AGB Audits of Great Britain, Ltd.

a.g.b. a/any good brand

A.G.B.I. Artists' General Benevolent Institution

AGC American Grassland Council; automatic gain control

AGCA automatic ground-controlled approach

AGCL automatic ground-controlled landing

agcy. agency

agd axial gear differential

agd. agreed

A.G.D.C. Assistant Grand Director of Ceremonies (freem.)

A.G.D.L. Attorney-General of the Duchy of Lancaster

AGE aerospace ground equipment; automatic guidance electronics

A.G.E. Admiralty Gunnery Establishment; Associate in General Education

AGEHR American Guild of English Handbell Ringers

agent-n. agent-noun

A.G.F. Adjutant-General to the Forces; army ground forces

ag.feb. L. *aggrediente febre*, when the fever increases (med.)

agg. aggregate

Aggie Agatha, Agnes

aggr. aggregate

Aggy Agatha, Agnes

A.G.H. Australian General Hospital

A.G.I. American Geographical/Geological Institute; Fr. *Année Géophysique Internationale*, Intern. Geophysical Year (1 July 1957–31 Dec. 1958); annual general inspection; Associate of the Institute of Certificated Grocers

A.G.I.P. It. *Agenzia Generale Italiana Petroli*, Nat. Italian Oil Co.

agit. L. *agitatum*, shaken

agit. ante sum. L. *agita ante sumendum*, shake before taking (med.)

agit-prop agitation and propaganda

agl above ground level

aglm. agglomerate

A.G.M. air to ground missile; American Guild of Musicians; annual general meeting; Award of Garden Merit (awarded by R.H.S. to flowers which have been proved excellent for ordinary garden or greenhouse use)

A.G.M.A. American Guild of Musical Artists; Athletic Goods Manufacturers' Association

agn. again; agnomen

Agⁿ. Augustin

agnos. agnostic

ago. It. *agosto*, August

A.G.O.R. Auxiliary General Oceanographic Research

A.G.P. Academy of General Practice; aviation general policy

AGPA American Group Psychotherapy Association

A.G.P.L. Port. *Administração-Geral do Pôrto de Lisboa*, Port of Lisbon Authority

agr. agreement; agriculture

A.G.R. advanced gas cooled reactor

A.G.R.A. Australian Garrison Royal Artillery

AGREE Advisory Group on Reliability of Electronic Equipment

AGRF American Geriatric Research Foundation

agric. agriculture

A.G.R.M. Adjutant-General, Royal Marines

A.G.S. Air Gunnery School; Alpine Garden Society; American Geographical Society

A.G.S.M. Associate of the Guildhall School of Music and Drama

AGSRO Association of Government Supervisors and Radio Officers

A.G.S.S. American Geographical and Statistical Society

agst. against

agt. agent; agreement

A.G.T. Art Gallery of Toronto; Associate in Glass Technology; Association of Geology Teachers (U.S.A.)

Ag.ᵗᵉTéc.ᵒEng.ᵃ Port. *Agente Técnico de Engenharia*, engineer possessing Industrial Institute Diploma

Agᵗᵒ It./Port./Sp. *agosto*, August

AGU American Geophysical Union

a.g.v. anilin gentian violet

A.G.V.A. American Guild of Variety Artists

AGVG Anglo-German variable geometry aircraft

a.g.w. actual gross weight

A.G.W.A.C. Australian Guided Weapons and Analogue Computer

agy. agency

AH *s* Arbroath (B.F.P.); *s* Norfolk (B.V.R.)

a.h. after hatch; ampère hour; armed helicopter

A.H. L. *Anno Hebraico*, in the Jewish Year; *Anno Hegirae*, the Mohammedan era, A.D. 622

A.H.A. American Heart/Historical/Hospital/Hotel/Humane Association; Associate of the Australian Institute of

16

Hospital Administration; Associate of the Institute of Hospital Administrators

AHAM Association of Home Appliance Manufacturers (U.S.A.)

AHAUS Amateur Hockey Association of the United States

A.H.C. Accepting Houses Committee; American Horticultural Council; Army Hospital Corps

ahd. ahead

A.H.D. *American Heritage Dictionary*

A.H.E. Associate of Home Economics

A.H.E.M. Association of Hydraulic Equipment Manufacturers

AHF anhydrous hydrofluoric acid; anti-haemophilic factor (med.)

AH & FITB Agricultural, Horticultural & Forestry Industry Training Board

AHGMR Ad Hoc Group on Missile Reliability

AHI American Health/Hospital Institute

AHIL Association of Hospital and Institutional Libraries (U.S.A.)

a.h.l. L. *ad hunc locum*, on this passage

A.H.M.C. Association of Hospital Management Committees

A.H.M.P.S. Association of Headmistresses of Preparatory Schools

A.H.M.S. American Home Mission Society

A.H.P. air horse-power; assistant house physician (med.)

A.H.P.R. Association of Health and Pleasure Resorts

A.H.Q. Air/Allied/Army Headquarters

ahr acceptable hazard rate

A.H.R.C. Australian Humanities Research Council

A.H.R.I.H.(N.Z.) Associate of Honour of the Royal New Zealand Institute of Horticulture

A.H.R.H.S. Associate of Honour of the Royal Horticultural Society

A.H.S. American Helicopter Society; American Humane Society; assistant house surgeon (med.)

A.H.S. L. *anno humanae salutis*, in the year of human salvation

AHSB authority, health and safety branch (UKAEA)

AHT acoustic homing torpedo; Animal Health Trust; Association of Highway Technicians

a.h.v. L. *ad hanc vocem*, at this word

A.H.W.A. Association of Hospital and Welfare Administrators

A.H.W.C. Associate of the Heriot-Watt College (Scot.)

AI *s* Meath (Rep. of Ireland V.R.)

A & I Agricultural and Industrial (U.S.A.)

a.i. L. *ad interim*, for the meantime

A.I. admiralty instruction; Admiralty Islands; Air India; Fr. *Altesse impériale*, Imperial Highness; American Institute; Anthropological Institute; army intelligence; artificial insemination

A.I. L. *anno inventionis*, in the year of the discovery

AIA Aerospace Industries Association, *formerly* Aircraft Industries Assn. (U.S.A.)

A.I.A. Abrasive Industries Association; American Institute of Aeronautics/ Architects/Architecture; American Inventors' Association; Anglo-Indian Association; Archeological Institute of America; Associate of the Institute of Actuaries; Association of International Accountants; Aviation Industry Association (N.Z.)

AIAA Aircraft Industries Association of America; American Institute of Aeronautics and Astronautics

A.I.A.A. Associate Architect Member of the Incorporated Association of Architects and Surveyors; Association of International Advertising Agencies

A.I.A.C. Air Industries Association of Canada; Associate of the Institute of Company Accountants; Fr. *Association internationale d'archéologie classique*, Intern. Assn. for Classical Archaeology

A.I.A.E. Associate of the Institution of Automobile Engineers

A.I.Agr.E. Associate of the Institution of Agricultural Engineers

A.I.A.L. Associate Member of the International Institute of Arts and Letters

A.I.A.N.Z. Associate of the Incorporated Institute of Accountants, New Zealand

A.I.Arb. Associate of the Institute of Arbitrators

A.I.A.S. Associate Surveyor Member of the Incorporated Association of Architects and Surveyors; Australian Institute of Agriculture and Science

A.I.A.S.Quan. Quantity Surveyor Member of the Incorporated Association of Architects and Surveyors

A.I.B. accidents investigation branch; American Institute of Banking; Associate of the Institute of Bankers; Associate of the Institute of Building; *Associazione Italiana Biblioteche*, Italian Library Assn.

A.I.B.A. Fr. *Association internationale de boxe amateur*, Intern. Amateur Boxing Assn.

A.I.B.C. Architectural Institute of British Columbia

A.I.B.D. Associate of the Institute of British Decorators and Interior Designers

A.I.B.E. Associate of the Institute of Building Estimators

A.I.B.M. Associate of the Institute of Baths Management; Fr. *Association internationale des bibliothèques musicales*, Intern. Assn. of Music Libraries

A.I.B.P. Associate of the Institute of British Photographers

A.I.B.S. American Institute of Biological Sciences; Associate of the Institute of Building Societies (S.Afr.)

A.I.C. Fr. *Académie internationale de la céramique*, Intern. Academy of Ceramics (Switz.); Agricultural Improvement Council for England and Wales; Agricultural Institute of Canada; American Institute of Chemists; artificial insemination centre; Art Institute of Chicago

A.I.C.A. Associate Member of the Commonwealth Institute of Accountants; Associate of the Institute of Company Accountants; Fr. *Association Internationale des Critiques d'Art*, Intern. Assn. of Art Critics

A.I.C.B. Fr. *Association Internationale Contre le Bruit*, Intern. Assn. Against Noise

AICBM anti-intercontinental ballistic missile

A.I.C.C. All-India Congress Committee

A.I.C.E. American Institute of Consulting Engineers; Associate of the Institution of Civil Engineers

A.I.C.E.A. Associate of the Association of Industrial and Commercial Executive Accountants

A.I.Ceram. Associate of the Institute of Ceramics

A.I.Ch.E., **A.I.Che.E.**, **A.I.C.E.** American Institute of Chemical Engineers

AICMA Fr. *Association internationale des constructeurs de matériel aérospatial*, Intern. Assn. of Aerospace Equipment Manufacturers

AICMR Fr. *Association internationale des constructeurs de matériel roulant*, Intern. Assn. of Rolling Stock Builders

AICPA American Institute of Certified Public Accountants

AICQ *Associazione Italiana per il Controllo della Qualita*, Italian Assn. for Quality Control

A.I.C.S. Associate of the Institute of Chartered Shipbrokers; Fr. *Association internationale du cinéma scientifique*, Intern. Scientific Film Assn.

A.I.C.T.A. Associate of the Imperial College of Tropical Agriculture (Trinidad)

AICV armoured infantry combat vehicle

AID Agency for International Development (U.S.A.)

A.I.D. Aeronautical inspection directorate covering airframes, power plants, and guided weapons; agricultural industrial development; aircraft intelligence department; American Institute of Decorators; army intelligence department; artificial insemination by donor; Fr. *Association internationale pour le développement*, Intern. Development Assn.

A.I.D.A. Fr. *Association internationale de droit africain*, Intern. African Law Assn.; Fr. *Association internationale de la distribution des produits alimentaires*, Intern. Assn. of Food Distribution

AIDD American Institute for Design and Drafting

A.I.D.E. Fr. *Association internationale des distributions d'eau*, Intern. Water Supply Assn.

AIDI *Associazione Italiana per la Documentazione e l'Informazione*, Italian Assn. for Documentation and Information

A.I.D.I.A. Associate of the Industrial Design Institute of Australia

A.I.D.I.S. Sp. *Asociación Interamericana de Ingenieria Sanitaria*, Inter-American Assn. of Sanitary Engineering

A.I.D.L. Auckland Industrial Development Laboratory (N.Z.)

A.I.D.P. Associate, Institute of Data Processing; Fr. *Association internationale de droit pénal*, Intern. Assn. of Penal Law

AIDS aircraft integrated data system; air force intelligence data handling system

A.I.D.T. Fr. *Association interparlementaire du tourisme*, Interparliamentary Assn. for Tourism

A.I.E.A. Fr. *Agence internationale de l'énergie atomique*, Intern. Atomic Energy Agency; Fr. *Association internationale des étudiants en agriculture*, Intern. Assn. of Agricultural Students

A.I.E.D. Fr. *Association internationale des étudiants dentaires*, Intern. Assn. of Dental Students

AIEE American Institute of Electrical Engineers, *now* IEEE

A.I.E.E. Associate of the Institution of Electrical Engineers; Fr. *Association des instituts d'études européennes*, Assn. of Institutes for European Studies

A.I.E.J.I. Fr. *Association internationale des éducateurs de jeunes inadaptés*, Intern. Assn. of Workers for Maladjusted Children

A.I.E.R.I. Fr. *Association internationale des études et recherches sur l'informa-*

tion, Intern. Assn. for Mass Communication Research

A.I.E.S.E.C. Fr. *Association internationale des étudiants en sciences économiques et commerciales*, Intern. Assn. of Students of Economics and Commercial Sciences

A.I.E.S.S. Fr. *Association internationale des écoles de service social*, Intern. Assn. of Schools of Social Work

A.I.E.S.T. Fr. *Association internationale des experts scientifiques du tourisme*, Intern. Assn. of Scientific Experts in Tourism

AIF It. *Agenzia Internazionale Fides*, Vatican City State news agency; Atomic Industrial Forum (U.S.A.)

A.I.F. Fr. *Alliance internationale des femmes*, Intern. Alliance of Women; Australian Imperial Forces

A.I.F.A. Associate of the International Faculty of Arts

A.I.Fire E. Associate of the Institution of Fire Engineers

A.I.F.M. Associate of the Institute of Factory Managers; Fr. *Association internationale des femmes médicins*, Intern. Assn. of Women Doctors

A.I.G. Adjutant/Assistant Inspector-General; assistant instructor of gunnery

A.I.G.A. American Institute of Graphic Arts; Fr. *Association internationale de géomagnétisme et d'aéronomie*, Intern. Assn. of Geomagnetism and Aeronomy

A.I.G.C.M. Associate of the Incorporated Guild of Church Musicians

A.I.G.M. Associate of the Institute of General Managers; Fr. *Association internationale de grands magasins*, Intern. Assn. of Department Stores

AIGS Agricultural Investment Grant Schemes

A.I.G.T. Association for the Improvement of Geometrical Teaching

A.I.H. all in hand; artificial insemination by husband; Fr. *Association internationale de l'hôtellerie*, Intern. Hotel Assn.

A.I.H.A. American Industrial Hygiene Association; Associate of the Institute of Hospital Administrators

A.I.H.S. Fr. *Association internationale d'hydrologie scientifique*, Intern. Assn. of Scientific Hydrology

A.I.Hsg. Associate of the Institute of Housing

A.I.H.V.E. Associate of the Institution of Heating and Ventilating Engineers

A.I.I. Air India International

A.I.I.A. Associate of the Indian Institute of Architects; Associate of the Institute of Industrial Administration; Associate of the Insurance Institute of America; Australian Institute of International Affairs

A.I.I.A.L. Associate of the International Institute of Arts and Letters

AIIE American Institute of Industrial Engineers

A.I.INF.SC. Associate of the Institute of Information Scientists

AIIP advanced industrial instrumentation project; Associate, Institute of Incorporated Photographers

A.I.I.S.U.P. Fr. *Association internationale d'information scolaire, universitaire et professionnelle*, Intern. Assn. for Educational and Vocational Information

A.I.I.Tech. Associate Member of the Institute of Industrial Technicians

A.I.J.D. Fr. *Association internationale des juristes démocrates*, Intern. Assn. of Democratic Lawyers

A.I.J.E. Fr. *Association des industries du jute européennes*, Assn. of European Jute Industries

A.I.L. Air Intelligence Liaison; American Institute of Laundering; Associate of the Institute of Linguists

A.I.L.A. Associate of the Institute of Land Agents; Associate of the Institute of Landscape Architects

AILAS automatic instrument landing approach system

A.I.L.C. Fr. *Association internationale de littérature comparée*, Intern. Comparative Literature Assn.; Association of Irish Laundererers and Cleaners

Ailie Alice, Alison and Helen, esp. in Scot.

A.I.L.O. air intelligence liaison officer

A.I.Loco.E. Associate of the Institution of Locomotive Engineers

A.I.M. Africa Inland Mission; American Institute of Management; Associate of the Institution of Metallurgists; Association of Industrial Machinery Merchants; Australian Inland Mission (Presby.)

a.i.m.a. as interest may appear

A.I.Mar.E. Associate of the Institute of Marine Engineers

A.I.M.E. American Institute of Mining, Metallurgical & Petroleum Engineers; Associate of the Institute of Municipal Entertainment

A.I.Mech.E. Associate of the Institution of Mechanical Engineers

A.I.M.I. Associate of the Institute of the Motor Industry

A.I.Min.E. Associate of the Institution of Mining Engineers

A.I.M.M. Australasian Institute of Mining and Metallurgy

A.I.M.O. Association of Industrial Medical Officers

A.I.M.P.A. Fr. *Association internationale de météorologie et de physique de l'atmosphère*, Intern. Assn. of Meteorology and Atmospheric Physics

A.I.M.P.E. Australian Institute of Marine and Power Engineers

AIMS Association for Improvement in Maternity Services

A.I.M.T.A. Associate of the Institute of Municipal Treasurers and Accountants

AIN American Institute of Nutrition

A.I.N.A., A.Inst.N.A. Associate of the Institution of Naval Architects, *now* A.R.I.N.A.

A.I.N.E.C. All-India Newspaper Editors' Conference

A.Inst.B.C.A. Associate of the Institute of Burial and Cremation Administration

A.Inst.C.E. Associate of the Institution of Civil Engineers

A.Inst.Ex.E. Associate of the Institute of Executive Engineers and Officers

A.Inst.H.E. Associate of the Institution of Highway Engineers

A.Inst.M.O. Associate of the Institute of Market Officers

A.Inst.M.S.M. Associate of the Institute of Marketing and Sales Management

A.Inst.P. Associate of the Institute of Physics

A.Inst.P.A. Associate of the Institute of Park Administration

A.Inst.R. Associate of the Institute of Refrigeration

A.Inst.S.P. Associate of the Institute of Sewage Purification

ain't am/are/is not *and sometimes* has/have not

A.I.Nuc.E. Associate of the Institution of Nuclear Engineers

A.I.O.B. Associate of the Institute of Building

A.I.P. American Institute of Physics/ Planners; *Associação Industrial Portuguesa*, Portuguese Industrial Assn.

A.I.P.A. Associate Member of the Institute of Practitioners in Advertising; Fr. *Association internationale de psychologie appliquée*, Intern. Assn. of Applied Psychology

A.I.P.C. Fr. *Association internationale de prophylaxie de la cécité*, Intern. Assn. for the Prevention of Blindness; Fr. *Association internationale des ponts et charpentes*, Intern. Assn. for Bridge and Structural Engineering

A.I.P.C.E.E. Fr. *Association des industries du poisson de la C.E.E.*, Assn. of Fish Industries of the E.E.C.

A.I.P.E. Associate of the Institution of Production Engineers, *now* A.I.Prod.E.

A.I.P.E.P.O. Fr. *Association internationale de presse pour l'étude des problèmes d'outre-mer*, Intern. Press Assn. for the study of Overseas Problems

A.I.Pet. Associate of the Institute of Petroleum

A.I.P.H.E. Associate of the Institution of Public Health Engineers

AIPO American Institute of Public Opinion

A.I.P.P.I. Fr. *Association internationale pour la protection de la propriété industrielle*, Intern. Assn. for the Protection of Industrial Property

A.I.Q. Associate of the Institute of Quarrying

A.I.Q.S. Associate of the Institute of Quantity Surveyors

AIR All India Radio, 73 stations operate under the auspices of AIR; American Institute of Refrigeration

AIRA air attaché (U.S.A.)

A.I.R.B.R. Fr. *Association internationale du registre des bateaux du Rhin*, Intern. Assn. for the Rhine Ships Register

AIRCENT Allied Air Forces, Central Europe

AIRCOM airways communications system

A.I.R.G. Agency for Intellectual Relief in Germany

A.I.R.H. Fr. *Association internationale de recherches hydrauliques*, Intern. Assn. of Hydraulic Research

A.I.R.I. Associate of the Institution of the Rubber Industry

Airmiss aircraft miss, reporting system established in 1962. Whenever a pilot considers that his aircraft may have been endangered by the proximity of another aircraft during flight within U.K. airspace to the extent that definite risk of collision existed, he makes an airmiss report

AIRPASS aircraft interception radar and pilots attack sight system

A.I.R.T.E. Associate of the Institute of Road Transport Engineers

A.I.S. agreed industry standard (packaging); Anglo-Italian Society; Associate of the Institute of Statisticians; Fr. *Association internationale de la soie*, Intern. Silk Assn.; Fr. *Association internationale de sociologie*, Intern. Sociological Assn.; Australian Illawarra Shorthorn

A.I.S.A. Associate of the Incorporated Secretaries Association

A.I.San.E. Associate of the Institution of Sanitary Engineers, *now* **A.I.P.H.E.**

A.I.S.E. Fr. *Association internationale des sciences économiques*, Intern. Economic Assn.

20

A.I.S.I. American Iron and Steel Institute; Associate of the Iron and Steel Institute

A.I.S.J. Fr. *Association internationale des sciences juridiques*, Intern. Assn. of Legal Science

A.I.S.M. Fr. *Association internationale de signalisation maritime*, Intern. Assn. of Lighthouse Authorities

A.I.S.P.I.T. Fr. *Association internationale de séismologie et de physique de l'intérieur de la terre*, Intern. Assn. of Seismology and Physics of the Earth's Interior

A.I.S.S. Fr. *Association internationale de la sécurité sociale*, Intern. Social Security Assn.

A.I.S.T. Associate of the Institute of Science and Technology

A.I.Struct.E. Associate of the Institution of Structural Engineers

A.I.T. Fr. *Alliance internationale de tourisme*, Intern. Tourist Alliance; American Technology Institute; Association of H.M. Inspectors of Taxes; Association of Investment Trusts

A.I.T.A. Fr. *Association internationale du théâtre d'amateurs*, Intern. Amateur Theatre Assn.

A.I.T.C. Fr. *Association internationale des traducteurs de conférence*, Intern. Assn. of Conference Translators; Association of Investment Trust Companies

A.I.U. Fr. *Alliance israélite universelle*, Universal Israel Alliance; Fr. *Association internationale des universités*, Intern. Assn. of Universities

A.I.V. Fr. *Association internationale de volcanologie*, Intern. Assn. of Volcanology; method of preserving fodder, named after its inventor Prof. A. I. Virtanen

AIW Atlantic-Intercoastal Waterway, Cape Cod to Florida Bay

A.I.W.C. All-India Women's Conference

A.I.W.E. Associate of the Institution of Water Engineers

AIWM American Institute of Weights and Measures

A.I.W.M.A. Associate Member of the Institute of Weights and Measures Administration

Aix Aix-en-Provence

AJ anti-jam; *s* Yorkshire, N. Riding (B.V.R.)

A.J. *Archaeological Journal*; Associate in Journalism

A.J.A. Anglo-Jewish Association; Australian Journalists' Association

A.J.A.G. Assistant Judge Advocate General

A.J.C. Australian Jockey Club (Sydney)

AJEX Association of Jewish Ex-Service Men and Women

A.J.P.M. L. *Ad Jesum per Mariam.* to Jesus through Mary

A.J.R. Association of Jewish Refugees; Australian Jurist Reports, Vic.

AJY Association for Jewish Youth, formed 1899 as the Jewish Athletic Assn., name changed, 1926

AK Alaska; *s* Bradford (B.V.R.)

A.K. above knee

a.k.a. also known as

Akad. Ger. *Akademie*, academy

A.K.C. American Kennel Club; Associate of King's College (Lond.)

A.K.C.(N.S.) Associate of the University of King's College, Nova Scotia

A.K.E.L. Gk. *Anorthotikon Komma Ergazomanou Laou*, Progressive Party of the Working People, successor to the Comm. Party (Cyprus)

AKFM *Antokon'ny Kongresy Ho An'ny Fahaleovantenan'i Madagasikara*, Congress Party for Malagasy Independence (Madag.)

A.K.O.E. Anti-killer Organization of Expatriates (Cyprus)

Akt, Aktb., Aktieb Swed. *Aktiebolaget*, joint stock company

Akt. Ges. Ger. *Aktiengesellschaft*, joint stock company or corporation

Al Alabama (*also* Al., Ala.); Alan; Albert; *s* aluminium (chem.)

AL Albania (I.V.R.); *s* Nottinghamshire (B.V.R.)

al. alcohol

a.l. allotment letter (fin.); Fr. *après livraison*, after delivery, of goods; autograph letter

A.L. Abraham Lincoln (1809–65), president of the U.S.A.; Admiralty letter; Sp. *América Latina*, Latin America; American Legion; army list

A.-L. Anglo-Latin

A.L. L. *anno lucis*, in the year of light

A.L.A. Air Licensing Authority; American Library Association; Associate in Liberal Arts; Associate of the Library Association; Association of Lecturers in Accountancy; Authors' League of America

A.L.A.A. Associate of Library Association of Australia; Associate of the London Association of Certified Accountants

ALACP American League to Abolish Capital Punishment

A.L.A.-I.S.A.D. American Library Association—Information Science and Automation Division

A.L.A.L.E. Fr. *Association latino-*

américaine de libre échange, Latin-American Free Trade Assn., LAFTA

A.L.A.M. Associate of the London Academy of Music

Alas. Alaska

A.L.A.S. Associate of the Land Agents' Society

Alb. Albania (*also* Alban.); Alberta (*also* Alba); Albion

Alban. L. *Albanensis*, of St. Albans, Eng. episcopal title, in bishop's signature

ALBM air-launched ballistic missile

Albq. Albuquerque (U.S.A.)

Albr. Albrecht

alc alcohol

a.l.c. Fr. *à la carte*

A.L.C. Agricultural Land Commission; Associate of Loughborough College of Advanced Technology

ALCA American Leather Chemists' Association

ALCAN Aluminium Company of Canada

A.L.C.D. Associate of the London College of Divinity

alch. alchemy

A.L.C.M. Associate of London College of Music

ald., aldm. alderman

ALDEV African Land Development

ALE Association for Liberal Education

Alec, Aleck, Alex Alexander

A-level Advanced level examination, *see* G.C.E.

ALF Arab Liberation Front, organized and supported by Baathist régime in Iraq

Alf. Alfonso; Alfred

Alf., ALF, A.L.F. Automatic Letter Facer, positions letters, checks stamps, identifies class of mail, postmarks and sorts into neat piles

Alfie Alfred

ALFSEA Allied Land Forces South-East Asia

Alg. algebra; Algeria; Algernon; Algiers

a.l.g. advanced landing ground

A.L.G.E.S. Association of Local Government Engineers and Surveyors

A.L.G.F.O. Association of Local Government Financial Officers

Algie, Algy Algernon

ALGOL Algorithmic Language, arithmetic language by which numerical sequences and procedures may be fed to a computer in standard format

A.L.H. Australian Light Horse

A.L.I. American Library Institute

ALIA Royal Jordanian Airlines

Alick Alexander

algn. alignment

Alitalia Italian international airline

A.L.J.R. *Australian Law Journal Reports*

alk. alkaline

Al.-L. Alsace-Lorraine

ALLA Allied Long Lines Agency

alleg. allegory

allg., allgn. Ger. *allgemein*, general

All H. All Hallows

Allie Alice

all'ingr. It. *all'ingrosso*, wholesale

allo. It. *allegro*, lively (mus.)

All'ott. It. *All'ottava*, direction to play an octave higher, usually 8va (mus.)

All S. All Souls

All SS. All Saints

Allu. aluminium

allus. allusively

Ally Alice, Alison

ALM Dutch *Antilliaanse Luchvaart Maatschappij*, Neth. Antilles Airlines

A.L.M. *Artium Liberalium Magister*, Master of the Liberal Arts

A.L.M.T. Association of London Master Tailors

ALNA Fr. *Armée de Libération Nationale d'Angola*, military arm of FNLA

A.L.O. air/allied liaison officer

A.L.O.E. A Lady of England, pseud. of Charlotte M. Tucker (1821 -93), author of *The Olive Branch*, 1875

ALP automated learning process; automated library program (U.S.A.)

Alp. alpine (bot.)

A.L.P. American Labor Party; Australian Labour Party, the oldest of present political parties in Aust.

ALPA Air Line Pilots' Association

Alph. alphabetical; Alphonse

A.L.P.O. Association of Land and Property Owners; Association of Lunar and Planetary Observers

A.L.P.S.P. Association of Learned and Professional Society Publishers

ALPURCOMS all-purpose communications system

alr. L. *aliter*, otherwise

A.L.R. *American Law Reports*

A.L.R.C. Anti-Locust Research Centre

ALRI airborne long-range input

ALS Agricultural Land Service; antilymphocyte serum; approach lighting systems system of lights to aid an instrument approach to airport

a.l.s. autograph letter signed

A.L.S. Agricultural Land Service; Associate of the Linnean Society

Alsat. Alsatian

al seg. It. *al segno*, to, or at, the sign (mus.)

ALSEP Apollo Lunar Surface Experiment Package

alt. alteration; alternate; alternative; alternator; altimeter; altitude

ALT *Aer Lingus*, Irish Air Lines; Agricultural Land Tribunal

Alt. Fr. *Altesse*, Highness

alt.dieb. L. *alternis diebus*, every other day (med.)

alter. alteration

alt.hor. L. *alternis horis*, every other hour (med.)

alt.noc. L. *alternis noctibus*, every other night (med.)

A.L.T.P.R. Association of London Theatre Press Representatives

A.L.T.U. Association of Liberal Trade Unionists

ALU arithmetic logic unit (computers)

alum. alumna; alumnae; alumni; alumnus

aM, a/M, a.M. Ger. *am Main*, on river Main

Am *s* americium (chem.)

A/m unit of magnetic field strength

AM administrative memorandum; amplitude modulation; *s* Wiltshire (B.V.R.)

A & M agricultural and mechanical (U.S.A.); Ancient and Modern (hymns)

Am. America; American; ammeter; ammunition

a.m. L. *ante meridiem*, before noon

A.M. Academy of Management; air mail; air marshal; air ministry; Albert medal; area manager; army manual; L. *Artium Magister*, Master of Arts; assistant manager; associate member; Award of Merit, to flowers (R.H.S.)

A.M. L. *Ave Maria*, Hail Mary

A.M. L. *anno mundi*, in the year of the world; L. *annus mirabilis*, 1666, the great fire of London, and Eng. successes over the Dutch

A.-M. Alpes-Maritimes (France)

A.M.A. Accumulator Makers' Association; against medical advice; American Machinery / Management / Marketing / Medical/Missionary Association; Incorporated Association of Assistant Masters in Secondary Schools, known as Assistant Masters' Assn.; Associate of the Museums Association; Auckland Mathematical Association; Australian Medical Association

A.M.A.B. Army Medical Advisory Board

Amad. Amadeus

AMAE American Museum of Atomic Energy

A.M.A.I.M.M. Associate Member of the Australasian Institute of Mining and Metallurgy

Amal. amalgamated

A.M.Am.I.E.E. Associate Member of the American Institute of Electrical Engineers

A.M.Am.Soc.H.R.A.E. Associate Member of American Society of Heating, Refrigeration and Air Conditioning Engineers

A.M.A.S.C.E. Associate Member of the American Society of Civil Engineers

Amat. amateur

A.M.Aus.I.M.M. Associate Member Australian Institute of Mining and Metallurgy

Amb. ambassador (*also* Ambas.); ambulance

A.M.B. air ministry bulletin; Airways Modernization Board (U.S.A.)

A.M.B.A.C. Associate Member of the British Association of Chemists

ambig. ambiguous

A.M.B.I.M. Associate Member of the British Institute of Management

A.M.Brit.I.R.E. Associate Member of the British Institution of Radio Engineers, *now* A.M.I.E.R.E.

AMC Aerospace Manufacturers' Council (U.S.A.); Agricultural Mortgage Corporation; Air/Army Materiel Command; American Motors Corporation; Army Missile/Mobility/Munitions Command (U.S.A.); Association of Management Consultants; Association of Municipal Corporations

A.M.C. Army Medical Corps, *now* R.A.M.C.; art master's certificate

A.M.C.A. Architectural Metal Craftsmen's Association

A.M.C.I.A. Associate Member of the Association of Cost and Industrial Accountants

A.M.C.I.B. Associate Member of the Corporation of Insurance Brokers

A.M.C.L. Association of Metropolitan Chief Librarians

AMCOS Aldermaston mechanized cataloguing and ordering system (UKAEA)

AMCS airborne missile control system

A.M.C.S.T. Associate of the Manchester College of Science and Technology

am. cur. L. *amicus curiae*, a friend of the court

AMD aerospace medical division; air movement data

A.M.D. Admiralty machinery depot; army medical department

A.M.D.B. Agricultural Machinery Development Board

A.M.D.E.A. Associated Manufacturers of Domestic Electrical Appliances

A.M.D.E.C. Agricultural Marketing Development Executive Committee; Associated Manufacturers of Domestic Electric Cookers

A.M.D.G. L. *ad majorem Dei gloriam,* for the greater glory of God

amdt., amend., amendt. amendment

A.M.E. African Methodist Episcopal

A.M.E.E. Admiralty Marine Engineering Establishment; Association of Managerial Electrical Executives

A.M.E.I.C. Associate Member of the Engineering Institute of Canada

A.M.E.M. African Methodist Episcopal Mission

Am. Emb. American Embassy

A.M.E.M.E. Association of Mining, Electrical and Mechanical Engineers

Amer. America; American

Amerind, Amer. Ind. American Indian

Amer. Std. American Standard

A.M.E.S. Air Ministry Experimental Station; Association of Marine Engineering Schools

A. Met. Associate of Metallurgy

A.M.E.W.A. Associated Manufacturers of Electric Wiring Accessories

Amex American Express; American Stock Exchange

A.M.E.Z.C. African Methodist Episcopal Zion Church

A.M.F. Australian Marine Force; Australian Military Forces

amg automatic magnetic guidance

amg. among

A.M.G., Amgot, AMGOT Allied Military Government of Occupied Territory, *usually* A.M.G.

A.M.G.O. Assistant Master-General of Ordnance

A.M.H.C.I. Associate Member of the Hotel and Catering Institute

ami advanced manned interceptor; air mileage indicator

A.M.I. American Meat/Military Institute; Ancient Monuments Inspectorate; Fr. *Association Montessori Internationale,* Intern. Montessori Assn., founded to further teaching methods of Dr. Maria Montessori (1870–1952), It. educationist

A.M.I.A. Associate Member of the Institute of Almoners

A .I.MA.E. Associate Member of the Institute of Automobile Engineers

A.M.I.A.M.A. Associate Member of the Incorporated Advertising Managers' Association

A.M.I.Brit.F. Associate Member of the Institute of British Foundrymen

A.M.I.C.E. Associate Member of the Institution of Civil Engineers

A.M.I.C.E.I. Associate Member of the Institution of Civil Engineers of Ireland

A.M.I.Chem.E. Associate Member of the Institution of Chemical Engineers

A.M.I.E.Aust. Associate Member of the Institution of Engineers, Australia

A.M.I.E.D. Associate Member of the Institution of Engineering Designers

A.M.I.E.E. Associate Member of the Institution of Electrical Engineers

A.M.I.E.I. Associate Member of the Institution of Engineering Inspection

A.M.I.E.(Ind.) Associate Member of the Institution of Engineers, India

A.M.I.E.R.E. Associate Member of the Institute of Electronic and Radio Engineers

A.M.I.Fire E. Associate Member of the Institution of Fire Engineers

A.M.I.Gas E. Associate Member of the Institution of Gas Engineers

A.M.I.H. Associate Member of the Institute of Housing

A.M.I.H.V.E. Associate Member of the Institution of Heating & Ventilating Engineers

A.M.I.I. Association of Musical Instrument Industries

A.M.I.I.A. Associate Member of the Institute of Industrial Administration

A.M.I.Loco.E. Associate Member of the Institution of Locomotive Engineers

A.M.I.Mar.E. Associate Member of the Institute of Marine Engineers

A.M.I.M.E. Associate Member of the Institution of Mining Engineers

A.M.I.Mech.E. Associate Member of the Institution of Mechanical Engineers

A.M.I.M.I. Associate Member of the Institute of the Motor Industry

A.M.I.Min.E. Associate Member of the Institution of Mining Engineers

A.M.I.M.M. Associate Member of the Institution of Mining and Metallurgy

A.M.I.Mun.E. Associate Member of the Institution of Municipal Engineers

Am. Ind. American Indian

A. Minls. Tech. Associate in Minerals Technology

A.M.Inst.B. & C.A. Associate Member of the Institute of Burial and Cremation Administration

A.M.Inst.B.E. Associate Member of the Institution of British Engineers

A.M.Inst.C.E. Associate Member of the Institution of Civil Engineers, *now* A.M.I.C.E.

Am.Inst.E.E. American Institute of Electrical Engineers

A.M.Inst.H.E. Associate Member of the Institution of Highway Engineers

A.M.Inst.P.C. Associate Member of the Institute of Public Cleansing

A.M.Inst.R. Associate Member of the Institute of Refrigeration

A.M.Inst.R.E.(Aust.) Associate Member of the Institution of Radio Engineers, Australia

A.M.Inst.T. Associate Member of the Institute of Transport

A.M.Inst.T.E. Associate Member of the Institution of Transport Engineers

A.M.Inst.W. Associate Member of the Institute of Welding

A.M.I.Nuc.E. Associate Member of the Institution of Nuclear Engineers

A.M.I.O.B. Associate Member of the Institute of Building

A.M.I.O.P. Associate Member of the Institute of Printing

A.M.I.P.A. Associate Member of the Institute of Park Administration

A.M.I.P.A. Associate Member of the Institute of Practitioners in Advertising

A.M.I.P.E. Associate Member of the Institution of Production Engineers

A.M.I.P.H.E. Associate Member of the Institution of Public Health Engineers

A.M.I.Plant.E. Associate Member of the Institution of Plant Engineers

A.M.I.P.M. Associate Member of the Institute of Personnel Management

A.M.I.Prod.E. Associate Member of the Institution of Production Engineers

A.M.I.Ptg.M. Associate Member of the Institute of Printing Management

A.M.I.R.E. Associate Member of the Rhodesian Institute of Engineers

A.M.I.(S.A.)C.E. Associate Member of the South African Institution of Civil Engineers

A.M.I.San.E. Associate Member of the Institution of Sanitary Engineers, *now* A.M.I.P.H.E.

A.M.I.S.P. Associate Member of the Institute of Sewage Purification

A.M.I.Struct.E. Associate Member of the Institution of Structural Engineers

A.M.I.T.A. Associate Member of the Industrial Transport Association

A.M.I.T.E. Associate Member of the Institute of Traffic Engineers (U.S.A.)

A.M.I.W.E. Associate Member of the Institution of Water Engineers

A.M.I.W.M. Associate Member of the Institution of Works Managers

A.M.J. Fr. *Assemblée mondiale de la jeunesse*, World Assembly of Youth

a.m.l. amplitude modulation with noise limiter

A.M.L. Admiralty materials laboratory; applied mathematics laboratory (N.Z.)

AMM anti-missile missile

A.M.M. assistant marketing manager; Fr. *Association médicale mondiale*, World Medical Assn.

ammeter *amp*ère plus *meter* (elec.)

A.M.M.I. American Merchant Marine Institute

ammo., amm., amn. ammunition

A.M.N.I.L.P. Associate Member of the National Institute of Licensing Practitioners

A.M.N.Z.I.E. Associate Member of the New Zealand Institution of Engineers

A.M.O. Air Ministry order; area milk officer; assistant medical officer (med.)

A.M.O.B. automatic meteorological oceanographic buoy

A.M.O.R.C. Ancient Mystical Order Rosae Crucis (Rosicrucian Order)

AMOS automatic meteorological observing station

amp. ampère; amplitude

A.M.P. Air Member for Personnel (R.A.F.); Associated Master Plumbers and Domestic Engineers; Australian Mutual Provident Society

A.M.P.A. Associate, Master Photographers' Association

A.M.P.A.S. Academy of Motion Picture Arts and Sciences (U.S.A.)

AMPC automatic message processing center (U.S.A.); auxiliary military pioneer corps

amph. amphibian; amphibious

AMPHIBEX amphibious exercise

Amp.-hr. Ampère-hour

ampl. It. *ampliata*, enlarged; amplifier

AMPS automatic message processing system

A.M.P.S.S. advanced manned precision strike system

A.M.Q. American medical qualification

AMR Atlantic Missile Range

A.M.R.I.N.A. Associate Member of the Royal Institution of Naval Architects

Amrit. Amritsar

A.M.R.O. Association of Medical Record Officers

A.M.R.S. Air Ministry radio station

A.M.S. Administration Management Society (U.S.A.); American Mathematical /Meteorological/Microscopical Society; Ancient Monuments Society; *Apollo* mission simulator; army map service; army medical service/staff; assistant military secretary; Association of Metal Sprayers; Australian medical services

AMSA advanced manned strategic aircraft

A.M.S.A.I.E.E. Associate Member of

South African Institution of Electrical Engineering

AMSAM anti-missile surface-to-air missile

Am. Sam. American Samoa

A.M.S.E. Associate Member of the Society of Engineers

A.M.S.E.F. anti-mine-sweeping explosive float

A.M.S.G.A. Association of Manufacturers and Suppliers for the Graphic Arts

A.M.S.H. Association for Moral and Social Hygiene

amsl above mean sea level

A.M.S.O. Air Member for Supply and Organisation (R.A.F.)

A.M.S.S.F.G. Association of Manufacturers of Small Switch and Fuse Gear

Amst. Amsterdam

Amt, amt. amount

A.M.T. Academy of Medicine, Toronto; air mail transfer; Air Member for Training (R.A.F.); Associate in Mechanical/Medical Technology; Association of Marine Traders

amtank amphibious tank

A.M.T.C. Academic Member of the Trinity College of Music; Art Master's Teaching Certificate

A.M.T.D.A. Agricultural Machinery Tractor Dealers' Association

A.M.Tech.I. Associate Member of the Technological Institute of G.B.

AMTI airborne moving target indicator

A.M.T.P.I. Associate Member of the Town Planning Institute

amtrac amphibious tractor

A.M.T.S. Associate Member of the Television Society

A.M.U. Associated Midwestern Universities (U.S.A.); Association of Master Upholsterers; atomic mass unit (phys.)

A.M.U.A. Associate of Music, University of Adelaide (Aust.)

A.Mus. Associate in Music

A.Mus.A. Associate of Music, Australia

A.Mus.L.C.M. Associate in Music, London College of Music

A.Mus.T.C.L. Associate in Music, Trinity College of Music, London

A.M.V. Fr. *Association mondiale vétérinaire*, World Veterinary Assn.

A.M.V.A.P. Associated Manufacturers of Veterinary and Agricultural Products

AMVERS automated merchant vessel report system

AMVETS American Veterans of World War 2 and Korea

A.M.W.I. Associate Member of the Institute of Welfare Officers

an' and

An. Annam

AN acid number; Anglo-Norman (*also* A.N., A.-N.); ante-natal; *s* London (B.V.R.); *s* Nicaragua (I.C.A.N.)

A/N advice note

an. anonymous; answer

an. L. *anno*, in the year; L. *ante*, before

a.n. above-named

A.N. Associate in Nursing

A. & N. Army and Navy Club/Stores

A.N.A. All Nippon Airways (Jap.); American Nature/Neurological/Newspaper/Numismatic/Nurses' Association; Associate National Academician (U.S.A.); Australian National Airways; Australian Natives' Association

anac., anacr. anacreon

anaes. anaesthesia; anaesthetic

anag. anagram

anal. analogy; analyse; analysis

ANAPO Sp. *Alianza Nacional Popular*, National Popular Alliance (Col.)

A.N.A.R.E. Australian National Antarctic Research Expedition

anat. anatomical; anatomy

ANC African National Congress, formerly led by Albert Luthuli and Nelson Mandela, banned 1960 (S. Afr.); African National Congress (Zamb.)

anc., anct. ancient

A.N.C. all numbers calling; Australian Newspapers Council

Ancap. Sp. *Administración Nacional de Combustibles, Alcohol y Portland* (Uru.)

A.N.C.U.N. Australian National Committee for the United Nations

AND Andorra (I.V.R.)

and. It. *andante*, moderate speed (mus.)

And., Andie, Andy Andrew

ANDB Air Navigation Development Board (U.S.A.)

A.N.E.C.Inst. Associate of the North-East Coast Institution of Engineers and Shipbuilders

anes. anesthetic

A.N.F. anti-nuclear factor; Atlantic Nuclear Force

ANG Australian New Guinea; Australian Newspaper Guild

ang. angle; angular

Ang. Anglesey

A.N.G.A.U. Australian New Guinea Administrative Unit

Angl. Fr. *Angleterre*, England; Anglican

Anglo-Fr.—Anglo-French;—**Ind.** Anglo-Indian; —**Ir.** Anglo-Irish; —**L.** Anglo-Latin; —**Sax.** Anglo-Saxon

ANGUS Air National Guard of the United States

anhyd., anhydr. anhydrous

ANI Port. *Agência de Notícias de Informações*, Portuguese news agency privately owned but officially supported by Ministry of Interior; Sp. *Agencia Nacional de Informaciones*, Uruguayan press agency; *Agência Nacional de Informações*, Nat. Information Agency (Port.)

a.n.i. Fr. *atmosphère normale internationale*, intern. normal atmosphere

A. & N.I. Andaman and Nicobar Islands

anim. It. *animato*, animated (mus.)

Ank. Ger. *Ankunft*, arrival

ANL Argonne National Laboratory; automatic noise limiting

A.N.L. *Archaeological News Letter*; National Library of Australia

Anm. Ger. *Anmerkung*, note

A.N.M. Admiralty Notices to Mariners

ANN all-figures numbers now (Post Office)

ann. Fr. *annales*, annals; It. *annali*, annals; annual; annuity (*also* anny)

ann. L. *anno*, in the year; L. *anni*, years

Ann. Ger. *Annalen*, annals

ANNA Army-Navy-NASA-Air Force satellite (U.S.A.)

anniv. anniversary

annot. annotate; annotation; annotator

annuit. annuitant

annul. annulment

Annunc. Annunciation

anon., Anon anonymous, used with capital as attribution of unknown authorship

ANP aircraft nuclear propulsion; *Algemeen Nederlands Persbureau*, independent news agency (Neth.); Australian Nationalist Party

A.N.P.A. American Newspaper Publishers' Association; Australian National Publicity Association

anr. another

anrac aids navigation radio control

A.N.R.C. American National Red Cross; Australian National Research Council

ANS American Nuclear Society; Army News/Nursing Service

ans. answer

a.n.s. autograph note signed

A.N.S.A. *Agenzia Nazionale Stampa Associata*, Italian Press Agency

A.N.S.L. Australian National Standards Laboratory

A.N.S.P. Academy of Natural Sciences of Philadelphia; Australian National Socialist Party

ant. antenna; antilog; antiquarian; antique (*also* antiq.); antiquity; antonym

Ant. Anthony; Antigua (*also* Antig.); Antrim

A.N.T.A. American National Theatre and Academy; Australian National Television Council; Australian National Travel Association

Antarc. Antarctic

anthol. anthology

anthrop. anthropological; anthropology

Ant. Lat. antique Latin

Ant. Ld. antique laid (paper)

Anto. Port. *Antonio*, Anthony

anton. antonym

Antr. Antrim

Ants. J. *Antiquaries Journal*

Ant. Wo. antique wove (paper)

A.N.U. Australian National University (Canberra)

anx. annex

ANZ Australia and New Zealand Bank

A.N.Z.A.A.S. Australian and New Zealand Association for the Advancement of Science

Anzac A Member of the Australian and New Zealand Army Corps, but loosely any Australian or New Zealand soldier serving in WW1

A.N.Z.A.M. Australia, New Zealand and Malaya

A.N.Z.A.M.R.S. Australian & New Zealand Association for Medieval and Renaissance Studies

A.N.Z.I.A. Associate of the New Zealand Institute of Architects

A.N.Z.I.C. Associate of the New Zealand Institute of Chemists

A.N.Z.L.A. Associate of the New Zealand Library Association

A.N.Z.U.K. task force comprising Australian, New Zealand and United Kingdom troops based on Singapore and Malaysia, estab. Nov. 1971

ANZUS Australian, New Zealand and U.S. Defence Pact, Pacific Security Treaty

aO, a/O, a.O. Ger. *an der Oder*, on river Oder

A/o, a/o account of

AO *s* Cumberland (B.V.R.)

A.O. accountant officer; air ordnance area office/officer; army order

A.O. L. *Anno Ordinis*, in the year of the order

AOA Accident Offices Association; American Ordnance/Orthopedic/Osteopathic/Overseas Association

A.O.A. Aerodrome Owners' Association; air officer in charge of administration; American Overseas Airlines Inc.

aob at or below

A.O.B. advanced operational base; Antediluvian Order of Buffaloes; any other business

A.O.C. air officer commanding; army ordnance corps; Artists of Chelsea

A.o.c. L. *Anno Orbis Conditi*, in the year of the Creation

A.O.C.-in-C. Air Officer Commanding-in-Chief

AOCM aircraft out of commission for maintenance (USAF)

A.O.D. Advanced/Army Ordnance Department/Depot; Ancient Order of Druids

A.O.E.R. Army Officers' Emergency Reserve

A.O.F. Fr. *Afrique Occidentale Française*, French West Africa; Ancient Order of Foresters; Australian Olympic Federation

A. of F. Admiral of the Fleet

A. of S. Academy of Science

A.O.G. Aircraft on Ground

A.O.H. Ancient Order of Hibernians

A.o.I. Aims of Industry

a.o.i.v. automatically operated inlet valve

A.O.L. absent over leave (U.S.A.); Admiralty oil laboratory; Atlantic Oceanographic Laboratories (ESSA); Atlantic Oceanographic Laboratory, Bedford Inst. of Ocean. (Can.)

AONB area of outstanding natural beauty

A.O.P. Association of Optical Practitioners

AOQ average outgoing quality

AOQL average outgoing quality limit

a/or, A/or and/or

aor. aorist

AORE Army Operational Research Establishment, *now* DOAE

AORG Army Operational Research Group, *now* DOAE

A.O.S. acquisition of signal (Space); American Opera/Ophthalmological/Oriental/Society; Ancient Order of Shepherds

A.O.S.E. American Order of Stationary Engineers

A.O.S.M. Associate of the Otago School of Mines

AOSO advanced orbiting solar observatory

A.O.S.S. L. *Americanae Orientalis Societatis Socius*, Fellow of the American Oriental Soc.

A.O.S.W. Association of Official Shorthand Writers

AP *Acción Popular*, Popular Action Party (Peru); *Adalet Partisi*, Justice Party founded 1961 (Turk.); airplane; air pollution; air publication (MOD); anti-personnel; Associated Press (U.S.A.); automotive products; *Det Norske Arbeiderpartiet*, a Labour Party founded in Norway, 1887; *s* Pakistan (I.C.A.M.); *s* Sussex, East (B.V.R.)

ap. apothecary; apparent

ap. L. *apud*, in the works of *or* according to

Ap. apostle; April

a.p. above proof; advanced post; arithmetical progression (*see* g.p.); author's proof

a.p. L. *ante prandium*, before a meal

A/P. authority to pay/purchase

A.P., A/P., a.p. additional premium (insce.)

A.P. Andhra Pradesh (India); armour-piercing; Associated Presbyterian; atomic power

A. & P. agricultural and pastoral

A.P.A. additional personal allowance (tax.); All Parties Administration (Aust.); American Philological/Physicists/Pilots/Press/Protestant/Psychiatric/Psychological/Pulpwood Association; Association for the Prevention of Addiction, formed by parents of addicted teenagers; Association of Public Analysts; Australian Physiotherapy Association; Ger. *Austria Presse Agentur*, newsagency jointly operated by Austrian newspapers and Austrian Broadcasting Company

A.P.A.C.L. Asian People's Anti-communist League

A.P.A.E. Association of Public Address Engineers

A.P.A.N.Z. Associate of the Public Accountants of New Zealand

apart. apartment

a.-part. alpha particle

APB all points bulletin

APBA American Power Boat Association

A.P.B.F. Accredited Poultry Breeders' Federation

A.P.B.S. Accredited Poultry Breeding Stations Scheme

APC All People's Congress founded 1960 (Sierra Leone); armoured personnel carrier; automatic phase control

A.P.C. American Philatelic Congress; assistant principal chaplain; Associated Portland Cement

A.P.C.A. Air Pollution Control Association (U.S.A.); Anglo-Polish Catholic Association

A.P.C.K. Association for Promoting Christian Knowledge, Ch. of Ireland

A.P.C.N. L. *anno post Christum natum*, in the year after the birth of Christ

A.P.C.O. Association of Pleasure Craft Operators

A.P.C.O.L. All-Pakistan Confederation of Labour

apd. approved

A.P.D. administrative planning division; air pollution division (U.S.A.); Army Pay Department

A.P.D.C. Apple and Pear Development Council

Ap. Deleg. Apostolic Delegate

APE Amalgamated Power Engineering; automatic photomapping equipment

APEX Association of Professional, Executive, Clerical and Computer Staff

apf acid-proof floor

A.P.F. Association for the Propagation of the Faith

A.P.F.C. Asia-Pacific Forestry Commission

APG Aberdeen/Air Proving Ground (USAF)

aph. aphorism

A.P.H. Sir Alan Patrick Herbert (1890–1971), Eng. novelist, poet and politician; Antepartum haemorrhage, bleeding during pregnancy or labour (med.); anterior pituitary hormone

A.P.H.A. American Public Health Association

aphet. aphetic

A.P.H.I. Association of Public Health Inspectors

A.P.I. air-position indicator; American Petroleum Institute; Association for the study of the arts and sciences connected with petroleum ind. (U.S.A.); Associate of the Plastics Institute; Fr. *Association phonétique internationale*, Intern. Phonetic Assn.

API Gravity arbitrary scale used for reporting the gravity of petroleum products. The degree Baume is an earlier form of the degree API and is based on a slightly different scale (U.S.A.)

A.P.I.S. Army Photographic Intelligence Service

ap.J.-C. Fr. *après Jésus-Christ* A.D.

APL Applied Physics Laboratory, Johns Hopkins Univ. (U.S.A.)

Apl. April

A.P.L.A. American Patent Law Association

A.P.L.E. Association of Public Lighting Engineers

A.P.M. Academy of Physical Medicine (U.S.A.); assistant paymaster; assistant provost-marshal

A.P.M.C. Allied Political and Military Commission

A.P.M.G. assistant postmaster-general

apmt. appointment

A.P.N. *Agentstvo Pechati Novosti*, News Press Agency (U.S.S.R.)

Apo., apo., apog. apogee

A.P.O. acting pilot officer; African People's Organization; armed forces/army post office; Asian Productivity Organization

Apoc. apocalypse

Apoc., Apocr. apocrypha; apocryphal

apos. apostrophe

APOTA automatic positioning telemetering antenna

apoth. apothecary

APP African People's Party, absorbed by KANU (Kenya)

app. apparatus (*also* appar.); apparent; appeal; appended; appendix; applied; appoint; apprentice; approval; approximate

App. Apostles; Ger. *Apparat*, apparatus

appd. approved

APPES American Institute of Chemical Engineers Physical Properties Estimation System

A.P.P.I.T.A., Appita Australian Pulp and Paper Industries Technical Association

appl. appeal; appellant; applicable; applied

appos. appositive

appr. apprentice

A.P.P.R. Army Package Power Reactor (U.S.A.)

appro. approbation; approval

approx. approximate; approximation

apps. appendices

appt. appoint; appointment

apptd. appointed

appurts. appurtenances

appx. appendix

apr. It. *aprile*, April

Apr. April

A.P.R. annual progress report

A.P.R.C. L. *anno post Roman conditam*, in the year after the foundation of Rome in 753 B.C.

A/Prin. assistant principal

A.P.R.S. acoustic position reference system (nav.); Association for the Preservation of Rural Scotland; Association of Professional Recording Studios

APS Fr. *Algérie Presse Service*

a.p.s. autograph poem signed

A.P.S. Aborigines' Protection Society (Aust.); American Peace/Physical/Physiological/Protestant Society; army postal service; assistant private secretary;

29

Associate of the Pharmaceutical Society of G.B.; Associate of the Philosophical Society of Eng.

A.P.S.A. Sp. *Aerolineas Peruanas S.A.*, Peruvian Airlines; American Political Science Association; Associate of the Photographic Society of America; Australian Political Studies Association

A.P.S.L. acting paymaster sub-lieutenant

A.P.S.W. Association of Psychiatric Social Workers

APT advanced passenger train; automatic picture transmission (NASA)

apt. apartment

A.P.T. after peak tank (shipping); alum-precipitated toxoid (med.); Association of Polytechnic Teachers/Printing Technologists/Private Traders

A.P.T.C. Army Physical Training Corps

Aptdo. Sp. *apartado*, post office box

A.P.T.I. Association of Principals of Technical Institutions

APTS Automatic Picture Transmission Subsystem (NASA)

A.P.T.U. African Postal and Telecommunications Union

A.P.U. Arab Postal Union; auxiliary power unit

A.P.U.C. Association for Promoting Unity of Christendom

A.P.W.A. All Pakistan Women's Association; American Public Welfare/Works Association

aq. aqueous

aq. L. *aqua*, water

Aq. aquatic (hort.)

A.Q. accomplishment / achievement quotient (psy.)

aq.bull. L. *aqua bulliens*, boiling water

A.Q.C. Associate of Queen's College, Lond.

aq.cal. L. *aqua calida*, warm water; — **com.** L. *aqua communis*, tap water; — **dest.** L. *aqua destillata*, distilled water; — **ferv.** L. *aqua fervens*, hot water; — **fluv.** L. *aqua fluvialis*, river water; — **font.** L. *aqua fontana*, spring water; — **frig.** L. *aqua frigida*, cold water; — **mar.** L. *aqua marina*, sea water; — **m.pip.** L. *aqua menthae piperitae*, peppermint water; — **niv.** L. *aqua nivalis*, snow water; — **pluv.** L. *aqua pluvialis*, rain water; — **pur.** L. *aqua pura*, pure water; — **tep.** L. *aqua tepida*, tepid water

A.Q.L. acceptable quality level

A.Q.M.G. Assistant Quartermaster-General

aque. aqueduct

a/r, A/r, A/r., a.r. all risks (insce.)

Ar *s* Argon (*also* A)

AR acrylic rubber, alkyl acrylate copolymer; *Agencja Robotnicza*, Workers' Press Agency (Pol.); Arkansas; *s* Ayr (B.F.P.); *s* Hertfordshire (B.V.R.)

A/R, AR account receivable

AR L. *argentum*, silver (numis.)

ar. arrival; arrive

Ar. Arabia; Arabian; Arabic; Aramaic

A.R. accomplishment / achievement ratio (psy.); acid resisting; advice of receipt; airman recruit (U.S.A.); Fr. *Altesse Royale*, Royal Highness; analytical reagent; *Annual Register of World Events*, first published 1758; annual report; annual return (tax.); army regulation; assistant resident; Associated Rediffusion; Augmented Roman

A.R. L. *Anna Regina*, initials of Anne Boleyn, queen of Henry VIII, carved in screen, King's College Chapel, Cambridge

A.R. L. *Anno Regni*, in the year of the reign

ARA Association of River Authorities

A.R.A. Aerial Ropeways Association; Aircraft Research Association; Army Rifle Association; Associate of the Royal Academy

Arab. Arabia; Arabian; Arabic

A.R.A.C. Associate of the Royal Agricultural College

arach. arachnology

A.R.A.C.I. Associate of the Royal Australian Chemical Institute

A.R.A.D. Associate of the Royal Academy of Dancing

A.R.Ae.S. Associate of the Royal Aeronautical Society

A.R.Ag.S. Associate of the Royal Agricultural Societies

A.R.A.I.A. Associate of the Royal Australian Institute of Architects

Aram. Aramaic, semitic dialect

A.R.A.M. Associate of the Royal Academy of Music

ARAMCO Arabian-American Oil Company

A.R.A.S. Associate of the Royal Astronomical Society

arb. arbiter; arbitrary; arbitration; arbitrator

A.R.B. Air Registration Board controlling contracts for civil aviation; Air Research Bureau

A.R.B.A. Associate of the Royal (Society of) British Artists

A.R.B.E. Fr. *Académie Royale des Beaux-Arts, École Supérieure des Arts Décoratifs et École Supérieure d'Architecture de Bruxelles*, Brussels Royal Academy of Fine Arts

A.R.B.M. Association of Radio Battery Manufacturers

arbor. arboriculture

A.R.B.S. Associate of the Royal (Society of) British Sculptors

Arc. It. *Arcato,* or *Coll'arco,* with the bow (mus.)

A.R.C. Aeronautical / Agricultural Research Council; American Red Cross; Arthritis and Rheumatism Council; automatic relay calculator

A.R.C.A. Associate of the Royal Cambrian Academy (*also* A.R.Cam.A.); Associate of the Royal Canadian Academy of Arts; Associate of the Royal College of Art

arch. archaic; archery; archipelago; architect; architectural; architecture

Arch. archbishop (*also* Archbp.); archdeacon; Archduke; Archibald (*also* Archie); Archipelago; Architecture

A.R.C.I. Associate of the Royal Colonial Institute

A.R.C.M. Associate of the Royal College of Music

A.R.C.O. Associate of the Royal College of Organists; — (CHM) diploma of choir master

ARCOS Anglo-Russian Co-operative Society

A.R.C.R.L. Agricultural Research Council Radiobiological Laboratory

A.R.C.S. Associate of the Royal College of Science (*also* A.R.C.Sc.); Associate of the Royal College of Surgeons of England; Australian Red Cross Society

A.R.C.S.T. Associate of the Royal College of Science and Technology (Glas.), *now* Univ. of Strathclyde

A.R.C.U.K. Architects' Registration Council of the United Kingdom

A.R.C.V.S. Associate of the Royal College of Veterinary Surgeons

A.R.D.C. Air Research and Development Command (U.S.A.)

A.R.E. Associate Member of the Royal Society of Painter-Etchers & Engravers

A.R.E.I. Associate of the Real Estate and Stock Institute of Australia

ARENA *Aliança Renovadora Nacional,* Nat. Renovating Alliance (Braz.)

aren't are not

A.R.F. Advertising Research Foundation; Aid to Russia Fund

ARFA Allied Radio Frequency Agency

Arg. argent; Argentine; Argentinian; Argyll; Argyllshire

a. Rh., a/Rh, a.R. Ger. *am Rhein,* on river Rhine

A.R.H.A. Associate of the Royal Hibernian Academy of Painting, Sculpture and Architecture

A.R.H.S. Associate of the Royal Horticultural Society

A.R.I.B.A. Associate of the Royal Institute of British Architects

A.R.I.C. Associate of the Royal Institute of Chemistry

A.R.I.C.S. Associate of the Royal Institution of Chartered Surveyors

ARIEL Automated Real-Time Investments Exchange Limited, London accepting houses computer company

A.R.I.N.A. Associate of the Royal Institution of Naval Architects

ARIS advanced range instrumentation ship

Arist. Aristotle (384–322 B.C.), Gk. philosopher

Aristoph. Aristophanes (*c.* 445–*c.* 380 B.C.), Gk. comic poet and playwright

arith. arithmetic; arithmetical; arithmetician

Ariz. Arizona

Ark. Arkansas

A.R.L. Admiralty/Aeronautical/Arctic Research Laboratory

ARM anti-radar missile; anti-radiation missile

Arm. Armagh; Armenia; Armenian; armoric

Ar. M. L. *Architecturae Magister,* Master of Architecture

A.R.M. Fr. *Alliance réformée mondiale,* Alliance of the reformed churches throughout the world holding the presbyterian order

A.R.M.C.M. Associate of the Royal Manchester College of Music

armd. armoured

A.R.M.I.T. Associate of the Royal Melbourne Institute of Technology

A.R.M.S. Associate of the Royal Society of Miniature Painters, Sculptors and Gravers

A.Rn.I. Association of Rhodesian Industries

A.R.O. army routine order; Asian Regional Organisation; Associate Member of the Register of Osteopaths

Arp. It. *Arpeggio,* notes of a chord played in rapid succession (mus.)

A.R.P. Air Raid Precautions; *Anti-Revolutionaire Partij,* Anti-Revolutionary Party (Neth.); Associated Reformed Presbyterian; Australian Republican Party

A.R.P.A. Advanced Research Projects Agency (U.S.A.)

A.R.P.O. Association of Resort Publicity Officers

A.R.P.S. Associate of the Royal Photographic Society

Arq.to Port. *Arquitecto,* Architect

arr. arrange; arrangement; arranger; arrivals; arrive

A.R.R. L. *anno regni Regis* or *Reginae*, in the year of the King's or Queen's reign

A.R.R.C. Associate of the Royal Red Cross

arron. Fr. *arrondissement*, admin. district

ARS American Records/Recreation /Rocket Society

A.R.S. Army Radio School

A.R.S. L. *Anno Reparatae Salutis*, in the year of our redemption

A.R.S.A. Associate of the Royal Scottish Academy; Associate of the Royal Society of Arts

A.R.San.I. Associate of the Royal Sanitary Institute, *now* A.R.S.H.

A.R.S.H. Associate of the Royal Society for the Promotion of Health

A.R.S.L. Associate of the Royal Society of Literature

A.R.S.M. Associate of the Royal School of Mines

ARSR Air Route Surveillance Radar, a long-range radar (approximately 150-mile radius) used to control air traffic between terminals

A.R.S.W. Associate of the Royal Scottish Society of Painting in Water Colours

Art Arthur

art. article; artificer; artificial; artillery; artist

Art. Artemis, Greek goddess, patroness of both chastity and childbirth, identified by the Romans with Diana; Ger. *Artikel*, article

A.R.T.C. air route traffic control; Associate of Royal Technical College (Glas.), *later* A.R.C.S.T.

artic articulated vehicle

artif. artificer

art.º Port. *artigo*, article

Art. Pf. artist's proof

A.R.T.S.M. Association of Road Traffic Sign Makers

arty. artillery

A.R.U. American Railway Union

A.R.V. American (Standard) Revised Version (Bible)

A.R.V.A. Associate of the Incorporated Association of Rating and Valuation Officers

A.R.V.I.A. Associate of the Royal Victorian Institute of Architects

A.R.W.A. Associate of the Royal West of England Academy

A.R.W.S. Associate Member of the Royal Society of Painters in Water Colours

As *s* arsenic (chem.); *s* astatine (chem.)

AS all sections (insce.); Anglo-Saxon (*also* A.S., AS., A.-S.); *s* Nairnshire (B.V.R.)

A/S Nor. *Aktjeselskap*, limited co.; Dan. *Aktieselskab*, jnt. stock co.

As. Asia; Asian; Asiatic

AS. air speed, a measure of air pressure set up by the motion of the craft and expressed in terms of speed needed to achieve that pressure under certain specified conditions (nav.)

A/S. account sales; after sight; alongside; anti-submarine (*also* AS); antisyphon

A.S. Academy of Science; Admiral Superintendent; air staff; assistant-secretary; assistant surgeon; *s* personal allowance, single (tax.)

A.S. It. *al segno*, to, or at, the sign (mus.)

A.s. L. *anno salutis*, in the year of salvation; L. *anno Salvatoris*, in the year of the Saviour

ASA Addiction Services Agency (U.S.A.); American Standards Association

A.S.A. Advertising Standards Authority; Amateur Swimming Association; American Standards/Statistical Association

A.S.A.A. Associate of the Society of Incorporated Accountants and Auditors, *now* amal. with A.C.A.

A.S.A.B. Association for the Study of Animal Behaviour

A.S.A.L.A. Associate of the South African Library Association

A.S.A.M. Associate of the Society of Art Masters

a.s.a.p. as soon as possible

asb aircraft safety beacon; asbestos

A.S.B. *Africaans Studentebond*, South African Union of Students; American Society of Bacteriologists

A.S.B.A.H. Association for Spina Bifida and Hydrocephalus

asc ascend/ascent, used by A.A. home routes

A. Sc. Associate in Science

A.S.C. Air Service Command (U.S.A.); American Society of Cinematographers; Anglo-Soviet Committee; Army Service Corps, *now* R.C.T.; Asian Socialist Conference

A.S.C.A.P. American Society of Composers, Authors and Publishers

A.S.C.C. Association of Scottish Climbing Clubs

A.S.C.E. American Society of Civil Engineers

A.S.C.E.A. American Society of Civil Engineers and Architects

A.S.C.M. Association of Steel Conduit Manufacturers; Australian Student Christian Movement

ASCU Association of State Colleges and Universities (U.S.A.)

A.Sc.W. Association of Scientific Workers

A.S.D. Admiralty salvage department; armament supply department

AsDB Asian Development Bank

A.S.D.C. Associate of the Society of Dyers and Colourists

ASDE airport surface detection equipment

a/s.de Fr. *aux soins de*, care of

ASDIC Anti-Submarine Detection Investigation Committee (U.K.); Armed Services Documents Intelligence Center (U.S.A.)

a.s.e. air standard efficiency

A.S.E. Admiralty signal department; Amalgamated Society of Engineers; American Stock Exchange; Army School of Education; Associate of the Society of Engineers; Association for Science Education, *formerly* A.W.S.T.

A.S.E.A. Association of South East Asia

A.S.E.A.N. Association of South-East Asian Nations, regional alliance of Indonesia, Malaysia, Philippines, Singapore and Thailand, *estab.* 1967

A.S.E.E. American Society of Engineering Education; Association of Supervising Electrical Engineers

asf ampères per square foot

A.S.F. Associate of the Institute of Shipping and Forwarding Agents

A.S.F.P. Association of Specialized Film Producers

A.S.G. acting/assistant secretary-general

A.S.G.B. Aeronautical Society of Great Britain; Anthroposophical Society in Great Britain

A.S.G.B.I. Anatomical Society of Great Britain and Ireland

asgd. assigned

asgmt. assignment

ASH Action on Smoking and Health, formed 1971 by Royal Coll. of Physicians

A. & S.H. Argyll and Sutherland Highlanders

ashp. airship

A.S.I. air speed indicator; Fr. *Association soroptimiste internationale*, Soroptimist Intern. Assn.

A.S.I.A. Airlines Staff International Association

A.S.I.C.A. Fr. *Association internationale pour le calcul analogique*, Intern. Assn. for Analogue Computation

A.S.I.F. Amateur Swimming International Federation

ASIRC Aquatic Sciences Information Retrieval Center, Rhode Island, (U.S.A.)

ASIS abort sensing and implementation system (NASA); American Society for Information Science

asl above sea level

A.S.L. acting sub-lieutenant; advanced student in law; American Association of State Libraries; Architectural Society of Liverpool; Assistant Scout Leader; Fr. *Association Syndicale Libre*, Free Syndical Association

ASLE American Society of Lubricating Engineers

A.S.L.E.C. Association of Street Lighting Erection Contractors

A.S.L.E.F. Associated Society of Locomotive Engineers and Firemen (T.U.)

ASLEP *Apollo* surface lunar experiments package

Aslib, ASLIB, A.S.L.I.B. Association of Special Libraries and Information Bureaux

ASLO American Society of Limnology and Oceanography; Australian Scientific Liaison Office

A.S.L.P. Amalgamated Society of Lithographic Printers

A.S.L.W. Amalgamated Society of Leather Workers

A.S.M. acting sergeant-major; air-to-surface missile; assistant sales manager; assistant scoutmaster; assistant stage manager; assistant station master

A.S.M.E. American Society of Mechanical Engineers

As. Mem. Associate Member

A.S.M.P. American Society of Magazine Photographers

A.S.N. army service number; average sample number

A.S.N.D.E. Associate of the Society of Non-Destructive Examination

A.S.N.E. American Society of Newspaper Editors

A.S.N.E.M.G.E. Fr. *Association des sociétés nationales européennes et méditerranéennes de gastro-entérologie*, Assn. of European and Mediterranean Societies for the Study of Gastro-enterology

A.S.O. air staff officer; American Symphony Orchestra

ASOS automatic storm observation service

ASP accelerated surface post; Aerospace Plane (USAF); Afro-Shirazi Party (Tanz.)

A.S.P. Fr. *accepté sous protêt*, accepted under protest; African Special

33

Project, of the International Union for the Conservation of Nature and Natural Resources; Astronomical Society of the Pacific

A.S.P.A. Australian Sugar Producers' Association

ASPAC Asian and Pacific Council

A.S.P.C. Fr. *accepté sous protêt, pour acompte*, accepted under protest for account; Association of Swimming Pool Contractors

A.S.P.C.A. American Society for Prevention of Cruelty to Animals

ASPEP Association of Scientists and Professional Engineering Personnel

A.S.P.F. Association of Superannuation and Pension Funds

ASR airport surveillance radar, can establish the location and bearing of aircraft within about 30 nautical miles; air-sea rescue

A.S.R.E. Admiralty Signal and Radar Establishment

A.S.R.S. Amalgamated Society of Railway Servants, *now* N.U.R.

A/S.R.S. air-sea rescue service

ass. assembly; Fr. *assessore*, alderman or assessor; assistant; association; assurance

A.S.S.A. Astronomical Society of South Australia

Ass.-Com.-Gen. assistant-commissary-general

A.S.S.E.T. aerothermodynamic-elastic structural systems environmental tests (USAF); Association of Supervisory Staffs, Executives and Technicians

A.S.S.G.B. Association of Ski Schools in Great Britain

assigt. assignment

assim. assimilate

A.S.S.M. Association of Shopfront Section Manufacturers

assmt. assessment

assn, assn., assocn. association

assoc. associate; association

Assoc. Eng. Associate of Engineering

Associate I.E.E. Associate of the Institution of Electrical Engineers

Assoc.I.Min.E. Associate of the Institute of Mining Engineers

Assoc.I.N.A. Associate of the Institute of Naval Architects

Assoc.Inst.P.C. Associate of the Institute of Public Cleansing

Assoc.I.S.I. Associate of the Iron and Steel Institute

Assoc. Met. Associate of Metallurgy

Assoc.M.Inst.Gas.E. Associate Member of the Institution of Gas Engineers, *now* M.I.Gas.E.

Assoc.R.C.A.T.S. Ordinary Associate

of the Royal College of Advanced Technology

Assoc.Sc., Assoc.Sci. Associate in Science

A.S.S.R. Autonomous Soviet Socialist Republic

asst., ass/t assistant

A.S.S.U. American Sunday School Union

ASSUC Fr. *Association des organisations professionnelles de commerce des sucres pour les pays de la C.E.E.*, Assn. of Sugar Trade Organizations for the E.E.C. Countries

assy. assembly

Assyr. Assyrian

A.S.T. air service training; Astronomical Society of Tasmania

A.S.T.A. American Society of Travel Agents; Auckland Science Teachers' Association (N.Z.)

A.S.T.C. Associate of the Sydney Technical College

ASTEC advanced solar turbo-electric conversion

A.S.T.E.O. *Association Scientifique et Technique pour l'Exploitation des Océans* (France)

A.S.T.I.A. Armed Services Technical Information Agency (U.S.A.)

ASTM American Society for Testing and Materials, for promoting knowledge of properties of engineering materials and standardizing specifications and methods of testing

A.S.T.M.S. Association of Scientific, Technical & Managerial Staffs

A.S.T.O.R. anti-submarine torpedo ordnance rocket

astr., astro., astron. astronomer; astronomy

astro. astronautics

A.S.T.R.O. Air Space Travel Research Organization (U.S.A.)

astrol. astrologer; astrology

astrophys. astrophysical

Ast. T. astronomical time

A.S.U. Arab Socialist Union

A.S.U.A. Amateur Swimming Union of the Americas

A.S.V. American Standard Version (Bible)

A.S.V.A. Associate of the Incorporated Society of Valuers and Auctioneers

A.S.V.U. Army Security Vetting Unit

A.S.W. Amalgamated Society of Wood Workers; anti-submarine warfare/work; Association of Scientific/Social Workers

A.S.W.D. and K.W. Amalgamated Society of Wire Drawers and Kindred Workers

34

A.S.W.E. Admiralty surface weapons establishment

Asyl. Asylum

aT attotesla (phys.)

At astatine; member of *A*uxiliary Territorial Service (colloq.)

AT antitank; *s* Kingston-upon-Hull (B.V.R.); *s* Royal Air Maroc

at. atomic; attorney

A t. It. *A tempo*, in the time (mus.)

At. attitude (nav.)

A.t. Atlantic time

A/T. American terms

A.T. achievement test; Ger. *Altes Testament*, Old Testament (Bible); *Angling Times*; apparent time

A.T.A. Air Transport Association; Air Transport Auxiliary; American Translators' Association; Amusement Trades Association; Animal Technicians' Association; Atlantic Treaty Association

A.T.A.C. Air Transport Advisory Council

A.T.A.E. Association of Tutors in Adult Education

A.T.A.F. Allied Tactical Air Force

A.T.A.M. Association for Teaching Aids in Mathematics

A.T.A.S. Air Transport Auxiliary Service

A.T.B. aeration test burner; Agricultural, Horticultural & Forestry Industry Training Board

atc. automatic temperature control

A.T.C. Air Traffic Control; Air Training Corps; annotated tax cases

A.T.C.C. air traffic control centre

A.T.C.D.E. Association of Teachers in Colleges and Departments of Education

ATCE ablative thrust chamber engine (NASA)

atchd. attached

A.T.C.L. Associate of Trinity College of Music, London

A.T.C.O. air traffic control officer

A.T.D. actual time of departure; Art Teacher's Diploma; Association of Tar Distillers; Australian Tax Decisions

ATDS Association of Teachers of Domestic Science

A.T.E. Amusement Trades Exhibition; Automatic Telephone and Electric Company

A.T.E.C. Air Transport Electronics Council

A temp. It. *A tempo*, in time (mus.)

ATEX Atlantic tradewind experiment

A.T.F.S. Association of Track and Field Statisticians

ath., athl. athlete; athletic

Athen. Athenian

A-300B Short haul air bus (aircraft)

A.T.I. Associate of the Textile Institute; Association of Technical Institutions

A.T.I.I. Associate of the Taxation Institute Incorporated

A. Tk. anti-tank

Atl. Atlantic

A.T.L.B. Air Transport Licensing Board

atm atmosphere (phys.)

A.T.M. Air Training Memorandum; Anti-tank Missile; Association of Teachers of Management/Mathematics

A.T.M.A. Adhesive Tape Manufacturers' Association

A.T.N.A. Australasian Trained Nurses' Association

At. No. atomic number

A.T.O. assisted take-off

A. to A. air-to-air

ATP Adenosine Triphosphate, a coenzyme of many reactions (biol.)

A.T.P. Air Technical Publications; Associated Theatre Properties

A.T.P.A.S. Association of Teachers of Printing and Allied Subjects

ATPE Association of Teachers in Penal Establishments

A.T.P.M. Association of Toilet Paper Manufacturers; Association of Touring and Producing Managers

ATR Association of Teachers of Russian

ATRAN automatic terrain recognition and navigation

a.t.r.i.m.a. as their respective interests may appear (leg.)

ATS Amalgamated Television Services (Aust.); anti-tetanus serum

a.t.s. at the suit of

A.T.S. American Temperance/Tract Society; American Travel Service; Army Transport Service (U.S.A.); Associate of Theological Study; Auxiliary Territorial Service, women's army organ. *now* W.R.A.C.

A.T.S.C. Associate of Tonic Sol-Fa College

att. attached; attention, *also* attn.; attorney, *also* atty.

Att.-Gen. attorney-general

A.T.T.I. Association of Teachers in Technical Institutions

attrib. attribute

atü Ger. *Atmosphärenüberdruck*, atmospheric excess pressure

A.T.U.C. African Trade Union Confederation

A.T.V. Associated Television

at. wt. atomic weight

A.Typ.I. Fr. *Association typographique internationale*, Intern. Typographic Assn.

Au *s* L. *aurum*, gold (chem.)

Åu Ångström unit employed in designating wave-length of light equal to 1/10th of a micromillimetre or 10⁻⁹mm. (phys.)

AU *s* Nottingham (B.V.R.)

A.U. Actors' Union (U.S.A.); all up, all set in type; astronomical unit

AUA *s* Austrian Airlines

A.U.A. American Unitarian Association; Associate of the University of Adelaide

A.U.B.C. Association of Universities of the British Commonwealth

A.U.B.T.W. Amalgamated Union of Building Trade Workers

A.U.C. Association of Underwater Contractors

A.U.C. L. *anno urbis conditae*, in the year from the foundation of the city, Rome, in 753 B.C.

AUCAS Association of University Clinical Academic Staff

auct. L. *auctorum*, of (other) authors, denoting in bot. that specific name of a plant is that given by others than Linnaeus; — *angl. anglice.* in English; — *Brit.* British; — *non L.*, not Linnaeus

aud. audit; auditor

Aud.-Gen. auditor-general

Aufl. Ger. *Auflage*, edition

A.U.F.W. Amalgamated Union of Foundry Workers

aug., augm. augmentative

Aug. August; Augustine

augm. Fr. *augmenté*, enlarged

A.U.L.L.A. Australasian Universities Language and Literature Association

A.U.M. air-to-underwater missile

A.U.M.L.A. Australian Universities Modern Language Association

a.u.n. L. *absque ulla nota*, with no identifying mark

A.U.O. African Unity Organisation

AUS Australia, including Papua and New Guinea (I.V.R.)

Aus., Aust. Australia (*also* Austl.); Australian (*also* Austl.); Austria; Austrian

A.U.S. Army of the United States; assistant under-secretary

A.U.S.A. Association of the United States Army

Ausg. Ger. *Ausgabe*, revised edition

Aussie Australian

Austin Augustine

aut. autograph (*also* autog.); It. *autore*, author

Aut. Fr. *Autriche*, Austria

A.U.T. Association of University Teachers

A.U.T.E.C. Atlantic underwater test evaluation center (USN)

auth. authentic; author; authoress; authority; authorize

Auth. Ver., A.V. Authorized Version, published 1611 (Bible)

auto. automatic; automobile; automotive

autobiog. autobiographical; autobiography

autom. It. *automobile*, motorcar; It. *automazione*, automation

automatic automatic revolver

AUT(S) Association of University Teachers (Scot.)

a.u.w. all-up-weight

A.U.W.E. Admiralty underwater weapons establishment

aux., auxil. auxiliary

AV *s* Aberdeenshire (B.V.R.)

AV L. *aurum*, gold (numis.)

av. avenue; average, *also* ave. (math.); avoirdupois, *also* avoir., avp.

Av. Port. *avenida*, avenue; average (insce.); Fr. *Avocat*, lawyer; Fr. *Avril*, April

a.v. asset value (fin.)

a.v. L. *ad valorem*, as valued (*also* a/v); L. *annos vixit*, he/she lived so many years

A.v. Atomic volume

A.V. acid value (chem.); artillery volunteers; audio-visual; Authorised Version; average value

AVA Audio Visual Aids

A.V.A. Alberta Veterinary Association (Can.); Amateur Volleyball Association of G.B.; Associate of Valuers' Association; Australian Veterinary Association

av.C. It. *avanti Cristo*, B.C.

A.V.C. American Veterans' Committee; Army Veterinary Corps, *now* R.A.V.C.; automatic volume control

AVCAT high flashpoint aviation turbine fuel

Av. Cert. Aviator's Certificate

A.V.D. Army Veterinary Department

avdp. avoirdupois

ave. avenue; average, *also* avg. (math.)

AVENSA Sp. *Aerovías Venezolanas*, Venezuelan airline

AVGAS aviation gasoline of high octane for piston type engine

Avge. average (cricket)

A.V.I. Association of Veterinary Inspectors

Avia. aviation

A.V.L.A. Audio Visual Language Association

A/Vm *s* unit of elec. conductivity

A.V.M. Air Vice-Marshal

A.V.M.A. Automatic Vending Machine Association

avn. aviation

36

A.V.O. administrative veterinary officer
A.V.R. Army Volunteer Reserve
A.V.R.I. Animal Virus Research Institute
AVRO A. V. Roe and Co.
AVRP audio visual recording and presentation
A.V.S. Anti-Vivisection Society
A.V.S.L. Assistant Venture Scout Leader
A.V.T.R.W. Association of Veterinary Teachers and Research Workers
AVWV Dutch *Antilliaans Verbond van Werknemers Verenigingen*, Antillean Confed. of Workers' Unions, Curaçao
AW *s* Shropshire (B.V.R.)
A/W actual weight; airworthy; artwork
a.w. all water (transp.); atomic weight
A.W. Armstrong Whitworth; atomic warfare
A.W.A. Amalgamated Wireless of Australasia
A.W.A.M. Association of West African Merchants
A.W.A.S. Australian Women's Army Service
A.W.A.S.M. Associate of the Western Australia School of Mines
aWb attoweber (phys.)
A.W.B. Agricultural Wages Board; Australian Wool Board
A.W.B.A. American World's Boxing Association
A.W.C. Allied Works Council; Army War College (U.S.A.)
A.Weld.I. Associate of the Welding Institute
A.W.G. American Wire Gauge; Art Workers' Guild

A.W.H.A. Australian Women's Home Army
awl, awol absent without leave *and* absence without official leave
A.W.L.C. Association of Women Launderers and Cleaners
A.W.M.C. Association of Workers for Maladjusted Children
A.W.N.L. Australian Women's National League
A.W.P. Amusements with prizes, term used in British Gaming Acts to cover certain forms of minor gaming
A.W.R. Association for the Study of the World Refugee Problem
A.W.R.A. Australian Wool Realization Agency
A.W.R.E. Atomic Weapons Research Establishment
A.W.S. Agricultural Wholesale Society; automatic warning system
A.W.S.A. American Water Ski Association
A.W.S.T. Association of Women Science Teachers, *now* A.S.E.
A.W.U. atomic weight unit; Australian Workers' Union
AX *s* Monmouthshire (B.V.R.)
ax. axiom
AY *s Finnair Aero O/Y*, Finnish airlines; *s* Leicestershire (B.V.R.)
A.Y.L.C. Association of Young Launderers & Cleaners
A.Y.L.I. *As You Like It* (Shake.)
A.Y.M. Ancient York Mason (freem.)
Ayr. Ayrshire
AZ *s Alitalia*, Italian airlines; Arizona; *s* Belfast (B.V.R.)
az. azimuth; azure
Az. Ld. azure laid (paper)
Azo. Azores
Az. Wo. azure wove (paper)

37

B

b barn (phys.); bloody; *s* blue sky, not more than quarter covered by cloud (met.); by (compass)

B a human blood type of the ABO group; baryon number; *s* Belfast (B.F.P.); *s* Belgium (I.V.R.); bishop (chess); *s* boron (chem.); *s* Formosa (I.C.A.M.); *s* Lancashire (B.V.R.); Soft (pencils); the second best or highest in quality or rank

B111 BAC one-eleven (aircraft)

B707 Boeing 707; —727; —737; —747 (aircraft)

3B soft pencil

4B very soft pencil

B/ *balboa*, currency (Pan.)

B/- bag-bale

B *Bass*, lowest note of chord, lowest member of any family of instruments, lowest male voice; It. *Basso*, bass voice or singer, double bass, bass part (mus.)

b. back, to engine (rail.); bag; bale; ball; base; bath; batsman; bay; beam; bedroom; before; bitch; blue sky (naut.); book; born; bound; bowels (med.); bowled (cricket); breadth; brother; bust; by; bye (cricket)

b. L. *bis.* twice

B. bachelor; Bacillus; Baptist; Baron; battle; Baumé; Belgium; Benediction; Bey; Bible; Bishop; Blessed; board; Boatswain; *bolivar*, currency (Ven.); bomber; British; brotherhood; building

B. *Bassoon* (mus.); L. *Beatus*, Blessed

ba balancing allowance (tax.); base line; blind approach

Ba *s* barium (chem.)

BA *s* Ballantrae (B.F.P.); *s* Ballina (Rep. of Ireland F.P.); *Biological Abstracts* (U.S.A.); *s* Salford (B.V.R.)

B.A. able-bodied seaman *generally* A.B.; Bachelor of Arts (L. *Baccalaureus Artium*); *Basses-Alpes* (France); Board of Agriculture; Fr. *Bombe Atomique*, atomic bomb; Booksellers' Association of Great Britain and Ireland; breathing apparatus; British Academy; British Airways (BEA, BOAC, Cambrian Northeast, Channel Island Airways and Scottish Airways); British America; British Association; bronchial asthma; Buenos Aires, cap. of Argen.

B.A.A. Bachelor of Art and Architecture; Booking Agents' Association of Great Britain; British Acetylene Association; British Airports Authority; British Archaeological Association; British Astronomical Association

B.A.A. & A. British Association of Accountants and Auditors

B.A.A.B. British Amateur Athletic Board

B.A.(Admin.) Bachelor of Arts in Administration; — (**Art**) Bachelor of Arts in Art

B.A.A.S. British Association for the Advancement of Science

Bab, Babs Barbara

Bab. Babylonia; Babylonian

Bac. L. *Baccalaureus*, bachelor

B.A.C. Boiler Availability Committee; British Aircraft Corporation; British Association of Chemists; British Atlantic Committee; British Automatic Company; Business Archives Council

B.A.C.A.H. British Association of

Consultants in Agriculture and Horticulture

B. Acc. Bachelor of Accountancy

B.A. & C.C. Billiards Association and Control Council

BACCHUS British Aircraft Corporation Commercial Habitat Under the Sea

bach. bachelor

B.A.Chem. Bachelor of Arts in Chemistry

B.A.C.I.E. British Association for Commercial and Industrial Education

Back. backwardation

B.A.C.M. British Association of Colliery Management

B.A.C.M.A. British Aromatic and Compound Manufacturers' Association

BACO British Aluminium Company Ltd.

bact. bacteria; bacterial; bacteriology

B.A.D. base air depot; British Association of Dermatology

B.A.D.A. British Antique Dealers' Association

BADGE base air defence ground environment

B.Admin. Bachelor of Administration

B.A.E. Badminton Association of England; Belfast Association of Engineers; Board of Architectural Education; Bureau of Agricultural Economics (U.S.A.)

B.A.E.A. British Actors' Equity Association

B.A.E.C. British Agricultural Export Council

B.A.(Econ.) Bachelor of Arts in Economics

B.A.(Ed.) Bachelor of Arts in Education

B.A.E.F. Belgian-American Educational Foundation

B.A.F. British/Burma Air Force

B.A.(Fine Art) Bachelor of Arts in Fine Art

B.A.F.M. British Association of Forensic Medicine

B.A.F.M.A. British and Foreign Maritime Agencies

B.A.F.O. British Air Forces of Occupation; British Army Forces Overseas

BAFS *Banque Americano - Franco - Suisse* (Casablanca)

B.A.F.S.C. British Association of Field and Sports Contractors

BAFSV British Armed Forces Special Vouchers

BAFTM British Association of Fishing Tackle Makers

B.A.G.A. British Amateur Gymnastics Association

B.A.G.D.A. British Advertising Gift Distributors' Association

B. Ag. Ec. Bachelor of Agricultural Economics

B. Agr. Bachelor of Agriculture

B. Agr.(Hort.) Bachelor of Agriculture (Horticulture)

B. Agr. Sc. Bachelor of Agricultural Science

Bah. Bahamas

B.A.H.O.H. British Association of the Hard of Hearing

B.A.(Home Arts) Bachelor of Arts (Home Arts); — (Home Science) B. of A. (Home Science); — (Household Arts) B. of A. (Household Arts)

B.A.H.S. British Agricultural History Society

B.A.I. L. *Baccalaureus Artis Ingeniariae*, Bachelor of Engineering; Book Association of Ireland

B.A.I.E. British Association of Industrial Editors

B.A.(J.) Bachelor of Arts in Journalism

bal. balance

Bal. Ballarat

B.A.L. British Anti-Lewisite

Baldie Archibald

BALKAN Bulgarian Airline, *formerly* TABSO

ball. ballast

Ball. Balliol College, Oxford, founded 1263; Ballistics

B.A.(L.P.) Bachelor of Arts in Latin Philosophy

B.A.L.P.A., BALPA, Balpa British Air Line Pilots' Association

B.-Alpes Basses-Alpes (France)

bals. balsam

Balt. Baltic; Baltimore

B.A.M. Bachelor of Ayurvedic Medicine

B.A.M.A. British Aerosol Manufacturers' Association; British Amsterdam Maritime Agencies; British Army Motoring Association

BAMBI ballistic missile boost intercept

BAMES *Banque Malagasy d'Escompte et de Crédit* (Madag.)

B.A.M.M.A.T.A. British Animal Medicine Makers' and Allied Traders' Association

B.A.M.S., B.A.M. & S. Bachelor of Ayurvedic Medicine and Surgery

B.A.M.T.M. British Association of Machine Tool Merchants

B.A.(Mus.) Bachelor of Arts in Music

B.A.M.W. British Association of Meat Wholesalers

Ban. Bangor; Bantu

B.A.N. British Association of Neurologists

B.A.N.C. British Association of National Coaches

Banc. Sup. L. *Bancus Superior*, King's/Queen's Bench (leg.)

B.A.N.S. British Association of Numismatic Societies

B.A.N.Z.A.R.E. British, Australian, New Zealand Antarctic Research Expedition

B.A.O. L. *Baccalaureus Artis Obstetricae*, Bachelor of Obstetrics; Bankruptcy Annulment Order; British American Oil

B.A. of E. Badminton Association of England, founded 1893

B.A.O.F.R. British Association of Overseas Furniture Removers

B.A.O.R. British Army of the Rhine

B.A.(Oriental Studies) Bachelor of Arts (Oriental Studies)

bap. baptize

Bap., Bapt. Baptist

b. à p. Fr. *billets à payer*, bills payable

B.A.P.A. British Airline Pilots' Association

BAPCO Bahrain Petroleum Company

B.A.(P.E.) Bachelor of Arts in Physical Education

B.A.P.M. British Association of Physical Medicine

B.App.Sc. Bachelor of Applied Science

B.A.P.S. British Association of Paediatric/Plastic Surgeons

B.A.P.T. British Association for Physical Training

BAR base address register (computer); Browning automatic rifle

bar. barley-corn; barometer; barometric; barrel

Bar. Barrister (*also* Barr.); Baruch

Bar. *Baritone* (mus.)

b. à r. Fr. *billets à recevoir*, bills receivable

B.A.R. *Book Auction Records*

Barb. Barbados

Barbie Barbara

B.A.R.C. British Automobile Racing Club

B. Arch. Bachelor of Architecture

B. Arch. & T.P. Bachelor of Architecture and Town Planning

barg. bargain

BARIC Baric Computing Services, owned by ICL and Barclays Bank

Barn, Barney Barnabas

B. Arp. Fr. *Bachelier en arpentage*, Bachelor of Surveying

B.A.R.S. British Association of Residential Settlements

Bart Bartholomew

Bart. Baronet (*also* Bt.); Bartholomew

Bart's St. Bartholomew's Hospital London

B.A.S. Bachelor in Agricultural Science; Bachelor of Applied Science; British Antarctic Survey

B.A.S.A. British Architectural Students' Association

B.A.S.A.F. British and South Africa Forum

B. A. Sc. Bachelor of Agricultural/Applied Science

B.A.(Sec. Cert.) Bachelor of Arts with Secretarial Certificate

BASEEFA British Approvals Service for Electrical Equipment in Flammable Atmospheres

B.A.S.F. *Badische Anilin und Soda-Fabrik*, German chemical co.

B.A.S.I. British Association of Ski Instructors

Basic 850-word British American Scientific International Commercial simplified Eng. vocabulary made for Basic English, a system invented by C. K. Ogden (1889–1957) for teaching Eng. as an international auxiliary language

B.A.S.M.A. Boot and Shoe Manufacturers' Association and Leather Trades Protection Society

BASOMED Basutoland Socio-Medical Services

Bass Double-Bass, largest and deepest toned instrument of the violin family (mus.)

B.A.(S.S.) Bachelor of Arts in Social Science

Bass. Con. It. *Basso continuo*, figured bass part for organ or pianoforte (mus.)

bat. battalion (*also* batt., battn.); battery (*also* batty.); battle

Bat. Batavia

B.A.T. British-American Tobacco Co.; Fr. *Bureau de l'assistance technique*, Technical Assistance Bureau

B.A.T.C. Brisbane Amateur Turf Club (Aust.)

bath., bth. bathroom

B.A.(Theol.) Bachelor of Arts in Theology

B.A.T.O. balloon assisted take-off

B.A.(T.P.) Bachelor of Arts in Town and Country Planning

Bats. British American Tobacco Co., stock exchange express.

B.A.U. British Association Unit

B.A.U.A. Business Aircraft Users' Association

B.A.U.S. British Association of Urological Surgeons

Bav., Bavar. Bavaria; Bavarian

b.à.v. Fr. *bon à vue*, good at sight (fin.)

40

B.A.W.A. British Amateur Wrestling Association

B.A.W.L.A. British Amateur Weight-Lifters' Association

B.A.W.R.A. British Australian Wool Realization Association

B.A.Y.S. British Association Young Scientists

bb books

BB *s* a standard size of lead shot measuring 0.18 in. diam.; *s* double black (pencils); *s* Newcastle upon Tyne (B.V.R.)

B/B butcher button (buttons)

Bb. bishops

b.b. ball bearing; bearer bonds; beer barrel; below bridges, meaning vessel will load or discharge below bridges, i.e. Lond. — below Lond. Br.

b. & b. bed and board/breakfast

BB. Certificate issued by U.K. Mercantile Marine Office when vessel reports inwards from foreign, stating that the vessel's articles, official log and crew lists have been examined and found in order

B.B. bail bond; balloon barrage; bank book; basket ball; bill book; *Blue Book*, H.M.S.O. ann. pub. which gives details of Nat. Income; B'nai B'rith, Jewish intern. fraternal soc.; Boys' Brigade; branch bill; Brigitte Bardot; Burton and Bitter (beer)

B.B.A. Bachelor of Business Administration; Big Brother of America; born before arrival (med. students); British Bankers' Association; British Bee-keepers' Association (*also* B.B.K.A.); British Bloodstock Association; British Bobsleigh Association

BBB bed, breakfast and bath; *s* treble black (pencils)

B.B.B. Bach, Beethoven and Brahms; Better Business Bureau (U.S.A.)

B.B.B.C. British Boxing Board of Control

BBC bromo-benzyl cyanide (chem.)

B.B.C. baseball club; British Broadcasting Corporation

B.B.C.F. British Bacon Curers' Federation

B.B.C.M. Bandmaster of Bandsmen's College of Music

B.B.C.M.A. British Baby Carriage Manufacturers' Association

B.B.C.S. *Bulletin of the Board of Celtic Studies*

B.B.F.C. British Board of Film Censors

B-B fraction butane-butene fraction

B.B.G.A. British Broiler Growers' Association

B.B.I. British Bottlers' Institute

B. Bibl. Fr. *Bachelier en bibliothéconomie*, Bachelor in Library Science

B.B.I.R.A. British Baking Industries' Research Association

B. Bisc. Bay of Biscay

bbl., bbl barrel

B. Bldg. Bachelor of Building Science (*also* B. Bld. Sc.)

Bbls/D barrels per day

B.B.M.A. Board / British / Brush / Button Manufacturers' Association

B.B.M.R.A. British Brush Manufacturers' Research Association

BBQ barbecue

B.B.S. Bachelor of Business Science; British Bryological Society

B.B.S.I. British Boot and Shoe Institution

B.B.S.R. Bermuda Biological Station for Research

B. Build. Bachelor of Building

BBW. Birmingham wire gauge

bc *s* sky partly clouded, approx. half covered (met.)

BC *s* Leicester (B.V.R.)

B/C Bills for Collection

B.C. Bachelor of Chemistry/Commerce/Surgery; bad character; badminton club; balancing charge (tax.); bank clearing; bankruptcy court; basketball club; battery commander; battle cruiser; bicycle/billiards club; bills for collection; bishop and confessor; board of control; boat/boating club; bomber command; borough council; bowling/bowls/boxing/boys' club; Bristol Channel; British Columbia (Can.); British Commonwealth; British Council, estab. 1934 to promote wider knowledge of Britain and Eng. lang. abroad; budgeted cost; Building Centre; Burnham Committee

B.C. It. *Basso continuo*, figured bass part for organ or pianoforte (mus.)

B.C. before Christ

BCA Boys' Clubs of America; British-Caribbean Association; British Casting Association (angling)

B.C.A. Bachelor of Commerce and Administration; British Chicken Association; British Chiropractors' Association; Bureau of Current Affairs

B.C.A.B. Birth Control Advisory Bureau

B.C.A.C. British Conference on Automation and Computation

B.C.A.R. British Civil Airworthiness Requirements; British Council for Aid to Refugees

B.C.A.S. British Compressed Air Society

B.C.B.C. British Cattle Breeders' Club

B.C.C. British Colour Council; British

41

Copyright Council; British Council of Churches; British Crown Colony; Fr. *Bureau central de compensation*, Central Bureau of Compensation

B.C.C.A. British Cyclo-Cross Association

B.C.C.C.U.S. British Commonwealth Chamber of Commerce in the United States

B.C.C.F. British Cast Concrete Federation

B.C.C.G. British Cooperative Clinical Group

BCD bad conduct discharge (U.S.A.); binary coded decimal (computer)

B.C.D. British Crop Driers

B.C.D.T.A. British Chemical and Dyestuffs Traders' Association

B.C.E. Bachelor of Chemical/Civil Engineering; Before the Christian Era; Board of Customs and Excise

B.C.E.C.C. British and Central-European Chamber of Commerce

BCF Bacon Curers' Federation; Bromochlorodifluoromethane, used for fire fighting (chem.); bulked continuous filament, yarns of certain man-made fibres

B.C.F. battle cruiser force; British Chess/Cycling Federation; Bureau of Commercial Fisheries (U.S.A.)

B.C.F.A. British-China Friendship Association

B.C.F.G.A. British Columbia Fruit Growers' Association

B.C.F.K. British Commonwealth Forces in Korea

B.C.F.S. British Columbia Forestry Society

B.C.G. Bacillus Calmette-Guérin, tuberculosis vaccine (med.)

B.C.G.A. British Commercial Gas Association; British Cotton Growing Association

Bch. branch; bunch

B.Ch., B.Chir. L. *Baccalaureus Chirurgiae*, Bachelor of Surgery

B.Ch.D. L. *Baccalaureus Chirurgiae Dentalis*, Bachelor of Dental Surgery

B.Ch.E., B.Chem.Eng. Bachelor of Chemical Engineering

B. Chrom. Bachelor of Chromatics

B.C.I.A. British Columbia Institute of Agrologists

BCIE *Banco Centroamericano de Integración Economica, see* Cabei

B.C.I.N.A. British Commonwealth International Newsfilm Agency

B.C.I.P.P.A. British Cast Iron Pressure Pipe Association

B.C.I.R.A. British Cast Iron Research Association

B.C.I.S. Fr. *Bureau Central Inter-national de Séismologie*, Intern. Central Bureau of Seismology

BCK s Buckie (B.F.P.)

B.C.L. Bachelor of Canon/Civil Law

B.C.M. Blackheath Conservatiore of Music; Boston Conservatory of Music (U.S.A.); *British Chess Magazine*; British Commercial Monomark; British Consular Mail

B.C.M.A. British Colour Makers' Association; British Columbia Medical Association

B.C.M.S. Bible Churchmen's Missionary Society

bcn. beacon

B.C.N. British Commonwealth of Nations

B.C.O.F. British Commonwealth Occupation Force

B.Col.P. British Columbia Pine

B. Com., B. Comm. Bachelor of Commerce

B.Com.Ed. Bachelor of Commerce in Education

B.Com.Sc., B.C.S. Bachelor of Commercial Science

BCP Basutoland Congress Party, strongly anti-apartheid and pan-Africanist in outlook (Lesotho); Bulgarian Communist Party founded in 1919

B.C.P. *Book of Common Prayer*

B.C.P.A. British Commonwealth Pacific Airlines Ltd.

B.C.P.C. British Crop Protection Council

B.C.P.I.T. British Council for the Promotion of International Trade

B.C.P.M.A. British Chemical Plant Manufacturers' Association

B.C.P.O. British Commonwealth Producers' Organization

B.C.R.A. British Ceramic Research Association; British Coke Research Association

B.C.R.C. British Columbia Research Council

B.C.R.D. British Council for the Rehabilitation of the Disabled

BCS British Calibration Service

B.C.S. Bachelor of Chemical Science; battle cruiser squadron; Bengal Civil Service; British Cardiac/Ceramic/Computer Society; Bureau of Criminal Statistics (U.S.A.)

B.C.S.A. British Constructional Steelwork Association

B.C.S.O. British Commonwealth of Nations Scientific Liaison Offices

bcst. broadcast

B.C.T. Belfast Chamber of Trade

B.C.T.A. British Canadian Trade Association; British Children's Theatre Association

B.C.T.C. British Cycle Tourist Competition

B.C.U. big close-up, a film shot where object indicated is as large as possible on the screen; British Canoe Union; British Commonwealth Union

B.C.U.R.A. British Coal Utilization Research Association

B.C.V.A. British Columbia Veterinary Association

B.C.W.A. British Cotton Waste Association

B.C.W.M.A. British Clock and Watch Manufacturers' Association

BD Bahrain dinar, currency of Bahrain; beaded border (numis.); s Bideford (B.F.P.); s Northamptonshire (B.V.R.)

2BD s Aberdeen (radio call-sign)

bd. board; bold; bond; bound; broad

b/d. bank draft; barrels per day; bill discounted; brought down

Bd. Ger. *Band*, volume; Fr. *Boulevard*

b.d. L. *bis die*, twice a day (med.)

B.D. Bachelor of Divinity; battle dress; bill discounted; bishop and doctor; bomb disposal; boom defence; Ger. *Bundesrepublik Deutschland*, German Federal Republic

B.D.A. Bachelor of Domestic / Dramatic Art; Bradford Dyers' Association; British Dental/Diabetic/Door/Association

b.d.c. bottom dead centre

B.D.C. Fr. *Bachelier en droit canonique*, Bachelor of Canon Law; Book Development Council; Fr. *Bureau international de documentation des chemins de fer*, Intern. Office of Railway Documentation

B.D.C.C. British Defence Co-ordinating Committee

B.D.D.A. British Deaf and Dumb Association

Bde. Brigade

B. Dent. Sc. Bachelor in Dental Science

B.D.F.A. British Dairy Farmers' Association

bd. ft. board foot

BDG binding (pub.)

BDG/ND binding, no date can be given (pub.)

B.D.H. British Drug Houses

b.d.i. bearing deviation indicator; both dates/days included

B. Di. Bachelor of Didactics

B.D.I. Ger. *Bundesverband der Deutschen Industrie*, Fed. of German Industries

bdl., bdle. bundle

B.D.L. British Drama League

B.D.M. births, deaths, marriages; bomber defence missile; branch delegates' meeting

B.D.M.A. British Disinfectant Manufacturers' Association

B.D.M.A.A. British Direct Mail Advertising Association

Bdmr. bandmaster

B.D.O. boom defence officer

BDP. breakdown pressure; Budapest

Bdr. bombardier; brigadier

B. Dr. Art Bachelor of Dramatic Art

BDS s Barbados (I.V.R.)

b.d.s. L. *bis in die sumendus*, to be taken twice a day (med.)

B.D.S. Bachelor of Dental Surgery; bomb damage survey; bomb disposal squad; British Deer/Display/Driving Society

BDSA Business and Defense Services Administration (U.S.A.)

B. D. Sc. Bachelor of Dental Science

B.D.S.T. British Double Summer Time

B.D.U. bomb disposal unit

Bdx. Bordeaux

Be s beryllium (chem.)

Bé Baumé scale (chem.)

BE s Barnstaple (B.F.P.); s Lincolnshire, Lindsey (B.V.R.)

2BE s Belfast (radio call-sign)

B/E bill of entry/exchange

be. Ger. *bezüglich*, regarding *or* with reference to

b.e. binding edge

b. & e. beginning and ending

B.E. Bachelor of Economics/Education/Engineering; Bank of England; Board of Education (*also* Bd. Ed.), *now* Dept. of Education and Science; borough engineer; British element; British Embassy; British Empire; Buddhist Era; Building Exhibition

Bea, Beattie, Beatty Beatrice

B.E.A. British East Africa; British Electricity Authority, *now* C E.A.; British Engineers' Association, *now* B.M.E.F.; British Esperanto Association; British European Airways

B.E.A.B. British Electrical Approvals Board

B.E.A.I.R.E. British Electrical and Allied Industries' Research Association

B.E.A.M.A. British Electrical & Allied Manufacturers' Association

bearb. Ger. *bearbeitet*, compiled, edited

BEC Bureau of Employees' Compensation (U.S.A.); Business Education Council

bec. because

B. Ec. Bachelor of Economics

B.E.C. British Employers' Confedera-

43

tion, *now* C.B.I.; Fr. *Bureau européen du café*, European Coffee Bureau

B.E.C.C. British Empire Cancer Campaign

B.E.C.G.C. British Empire and Commonwealth Games Council

Bech. Bechuanaland, *now* Botswana

B. E. (Chem.) Bachelor of Chemical Engineering

Beck, Becky Rebecca

B.E.C.M. British Electric Conduit Manufacturers

B.E.C.M.A. British Electro-Ceramic Manufacturers' Association

BECO booster-engine cut-off

B. Econ. Bachelor of Economics; — **(I.A.)** Bachelor of Economics in Industrial Administration; — **(P.A.)** Bachelor of Economics in Public Administration

B.E. & C.W.L.C. British Empire and Commonwealth Weight-Lifting Council

B. Ed. Bachelor of Education; — **(Agr., Agri., Agric.)** Bachelor of Education in Agriculture; — **(Com.)** Bachelor of Education in Commerce; — **(H. Ec.)** Bachelor of Education in Home Economics; — **(N.)** Bachelor of Education in Nursing; — **(P.E.)** Bachelor of Education in Physical Education; — **P.R.** Bachelor of Physical and Recreational Education; — **(Sc.)** Bachelor of Education in Science/Educational Science

B.E.D.A. British Electrical Development Association

beds. bedrooms

Beds. Bedfordshire

B.E.E. Bachelor of Electrical Engineering

B.E.E.P. Fr. *Bureau européen de l'éducation populaire*, European Bureau of Adult Education

bef. before

B.E.F. British Expeditionary Force

BEFA British Emigrant Families Association

beg. beginning

B.E.H.A. British Export Houses Association

B.E.I. Bachelor of Engineering (Dublin); Fr. *Banque européenne d'investissement*, European Investments Bank

B.E.I.A. Fr. *Bureau d'éducation ibéro-américain*, Ibero-American Bureau of Education

Beibl. Ger. *Beiblatt*, supplement

beigeb. Ger. *beigebunden*, bound, in with something else

beil. Ger. *beiliegend*, enclosed

B.E.I.S. British Egg Information Service

B.E.L. British Electrotechnical Committee

B. Elec. & Tel. E. Bachelor of Electronics and Tele-Communication Engineering

bel. ex. Fr. *bel exemplaire*, a fine copy of book or engraving

Belf. Belfast

Belg. Belgian; Belgic; Belgium

Bell, Bella, Belle Arabella/Isabella

B.E.L.R.A. British Empire Leprosy Relief Association

B.E.M. British Empire Medal; bug-eyed monster (sci. fiction)

B.E.M.A. Bristol and West of England Engineering Manufacturers' Association; British Essence Manufacturers' Association; Business Equipment Manufacturers' Association

B.E.M.A.C. British Exports Marketing Advisory Committee

B.E.M.B. British Egg Marketing Board

B.E.M.S.A. British Eastern Merchant Shippers' Association

Ben. Benedict; Benjamin (*also* Benj, Benjy, Benny); Bennet

Ben. L. *benedictio*, blessing

Bend. Bendigo

B. en Dr. Fr. *Bachelier en droit*, Bachelor of Laws

Bened. Benedict

Benef. Benefice

BENELUX Belgium, Netherlands, Luxembourg; a customs union between these countries came into force 1948 and full economic union 1960

Bene't Benedict

Benev. benevolent

Beng. Bengali; Bengalis

B. Eng. Bachelor of Engineering (*also* **B. Engin.**);—**(Tech.)** Bachelor of Engineering in Technology; — **Sc.** Bachelor of Engineering in Science

B. en H. Fr. *Bachelier en Humanidades*, Bachelor of Humanities

B. Ep. A. British Epilepsy Association

B.E.P.C. British Electrical Power Convention

B.E.P.O. British Experimental Pile O

beq. bequeath

beqt. bequest

ber. Ger. *berechnen*, compute

Ber., Berl. Berlin

BERCO British Electric Resistance Company

berg iceberg

Berk. Berkeley (bot.)

Berks. Berkshire

Berm. Burmuda

Bernie Bernard

44

Bert Albert/Bertram/Herbert/Hubert/ Robert

Bertie, Berty Albert/Alberta/Bertha/ /Herbert/Robert/Roberta

Berw. Berwickshire

bes. Ger. *besonders*, especially

B.E.S. Bachelor of Environmental Studies; British Ecological Society

B. ès A. Fr. *Bachelier ès arts*, Bachelor of Arts

B.E.S.A. British Engineering Standards Association, *now* B.S.I.; British Esperanto Scientific Association

B.E.S.I. bus electronic scanning indicator

B. ès L. Fr. *Bachelier ès lettres*, Bachelor of Letters

B.E.S.L. British Empire Service League

B.E.S.O. British Executive Service Overseas

Bess, Bessie, Bessy, Bet, Beth, Betsy, Betty Elizabeth; Elisabeth; Eliza

B. ès S. Fr. *Bachelier ès sciences*, Bachelor of Science

B.E.S.S. Bank of England Statistical Summary; bottom environmental sensing system

Best. Ger. *Bestellung*, order

bet., betw. between

B.E.T. Fr. *Baccalauréat en enseignement technique*, Bachelor in Technical Teaching; British Electric Traction Company

B.E.T.A. Business Equipment Trades' Association

B.E.T.A.A. British Export Trade Advertising Association

Betr. Ger. *Betreff*; *betrifft*, subject

B.E.T.R.O. British Export Trade Research Organization

B.E.U. Benelux Economic Union; British Empire Union, *now* B.C.U.

BeV Billion electron volts; the abbrev. GeV is preferable for standard intern. use (phys.)

bev. bevel

Bev. Beverley

bez. Ger. *bezahlt*, paid; Ger. *bezüglich*, with reference to

bezw. Ger. *beziehungsweise*, respectively

BF *s* Banff (B.F.P.); *s* Staffordshire (B.V.R.)

B/F, b/f, b.f. brought forward

bf. brief

b.f. bankruptcy fee; base frequency; beer firkin; bloody fool; bold face (typ.)

b.f. L. *bona fide*, genuinely or sincerely

B/F bring forward, date on correspondence for follow up

B.F. Fr. *Banque de France*; Belgian francs; British Funds

B.F.A. Bachelor of Fine Arts; British Fellmongers' Association; British Film Academy

B.F.A.P. British Forces Arabian Peninsula

B.F.B.P.W. British Federation of Business and Professional Women

B.F.B.S. British and Foreign Bible Society *also* B. & F.B.S.; British Forces Broadcasting Service, organized in WW2 to entertain, inform and maintain morale of servicemen

B.F.C.A. British Federation of Commodity Associations

B.F.C.S. British Friesian Cattle Society

B.F.E.B.S. British Far Eastern Broadcasting Service

B.F.F.A. British Film Fund Agency

BFFC British Federation of Folk Clubs

B.F.H.M.F. British Felt Hat Manufacturers' Federation

B.F.I. British Film Institute

B.F.I.A. British Flower Industry Association

BFL Bahamas Federation of Labor

B.F.M.A. British Farm Mechanization Association

B.F.M.F. British Federation of Music Festivals; British Footwear Manufacturers' Federation

B.F.M.I.R.A. British Food Manufacturing Industries' Research Association

B.F.M.P. British Federation of Master Printers

Bfn. Bloemfontein

B.F.N. British Forces Network

B.F.O. beat-frequency oscillator

B. For. Bachelor of Forestry; — Sc. Bachelor of Forestry Science

B.F.P.A. British Film Producers' Association

B.F.P.C. British Farm Produce Council

B.F.P.M. British Federation of Plumbers' Merchants, *now* N.F.B.P.M.

B.F.P.O. British Forces Post Office

B.F.S. British Fuchsia Society

B.F.S.A. British Fire Services' Association

B.F.S.S. British and Foreign Sailors' Society; British Field Sports Society, founded 1930

B.F.T.A. British Fur Trade Alliance

B.F.U.W. British Federation of University Women

BG *s* Birkenhead (B.V.R.); *s* Bulgaria (I.V.R.)

bg. bag

b/g. bonded goods
b.g. bay gelding (horse-racing)
B.G. Birmingham gauge; blood group; brigadier general (*also* B. Gen.); British Guiana, *now* Guyana
B.G.A. Better Government Association (U.S.A.); British Gliding/Graduates Association
BGB Ger. *Bürgerliches Gesetzbuch*, code of civil law
B.G.B. Booksellers' Association of Great Britain and Ireland
BGC bank giro credit (fin.)
BGEA Billy Graham Evangelistic Association
B.G.F. Banana Growers' Federation (Aust.)
B.G.G.A. British Golf Greenkeepers' Association
B.G.G.R.A. British Gelatine and Glue Research Association
B.G.I.R.A. British Glass Industry Research Association
bgl below ground level
bglr. bugler
B.G.L. Bachelor of General Laws
B.G.M. Bethnal Green Museum
B.G.M.A. British Gear Manufacturers' Association
B.G.S. British Geriatrics/Goat/Grassland Society; Brothers of the Good Shepherd
B.G.S.A. British Gas Staff Association, *now* merged with N.A.L.G.O.
bgt. bought
BG-TUC British Guiana Trades' Union Council
bh barrels per hour; bloody hell; Brinell hardness (metal.)
BH *s* Blyth (B.F.P.); *s* British Honduras (I.V.R.); British Hovercraft; *s* Buckinghamshire (B.V.R.)
b.h. Fr. *bougie-heure*, candle-hour
B/H bill of health
B.H. base hospital; British Honduras; Burlington House (Lond.), home of the Royal Academy
B.H.A. British Homeopathic/Humanist Association
B.H.A.F.R.A. British Hat and Allied Feltmakers' Research Association
B'ham. Birmingham, *also* Bhm.
B.H.B. British Hockey Board
BHC Benzene hexachloride or hexachlorocyclohexane, obtained by additive chlorination of benzene, an insecticide; British Hovercraft Corporation
B.H.C. British High Commissioner
B. H. Cross Brotherhood of the Holy Cross
B.H.C.S.A. British Hospitals Contributory Scheme Association

bhd. beachhead; billhead; bulkhead
B.H.E. Bachelor of Home Economics, *also* B. H. Ec.
B'head Birkenhead
Bhf. Ger. *Bahnhof*, railway station
B.H.I. British Horological Institute; Fr. *Bureau hydrographique internationale*, Intern. Hydrographic Bureau
B(H)L Borax (Holdings) Limited
B.H.M.R.A. British Hydromechanics' Research Association
Bhn., B.H.N. Brinell number (metal.)
B. Hort. Bachelor of Horticulture; — **Sc.** Bachelor of Horticultural Science
b.h.p. brake horsepower; — **hr.** brake horsepower hour
B.H.P. Broken Hill Proprietary Company Limited (Aust.)
bhpric. bishopric
B.H.Q. Brigade Headquarters
BHRA British Hotels and Restaurants Association; British Hydromechanics' Research Association
B.H.S. boys' high school; British Home Stores; British Horse Society
B. H. Sc. Bachelor of Home/Household Science
B.H.T.A. British Herring Trade Association
Bhu. Bhutan
B. Hy. Bachelor of Hygiene/Public Health
Bi *s* bismuth (chem.)
BI *s* Monaghan (B.V.R.)
B.I. background information; Bahama/Balearic Islands; base ignition; Bermuda Islands; bodily injury; bulk issue
B.I.A. British Institute of Acupuncture; British Insurance/Ironfounders' Association
B.I.A.A. British Industrial Advertising Association
B.I.A.C. Business & Industry Advisory Committee, advisory body on management and trade union sides of industry, in assn. with OECD
B.I.A.D. Fr. *Bureau international d'anthropologie différentielle*, Intern. Bureau of Differential Anthropology
B.I.A.E. British Institute of Adult Education
BIAS Bristol Industrial Archeological Society
B.I.A.T.A. British Independent Air Transport Association
bib. Fr. *bibliothèque*, library
bib. L. *bibe*, drink (med.)
Bib. bible; biblical, *also* **bibl.**
b.i.b., BIB baby incendiary bomb
B.I.B.C. British Isles Bowling Council

B.I.B.F. British and Irish Basketball Federation

bibl., bibliog. bibliographer; bibliographical; bibliography

B.I.B.R.A. British Industrial Biological Research Association

B.I.C. Bahá'í International Community; Fr. *Bureau international des containers,* Intern. Container Bureau; Fr. *Bureau international du cinéma,* Intern. Cinema Bureau

bicarb. bicarbonate of soda

B.I.C.C. Berne International Copyright Convention; British Insulated Callender's Cables

B.I.C.E. Fr. *Bureau international catholique de l'enfance,* Intern. Catholic Child Bureau

B.I.C.E.M.A. British Internal Combustion Engine Manufacturers' Association

B.I.C.E.P. British Industrial Collaborative Exponential Programme

B.I.C.E.R.A. British Internal Combustion Engine Research Association

bichrome sodium bichromate

B.I.C.S. British Institute of Cleaning Science

B.I.C.T.A. British Investment Casters' Technical Association

b.i.d. L. *bis in die,* twice daily (med)

B.I.D. Bachelor of Interior Design; Fr. *Banque interaméricaine de développement,* Inter-American Development Bank; brought in dead (med.); Building Industry Distributors, *now* N.F.B.P.M.

Biddy Bridget

B.I.E. Bachelor of Industrial Engineering; Fr. *Bureau international d'éducation,* Intern. Bureau of Education; Fr. *Bureau international des expositions,* Intern. Exhibition Bureau

B.I.E.M. Fr. *Bureau international de l'édition mécanique,* Intern. Bureau for Mechanical Reproduction

bien. biennial

B.I.E.T. British Institute of Educational/Engineering Technology

B.I.F. British Industries Fair

B.I.F.A. British Industrial Film Association, *now* part of B.I.S.F.A.

B.I.F.U.S. British, Italian, French and United States

Big D Dallas, Texas (U.S.A.)

B.I.H.A. British Ice Hockey Association

bike bicycle

Bill, Billie, Billy William

bim. It. *bimestre, bimestrale,* a two-month period, bi-monthly

B.I.M. Bachelor of Indian Medicine; British Institute of Management; British Insulin Manufacturers

B.I.M.C.A.M. British Industrial Measuring and Control Apparatus Manufacturers' Association

bin. binary (math.)

B.I.N. *Bulletin of International News*

B.I.N.C. Building Industries' National Council

bind. binding

B.I.O. Bedford Institute of Oceanography (Can.)

biochem. biochemistry

biog. biograph; biographer; biographic; biographical; biography

biogeog. biogeography

biol. biological; biologist; biology

BIOS, bios biological satellite (NASA)

B.I.O.S. Biological Investigations of Space; British Intelligence Objectives Sub-Committee

BIP Botswana Independence Party (Botswana)

B.I.P. British Industrial Plastics; British Institute in Paris

B.I.P.C.A. Fr. *Bureau international permanent de chimie analytique pour les matières destinées à l'alimentation de l'homme et des animaux,* Permanent Intern. Bureau of Analytical Chemistry of Human and Animal Food

B.I.P.L. Burmah Industrial Products Limited

B.I.P.M. Fr. *Bureau international des poids et mésures,* Intern. Bureau of Weights and Measures

B.I.P.P. Bismuth, iodoform, paraffin paste, used for packing septic cavities (med.); British Institute of Practical Psychology

B.I.R. Board of Inland Revenue; British Institute of Radiology

B.I.R.D. Fr. *Banque internationale pour le reconstruction et le développement,* Intern. Bank for Reconstruction and Development

B.I.R.E. British Institution of Radio Engineers

B.I.R.F. Brewing Industry Research Foundation

Birm. Birmingham

B.I.R.M.O. British Infra-Red Manufacturers' Organization

BIRPI Fr. *Bureaux internationaux réunis pour la protection de la propriété intellectuelle,* United Intern. Bureaux for the Protection of Intellectual Property, *now* W.I.P.O.

B.I.R.S. British Institute of Recorded Sound

bis. bissextile

B.I.S. Bank for International Settlements; British Information Services; British Interplanetary/Iris Society; Fr.

Bureau international du scoutisme, Boy Scouts Intern. Bureau

B.I.S.A.K.T.A. British Iron, Steel and Kindred Trades Association

Bisc. Biscayan

B.I.S.F. British Iron and Steel Federation

B.S.F.A. British Industrial and Scientific Film Association; Fr. *Bureau international pour la standardisation de la rayonne et des fibres synthétiques*, Intern. Bureau for the Standardization of Man-Made Fibres

bish. bishop

bis. ind. L. *bis in dies*, twice a day (med.)

bis in 7d. L. *bis in septem diebus*, twice a week (med.)

B.I.S.I.T.S. British Iron and Steel Industry Translation Service

B.I.S.R.A. British Iron and Steel Research Association

BIT *bi*nary dig*it* (computer)

B.I.T. Fr. *Bureau international du travail*, Intern. Labour Office

B.I.T.A. British Industrial Truck Association

B.I.T.O. British Institution of Training Officers

B.I.T.U. Bustamante Industrial Trade Union (Jamaica)

bitum., bitm. bituminous

BIU Bermuda Industrial Union

B.I.U. Fr. *Bureau international des universités*, Intern. Univ. Bureau

biv. bivouac

B.I.W.F. British-Israel World Federation

B.I.W.S. Bureau of International Whaling Statistics

biz business; show business (theatre)

B.I.Z. Ger. *Bank für Internationalen Zahlungsausgleich*, Bank for Intern. Settlements

BJ *s* Suffolk, East (B.V.R.)

B.J. Bachelor of Journalism

B.J.A. British Judo Association

B.J.C.E.B. British Joint Communications Electronics Board

B. JONS. Ben Jonson (*c.* 1573–1637), poet and dramatist

BJOS *British Journal of Occupational Safety*

B.J.S.M. British Joint Services Mission

B.J.T.R.A. British Jute Trade Research Association

B. Jur., B. Juris. Bachelor of Jurisprudence

Bk *s* berkelium (chem.)

BK *s* Berwick-on-Tweed (B.F.P.); *s* Portsmouth (B.V.R.)

bk. backwardation; bank; bark; barrack; black; block; book; break

bkble bookable

BKC benzalkonium chloride

bkcy. bankruptcy

bkd. blackboard

bkg. banking; booking; book-keeping, *also* **bkkg.**

bkgd. background

BKH security police (Hungary)

bklr. black letter (typ.)

bklt. booklet

Bklyn. Brooklyn (U S A.)

bkm. buckram

bkpt., bkrpt. bankrupt

B.K.S. British Kinematograph Society

bkt. basket; bracket

BL *s* Berkshire (B.V.R.); *s* Bristol (B.F.P.)

B/L, B./L., b.l. bill of lading, receipt given on behalf of shipowner for goods shipped

bl. bale; barrel; black; blue

Bl. Ger. *Blat*, newspaper; blessed; Turk. *Bölük*, company

Bl. Ger. *Bläser*, performer(s), on wind instruments (mus.)

B.L. Bachelor of Law/Letters/Literature; barrister-at-law; base line; bill lodged; black letter; boatswain lieutenant; Bodleian Library, Oxford; breaking load; breech-loader; breech-loading; British Legion, *now* R.B.L.

B.L.A. Bachelor of Landscape Architecture/Liberal Arts; British Liberation Army, early form of B.A.O.R.

B.L.A.C.C. British and Latin American Chamber of Commerce

B.L.B. nasal oxygen mask Boothby, Lovelace and Bulbulian nasal oxygen mask

B.L.C. British Lighting Council

bld. bold; boldface

bldg. building

Bldg. E. building engineer

B.L.E. Brotherhood of Locomotive Engineers (U.S.A.)

B.L.E.S.M.A. British Limbless Ex-Servicemen's Association

B.L.E.U. Belgo-Luxembourg Economic Union; blind landing experimental unit

B.L.F. & E. Brotherhood of Locomotive Firemen and Enginemen (U.S.A.)

B.L.G. *Burke's Landed Gentry*

B.L.H. British Legion Headquarters

B.L.H.A. British Linen Hire Association

BLI British Lighting Industries

B. Lib., B. Lib. Sc. Bachelor of Library Science

B.L.I.C. Fr. *Bureau de liaison des*

industries du caoutchouc de la C.E.E., Rubber Industries Liaison Bureau of the EEC

B. Lit., B. Litt. L. *Baccalaureus Literarum*, Bachelor of Literature

blitz Ger. *Blitzkreig*, lightning war

blk. black (typ.); blank; block; bulk

B. LL. Bachelor of Laws

B.L.M. Bachelor of Land Management; blind landing machine; Bureau of Land Management (U.S.A.)

B.L.M.A. British Lead Manufacturers' Association

B.L.M.A.S. Bible Lands Missions' Aid Society

B.L.M.C. British Leyland Motor Corporation

B.L.M.R.A. British Leather Manufacturers' Research Association

B.L.O.F. British Lace Operatives' Federation

blotch blotting-paper

BLP Barbados Labour Party, founded in 1938, is the oldest of the existing political parties

b.l.r. breech-loading rifle

B.L.R.A. British Launderers' Research Association

B.L.S. Bachelor of Library Science/Service; Branch Line Society; Bureau of Labor Statistics (U.S.A.)

B.L.S. L. *Benevolenti lectori salutem*, greeting to the well-wishing reader

B.L.S.G.M.A. British Lampblown Scientific Glassware Manufacturers' Association

blt. built

B.L.V. British Legion Village

blvd. boulevard

B.L.W.A. British Laboratory Ware Association

BM *s* Bedfordshire (B.V.R.); *s* Brixham (B.F.P.)

6BM *s* Bournemouth (radio call-sign)

b.m. black mare (horse-racing); board measure; bowel movement; breech mechanism; broad measure

b.m. L. *bene merenti*, to the well-deserving

B.M. Bachelor of Medicine/Music; bandmaster; bench mark (survey); bending moment; binding margin; bishop and martyr; brigade major; British Monomark; British Museum; Bronze Medallist; Bureau of Mines (U.S.A.)

B.M. L. *beatae memoriae*, of blessed memory; L. *Beata Maria*, the Blessed Virgin; L. *Bonae Memoriae*, of happy memory

B.M.A. British Manufacturers' Association; British Medical Association

B. Math. Bachelor of Mathematics

B.M.C. British Match Corporation; British Medical Council; British Metal Corporation; British Motor Corporation, *now* B.L.M.C.; British Mountaineering Council; Catalogue of books printed in XV cent. at British Museum

BMD ballistic missile defence

B.M.D. Births, Marriages and Deaths

B.M.D.M. British Museum Department of Manuscripts

bmdr. bombardier (mil.)

B.M.E. Bachelor of Mechanical/Mining Engineering

B.M.E.C. British Marine Equipment Council

B. Med. Bachelor of Medicine; — **Biol.** Bachelor of Medical Biology; — **Sc.** Bachelor of Medical Science

B.M.E.F. British Mechanical Engineering Federation, *formerly* B.E.A.

B.M.E.G. Building Materials Export Group

b.m.e.p. brake mean effective pressure

B. Met. Bachelor of Metallurgy; — **E.** Bachelor of Metallurgical Engineering

B.M.E.W.S. ballistic missile early warning station/system

BMFA Boston Museum of Fine Arts (U.S.A.)

B.M.I. ballistic missile interceptor; Birmingham and Midland Institute; Broadcast Music Incorporated

B.M.J. *British Medical Journal*

B.M.L. Bachelor of Modern Languages; British Museum Library

B.M.M.A. British Mantle Manufacturers' Association

b.m.o. business machine operator

B'mouth Bournemouth

b.m.p. brake mean power

B.M.P.A. British Metalworking Plantmakers' Association

B.M.P.S. British Musicians' Pension Society

B.M.R. basal metabolic rate (biol.)

B.M.R.A. British Manufacturers' Representatives' Association (S. Afr.)

B.M.R.B. British Market Research Bureau

B.M.R.M.C. British Motor Racing Marshals' Club

B.M.S. Baptist Missionary Society; British Mycological Society

B.M.S.E. Baltic Mercantile and Shipping Exchange

B.M.T. British Mean Time

B.M.T.A. British Motor Trade Association

B.M.T.F.A. British Malleable Tube Fittings Association

49

B. Mus. Bachelor of Music; — **Ed.** Bachelor of Music Education

B.M.V. Blessed Mary the Virgin

BMW Ger. *Bayerische Motoren Werke*, Bavarian motor works

B.M.W.S. ballistic missile weapon system

BN s Bolton (B.V.R.); s Boston (B.F.P.)

bn. battalion; beacon; been; born

Bn. Baron

Bn. *bassoon* (mus.)

B.N. Bachelor of Nursing; bank note

BNA British Naturalists' Association, founded by F. Kay Robinson in 1905. The initial letters form the assn.'s motto *Beatus* [*est*] *Naturae Amor*

B.N.A. British North America; British North Atlantic, defines N. Atl. Institute Insce. Warranty limits, i.e. latitude 43° 40′ N.—North America, above which extra premium becomes payable

B.N.A.F. British North Africa Force

BNAU Bulgarian National Agrarian Union

B.N.B. *British National Bibliography*; British North Borneo

B.N.B.C. British National Book Centre

B.N.C. Brasenose College, Oxford, founded 1509

B.N.C.C. British National Committee for Chemistry

BNCI Fr. *Banque Nationale pour le Commerce et l'Industrie* (Madag.)

B.N.C.M. Fr. *Bibliothèque Nationale du Conservatoire de Musique*, Nat. Library of Music, Paris

B.N.C.S. British National Carnation Society

B.N.C.S.A.A. British National Committee on Surface Active Agents

B.N.C.S.R. British National Committee for Scientific Radio/on Space Research

B/ND binding, no date given (pub.)

B.N.D.D. Bureau of Narcotics and Dangerous Drugs (U.S.A.)

Bndr. S. L. Bandmaster Sub-Lieutenant

BNEC British National Export Council

B.N.E.C. British Nuclear Energy Conference

B.N.E.S. British Nuclear Energy Society

BNF Botswana National Front; Braniff International Airways

B.N.F. British National Formulary

B.N.F.C. British National Film Catalogue

BNFL British Nuclear Fuels Limited

B.N.F.M.F. British Non-Ferrous Metals Federation

B.N.F.M.R.A. British Non-Ferrous Metals Research Association

B.N.F.S.A. British Non-Ferrous Smelters' Association

B.N.G.A. British Nursery Goods Association

B.N.G.M. British Naval Gunnery Mission

BNHQ battalion headquarters

Bnkg. banking

BNL It. *Banca Nazionale del Lavoro* (Italy)

BNM Fr. *Banque Nationale Malagasy de Développement*, Madagascar

B.N.O.C. British National Opera Company

BNP Fr. *Banque Nationale de Paris*; Barbados National Party; Basutoland National Party (Lesotho)

B.N.S. Bachelor of Natural Science; Bathymetric Navigation System; British Numismatic Society; British Nylon Spinners

B.N.Sc. Bachelor of Nursing Science

Bnst. *bassoonist* (mus.)

BNX British Nuclear Export Executive

bnzn. benzoin

BO s Borrowstounness, Bo'ness (B.F.P.); s Cardiff (B.V.R.)

b/o. back order; brought over

b.o. blackout; body odour; bowels open; box office; branch office; broker's order; buyer's option

B.O. Bachelor of Oratory

B.O.A. British Olympic/Optical/Orthopaedic/Osteopathic Association

B.O.A.C. British Overseas Airways Corporation

BOADICEA British Overseas Airways Corporation digital information computer for electronic automation

B.O.A.(Disp.) British Optical Association, Dispensing Certificate

B.O.A.F.G. British Order of Ancient Free Gardeners

Bob, Bobbie, Bobby Robert

B.O.B.A. British Overseas Banks' Association

B.O.B.M.A. British Oil Burner Manufacturers' Association

B.O.C. British Oxygen Company; Burmah Oil Company

B. Occup. Thy. Bachelor of Occupational Therapy

B.O.C.E. Board of Customs and Excise

BOCI Sp. *Bloque de Obreros, Campesinos e Intelectuales*, Bloc of Workers, Peasants and Intellectuals (Costa Rica)

50

B.O.C.M. British Oil and Cake Mills Limited

bod Sp. *bodega*, wine cellar; body, service slang for a person

Bod., Bodl., Bodley Bodleian Library, Oxford

B.O.D. biochemical oxygen demand of effluent in sewage treatment

B.O.E. Board of Education

B.O.F. British Orienteering Federation, formed 1967; British Overseas Fairs

B. of E. Bank of England

B. of H. Band of Hope Union

Boh. Bohemia; Bohemian

B.O.H.S. British Occupational Hygiene Society

bol. L. *bolus*, large pill (med.)

Bol. Bolivar; Bolivia; Bolivian

B.O.L. Bachelor of Oriental Learning

bolshie bolshevik

Bom. Bombay, India

Bomb. bombardier

Bomb. C. S. Bombay Civil Service

Bomb. S. C. Bombay Staff Corps

BOMEX Barbados Oceanographic and Meteorological Experiment

bon. Fr. *bataillon*, battalion

B.O.N. acid beta-oxynaphthoic acid

Boney Napoleon Bonaparte

Bop Bebop, a kind of syncopated music

B.O.P. *Boy's Own Paper*

B. Optom. Bachelor of Optometry

B.O.P.W. Bristol Old People's Welfare

BOQ bachelor/base officers' quarters

Bor., Boro. Borough

B. Or. Bachelor of Orientation

B.O.R.A.D. British Oxygen Research and Development Association

bos'n. boatswain

Bos. Pops. Boston Pops Orchestra (U.S.A.)

BOSS Bio-astronautic Orbiting Space Station

B.O.S.S. Bureau of State Security (S.Afr.)

BoT, B. of T., BOT Board of Trade, first Committee of Privy Council established to deal with trade problems set up 1621. BoT was reconstituted 1786 and was charged with 'consideration of all matters relating to trade and foreign plantations'

bot. botanic; botanical; botanist; botany; bottle; bottom; bought

B.O.T. Bachelor of Occupational Therapy

B.O.T.A.C. Board of Trade Advisory Committee

B.O.T.U. Board of Trade Unit

B.O.U. British Ornithologists' Union

boul. boulevard

Boulmich Boulevard St. Michel (Paris)

B.O.V. brown oil of vitriol, commercial sulphuric acid of approx. 78% strength

B.O.W.O. brigade ordnance warrant officer

BP *Boerenpartij*, Farmers' Party (Neth.); *s* Sussex, West (B.V.R.)

B/P bills payable

bp. baptized; birthplace; bishop

b/p. blueprint

b.p. below proof; bill of parcels; blood pressure (med.); boiling point

b.p. L. *bonum publicum*, the public good

B.P. Bachelor of Painting/Pharmacy /Philosophy; back projection; Robert Baden-Powell (1857–1941), founder of Scout and Guide movement (*also* B.-P.); beach party (mil.); behaviour pattern; between perpendiculars; Borough Polytechnic, Lond.; British Patent; British Petroleum; British Pharmacopoeia; British Public

B.-P. *Basses-Pyrénées* (France)

B.P.A. Ger. *Bahnpostamt*, railway post office; *Banco Português do Atlântico*, Portuguese Atl. Bank; Bicycle Polo Association; Biological Photographic Association (U.S.A.); Bookmakers' Protection Association; British Paediatric/ Philatelic/Ploughing Association; Business Publications Audit of Circulation (U.S.A.)

B.P.A.A. British Poster Advertising Association

B. Paed. Bachelor of Paediatrics

B.P.A.G.B. Bicycle Polo Association of Great Britain

b.p.b. bank post bills

B.P.B.F. British Paper Box Federation

B.P.B.I.R.A. British Paper and Board Industry Research Association

B.P.B.M.A. British Paper and Board Makers' Association

B.P.C. Book Prices Current; British Pharmaceutical Codex; British Pharmacopoeia Commission; British Printing Corporation; British Productivity Council; Business and Professional Code (U.S.A.)

b.p.c.d. barrels per calendar day (U.S.A.)

B.P.C.F. British Precast Concrete Federation

BPCR Brakes on Pedal Cycle Regulations

B.P.C.R.A. British Professional Cycle Racing Association

b.p.d. barrels per day (U.S.A.)

B. Pd. Bachelor of Pedagogy, *also* B. Pe., B. Ped.

B.P.D. Boots Pure Drug Company

B.P.E. Bachelor of Physical Education, *also* B. P. Ed.

b.p.f. Fr. *bon pour francs*, value in francs

B.P.F. Fr. *Bachelière en pédagogie familiale*, Bachelor of Family Pedagogy; bottom pressure fluctuation; British Plastics Federation; British Polio Fellowship

B.Ph. Bachelor of Philosophy

B.Pharm. Bachelor of Pharmacy

B.P.H.E. Bachelor of Physical and Health Education

B. Phil. Bachelor of Philosophy

B.Phys.Ed. Bachelor of Physical Education

B.Phys.Thy. Bachelor of Physical Therapy

bpi bits per inch (computer)

B.P.I. Booksellers' Provident Institution; British Pacific Islands

B.P.I.C.A. Fr. *Bureau permanent international des constructeurs d'automobiles*, Intern. Permanent Bureau of Motor Manufacturers

bpl., b.pl. birthplace

Bpl. Barnstaple

b.p.m. barrels per minute (U.S.A.)

B.P.M.A. British Pump Manufacturers' Association

B.P.M.F. British Pottery Manufacturers' Federation

B.P.M.S. blood pressure measuring system

B.P.N.M.A. British Plain Net Manufacturers' Association

B.P.O. base post office; Berlin Philharmonic Orchestra

B.P.O.E. Benevolent and Protective Order of Elks (U.S.A.)

B.P.P. Bechuanaland, *now* Botswana, People's Party

B.P.P.M.A. British Power-Press Manufacturers' Association

B.P.R.A. Book Publishers' Representatives' Association

BPRO Blind Persons Resettlement Officer

B. Ps. Bachelor in Psychology

B.P.S. border patrol sector/station; British Pharmacological / Phrenological Society

b.p.s.d. barrels per steam day (U.S.A.)

B. Ps. S. British Psychological Society

Bp. Suff. Bishop Suffragan

B. Psych. Bachelor of Psychology

b. pt. boiling point

B.P.T. Bachelor of Physiotherapy;

battle practice target; British Petroleum Tanker

B-Pyr. *Basses-Pyrénées* (France)

bq., bque. barque

B.Q. L. *Bene quiescat*, may he/she repose well

B.Q.M.S. battery quartermaster-sergeant

Br *s* bromine (chem.)

BR Block release; *s* Brazil (I.V.R.); *s* Bridgwater (B.F.P.); *s* Sunderland (B.V.R.)

B/R bills receivable; Bordeaux or Rouen (grain trade); builders' risks

br. bearing; bombardier; branch; bridge; brief; brig; bronze; brother; brown; bugler

Br. Brazil; Brazzaville (Congo); Breton; Britain; British

Br. Ger. *Bratsche*, viola (mus.)

b.r. bank rate; bills receivable; block release; breeder reactor

B.R. book of reference; British Rail, *formerly* British Railways; (poly)butadiene rubber

B.R. L. *Bancus Reginae*, Queen's Bench (leg.); L. *Bancus Regis*, King's Bench (leg.)

bra brassière

B.R.A. Beef Recording Association; Bee Research Association; Brigadier Royal Artillery; British Radiesthesia/Records/Refrigeration/Rheumatism and Arthritis Association

Bra. Cur. Brazil current

Brad. Bradford

Br. Am. British America

BRAS ballistic rocket air suppression

Braz., Bras. Brazil; Brazilian

Brazza. Brazzaville, Congo

B.R.B. British Rail Board

Br. C. British Columbia

B.R.C. base residence course (U.S.A.); Biological Records Centre, Nature Conservancy; British Rabbits Council; British Radio Corporation; Brotherhood of Railway Car Men (U.S.A.)

Brch. branch

B.R.C.M.A. British Radio Cabinet Manufacturers' Association

B.R.C.S. British Rail Catering Service; British Red Cross Society, formed 1870 as National Society for Aid to the Sick and Wounded in War

BRD *s* Broadford (B.F.P.)

B.R.D. Building Research Division, National Bureau of Standards (U.S.A.); *Bundesrepublik Deutschland*, German Federal Rep.

B.R.D.C. British Racing Drivers' Club

brdcst. broadcast

B.R.E. Bachelor of Religious Education

Brec. Brecknockshire; Brecon

b. rec. bills receivable

B.R.E.M.A. British Radio Equipment Manufacturers' Association

Br'er brother

Bret. Breton

brev. brevet; Fr. *breveté*, patent; It. *brevetto*, patent

brew. brewer; brewery; brewing

brf. brief (leg.)

B.R.F. Bible Reading Fellowship; British Road Federation

BRFC British Record (rod-caught) Fish Committee (angling)

BRG *s* Guyana, *formerly* British Guiana (I.V.R.)

brg. bearing

br. g. brown gelding (horse-racing)

Br. Gu., Br. G. British Guiana, *now* Guyana

Br. Hond., Br. Hon. British Honduras

Br. I. British India; British Isles

B.R.I. Fr. *Banque des règlements internationaux*, Bank for Intern. Settlements; Biological/Brain Research Institute (U.S.A.)

Brig. brigade; brigadier

Brig.-Gen. brigadier-general

Brill. It. *brillante*, brilliant (mus.)

BRIMAFEX British Manufacturers of Malleable Tube Fittings Export Group

BRIMEC British Mechanical Engineering Confederation

BRINCO British Newfoundland Corporation Limited

Brisb. Brisbane

Brist. Bristol

Brit. Britain; Britannia; Britica; Briticus; British; Briton; — **I.R.E.** British Institution of Radio Engineers, *now* I.E.R.E.; — **Mus.** British Museum; — **N. Amer.** British North America; — **Pat.** British patent

Britt. Britanniarum (numis.)

Britt. L. *Britannorum*, of the Britons

brk. brick

brkt. bracket

brkwtr. breakwater

BRL Ballistic Research Laboratory; Bible Research Library (U.S.A.)

brl. barrel

B.R.M. British Racing Motors

B.R.M.A. Board of Registration of Medical Auxiliaries; British Rubber Manufacturers' Association

B.R.M.C.A. British Ready Mixed Concrete Association

B.R.M.F. British Rainwear Manufacturers' Federation

BRN *s* Bahrain (I.V.R.); Bulgarian River Navigation

brn. brown

brng. bearing (nav.); burning

Bro. brother; brotherhood

B.R.O. brigade routine order

BROILER, Broiler Biopedagogical Research Organization on Intensive Learning Environment Reactions

Brom. bromide

bros. brothers

brosch. Ger. *broschiert*, stitched

brot. brought

B.R.S. British Record Society; British Road Services; Brotherhood of Railway Signalmen (U.S.A.); Building Research Station

B.R.S.A. British Rail Staff Association

B.R.S.C.C. British Racing and Sports Car Club

BRT Ger. *Brutto - Register - Tonnen*, gross register tons

brt. bright

Br. T. British Time

B.R.T.A. British Racing Toboggan Association; British Regional Television Association; British Road Tar Association

BRU *s* Brunei (I.V.R.)

Brum. Birmingham

brunch *br*eakfast/l*unch*eon

Brunsw. Brunswick

B. Rur. Sc. Bachelor of Rural Science

Brute British Universal Trolley Equipment

Brux. *Bruxelles*, Brussels

B.R.V.M.A. British Radio Valve Manufacturers' Association, *also* B.V.A.

B.R.W. British Relay Wireless

bry., bryol. bryology

brz. bronze

BS *s* Bahamas (I.V.R.); *s* Beaumaris (B.F.P.); breaking strain of line (angling); *s* Orkney (B.V.R.)

B/S balance sheet; bill of sale

bs. bags; bales

B$. *bolivar*, mon. unit of Venezuela; *bolivianos*, mon. unit of Bolivia

b.s. back stage; balance sheet (*also* B/S); bill of sale, *also* B/S

b. & s. brandy and soda

B.S. Bachelor of Science/Surgery; battleship/squadron; below specification; sub-standard; Bibliographical Society; bill of sale; Biochemical/Biometric Society; Biological Society (U.S.A.); Blackfriars Settlement; Blessed Sacrament; boiler survey; Boy Scouts; Bristol Siddeley; British Standard; Budgerigar/Building Society

B.S.A. Bachelor of Secretarial Arts; Bachelor of Science in Agriculture; Bibliographical Society of America; Birmingham Small Arms; Botanical Society of America; bovine serum albumin; Boy Scouts' Association; Boy Scouts of America; British School at Athens; British Shipbreakers' Association; British Society of Aesthetics; British South Africa; British Speleological Association; Building Societies' Association; Ger. *Bund Schweizer Architekten*, Fed. of Swiss Architects

B.S.A.A. British School of Archaeology at Athens; British South American Airways Corporation, *now* part of B.O.A.C.

B.S.A.C. British Sub-Aqua Club

B.S.A.F. British Sulphate of Ammonia Federation

B.S.A.M. Bachelor in Suddha Ayurvedic Medicine

B.S.A.P. British Society of Animal Production; British South Africa Police

B.S.A.S. British Ship Adoption Society

BSAVA British Small Animals Veterinary Association

Bsb. Brisbane

B.S.B. British Standard Beam

B.S.B.A. British Starter Battery Association

B.S.B.C. British Social Biology Council

B.S.B.I. Botanical Society of the British Isles

BSBSPA British Sugar Beet Seed Producers' Association

bsc. basic

B. Sc. Bachelor of Science; — **(Acc.)** Bachelor of Science in Accounting; — **(Ag.), (Agri.), (Agric.)** Bachelor of Science in Agriculture; — **(Ag. & A.H.)** Bachelor of Science in Agriculture and Animal Husbandry; — **(Ag. E.), (Ag. Eng.)** Bachelor of Science in Agricultural Engineering; — **(Ag. Econ.)** Bachelor of Science in Agricultural Economics; — **(Ag. Eng. & Tech.)** Bachelor of Science in Agricultural Engineering and Technology; — **(Agric. Biol.)** Bachelor of Science in Agricultural Biology; — **(Arch.)** Bachelor of Science in Architecture; — **(Bus.)** Bachelor of Science in Business Administration; — **(C.E.)** Bachelor of Science in Civil Engineering; — **(Chem. Eng.)** Bachelor of Science in Chemical Engineering; — **(D.), (Dent.)** Bachelor of Science in Dentistry; — **(Dom. Sc.)** Bachelor of Science in Domestic Science; — **(Econ.)** Bachelor of Science in Economics; — **(Ed.)** Bachelor of Science in Education; — **Ed. Inf.** *Bachelière en sciences de l'éducation des infirmières*, Bachelor of Science in Nursing Education; — **(E.E.), (Elec. Eng.)** Bache-

lor of Science in Electrical Engineering; — **El. Ed.** Bachelor of Science in Elementary Education; — **(Eng.), (Engg.), (Engin.)** Bachelor of Science in Engineering; — **(Est. Man.)** Bachelor of Science in Estate Management; — **(F.), (For.)** Bachelor of Science in Forestry; — **(Fam.)** *Bachelier ès sciences familiales*, Bachelor of Science in Home Economics; — **(Fisheries)** Bachelor of Science in Fisheries; — **(Food Scis.)** Bachelor of Science in Food Sciences; — **(Gen. Sc.)** Bachelor of Science in General Science; — **(H. Ec.), (Home Econ.)** Bachelor of Science in Home Economics; — **(Hort.)** Bachelor of Science in Horticulture; — **(Hosp.)** *Bachelier en sciences hospitalières*, Bachelor of Nursing; — **(H. Sci.), (Home Sci.)** Bachelor of Science in Home Science; — **(L.A.)** Bachelor of Science (Laboratory Assistant); — **(M.E.), (Mech. Engg.)** Bachelor of Science in Mechanical Engineering; — **(Med.)** Bachelor of Science in Medicine; — **(Med. Lab. Tech.)** Bachelor of Science in Medical Laboratory Technology; — **(Med. Sci.)** Bachelor of Science in Medical Sciences; — **(Met.)** Bachelor of Science in Metallurgy; — **(Min.)** Bachelor of Science in Mining; — **(M.L.S.)** Bachelor of Science in Medical Laboratory Science; — **(M.R.)** Bachelor of Science in Medical Rehabilitation; — **(N.)** Bachelor of Science in Nursing; — **(Nutr.)** Bachelor of Science in Nutrition; — **(O.T.)** Bachelor of Science in Occupational Therapy; — **(P. and O.T.)** Bachelor of Science in Physical and Occupational Therapy; — **(P.E.), (P. Ed.)** Bachelor of Science in Physical Education; — **(Pharm.)** Bachelor of Science in Pharmacy; — **(Pol.)** Bachelor of Science in Political Science; — **(Q.S.)** Bachelor of Science in Quantity Surveying; — **Rel.** *Bachelier en sciences religieuses*, Bachelor of Religious Science; — **(R.S.)** Bachelor of Science in Rural Science; — **(R.T.)** Bachelor of Science in Radiologic Technology; — **(Soc.)** Bachelor of Science in Social Science(s)/Sociology; — **(S.P.)** *Bachelier ès sciences sociales et politiques*, Bachelor of Social and Political Science; — **S.S.** Bachelor of Science in Secretarial Studies; — **(Sur.)** Bachelor of Science in Land Surveying; — **(T.E.)** Bachelor of Science in Textile Engineering; — **(Tech.)** Bachelor of Technical Science /Technology; — **(Text.)** Bachelor of Science in Textiles; — **(Vet.)** Bachelor of Science in Veterinary Science; — **(Vet. Sc. & A.H.)** Bachelor of Science in Veterinary Science and Animal Husbandry

B.S.C. Bengal Staff Corps; Bethlehem Steel Corporation; Bibliographical Society of Canada; Biological Stain Commission (U.S.A.); Biomedical Sciences Corporation; British Safety Council; British Shoe Corporation; British Society of Cinematographers/Commerce; British Standard Channel; British Stationery Council; British Steel/Sugar Corporation; British Supply Council

B.S.C.A. British Sulphate of Copper Association; British Swimming Coaches' Association; Bureau of Security and Consular Affairs (U.S.A.)

B.Sc. App. Bachelor of Applied Science

BSCC British Society for Clinical Cytology; British Synchronous Clock Conference

BSCP *British Standard Code of Practice*, published by B.S.I.

B.S.C.R.A. British Steel Castings Research Association

bsd barrels per steam day (U.S.A.)

BSD ballistic system division

B.S.D. British Society of Dowsers; British Space Development

B.S.D.A. British Spinners' and Doublers' Association

b.s.d.l. boresight datum line

bse base support equipment

B.S.E. Bachelor of Sanitary Engineers; Bachelor of Science Education; Bachelor of Science in Education; Bachelor of Science in Engineering

B. S. Ed. Bachelor of Science in Education

B. Serv. Soc. Fr. *Bachelier en service social*, Bachelor of Social Service

B.S.E.S. British Schools Exploring Society, founded by Surg.-Cdr. Murray Levick (1932). Ann. expeditions have been made to Arctic Norway, Labrador, N. Quebec and Iceland

B.S.F. Bachelor of Science in Forestry; blade slap factor; British Salonica Force; British Slag Federation; British Standard Fine; British Stone Federation

B.S.F.A. British Sanitary Fireclay Association; British Steel Founders' Association

b.s.f.c. brake specific fuel consumption

B.S.F.(L.) British Shipping Federation (Limited)

B.S.F.S. Bachelor of Science in Foreign Service; British Soviet Friendship Society

B.S.G. British Standard Gauge

b.s.g.d.g. Fr. *breveté sans garantie du gouvernement*, patented without government guarantee

bsh. bushel

B.S.H. British Society of Hypnotherapists; British Standard Hardness

B.S.H.Ec. Bachelor of Science in Home Economics

B.S.H.S. British Society for the History of Science

B.S.I. British Sailors' Institute; British Standards Institution; Building Societies' Institute

B.S.I.A. Better Speech Institute of America

B.S.I.B. Boy Scouts International Bureau; British Society for International Bibliography, *now* A.S.L.I.B.

B.S.I.C. British Ski Instruction Council responsible for co-ordination of standards of ski instruction

B.S.I.P. British Solomon Islands Protectorate

B.S.I.R.A. British Scientific Instrument Research Association

B.S.I.U. British Society for International Understanding

B.S.J.A. British Show Jumping Association

bsk., bskt. basket

B.S.L. Blue Star Line (ship.); boatswain sub-lieutenant; Botanical Society of London

B. S. Litt. Bachelor of Sacred Letters

B.S.L.S. Bachelor of Science in Library Science/Library Service

B.S.M. battery sergeant-major; branch sales manager; bronze star medal (U.S.A.)

B.S.M.A. British Skate Makers' Association

B.S.M.G.P. British Society of Master Glass-Painters

bsmt. basement

bsn. *bassoon* (mus.)

B.S.N. Bachelor of Science in Nursing

B.S.O. base supply officer; Boston/Bournemouth Symphony Orchestra; Business Statistics Office estab. 1969 by BoT Census Office

B. Soc. Sc. Bachelor of Social Science; — St. Bachelor of Social Studies; — Wk. Bachelor of Social Work

B.S.P. Bachelor of Science in Pharmacy; Bering Sea Patrol; Birmingham School of Printing; bleached sulphite pulp (paper); British Standard pipe-thread; Fr. *Bureau sanitaire panaméricain*, Pan-American Sanitary Bureau

B.S.P.A. Basic Slag Producers' Association

BSPP Burmese Socialist Program Party (Burma)

B. Sp. Thy. Bachelor of Speech Therapy

B.S.R. Bachelor of Science in Rehabilitation; Birmingham Sound Reproducers; British School at Rome; British Society of Rheology

B.S.R.A. British Ship Research Association; British Society for Research on Ageing; British Sound Recording Association

B.S.R.A.E. British Society for Research in Agricultural Engineering

B.S.R.C. Biological Serial Record Center (U.S.A.)

b.s.r.f. brain stem reticular formation

B.S.S. Bachelor of Sanitary Science/ of Science in Science/of Secretarial Science/of Social Sciences; Fr. *Bibliothèque Saint-Sulpice*, Montreal (Can.); British Sailors' Society; British Standard Sizes/Specification

b. ssa It. *baronessa*, baroness

B.S.S.A. Bachelor of Science in Secretarial Administration

B. S. Sc. Bachelor of Sanitary/Social Science

B.S.S.G. Biomedical Sciences Support Grant (U.S.A.)

B.S.S.O. British Society for the Study of Orthodontics

B.S.S.S. British Society of Soil Science

B/St. bill of sight

B.S.T. Bachelor of Sacred Theology; British Standard/Summer Time

B.S.T.A. British Surgical Trades' Association

BSTC British Student Travel Centre

bstd. bastard

bstr. booster; — **rkt.** booster rocket

B. Surv. Bachelor of Surveying

b.s.w. barrels of salt water

B.S.W. Bachelor of Social Work; British Standard Whitworth (engn.)

B.S. & W. basic sediment and water; bottom settling and water

B.S.W.B. Boy Scouts World Bureau

B.S.W.E. British Scouts in Western Europe

B.S.W.I.A. British Steel Wire Industries' Association

BT *s* Yorkshire, E. Riding (B.V.R.)

bt. bathythermograph; beat; benefit; bent; bought

Bt. baronet, *also* **Bart.**; brevet

B.T. Bachelor of Teaching/Theology; basic trainer; bishop's transcript

B.T.A. Billiards Trade Association; Blood Transfusion Association (U.S.A.); British Tourist Authority; British Travel Association; British Troops in Austria; Bulgarian Telegraph Agency

B.T.A.S.A. Book Trade Association of South Africa

Btb. *bass tuba* (mus.)

B.T.B.A. British Ten Pin Bowling Association

B.T.B.S. Book/Boot Trade Benevolent Society

B.T.C. Bachelor of Textile Chemistry; Bankers' Trust Company (U.S.A.); basic training center (U.S.A.); Bethlehem Transportation Company (U.S.A.); Bicycle Touring Club, founded 1878, since 1883 known as C.T.C.; British Textile Confederation; British Transport Commission

btca. Sp. *biblioteca*, library

B.T.C.C. Board of Transportation Commissioners of Canada

B.T.C.P. Bachelor of Town and Country Planning

BTCV British Trust for Conservation Volunteers

b.t.d. bomb testing device

B.T.D.B. Bermuda Trade Development Board; British Transport Docks Board

b.t.d.c. before top dead centre

bté. Fr. *breveté*, patent

B.T.E. British troops in Egypt

B. Tech. Bachelor in Technology; — **Ed.** Bachelor of Technical Education / of Technology in Education; — **(Food)** Bachelor of Food Technology

B.T.E.F. Book Trade Employers' Federation

B. Tel. E. Bachelor of Telecommunication Engineering

B.T.E.M.A. British Tanning Extract Manufacturers' Association

B. Text. Bachelor of Textiles; — **(Eng.)** Bachelor of Textile Engineering; — **(Tech.)** Bachelor of Textile Technology

b.t.f. barrels of total fuel; bomb tail fuse

B.T.F. British Tarpaviors'/Trawlers /Turkey/Federation

bth. bath; bathroom; berth

B. Th. Bachelor of Theology

B.T.H. British Thomson-Houston Company

B.T.H.A. British Travel and Holidays Association, *now* B.T.A.

B. Th. U. British thermal unit

B.T.I. *British Technology Index*

B.T.I.A. British Tar Industries' Association

btk. buttock

btl. bottle

BTM bromotrifluoromethane, used for fire fighting

b.t.m. bottom

B.T.M.A. British Toy/Typewriter Manufacturers' Association

btn. baton; button

B.T.N. Brussels Tariff Nomenclature

B.T.O. big time operator; British Trust for Ornithology

B.T.P. Bachelor of Town Planning

B.T.R. *British Tax Review*; British Telecommunications Research

B.T.R.A. Bombay Textile Industry's Research Association

B.T.R.P. Bachelor of Town and Regional Planning

btry. battery

B.T.S. Blood Transfusion Service

Btu, BTU, B.t.u., B.T.U. Board of Trade unit; British thermal unit, the quantity of heat required to raise the temperature of 1 lb. of water through 1°F. (elec.)

B.T.U.C. Bahamas Trade Union Congress

btwn. between

B.T.X. benzene, toluene and xylene (chem.)

bty. battery

B-type Basedow type (psy.)

BU *s* Burntisland (B.F.P.); *s* Oldham (B.V.R.)

bu. base unit; bureau; bushel

B.U. Baptist Union of Great Britain and Ireland; Brown University, Rhode Island (U.S.A.)

B.U.A. British United Airways

BuAer Bureau of Aeronautics (USN)

B.U.A.F. British United Air Ferries

B.U.A. of E. Badminton Umpires' Association of England

B.U.A.V. British Union for the Abolition of Vivisection

BUC Bangor University College (Wales)

buck. buckram

Buck House Buckingham Palace, London home of the Brit. monarch

Bucks. Buckinghamshire

B.U.C.O.P. *British Union Catalogue of Periodicals*

bud. budget

Budd., Bud. Buddhism; Buddhist

BuDocks Bureau of Yards and Docks (USN)

Budpst. Budapest

bue built up edges

B.U.F. British Union of Fascists

Bug. Bugatti

BUIC back-up Interceptor Control

B.U.J. L. *Baccalaureus utriusque juris*, Bachelor of Canon and Civil Law

bul., bull. bulletin

Bulg. Bulgaria; Bulgarian

bull. L. *bulla*, lead seal used on papal documents; L. *bulliat*, let it boil (med.)

buloga business logistics game

B.U.L.V.A. Belfast and Ulster Licensed Vintners' Association

BuMed Bureau of Medicine and Surgery (USN)

B.U.M.S., B.U.M. & S. Bachelor of Unani Medicine and Surgery

buna butadiene+natrium, kind of synthetic rubber

BUNAC British Universities North America Club, organizing student reduced fare travel to and from U.S.A. and internally in U.S.A., also helps provide employment and visas

Bunty Barbara

BuOrd Bureau of Ordnance (USN)

B.U.P. British United Press

B.U.P.A. British United Provident Association

BuPers Bureau of Naval Personnel (USN)

Bu. Pub. Aff. Bureau of Public Affairs (U.S.A.)

BUR *s* Burma (I.V.R.)

bur. bureau; buried

Bur., Burm. Burma; Burmese

BuRec Bureau of Reclamation (U.S.A.)

burg. burgess; burgomaster

burger hamburger

burl. burlesque

Burs. Bursar

bus. bushel (*also* bush.); business

BuSandA Bureau of Supply and Accounts (USN)

B.U.S.F. British Universities' Sports Federation

BuShips Bureau of Ships (USN)

Bus. Mgr. business manager

but butter; button

BuWeps Bureau of Naval Weapons (USN), *now* NOSC

buy buyer; buying

BV *s* BEA Helicopters Limited; *s* Blackburn (B.V.R.)

b.v. balanced voltage; book value; break-up (fin.); Dutch *bij voorbeeld*, for example

b.v. L. *bene vale*, farewell

B.V. Bible Version, of Psalms; blood volume; Port. *Bombeiros Voluntarios*, Voluntary Firefighting Service

B.V. L. *Beata Virgo*, Blessed Virgin; L. *Beatitudo Vestra*, Your Holiness

B.V.A. British Radio Valve Manufacturers' Association; British Veterinary /Vigilance Association

B. Vet. Med., B.V.M. Bachelor of Veterinary Medicine

B. Vet. Sc., B.V.Sc. Bachelor of Veterinary Science

B.V.H. British Van Heusen Corporation

B.V.I. British Virgin Islands

B.V.J. *British Veterinary Journal*

B.V.K. *Bundesverdienstkreuz*, Federal Cross of Merit, West Germany

B.V.M. L. *Beata Virgo Maria*, Blessed Virgin Mary

B.V.M.A. British Valve Manufacturers' Association

B.V.M.S., B.V.M. & S. Bachelor of Veterinary Medicine and Surgery

B.V.O. *Bundesverdienstorden*, Federal Order of Merit, West Germany

B.V.P. British Volunteer Programme

B.V.S. Bachelor of Veterinary Surgery

B.V.Sc. & A.H. Bachelor of Veterinary Science and Animal Husbandry

bvt. brevet

BW *s* Barrow (B.F.P.); *s* Oxfordshire (B.V.R.)

B/W black and white; black to white

B & W Babcock & Wilcox; black & white

b.w. biological warfare; Ger. *bitte wenden*, please turn over; bridleways

B.W. Bath and Wells, episcopal see; Black Watch; Board of Works; bonded warehouse; Borg-Warner; British Waterways; Business Week

B.W.A. backward wave amplifier; Baptist World Alliance; British Waterworks Association; British West Africa

B-way Broadway, N.Y. (U.S.A.)

B.W.B. British Waterways Board

B.W.C. British War Cabinet

B.W.C.C. British Weed Control Conference

b.w.-c.w. biological warfare-chemical warfare

bwd. backward

b.w.d. bacillary white diarrhoea; barrels of water per day

B. & W.E. Bristol and West of England

B.W.F. British Whiting/Wool Federation

B.W.G., B.w.g. Birmingham wire gauge

B.W.I. British West Indies; British Workmen's Institute

B.W.I.A. British West Indian Airways

B.W.I.R. British West India Regiment

B.W.I.S.A. British West Indies Sugar Association

bwk. brickwork; bulwark

B.W.M. British War Medal

B.W.M.A. British Woodwork Manufacturers' Association

B.W.M.B. British Wool Marketing Board

B.W.O. backward wave oscillator

B.W.P. basic war plan

B.W.P.A. backward wave power amplifier; British Waste Paper Association; British Word Preserving Association

b.w.p.d. barrels of water per day

b.w.p.h. barrels of water per hour

B.W.P.U.C. British Wastepaper Utilisation Council

b.w.r., B.W.R. boiling water reactor

B.W.R.A. British Welding Research Association, *now* part of Welding Institute

B.W.S. British Water-colour Society

B.W.S.F. British Water Ski Federation

B.W.T.A. British Women's Temperance Association

bw-tv black and white television

BWU Barbados Workers' Union

bwv back water valve

B.W.V.A. British War Veterans of America

B.W.W.A. British Waterworks Association

BX *s* Carmarthenshire (B.V.R.)

bx. box

Bx. Beatrix

B.X. Base Exchange (USAF); British Xylonite

b—y bloody

BY *s* London (B.V.R.)

By. Barony

B.Y. brilliant yellow, test paper for detecting alkalinity

Bye. Byelorussia; Byelorrussian

Byo. Bulawayo

b.y.o.b. bring your own beer

b.y.o.g. bring your own girl

B.Y.T. bright young things

Byz. Byzantine

Bz Benzene (chem.)

BZ *s* Down (B.V.R.); British Zone

BZ. B'nai Zion; Brazil; Brazilian

bzw. Ger. *beziehungsweise*, respectively

C

c   _s_ candle (phys.); _s_ constant (math.); _s_ generally cloudy (met.); _s_ velocity of light _in vacuo_

c/   Port. _com_, with

c/-   case; coupon; currency

C   _s_ capacitance (elec.); _s_ carbon (chem.); Command paper; — **(1st series)** Command paper, 1833–68/69; — **(2nd series)** Command paper, 1870–99 (published by H.M.S.O.); _s_ Cork (Rep. of Ireland F.P.); _s_ Cuba (I.V.R.); _s_ heat capacity per mole; one hundred (Roman); _s_ shear modulus (engn.); _s_ Yorkshire, West Riding (B.V.R.)

C3   of low physical standard (A1, high)

C4   crown quarto, 7½ in. by 10 in. (paper)

C8   crown octavo, 5 in. by 7½ in. (paper)

C-   Cargo transport, followed by a number to designate model of U.S. Army airplane designed to carry cargo or troops

C°   degree Celsius/Centigrade

©   Copyright. _s_ indicating protection in all countries subscribing to Universal Copyright Convention, 1952, must appear in books claiming protection in U.S.A. on reverse of title-page. Introduced in U.K. 1957

Ɔ   500 (Roman)

₡   _colón_, _colónes_, currency of Costa Rica and El Salvador

C   L. _congius_, gallon (phar.); _quadruple_ (4-4), _or common time_ (mus.)

c.   capacity; cape; carat; carton; case; catcher (baseball); cathode; cattle; caught (cricket); cent; centavo; centigram; cen-

time; centimetre; central; centre; century; chairman; chairwoman; chapter; charge; chest; child; church; city; class; cloudy (naut.); club; cold; collected; colt (horse-racing); compound; conductor; constable; consul; contrast; convection; copy; copyright; corps; coupon; court; cousin; creation; crowned; cubic; cup; currency; current (elec.); cycle

c.   L. _caput_, chapter; L. _centum_, a hundred; L. _cibus_, meal; L. _circa_, about; L. _circiter_, approximately; L. _circum_, around; L. _contra_, against; L. _cum_, with

C.   Sp. _Caballeros_, gentlemen; Caesar; It. _caldo_, hot; Sp. _caliente_, hot; Sp. _calle_, street; calorie; calyx, the cup of a flower (bot.); candle; canon; canto (poetry); captain; cardinal; case, followed by numerals I to VII (tax.); catechism; catholic; Celtic; centigrade, having 100 degrees; chancellor; Chancery, Eng. court of equity, since 1875 a div. of the High Court of Justice; charge conjugation (phys.); Fr. _chaud_, hot; chief; Christ; Christian; circuit; Sp. _ciudad_, town; Colorado, indicating shade of wrapper (cigars); commander; commended; commodore; common metre (poetry); Companion, style of members of the lowest grade in certain Brit. Orders of Chivalry; computer; confessor; confidential; congregation; congregational; congress; conservative; contract; coulomb, unit of electric charge; council; count; county; coupon; cross; crown, applied to size of book; cruiser; curacy; curate

C.   _contralto_, lowest of female voices

(mus.); *counter-tenor*, male alto voice (mus.)

Ca *s* calcium (chem.)

CA, Ca., Calif. California (U.S.A.); *s* Cardigan (B.F.P.)

CA cellulose acetate; *s* Denbighshire (B.V.R.)

C/A, C.A. capital/credit/current account

C & A Clemens and August (Breeninkmeyer), brother-founders in the 1860s at Sneek, Neth. ,of the now intern. fashion house C & A

ca. cases (leg.); cathode; centiare

ca. L. *cirva*, about, also *c*

Ca. Canada; Canadian; It. *Compagnia*, company

Cª Port. *Companhia*, company; Sp. *Compañía*, company

C/ª. Sp. *cuenta abierta*, open account

c.a. capital asset; close annealed; Fr. *courant alternatif*, alternating current (elec.)

C.a. It. *Coll'arco*, with the bow (mus.)

C.A. Canadian army; capital allowances (tax.); Caterers' Association, formed in U.K., 1917; Catholic Association; Central America; certificate of airworthiness; Fr. *Chargé d'Affaires*; Chartered Accountant (Can.); Chartered Accountant (Member, Institute of C.A., Scot.); *Chemical Abstracts*; chief accountant; child allowance (tax.); chronological age, usually taken in months in calculating I.Q. (psy.); Church Army, mission of Church of England, estab. 1883 by Prebendary Wilson Carlile; Church Assembly; city architect/attorney; civil affairs/aviation; Classical Association; coast artillery; College of Arms; command accountant; commercial agent; community association; Companies Act; Confederate Army, formed in 1860 by S. States of America to fight Unionists of the N. (U.S.A.); Constituent Assembly; consular agent; Consumers' Association; controller of accounts; Fr. *Corps d'Armée*, Army Corps; Sp. *corriente alterna*, alternating current (elec.); county alderman/architect; Court of Appeal, branch, in civil div. of U.K. Supreme Court of Judicature and, in criminal div. of High Court of Justice, replacing (1968) the Court of Criminal Appeal; Croquet Association; Crown Agent; Cruising Association; current assets

CAA Community Action Agency (U.S.A.); County Agricultural Adviser

C.A.A. Canadian Authors' Association; Capital Allowances Act; Central African Airways Corporation; Chemists' Assistants' Association; Civil Aviation/Aeronautics Administration / Administrator / Authority; Cold Asphalt Association; Concert Artists' Association; Cost Accountants' Association; Cremation Association of America

C.A.A.A. Canadian Association of Advertising Agencies

C.A.A.B.U. Council for the Advancement of Arab-British Understanding

CAAC Civil Aviation Authority of China (Taiwan)

CAADRP civil aircraft airworthiness data recording programme

C.A.A.E. Canadian Association of Adult Education

C.A.A.E.O. Fr. *Commission des affaires d'Asie et d'Extrême-Orient de la chambre de commerce internationale*, Commission on Asian and Far Eastern Affairs of the Intern. Chamber of Commerce

CAAIS computer assisted action information systems

CAAR compressed air accumulator rocket

C.A.A.R.C. Commonwealth Advisory Aeronautical Research Council

C.A.A.S. Ceylon Association for the Advancement of Science

CAAT College of Applied Arts and Technology (Can.)

C. A. Att. Civil Air Attaché

C.A.A.V. Central Association of Agricultural Valuers

cab cabriolet, taxi (meter) cab

CAB cellulose acetate butyrate

cab. cabalistic; cabin; cabinet (*also* Cabt.); cable

C.A.B. Canadian Association of Broadcasters; captive air bubble; Citizens' Advice Bureau; Civil Aeronautics Board (U.S.A.); Commonwealth Agricultural Bureaux; Critical Air Blast, test for coke reactivity towards air

Cabal from Heb. *cabbala*, something conceived in secret. Term was applied to secret councillors of James I; fortuitous acronym of initials of intriguing ministers of Charles II, Clifford, Ashley, Buckingham, Arlington and Lauderdale forming the so-called Cabal Ministry of 1671

Cabal glasses glasses of the calcium oxide-boric oxide-alumina system

C.A.B.A.S. City and Borough Architects' Society

C.A.B.E.I. Cabei. Central American Bank for Economic Integration, Sp. *Banco Centroamericano de Integracion Economica*, *alt.* BCIE

C.A.B.M. Commonwealth of Australia Bureau of Meteorology

C.A.B.M.A. Canadian Association of British Manufacturers and Agencies

CABRA Copper and Brass Research Association (U.S.A.)

cabtmkr. cabinet maker

C.A.C. Canadian armoured corps; Central Advisory Committee; Colonial Advisory Council; Fr. *Comité administratif de co-ordination* (*des Nations Unies*), Admin. Co-ordination Committee (U.N.O.); Consumer Advisory Council (U.S.A.); Corrective Action Commission /Committee (U.S.A.); County Agricultural Committee

C.A.C.A. Canadian Agricultural Chemicals Association; Cement and Concrete Association; Central After-Care Association

C.A.C.C. Civil Aviation Communications Centre

CACD computer-aided circuit design

C.A.C.E. Central Advisory Council for Education

Cacex Port. *Carteira do Comercio Exterior, Banco do Brasil*

CACM Central American Common Market

C.A.C.T.M. Central Advisory Council of Training for the Ministry, *now* Central Advisory Council for the Ministry

CACUL Canadian Association of College and University Libraries

CAC&W Continental Aircraft Control and Warning

c-à-d Fr. *c'est-à-dire*, that is to say

cad. It. *cadauno*, each; cadet; cadger, *hence* derogatory noun

cad. It. *cadenza*, final flourish, orig. a cadence (mus.)

Cad. Cádiz (Sp.)

c.a.d. cash against disbursements/ documents; contract award date

C.A.D. civil air defense (U.S.A.); Fr. *Comité d'aide au développement*, development assistance committee; computer-aided design; crown agent's department

C.A.D.A. Fr. *Centre d'Analyse Documentaire pour l'Archéologie*, Document analysis centre, archaeology

cadav., cad. cadaver, dead/sickly looking (med.)

CADC central air data computer; colour analysis display computer

CADE computer assisted data evaluation

C.A.D.C. Commutated Antenna Direction Finder

CADIN continental air defense integration north (U.S.A.)

CADO central air documents office (USAF)

CADORIT Caribbean area division of ORIT

CADPO communications and data processing operation

C.A.E. Canadian Aviation Electronics; chartered automobile engineer; Sp. *Cóbrese al Entregar*, cash on delivery

C.A.E.A. Central American Economics Association

C.A.E.A.I. Chartered Auctioneers' and Estate Agents' Institute

C.A.E.C. County Agricultural Executive Committee

C.A.E.M. Fr. *Conseil d'assistance économique mutuelle*, Council for Mutual Economic Aid

Caern., Caerns. Caernarvonshire (Wales)

Caes. Caesar, Rom. cognomen

caf. café; cafeteria

C.A.F. cardiac assessment factor (med.); Central African Federation; Ceylon Air Force; charities aid fund; Clergy/ Curates' Augmentation Fund; clerical, administrative and fiscal; cost, assurance and freight; Fr. *Coût, Assurance, Fret*, cost, assurance, freight

C.A.F.E.A.-I.C.C. Commission on Asian and Far Eastern Affairs of the International Chamber of Commerce

C.A.F.I.C. Combined Allied Forces Information Centre

c.a.f.m. commercial air freight movement

C.A.F.M.N.A. Compound Animal Feedingstuffs Manufacturers' National Association

C. Afr. Fed. Central African Federation

CAFU civil aviation flying unit

CAG carrier air group (USN); civil air guard (U.S.A.)

C.A.G. Canadian Association of Geographers; Commercial Artists' Guild; Composers'-Authors' Guild; Concert Artists' Guild

CAGI Compressed Air and Gas Institute (U.S.A.); Consultative Association of Guyanese Industry

CAH cyanacetic hydrazide (chem.)

Cai. Caius (properly Gonville and Caius) College, Camb., founded 1348 by Edmund Gonville; royal charter obtained 1557 by John Caius

C.A.I. Canadian Aeronautical Institute; It. *Club Alpino Italiano*, Italian Alpine Club

C.A.I.B. Certified Associate of the Institute of Bankers

CAIRC Caribbean Air Command (USAF)

C.A.I.S.M. Central Association of Irish Schoolmistresses

Caith., Cai. Caithness (Scot.)

CAL Continental Airlines; Cornell (Univ.) Aeronautical Laboratory

cal. calendar; calibre; calorie, small heat unit

cal. It. *calando*, calming (mus.)

Cal. Calcutta; Caledonia; Calends; California; Calorie, large heat unit

C.A.L. conversational algebraic language

C.A.L.A. Civil Aviation (Licensing) Act

CALANS Caribbean and Latin American News Service

calc. calculate; calculus

Calc. Calcutta

Calç. Port. *Calçada*, street

CALCOFI California Co-operative Oceanic Fisheries Investigations (U.S.A.)

cald. calculated

Cald. Calderón de la Barca, Don Pedro (1600–81), Sp. poet and dramatist

C.A.L.E. Canadian Army Liaison Executive

Caled., Caley Caledonia(n) (Railway Co.)

calg. calculating

Calg. Calgary (Can.)

calibr. calibrate; calibration

Calif. California; — **cur.** California current

caln. calculation

calo. It. *calando*, gradually diminishing (mus.)

CALPA Canadian Air Line Pilots' Association

C.A.L.R.I. Central Artificial Leather Research Institute (U.S.A.)

Caltex California-Texas Petroleum Corporation

Calv. Calvin; Calvinism

Calz. Sp. *Calzada*, boulevard

CAM communication, advertising and marketing

cam. camber; camouflage

Cam. Cambodia, *now* Khmer Republic; Cambrian; Cambridge; Cameroun

C.A.M. commercial air movement

C.A.M.A. Civil Aerospace Medical Association; Coated Abrasives Manufacturers' Association

CAMAL continuous airborne missile-launched and low-level system

Camb. Cambrian; Cambridge; Cambridgeshire

Cambrian Cambrian Airways

Cambs. Cambridgeshire

C.A.M.C. Canadian Army Medical Corps

C.A.M.D.A. Car and Motorcycle Drivers' Association

Camd. Soc. Camden Society, name from Wm. Camden (1551–1623), antiquary, historian, Master of Westminster School

C.A.M.E. Conference of Allied Ministers of Education

Camn. Highrs. Cameron Highlanders (mil.)

Camp. Campion Hall, Oxford, Jesuit house of studies, founded 1896 and now a Permanent Private Hall of the Univ.

CAN customs assigned numbers

can. canal; cancel; cannon; canton

Can. Canada; Canadian; canal; Canberra (Aust.); canon; canonically; canonry

Can. It. *Canto*, song, melody (mus.); L. *Cantoris*, the side in a choir upon which the precentor sits, usually the north side

Canad. Canada; Canadian

canc. cancellation; cancelled

Canc. L. *Cancellarius*, Chancellor

CANCIRCO Cancer International Research Co-operative

cand. candidate

CANDU Canadian Deuterium Uranium Reactor

CANEL Connecticut Advanced Nuclear Engineering Laboratory (U.S.A.)

Can. Fr. Canadian French

C.A.N.G.O. Committee for Air Navigation and Ground Organization

Can. I. Canary Islands

Can. Pac. Canadian Pacific

C.A.N.S.G. Civil Aviation Navigational Services Group

can't cannot

Cant. Canterbury; Canticles; Cantonese

Cantab. L. *Cantabile*; L. *Cantabrigia*, Cambridge; L. *Cantabrigiensis*, of Cambridge

CANTAT telephone cable, from Scot. to Can., opened 1961

cant. b. cantilever bridge

Canton. cantonment

CANTRAN cancel in transmission

Cantuar. L. *Cantuariensis*, *Cantuarius*, of Canterbury, Eng. archiepiscopal title used in archbishop's signature

CANUKUS Canada, United Kingdom, United States

CANUSPA Canada, Australia, New Zealand and U.S.A. Parents' Association

canv. canvas

C.A.O. Canadian Association of Optometrists; Chief Accountant/Administrative Officer; County Advisory/Agricultural Officer; Crimean Astrophysical Observatory (U.S.S.R.)

CAOBISCO Fr. *Association d'industries de produits sucrés de la C.E.E.*, Assn. of the Confectionery Industries of the E.E.C.

C.A.O.R.B. Civil Aviation Operational Research Branch

C.A.O.R.G. Canadian Army Operational Research Group

C.A.O.T. Canadian Association of Occupational Therapy

CAP civil/combat air patrol (U.S.A.); Common Agricultural Policy, of the E.E.C.

cap. capacity; capitalize; capital, chief city; capital letter; foolscap

cap. L. *capiat*, let him take (med.); L. *capitulum*, a small head or knob; L. *caput*, head

Cap. It. *capitolo*, chapter; Captain, also Capn./Capt.

c.a.p. It. *codice di avviamento postale*, mail code number

C.A.P. Canadian Association of Physicists; chlor-aceto-phenone, a gas; Code of Advertising Practice; College of American Pathologists; Community Action Program (U.S.A.)

C.A.P.A. Canadian Association of Purchasing Agents

C.A.P.A.C. Composers' Authors' and Publishers' Association of Canada

CAPCOM command communicator, Houston (space)

C.A.P.I.E.L. Common Market Association for Switchgear & Control Devices

Capn. Sp. *Capitán*, captain

C.A.P.O. Canadian Army Post Office

Capric. Capricorn

caps. capital letters (typ.); capsule

capt. caption

CAR Civil Air Regulations; cloudtop altitude radiometer

car. carat

Car. Carlow

Car. L. *Carolus*, Charles

C.A.R. Canadian Association of Radiologists; Central African Republic, *République Centrafricaine*; *Commonwealth Arbitration Reports* (Aust.)

CARA combat air rescue aircraft

C.A.R.A.C. Civil Aviation Radio Advisory Committee

Carav. Fr. *Sud-Aviation Caravelle*, (aircraft)

Carb. carbon; carbonate

Card. Cardiganshire (*also* Cards.); cardinal

C.A.R.D. Campaign Against Racial Discrimination; compact automatic retrieval device/display; computer augmented road design

CARDAN Fr. *Centre d'Analyse et de Recherche Documentaires pour l'Afrique Noire*, Documentary Analysis and Research Centre for Black Africa

C.A.R.D.E. Canadian Armament Research and Development Establishment

Card. num. cardinal number (math.)

C.A.R.E. continuous aircraft reliability evaluation; Co-operative for American Relief (*formerly* Remittances) Everywhere, a nonprofit organization set up after WW2 to send packages of food and clothing to needy people overseas

Carib. Caribbean; — **Cur.** Caribbean current

Carifta, CARIFTA Caribbean Free Trade Area/Association

Carm., Carms. Carmarthenshire

Carn. Caernarvonshire

Caro, Carol Caroline

carp. carpenter; carpentry

Carp. Carpathian mountains; Carpentaria (Aust.)

CARPAS *Comisión Asesora Regional de Pesca el Atlantico Sud-Occidental*, Regional Fisheries Advisory Commission for the Southwest Atlantic (FAO)

carr. carriage

Carrie Caroline

CARRIS *Companhia Carris de Ferro de Lisboa*, Lisbon Tram Co. (Port.)

C.A.R.S. Canadian Arthritis and Rheumatism Society

cart. cartage

C.A.R.T. collision avoidance radar trainer (aircraft)

Carth. Carthage

Cartog. cartographer; cartography

CAS Carib Advertising Services (Guyana); collision avoidance system; controlled airspace

cas. casual; casualty

Cas. Caracas (Ven.); castle

C.A.S. Cambridge Antiquarian Society; Cathcart Art Society; Centre for Administrative Studies; Chemical Abstracts Service; Chief of the Air Staff; Children's Aid Society; collision avoidance system; *Connecticutensis Academiae Socius*, Fellow of the Connecticut Academy of Arts and Sciences

CASA Canadian Automatic Sprinkler Association

ca.sa. L. *capias ad satisfaciendum*, a writ of execution

C.A.S.A. Contemporary Art Society of Australia

C.A.(S.A.) Member of the Accountants' Society (South Africa)

C.A.S.E. Centre for Advanced Studies in Environment, of the Arch. Assn.; Committee on Academic Science and Engineering (U.S.A.); Confederation for the Advancement of State Education

Cash. cashier

CASI Canadian Aeronautics and Space Institute

CASIG Careers Advisory Service in Industry for Girls

Ca. S.L. Catering Sub-Lieutenant

C.A.S.L.E. Commonwealth Association of Surveying and Land Economy

CASL-HV Fr. *Confédération Africaine des Syndicats Libres de la Haute Volta*, African Confed. of Free Trade Unions of the Upper Volta

Caspar, CASPAR Cambridge analog simulator for predicting atomic reactions

CAST Consolidated African Selection Trust

Cast. Castile; Castilian

C.A.S.T.E. Civil Aviation Signals Training Establishment

CAST-FO-Chad Fr. *Confédération Africaine des Syndicats Libre—Force Ouvrière*, African Confed. of Free Trade Unions—Workers' Force—Chad

C.A.S.U. Co-operative Association of Suez Canal Users

C.A.S.W. Council for the Advancement of Scientific Writing (U.S.A.)

CAT computer of average transients

cat. catalogue; catamaran; cataplasma, a poultice (med.); catapult; catechism; caterpillar tractor; cattle

Cat. Catalan, of Catalonia (*also* Catal.); catholic; Catullus, Gaius Valerius (*c.* 84–54 B.C.), Lat. poet

C.A.T. Child's Apperception Test; Civil Air Transport; clear air turbulence; College of Advanced Technology; Fr. *Comité de l'assistance technique de l'O.N.U.*, Technical Assistance Committee, U.N.O.; Fr. *Compagnie Air Transport*, French Air Line; compressed air tunnel; computer aided typesetting

catachr. catachrestic

C.A.T.C. Commonwealth Air Transport Commission/Council

CATCC Canadian Association of Textile Colorists and Chemists

Cath, Cathie, Cathy Catherine; Katherine

cath. cathedral; cathode; catholic

catk counter attack

C.A.T.O.R. Combined Air Transport Operations Room

C.A.T.R.A. Cutlery and Allied Trades Research Association

CATVs cable televisions systems

caus. causation; causative

CAV C.A.Vandervell, founder of firm now subsidiary of Joseph Lucus (elec.)

cav. cavalier; cavalry

cav. L. *caveat*, a form of writ

Cav. It. *Cavaliere*, Knight

c.a.v. L. *curia advisare vult*, the court desires to consider (leg.)

C.A.V. Construction Assistance Vehicle (undersea)

C.A.V.D. Completion, Arithmetic Problems, Vocabulary, Following Directions, Thorndike's intelligence test (psy.)

C.A.V.I. Fr. *Centre audio-visuel international*, Intern. Audio-Visual Centre

C.A.W.U. Clerical and Administrative Workers' Union

Cay. Cayenne; Cayman

CB *s* Blackburn (B.V.R.); *s* Bolivia (I.C.A.M.); chlorobromomethane gas, used for fire extinction

Cb. *s* columbium (chem.)

Cb. Fr. *Contre-basse*, double bass (mus.)

c.b., C.B., C/B cash book; cast brass; circuit breaker; compass bearing; continuous breakdown

c./b. caught and bowled (cricket)

C.B. Cape Breton; Fr. *Carte Blanche*, full discretion (*also* C. bl.); cavalry brigade; census bureau (U.S.A.); centre of buoyancy; chief baron; Coal Board; Common Bench; Companion of the Most Honourable Order of the Bath; confidential book (naval); confined to barracks; cost benefit; country bill; county borough; currency bond

C.B. It. *Col basso*, with the bass (mus.); It. *Contrabasso*, double bass (mus.)

C.B.A. Caribbean Atlantic Airways; *Chemical-Biological Activities*; Commercial Bank of Australia; Community Broadcasters' Association (U.S.A.); Concrete Block Association; cost benefit analysis; Council for British Archaeology

CBAA Canadian Business Aircraft Association

C.B.A.T. Central Bureau for Astronomical Telegrams

CBB Campaign for Better Broadcasting; *Centre Belge du Bois*, Belgian Timber Research Centre

CBBI Cast Bronze Bearing Institute (U.S.A.)

cbc combined blood count

CBC Caribbean Broadcasting Company; Children's Book Council (U.S.A.)

C.B.C. Canadian Broadcasting Corporation; Christian Brothers' College (Aust.); county borough council

C.B.C.S. Commonwealth Bureau of Census and Statistics (Aust.)

c.b.d. cash before delivery

C.B.E. chemical, biological and environmental; Commander of the Order of the British Empire; Council for Basic

Education; Conference/Council of Biology Editors

C.B.E.L. *Cambridge Bibliography of English Literature*; current balance earth leakage

CBEMA Canadian Business Equipment Manufacturers' Association

C.B.F. central board of finance; cerebral blood flow

c.b.i. complete background investigation

C.B.I. Cape Breton Island; Central Bureau of Identification (U.S.A.); China, Burma, India; computer-based information; Confederation of British Industries, founded 1965 to promote prosperity of Brit. industry. Amal. of the B.E.C., the F.B.I. and N.A.B.M.; Cumulative Book Index (U.S.A.)

C.B.I.S. computer-based information system

C.B.J.O. Co-ordinating Board of Jewish Organizations

cbk. cheque book

cb/l commercial bill of lading

cbl. cable

cbm Ger. *kubikmeter*, cubic metre

C.B.M.C. Fr. *Communauté de travail des brasseurs du marché Commun*, Working Committee on Common Market Brewers

C.B.M.I.S. computer-based management information system

C.B.M.M. Council of Building Materials Manufacturers

C.B.M.P.E. Council of British Manufacturers of Petroleum Equipment

C.B.M.S. Conference Board of Mathematical Sciences (U.S.A.)

CBNM Central Bureau of Nuclear Measurements (EURATOM)

Cbo. Colombo (Ceylon)

C.B.O. Conference of Baltic Oceanographers; counter-battery officer

C-bomb cobalt bomb

CBP *Centro de Biologia Piscatória*, Fisheries Biological Centre, Lisbon (Port.)

C.B.P.C. Canadian Book Publishers' Council

CB & PGNCS circuit breaker and primary guidance navigation control system

CBQ civilian bachelor quarters

C.B.R. Center for Brain Research (U.S.A.); chemical, biological, radiological (mil.); cloud base recorder

C.B.R.I. Central Building Research Institute (India)

C.B.S. Canadian Biochemical Society; *Centraal Bureau voor de Statistiek*, Central Statistical Bureau (Neth.); Columbia Broadcasting System (U.S.A.); Confra-

ternity of the Blessed Sacrament; Church Building Society

C.B.S.O. City of Birmingham Symphony Orchestra

CBT *Centre Belge de Traductions*, Belgian Translations Centre

c.b.u. clustered bomb unit

C.B.W. chemical and biological warfare

C/c, c/c, c.c. It. *conto corrente*, current account

CC *s* Caernarvonshire (B.V.R.); *s* Chile (I.C.A.M.); concave; 200 (Roman)

cc. centuries; chapters; copies

c/c., c.c. Fr. *compte courant*, current account

Cc. L. *capita*, chapters (typ.); L. *confessores*, confessors

c.c. carbon copy; cash credit; change course; chronometer correction; close control; colour code; contra credit; Fr. *courant continu*, direct current (elec.); cubic centimetre (millilitre) / contents

c. & c. carpets and curtains

C.C. Caius College, Cambridge (*also* Cai.); Cape Colony; Caribbean Commission; catholic clergyman; central committee; Chamber of Commerce (*also* C. of C.); Charity Commission; chess club;˙ chest complaint; circuit court; city council; city councillor; civil commotion; civil court; common councillor; common councilman; community council; Fr. *Compagnon de l'Ordre du Canada*; Companion, Order of Canada; compass course; confined to camp; consular clerk; continuation clause; control computer; Sp. *corriente continua*, direct current (elec.); country cheque/clearing; Countryside Commission; county clerk/commissioner / council / councillor / court; credit card; cricket/croquet club; crown clerk; cruising club; curate in charge (*also* C. in C.); cushion craft; cycling club

CCA carrier-controlled approach (USN); continental control area

C.C.A. Canadian Construction Association; Cement and Concrete Association; Chief Clerk of the Admiralty; Circuit Court of Appeals (U.S.A.); Commonwealth Correspondents' Association; Consumers' Co-operative Association (U.S.A.); Copper Conductors' Association; Council for Colored Affairs (U.S.A.); County Councils' Association; Court of Criminal Appeal, *now* Court of Appeal (Criminal Division); Covered Conductors' Association

C.C.A.B. Canadian Circulations Audit Board

CCAHC Central Council for Agricultural and Horticultural Co-operation

CCAM Canadian Congress of Applied Mechanics

c.c.b. cubic capacity of bunkers

C.C. black conductive channel black, filler in rubber compounding

C.C.B.M. Copper Cylinder and Boiler Manufacturers' Association

C.C.B.N. Central Council for British Naturism

C.C.B.V. Fr. *Comité professionnel des co-opératives des pays du marché commun pour le bétail et la viande*, Committee of Cattle and Meat Co-operatives in the Common Market Countries

C.C.B.W. Committee on Chemical and Biological Warfare

CCC Civilian Conservation Corps (U.S.A.); Commodity Credit Corporation; Craftsmen's Co-ordinating Committee, Steel Industry; 300 (Roman)

CCCP *s* Soviet Union (I.C.A.M.)

C.C.C. Canadian Chamber of Commerce; canoe camping club; Central Control Commission; Central Criminal Court, also known as Old Bailey, estab. 1834 for trial of treasons, murders and other crimes committed within the City of London and county of Middlesex and in certain areas of Essex, Kent and Surrey; Christ's College, Cambridge, founded 1505; Club Cricket Conference; Fr. *Conseil de co-opération culturelle*, European Council for Cultural Co-operation; Corpus Christi College, founded Camb. 1352 and Oxford 1517; Council for the Care of Churches; county cricket club; cross country club; Customs Co-operation Council

C.C.C.A. Corps Commander, Coast Artillery

CCCC 400 (Roman), *also* CD

C.C.C.C. Central Council for the Care of Cripples; Corpus Christi College, Cambridge, founded 1352

C.C.C.P. *Soyuz Sovietskikh Sotsialisticheskikh Respublik*, Union of Soviet Socialist Republics

C.C.C.S. Colonial / Commonwealth and Continental Church Society

C.C.D. Fr. *Conseil de coopération douanière*, Customs Co-operation Council

CCDA Commercial Chemical Development Association (U.S.A.)

C.C.E. carbon-chloroform extract; *Casa de la Cultura Ecuatoriana*, House of Ecuadorian Culture; Fr. *Conseil des communes d'Europe*, Council of European Municipalities; Council of Construction Employers (U.S.A.)

c.c.e.i. composite cost effectiveness index

C.C.E.T. Carnegie Commission on Educational Television

C.C.F. chronic cardiac failure; Combined Cadet Force; Common Cold Foundation; concentrated complete fertilizer; Co-operative Commonwealth Federation (Can.)

C.C.F.A. Combined Cadet Force Association

C.C.G. Control Commission, Germany; — **(B.E.)** Control Commission, Germany, British Element

C.C.G.B. Cycling Council of Great Britain

c.c.h. commercial clearing house; cubic capacity of holds

C.C.H.E. Central Council for Health Education

CCHF Children's Country Holidays Fund

CCHMS Central Committee for Hospital Medical Services

cc. hr. cubic centimetres per hour

C.C.I. *Central Campesina Independiente*, Independent Peasant Central (Mexico); Fr. *Chambre de commerce internationale*, Intern. Chamber of Commerce

C.C.I.A. Commission of the Churches on International Affairs

C.C.I.C. Fr. *Comité consultatif international du coton*, Intern. Cotton Advisory Committee

C.C.I.R. Catholic Council for International Relations; Fr. *Comité Consultatif International des Radiocommunications*, Intern. Telecommunications Consultative Committee

CCIS command control information system

C.C.I.T.T. Fr. *Comité Consultatif International Télégraphique et Téléphonique*, Intern. Telegraph and Telephone Consultative Committee

C.C.J. circuit/county court judge

C.C.J.O. Consultative Council of Jewish Organizations

C.C.L. Caribbean Congress of Labour

ccm Ger. *Kubikzentimeter*, cubic centimetre

CCM constant current modulation; controlled carrier modulation

c. cm. cubic centimetre

C.C.M.A. Canadian Council of Management Association; Commander, Corps Medium Artillery

C.C.M.D. Carnegie Committee for Music and Drama; continuous current monitoring device

cc./min. cubic centimetres per minute

C.C.M.T.C. Crown Cork Manufacturers' Technical Council

CCN command control number; contract change notice/notification; *Cruzada Civica Nacionalista*, Nat. Civic Crusade (Ven.)

CCNDT Canadian Council for Non-Destructive Technology

CCNR Consultative Committee for Nuclear Research, Council of Europe

CCNSC Cancer Chemotherapy National Service Center (U.S.A.)

C.C.N.Y. Carnegie Corporation of New York; City College of the City Univ. of New York

C.C.O. central coding office; country clearing office; current-controlled oscillator

C.C.O.A. County Court Officers' Association

C.C.O.F.I. California Co-operative Oceanic Fisheries Investigations (U.S.A.)

CCP critical compression pressure

c.c.p. It. *conto corrente postale*, current postal account; credit card purchase

C.C.P. Chinese Communist Party, *Chung-kuo Kung-ch'an Tang*; Code of Civil Procedure; Committee on Commodity Problems (FAO); Commonwealth Centre Party (Aust.); Court of Common Pleas

C.C.P.E. Canadian Council of Professional Engineers

C.C.P.F. Fr. *Comité central de la propriété forestière de la C.E.E.*, Central Committee on Forest Property for the E.E.C.

C.C.P.I.T. China Committee for the Promotion of International Trade

C.C.P.O. Fr. *Comité central permanent de l'opium*, Permanent Central Opium Board

C.C.P.R. Central Council of Physical Recreation, founded 1935. Crystal Palace National Sports Centre, managed by C.C.P.R. for G.L.C.

C.C.P.S. Consultative Committee for Postal Studies (UPU)

C.C.P.W. Catholic Council for Polish Welfare

CCR coherent crystal radiation; critical compression ratio

C.C.R. Fr. *Commission centrale pour la navigation du Rhin*, Central Commission for the Navigation of the Rhine; Commission of Civil Rights (U.S.A.); Common Centre of Research; contract change request

C.C.R.A. Commander Corps Royal Artillery

C. Cr. P. Code of Criminal Procedure

C.C.R.T.D. Committee for Coordination of Cathode Ray Tube Development

CCRU Common Cold Research Unit (U.S.A.)

CCS collective call sign; combined chiefs of staff (U.S.A.)

C.C.S. Canadian Cancer / Ceramic Society; casualty clearing station; Ceylon Civil Service; child care service; controlled combustion system

C.C.S.A. Canadian Committee on Sugar Analysis

C.C.S.A.T.U. Co-ordinating Council of South African Trade Unions

cc./sec. cubic centimetres per second

CCSL *Confédération Congolaise des Syndicats Libres*, Congolese (Brazzaville) Confed. of Free Trade Unions

CCST Center for Computer Sciences and Technology (U.S.A.)

CCT *Confederación Costarricense del Trabajo*, Costa Rican Confed. of Workers

C.C.T. *Comité de Co-ordination des Télécommunications*, French Standardization Committee; correct corps time

C.C.T.A. Fr. *Commission de coopération technique pour l'Afrique*, Commission for Tech. Co-operation in Africa; Co-ordinating Committee of Technical Assistance

c.c.tks. cubic capacity of tanks

CCTS Canaveral Council of Technical Societies (U.S.A.); combat crew training squadron

CCTV closed circuit television

c.c.u. chart comparison unit

CCUS Chamber of Commerce of the United States

c.c.w. counter clockwise

CCWU Clerical and Commercial Workers' Union (Guyana)

cd candela, unit of luminous intensity;
— **/ft.²** candela per square foot;
— **/m²** candela per square metre

c/d carried down (accy.)

c & d collection and delivery

Cd *s* cadmium (chem.)

CD *s* Brighton (B.V.R.); certificate of deposit (fin.); contracting definition; 400 (Roman)

C/D customs declaration

cd. Turk. *cadde*, street; cord; could

Cd. Sp. *ciudad*, city; command; Command Paper, published by H.M.S.O. 1900–1918; commissioned

c.d. carried down; cash discount; cum dividend (fin.)

C/D consular declaration

C.D. Canadian Forces Decoration; Chancery Division (leg.); chemist and druggist; Civil Defence/Defense; clearance diving; college diploma; Commercial dock (Lond.); Fr. *Commission du Danube*, Danube Commission; confidential document; contagious disease; Fr. *Corps Diplomatique*, diplomatic corps; count down; county development; court of deliberation (freem.)

C.D. It. *Colla destra*, with the right hand (mus.)

C.D.A. Canadian Dental/Dietetic Association; Civil Defence Act; College Diploma in Agriculture; Colonial Dames of America; Conference of Defence Associations (Can.); Copper Development Association

C.D.A.A.A. Committee to Defend America by Aiding the Allies

C.D. Acts Contagious Diseases Acts

Cd. A. Eng. commissioned air engineer

Cd. Armn. commissioned airman

C.D.A.S. Civil Defence Ambulance Service

Cd. B. commissioned boatswain

cdbd. cardboard

Cd. Bndr. commissioned bandmaster

Cd. B. (P.R.) commissioned boatswain (plotting and radar)

CDC Canada Development Corporation; Caribbean Defence Command/Commander; Combat Development Command (U.S.A.); command and data-handling console (computer); common development cycle (computer)

C.D.C. Commissioners of the District of Columbia; Commonwealth Development Corporation, originally estab. as a public corp. 1948, as Colonial Dev. Corp.; cost determination committee

Cd. Cmy. O. commissioned commissary officer

Cd. C. O. commissioned communication officer

Cd. Con. commissioned constructor

CDD certificate of disability for discharge (U.S.A.)

C.D.E.E. Chemical Defence Experimental Establishment

C. de G. *Croix de Guerre*, war cross, Belgium/France

Cd. El. O. commissioned electrical officer

Cd. Eng. commissioned engineer

C.D.F.C. Commonwealth Development Finance Company

cd. fwd. carried forward

Cdg. Cardigan; Cardiganshire (Wales)

Cd. Gr. commissioned gunner

CDH constant delta height

C.D.H. College Diploma in Horticulture

C.Dip.F.A. Certified Diploma in Finance and Accounting

Cd. In. O. commissioned instructor officer

c. div. cum dividend (fin.)

Cdl. cardinal

C.D.L. central dockyard laboratory (MOD); Council of the Duchy of Lancaster; Country and Democratic League (Aust.)

Cd. M.A.A. commissioned master-at-arms

CDN *s* Canada (I.V.R.); *Chicago Daily News*

Cd. O. commissioned officer

Cd. Obs. commissioned observer

Cd. O.E. commissioned ordnance engineer

Cd. O.O. commissioned ordnance officer

C.D.P.E. continental daily parcels express

Cdr. commander (*also* CDR, Cdmr.); conductor

C.D.R. Committee for the Defence of the Revolution (Cuba); critical design review

C.D.R.A. Committee of Directors of Research Associations

Cd. Rad. O. commissioned radio officer

C.D.R.B. Canadian Defence Research Board

C.D.R.C. Civil Defence Regional Commissioner

Cdre. commodore

C.D.R.F. Canadian Dental Research Foundation

C.D.R.I. Central Drug Research Institute (India)

C.D.R.S. civil defence rescue service

C.D.S. Chief of the Defence Staff; Civil Defence Services

Cd. S. B. commissioned signals boatswain

CDSE computer-driven simulation environment

Cd. Sh. commissioned shipwright

Cd. S. O. commissioned stores/supply officer

C.D.S.O. Companion of the Distinguished Service Order, *usually* D.S.O.

Cdt. cadet; commandant, *also* Cmdt.

C.D.T. Carnegie Dunfermline Trust

Cdt. Mid. cadet midshipman

CDU *Christlich-Demokratische Union*, Christian Democratic Union, West Ger.; *Christlich-Demokratische Union Deutschlands*, Christian Democratic Union of Germany, East Ger.

C.D.U.C.E. Christian Democratic Union of Central Europe

c.d.v. Fr. *carte-de-visite*, visiting card

C.D.V. Civil Defence Volunteers

c.d.w. chilled/cold drinking water

C.D. & W. Colonial Development and Welfare

Cd. Wdr. commissioned wardmaster

Cd. W. O. commissioned writer officer

C.D.W.S. Civil Defence Wardens' Service

Cdz. Cádiz (Spain)

Ce *s* cerium (chem.)

CE *s* Cambridgeshire (B.V.R.); *s* Coleraine (B.F.P.)

c.e. critical examination

c.e. **L.** *caveat emptor*, let the buyer beware (leg.)

C.E. Canada East; carbon equivalent; centre of effort (naval arch.); Chancellor of the Exchequer; chemical/chief engineer; Christian Endeavour; Church of England (*also* C. of E.); circular error; civil engineer; common era; compass error; compression engine; Council of Europe; counter-espionage

C. & E. Customs & Excise, board formed in 1909 to manage duties (customs) on imported and exported goods and (excise) on home-produced goods and services

C.E.A. Canadian Electrical Association; Central Electricity Authority; Cinematograph Exhibitors Association; Combustion Engineering Association; Fr. *Comité européen des assurances*, European Insurance Committee; commodity exchange authority; Fr. *Confédération des éducateurs américains*, Confed. of Latin American Educators; Fr. *Confédération européenne de l'agriculture*, European Confed. of Agric.; Conference of Educational Associations; control electronics assembly; Council for Educational Advance; Council of Economic Advisers (U.S.A.)

C.E.A.A. Center for Editions of American Authors; Fr. *Centre européen d'aviation agricole*, European Agricultural Aviation Centre; Council of European-American Associations

C.E.A.C. Fr. *Commission européenne de l'aviation civile*, European Civil Aviation Commission

C.E.A.F. Fr. *Comité européen des associations de fonderies*, European Committee of Foundry Assns.

C.E.B. Central Electricity Board; Fr. *Confédération européenne de billard*, European Billiards Confed.

CEBAR chemical, biological, radiological warfare

C.E.C. Canadian Electrical Code, of Standardization; Fr. *Centre européen de la culture*, European Cultural Centre; Church Education Corporation; Civil Engineering Corps; Clothing Export

Council; Commonwealth Economic Committee; Commonwealth Education Conference; Commonwealth Engineering Conference; Council for Exceptional Children

C.E.C.A. Fr. *Communauté européenne du charbon et de l'acier*, European Coal and Steel Community

C.E.C.B. Fr. *Conseil européen du cuir brut* (*Comité des Six*), European Hide Council (Six Countries Committee)

C.E.C.C. Fr. *Communauté européenne de crédit communal*, European Municipal Credit Community

C.E.C.E. Committee for European Construction Equipment

C.E.C.H. Fr. *Comité européen de la culture du houblon*, European Hops Culture Committee

C.E.C.L.E.S. Fr. *Conseil européen pour la construction de lanceurs d'engins spatiaux*, European Launching Development Organization

CECOMAF Fr. *Comité européen des constructeurs de matériel frigorifique*, European Committee of Manufacturers of Refrigeration Equipment

C.E.C.S. Church of England Children's Society; civil engineering computing system; Communications Electronics Coordination Section

C.E.C.T. Fr. *Comité européen de la chaudronnerie et de la tôlerie*, European Committee for Boilermaking and Kindred Steel Structures

CED carbon equivalent difference; computer entry device; Council for Economic Development (U.S.A.)

C.E.D. Committee for Economic Development

C.E.D.A. Committee for Economic Development of Australia

C.E.D.I. Fr. *Centre européen de documentation et d'information*, European Documentation and Information Centre

CEDIC Church Estates Development and Improvement Company

CEDO Centre for Educational Development Overseas

C.E.E. Central Engineering Establishment; Certificate of Extended Education; Fr. *Commission économique pour l'Europe*, Economic Commission for Europe; Fr. *Commission internationale de réglementation en vue de l'approbation de l'équipement électrique*, Intern. Commission on Rules for the Approval of Electrical Equipment; Common Entrance Examination; Fr. *Communauté économique européenne*, European Economic Community; Port. *Comunidade Económica Europeia*, European Economic Community

69

C.E.E.A. Fr. *Communauté européenne de l'énergie atomique*, European Atomic Energy Community, also EURATOM

C.E.E.C. Council for European Economic Co-operation

C.E.E.P. Fr. *Centre européen d'études de population*, European Centre for Population Studies

C.E.F. Canadian/Chinese Expeditionary Force

C.E.F.A.C.D. Fr. *Comité européen des fabricants d'appareils de chauffage et de cuisine domestiques*, European Committee of Manufacturers of Domestic Heating and Cooking Appliances

C.E.F.I.C. Fr. *Centre européen des fédérations de l'industrie chimique*, European Centre of Chemical Manufacturers' Federations

C.E.F.S. Fr. *Comité européen des fabricants de sucre*, European Committee of Sugar Manufacturers

CEFTRI Central Food Technological Research Institute (India)

C.E.G. Catholic Evidence Guild; *collèges d'Enseignement Général*, colleges of general education (France)

C.E.G.B. Central Electricity Generating Board created by Electricity Act, 1957, to provide an efficient co-ordinated economic supply of elec. to Area Boards with due regard to natural beauty of countryside

C.E.G.G.S. Church of England Girls' Grammar School

CEGOC *Centro de Estudos de Gestão e Organização Científica*, Business Management and Organization Study Centre (Port.)

CEGROB Fr. *Communauté européenne des associations du commerce de gros de bière des pays membres de la C.E.E.*, European Community of Assns. of the Wholesale Beer Trade for the E.E.C. Countries

C.E.G.S. Church of England Grammar School

C.E.H. Fr. *Conférence européenne des horaires des trains de voyageurs*, European Passenger Time-Table Conference

C.E.I. *Centre d'Etudes Industrielles*, Centre for Industrial Studies (Switz.); *Comitato Elettrotecnico Italiano*, Italian Electrotechnical Committee; Fr. *Commission électrotechnique internationale*, Intern. Electrotechnical Commission; communications-electronics instructions; cost effectiveness index; Council of Engineering Institutions *formerly* E.I.J.C.

C.E.I.Bois Fr. *Confédération européenne des industries du bois*, European Confed. of Woodworking Industries

C.E.I.F. Council of European Industrial Federations, having same membership as O.E.C.D. less Canada and U.S.A.

C.E.I.R. Corporation for Economic and Industrial Research

CEL Constitutional Educational League (U.S.A.)

cel. celebrate; celebration; celery; celibate

Cel., Cels. Celsius, temperature scale as centigrade

C.E.L.A. Council for Exports to Latin America, of B.N.E.C.

CELAM Fr. *Conseil épiscopal latino-américain*, Latin-American Episcopal Council

C.E.L.C. Commonwealth Education Liaison Committee

CELESCOPE celestial telescope

'cellist violoncellist (mus.)

'cello It. *violoncello*, bowed 4-stringed instrument one of family of which principal member is violin (mus.)

Celt. Celtic; Celticism

Cem. cement; cemetery

C.E.M. cost and effectiveness method; Council of European Municipalities

CEMA Catering Equipment Manufacturers' Association

C.E.M.A. Canadian Electrical Manufacturers' Association; Conveyor Equipment Manufacturers' Association (U.S.A.); Council for Economic Mutual Assistance; Council for the Encouragement of Music and the Arts, *now* Arts Council of Great Britain

C.E.M.A.C. Committee of European Associations of Manufacturers of Active Electronic Components

C.E.M.A.P. Fr. *Commission européenne des méthodes d'analyse des pesticides*, Collaborative Pesticides Analytical Committee

Cemb. It. *cembalo*, harpsichord (mus.)

Cembalo It. *Clavicembalo*, harpsichord (mus.)

C.E.M.F. counter-electro-motive force (elec.)

C.E.M.L.A. Sp. *Centro de Estudios Monetarios Latino-americanos*, Latin-American Centre for Monetary Studies

C.E.M.S. Church of England Men's Society

C.E.M.T. Fr. *Conférence européenne des ministres des transports*, European Conference of Ministers of Transport

cen. center; central (*also* centr.); centre; century

Cen. Eccl. L. *Censura Ecclesiastica*, Ecclesiastical Censure

C.E.N.E.L. European Electrical Standards Co-ordinating Committee

CENFAM *Centro Nazionale di Fisica dell Atmospera e Meteorologia*, Nat. Centre of Physics of the Atmosphere and Meteorology (Italy)

C. Eng. Chartered Engineer

cens. censor; censorship

cent. centavo; centesimo; centigrade; centime; central; centrifugal; century

cent. L. *centum*, hundred

CENTAG Central (European) Army Group (NATO)

Centig. centigrade

CENTO, CENTRO Central Treaty Organization, known as the Baghdad Pact until 1959

Centr. Afr. Central Africa

C.E.O. Chief Education Officer; Confederation of Employee Organisations

C.E.O.A. Central European Operating Agency (NATO)

CEP circular error probability (computer)

C.E.P.C. Central European Pipeline Committee; Fr. *Comité éuropéen pour les problèmes criminels*, European Committee on Crime Problems

C.E.P.C.E.O. Fr. *Comité d'étude des producteurs de charbon d'Europe occidentale*, Western European Coal Producers' Assn.

C.E.P.E. Central Experimental and Proving Establishment (R.C.A.F.)

C.E.P.E.C. Committee of European Associations of Manufacturers of Passive Electronic Components

C.E.P.E.S. Fr. *Comité européen pour le progrès économique et social*, European Committee for Economic and Social Progress

C.E.P.O. Central European Pipeline Office

CEPS Central European Pipeline System

C.E.P.S. Cornish Engine Preservation Society

C.E.P.T. Fr. *Conférence européenne des administrations des postes et des télécommunications*, European Conference of Postal and Telecommunications Administrations

Cer., ceram. ceramic

CERBOM *Centre d'Études et de Recherches de Biologie et d'Océanographie Médicale*, Centre for Investigations and Biological Research and Medical Oceanography (France)

C.E.R.C.A. Commonwealth and Empire Radio for Civil Aviation

C.E.R.I. Centre for Educational Research and Innovation

C.E.R.L. Central Electricity/Coastal Engineering Research Laboratories

C.E.R.N. Fr. *Centre Européen de Recherches Nucléaires*, European Organization (*formerly* Council) for Nuclear Research

C.E.R.P. Fr. *Centre européen des relations publiques*, European Centre of Public Relations

cert. (a) certainty (gambling); certain; certificate (*also* certif.); certification; certified; certify

cert. inv. certified invoice

Cert-CAM Certificate in Communication, Advertising and Marketing

Cert. T. M. Fr. *Certificat en Technologie médicale*, Certificate in Medical Technology

C.E.R.U. Fr. *Comité des Études Régionales et Urbaines*, Committee of Regional and Urban Studies

cerv. cervical

C.E.S. Christian Evidence Society; *collèges d'Enseignement Secondaire*, colleges of secondary education (France)

C. esp. It. *con espressione*, with expression (mus.)

C.E.S.S.A.C. Church of England Soldiers', Sailors' and Airmen's Clubs

C.E.S.S.I. Church of England Sunday School Institution

Cestr. L. *Cestrensis*, of Chester, Eng. episcopal title in signature of bishop

CET *Collèges d'Enseignement Technique*, colleges of technical education (France)

C.E.T. Central European Time; common external tariff

Četeka *Československá Tisková Kancelár*, Czechoslovak Press Bureau

CETEX Committee on Extra-Terrestrial Exploration

CETI Communication with Extra-Territorial Intelligence

C.E.T.O. Centre for Educational Television Overseas

cet. par. L. *ceteris paribus*, other things being equal

C.E.T.S. Church of England Temperance Society

C.E.U. Christian Endeavour Union; Constructional Engineering Union

C.E.U.S.A. Committee for Exports to the United States of America

C.E.W.M.S. Church of England Working Men's Society

Cey., Ceyl. Ceylon

CEYC Church of England Youth Council

C.E.Z.M.S. Church of England Zenana Missionary Society

cf. L. *confer*, compare

Cf *s* californium (chem.)

CF _s_ Canada (I.C.A.M.); _s_ Cardiff (B.F.P.); _s_ Suffolk, West (B.V.R.)

cf., Cf. calf (binding)

c/f., c.f. carried forward (accy.)

Cf. confessions

c.f. centre field; center fielder (baseball); centre forward (football); Fr. _chemin-de-fer_, railway; communication factor; context free; cost and freight (_also_ c. & f.); cubic feet

C.F. centre of flotation; Chaplain to the Forces; Fr. _Comédie Française_; Commonwealth Fund; Corresponding Fellow

C.F. It. _canto fermo_, fixed song (mus.); L. _cantus firmus_, fixed song (mus.)

C.F.A. Canadian Federation of Agriculture; Canadian Field Artillery; Canadian/Commonwealth Forestry Association; Chartered Financial Analyst (U.S.A.); _Colonies Françaises d'Afrique_, French African Colonies; Commission of Fine Arts; Cookery and Food Association (_also_ C. & F.A.); Council of Foreign Affairs; Council of Iron-foundry Associations; cross field amplifier

C factor cleverness factor, factor in mental ability (psy.)

C.F.A.E. Fr. _Centre de formation en aérodynamique expérimentale_, Training Centre for Experimental Aerodynamics

C.F.A.L. Current Food Additives Legislation

C.F.A.P. Canadian Foundation for the Advancement of Pharmacy

CFAR constant false alarm rate

C.F.A.T. Carnegie Foundation for the Advancement of Teaching

C.F.B. Consumer Fraud Bureau (U.S.A.); Council of Foreign Bondholders

C.F. black conductive furnace black, filler in rubber compounding

C.F.B.S. Canadian Federation of Biological Sciences

C.F.C. Ceylon Fisheries Corporation; L. _Congregatio Fratrum Christianorum_, Congregation of Christian Brothers; consolidation freight classification

C.F.C.E. Fr. _Conseil des fédérations commerciales d'Europe_, Council of European Commercial Federations

c.f.d. cubic feet per day

CFDC Canadian Film Development Corporation; Cane Farming Development Corporation (Guyana)

CFE College of Further Education

C.F.E. Central Fighter Establishment

C.F.F. _Chemins de fer fédéraux Suisses_, Swiss Nat. Railway; critical flicker/fusion frequency

c.f.g. cubic feet of gas; — **d.** cubic feet of gas per day; — **h.** cubic feet of gas

per hour; — **m.** cubic feet of gas per minute

c.f.h. cubic feet per hour

c.f.i., C.F. & I. cost, freight and insurance

C.F.I. chaplain to foreign immigrants; chief flying instructor

C.F.L. Carnegie Free Library; ceasefire line; Central Film Library (COI)

cfm. confirm; confirmation

c.f.m. cubic feet per minute/month

C.F.M. Cadet Forces Medal; Council of Foreign Ministers

C.f.o. calling/channel for orders; coast for orders (shipping)

C.F.O. Central Forecasting Office, of Met. Office; chief fire officer

C.F.O.A. Chief Fire Officers' Association

CFOD Catholic Fund for Overseas Development

CFP _Concentración de Fuerzas Populares_, Concentration of Popular Forces (Ecu.)

C.F.P. _Colonies Françaises du Pacifique_, French Pacific Colonies; _Compagnie Française des Pétroles_, French Petroleum Co.

CFR commercial fast reactor

cfr. chauffeur; It. _confronta_, compare, _also_ cf.

C.F.R. code of federal regulations (U.S.A.); Council on Foreign Relations

C.F.R. engine Standard single-cylinder variable compression engine developed by Co-operative Fuel Research Council, determines anti-knock value of motor gasolines/ignition quality of diesel fuels

c.f.s. cubic feet per second

C.F.S. Central Flying School; Clergy Friendly Society

CFSG cometary feasibility study group (ESRO)

CFSTI Clearinghouse for Federal Scientific and Technical Information (U.S.A.)

cft. craft

c. ft. cubic feet (or foot)

C.F.T. _Compagnie Française de Télévision_, French television co.

C.F.T.A. Cattle Food Trade Association Inc.

C.F.T.B. Commonwealth Forestry and Timber Bureau

cftmn. craftsman

CFWI County Federation of Women's Institutes. C is sometimes replaced by initial letter of county

C.F.X. L. _Congregatio Fratrum Xaverianorum_, Congregation of Xaverian Brothers

CG Commanding General, prefix applied to abbreviations of U.S. Army/ Marine Corps commands only; *s* Hampshire (B.V.R.)

CG It. *cassa grande*, bass drum (mus.)

cg. centigram

c.g. centre of gravity

C.G. captain-general; Captain of the Guard; coastguard; Coldstream Guards; commanding general; Fr. *commerce en gros*, wholesale trade; commissary general; consul general; *Croix de Guerre*, Belg. and Fr. war decoration

C.-G., Chap.-Gen. chaplain-general

C.G.A. Canadian Gas Association; cargo's proportion of general average; certified general accountant; Coast Guard Academy (U.S.A.); coast guard auxiliary; Community of the Glorious Ascension; Compressed Gas Association (U.S.A.); Country Gentlemen's Association

C.G.C. coast guard cutter (U.S.A.)

cge. carriage; — **fwd.** carriage forward; — **pd.** carriage paid; charge

CGEC *Confederación General de Empleados de Comercio*, General Confed. of Commercial Employees (Argen.)

C.G.H., C. of G.H. Cape of Good Hope (S. Afr.)

c.g.i. corrugated galvanized iron

C.G.I. chief ground/gunnery instructor; City and Guilds Institute

C.G.I.A. City and Guilds of London Insignia Award

C.G.I.L. *Confederazione Generale Italiana del Lavoro*, Italian Fed. of Trade Unions

C.G.L.I. City and Guilds of London Institute, founded 1878 for advancement of tech. educ., examines in 200 industrial subjects mainly for operatives, craftsmen and technicians

cgm. centigramme

C.G.M. Conspicuous Gallantry Medal

C.G.M.W. Commission for the Geological Map of the World

CGO *s* Congo *now* Zaire (Kinshasa) (I.V.R.)

cgo. cargo; contango (fin.)

C.G.O.U. Coast Guard Oceanographic Unit (U.S.A.)

C.G.P. College of General Practitioners; Fr. *Commissariat Général du Plan d'Équipement et de la Productivité*, Commissariat General for Equipment and Productivity Planning

CGPM Fr. *Conférence Général des Poids et Mésures*, General Conference on Weights and Measures

C.G.P.M. Fr. *Conseil général des pêches pour la Méditerranée*, General Fisheries Council for the Mediterranean

C.G.P.S. Canadian Government Purchasing System

C.G.R.A. Canadian Good Roads Association

C.G.R.I. Central Glass and Ceramic Research Institute (India)

C.G.R.M. Commandant General, Royal Marines

cgs, C.G.S. centimetre-gram/gramme second, unit system of length, mass and time

CGS Coast and Geodetic Survey; *Confederación General de Sindicatos*, General Confed. of Unions (El Salvador)

C.G.S. Canadian Geographical Society, *now* R.C.G.S.; central gunnery school; Chief of General Staff; Commissary General of Subsistence

C.G.S.B. Canadian Government Specifications Board

c.g.s.e. centimetre gramme second electromagnetic

CGSUS Council of Graduate Schools in the United States

CGT *Confederación General del Trabajo*, General Fed. of Workers (Argen.); *Confédération Générale du Travail*, largest French labour organization; *Confédération Générale du Travail*, General Confed. of Labour (Lux.)

c.g.t. capital gains tax (fin.)

C.G.T. *Compagnie Générale Transatlantique*, French Line (ship.)

C.G.T.B. Canadian Government Travel Bureau

CGT-FO *Confédération Général du Travail—Force Ouvrière*, General Confed. of Labour—Workers' Force (France); Fr. *L'Union Territoriale des Syndicats Confédération Général du Travail—Force Ouvrière*, Territorial Fed. of Trade Unions General Confed. of Labour—Workers' Force (New Caledonia)

c.g.u. ceramic glazed units

CH *s* Chester (B.F.P.); L. *Confederatio Helvetico*, Swiss Confederation; *s* Derby (B.V.R.); *s* Switzerland (I.V.R.)

ch. chain (crochet); chain (length); chaldron; Fr. *chambre*, room; chaplain; chapter; chart; check; cheese; chemical; chemistry; chestnut (horse racing); Fr. *chevaux*, horses; chief; child; children; chirurgeon; choice; choir; choke; church

Ch. chairman; Chaldean; chamber; champion; chancellor; chancery; Charles (*also* Chas.); Chile; Chilean; China; Chinese; Christ

Ch. L. *Chirurgiae*, of surgery

c.h. candle hour; central heating; centre half (sport); Fr. *cheval-vapeur*, horsepower; clearing/club/court/customs house; compass heading

C.H. Captain of the Horse (mil.); Captain of the Host (freem.); Carnegie Hall; chapter house; Christ's Hospital; Companion of Honour, an order of chivalry of one class which carries no title, instituted 4 June 1917. The number of awards is limited to 65

CHA Country-wide Holidays Association, pioneer open-air holidays organization founded as Co-operative Holidays Assn. by T. A. Leonard in 1893

C.H.A. Catholic Hospital Association; Chest and Heart Association; Community Health Association

chacom chain of command

chal. chaldron; Fr. *chaleur*, heat; challenge

Chald., Chal. Chaldaic; Chaldaism; Chaldean; Chaldee

chamb. chamberlain

Chamb. chambers

Chamb. Ency. *Chambers's Encyclopaedia*

champ champion

champers champagne

chan. channel

Chan., Chanc. chancellor; chancery

CHANCOM Channel Committee (NATO)

change produce/stock exchange

chap. chapel; chaplain; chaplaincy; chapter

Chap. chaplain; — -**Gen.** chaplain-general

Chap. St. J. Chaplain of the Order of Saint John of Jerusalem, *now* Ch. St. J.

char. character; characteristic; characterize (*also* charact.); charity; charter; charwoman

charc. charcoal

Charlie, Charley, Chas. Charles

Chauc. Geoffrey Chaucer (*c.* 1340–1400), English poet

ChB Chief of the Bureau (U.S.A.); — **Aer.** Ch. of the Bu. of Aeronautics; — **Docks** Ch. of the Bu. of Yards and Docks; — **Med.** Ch. of the Bu. of Medicine and Surgery; — **Ord.** Ch. of the Bu. of Ordnance; — **Pers.** Ch. of the Bu. of Naval Personnel; — **Sanda.** Ch. of the Bu. of Supplies and Accounts; — **Ships** Ch. of the Bu. of Ships; — **Weps.** Ch. of the Bu. of Weapons

Chb. Cherbourg (France)

Ch. B. *Baccalaureus Chirurgiae*, Bachelor of Surgery

Ch. B. S. Incorporated Church Building Society

CHC choke coil; cyclohexylamine carbonate

C.H.C. Clerk to the House of Commons; Confederate High Command

ch. cent. Fr. *chauffage central*, central heating

Ch. Ch. Christ Church, Oxford

Ch. Clk. chief clerk

Ch. Coll. Christ's College, Cambridge

Ch. D. Chancery Division (leg.); Doctor of Chemistry

C.H.D. coronary heart disease

Ch. E. chemical/chief engineer

CHEAR Council on Higher Education in the American Republics

CHEKA *Chrezvychainaya Kommissia*, All Russian Extraordinary Commission for Fighting Counter-Revolution and Sabotage, set up in 1917, changed to GPU in 1922

C.H.E.L. *Cambridge History of English Literature*

Chelm. Cheltenham, Glos.

chem. chemical; chemically; chemist; chemistry

Chem. E. chemical engineer

Chem. war. chemical warfare

CHENOP *Companhia Hidro-Eléctrica do Norte de Portugal*, Northern Hydro-Electric Company of Portugal

Ches. Cheshire

chev. chevron

Chev. Fr. *chevalier*, knight; Chevrolet (auto.)

chf. chief

Ch. F., Ch. of the F. chaplain of the fleet

C.H.F. Carnegie Hero Fund; — **C.** Carn. Hero F. Commission; — **T.** Carn. Hero F. Trust

Ch. fwd. charges forward

chg. change; charge

Chg. Chi Hagong (Bangladesh)

chgd. charged (accy.)

chgph. choreographer; choreographic; choreography

Ch. Hist. church history

Chi. Chicago (*also* Chic.); China; Chinese

Chich. Chichester, Sussex

chick chicken

Chicom Chinese communist

Chicos Chinese communists

chim. It. *chimica*, chemistry; It. *chimico*, chemical

chimp. chimpanzee

Chin. China; Chinese

chir. It. *chirurgia*, surgery

Chi. Trib. *Chicago Tribune*

Chiv. chivalry

Ch. J. chief justice

chk. check

Ch. K. Christ the King

chkr. checker

chl., chlo. chloride; chloroform

ch.-l. Fr. *chef-lieu*, chief town

C.H.L. Cambridge Higher Local (exam.)

Ch. Lbr. chief librarian

chm. chairman (*also* chmn.); checkmate (chess); choirmaster

Ch. M. L. *Chirurgiae Magister*, Master of Surgery

C.H.M. Diploma of Choir Master of the Royal College of Organists

cho., chor. choral; chorister; chorus

C.H.O. crop husbandry officer

choc. chocolate

Ch. of S. Chamber of Shipping

Chogyal title of rulers of Sikkim, from *Cho*, religion and *Gyalpo*, King

CHP *Cumhuriyet Halk Partisi*, Republican People's Party, founded by Kemal Atatürk 1923 (Turk.)

C.H.P. *Certificat en hygiène publique*, Certificate in Public Health (France)

Ch. ppd. charges prepaid

chq. cheque

C.H.Q. Commonwealth Headquarters, central office of Girl Guides Association, U.K. and Commonwealth

Chr. Christ

Chr., Chris Christian; Christianity; Christmas; Christopher

c. hr. candle hour

Chr. Coll. Cam. Christ's College, Cambridge, founded 1505, *also* C.C.C.

Chris, Chrissie Christiana; Christine; Christopher

christie Christiania turn (skiing)

chrm. chairman

chrmg. charming

chron. chronicle; chronological; chronologically; chronology; chronometry

1 Chron., 2 Chron. First/Second Book of Chronicles (Bible)

Chrs. chambers

CHS charges on account (accy.)

C.H.S. Canadian Hydrographic Service; Church Historical Society

ch'ship championship

Ch. Skr. chief skipper

Ch. St. J. Chaplain of the Order of Saint John of Jerusalem

c.h.t. cylinder head temperature

chtg. charting

CHU *Christelijk-Historische Unie*, Christian Historical Union, political party (Neth.)

C.H.U. centigrade heat unit

Chunnel Channel Tunnel, proposed for railed motor traffic, Straits of Dover, England–France

chute parachute

ch. v. check valve

c.h.w. constant hot water

chwdn. churchwarden

C. Hy. Commission for Hydrometeorology (WMO)

chyd. churchyard

Chy. Div. Chancery Division (leg.)

Ci *s* curie, a unit of radioactivity

CI *s* Ivory Coast (I.V.R.); *s* Laoighis (Rep. of Ireland V.R.)

c.i. cast iron; compression ignition (mech.); configuration inspection

c. & i. cost and insurance; cowboys and indians

C.I. Channel Islands; Chapter of Instruction (freem.); chemical inspectorate (MOD); chief inspector/instructor; colour index; Commonwealth Institute; Communist International; consular invoice; counter intelligence; (Imperial Order of the) Crown of India, honour instituted for ladies 1877, carrying no rank or title. No conferments have been made since 1947

C. & I. cost and insurance

CIA Chemical Industries' Association

Cia. It. *Compagnia*, company; Port. *Companhia*, company; Sp. *Compañia*, company

C.I.A. Central Intelligence Agency (U.S.A.); Chief Inspector of Armaments; Fr. *Comité international d'Auschwitz*, Intern. Auschwitz Committee; Fr. *Confédération internationale des accordéonistes*. Intern. Confed. of Accordionists; Fr. *Conseil international des archives*, Intern. Council on Archives; Corporation of Insurance Agents; Culinary Institute of America

C.I.A.A. Fr. *Centre international d'aviation agricole*, Intern. Agricultural Aviation Centre; Co-ordinator Inter-American Affairs

C.I.A.B. Fr. *Conseil international des agences bénévoles*, Intern. Council of Voluntary Agencies

C.I.A.I. Fr. *Comité international d'aide aux intellectuels*, Intern. Relief Committee for Professional Workers; Commerce and Industry Association Institute

C.I.A.L. Fr. *Communauté internationale des associations de la librairie*, Intern. Community of Booksellers' Assns.; Corresponding Member of the International Institute of Arts and Letters

C.I.A.O. Fr. *Conférence internationale des africanistes de l'ouest*, Intern. West African Conference

C.I.A.P.G. Fr. *Confédération internationale des anciens prisonniers de guerre*, Intern. Confed. of Former Prisoners of War

C.I.A.S. Conference of Independent African States

CIB Central Intelligence Board; Corporation of Insurance Brokers

C.I.B. Fr. *Communauté internationale Baha'ie*, Baha'i Intern. Community; Fr. *Conseil international du bâtiment pour la recherche, l'étude et la documentation*, Intern. Council for Building Research, Studies and Documentation; Criminal Investigation Branch

C.I.B.E. Fr. *Confédération internationale des betteraviers européens*, Intern. Confed. of European Sugar-Beet Growers

C.I.B.E.P. Fr. *Section des six pays du commerce international de bulbes à fleurs et de plantes ornementales*, Intern. Flower, Bulb and Ornamental Plant Trade Section for the Six Countries

CIC *Centre d'Information de la Couleur*, Colour Information Centre (France); Chemical Industry of Canada; — **MHE** College-Industry Committee on Material Handling Education (U.S.A.); Fr. *Conseil internationale de la chasse*, Intern. Hunting Council; Counter-Intelligence Corps (U.S.A.)

Cic. Marcus Tullius Cicero (106–43 B.C.) Roman orator

C.I.C. Capital Issues Committee; Chemical Institute of Canada; Combat Intelligence Center (U.S.A.); Commander-in-Chief; Command Information Center (U.S.A.); Commercial Instruments Conference; Commonwealth Information Centre; Fr. *Confédération internationale de la coiffure*, Intern. Confed. of the Hairdressing Trade; Fr. *Confédération internationale des cadres*, Intern. Confed. of Executive Staffs; Fr. *Conseil international de la chasse*, Intern. Hunting Council; Fr. *Conseil international des compositeurs*, Intern. Council of Composers; Counter Intelligence Corps (U.S.A.); Critical Issues Council (U.S.A.)

C.I.C.A. Canadian Institute of Chartered Accountants; Fr. *Confédération internationale du crédit agricole*, Intern. Confed. for Agricultural Credit

C.I.C.A.E. Fr. *Confédération internationale des cinémas d'art et d'essai*, Intern. Experimental and Art Film Theatres Confed.

CICAR Co-operative Investigations of the Caribbean and Adjacent Regions

C.I.C.C. Fr. *Conférence internationale des charités catholiques*, Intern. Conference of Catholic Charities

Cicestr. L. *Cicestrensis*, of Chichester, Eng. episcopal title in bishop's signature

C.I.C.G. Fr. *Centre international du commerce de gros*, Intern. Centre for Wholesale Trade

C.I.C. hut Charles Inglis Clark memorial hut of S.M.C. on Ben Nevis

C.I.C.I.A.M.S. Fr. *Comité internationale catholique des infirmières et assistantes médico-sociales*, Intern. Committee of Catholic Nurses

C.I.C.I.H. Fr. *Confédération internationale catholique des institutions hospitalières*, Intern. Catholic Confed. of Hospitals

C.I.C.J. Fr. *Comité international pour la coopération des journalistes*, Intern. Committee for Co-operation of Journalists

CICP Committee to Investigate Copyright problems (U.S.A.)

C.I.C.P. Sp. *Comisión Internacional para la Coopéración de los Periodistas*, Intern. Committee for the Co-operation of Journalists; Fr. *Confédération internationale du crédit populaire*, Intern. Confed. for Small-Scale Credit

C.I.C.R. Fr. *Comité international de la Croix Rouge*, Intern. Committee of the Red Cross

C.I.C.R.C. Fr. *Commission internationale contre le régime concentrationnaire*, Intern. Commission Against Concentration Camp Practices

C.I.C.R.I.S. Co-operative Industrial and Commercial Reference and Information Service

CICS committee for index cards for standards

C.I.C.T. Fr. *Conseil international du cinéma et de la télévision*, Intern. Film and Television Council

C.I.C.Y.P. Sp. *Consejo Interamericano de Comercio y Producción*, Inter-American Council of Commerce and Production

C.I.D. Fr. *Comité international de Dachau*, Dachau Intern. Committee; Committee for Imperial Defence; Council of Industrial Design; Criminal Investigation Department

C.I.D.A. Sp. *Comisión Interamericano de Desarrollo Agricola*, Inter-American Committee for Agricultural Development; Fr. *Comité intergouvernemental du droit d'auteur*, Inter-governmental Copyright Committee

CIDADEC Fr. *Confédération internationale des associations d'experts et de conseils*, Intern. Confed. of Assns. of Experts and Consultants

CIDALC Fr. *Comité international du cinéma d'enseignement et de la culture*, Intern. Committee of Film Education and Culture

Cide., CIDE *Comisión de Inversion y Desarrollo Economico*, Commission for

Investment and Economic Development (Uruguay)

C.I.D.E.S.A. Fr. *Centre international de documentation économique et sociale africaine*, Intern. Centre for African Social and Economic Documentation

CIDESCO Fr. *Comité international d'esthétique et de cosmétologie*, Intern. Committee for Beauty Culture and Cosmetology

CIDLA Port. *Combustíveis Industriais e Domésticos S.A.R.L.*, Industrial and Domestic Fuel Company

CIDOC Centre for Intercultural Documentation (Mexico)

C.I.D.S.S. Fr. *Comité international pour la documentation des sciences sociales*, Intern. Committee for Social Sciences Documentation

Cie. Fr. *compagnie*, company

C.I.E. captain's imperfect entry; Fr. *Centre international de l'enfance*, Intern. Children's Centre; Fr. *Commission internationale de l'éclairage*, Intern. Commission on Illumination; Companion of the Most Eminent Order of the Indian Empire; *Coras Iompair Eireann*, Transport Organization of Ireland

C.I.E.C. Fr. *Centre international d'études criminologiques*, Intern. Centre of Criminological Studies; Fr. *Commission internationale de l'état civil*, Intern. Commission on Civil Status; Sp. *Confederación Interamericana de Educación Católica*, Inter-American Confed. of Catholic Education; Fr. *Conseil international des employeurs du commerce*, Intern. Council of Commerce Employers

C.I.E.E. Companion of the Institution of Electrical Engineers

C.I.E.M. Fr. *Conseil international pour l'exploration de la mer*, Intern. Council for the Exploration of the Sea

C.I.E.N. Fr. *Commission interaméricaine d'énergie nucléaire*, Inter-American Nuclear Energy Commission

C.I.E.O. Catholic International Education Office

C.I.E.P.S. Fr. *Conseil international de l'éducation physique et sportive*, Intern. Council of Sport and Physical Education

C.I.E.S. Fr. *Comité international des entreprises à succursales*, Intern. Assn. of Chain Stores

C.I.E.S.M.M. Fr. *Commission Internationale pour l'Exploration Scientifique de la Mer Méditerranée*, Intern. Commission for the Scientific Exploration of the Mediterranean sea

C.I.E.T.A. Fr. *Centre international d'études des textiles anciens*, Intern. Research Centre on Ancient Textiles

c.i.f., C.I.F., C.I. & F. cost, insurance and freight

C.I.F. Canadian Institute of Forestry; *Clube Internacional de Futebol*, Intern. Football Club (Port.); Fr. *Commission interaméricaine des femmes*, Inter-American Commission of Women; Fr. *Conseil international des femmes*, Intern. Council of Women

c.i.f. & c. cost, insurance, freight and commission

C.I.F.C. Centre for Inter-Firm Comparison

c.i.f.c.&i. cost, insurance, freight, commission and interest

c.i.f.&e. cost, insurance, freight and exchange

C.I.F.E. Fr. *Conseil des fédérations industrielles d'Europe*, Council of European Industrial Feds.; Fr. *Conseil international du film d'enseignement*, Intern. Council for Educational Films

c.i.f.&i. cost, insurance, freight and interest

C.I.F.J. Fr. *Centre international du film pour la jeunesse*, Intern. Centre of Films for Children

c.i.f.L.t. cost, insurance and freight, London terms

Cifra Spanish news agency

cig. cigarette

C.I.G. Fr. *Comité international de géophysique*, Intern. Geophysical Committee

C.I.G.A. It. *Compagnia Italiana dei Grandi Alberghi*, Italian hotel group

C.I.G.B. Fr. *Commission internationale des grands barrages de la Conférence mondiale de l'énergie*, Intern. Commission of Large Dams of the World Power Conference

C.I.G.R. Fr. *Commission internationale du génie rural*, Intern. Commission of Agricultural Engineering

C.I.G.R.E. Fr. *Conférence internationale des grands réseaux électriques*, Intern. Conference on Large Electric Systems

C.I.G.S. Chief of the Imperial General Staff

C.I.H.A. Fr. *Comité international d'histoire de l'art*, Intern. Committee on the History of Art

C.I.I. Centre for Industrial Innovation (Univ. of Strathclyde); Chartered Insurance Institute; Fr. *Conseil international des infirmières*, Intern. Council of Nurses

C.I.I.A. Canadian Institute of International Affairs; Fr. *Commission internationale des industries agricoles*, Intern. Commission for Agricultural Industries

77

CIIR Catholic Institute for International Relations

C.I.J. Fr. *Commission internationale de juristes*, Intern. Commission of Jurists

C.I.L.B. Fr. *Commission internationale de lutte biologique contre les ennemis des plantes*, Intern. Commission for Biological Control

C.I.L.C. Fr. *Confédération internationale du lin et du chanvre*, Intern. Linen and Hemp Confed.

CILECT Fr. *Centre International de Liaison des Écoles de Cinéma et de Télévision*, Intern. Assn. of National Film Schools

CILG Construction Industry Information Liaison Group

Cilla Priscilla

C.I.L.P.E. Fr. *Conférence internationale de liaison entre producteurs d'énergie électrique*, Intern. Liaison Conference for Producers of Electrical Energy

C.I.M. Canadian Institute of Mining; China Inland Mission; Fr. *Comité International de Mini-Basketball*, Intern. Mini-Basketball Committee; Commission for Industry and Manpower; Fr. *Conférence islamique mondial*, World Muslim Conference; Fr. *Conseil international de la musique*, Intern. Music Council; Sp. *Consejo Internacional de Mujeres*, Intern. Council of Women; Fr. *Convention internationale concernant le transport des merchandises par chemins de fer*, Intern. Convention Concerning the Carriage of Goods by Rail

CIMA Construction Industry Manufacturers' Association (U.S.A.)

C.I.M.A.C. Fr. *Congrès international des machines à combustion*, Intern. Congress on Combustion Engines

C.I. Mar. E. Companion of the Institute of Marine Engineers

CIMAS continuous iron-making and steel-making, a smelting process for iron and steel

C.I.M.C.E.E. Fr. *Comité des industries de la moutarde de la C.E.E.*, E.E.C. Committee for the Mustard Industries

C.I.M.E. Fr. *Comité intergouvernemental pour les migrations européennes*, Intergovernmental Committee for European Migration; Council of Industry for Management Education

C.I. Mech. E. Companion of the Institution of Mechanical Engineers

C.I.M.M. Canadian Institute of Mining and Metallurgy

C.I.M.P. Fr. *Conseil international de la musique populaire*, Intern. Folk Music Council

C.I.M.P.M. Fr. *Comité international*

de médecine et de pharmacie militaires, Intern. Committee of Military Medicine and Pharmacy

C.I.M.S.C.E.E. Fr. *Comité des industries des mayonnaises et sauces condimentaires de la C.E.E.*, Committee of the Mayonnaise and Sauce Industries of the E.E.C.

C.I.M.T.P. Fr. *Congrès international de médecine tropicale et de paludisme*, Intern. Congress of Tropical Medicine and Malaria

C.I.N. Fr. *Commission internationale de numismatique*, Intern. Numismatic Commission

C.-in-C. commander-in-chief (*also* CINC); curate-in-charge

CINCAFMED Commander-in-Chief Allied Forces Mediterranean

CINCEASTLANT Commander-in-Chief Eastern Atlantic Area

CINCENT Commander-in-Chief Allied Forces Central Europe

CINCEUR Commander-in-Chief, Europe

CINCHAN Commander-in-Chief Channel and South North Sea

CINCLANT Commander-in-Chief Atlantic Fleet

CINCLANTFLT Commander-in-Chief, Atlantic Fleet (USN)

CINCMED Commander-in-Chief British Naval Forces in the Mediterranean

CINCNELM Commander-in-Chief U.S. Naval Forces in Europe, the East Atlantic, and the Mediterranean

CINCNORTH Commander-in-Chief Allied Forces Northern Europe

CINCPAC Commander-in-Chief Pacific Fleet

CINCPACFLT Commander-in-Chief, Pacific Fleet (USN)

CINCSOUTH Commander-in-Chief Allied Forces Southern Europe

CINCWESTLANT Commander-in-Chief Western Atlantic Area

Cine cinema

CINECA Co-operative Investigation of the Northern Part of the Eastern Central Atlantic

Cinerama cine plus panorama, form of 3-dimensional film

CINFO chief of information

Cinn. Cincinnati

cinna. cinnamon

C.I.N.O. Chief Inspector of Naval Ordnance

C.I.N.O.A. Fr. *Confédération internationale des négociants en œuvres d'art*, Intern. Confed. of Art Dealers

C. Inst. R. Companion of the Institute of Refrigeration

C. Inst. R.E. (Aust.) Companion of the Institution of Radio Engineers (Aust.)
CIO Congress of Industrial Organizations (Liberia)
C.I.O. Church Information Office; Fr. *Comité international olympique*, Intern. Olympic Committee; Fr. *Commission internationale d'optique*, Intern. Commission for Optics; Congress of Industrial Organisations, *now* A.F.L.-C.I.O.
C.I.O.M.S. Council for International Organizations of Medical Sciences
CIOS Fr. *Conseil International pour l'Organisation Scientifique*, Intern. Committee of Scientific Management
C.I.O.S. combined intelligence objectives sub-committee; Fr. *Comité international de l'organisation scientifique*, Intern. Committee of Scientific Management
C.I.O.S.L. Sp. *Confederación Internacional de Organizaciones Sindicales Libres*, Intern. Confed. of Free Trade Unions
C.I.O.S.T.A. Fr. *Commission internationale pour l'organisation scientifique du travail en agriculture*, Intern. Agricultural Labour Science Group
C.I.O.T.F. Fr. *Conseil international des organismes de travailleuses familiales*, Intern. Council of Home-Help Services
C.I.P. *Centre d'Information de la Presse*, Catholic news agency (Belgium); Fr. *Collège international de podologie*, Intern. College of Podology; Fr. *Comité international de photobiologie*, Intern. Committee of Photobiology; Fr. *Commission internationale du peuplier*, Intern. Poplar Commission; Fr. *Commission Internationale Permanente pour l'Épreuve des Armes à Feu*, Intern. Proof Commission for Firearms
C.I.P.A. Canadian Industrial Preparedness Association; Chartered Institute of Patent Agents
CIPASH Committee for International Program in Atmospheric Sciences and Hydrology (U.N.O.)
C.I.P.B.C. Church of India, Pakistan, Burma and Ceylon
C.I.P.C. Fr. *Comité international permanent de la conserve*, Permanent Intern. Committee on Canned Foods
C.I.P.C.E. Fr. *Centre d'information et de publicité des chemins de fer européens*, Information and Publicity Centre of the European Railways
C.I.P.E. Sp. *Consejo Internacional de la Película de Enseñanza*, Intern. Council for Educational Films
C.I.P.L. Fr. *Comité international permanent de linguistes*, Permanent Intern. Committee of Linguists

CIPM Council for International Progress in Management (U.S.A.)
C.I.P.O. Fr. *Comité international pour la préservation des oiseaux*, Intern. Committee for Bird Preservation
C.I.P.P. Fr. *Conseil indo-pacifique des pêches*, Indo-Pacific Fisheries Council
C.I.P.R. Fr. *Commission internationale de protection contre les radiations*, Intern. Commission on Radiological Protection
CIPRA Cast Iron Pipe Research Association
C.I.P.S.H. Fr. *Conseil international de la philosophie et des sciences humaines*, Intern. Council for Philosophy and the Humanities
CIR Commission on Industrial Relations; *Convention des Institutions Républicaines*, Republican Institutions Convention (France)
cir., circ. circle; circuit; circular; circulation; circumference; circus
cir., circ. L. *circa*, about
C.I.R. Canada India reactor; Commissioners of Inland Revenue; Commission/Committee/Council on Industrial Relations; cost information report
CIRA Committee on International Reference Atmosphere; Conference of Industrial Research Associations
C.I.R.C.C.E. Fr. *Confédération internationale de la représentation commerciale de la Communauté européenne*, Intern. Confed. of Commercial Representation in the European Community
circs. circumstances
circum. circumference
C.I.R.F. Fr. *Centre international d'information et de recherche sur la formation professionelle*, Intern. Vocational Training Information and Research Centre; Corn Industries Research Foundation
C.I.R.F.S. Fr. *Comité international de la rayonne et des fibres synthétiques*, Intern. Rayon and Synthetic Fibres Committee
C.I.R.I.A. Construction Industry Research and Information Association, *formerly* C.E.R.A.
C.I.R.I.E.C. Fr. *Centre international de recherches et d'information sur l'économie collective*, Intern. Centre of Research and Information on Collective Economy
C.I.R.P. Fr. *Collège international pour l'étude scientifique des techniques de production mécanique*, Intern. Institution for Production Engineering Research
cis, CIS cataloguing in source
Cis, Cissie, Cissy Cecilia
CIS Catholic Information Society (U.S.A.); Center for International Studies, MIT (U.S.A.); Central Information Ser-

vice on Occupational Health and Safety (RoSPA)

C.I.S. Chartered Institute of Secretaries; Coal Industry Society; Conference of Internationally-Minded Schools

CISA Canadian Industrial Safety Association; It. *Centro Italiano Studi Aziendali*, Italian Centre for Business Studies

C.I.S.A.C. Fr. *Confédération internationale des sociétés d'auteurs et compositeurs*, Intern. Confed. of Societies of Authors and Composers

C.I.S.B.H. Fr. *Comité international de standardisation en biologie humaine*, Intern. Committee for Standardization in Human Biology

C.I.S.C. Fr. *Confédération internationale des syndicats chrétiens*, Intern. Fed. of Christian Trade Unions; Fr. *Conférence internationale du scoutisme catholique*, Intern. Catholic Scouters Conference

Cisco San Francisco

C.I.S.F. Fr. *Confédération internationale des sages-femmes*, Intern. Confed. of Midwives

C.I.S.H. Fr. *Comité international des sciences historiques*, Intern. Committee of Historical Sciences

C.I.S.I.R. Ceylon Institute of Scientific and Industrial Research

C.I.S.J.A. Fr. *Comité international de solidarité avec la jeunesse algérienne*, Intern. Solidarity Committee with Algerian Youth

C.I.S.L. Fr. *Confédération internationale des syndicats libres*, Intern. Confed. of Free Trade Unions; *Confederazione Italiana Sindacati Lavoratori*, Fed. of Italian Trade Unions

Cislunar nav earth–moon distance measurement

C.I.S.M. Fr. *Conseil international du sport militaire*, Intern. Military Sports Council

C.I.S.N.A.L. *Confederazione Italiana dei Sindacati Nazionali dei Lavoratori*, National Italian Confed. of Workers' Trade Unions

C.I.S.O. Fr. *Comité international des sciences onomastiques*, Intern. Committee of Onomastic Sciences

C.I.S.P.M. Fr. *Confédération internationale des sociétés populaires de musique*, Intern. Confed. of Popular Music Societies

C.I.S.P.R. Fr. *Comité international spécial des perturbations radioélectriques*, Intern. Special Committee on Radio Interference

C.I.S.S. Fr. *Comité international des sports silencieux*, Intern. Committee for Silent Games; Fr. *Conférence internationale de service social*, Intern. Confer-

ence of Social Work; Sp. *Conferencia Interamericano de Seguridad Social*, Inter-American Conference on Social Security; Fr. *Conseil international des sciences sociales*, Intern. Social Science Council

Cist. Cistercian

C.I.S.V. Children's International Summer Village Association

cit. citadel; citation; cited; citizen; citrate

c.i.t. compression in transit

C.I.T. California/Carnegie Institute of Technology (U.S.A.); Fr. *Comité international des transports par chemins de fer*, Intern. Railway Transport Committee; Fr. *Conseil international des tanneurs*, Intern. Council of Tanners

C.I.T.A. Sp. *Confederacion Internacional de Ingenieros y Técnicos de la Agricultura*, Intern. Confed. of Technical Agriculturalists

C.I.T.B. Construction Industry Training Board

C.I.T.C. Canadian Institute of Timber Construction; Construction Industry Training Centre

C.I.T.C.E. Fr. *Comité international de thermodynamique et de cinétique électrochimiques*, Intern. Committee of Electro-Chemical Thermodynamics and Kinetics

cite compression ignition and turbine engine

CITEL Committee for the Inter-American Telecommunications

C.I.T.E.N. Fr. *Comité international de la teinture et du nettoyage*, Intern. Committee for Dyeing and Dry Cleaning

C.I.T.I. Fr. *Confédération internationale des travailleurs intellectuels*, Intern. Confed. of Professional and Intellectual Workers

cito disp. L. *cito dispensetur*, let it be dispensed quickly (med.)

C.I.T.S. Fr. *Commission internationale technique de sucrerie*, Intern. Commission of Sugar Technology

C.I.T.T.A. Fr. *Comité international des fabricants de tapis et de tissues d'ameublement*, Intern. Committee of Manufacturers of Carpets and Furnishing Fabrics

C.I.U.S. Fr. *Conseil international des unions scientifiques*, Intern. Council of Scientific Unions

C.I.U.S.S. Catholic International Union for Social Service

civ. civil; civilian; civilization; civilize

C.I.V. City Imperial Volunteers; Fr. *Commission internationale du verre*, Intern. Glass Commission; Fr. *Convention internationale concernant le transport des voyageurs et des bagages par chemins de* *fer*, Intern. Convention Concerning the Carriage of Passengers and Baggage by Rail

Civ. E.   civil engineer/engineering

civvies   civilian clothes

civvy   civilian

C.I.W.   Carnegie Institute of Washington (U.S.A.)

CJ   *s* Herefordshire (B.V.R.)

C & J   clean and jerk (weight-lifting)

cj.   conjectural

C.J.   chief justice

C.J.B.   Constructors John Brown

C.J.C.C.   Commonwealth Joint Communications Committee

C.J.M.   Fr. *Code de justice militaire*, Code of Military Justice; Congregation of Jesus and Mary (Eudist Fathers); Fr. *Congrès juif mondial*, World Jewish Congress

CK   *s* Colchester (B.F.P.); *s* Preston (B.V.R.)

ck.   cask; check; cook

C.K.   Cape Kennedy (U.S.A.)

c.k.d.   completely knocked down

CKMP   *Cumhuriyet Koylu Millet Partisi*, Republic Peasant Nation Party (Turk.)

CKMTA   Cape Kennedy Missile Test Annex

ckpt   cockpit

C.K.R.A.   Council of the Knights of the Red Cross (freem.)

ckw.   clockwise

Cl   *s* chlorine (chem.)

CL   *s* Carlisle (B.F.P.); *s* Ceylon (I.V.R.); *s* Norwich (B.V.R.)

cl.   carload; centilitre; claim; class; classical; classics; classification; clause; clearance; clergy; clergyman; clerk; climb; close; closet; closure; cloth; clove; council

c/l.   cash letter; craft loss

Cl.   *clarinet* (mus.)

c.l.   carload; centre line; common law; compiler language; cut lengths; cutter location

C.L.   calendar line; civil law/lord; Commander of the Order of Leopold (Belg.); common law; communication lieutenant; craft loss; critical list

Cla., Clack.   Clackmannan

C.L.A.   Canadian Library/Lumbermen's Association; Central/Country Landowners' Association; centre line average

C.L.A.I.R.A.   Chalk Lime and Allied Industries Research Association

CLAM   chemical ramjet low-altitude missile

CLAO   Latin American Council on Oceanography

clar.   clarendon type

Clar.   Clarenceux, King of Arms; Clarendon

Clar.   *clarinet* (mus.)

C.L.A.R.C.   Sp. *Consejo Latino-Americano de Radiación Cósmica*, Latin-American Council for Cosmic Rays

Clarrie   Clarice; Clarissa

C.L.A.S.   Chartered Land Agents Society

C.L.A.S.P.   Consortium of Local Authorities Special Programme

class.   classic; classical; classification; classify

C.L.A.S.S.   Computer-based Laboratory for Automated School Systems

C.L.A.T.A.   Co-operative Laundry and Allied Trades Association

Clav.   *clavier* (mus.)

C.L.B.   Church Lads' Brigade, founded in 1891 to encourage young people to become faithful members of the C. of E.

CLC   Canadian Labour Congress, *Congrès du travail du Canada*; Central Liaison Committee (Guyana)

C.L.C.   chartered life underwriter of Canada; Commonwealth Liaison Committee

C.L.C.B.   Committee of London Clearing Bankers

C.L.C.C.R.   Fr. *Comité de liaison de la construction de carrosseries et de remorques*, Liaison Committee of Coachwork and Trailer Builders

C.L.Cert. (B.O.A.)   Supplementary Contact Lens Diploma of British Optical Association

C.L.Cert.(S.M.C.)   Supplementary Contact Lens Certificate of Worshipful Company of Spectacle Makers

C. L. Cr.   communication lieutenant-commander

cld.   called; cancelled; cleared; coloured; cooled; could

C.L.D.   Doctor of Civil Law

CLE   Council of Legal Education

C.L.E.A.P.S.E.   Consortium of Local Education Authorities for the Provision of Science Equipment

Clem   Clement; Clementina; Clementine

CLEPA   Fr. *Comité de liaison de la construction d'équipements et de pièces*, Liaison Committee for the Manufacture of Equipment and Spare Parts

cler.   clerical

cl. gt.   cloth gilt (bookbinding)

C.L.H.   Fr. *Croix de la Légion d'Honneur*, Cross of the Legion of Honour

C.L.I.   Conference of the Electronics Industry

Cliff   Clifford

clim.   climate; climatic

C.L.I.M.M.A.R. Fr. *Centre de liaison international des marchands de machines agricoles et réparateurs*, Intern. Liaison Centre for Agricultural Machinery Distributors and Maintenance

clin. clinic; clinical

C. Litt. Companion of Literature

C.L.J. *Cambridge Law Journal*

clk. clerk; clock

clkw. clockwise

cl. L. classical Latin

Cllr. councillor

clm. column

C.L.M.L. Contact Lens Manufacturers' Association; *Current List of Medical Literature*

clo. closet; clothing

C.L.O. chief liaison officer; cod liver oil

C.L.P.A. Common Law Procedure Acts

clr. clear; colour; cooler

C.L.R. Central London (Underground) Railway; Centre of Lateral Resistance (naval arch.); City of London Rifles; Council on Library Resources (U.S.A.)

clrm. classroom

C.L.R.U. Cambridge Language Research Unit

C.L.S. Certificate in Library Science; Christian Literature Society; Courts of London Sessions

C.L.S.G. Contact Lens Study Group

Clst. clarinettist (mus.)

C.L.T. *Canadian Law Times*

C.L.Tech.(A.D.O.) Contact Lens Diploma of the Association of Dispensing Opticians

C.L.U. chartered life underwriter

Clydeport Clyde Port Authority

cm Ger. *Zentimeter*, centimetre

c'm come

Cm *s* curium (chem.)

CM *s* Birkenhead (B.V.R.)

cm. centimetre; **cm²** square centimetre; **cm³** cubic centimetre

c.m. central meridian; centre of mass; Fr. *classes moyennes*, middle classes; court martial

c.m. L. *causa mortis*, by reason of death; L. *cras mane*, tomorrow morning (med.)

C.M. Canadian Militia; Catholic Mission; Certificate of Merit (*also* C. of M.); certificated/certified master/mistress; *Chirurgiae Magister*, Master of Surgery; church mission/missionary; circulation manager; Common Market; Congregation of the Mission, Vincentian Fathers; corporate membership; corresponding member; Fr. *Membre de l'Ordre du Canada*, Member of the Order of Canada

C.M. common metre (mus.)

CMA Catering Managers' Association; civil-military affairs

C.M.A. Cable Makers' Association; Canadian Medical Association; Church Music Association; Commonwealth Medical Association; Corset Manufacturers' Association; Court of Military Appeals

C.M.A.C. Catholic Marriage Advisory Council

C.M.A.C.P. Fr. *Conseil mondial pour l'assemblée constituante des peuples*, World Council for the People's World Convention

C.M.A.S. Clergy Mutual Assurance Society; Fr. *Confédération mondiale des activités subaquatiques*, World Underwater Fed.

C.M.B. Central Medical/Midwives Board; Chase Manhattan Bank; coastal motor boat

C.M.B.H.I. Craft Member of the British Horological Institute

C.M.B.I. Caribbean Marine Biological Institute

cmbt. combat

CMC carboxymethyl cellulose; Commandant, Marine Corps

C.M.C. Canadian Marconi Company; Canadian Music Council; Collective Measures Committee (U.N.O.); Fr. *Groupement des producteurs de carreaux céramiques du Marché Commun*, Common Market Group of Ceramic Tile Producers

C.M.C.W. Calvinistic Methodist Church of Wales

Cmd. *Command Paper* published by H.M.S.O. 1919–56

C.M.D. common metre double (mus.)

cmdg. commanding

Cmdr. commander

Cmdre. commodore

Cmdt. commandant

C.M.E. Fr. *Conférence mondiale de l'énergie*, World Power Conference

C.M.E.A. Council for Mutual Economic Aid/Assistance

C.M.F. Cement Makers' Federation; Central Mediterranean Force; Ceylon Military Force; coherent memory filter; Commonwealth Military Force

C.M.F. L. *Cordis Mariae Filii*, Missionary Sons of the Immaculate Heart of Mary

C.M.G. Commission on Marine Geology; Companion of the Most Distinguished Order of St. Michael and St. George; Computer Management Group

C.M.H. combined military hospital; Congressional Medal of Honor (U.S.A.)

82

C.M.H.A. Canadian Mental Health Association

CMHC Central Mortgage and Housing Corporation (Can.)

C.M.I. Christian Michelsen's Institute (Norway); Fr. *Comité maritime international*, Intern. Maritime Committee; Fr. *Commission mixte internationale pour la protection des lignes de télécommunication et des canalisations*, Joint Intern. Committee for the Protection of Telecommunication Lines and Ducts; Commonwealth Mycological Institute

C.M.I.A. Coal Mining Institute of America

C.M.J. Church's Ministry among the Jews

cml. commercial

C.M.L. *Câmara Municipal de Lisboa*, Lisbon Town Council (Port.); Central Music Library

C.M.M. Fr. *Commandeur de l'Ordre du Mérite Militaire*, Commander of the Order of Military Merit (Can.); Commission for Maritime Meteorology (WMO); Congregation of the Missionaries of Mariannhill

C.M.M.A. Concrete Mixer Manufacturers' Association

cmn. commission

Cmnd. *Command Paper* published by H.M.S.O. from 1956

cmnr. commissioner

CMO Central Merchandising Office (Zambia)

C.M.O. chief medical officer

C.M.O.P.E. Fr. *Confédération mondiale des organisations de la profession enseignante*, World Confed. of Organizations of the Teaching Profession

CMP command module pilot; cost of maintaining project

cmp. compromise

C.M.P. Commissioner of the Metropolitan Police; Corps of Military Police, *now* C.R.M.P.

cmpd. compound; compounded

cm. pf. cumulative preference/preferred shares

cm.p.s. centimetres per second

CMR common mode rejection

C.M.R. Cape Mounted Rifles

C.M.R.A. Chemical Marketing Research Association

C.M.R.O. County Milk Regulations Officer

C.M.R.S.S. Fr. *Conseil méditerranéen de recherches en sciences sociales*, Mediterranean Social Sciences Research Council

c.m.s. L. *cras mane sumendus*, to be taken tomorrow morning (med.)

C.M.S. Center for Measurement of Science (U.S.A.); Church Missionary Society

C.M.S.C. Common Market Safeguards Campaign

C.M.S.E.R. Commission on Marine Science, Engineering and Resources (U.S.A.)

cmsgt chief master sergeant (U.S.A.)

CM/SM command module service module

cmt. cement

C.M.Z.S. Corresponding Member of the Zoological Society

cN centinewton (phys.)

CN *s* Campbeltown (B.F.P.); cellulose nitrate (celluloid); chloracetophenone; *s* Gateshead (B.V.R.)

C/N circular/consignment/contract/country/cover/credit note

Cn. canon

c.n. L. *cras nocte*, tomorrow night (med.)

C.N. Chinese Nationalists; Fr. *Code Napoléon*; common network; Confederate navy

CNA Central News Agency, *Chungyang T'ung-hsün She* (Taiwan)

C.N.A. Canadian Nuclear Association; Center for Naval Analyses (USN); Chemical Notation Association (U.S.A.); cosmic noise absorption

C.N.A.A. Council for National Academic Awards

CNADS Conference of National Armaments Directors (NATO)

C.N.A.S. Chief of Naval Air Services

C.N.A.T. Fr. *Commission Nationale de l'Aménagement du Territoire*, National Territorial Planning and Development Commission

Cncl. council

Cnclr. councillor, *also* cllr.

CNCMH Canadian National Committee for Mental Hygiene

cncr. concurrent

C.N.D. Campaign for Nuclear Disarmament, organization formed 1958 to campaign for Britain's unilateral nuclear disarmament, and ultimately, for world nuclear disarmament. Under its auspices Aldermaston marches took place 1958–1963

C.N. (Eng.) O. chief naval engineering officer

CNEXO *Centre National pour l'Exploration des Océans* (France)

C.N.I. Chief of Naval Information

CNIP *Centre National des Indépendants et Paysans*, Nat. Centre of Independents and Peasants (France)

C.N.I.P.A. Committee of National Institutes of Patent Agents
cnl. cancel
C.N.L. Canadian National Library; Commonwealth National Library (Aust.)
C.N.L.A. Council of National Library Associations (U.S.A.)
C.N.M.A. Cordage and Net Manufacturers' Association
C.N.N. *Companhia Nacional de Navegação*, Nat. Shipping Co. (Port.)
C.N.O. Chief of Naval Operations
C.N.P. Chief of Naval Personnel
CNR *Conseil National de la Révolution*, Nat. Council of the Revolution (Congo, Br.)
cnr. corner
C.N.R. Canadian National Railway, has 23,763 m. of track and is the greatest railway system of N. America; Civil Nursing Reserve; *Consiglio Nazionale delle Ricerche*, Italian Nat. Research Council
C.N.S. central nervous system; Chief of the Naval Staff; Congress of Neurological Surgeons
CNSG consolidated nuclear steam generator
C.N.S.S.O. Chief Naval Supply and Secretariat Officer
CNT celestial navigation trainer; *Confederación Nacional de Trabajadores*, Nat. Confed. of Workers (Chile); *Confederación Nacional de Trabajo*, Nat. Confed. of Labour (Sp.)
C.N.T. Canadian National Telegraphs
CNTC *Confederação Nacional dos Trabalhadores no Comercio*, Nat. Confed. of Commercial Workers (Brazil)
CNTG Fr. *Confédération Nationale des Travailleurs Gabonais*, Nat. Confed. of Gabonian Workers
CNTI *Confederação Nacional dos Trabalhadores na Industria*, Nat. Confed. of Industrial Workers (Brazil)
cntn. contain
cntr. container; contribute; contribution
CNTTT *Confederação Nacional dos Trabalhadores em Transportes Terrestres*, Nat. Confed. of Land Transport Workers (Braz.)
cnvt. convict
c/o care of; carried over; cash order; change over
Co *s* cobalt (chem.); columbium
CO *s* Caernarvon (B.F.P.); *s* Colombia (I.V.R.); Colorado; conscientious objector, generally referring to military service; *s* Plymouth (B.V.R.)
co. company; county
Co. colon; course (nav.)

Co. *'cello*, violoncello (mus.)
C/O. case oil; certificate of origin
C.O. cabinet/central office; chief/clerical officer; Colonial Office, now amalgamated with Foreign and Commonwealth Office; commanding officer; command order; commissioner of oaths, comm. to administer oaths in supreme court; Commissioner's office, comm. of Metropolitan Police, Scotland Yard; Fr. *Compte Ouvert*, open account; criminal offence; Crown Office
C.O.A. College of Aeronautics, *now* Cranfield Institute of Technology; condition on admission
coad. coadjutor
Coal. coalition; — govt. coalition government
C.O.A.S. Council of the Organization of American States
c.o.b. close of business
C.O.B.C.C.E.E. Fr. *Comité des organisations de la boucherie et charcuterie de la C.E.E.*, Committee of Meat Trade Organizations of the E.E.C.
COBOL common/computer business oriented language
c.o.b.q. L. *cum omnibus bonis quiescat*, may he or she rest with all good souls
coc. cocaine
C.O.C. Chamber of Commerce; Clerk of the Chapel; combat operations center (U.S.A.); Corps of Commissionaires
C.O.C.A.S.T. Council for Overseas Colleges of Arts, Science and Technology
C.O.C.E.M.A. Fr. *Comité des constructeurs européens de matériel alimentaire*, Committee of European Machinery Manufacturers for the Food Industries
coch., cochl. L. *cochleare*, spoonful; — *amp. cochleare amplum*, tablespoonful; — *infant. cochleare infantis*, teaspoonful; — *mag., magn. cochleare magnum*, tablespoonful; — *med. cochleare medium*, dessertspoonful; — *mod. cochleare modicum*, dessertspoonful; — *parv. cochleare parvum*, teaspoonful (*all* med.)
COCI Consortium on Chemical Information
COCOM Coordinating Committee Controlling East-West Trade, *also* Coordinating Committee for Export to Communist Areas
C.O.C.O.S. Co-ordinating Committee for Manufacturers of Static Convertors in the Common Market Countries
COCOSEER Co-ordinating Committee on Slavic and East European Library Services
c.8va It. *coll'ottava*, in octaves (mus.)
COD chemical oxygen demand
cod. codex; — memb. codex membran-

acius, book written on skin/vellum; codicil; codification

c.o.d. cargo on deck; cash/collect on delivery

C.O.D. Chamber of Deputies; *Concise Oxford Dictionary*

C.O.D.A.G. combined diesel and gas turbine (ship propulsion)

CODATA Standing Committee for Data on Science and Technology

codd. codices

CODIPHASE coherent digital phased array system (computer)

C.O.D.O.G. combined diesel or gas turbine (ship propulsion)

CODOT Classification of Occupations and Directory of Occupational Titles, lists published by the Dept. of Employment classifying almost every known occupation in U.K.

COE Corps of Engineers (U.S.A.)

C.O.E. Fr. *Conseil œcuménique des églises*, World Council of Churches

COED computer operated electronic display

co-ed. co-editor; co-education

C.O.E.D. *Concise Oxford English Dictionary*

coeff. coefficient

CoEnCo Committee for Environmental Conservation

COESA Committee on Extension to the Standard Atmosphere (U.S.A.)

C.O.F. Fr. *Comité Olympique Française*, French Olympic Committee

C. of A. Certificate of Airworthiness; College of Arms

COFALEC Fr. *Comité des fabricants de levure de panification de la C.E.E.*, Committee of Bread Yeast Manufacturers of the E.E.C.

C. of B. confirmation of balance

C. of C. chamber of commerce; coefficient of correlation

C. of E. Church of England; coefficient of elasticity; Council of Europe

C. of E.C.S. Church of England Children's Society

C. of F. chaplain of the fleet; chief of finance; coefficient of friction

c. of g. centre of gravity

COFI Committee on Fisheries (FAO)

C. of I. Church of Ireland

C. of L. City of London

C. of S. chief of staff; Church of Scotland; conditions of service

cog. cognate; cognisant; cognomen

c.o.g. centre of gravity

C.O.G. Cleansing Officers' Guild

C.O.G.A.G. combined gas and gas turbine (ship propulsion)

COGECA Fr. *Comité général de la*

coopération agricole des pays de la C.E.E., General Committee for Agricultural Co-operation in the E.E.C. Countries

cogn. w. cognate with

COGS continuous orbital guidance system

coh. coheir

c.o.h. cash on hand

COHO coherent oscillator

C.O.H.S.E. Confederation of Health Service Employees

C.O.I. Central Office of Information; certificate of origin and interest; Fr. *Commission océanographique intergouvernementale*, Inter-governmental Oceanographic Commission

C.O.I.C. Canadian Oceanographic Identification Centre

COID, CoID, C.O.I.D. Council of Industrial Design

COIN counter-insurgency

COINS Committee on Improvement of National Statistics (U.S.A.)

C.O.J.O. Conference of Jewish Organizations

Coke abbrev. (1909) of trade name, Coca-Cola, for a beverage, *coca* and *cola* being names of vegetable products from which stimulants are extracted

col. cola (strain); collect; collected; collection; collector; college; collegiate; colonial; colony; colour; coloured; column

Col. Colombia; colon; colonel; Colorado (*also* Colo.); Colossians

Co. L. Coalition Liberal

4 Col.P. 4-colour page (advert.)

C.O.L. cost of living; — **B.** cost of living bonus

Col c. It. *Col canto*, with vocal part, or with melody (mus.)

Col. Comdt. colonel commandant

cold. coloured

Colette Nicola

COLIDAR coherent light detection and ranging

COLIPED Fr. *Commission de liaison des pièces et équipements de deux roues*, Liaison Committee for Motor Cycle and Bicycle Equipment and Spare Parts

coll. collateral; colleague; collect; collection; collector (*also* collr.); college; collegiate; colloquial; colloquialism

Coll. collateral, *also* collat.

collab. collaborate; collaborator

collect. collective; collectively

Coll. of F.E. College of Further Education

Coll'ott. It. *Coll'ottava*, with the octave, to be played in octaves (mus.)

colly. colliery

colog. cologarithm

Col. P. colour page, publishers selection (advert.)

COLS communications for on line systems (computer)

cols. columns

Col.-Sergt., Col.-Sgt. colour-sergeant

COM commander, prefix applied to abbrev. of US naval commands

com. comedy; comic; comma; commentary; commerce; commercial; commission; commissioner; committee; common; commoner; commonly; commune; communicate; communicated; communication; community

Com. Commander; commissary, *also* commiss. / commy.; commodore; Commonwealth; commune; communist

C.O.M.A. Coke Oven Managers' Association

COMACA Corresponding Member of the Academy of Arts of the U.S.S.R.

COMACH *Confederación Marítima de Chile*, Maritime Confed. of Chile

COMAF Fr. *Comité des constructeurs de matériel frigorifique de la C.E.E.*, Committee of Refrigerating Plant Manufacturers of the E.E.C.

COMAIRCENTLANT Air Commander Central Atlantic Sub-area

COMAIRCHAN Maritime Air Commander Channel

COMAIREASTLANT Air Commander Eastern Atlantic Area

COMAIRLANT Commander Air Force, Atlantic (U.S.A.)

COMAIRNORLANT Air Commander Northern Atlantic Sub-area

COMART Commander, Marine Air Reserve Training

comb. combination; combine; combustible

combine combined harvester (agric.)

COMBISLANT Commander Bay of Biscay Atlantic Sub-area

Combo combination (mus.)

COMBQUARFOR Combined Quarantine Force (U.S.A., Ven., Dom. Rep., Argen.)

combs. combinations (clothing)

combu. combustion

COMCANLANT Commander Canadian Atlantic Sub-area

COMCENTLANT Commander Central Atlantic Sub-area

COMCRULANT Commander Cruisers, Atlantic (U.S.A.)

comd. command; commanding

Comd. commander, *also* Cdr., Cmdr., Comdr.

COMDEV Commonwealth Development Finance Company

comdg. commanding

Comdt. commandant

C.O.M.E. Chief Ordnance Mechanical Engineer

COMECON Council for Mutual Economic Aid/Assistance (E. European)

Com. Err. *The Comedy of Errors* (Shake.)

Comet Committee for Middle East Trade, *also* COMET; de Havilland Comet 4B (aircraft)

COMET computer-operated management evaluation technique

COMETEC-GAZ Fr. *Comité d'études économiques de l'industrie du gaz*, Economic Research Committee of the Gas Industry

COMEXO Committee for Exploitation of the Oceans

comfy comfortable

Com.-Gen. commissary-general

COMIBOL *Corporación Minera de Bolivia*, Bolivian state industry mining corp.

Cominform Communist Information Bureau

COMINT communications intelligence

Comintern Communist International

COMISCO Committee of International Socialist Conference

coml. commercial

COMLOGNET combat logistics network (USAF)

comm. commentary; commerce; commercial; It. *commerciale*, commercial; commercially; It. *commercio*, trade; communication

Comm. commodore

commd. commissioned

commem. commemoration day/week; commemorative

Commiss. commissary

commissr., commr. commissioner

commn. commission

commun. communication; community

commy. commissary; communist

COMNAVNORTH Commander Allied Naval Forces Northern Europe

COMNORASDEFLANT Commander North American Anti-Submarine Defence Force Atlantic

COMNORLANT Commander Northern Atlantic Sub-area

Como. commodore

COMOCEANLANT Commander Ocean Atlantic Sub-area

comp. companion; comparative; compare; comparison; compass, an instrument or equipment that measures direction in the horizontal plane (nav.); compensation; compete; competitive; competitor; compilation; compile; compiler;

complete; compose; composer (*also* compr.*); composite; composition; compositor; compound; comprehensive; compression; comprising
   comp. L. *compositus*, compounded of (med.)
   COMPAC Commonwealth Trans-Pacific Telephone Cable, opened 1963
   compar. comparative; comparison
   compd. compound
   Comp. Gen(l). comptroller-general
   compl. complement; complete; compliment; complimentary
   complt. complainant; complaint
   compo. composition
   compr. compressive
   Comp. S. comprehensive secondary (educ.)
   compt. compartment
   Comptr. comptroller
   Comr. commissioner
   Com. Rom. Common Romanic
   Comsat, COMSAT communications satellite
   COMSER Commission on Marine Science and Engineering Research (U.N.O.)
   Com.-Serj. common serjeant
   COMSTRIKEFLTLANT Commander Striking Fleet Atlantic
   COMSUBEASTLANT Commander Submarine Force Eastern Atlantic
   Com. Teut. Common Teutonic
   Com. Ver. Common Version (Bible)
   Com. WGer. Common West Germanic
   Comy.-Gen. commissary-general
   con L. *contra*, in opposition to
   con. concentration; concerning; conclusion; confidence; conformist; conics; con-man, person who gains conf. by false pretences; connection; consolidate; consols; consul; continued; convenience; conversation
   con. It. *concerto* (mus.); L. *conjunx*, wife
   Con. It. *contralto*, lowest of female voices (mus.)
   CONAC Continental Air Command (USAF)
   CONAD Continental Air Defense Command (U.S.A.)
   CONARC Continental Army Command (U.S.A.)
   CONATRAL *Confederación Nacional de Trabajadores Libres*, Nat. Confed. of Free Workers (Dominican Rep.)
   conbd. contributed
   conc. concentrate; concentration
   Conc. It. *Concerto* (mus.)
   Con. C. constructor captain
   Con Carbon Conradson carbon residue
   concd. concentrated

   concg. concentrating
   conch. conchology
   conchie, conchy conscientious objector, gen. referring to mil. service
   concn. concentration
   CONCP *Conferência das Organizações Nacionais deas Colónias Portuguesas*, Central directorate of the nationalist organizations in Portuguese Guinea, Angola, Mozambique and São Tomé; founded 1961, Brazzaville, Congo Rep.
   concr. concrete
   Con. cr. contra credit
   Con. Cr. constructor commander
   cond. condense; condenser; condition; conditional; conduct; conductivity; conductor, *also* condr.
   Conductimetric conductance + metric (chem.)
   CONELRAD control of electromagnetic radiation
   con. esp., con. espr. It. *con espressione*, with expression (mus.)
   conf. confectionery; conference; confessor
   conf. L. *confer*, compare
   confab. confabulation
   Confd., Confed. confederated; confederation
   Confed. Confederation of Shipbuilding and Engineering Union, alt. form CSEU
   Conf. Industria *Confederazione Generale dell'Industria Italiana*, Italian Manufacturers' Assn.
   Conf. Pont. L. *Confessor Pontifex*, Confessor and Bishop
   cong. congregation; congregational; congregationalist; congregationist; congress; congressional
   cong. L. *congius*, gallon (med.)
   con-game confidence trick
   Cong. R., Cong. Rec. *Congressional Records* (U.S.A.)
   congrats. congratulations
   Cong. U. Congregational Union of England and Wales
   C.O.N.G.U. Council of National Golf Unions
   C.O.N.I. *Comitato Olimpico Nazionale Italiano*, Italian National Olympic Committee
   conj. conjugation, *also* conjug.; conjunction; conjunctive
   Con. L. constructor lieutenant; — **Cr.** constructor lieutenant-commander
   conn. connected; — **w.** connected with; connection; connotation
   Conn. Connecticut
   Connie, Conny Constance
   conq. conquer; conqueror
   cons. consecrate; consecration; con-

secutive; consequence; conservation; consigned; consignment; consolidated (*also* consol.); consonant; constable; constitution; constitutional; construction; consult

Cons. conservative; conservatoire; conservatorio; conservatorium; conservatory; consul

con. sec. conic sections

Conserv. conservatoire; conservatory

cons. et prud. L. *consilio et prudentia*, by counsel and prudence

consgt. consignment

consid. consideration

Con. S. L. constructor sub-lieutenant

Consols. Consolidated Funds, a right to a perpetual annuity/annual payment of interest (since 1905, $2\frac{1}{2}\%$) but can be sold at a price reflecting yield in comparable securities

const. constable; constant; constituency; constitution (*also* constn.); constitutional (*also* constl.); construction

constr. construct; construction (*also* constrn.); construe

cont. containing; contents; continent; continue; continuum; contract (*also* contr.); contraction; control; controller

cont. L. *contra*, against

Cont. It. *Contano*, expression indicates that certain parts are silent (mus.)

contag. contagious

contbd. contraband

contbg. contributing

cont. bon. mor. L. *contra bonos mores*, contrary to good manners

contd. contained; continued

contemp. contemporary

contempt. in contemptuous use

contg. containing

contn. continuation

contr. contract; contracted; contraction; contracts; contrary; control

Contr. It. *contralto*, lowest of female voices (mus.)

contrail condensation + trail, a vapour trail (aircraft)

contraprop contra + first part of propeller, a coaxial oppositely rotating airscrew (aircraft)

contr. bon. mor. L. *contra bonos mores*, contrary to good manners

cont. rem. L. *continuantur remedia*, let the medicines be continued (med.)

contrib. contributed; contribution; contributor

conurbation group of adjacent towns which by expansion have merged into single community, con + urbs. city

CONUS Continental United States

conv. convenient; convent; convention; conventional; conversation; converter; convertible

Conv. convocation

convce. conveyance

C.O.O.C. contact with oil or other cargo (insce.)

Co-op Co-operative Society

co-op. co-operation; co-operative

Co-Op. U. Co-operative Union

co-ord. co-ordinate; co-ordination

COORS communications outage restoral section

cop. copper, policeman; copulative; copyright, *also* copr.

Cop. Copernica; Coptic, *also* Copt.

C.O.P. custom of port

C.O.P.A. Fr. *Comité des organisations professionnelles agricoles de la C.E.E.*, Committee of Agricultural Organizations in the E.E.C.

Copec Conference on Christian Politics, Economics and Citizenship

COPEI *Comite Organizador del Partido Electoral Independiente*, Social Christian Party (Ven.)

COPERS Preparatory Commission for European Space Research, *now* E.S.R.O.

COPMEC Fr. *Comité des petites et moyennes entreprises commerciales des pays de la C.E.E.*, Committee of Small and Medium Sized Commercial Enterprises of the E.E.C. Countries

C.O.P.P.S.O. Conference of Professional and Public Service Organisations

C.O.P.R.A.I. *Comissão de Produtividade da Associação Industrial Portuguesa*, Portuguese Industrial Assn. Productivity Commission

copter helicopter

co.-ptr. co-partner

coq. L. *coque*, boil

cor. corner; coroner; correct; correction; correlative; correspondence; correspondent; corresponding; corrupt

cor. cornet, brass wind instrument, *also* organ mixture stop (mus.); L. *corpus*, the body

Cor. St. Paul's Epistles to the Corinthians (Bible); *Coriolanus* (Shake.); Cornelia; Cornelius

Cor. It. *corno*, horn (mus.)

Corat Christian Organizations Research and Advisory Trust

CORC Cornell computing language

CORD computer with on-line remote devices

CORDS Civil Operations and Revolutionary Development Support (Vietnam)

cords. corduroy trousers

C.O.R.E. Congress of Racial Equality (U.S.A.)

COREMO *Comité Revolucionário de*

Moçambique, Revolutionary Committee of Mozambique based in Zambia

CORESTA Fr. *Centre de coopération pour les recherches scientifiques rélative au tabac*, Co-operation Centre for Scientific Tobacco Research

CORGI Confederation for Registration of Gas Installers

Cor. Mem. corresponding member

Corn. Cornish; Cornwall

Cornh. *Cornhill Magazine*

Coro., Coron Convair 990 Coronado (aircraft)

corol., coroll. corollary

corp. corporal (*also* cpl.); corporation, *also* corpn.

Corp. Corpus Christi College, Oxford, founded 1517

corr. correct; correction; corrective; correlative; It. *corrente*, current; correspond; correspondence; correspondent; It. *corretto*, corrected; It. *corrispondenza*, correspondence; corrugated; corrupt; corruption

Corr. corrigenda

C.O.R.R.A. Combined Overseas Rehabilitation Relief Appeal

correl. correlative

corresp. corresponding

Corr. Mem. corresponding member

corrupt. corruption

Cors. Corsica; Corsican

C.O.R.S. Chief of the Regulating Staff

Cor. Sec. corresponding secretary

cort. cortex

C.O.R.T. Conference/Council of Repertory Theatre

cos cosecant; cosine

COs career officers

Cos. consul. highest ordinary magistrate of republican Rome; counties

c.o.s. cash on shipment

C.O.S. Chamber of Shipping; Charity Organization Society, *now* F.W.A.; Chief of Staff

co. sa. It. *come sopra*, as above

C.O.S.A.G. combined steam turbine and gas turbine (ship propulsion)

COSAR compression scanning array radar

COSATI Committee on Scientific and Technical Information

COSBA Computer Services (and) Bureaux Association

COSEC Co-ordinating Secretariat of the National Unions of Students

cosec. cosecant

C.O.S.F.P.S. Commons, Open Spaces, Footpaths Preservation Society

cosh hyperbolic cosine (math.)

COSINE Committee on Computer Science in Electrical Engineering Education, Assn. for Computer Machinery (U.S.A.)

COSIRA Council for Small Industries in Rural Areas, *also* CoSIRA

C.O.S.M.D. Combined Operations Signals Maintenance Division

cosmog. cosmogony; cosmographical; cosmography

COSMOS Coast Survey Marine Observation System; computer optimization and simulation modelling for operating supermarkets (computer)

co. so. It. *come sopra*, as above

COSPAR Committee on Space Research

coss. L. *consules*, consuls

C.O.S.S.A.C. Chief of Staff to Supreme Allied Commander

C.O.S.T. Committee for Overseas Science and Technology (Royal Society)

COSVN Central Office for South Vietnam

cot cotangent

COT card or tape reader (computer)

C.o.T. college of technology

C.O.T.A.L. Fr. *Confédération des organisation touristiques de l'Amérique latine*, Latin American Confed. of Travel Organizations

C.O.T.C. Canadian Overseas Telecommunications Corporation

coth hyperbolic cotangent

COTR contracting officers' technical representative (U.S.A.)

C.O.T.T. Central Organization for Technical Training (S. Afr.)

CO² carbon dioxide, used in fire fighting/industry

Co. U. Coalition Unionist

couch. couchant (heraldry)

couldn't could not

Coun. council; councillor; counsellor

cour. Fr. *courant*, of the current month

COV concentrated oil of vitriol, a grade of sulphuric acid

cov. covenant

Cov. Coventry; — **pt.** cover point (cricket)

C.O.V. cross-over value (biol.)

cow cold war game

COWAR Committee on Water Research

Cox. coxswain

coy. company

coz. cousin

COZI communications zone indicator

cP, cp. centipoise

Cp cassiopeium (chem.)

CP Congress Party (Gambia); *s* Halifax (B.V.R.)

cp. compare

Cp. compline

c.p. candle power; carriage paid; centre of pressure; chemically pure; common pleas; condensation product; constant pressure

c. & p. carriage and packing; collated and perfect

C.p. It. *Colla parte*, with the solo part (mus.)

C/P. custom of ports

C.P. Book of Common Prayer; Canadian Press, news agency; Cape Province (S. Afr.); Captain of the Parish (I. of Man); cardinal point; Carter Paterson; It. *Casella Postale*, post office box; Central Provinces, *now* Madhya Pradesh (India); cerebral palsy; charter party (*also* C/P); chemical practitioner; chief of police; chief patriarch; civil power/procedure; Clarendon Press; clerk of the peace; code of procedure; It. *Codice Penale*, penal code; College of Preceptors; command post; Common Pleas; Communist Party; *Companhia dos Caminhos de Ferro Portugueses*, Port. Railway Co.; concert party; conference paper/proceedings; convict prison; Court of Common Pleas; Court of Probate; current paper

C.P. L. *Congregatio Passionis*, Congregation of the Passion (Passionists)

CPA Clyde Port Authority; Communist Party of Australia; cost planning and appraisal

C.P.A. Calico Printers' Association; Canadian Pacific Air Lines Ltd.; Canadian Pharmaceutical/Psychological Association; Certified Public Accountant (U.S.A.); chartered patent agent; Chick Producers' Association; Church Pastoral-Aid Society; Commonwealth Parliamentary Association; Construction/Contractors' Plant Association; contract price adjustment; critical path analysis (computer)

C.P.A.C. Collaborative Pesticides Analytical Committee

C.P.A.G. Child Poverty Action Group; Collision Prevention Advisory Group (U.S.A.)

C.P.A.I. Canvas Products Association International

C. Pal. Crystal Palace

CPAM Committee of Purchasers of Aircraft Material, consortium of 15 airlines

C.P.A.S. Catholic Prisoners' Aid Society; Church Pastoral-Aid Society

C.P.B. casual payments book; *Centraal Planbureau*, Central Planning Bureau (Neth.)

C.P.C. city planning commission (U.S.A.); city police commissioner; Clerk

of the Privy Council; Clinical Pathological Conference; Conservative Political Centre

C.P.C.I.Z. Fr. *Comité permanent des congrès internationaux de zoologie*, Permanent Committee of Intern. Zoological Congresses

C.P.C.U. Chartered Property and Casualty Underwriter

cp cycle constant pressure cycle

cpd. compound

c.p.d. charterers pay dues (ship.)

CPDL Canadian Patents and Developments Limited

C.P.E. *Centre de Prospective et d'Evaluation*, Feasibility and Evaluation Centre (France); Certified Property Exchanger (U.S.A.); Certificate/College of Physical Education; *Companhia Portuguesa de Electricidade S.A.R.L.*, Port. Electricity Co.; Fr. *Congrès du peuple européen*, Congress of European People; contractor performance evaluation

C.P.E.A. Catholic Parents' and Electors' Association; Co-operative Program for Educational Administration (U.S.A.)

c. pén. Fr. *code pénal*, penal code

C.P.E.Q. Corporation of Professional Engineers of Quebec (Can.)

C.P.F. contributory pension fund

CPFF cost plus fixed fee

C.P.F.S. Council for the Promotion of Field Studies

C.P.G.B. Communist Party of Great Britain

c.p.h. cycles per hour

C.P.H. Certificate in Public Health

C.P.H.A. Canadian Public Health Association

CPI consumer price index; Communist Party of India, pro U.S.S.R;— **(M)** Communist Party of India, Marxist (formed 1964 after split with CPI, influenced by China);—**(M-L)** Communist Party of India, Marxist-Leninist (formed) 1969 after several splits with other 2 communist parties)

C.P.I. chief pilot instructor; Fr. *Commission permanente internationale de l'acétylène, de la soudure autogène et des industries qui s'y rattachent*, Permanent Intern. Committee on Acetylene, Oxy-Acetylene Welding and Allied Industries; consumer price index (U.S.A.)

C.P.I.T.U.S. Fr. *Comité permanent international des techniques et de l'urbanisme souterrains*, Permanent Intern. Committee of Underground Town Planning and Construction

C.P.I.U.S. Sp. *Comité permanent Internacional de Tecnicos y de Urbanismo Subterráneo*, Permanent Intern. Committee of Underground Town Planning and Construction

C.P.J.I. Fr. *Cour permanente de justice internationale*, Permanent Court of Intern. Justice

Cpl. corporal

C.P.L. central public library; Colonial Products Laboratory

cpm cards per minute (computer)

CPM Communist Party of Malaya; critical path method

c.p.m. cycles per minute

C.P.M. Certified Property Manager (U.S.A.); critical path method

C.P.M. *common particular metre* (mus.)

CPN *Communistische Partij van Nederland*, Neth. Communist Party

cpn. coupon

Cpnhgn., Cpn. Copenhagen

CPNZ Communist Party of New Zealand

CPO compulsory purchase order; county planning officer

C.P.O. chief petty officer; command pay office; Commonwealth Producers' Organization

c.p.p. controllable pitch propeller

C.P.P. Convention People's Party (Ghana)

C.P.P.A. Canadian Pulp and Paper Association

C.P.P.C.C. Chinese People's Political Consultative Conference

CPPS critical path planning and scheduling

C.PP.S. L. *Congregatio Pretiosissimi Sanguinis*, Congregation of the Most Precious Blood

C.P.P.S. *Comisión permanente para la Explotación y Conservación de las Riquezas Marítimas del Pacífico Sur*, Permanent Commission for the Conservation of the Maritime Resources of the South Pacific

cpr. copper

C.P.R. Canadian Pacific Railway

C.P.R.C. central price regulation committee

CPRE Council for the Protection of Rural England, *formerly* Council for the Preservation of Rural England, name changed 1970

C.P.R.W. Council for the Protection of Rural Wales

cps characters per second (computer); cycles per second

CPS Communist Party of Syria

C.P.S. Church Patronage Society; Clerk of Petty Sessions; Committee for Penicillin Sensitivity; Commonwealth Public Service; Congregational Publishing Society

C.P.S. L. *Custos Privati Sigilli*, Keeper of the Privy Seal

C.P.S.A. Civil and Public Services Association; Clay Pigeon Shooting Association

C.P.S.S. Certificate in Public Service Studies

C.P.S.U. Communist Party of the Soviet Union, *Kommunisticheskaya Partiya Sovetskovo Soyuza*, founded in 1903 by V. I. Lenin

cpt cockpit; counterpoint

CPT *Confederación Paraguaya de Trabajadores, en-el-Exilio*, Confed. of Paraguayan Workers, in Exile; critical path technique

Cpt. captain

C.P.T. Canadian Pacific Telegraphs

C.P.T.B. Clay Products Technical Bureau

C.P.U. central packaging/processing unit; collective protection unit; Commonwealth Press Union

CPVC critical pigment volume concentration

CPWC Central People's Workers' Council (Burma)

CQ call to quarters, code letters used at beginning of radio messages intended for all receivers

C.Q. conditionally qualified

C.Q.M. chief/company quartermaster

C.Q.M.S. company quartermaster-sergeant

C.Q.P.P.A. Council of Quality Pig Producers Associations

C.Q.R. *Church Quarterly Review*

C.Q.S. Court of Quarter Sessions

C.Q.S.W. Certificate of Qualification in Social Work

Cr *s* chromium (chem.)

CR Celanese-resist, does not dye/ stain acetate rayon; *s* Costa Rica (I.V.R.); *s* Portugal and colonies (I.C.A.N.); *s* Southampton (B.V.R.)

cr. created; credit; creditor; creek; crew; crimson; crown; cruise

cr. It. *crescendo* (mus.); L. *crux*, cross

c/r. company's risk

Cr. commander; Contador; cruiser

c.r. It. *con riserva*, with reservations; cum rights, with rights issue (fin.)

C.R. carrier's risk; central railway/ registry; chief ranger; coin return, amusement machine which returns to succcessful player coin which had been inserted to operate machine; Commendation Ribbon (U.S.A.); Community of the Resurrection; company's risk; compression ratio; conditioned reflex; conference report; congo red (test paper for detecting acid-

91

ity); control relay; crease-resist (resin); credit rating; current rate

C.R. L. *Carolina Regina*, Queen Caroline; L. *Carolus Rex*, King Charles; L. *Civis Romanus*, Roman citizen; L. *Custos Rotulorum*, Keeper of the Rolls

CRA Civil Rights Association (N. Ireland); Conzinc Riotinto of Australia Limited

C.R.A. California Redwood Association; Canadian Rheumatism Association; Commander, Royal Artillery; Commercial Rabbit Association; composite research aircraft

Cr. A.A. commander-at-arms

CRAC Careers Research and Advisory Centre; Construction Research Advisory Council

C.R.A.C. Central Religious Advisory Committee

C.R.A.D. Committee for Research into Apparatus for the Disabled

CRAF Civil Reserve Air Fleet (U.S.A.)

C.R.A.M. card random access memory

Cran., craniol. craniology

craniom. craniometry

C.R.A.S.C. Commander, Royal Army Service Corps

C.R.B. central radio bureau

CRC Co-ordinating Research Council Inc.; Cycle Racing Club

C.R.C. Civil Rights Commission; coal rank code, systems of classifying coals for commercial purposes (N.C.B.); composing room chapel (typ.)

C.R.C.C. Canadian Red Cross Committee

C.R.D. Fr. *Centre de recherches et de documentation*, Research and Documentation Centre of the WEA; chronic respiratory disease; computer read-out device; crop research division

C.R.D.F. cathode-ray direction-finding

C.R.E. Coal Research Establishment; Commander, Royal Engineers

CREFAL *Centro Regional de Educación Fundamental para la América Latina*, training school for teachers of fundamental educ. in under-developed rural communities, estab. by UNESCO and Mexican govt. 1951 at Patzcuaro, Michoacán

C. Rep. coin repeat, amusement machine which returns coin to a successful player, and also allows a further free game, thus giving chance to win further coin

cres., cresc. It. *crescendo*, increasing (mus.)

Cres. crescent

C.R.F. capital recovery factor

crg. carriage

C.R.G. Cave Research Group of Great Britain

C.R.G.E. *Companhias Reunidas Gás e Electricidade S.A.R.L.*, United Gas and Electricity Co., Lisbon (Port.)

Cri, The Criterion restaurant

C.R.I. Caribbean Research Institute; Coconut Research Institute (Ceylon); *Croce Rossa Italiana*, Italian Red Cross

crib cribbage, card game

C.R.I.C. Canon Regular of the Immaculate Conception

C.R.I.E.P.I. Central Research Institute of the Electrical Power Industry (Jap.)

C.R.I.L.C. Canadian Research Institute of Launderers and Cleaners

crim. con. criminal conversation, adultery (leg.)

Criminol. criminology

crimp. crimplene (tex.)

CRIS command retrieval information system; current research information system

crit. criterion; critic; critical; critically; criticism

Crk. Cork (Rep. of Ireland)

C.R.L. Canon Regular of the Lateran; Certified Record/Reference Librarian; Chemical Research Laboratory

CRM counter radar missile; count rate meter; cruise missile

C.R.M.A. Cotton and Rayon Merchants' Association

C.R.M.P. Corps of Royal Military Police, *formerly* C.M.P.

crn. crane; crown

C.R.N.S.S. Chief of the Royal Naval Scientific Service

CRO cathode-ray oscillograph/oscilloscope; compulsory rights order

C.R.O. chief recruiting officer; Commonwealth Relations Office; Criminal Records Office

Croat. Croatia; Croatian

croc. crocodile, a file of children walking two by two

'crosse lacrosse stick used by players

Cr. P. criminal procedure

C.R.P. Canons Regular of Prémontré (Premonstratensians)

C.R.P. L. *Calendarium Rotulorum Patentium*, Calendar of the Patent Rolls

C.R.P.L. Central Radio Propagation Laboratory (U.S.A.)

C.R.R. constant ratio rule; Curia Regis Roll

C.R.S. Catholic Record Society; Cereals Research Station; cold-rolled steel

C.R.S.A. Cold Rolled Sections Association; Concrete Reinforcement Steel Association

C.R.S.I. Concrete Reinforcing Steel Institute (U.S.A.)

Cr'slt 4 with bar, crosslet (numis.)

Crt. court

C.R.T. cathode ray tube; combat readiness training

CRTC Canadian Radio-Television Commission

crtkr. caretaker

C.R.T.S. Commonwealth Reconstruction Training Scheme

CRU control register, user

C.R.U. civil resettlement unit; Collective Reserve Union; Composite Reserve Unit

CRUDESPAC Cruiser-Destroyer Forces, Pacific (USN)

CRULANT Cruiser Forces, Atlantic (USN)

Cruz. *Cruzeiro*, Brazilian currency

C.R.W.P.C. Canadian Radio Wave Propagation Committee

Crypto. cryptographic; cryptography

cryst. crystal; crystalline

crystal., crystallog. crystallography

crystd. crystallized

crystn. crystallization

Cs *s* caesium (chem.)

C/s cases

CS *s* Ayrshire (B.V.R.); Cambrian Airways; casein; Christian Social Party (Belg.); *s* Cowes (B.F.P.); credit sales; *s* Czechoslovakia (I.V.R.); *s* Portugal and colonies (I.C.A.M.)

C/S channel shank (buttons); cycles per second

cs. cases; census; consul

Cs. Fr. *cours*, market price/rate

c.s. It. *come sopra*, as above

C/S. colliery screened (coal trade)

C.S. calcium silicate; capital stock; carbon/cast steel; Certificate in Statistics; Chemical Society; chief of staff; chief secretary; Christian Science/Scientist; city surveyor; civil servant/service; Clerk of Session; Clerk to the Signet; close shot/support; College of Science; colliery screened (coal trade); commissary of subsistence; Common Serjeant; Conchological Society of Great Britain and Ireland; Congregation of Salesians; Co-operative Society; cotton seed; county surveyor; Court of Session; cruiser squadron

C.S. It. *Colla sinistra*, with left hand (mus.); L. *Custos Sigilli*, keeper of the seal

C.S.A. Canadian Standards Association; *Československé Aerolinie*, Czechoslo-

vak Air Line; Commonwealth Sugar Agreement; Computer Science Association (Can.); Confederate States Army; Confederate States of America

CSAA Child Study Association of America

C.S.A.E. Canadian Society of Agricultural Engineering

C.S.A.P. Canadian Society of Animal Production

CSAR Communication Satellite Advanced Research

C.S.B. Bachelor of Christian Science; calcium silicate brick; Central Statistical Board; chemical stimulation, of the brain

C.S.B.G.M. Committee of Scottish Bank General Managers

csc. cosecant

C.S.C. Charles Stuart Calverley (1831–84), Eng. poet and parodist; Civil Service Commission; Commonwealth Scientific Committee; Comprehensive Schools Committee; Conspicuous Service Cross, *now* D.S.C.

C.S.C.A. Civil Service Clerical Association

C.S.C.B.S. Commodore Superintendent Contract Built Ships

C.S.C.C. Civil Service Commission of Canada; Council of Scottish Chambers of Commerce

csch. hyperbolic constant/cosecant

C.S.D. Civil Service Department; Commonwealth Society for the Deaf; constant speed drive; Doctor of Christian Science

C.S.D.E. Central Servicing Development Establishment (R.A.F.)

Cse. course

C.S.E. Central Signals Establishment; Certificate of Secondary Education; Council of the Stock Exchange, Lond.

CSED co-ordinated ship electronics design (USN)

C.S.E.U., C.S. & E.U. Confederation of Shipbuilding and Engineering Unions

C.S.F. cerebrospinal fluid (biol.); Coil Spring Federation

C.S.F.A. Canadian Scientific Film Association

C.S.F.E. Canadian Society of Forest Engineers

CSG *Consejo Sindical de Guatemala*, Trade Union Council of Guatemala

C.S.G. Catholic Social Guild

C.S.G.A. Canadian Seed Growers' Association

C.S.H. calcium silicate hydrate

CSI coelliptic sequence initiation

C.S.I. Chartered Surveyors' Institution; Church of South India; Fr. *Commission séricicole internationale*, Intern.

Sericultural Commission; Fr. *Commission Sportive Internationale*, Intern. Sporting Commission of Intern. Motorcycle Fed.; Companion of the Most Exalted Order of the Star of India; Construction Specifications Institute (U.S.A.)

C.S.I.C.C. Canadian Steel Industries Construction Council

C.S.I.E.J.B. Certificate of the Sanitary Inspectors Examination Joint Board

C.S.I.R. Council for Scientific and Industrial Research (India/S. Afr.)

C.S.I.R.A. Council for Small Industries in Rural Areas

C.S.I.R.O. Commonwealth Scientific and Industrial Research Organization (Aust.)

C.S.I.T. Fr. *Comité sportif international du travail*, Intern. Workers Sport Assn.

CSJ *Christian Science Journal*

csk. cask; countersink

C.S.K. Co-operative Study of the Kuroshio and Adjacent Regions

CSL computer simulation language; It. *Confederazione Somali Dei Lavoratori*, Somali Confed. of Labor

C.S.L. Commonwealth Serum Laboratories (Aust.); communication sublieutenant; cub scout leader

C.S.L.A.T.P. Canadian Society of Landscape Architects and Town Planners

C.S.L.O. Canadian Scientific Liaison Office; combined services liaison officer

C.S.L.T. Canadian Society of Laboratory Technologists

C.S.M. cerebro-spinal meningitis; *Christian Science Monitor*; Christian Socialist Movement; command service module (space); Commission for Synoptic Meteorology (WMO); company sergeant-major; corn-soya-milk mixture, supplied for Nigerian relief during civil war, 1968–70

C.S.M.A. Chemical Specialities Manufacturers' Association; Civil Service Motoring Association

C.S.M.M.G. Chartered Society of Massage and Medical Gymnastics

C.S.N. Confederate States Navy

C.so It. *corso*, Street

C.S.O. Central Selling Organization; Central Statistical Office; chief signal officer; chief staff officer; colonial secretary's office; command signals officer; Commonwealth Scientific Office

C.S.P. Chartered Society of Physiotherapists/Physiotherapy; Civil Service of Pakistan; Congregation of Saint Paul; continuous sampling plan; Council for Scientific Policy, *formerly* A.C.S.P.

C.S.P.A.A. Fr. *Conférence de solidar-ité des pays afro-asiatiques*, Afro-Asian People's Solidarity Conference

C.S.P.C.A. Canadian Society for the Prevention of Cruelty to Animals

C.S.P.Co. Caledonian Steam Packet Company

CSPR chlorosulphonated polyethylene rubber

C.S.R. Colonial Sugar Refining Company Limited; Czechoslovak Socialist Republic

C.S.S. computer systems simulator; Councils of Social Service

C.S.S.A. Civil Service Supply Association

C.S.S.B. Civil Service Selection Board

CSSDA Council for Social Science Data Archives (U.S.A.)

C.S.S.M. Children's Special Service Mission; compatible single-sideband modulation system

C.SS.R. L. *Congregatio Sanctissimi Redemptoris*, Congregation of the Most Holy Redeemer (Redemptorists)

CSSS Canadian Soil Science Society

C.SS.S. L. *Congregatio Sanctissimi Salvatoris*, Congregation of the Most Holy Saviour (Brigittines)

cSt centistokes

Cst. *cellist*, violoncellist (mus.)

C.S.T. central standard time; College of Science and Technology

C.S.T.A. Canadian Society of Technical Agriculturists; Canterbury Science Teachers' Association (N.Z.)

C.S.T.I. Council of Science and Technology Institutes

C. St. J. Commander of the Order of Saint John of Jerusalem

CSU Christian Democrats (W. Ger.); *Confederación Sindical del Uruguay*, Confed. of Uruguayan Trade Unions

C.S.U. Central Statistical Unit; *Christlich-Soziale Union*, Christian Social Union (W. Ger.); Civil Service Union; constant speed unit

C.S.U.C.A. Sp. *Consejo Superior Universitario Centroamericano*, Supreme Council of the Central American Universities

CSV community service volunteer

C.S.V. Congregation of St. Victor

C.S.W. Ger. *Christlicher Studenten-Weltbund*, World Student Christian Federation; continuous seismic wave

CT *s* Castletown (B.F.P.); *s* Lincolnshire (B.V.R.)

ct. carat, gold content; caught; cent; certificate; circuit; Fr. *courant*, the present month; court; credit; current

ct. L. *centum*, hundred

94

Ct. Canton; Connecticut, U.S.A. (*also* CT); Count

C/T. Californian Terms (grain trade)

C.T. cable transfer; Candidate in Theology; Cape Town; central time; certificated/certified teacher; circuit theory; Civic Trust; code telegrams; college of technology; commercial traveller; It. *Commissario Tecnico*, coach (sport); corporation tax

CTA Catering Teachers' Association; cellulose triacetate

c.t.a., L. *cum testamento annexo*, with will annexed

C.T.A. Camping Trade Association; Canadian Tuberculosis Association; Caribbean Technical Assistance; Caribbean Tourist Association; Chain Testers' Association of Great Britain; Channel Tunnel Association; Chaplain Territorial Army; Chicago Transit Authority; Commercial Travellers' Association

C.T.A.B. cetyl trimethyl ammonium bromide

C.T.A.U. Catholic Total Abstinence Union

C.T.B. *Centre Technique de Bois*, Wood Research Centre (France); Commonwealth Telecommunications Board

CTBT Comprehensive Test Ban Treaty

CTC carbon tetra chloride (tetrachloromethane), a harmful substance used in industry and for firefighting; centralized traffic control; *Confederación de Trabajadores de Colombia*, Confed. of Colombian Workers; Fr. *Congrès du Travail du Canada*, Canadian Labour Congress, *also* CLC

C.T.C. Canadian Transport Commission; Central Training Council; Civil Technical Corps; corn trade clauses; Cyclists' Touring Club, founded 1878 as Bicycle Touring Club (B.T.C.) name changed 1883

CTCB *Confederación de Trabajadores de Comercio de Bolivia*, Confed. of Commercial Workers of Bolivia

ctd. crated

C.T.D. central training depot; classified telephone directory

Cte. Fr. *Comte*, Count

CTEB Council of Technical Examining Bodies

Ctesse. Fr. *Comtesse*, Countess

C.T.E.T.O.C. Council for Technical Education and Training for Overseas Countries

ctf. certificate; certify

C.T.F. Chaplain to the Territorial Forces; coal tar fuel

ctge. cartage; cottage

C.T.H. Corporation of Trinity House,

received first royal charter 1514, maintains lighthouses, lightships, etc., round coasts of England and Wales

C. Theod. L. *Codex Theodosianus*, Theodosian Code

CTK *Ceskoslovenská Tisková Kancelář*, Czechoslovak Press Bureau

ctl. central

C.T.L. constructive total loss, a total loss as cost of retrieving and/or repair exceeds recovered/repaired value (insce.)

CTM *Confederación de Trabajadores de México*, Confed. of Mexican Workers

C.T.M.A. Collapsible Tube Manufacturers' Association

CTN confectioner, tobacconist, newsagent

ctn. carton; cotangent

Cto. It. *concerto* (mus.)

C.T.O. Central Telegraph Office; Central Tractor Organisation (India); Central Treaty Organization; chief technical officer

c. to c. centre to centre

CTOL conventional take-off and landing

CTP *Confederación de Trabajadores del Peru*, Peruvian Confed. of Labor

Ctpt. *counterpoint*, art of combining 2 or more independent melodic lines (mus.)

Ctptal. *contrapuntal*, adjective derived from 'counterpoint' (mus.)

Ctptst. *contrapuntist*, one skilled in counterpoint (mus.)

ctr. center/centre

Ctr. contribution; contributor

C.T.R. certified test record; controlled thermonuclear reaction

C.T.R.A. Coal Tar Research Association

CTRP *Confederación de Trabajadores de la República de Panama*, Confed. of Workers of the Rep. of Panama

C.T.R.U. Colonial Termite Research Unit

CTS Consolidated Tin Smelters

C.T.S. Incorporated Catholic Truth Society

C.T.S.A. Crucible and Tool Steel Association

CTT *Correios e Telecommunicações de Portugal*, Post and Telegraph Services (Port.)

C.T.T.B. Central Trade Test Board (R.A.F.)

C'ttee., Cttee. committee

C.T.T.S.C. Certificate in the Teaching and Training of Subnormal Children

C.T.U.S. Carnegie Trust for the Universities of Scotland

CTV *Confederación de Trabajadores*

95

Venezolanos, Confed. of Venezuelan Workers

Cty. city

Cu *s* L. *cuprum*, copper (chem.)

CU *s* Cuba (I.C.A.M.); *s* South Shields (B.V.R.)

cu. cubic (*also* cub.); cumulus

C.U. Cambridge University; Church Union; close-up (photog.); Congregational Union of England and Wales; Co-operative Union; Cornell University (U.S.A.); customs union

C.U.A. Canadian Underwriters' Association; Catholic University of America; Colour Users' Association

C.U.A.C. Cambridge University Athletic Club

C.U.A.F.C. Cambridge University Association Football Club

C.U.A.S. Cambridge University Agricultural Society; Cambridge University Air Squadron

Cubana *Cubana de Aviación*, Cuba state airline

C.U.B.C. Cambridge University Boat Club; Cambridge University Boxing Club

C.U.C. Canberra University College; Coal Utilization Council

C.U.C.C. Cambridge University Cricket Club

cu. cm. cubic centimetre

C.U.D.S. Cambridge University Dramatic Society

C.U.E.W. Congregational Union of England and Wales

CUF *Companhia União Fabril*, Union Manufacturing Co. (Port.)

C.U.F. L. *Catholicarum Universitatum Foederatio*, Fed. of Catholic Univs.

cu. ft. cubit feet/foot

C.U.G.C. Cambridge University Golf Club

C.U.H.C. Cambridge University Hockey Club

cu. in. cubic inch

cuis. cuisine

C.U.K.T. Carnegie United Kingdom Trust

Cul. culinary

C.U.L. Cambridge University Library

C.U.L.T.C. Cambridge University Lawn Tennis Club

cum. cumulative (fin.)

C.U.M. Cambridge University Mission

Cumb. Cumberland

cum. div., cum. d. cum dividend, with dividend (fin.)

cum. pref. cumulative preference (fin.)

C.U.M.S. Cambridge University Musical Society

C.U.N.A. Credit Union National Association

C.U.O.G. Cambridge University Opera Group

C.U.P. Cambridge University Press

cuppa cup of tea; — **cha** cup of tea

Cupper cup-tie+-er, a series of intercollegiate matches played for a cup (Oxford Univ.)

cur. currency; current

CURAC Coal Utilization Research Advisory Committee (Aust.)

C.U.R.E. care, understanding, research, organization for the welfare of drug addicts

C.U.R.F.C. Cambridge University Rugby Football Club

curt. current, Scottish equivalent of English 'instant'

CURV cable controlled undersea recovery vehicle (USN)

C.U.S. Catholic University School

cusec, cu.sec. cubic feet per second

C.U.S.R.P.G. Canada-United States Regional Planning Group (NATO)

custod. custodian

CUT *Comité de l'Unité Togolaise*, Committee for Togolese Unity

C.U.T.F. Commonwealth Unit Trust Fund

CV *s* Cornwall (B.V.R.)

cv. Port. *cave*, basement

c.v. Fr. *cheval-vapeur*, horse-power; chief value

c.v. L. *cras vespere*, tomorrow evening (med.); L. *cursus vitae*, course of life

C.V. calorific value; It. *cavallo vapore*, horse-power (H.P.); Port. *cavalos vapor*, horse-power; common valve; common version. Fr. *Croix de la Vaillance*, Cross of Valour (Can.)

C.V.A. cerebro-vascular accident/stroke

c.v.d. It. *come volevasi dimostrare*, which was to be demonstrated

C.V.D. common valve development

C.V.E. Council for Visual Education

CVF. *Corporación Venezolana de Fomento*, State Development Corporation (Ven.)

C.V.K. centre vertical keel

C.V.M. Company of Veteran Motorists

C.V.O. Commander of the Royal Victorian Order

C. voc. It. *Colla voce*, with the voice (mus.)

CVP. *Corporación Venezolana del Petróleo*, Venezuelan Petroleum Corporation

CVR controlled visual rules

cvt. convertible (fin.)

Cvt. Gdn. Covent Garden

CVWS combat vehicle weapons system

c/w chainwheel (cycling)

CW *s* Burnley (B.V.R.); Common Wealth Party; control word

c.w. carrier wave; continuous wave/weld

C.W. Canada West; chemical warfare; child welfare; clerk of works; commercial weight; Commissions and Warrants Department of the Admiralty; continuous wave

C. & W. country and western

C.W.A. Catering Wages Act; Civil Works Administration (U.S.A.); Country Women's Association (Aust.); Crime Writers' Association

CWAEC County War Agricultural Executive Committee

C.W.B. Canadian Wheat Board; Central Wages Board

CWBW chemical warfare-bacteriological warfare

CWC Ceylon Workers' Congress

C.W.C. Catering Wages Commission; Commonwealth of World Citizens

C & W Ck caution and warning system check

C.W.D. civilian war dead

C'wealth Commonwealth

C.W.G.C. Commonwealth War Graves Commission

C.W.I.N.C. Central Waterways, Irrigation and Navigation Commission (India)

C.W.L. Catholic Women's League

C.W.M.E. Commission on World Mission and Evangelism of the World Council of Churches

C.W.N.A. Canadian Weekly Newspapers Association

c.w.o. cash with order; chief warrant officer

C.W.O.I.H. Conference of World Organisations Interested in the Handicapped

CWP Christian Workers' Party (Malta)

C.W.R. continuous welded rail

CWS Co-operative Wholesale Society Limited

C.W.S. Canadian Welding Society; Chemical Welfare Service (U.S.A.)

cwt. hundredweight

C.W.T. central war time

C.W.U. Chemical Workers' Union

CX *s* Huddersfield (B.V.R.); *s* Uruguay (I.C.A.M.)

cx. convex

CXT Common External Tariff of the European Community

Cy cyanide

CY *s* Castlebay (B.F.P.); *s* Cyprus (I.V.R.); *s* Swansea (B.V.R.)

cy. capacity; currency

cyath. L. *cyathus*, glassful (med.)

cyath. vinos. L. *cyathus vinosus*, wineglassful (med.)

Cyber. cybernetics

cyc. cycles; cycling; cyclopedia; cyclopedic

C.Y.C.A. Clyde Yacht Clubs Association

cycle bicycle

Cyclo. cyclopaedia

CYEE Central Youth Employment Executive

C.Y.F.A. Club for Young Friends of Animals

cyl. cylinder; cylindrical

Cym. Cymric

Cymb. *Cymbeline* (Shake.)

C.Y.M.S. Catholic Young Men's Society

CYO Catholic Youth Organization (U.S.A.)

Cyp. Cyprian; Cyprus

CZ *s* Belfast (B.V.R.); *s* Principality of Monaco (I.C.A.M.)

Cz., Czech. Czechoslovakia

C.Z. canal zone

czy. crazy

D

d deci, 10^{-1}; deuteron (phys.); *s* drizzle (met.); penny (pence); do, doh, name for the Tonic note in any key in Sol-fa

¼d farthing
½d halfpenny
6d sixpence
'd abbreviated spelling, had/would
δ *deleatur*, delete/cancel (typ.)
D 500; democrat; democratic; deuterium (chem.); *s* Dublin (Rep. of Ireland F.P.); *s* Germany (I.C.A.M. and I.V.R.); *s* heavy hydrogen; *s* Kent (B.V.R.)
D '66 Democrats '66, political party (Neth.)
2,4-D 2,4- dichlorophenoxyacetic acid, herbicide used as a defoliant
3-D three-dimensional
D' De
d. damn; date; daughter; day; deacon; dead; deceased; deciduous; decision; decree; degree; deliver; delivery; delta; L. *denarius*, penny/tenth; density; depart; department; depth; deputy; desert; deserter; It. *destra*, right hand; dextrorotatory; diameter; diamonds (playing cards): died; dime; diopter, dioptral (optics); discharge; distance; dollar; dose; Fr. *douane* (customs); *drachma*, Greek currency; drama; Fr. *droite*, the right hand; dump
D. Ger. *Damen*, ladies; December; demy (paper); destroyer; *Deutschland*, Germany; *Diretto*, slow train (Italy); distinguished; doctor; It. *dogana*, customs/custom house; *Dom*, hereditary title of nobility in male line/high ecclesiastical title (Port.), also style of Benedic-

tine monks, and Cistercian abbots; *Don*, Sp. title; Fr. *Douane*, customs/custom house; Dowager; Fr. *droite*, right; Duchess; Duke; Dutch
D. L. *Deus*, God; L. *Dominus*, Lord
da deca, 10^1
Da davyum (chem.)
DA delayed action (bomb); *dinar*, Algerian currency; *s* Drogheda (Rep. of Ireland F.P.); *s* Wolverhampton (B.V.R.)
D/A days after acceptance; delivery/documents against/on acceptance
Da., Dan. Danish
D/a. discharge afloat
d. Ä. Ger. *der Ältere*, senior
D.A. Daughters of America; Defence Act; deposit account (*also*, D/A); deputy advocate/assistant; Diploma in Anaesthesia/Anaesthetics; dissolved acetylene; district attorney (U.S.A.); Doctor of Arts; doesn't answer
D.A.A. Fr. *Défense anti-aérienne*, antiaircraft defence; diacetone acrylamide/alcohol; Diploma of the Advertising Association
D.A.A.G. deputy assistant adjutantgeneral
D.A.A. & Q.M.G. deputy assistant adjutant and quartermaster general
DAAT Draughtsmen and Allied Technicians
D.A.B. daily audience barometer; *Deutsches Apothekerbuch*, German Pharmacopoeia; *Dictionary of American Biography*
d.a.c. deductible average clause (insce.); digital to analogue converter (computer); direct air cycle

98

D.A.C. data analysis and control; Development Assistance Committee (OECD)

D.A.C.C. Dangerous Air Cargoes Committee

D.A.C.G. deputy assistant chaplain general

dacr. dacron (tex.)

D.A.D. deputy assistant director; **—G.** deputy assistant director general; **—G.M.S.** deputy assistant director general of medical services; **—M.E.** deputy assistant director of military engineering; **—M.S.** deputy assistant director of medical services; **—O.S.** deputy assistant director of ordnance services; **—Q.** deputy assistant director of quartering; **—S.** deputy assistant director of supplies; **—S.T.** deputy assistant director of supplies and transport

D.A.E. *Dictionary of American English*; Diploma in Advanced Engineering; Director of Army Education

D.A.E.P. Division of Atomic Energy Production

D.A.E.R. Department of Aeronautical and Engineering Research

daf *Doorn Automobielfabriek*, the daf gearless car (Neth.)

DAF department of the air force

d.a.f. described as follows; dry ash free, basis for analysis of coals/cokes

daff, daffy daffodil

D.A.F.S. Department of Agriculture and Fisheries for Scotland

DAG *Deutsche Angestellten-Gewerkschaft*, Trade Union of German Employees

dag. decagram

D.A.G. deputy adjutant-general; development assistance group

D.Agr. Doctor of Agriculture

D.Agr.Sc. Doctor of Agricultural Science

Dah. Dahomey

D.A.H. disordered action of the heart

d.a.i. death from accidental injuries

daily daily domestic servant

D.A.J.A.G. deputy assistant judge advocate general

Dak. Dakota

dal. decalitre

Dal.S. It. *Dal segno*, from the sign (mus.)

dam. decametre

D.A.M. Diploma in Ayurvedic Medicine

DAMP downrange anti-missile measurement project

DAMS defense against missiles systems (U.S.A.)

D.A.M.S. deputy assistant military secretary

Dan, Danny Daniel

Dan. Book of Daniel (Bible)

Dand, Dandie Andrew

Danl. Daniel

D.A.O. district advisory officer

D.A.O.T. Director of Air Organization and Training

d.a.p. data automation proposal; do anything possible; documents against payment

D.A.P. Director of Administrative Planning

D.A.P. & E. Diploma in Applied Parasitology and Entomology

D.A.P.H.N.E. Dido and Pluto Handmaiden for Nuclear Experiments

D.A.P.M. deputy assistant provost-marshal

D.App.Sc. Doctor of Applied Science

D.A.P.S. Director of Army Postal Services

D.A.Q.M.G. deputy assistant quartermaster general

D.A.R. Daughters of the American Revolution, society of women formed in 1890 for patriotic and charitable purposes; Directorate of Atomic Research (Can.)

D.Arch. Doctor of Architecture

D.A.R.D. Directorate of Aircraft Research and Development

daren't dare not

DART development advanced rate techniques

d.a.s. delivered alongside ship

D.A.S. development advisory service; director of armament supply; Dramatic Authors' Society

DASA Defense Atomic Support Agency (U.S.A.)

DASC Direct Air Support Center (U.S.A.)

D.A.Sc. Doctor in/of Agricultural Science/Sciences

D.A.S.D. director of army staff duties

DASH drone anti-submarine helicopter

D.A.S.M. delayed action space missile

DAST division for advanced systems technology

DASTARD destroyer anti-submarine transportable array detector

dat. dative; datum

D.A.T.A. Draughtsmen's and Allied Technicians' Association

D.A.T.A.C. Development Areas Treasury Advisory Committee

DATEL data + telecommunications

dau. daughter

Dav, Dave, Davie, Davy David

DAV Disabled American Veterans
D.A.W.S. Director of Army Welfare Services
D.Ay.M. Doctor of Ayurvedic Medicine
d/b double-butted, cycle wheel spoke
dB decibel, unit of noise measurement
DB *Deutsche Bundesbahn*, German Federal Railway (W. Ger.); *s* Stockport (B.V.R.)
D/B, d.b. day book
db. *double bass* (mus.)
d.b. double bed; double-breasted; draw bar
D.B. dark blue; day book; deals and battens; L. *Divinitatis Baccalaureus*, Bachelor of Divinity; dock brief; *Domesday Book*, survey of Eng. made by William the Conqueror 1085-6; double-barrelled; Dresdner Bank (W. Ger.)
D.-B. Daimler-Benz
D. & B. Dun and Bradstreet
d.b.a. doing business as/at
D.B.A. Doctor of Business Administration
D.B.B. deals, battens and boards, lightwood goods (timber)
DBD *Demokratische Bauernpartei Deutschlands*, Democratic Peasants' Party of Germany (E. Ger.)
D.B.E. Dame Commander of the Order of the British Empire
D.B.E.A.T.S. dispatch payable both ends all time saved; —L.T.S. dispatch payable both ends on lay time saved
d.b.h. diameter at breast height (timber)
D. Bib. Douay Bible
D.B.I.U. Dominion Board of Insurance Underwriters (Can.)
dbk. debark; drawback
dbl., dble. double
D.B.M. Diploma in Business Management
Dbn. Durban (S. Afr.)
D.B.O. Diploma of the British Orthoptic Board
dbre. Sp. *diciembre*, December
D.Bs. double bottoms
D.B.S.T. double British summer time
DC 600 (Roman); *Democrazia Cristiana*, Christian Democratic Party (Italy); District of Columbia; District (War Agricultural) Committee; *s* Middlesbrough (B.V.R.)
DC4 Douglas DC4; —8; —9 (aircraft)
D/C deviation clause
d.c. dead centre; direct current (elec.); double column; double crochet; drift correction (nav.); It. *da capo*, repeat from the beginning (mus.)

d.C. Port. *depois de Cristo*, after Christ, A.D.; It. *dopo Cristo*, after Christ, A.D.
DC. de Candolle (bot.)
D.C. death certificate; decimal classification/currency; depth charge; deputy chief/commissioner/consul/counsel; diagnostic centre; diplomatic corps; Disarmament Conference; Disciples of Christ; District Commissioner/Court; District of Columbia; Doctor of Chiropractics; Douglas Aircraft (followed by numbers to signify different types, i.e. DC8)
D. and C. dilatation and curettage of the uterus
D. & C. dean and chapter
DCA Defense Communications Agency (U.S.A.); Department of Civil Aviation (Aust.); Digital Computer Association
D.C.Ae. Diploma of the College of Aeronautics
D.C.A.O. Deputy County Advisory Officer
d. cap. double foolscap (paper)
DCAS Data Collection and Analysis System (NASA)
D.C.A.S. Deputy Chief of the Air Staff (Air Council)
D.C.B. Dame Commander of the Most Honourable Order of the Bath
DCC driving other cars (insce.)
D.C.C. Diocesan Consistory Court
D.C.C.C. Domestic Coal Consumers' Council
D.C.C.P. Directorate of Communications Components Production
D.C.D. Diploma in Chest Diseases; Directorate of Communications Development
dcdr. decoder
DCE Directorate of Communications-Electronics; domestic credit expansion
D.C.E. Diploma in Chemical Engineering; Doctor of Civil Engineering
D.C.E.P. Diploma of Child and Educational Psychology
D.C.F., d.c.f. discounted cash flow, technique used to assess profitability of capital projects which is achieved by calculating capital investments and time scales; calculating incomes from investments and time scales; adjusting these for taxation and grant purposes. The resultant interest rate is guide to profitability of enterprise (fin.)
DCFEM dynamic crossed-field electron multiplication
DCG *Democracia Cristiana Guatemalteca*, Christian Democratic Party of Guatemala
dcg. dancing; decigramme

D.C.G. deputy chaplain-general
D.C.G.S. deputy chief of the general staff
D.Ch. Doctor of Surgery
D.C.H. Diploma in Child Health
D.Ch.O. Diploma in Ophthalmic Surgery
D.C.I. directorate of chemical inspection; double column inch (advert.)
DCIC Defense Ceramic Information Center (U.S.A.)
D.C.I.G.S. Deputy Chief of the Imperial General Staff
D.C.I.I. defense central index of investigation (U.S.A.)
D.C.J. district court judge (U.S.A.)
dcl. decalitre; declaration
D.C.L. Distillers' Company Limited; Doctor of Canon/Civil Law
D.C.L.I. Duke of Cornwall's Light Infantry
D.C.L.P. Contact Lens Certificate of Scottish Association of Opticians; Higher Contact Lens Diploma of British Optical Association
D.Cl.Sc. Doctor of Clinical Science
DCM Directorate for Classification Management
dcm. decametre
D.C.M. Department of Coins and Medals, British Museum; Distinguished Conduct Medal; district court-martial; Doctor of Comparative Medicine
D.C.M.G. Dame Commander of the Most Distinguished Order of St. Michael and St. George
D.C.M.S. deputy commissioner medical services
D.C.N.I. Department of the Chief of Naval Information
D.Cn.L. Doctor of Canon Law
D.C.N.S. deputy chief of naval staff
D.C.O. Dominion, Colonial and Overseas, *now* International (Barclays Bank); Duchy of Cornwall Office
D. & coh. daughter and co-heiress
D.C. of S. deputy chief of staff
d. col. double column (advert.)
D.Com.L. Doctor of Commercial Law
D.Comm. Doctor of Commerce
D. Comp. L. Doctor of Comparative Law
D.C.P. Diploma of Clinical Pathology /Psychology; disaster control plan
D.C.R. district chief ranger, Ancient Order of Foresters
D.C.R.E. Deputy Commandant, Royal Engineers
D.C.R.O. Dyers and Cleaners Research Organisation
D.C.S. deputy chief of staff; deputy

clerk of session; Doctor of Christian/ Commercial Science
D.C.S.L. district cub scout leader
D.C.S.O. deputy chief scientific officer
D.C.S.T. deputy chief of supplies and transport
dct. document
D.C.T. Port. *Defesa Civil do Território*, civil defence; depth-charge thrower; Doctor of Christian Theology; Drapers' Chamber of Trade
D.C.T.(Batt.) Diploma of the Battersea College of Technology
D.C.T.D. Diploma in Chest and Tuberculous Diseases
D.C.V.O. Dame Commander of the Royal Victorian Order
DCW dead carcase weight
d . . . d damned
DD direct debit (fin.); *s* Gloucestershire (B.V.R.); dichloropropylene and dichloropropane, soil fumigant
D/D days after date; demand draft
DD2 Second Development Decade, 1971–80
dd. dated; dedicated; delivered; drilled
d.d. day's date; definite decoding; delayed delivery; delivered dry/dock; detergent dispersant; due date/day
d.d. L. *dono dedit*, given as a gift
d. and d. drunk and disorderly
D.d. delivered docks, indicates that seller of goods pays all charges to the dock
D.d. L. *Deo dedit*, gave to God
D.D. Department of Defense (U.S.A.); deputy director; Diploma in Dermatology; *direttissimo*, fast train (Italy); discharged dead; dishonourable discharge; L. *Divinitatis Doctor*, Doctor of Divinity; double demy (paper)
D.½ D. dispatch money payable at half demurrage rate
dda digital differential analyser
D.D.A. Dangerous Drugs Act; Disabled Drivers' Association
D-day first day of Allied invasion of Europe, 6 June 1944, WW2
D. Day decimal day, 15 Feb. 1971 (U.K.)
D.D.C. deck decompression chamber (diving); Dewey Decimal Classification; Fr. *Docteur en droit canonique*, Doctor of Canon Law
D.D.D. deadline delivery date; direct distance dialling
D.D.D. L. *dat, dicat, dedicat*, he gives, devotes, and dedicates; L. *dono dedit dedicavit*, he gave and consecrated as a gift
D.D.D.S. deputy director of dental services

D.D.E. Dwight David Eisenhower (1890–1969), pres. of U.S.A.

D. de l'U. Doctor of the University (of Paris)

D.D.E.M. directorate of design of equipment and mechanization

D.D.G. deputy director-general

D.D.G.S.E. deputy director-general of signals equipment

D.D.G.S.R. division of the director-general of scientific research

D.D.H. Diploma in Dental Health

D.D.I. divisional detective inspector

d.d.in d. L. *de die in diem*, from day to day (med.)

DDL Danish Air Lines, Danish part of SAS

D.D.L. deputy director of labour

D.D.M. difference in depth modulation; Diploma in Dermatological Medicine; Doctor of Dental Medicine

D.D.M.C. Disabled Drivers' Motor Club

D.D.M.E. deputy director of mechanical engineering

D.D.M.I. deputy director of military intelligence

D.D.M.O.I. deputy director of military operations and intelligence

D.D.M.S. deputy director of medical services

D.D.M.T. deputy director of military training

D.D.N.I. deputy director of naval intelligence

D.D.O. dispatch money payable discharging only (ship.); Diploma in Dental Orthopaedics

D.D.O.S. deputy director of ordnance services

D.D.P. declaration of design performance; Department of Defense Production (Can.)

D.D.P.H. Diploma in Dental Public Health

D.D.P.R. deputy director of public relations

D.D.P.S. deputy director of personal/postal services

D.Dr. Ger. *Doktor/Doktor*, double doctorate

DDR direct debit (fin.)

D.D.R. *Deutsche Demokratische Republik*, German Democratic Republic (E. Ger.); Diploma in Diagnostic Radiology

D.D.R.A. deputy director, Royal Artillery

D.D.R.D. deputy directorate of research and development

DDRE director of defense research and engineering (U.S.A.)

D.D.R.M. deputy directorate of repair and maintenance

DDRR directional discontinuity ring radiator

dd/s. delivered sound

D.D.S. deep diving system; deputy directorate of science; director of dental services; Doctor of Dental Science/Surgery

D.D.Sc. Doctor of Dental Science

D.D.S.D. deputy director of staff duties

D.D. & Shpg. dock dues and shipping

D.D.S.R. deputy directorate of scientific research

D.D.S.T. deputy director of supplies and transport

D.D.T. dichloro-diphenyl-trichloroethane, chlorinated hydrocarbon used as insecticide

D.D.V.S. deputy director of veterinary services

D.D.W.E. & M. deputy director of works, electrical and mechanical

D.D.Y. *Devlet Demiryollari*, Turkish Railways

DE Delaware; Department of Employment; *s* Dundee (B.F.P.); *s* Pembrokeshire (B.V.R.)

2DE *s* Dundee (radio call-sign)

d.e. deckle edge; diesel-electric; direct elimination (fencing); double end/entry

D.E. Dáil Éireann, House of Representatives (Rep. of Ireland); deflection error; destroyer escort; digestible energy; Doctor of Engineering/Entomology; double elephant (paper); dynamical/dynamite engineer

DEA diethanolamine (chem.)

Dea. deacon; dean

D.E.A. Dairy Engineers' Association; Davis escape apparatus; Department of Economic Affairs, *now* disbanded; Department of External Affairs

D.E.A.U.A. Diesel Engineers' and Users' Association

deaur. pil. L. *deaurentur pilulae*, let the pills be gilded (med.)

Deb, Debbie, Debby Deborah

deb. debenture; debit; début; Fr. *débutante*

de Bc. Honoré de Balzac (1799–1850), Fr. novelist

deb. stk. debenture stock (fin.)

D.Ec. Doctor of Economics

dec. deceased; decimal; decimetre; declaration; declare; declared; declension; declination; decoration; decorative; decrease

dec. It. *decrescendo*, becoming softer (mus.)

dec. Fr. *décembre*, December

Dec. December
Dec. L. *Decani*, side of choir upon which the dean sits, usually the south side; L. *Decanus*, dean
D.E.C. Dollar Export Council
decd. deceased
decid. deciduous
decim. decimetre
decl. declension
decn. decontamination
decomp. decomposition
D. Econ. Doctor of Economics
D. Econ. Sc. Doctor of Economic Science
Decr. It. *Decreto*, decree/ordinance
Decres., Decresc. It. *decrescendo*, subsiding (mus.)
DECUS Digital Equipment Computer Users' Society
ded. dedicate; dedication; deduce; deduct; deduction, *also* deduct.
D.Ed. Doctor of Education
de d. in d. L. *de die in diem*, from day to day continuously
D.E.E. Diploma in Electrical Engineering
dee jay disc jockey, *also* D.J.
def. defecate; defecation; defect; defection; defective; defector; defence; defendant; deferred (fin.); defense; deficit; define; definite; definition; deflagrate; deflect; deflection; defoliate; defrost; defunct
def. L. *defunctus*, deceased
D.E.F. defence specification prefix
def.art. definite article
defl. deflate; deflation; deflect; deflection
deft. defendant; deflection
deg. degree
D. & E.G. Development and Engineering Group
D.E.I. Dutch East Indies
DEK *Demokratikon Ethnikón Kómma*, Democratic National Party (Cyprus)
dekag. dekagramme
dekal. dekalitre
dekam. dekametre
del. delegate; delegation; delete; delivery
del. L. *delineavit*, he/she drew it
deld. delivered
deleg. delegate; delegation
Del. Delaware; Delhi
DELIMCO Liberian-German Mining Company (Liberia)
D. Elo. Doctor of Elocution
DELTA detailed labor and time analysis (U.S.A.)
DELTIC delay line time compression
delv. deliver
dely. delivery

dem. demand; demerara; democracy; democratic; demurrage; demy (paper)
Dem. Democrat
D.E.M.E. Diesel Engine Manufacturers' Association; director of electrical and mechanical engineering
demo. demonstration
demob. demobilize
demon. demonstrate; demonstrative;
— **pro.** demonstrative pronoun
D.E.M.S. defensively equipped merchant ship/shipping
demur. demurrage
den. denier; denotation; denotative; denouement; dental; dentist; dentistry
Den. Denbighshire (Wales); Denmark; Denver (U.S.A.)
D. En. Doctor of English
D. en D. Fr. *Docteur en droit*, Doctor of Laws
dend., dendrol. dendrology
D. Eng., D. Engg. Doctor of Engineering
D. en M., D. en. Med. Fr. *Docteur en médecine*, Doctor of Medicine
Denny Denis; Dennis
denom. denomination
DENROREN *Zenkoku Denryoku Rodo Kumiai Rengokai*, National Fed. of Electric Power Workers' Unions (Jap.)
dens. density
dent. dental; dentist; dentistry; denture
D. Ent. Doctor of Entomology
dep. depart; department; departure; dependency; dependant; dependent; de-; ponent; depose; deposit; depositor; depot; Fr. *depuis*, since; deputy
dép. Fr. *département*, equiv. to Brit. county; Fr. *député*, deputy
D.E.P. deflection error, probable; Department of Employment and Productivity, *formerly* Ministry of Labour; director of equipment and policy
Dep.-Dir. deputy-director
dept. department; deponent; deputy
Dept. of A. Department of Agriculture
deputn. deputation
der. Sp. *derecha*, right; derivation; derivative; derive; Fr. *dernier*, last
Derby., Derbys. Derbyshire
Derek, Derrick Theodoric
deriv. derivation; derivative; derive
derm. dermatitis; dermatology, *also* dermat.
D.E.R.R. Duke of Edinburgh's Royal Regiment
D.E.R.V. diesel-engined road vehicle
Derry Londonderry
Des Desmond
des. desert; design; designate; designation; designer; desire; dessert

D.E.S. Department of Education and Science; director of educational services; director of engineering stores

DESC Defense Electronics Supply Center (U.S.A.)

desc. descend; descendant; descent; describe

desid. L. *desideratum,* wanted

desig. designate

D. ès L. *Docteur ès lettres,* Doctor of Letters

DESLANT destroyer forces, Atlantic (USN)

desp. despatch

Des.R.C.A. Designer of the Royal College of Art

D.ès S., D.ès Sc. Fr. Doctor of Science

D.ès Sc.Pol. Fr. Doctor of Political Science

dest. destroyer

destn. destination

det. detach; detachment; detail; determine

det. L. *detur,* let it be given (med.)

Det. Detective; — **Con.** Detective Constable; — **Insp.** Detective Inspector; — **Sgt.** Detective Sergeant; — **Sup., Supt.** Detective Superintendent

detn. determination

DEU data exchange unit

D.E.U.A. Diesel Engineers' & Users' Association

D.E.U.C.E. digital electronic universal computing engine

Deut. Deuteronomy (Bible)

dev. develop; developer; development; deviate; deviation (nav.)

Dev., Devon. Devonshire

dev.mo It. *devotissimo,* yours truly

devp. develop

devpt. development

devs. devotions

D.E.W. distant early warning

DEXAN digital experimental airborne navigator

dez. Port. *dezembro,* December

Dez. Ger. *Dezember,* December

DF s Gloucestershire (B.V.R.)

df. draft

d.f. dead freight; decontamination factor; drinking fountain

D.F. dean of faculty; direction-finder; direction-finding; Doctor of Forestry; double foolscap (paper); drop forging

D.F. L. *defensor fidei,* defender of the faith, title conferred on Henry VIII by Pope Leo X

D.F.A. Dairy Farmers' Association; Department of Foreign Affairs; Diploma in Foreign Affairs; Doctor of Fine Arts

D.F.C. Distinguished Flying Cross

D.F.D.S. *Det Forende Dampskibsselskab,* United Steamship Co. (Den.)

D.F.E. double fish eye (buttons)

D.F.H. Diploma of the Faraday House Engineering College

D.F.I. directorate of food investigation

D.fl. Dutch florins, currency

D.F.L.S. day fighter leaders' school

D.F.M. Diploma in Forensic Medicine; Distinguished Flying Medal

D.F.M.S. Domestic and Foreign Missionary Society

dfndt., dft. defendant

DFP diisopropylphosphorofluoridate (chem.)

DFPA Douglas Fir Plywood Association

D.F.R. decreasing failure rate; Dounreay fast reactor

D.F.R.A. Drop Forging Research Association

D.F.Sc. Doctor of Financial Science

dft. draft

D.F.W. director of fortifications and works

DG s Gloucestershire (B.V.R.)

dg. decigramme

DG. directional gyro (nav.)

D-G. director-general

D.G. Fr. *Déclaration de guerre,* declaration of war; Dragoon Guards

D.G. L. *Dei gratia,* by the grace of God; L. *Deo gratias,* thanks to God

D.G.A. director general aircraft; Directors Guild of America

D.G.A.A. Distressed Gentlefolk's Aid Association

D.G.A.M.S. director general of army medical services

D.G.B. Ger. *Deutscher Gewerkschaftsbund,* German Fed. of Trade Unions

D.G.C. Diploma in Guidance and Counselling

D.G.C.A. director general of civil aviation

D.G.C.E. directorate general of communications equipment

D.G.C.St.J. Dame Grand Cross of the Order of Saint John of Jerusalem

D.G.D. director gunnery division

D.G.D.C. deputy grand director of ceremonies (freem.)

D.G.D. & M. director general dockyards and maintenance

D.G.E. directorate general of equipment

DGG. *Deutsche Grammophon Gesellschaft,* German Gramophone Record Company

D.G.I. director general of information /inspection

D.G.M. Diploma in General Medicine; director general of manpower

D.G.M.S. director general of medical services

D.G.M.T. director general of military training

D.G.M.W. director general of military works

Dgn. dragoon

D.G.D. Diploma in Gynaecology and Obstetrics

D.G.P. Director General of Personnel /Production

D.G.P.S. Director General of Personal Services and Officer Appointments

d. Gr. Ger. *der Grosse*, the great

D.G.R. director of graves registration

D.G.S. Diploma in General Surgery; director general, ships; directorate general of signals

D.G.S.R.D. directorate general of scientific research and development

D.G.St.J. Dame of Grace of the Order of Saint John of Jerusalem, *now* **D.St.J.**

D.G.T. director general of training

D.G.T.A. Dry Goods Trade Association

D.G.W. director general of weapons/ works

DH *s* Dartmouth (B.F.P.); *dirham*, Moroccan currency; *s* Walsall (B.V.R.)

d.h. Ger. *das heisst*, that is to say; dead heat

D.H. De Havilland; Doctor of Humanities

dha. Sp. *dicha*, good luck

D. & H.A.A. Dock and Harbour Authorities' Association

D.H.D.P. Fr. *Diplôme en hygiène publique dentaire*, Diploma in Dental Public Health

D.H.E.W. Department of Health, Education and Welfare (U.S.A.)

D.H.I. *Deutsches Hydrographisches Institut*, German Hydrographic Institute, Hamburg

D.H.L. Doctor of Hebrew Literature; Doctor of Humane Letters

D.H.M. Diocesan Home Missionary

D.H.M.P.G.T.S. Department of Her/ His Majesty's Procurator General and Treasury Solicitor

D.H.M.S.A. Diploma in the History of Medicine

dho. Sp. *dicho*, said

D.H.O. Downhill Only Ski Club, formed 1925, Wengen (Switz.)

D.H.P. developed horse power; Fr. *Diplôme en hygiène publique*, Diploma in Public Health

D.H.Q. district/divisional headquarters

D.H.S. Diploma in Horticultural Science; district high school; Doctor of Health Sciences

D.H.S.S. Department of Health and Social Security

D.Hum.Lit. Doctor of Humane Letters

D.H.V.P. Fr. *Diplôme en hygiène publique vétérinaire*, Diploma in Veterinary Public Health

D.Hy. Doctor of Hygiene

Di Diana; Dinah; didymium (chem.)

DI *s* Roscommon (Rep. of Ireland V.R.)

di. diameter

Di. *dinar* (currency)

d.i. daily inspection; Ger. *das ist*, that is; de-ice; diplomatic immunity; document identifier

D.I. defence intelligence; director of infantry; detective/district/divisional inspector; double imperial (paper); drill instructor

DIA Defense Intelligence Agency (U.S.A.)

dia. diagram; dialect; diameter

D.I.A. Design and Industries Association; Diploma in International Affairs

diag. diagnose; diagonal; diagram

dial. dialect; dialectal; dialectic; dialectical; dialogue

Dial. diallyl-barbituric acid, white crystalline powder used as hypnotic

diam. diameter

DIAMANG Port. *Companhia de Diamantes de Angola*, Angolan Diamond Co.

DIANE digital integrated attack and navigation equipment

diap. *diapason*, foundation stops of organ in Eng. version (mus.); Fr. *diapason*, tuning fork/pitch (mus.); Gk. *diapason*, octave/constant harmony (mus.)

diaph. diaphragm

dic. It. *dicembre*, December; Sp. *diciembre*, December

D.I.C. Diploma of Membership of the Imperial College of Science and Technology (Lond.)

D.I.Chem. Diploma of Industrial Chemistry

dick detective

Dick, Dickie, Dickon, Dicky Richard

dict. dictate; dictation; dictator; dictionary

dicta. dictaphone

Dict. Amer. Slang *Dictionary of American Slang*

D.I.C.T.A. Diploma of the Imperial College of Tropical Agriculture (Trinidad)

Did. didactics

D.I.D.A.S. dynamic instrumentation data automobile system

didn't did not

D.I.E. Diploma in Industrial Engineering; Diploma of the Institute of Engineering

dieb.alt. L. *diebus alternis*, on alternate days (med.)

D.I.E.M.E. directorate of inspection of electrical and mechanical equipment

diet. dietary; dietetics; dietician

dif., diff. differ; difference; different; differential

D.I.F. district inspector of fisheries

diffs. axle differential gearing boxes

dig. digest; digestion; digestive; digit; digital

D.I.G. deputy inspector-general; disablement income group

digs. diggings, lodgings

D.I.H. Diploma in Industrial Health

Dij. Dijon (France)

dil. dilute; dilution

dil. L. *dilue*, dilute (med.)

dilet. dilettante

diln. dilution

dim. dimension; diminish; diminutive

dim. L. *dimidium*, one-half; It. *diminuendo*, becoming softer (mus.)

Dim. Fr. *Dimanche*, Sunday

D.I.M. Diploma in Industrial Management

dimin. diminutive

DIMPLE deuterium moderated pile low energy

din. *dinar* (currency); dining-room; dinner

Din. Dutch *Dinsdag*, Tuesday

D.I.N. Ger. *Das ist Norm*, this is normal/standard; Ger. *Deutsche Industrie-Norm*, German Industrial Standards, *also* **Din**

D.Ing. *Doctor Ingeniariae*, Doctor of Engineering

D.Inst.P.A. Diploma of the Institute of Park Administration

D.I.O. district intelligence officer

dioc. diocese; diocesan; — **syn.** diocesan synod

D.I.O.P. di-*iso*-octyl phthalate, plasticizer for P.V.C.

Dip. Diploma; — **A.D.** Dip. in Art and Design; — **Agr.** Dip. in Agriculture; — **A.Ling.** Dip. in Applied Linguistics; — **A.M.** Dip. in Applied Mechanics; — **App.Sc.** Dip. of Applied Science; — **Arch.** Dip. of Architecture; — **Arts** Dip. in Arts; — **Ass.Sc.** Dip. in Association Science; — **Bac.** Dip. in Bacteriology; — **B.M.S.** Dip. in Basic Medical Sciences; — **C.A.M.** Dip. in Communication, Advertising and Marketing; — **Card.** Dip. in Cardiology; — **C.D.** Dip. of Civic Design; — **Com.** Dip. in/of Commerce; — **D.Hus.** Dip. in Dairy Husbandry; — **D.P.** Dip. in Drawing and Painting; — **D.S.** Dip. in Dental Surgery; — **Econ.** Dip. in/of Economics; — **Ed.** Dip. in/of Education; — **Eng.** Dip. in Engineering; — **F.A.** Dip. in Fine Arts; — **For.** Dip. of Forestry; — **G.T.** Dip. in Glass Technology; — **H.A.** Dip. in Hospital Administration; — **H.E.** Dip. in Highway Engineering; — **H.Sc.** Dip. in Home Science; — **J** Dip. of Journalism; — **L.** Dip. in Languages; — **Lib.** Dip. of Librarianship; — **L.Sc.** Dip. of Library Science; — **Mech. E.** Dip. of Mechanical Engineering; — **M.F.O.S.** Dip. in Maxial, Facial and Oral Surgery; — **Mus.Ed.** Dip. in Musical Education; — **N.A. & A.C.** Dip. in Numerical Analysis and Automatic Computing; — **N.Ed.** Dip. in Nursery School Education; — **N.Z.L.S.** Dip. of the New Zealand Library Service; — **O. & G.** Dip. in Obstetrics and Gynaecology; — **O.L.** Dip. in Oriental Learning; — **Orth.** Dip. in Orthodontics; — **P.A.** Dip. in Public Administration; — **Pharm.** Dip. in Pharmacy; — **P.Hus.** Dip. in Poultry Husbandry; — **Phys.Ed.** Dip. in Physical Education; — **P. & O.T.** Dip. in Physiotherapy and Occupational Therapy; — **Q.S.** Dip. in Quantity Surveying; — **R.A.D.A.** Dip. of the Royal Academy of Dramatic Art; — **R.S.A.M.** Dip. of the Royal Scottish Academy of Music; — **S. & P.A.** Dip. in Social and Public Administration; — **S.S.** Dip. in Social Studies; — **S.W.** Dip. in Social Work; — **T.** Dip. in Teaching; — **T.C.P.** Dip. in Town and Country Planning; — **Tec./Tech.** Dip. in Technology; — **T.E.F.L.** Dip. in the Teaching of English as a Foreign Language; — **Th.** Dip. in Theology; — **T.P.** Dip. in Town Planning; — **V.F.M.** Dip. in Valuation and Farm Management

diphth. diphthong

dipl. diplomacy; diplomat; diplomatic; diplomatist

Dipl. Ger. *Diplom*, diploma; diploma

dipso. dipsomaniac

dir. direct; direction; director

Dir. *Dirham*, Moroccan currency

Dir. Gen. It. *Direttore Generale*, general manager

Dir.-Genl. director-general

DIS Defense Intelligence School (U.S.A.)

dis. discharge; disciple; discipline; disconnect; discontinue; discount; dispense;

distance; distant; distribute or break-up type

D.I.S. Dairy Industry Society (U.S.A.)

disab., disabl. disability

disco. discothèque

disb. disbursement

disc. disciple; discipline; discount; discover; discoverer; discovery

disch. discharge

disct. discount

dishon. dishonourable; dishonourably

dismd. dismissed

disp. dispensary; dispensation; dispense; disperse; dispersion

displ. displacement

diss. dissenter; dissertation; dissolve

dist. distance; distant; distilled; distinguish; district; — **atty.** district attorney (U.S.A.)

Dis.T.P. Distinction in Town Planning

distr. distribution; distributor

DISTRAM digital space trajectory measurement system

distrib. distributive

DISTRIPRESS F. *Fédération internationale des distributeurs de presse*, Intern. Assn. of Wholesale Newspaper, Periodical and Book Distributors

D.I.T. Detroit Institute of Technology

D.Iur. Doctor of Law

D.Iur.Utr. Doctor of Canon/Civil Law

div. divergence; diversion; divide; dividend; divine; division; divisor; divorce

Div. divine; divinity

divde. Fr. *dividende*, dividend

divi., divvy dividend

div. in p. aeq. L. *divide in partes aequales*, divided into equal parts (med.)

divn. division

divnl. divisional; — **S.M.** divisional sales manager

D.I.Y. do it yourself

diz. It. *dizionario*, dictionary

Dizzy Benjamin Disraeli, Lord Beaconsfield (1804–81), Brit. statesman and man of letters

DJ *s* St Helens (B.V.R.)

d. J. Ger. *der Jüngere*, junior; Ger. *dieses Jahres*, of this year

D.J. department of journalism; dinner jacket; Diploma in Journalism; disc jockey; Divorce Judge; Dow Jones (fin.); dust jacket

D.J.A.G. deputy judge advocate-general

D.J.I.A. Dow Jones Industrial Average

D.J.St.J. Dame of Justice of the Order of Saint John of Jerusalem, *now* D.St.J.

D.Jur. Doctor of Jurisprudence

DK *s* Denmark, including Faroe Islands and Greenland (I.V.R.); *s* Dundalk (Rep. of Ireland F.P.); *s* Rochdale (B.V.R.)

dk. dark; deck; dock; duck

dkg. decagramme

dkl. decalitre

dkm. decametre

DKP *Deutsche Kommunistische Partei*, Communist Party (W. Ger.)

D.K.S. Deputy Keeper of the Signet

dkt. docket

dkyd. dockyard

d . . . l devil

dl decalitre

DL *s* Deal (B.F.P.); Democratic League (Finland); difference limen/threshold (psy.); *s* Isle of Wight (B.V.R.)

D/L data link; demand loan

D.L. Department of Labor (U.S.A.); Deputy Lieutenant; *Doctor Legum*, Doctor of Laws; dog/driving licence; double ledger

D.L.A. Decorative Lighting Association

DLAS Defence of Literature and the Arts Society

D.Lat. difference of latitude

dlc direct lift control

DLC divisional land commissioner

D.L.C. Diploma of the Loughborough College of Technology; Doctor of Celtic Literature

dld. deadline date; delivered

D.L.E.S. Doctor of Letters in Economic Studies

D. Lett. Fr. *Docteur en Lettres*, Doctor of Letters

D.L.G. David Lloyd George (1863–1945), Brit. statesman and orator

D.L.G.A. Decorative Lighting Guild of America

DLH *Deutsche Lufthansa*, W. German airline

DLI Defense Language Institute (U.S.A.)

D.L.I. Durham Light Infantry

D.-Lib. Liberal Democrat (U.S.A.)

D.L.I.S. Desert Locust Information Service

D.Lit., D.Litt. Doctor of Letters/Literature

D.Litt.S. Doctor of Sacred Letters

D.L.J. Dame of Justice of the Order of Saint Lazarus of Jerusalem

d.l.M. Ger. *des laufenden Monats*, of the current month

D.L.M.A. Decorative Lighting Manufacturers' Association

d.l.o. dispatch loading only

D.L.O. dead letter office, *now* returned letter office; dispatch money payable loading only; Diploma in Laryngology and Otology/Otorhinolaryngology; divisional legal officer (Aust.)

D.Long. difference of longitude

D.L.O.Y. Duke of Lancaster's Own Yeomanry

DLP Democratic Labour Party (Barbados); Democratic Labour Party (Trinidad and Tobago)

D.L.P. double large post

dlr. dealer

D.L.R. Driving Licences Regulations; *Dominion Law Reports*

dls. dollars

D.L.S. debt liquidation schedule; Doctor of Library Science/Service; Dominion Land Surveyor

D.L.Sc. Doctor of Library Science

DLTP dilauryl thiodipropionate, antioxidant for rubber

dlvr. deliver

dlvy. delivery

D.L.W. Diploma in Labour Welfare

dly. daily

DM adamsite (chem.); *Deutsche Mark*, W. German currency; *s* Flintshire (B.V.R.)

dm. decimetre

d.M. Ger. *dieses Monats*, instant

D.M. *Daily Mail*; data manager; delta modulation; deputy master; design manual; director of music; district manager; Fr. *Docteur en Médecine*, Doctor of Medicine; Doctor of Mathematics/Medicine/Music; double medium

D.M.A. Diploma in Municipal Administration

D.M.A.A. Direct Mail Advertising Association

D.M.A.P. dimethyl amino-pyridine, modifier for urethane foams

D.Math. Doctor of Mathematics

DMC digital micro-circuit; direct manufacturing costs; dough moulding compound

D.M. & C.W. Diploma in Maternity and Child Welfare

D.M.D. Doctor of Dental Medicine; Doctor of Mathematics and Didactics; Doctor of Medical Dentistry

D.M.E. Diploma in Mechanical Engineering; director of mechanical engineering; distance-measuring equipment

D.Med. Doctor of Medicine

D.Met. Doctor of Metallurgy/Meteorology

D.M.E.T. directorate of marine engineering training (India)

D.M.F. Decorative Marble Federation; Dyers of Man-Made Fibre Fabrics Federation

D.M.F.O.S. Diploma in Maxillofacial and Oral Surgery

dmg. damage

DMG Defense Marketing Group (U.S.A.)

D.M.G.O. divisional machine-gun officer

D.M.H.S. director of medical and health services

D.M.I. director of military intelligence

D.M.I.C. Defense Metals Information Center (U.S.A.)

D.Miss. Doctor of Missiology

D.M.J. Diploma in Medical Jurisprudence

D.M.K. *Dravida Munnetra Kazhagam*, Dravidian Progressive Forum (India)

dml. demolish

D.M.L. Defence Medal for Leningrad (U.S.S.R.); Doctor of Modern Languages

D.M.L.T. Diploma in Medical Laboratory Technology

D.M.M. Defence Medal for Moscow (U.S.S.R.)

d.m.m.f. dry mineral matter free, basis for analysis of coals and cokes

dmn. dimension; dimensional

Dmn. Fst. *Damnation of Faust*

D.M.O. Defence Medal for Odessa (U.S.S.R.); director of military operations; district medical officer

D.M.O. & I. director military operations and intelligence

D.M.P. Diploma in Medical Psychology; director of manpower planning

D.M.P.A. Dublin Master Printers' Association

D.M.P.B. Diploma in Medical Pathology and Bacteriology

D.M.P.I. desired mean point of impact

dmpr. damper

D.M.R. Diploma in Medical Radiology; director of materials research

D.M.R.D. Diploma in Medical Radio-Diagnostics; directorate of materials research and development

D.M.R.E., D.M.R. & E. Diploma in Medical Radiology and Electrology

D.M.R.(T.) Diploma in Radiotherapy

D.M.S. data management system; Diploma in Management Studies; directorate of military survey; director of medical services; Doctor of Medical Science; documentation of molecular spectroscopy

D.M.S. L. *Dis manibus sacrum*, consecrated to the souls of the departed

D.M.Sc. Doctor of Missionary Science

D.M.S.C. Defence Material Standardization Committee (MOD)

DMSO dimethylsulfoxide (chem.)

D.M.S.S. director of medical and sanitary services

dmst. demonstrate; demonstration

dmstn. demonstration

dmstr. demonstrator

D.M.S.V. Defence Medal for Sevastopol (U.S.S.R.)

D.M.T. director of military training

D.M.T.R. Dounreay Materials Testing Reactor

D.M.T.S. Department of Mines and Technical Surveys (Can.)

D.Mus. Doctor of Music

D.M.V. Fr. *Docteur en médecine vétérinaire,* Doctor of Veterinary Medicine

DMZ demilitarized zone

d . . . n damn

DN *s* York (B.V.R.)

dn. deacon; down; dozen

Dn. Dragoon

Dⁿ. Sp. *Don* (title)

D.N. debit note; Diploma in Nursing/Nutrition

D.N. L. *Dominus noster,* our Lord

Dⁿᵃ. Sp. *Doña* (title)

D.N.A. deoxyribo-nucleic acid; *Deutscher Normen Ausschuss,* W. German Standards Institute; director of naval accounts; District Nursing Association

D.N.A.D. director of naval air division

D.N.A.R. director of naval air radio

D.N.B. departure from nucleate boiling; *Deutsches Nachrichten Büro,* German news agency during Nazi period; *Dictionary of National Biography*

D.N.C. director of naval construction

DNCCC Defense National Communications Control Center (U.S.A.)

D.N.C.L. Diploma of the Northampton College of Advanced Technology (Lond.)

D.N.D. Department of National Defense (Can.); director of navigation and direction

dne. Fr. *douane,* customs

D.N.E. Diploma in Nursing Education; director of naval equipment

D.N.E.S. director of naval education service

D.N.I. *Dana Normalisasi Indonesia,* Indonesian Standards Institute; director of naval intelligence

D.N.J. *Det Norske Justervesen,* Norwegian Weights and Measures Bureau

D.N.J.C. L. *Dominus noster Jesus Christus,* Our Lord Jesus Christ

DNL *Det Norske Luftartselkap,* Norwegian airline, part of SAS

D.N.M.S. director of naval medical services

D.N.O. director of naval ordnance; district naval officer

D. note $500 note (U.S.A.)

D. notices defence notices

DNP di-iso-octyl phthalate (chem.)

D.N.P. declared national programme

D.N.P.P. L. *Dominus Noster Papa Pontifex,* Our Lord the Pope

D.N.R. director of naval recruiting

dns. downs (cartog.)

D.N.S.A. Diploma in Nursing Service Administration

D.N.T. director of naval training

D.N.W.S. director of naval weather service

DO *s* Douglas (B.F.P.); *s* Lincolnshire, the part called Holland (B.V.R.)

D/O delivery/direct order

do. It. *ditto,* the same

D.O. defence/defense order; deferred ordinary shares (fin.); Diploma in Ophthalmology; Diplomate of Osteopathy; district office/officer; divisional office/officer; Doctor of Ophthalmology/Optometry/Oratory/Osteopathy; drawing office

DOA Department of the Army (U.S.A.)

D.O.A. date of availability; dead on arrival; dissolved oxygen analyser

DOAE Defence Operational Analysis Establishment (MOD)

d.o.b. date of birth

DOC Department of Commerce (U.S.A.); direct operating cost

doc. doctor; document

D.O.C. Department of Communications (Can.); district officer commanding

d.o.c.a. date of current appointment

d.o.c.e. date of current enlistment

Doc. Eng. Doctor of Engineering

Doc.rer.pol. Doctor of Political Science

Doct. L. *Doctor,* doctor

docu. document; documentary; documentation

Dod, Doddy George

DOD Department of Defense (U.S.A.)

d.o.d. date of death; died of disease

D.o.E. director of education

D.Œ. Diploma in Economics

D.Oec. Gk. *Doctor Oeconomiae,* Doctor of Economics

doesn't does not

D. of Corn. L.I. Duke of Cornwall's Light Infantry

D. of H. degree of honour

DOFL diamond ordnance fuze laboratory

D. of L. Duchy of Lancaster

D. of P. director of plans division

D. of S. director of stores

dogm. dogmatic

d.oh.c. double/dual overhead cam

DOI descent orbit insertion (space)

D.O.I. Department of Industry (Can.); died of injuries; director of information

dol. It. *dolce*, sweet (mus.)

D.O.L. Doctor of Oriental Learning

dolciss. It. *dolcissimo*, very sweetly (mus.)

Doll, Dolly Dorothy

Dolly Basil D'Oliveira (cricket)

Dom Dominic/Dominick

DOM *s* Dominican Republic (I.V.R.)

dom. It. *domenica*, Sunday; domestic; domicile; dominant; Sp./Port. *domingo*, Sunday; dominion

Dom. Dominical; Dominican

Dom. L. *Dominus*, Lord/Master

D.O.M. L. *Deo optimo maximo*, to God the best and greatest; L. *Dominus omnium magister*, God the Lord/Master of all

Dom. Bk. *Domesday Book*

Dom. Econ. domestic economy/home economics

DOMEI-KAIGI *Zen Nihon Rodo Sodomei Kumiai Kaigi*, Japanese Confed. of Labour

D.O.M.M.D.A. Drawing Office Material Manufacturers' and Dealers' Association

D.O.M.O. Dispensing Opticians' Manufacturing Organisation

Dom.Proc. L. *Domus Procerum*, House of Lords (leg.)

D.O.M.S. Diploma in Ophthalmic Medicine and Surgery

Dom. Sc. domestic science

Don, Donnie Donald

DON Department of the Navy (U.S.A.)

don. L. *donec*, until

Don., Doneg. Donegal

don't does not; do not

DOO Director, Office of Oceanography (UNESCO)

DOP di-octylphthalate (chem.)

D.O.P. developing-out paper

D.O.P.B.M. Department of Oriental Printed Books and Manuscripts, British Museum

Dopp.ped. It. *Doppio pedale*, in organ music, the pedal part to be played in octaves (mus.)

D.Opt. Diploma in Ophthalmics

Dor Dorian

Dor. Doric

D.Or. Doctor in Orientation

D.O.R. directorate of operational research

Dora Dorothy

DORA, D.O.R.A. Defence of the Realm Act, First Consolidated Act, 27 Nov. 1914

DORDEC Domestic Refrigerator Development Council

dorm. dormitory

Dorna desoxyribose nucleic acid (chem.)

Dors. Dorset

D.Orth. Diploma in Orthodontics/Orthoptics

D.O.S. day of sale; di-octyl sebacate; Diploma in Orthopaedic Surgery; directorate of overseas surveys; director of ordnance services

D.O.S.T. *Dictionary of the Scottish Tongue*

D.O.S.V. deep ocean survey vehicle

Dot Dorothy

DOT Department of the Treasury (U.S.A.); Department of Transportation (U.S.A.); Diploma in Occupational Therapy

dot. dotation

D.o.T. Department of Telecommunications

D.O.T. Department of Overseas Trade; Department of Transport (Can.); Diploma in Occupational Therapy

D.O.T.G. di-ortho-tolyl guanidine, vulcanization accelerator

D.O.T.I.P.O.S. Deep Ocean Test Instrument Placement and Observation System

dott. It. *dottore*, doctor

Doug Dougal; Douglas, *also* Dougie

D.O.V. double oil of vitriol, commercial sulphuric acid

DOVAP doppler velocity and position

dow. dowager

D.O.W. died of wounds

D.O.W.B. deep ocean work boat

doz. dozen

DP Democratic Party, *Stronnictwo Demokratyczne* (Pol.); Democratic Party (Uganda); *s* Reading (B.V.R.)

D/P delivery/documents against/on payment

dp. deep

d.p. damp proof; damp proofing; deep penetration; departure point; depreciation percentage (fin.); direct port; double paper; dry powder

d.p. L. *directione propria*, with proper direction (med.)

d. and p. development and printing

D.P. by direction of the president; delivery point; Democratic Party (Aust.); diametral pitch; Diploma in Psychiatry; disabled person; displaced person, refugee; Doctor of Philosophy; domestic prelate; durable press; duty paid

D.P. L. *Domus Procerum*, House of Lords (leg.)

d.p.a. deferred payment account

D.P.A. *Deutsche Presse-Agentur*, (W.) German Press Agency; Diary Publishers' Association; Diploma/Doctor in/of Public Administration; Discharged Prisoners' Aid

D.Paed. Doctor of Pedagogy

D.P.A.S. Discharged Prisoners' Aid Society

D.P.B. Department of Printed Books (British Museum); deposit pass book

D.P.D. Department of Prints and Drawings (British Museum); Diploma in Public Dentistry

Dpe. Dieppe (France)

D.P.E. Diploma/Doctor in Physical Education

D.P.Ec. Doctor of Political Economy

D.Ped. Doctor of Pedagogy

D.Péd. Fr. *Docteur en Pédagogie*, Doctor of Pedagogy

DPf. *Deutsch pfennig*, Ger. currency

D.Ph., D.Phil. Doctor of Philosophy

D.P.H. Department/Diploma/Doctor of Public Health; diamond pyramid hardness

D.Pharm. Doctor of Pharmacy

D.P.H.D. Diploma in Public Health Dentistry

D.P.H.N. Diploma in Public Health Nursing

D.P.I. department of public information; director of public instruction

dpl. diploma; diplomat; duplex

D.P.M. deputy prime minister; deputy provost marshal; Diploma in Psychological Medicine; Doctor of Pediatric Medicine

DPMA Data Processing Management Association

D.P.O. distributing post office; district pay office

d.p.o.b. date and place of birth

D.Pol.Sc. Doctor of Political Science

D.P.P. Diploma in Plant Pathology; director of public prosecutions

D.P.R. director of public relations

DPRI Disaster Prevention Research Institute

DPRGR *Dewan Perwakilan Ratjat-Gotong Rojong*, Mutual Co-operation House of Representatives (Indonesia)

D.P.R.K. Democratic People's Republic of Korea (N. Korea), *Choson Minch-Shui Inmin, Konghwa-Guk*

DPS descent propulsion system

D.P.S. department of political science; director of personal/postal services

D.P.S.A. Data Processing Supplies Association (U.S.A.); Diploma in Public and Social Administration

D.P. & S.P.A. Display Producers' and Screen Printers' Association

D.Ps.Sc. Doctor of Psychological Science

D.Psy. Fr. *Docteur en Psychologie*, Doctor of Psychology

D. Psych. Diploma of Psychiatry; Doctor of Psychology

dpt. department; deponent; deposit; depot

d.p.t. distributed profit tax

Dpty. deputy

D.P.W. Department of Public Works (Can.)

dpx. duplex

d.q. direct question

D.Q.M.G. deputy quartermaster-general

D.Q.M.S. deputy quartermaster-sergeant

DR *s* Dover (B.F.P.); *s* Plymouth (B.V.R.)

D/R deposit receipt

dr. debit; debtor; door; drachm; drachma; dram; drama; draw; drawer; drawn; dresser; drive; driver; drum; drummer

Dr. director; doctor; Ger. *Doktor*, doctor; Port. *Doutor*, doctor

d.r. data report; dead reckoning (nav.); deficiency report; design requirements; development/document report

D/R. deposit receipt

D.R. Daughters of the Revolution (U.S.A.); defence regulation; dependent relative allowance (tax.); dispatch rider; *Deutsches Reich*, German Empire; Diploma in Radiology; district railway/registry; double royal (paper); Dutch Reformed; dynamic relaxation

DRA dead reckoning analyser

Dr.ª Sp. *Doctora*, doctor (fem.); Port. *Doutora*, doctor (fem.)

D.R.A. de-rating appeals

D.R.A.C. Director Royal Armoured Corps

Dr. Agr. Doctor of Agriculture

DRAI dead reckoning analogue/analyser indicator

dram. drama; dramatic; dramatist

dram. pers. L. *dramatis personae*, characters represented in the drama

dr.ap. apothecaries' dram

Drav. Dravidian

dr.avdp. avoirdupois dram

D.R.B. Defence Research Board (Can.)

Dr.Bus.Admin. Doctor of Business Administration

D.R.C. Dutch Reformed Church
Dr.Chem. Doctor of Chemistry
D.R.C.O.G. Diploma of the Royal College of Obstetricians and Gynaecologists
DRDO Defence Research and Development Organization (India)
D.R.E. directorate of radio equipment; Doctor of Religious Education, *also* D.Rel.Ed.
Dr.Eng. Doctor of Engineering
DREO Defense Research Establishment, Ottawa (Can.)
DREP Defense Research Establishment, Pacific (Can.)
DRES Defense Research Establishment, Suffield (Can.)
DRET Defense Research Establishment, Toronto (Can.)
DREV Defense Research Establishment, Valcartier (Can.)
Drew Andrew
DREWS direct readout equatorial satellite (space)
drg. drawing
D.R.G.M. *Deutsches Reichsgebrauchs muster*, German registered design
Dr.h.c. L. *Doctor honoris causa*, Honorary Doctor
Dr.Ing. Ger. *Doktor Ingenieur*, Doctor of Engineering
Dr. jur. Ger. *Doktor der Rechte*, Doctor of Laws
DRK *Deutsches Rotes Kreuz*, German Red Cross
D.R.L.S. dispatch rider letter service
D.R.M. Diploma in Resource Management
Dr. med. Ger. *Doktor der Medizin*, Doctor of Medicine
Dr. Med. Doctor of Medicine
drn. drawn
DRNA desoxyribose nucleic acid (chem.)
Dr.Nat.Sci. Doctor of Natural Science
D.R.O. daily routine order; disablement resettlement officer; divisional routine order
Dr.Oec.(Publ.) Doctor of Public Economy
'drome aerodrome
DRP Democratic Republican Party (South Korea), *Minchu Kong Hwa Dang*
D.R.P. *Deutsches Reichs-patent*, German patent; directorate of radio production
D.R.P.C. Defence Research Policy Committee
Dr.P.H. Doctor of Public Health
Dr. phil. Ger. *Doktor der Philosophie*, Doctor of Philosophy

Dr.Phil. Doctor of Philosophy
Dr.Pol.Sci. Doctor of Political Science
D.R.P.P. directorate of research programmes and planning
Dr.re.nat. Doctor of Natural Science
Dr.rer.pol. Doctor of Political Science
D.R.S.A.M. Diploma of the Royal Scottish Academy of Music
DRSC direct radar scope camera
dr.t. troy dram
Drt. Dartmouth
D.R.T. dead reckoning tracer; diagnostic rhyme test (psy.)
D.R.T.C. Documentation Research and Training Centre (India)
D.R.T.E. Defense Research Telecommunications Establishment (Can.)
Dr.Theol. Doctor of Theology
Dr.Univ.Par. Doctor of University of Paris
D.Rur.Sc. Doctor of Rural Science
Dr. u. Vrl., Dr. und Vrl. Ger. *Druck und Verlag*, printed and published (by)
D.R.V. Democratic Republic of Vietnam, *Viet-Nam Dan-chu Cong Hoa* (N. Vietnam)
drx. *drachma*, Greek currency
DS *s* Dumfries (B.F.P.); *s* Peeblesshire (B.V.R.)
ds. It. *destro*, right
Ds. L. *Deus*, deity; L. *dominus*, Cambridge Univ. degree of B.A.; L. *Dominus*, Lord/Master
d.s. date of service; daylight saving; days after sight; day's sight; document signed
d.s. It. *dal segno*, from the sign (mus.)
d. & s. demand and supply
D.S. *Danske Standardiseringsraad*, Danish Standards Institute; debenture stock (fin.); dental surgeon; Department of State; deputy secretary; Doctor of Science/Surgery; double stout (brewing)
DSA Dante Society of America; Defense Supply Agency (U.S.A.)
D.S.A. Diploma in Social Administration; Fr. *Docteur en sciences agricoles*, Doctor of Agriculture
dsable. disable; disability
D.S.A.O. Diplomatic Service Administration Office
DSAP Data Systems Automation Program (U.S.A.)
D.S.A.S.O. deputy senior air staff officer
d.s.b. double sideband
D.S.B. Defense Science Board (U.S.A.); Drug Supervisory Body (U.N.O.)
d.s.c. down stage centre
D.Sc. Doctor of Science; — A. Fr. *Docteur en sciences agricoles*, Doctor of

Agriculture; Fr. *Docteur en sciences appliquées*, Doctor of Sciences; — **Adm.** Fr. *Docteur en Sciences administratives*, Doctor of Science (Administration); — **(Agr.)**, **(Agric.)** Doctor of Science in Agriculture; — **Bus. Ad.** Doctor of Science in Business Administration; — **Com.** Fr. *Docteur en Sciences commerciales*, Doctor of Commercial Science; — **D.** Doctor of Science and Didactics; — **Econ. (Econ.)** Fr. *Docteur en Sciences économiques*, Doctor of Science (Economics); — **Eng.**, **(Eng.)** Doctor of Science in Engineering; — **For.** Doctor of Science in Forestry; — **Mil.** Doctor of Military Science; — **(P.H.)** Doctor of Science (Public Health); — **Pol.** Fr. *Docteur ès sciences politiques*, Doctor of Political Sciences; — **Soc.** Fr. *Docteur en Science sociale*, Doctor of Social Science; — **Tech.** Doctor of Technical Science

D.S.C. Distinguished Service Cross; district scout council; Doctor of Surgical Chiropody

D.S.C.M. Diploma of the Sydney Conservatorium of Music

D.Scn. Doctor of Scientology

DSCS Defense Construction Supply Center (U.S.A.)

D.S.D. director of signals division; director of staff duties

D.S.E. Derby Society of Engineers; Doctor of Science in Economics

Dsf. Düsseldorf (W. Ger.)

dsgn. design; designer

D.S.I. Dairy Society International

DSIF deep space instrumentation facility

D.S.I.R. Department of Scientific and Industrial Research, *now* S.R.C.

D.Sk. *Daily Sketch*

D.Site. Decoy Site (mil.)

D.S.L. deep scattering layer (of the ocean); district scout leader

dsl. elec. diesel-electric

D.S.M. directorate of servicing and maintenance; Distinguished Service Medal

dsmd. dismissed

DSN deep space network

D.S.O. Companion of the Distinguished Service Order; district staff officer; Doctor of the Science of Oratory

D.Soc.S., D.Soc.Sc., D.Soc.Sci. Doctor of Social Science

D.Soc.Sc. Doctor of Social Sciences

DSP Democratic Socialist Party, *Min-chu She-hui Tang* (Taiwan)

d.s.p. L. *decessit sine prole*, died without issue

D.S.P. Democratic Socialist Party, *Minshu-Shakaito* (Jap.); director of selection of personnel

dspl. disposal

d.s.p.l. L. *decessit sine prole legitima*, died without legitimate issue

d.s.p.m. L. *decessit sine prole mascula*, died without male issue

d.s.p.m.s. L. *decessit sine prole mascula superstite*, died without surviving male issue

dspn. disposition

d.s.p.s. L. *decessit sine prole superstite*, died without surviving issue

d.s.p.v. L. *decessit sine prole virile*, died without male issue

d.s.q. discharged to sick quarters

D.S.R. director of scientific research

D.S.R.D. directorate of signals research and development

D.S.R.V. deep submergence rescue vehicle

D.S.S. Dental Students' Society; L. *Doctor Sacrae Scripturae*, Doctor of Holy/Sacred Scripture

D.S.Sc. Diploma in Sanitary Science; Doctor of Social Science

D.S.S.V. deep submergence search vehicle

D.S.T. daylight saving time, normally one hour in advance of local standard time which is observed by some countries for part of the year; director of supplies and transport; Doctor of Sacred Theology; double summer time

D.St.J. Dame of Justice/Grace of the Order of Saint John of Jerusalem

dstl. distil

dstn. destination

D.S.U.E. *Dictionary of Slang and Unconventional English*

D.S. Vehicle driver seated vehicle

D.S.W. Doctor of Social Work

DT *s* Doncaster (B.V.R.)

d.t. double throw; double time

d.t. L. *delirium tremens*

D.T. *Daily Telegraph*; daylight time; deep tank; dental technician; Department of Transportation/Treasury (U.S.A.); Fr. *Directoire Technique*, the body responsible for organizing a fencing championship; director of transport; L. *Doctor Theologiae*, Doctor of Divinity/Theology

D.T.A. Dance Teachers' Association; differential thermal analysis; Diploma in Tropical Agriculture; Distributive Trades' Alliance

D.T.A.S.W. department of torpedo and anti-submarine warfare

D.T.C. department of technical co-operation; Diploma in Textile Chemistry

D.T.C.D. Diploma in Tuberculosis and Chest Diseases

dtd. dated

113

d.t.d. L. *detur talis dosis*, let such a dose be given (med.)

D.T.D. Dutch *Dekoratie voor Trouwe Dienst*, Decoration for Distinguished Service; Diploma in Tuberculosis/Tuberculous Diseases; Director of Technical Development

DTDP ditridecyl phthalate, plasticizer for P.V.C.

D.Tech. Doctor of Technology

D.Ter. Dakota Territory, *now* N. and S. Dakota

D.T.F. Dental Traders' Federation; Domestic Textiles Federation

Dtg. Ger. *Dienstag*, Tuesday

D.Th., D.Theol. Doctor of Theology

D.T.H. Diploma in Tropical Hygiene

D.Th.P.T. Diploma in Theory and Practice of Teaching

DTI Department of Trade and Industry formed 1970, unified trade and industrial policy functions formerly carried on separately by the BoT and MinTech

D.T.L. Dictograph Telephone Limited; Down the Line, form of competitive clay pigeon shooting

Dtm. Dortmund (W. Ger.)

D.T.M. Diocesan Travelling Mission; Diploma/Doctor in Tropical Medicine

DTMB David Taylor Model Basin

D.T.M.&H. Diploma in Tropical Medicine and Hygiene

DTMS defense traffic management service (U.S.A.)

dt.⁰ Port. *direito*, right

D.T.O. *Dansk Teknisk Oplysningstjeneste*, Danish Technical Information Service

D.T.O.D. director of trade and operations division

D.T.R. Diploma in Therapeutic Radiology; double taxation relief

D.T.R.P. Diploma in Town and Regional Planning

DTU Dominica Trade Union

D.T.V.M. Diploma in Tropical Veterinary Medicine

D.T.W.P. director of tactical and weapons policy division

Dtz., Dtzd. Ger. *Dutzend*, dozen

DU *s* Coventry (B.V.R.)

Du. Ducal; Duchy; Duke; Dutch

D.U. died unmarried; Doctor of the University

dub. dubious

dub. L. *dubitans*, doubting; L. *dubius*, dubious

Dub., Dubl. Dublin

D.U.B.C. Durham University Boat Club

D.U.C. Doctor of the University of Calgary (Can.)

Dud Dudley

DUK Order of Merit (Kedah, Malaysia)

Duke Marmaduke

Dul. Duluth (Can.)

Dulag. Ger. *Durchgangslager*, transit camp, prisoners of war

D.U.M. Dublin University Mission

Dumb. Dumbarton

Dumf. Dumfries

dun. dunnage

Dun. Dundee; Dunedin (N.Z.)

DUNC deep under-water nuclear counting

Dunelm. L. *Dunelmensis*, of Durham, Eng. episcopal title, in bishop's signature

D. Univ. Doctor of the University

duo. duodecimo (paper)

DUP Democratic Unionist Party (Sudan)

dup. duplicate

D.U.P. Fr. *Docteur de l'Université de Paris*, Doctor of the Univ. of Paris

Dur. Durban (S. Afr.); Durham

D.U.S. Diploma of the University of Southampton

D.U.S.A. Defense Union of South Africa

DUSC deep underground support center (USAF)

D.U.S.W. director of undersurface warfare division

Dut. Dutch

DV *s* Devon (B.V.R.)

D.V. defective/direct vision; Diploma in Venereology; distinguished visitor; district valuer; Douay Version (Bible); double vision

D.V. L. *Deo volente*, God willing

D.V. & D. Diploma in Venereology and Dermatology

D. Verf. Ger. *der Verfasser*, the author

D.V.H. Diploma in Veterinary Hygiene

d.v.m. L. *decessit vita matris*, died in the lifetime of the mother

D.V.M. Doctor of Veterinary Medicine

D.V.M. & S. Doctor of Veterinary Medicine and Surgery

Dvnport. Devonport

D.V.O. divisional veterinary officer

d.v.p. L. *decessit vita patris*, died in the lifetime of the father

D.V.P.H. Diploma in Veterinary Public Health

Dvr. driver

D.V.S. Director of Veterinary Science/Services/Surgery

D.V.Sc., D.V.Sci. Doctor of Veterinary Science

D.V.S.L. district venture scout leader

D.V.S.M. Diploma in Veterinary State Medicine

d/w dust wrapper

DW *s* Newport, Mon. (B.V.R.)

D/W dead weight; dock warrant

d.w. delivered weight

d.w.c. deadweight capacity

dwg. drawing; dwelling, *also* dwel.

D.W.I. descriptive word index; Dutch West Indies

dwr. drawer

D.W.R. Duke of Wellington's Regiment

dwt deadweight ton

dwt. pennyweight, *denarius*+weight

d.w.z. Dutch *dat wil zeggen*, that is to say

DX *s* Ipswich (B.V.R.)

D.X. distance; distant (in radio)

DXDA-MC ductile metals experimental diamond abrasive, metal clad

D.X.R. deep X-ray; — **T.** deep X-ray therapy

Dy *s* dysprosium (chem.)

DY *s* Dahomey (I.V.R.); *s* Hastings (B.V.R.)

dy. delivery

Dy. demy (paper)

D.Y., Dyd. dockyard

dyn dyne (phys.)

dyn. dynamics; dynamite; dynamo

Dyn. dynasty

DYNAMO dynamic action management operations

D.Y.S. Duke of York's Royal Military School

DZ *s* Algeria (I.V.R.); *s* Antrim (B.V.R.)

dz. dozen; It. *dozzina*, dozen

d.Z. Ger. *der Zeit*, of the time

D.Z. department/Doctor of Zoology; dropping zone

D.Z.F. *Deutsche Zentrale für Fremdenverkehr*, German Central Tourist Assn.

dzne. Fr. *douzaine*, dozen

D.Zool. Doctor of Zoology

D.-Zug *ᵍDurchgang-Zug*, through train (Ger.)

E

e *s* base of natural (Napierian) system of logarithms (math.); *s* coefficient of elasticity (dyn.); *s* eccentricity of ellipse; *s* electromotive force of cell (elec.); *s* wet air (met.)

E einsteinium (chem.); English shilling (numis.); erbium (chem.); *s* Exeter (B.F.P.); illumination (lighting); *s* Spain, including Spanish Guinea and Spanish Sahara (I.V.R.); *s* Staffordshire (B.V.R.)

e. east; easterly; eastern; eccentricity; economics; edition; educated; elasticity; elder; eldest; electric; electricity; electromotive; electron; *en*, in (Dutch/Port./Sp.); engineer; engineering; error (baseball); *est*, east (Fr./It.); *este*, east (Port./Sp.); excellence; excellent

E. earl; earth; Easter (prayer bk.); Eastern postal district (Lond.); Edinburgh; efficiency; Egypt; Egyptian; eighth of a page, type area (advert.); elocution; eminence; enemy; engineer; engineering; England; English; envoy; equator; *Espagne*, Spain; evening; evensong (prayer bk.); *s* second-class merchant ship, Lloyd's

EA ethylacrylate; *s* West Bromwich (B.V.R.)

ea. each

E/A. enemy/experimental aircraft

E.A. East Anglia; economic adviser; educational age; electrical artificer; It. *Ente Autonomo*, Autonomous Corporation; Entered Apprentice (freem.); Evangelical Alliance

EAA ethylene acrylic acid

E.A.A. Electrical Appliance Association; Engineers' and Architects' Association (U.S.A.)

E.A.A.A. European Association of Advertising Agencies

E.A.A.C. East African Airways (Kenya); European Agricultural Aviation Centre

E.A.A.F.R.O. East African Agriculture and Forestry Research Organisation (Kenya)

E.A.A.P. European Association for Animal Production

EAC Educational Advisory Committee

E.A.C. Engineering Advisory Council

E.A.C.A. *East Africa Court of Appeal Reports*

E.A.C.C. East Asia Christian Conference

E.A. content effective agent content

E.A.C.S.O. East African Common Services Organisation

E.A.D.R. pseudonym of unknown author of *Mary Brunton and her one Talent, c* 1885

E.A.E.G. European Association of Exploration Geophysicists

E.A.E.N.F. Engineering and Allied Employers' National Federation, *now* E.E.F.

E.A.E.S. European Atomic Energy Society

e.a.f. emergency action file

E.A.F.F.R.O. East African Fresh-water Fisheries Research Organisation, Jinja, *sometimes* E.A.F.R.O.

EAG Economists Advisory Group

E.A.G.G.F. European Agricultural Guidance and Guarantee Fund

116

E.A.H.C. East African High Commission

EAK s Kenya (I.V.R.)

EAL Eastern Air Lines

E.A.M.F. European Association of Music Festivals

E.A.M.F.R.O. East African Marine Fisheries Research Organisation (Zanzibar)

E.A.M.P.A. East Anglian Master Printers' Alliance

E.A.M.S. Empire Air Mail Scheme

E.A.M.T.C. European Association of Management Training Centres

e.a.o.n. except as otherwise noted

E.A.P. East Africa Protectorate; Edgar Allan Poe (1809–49), American poet, story writer and critic

E.A.P.R. European Association for Potato Research

E.A.R. employee attitude research; energy absorbing resin

E.A.R.C.C.U.S. East African Regional Committee for Conservation and Utilisation of Soil

E.A.R.O.P.H. East Asia Regional Organization for Planning and Housing

E.A.S. equivalent air speed, measure of lift derived from rectified air speed corrected for compressibility (nav.); estimated air speed

E.A.S.A. Electrical Apparatus Service Association (U.S.A.); Entertainment Arts Socialist Association

EASELEC Eastern Electricity Board (trade mark)

EASEP Early Apollo Scientific Experiments Package

EASHP European Association of Senior Hospital Physicians

east. eastern

East L. East Lothian

EASTROPAC Eastern Tropical Pacific

EAT s Tanganyika, Tanzania (I.V.R.)

e.a.t. earliest arrival time

E.A.T.R.O. East African Trypanosomiasis Research Organisation

EAU s Uganda (I.V.R.)

E.A.V.R.O. East African Veterinary Research Organisation

E.A.W. Electrical Association for Women; equivalent average words

E.A.W.L.A. East Anglian Women's Lacrosse Association

EAX electronic automatic exchange

EAZ s Zanzibar, Tanzania (I.V.R.)

Eb Ebenezer, *also* Eben; erbium (chem.)

EB s Cambridge (B.V.R.)

eb. Fr. *point d'ébullition*, boiling point

E.B. electricity board; *Encyclopaedia Britannica*

E.B.A. English Bowling Association, founded 1903

e.b.a.r. edited beyond all recognition

E.B.C. European Billiards Confederation; European Brewery Convention

EBICON electron bombardment induced conductivity

E.B.L. European Bridge League

E.B.M.C. English Butter Marketing Company

E-boat *Eil*, fast/enemy boat, Ger. motor torpedo-boat, WW2

Ebor. L. *Eboracensis*, of York, Eng. archiepiscopal title, in archbishop's signature

E.B.R. experimental breeder reactor

E.B.R.A., E.B. & R.A. Engineer Buyers' and Representatives' Association

E.B.S. Emergency Bed Service; English Bookplate Society

E.B.U. English Bridge Union; European Badminton/Boxing/Broadcasting Union

EBWR experimental boiling water reactor

E.B.Y.C. European Bureau for Youth and Childhood

E. by N. east by north

E. by S. east by south

EC s Ecuador (I.V.R.); European Community, *generally* European Economic Community; s Spain (I.C.A.M.); s Westmorland (B.V.R.)

Ec., Ecua. Ecuador

e.c. earth closet; enamel coated/covered; error correction; extended coverage; extension course

e.c. L. *exempli causa*, for example

E.C. east coast; Eastern Central postal district (Lond.); Eastern Command; Ecclesiastical Commissioner; education/educational committee; electricity council; electrolytic corrosion; electronic computer; emergency commission; engineer captain; Episcopal/established church; Fr. *Etoile du Courage*, Star of Courage (Can.); executive committee

E.C.A. Early Closing Association; Economic Commission for Africa, estab. 1958 (U.N.O.); Educational Centres Association; Electrical Contractors' Association; European Confederation of Agriculture; European Congress of Accountants

ECAC Electromagnetic Compatibility Analysis Center (U.S.A.); Engineering College Administrative Council

E.C.A.C. European Civil Aviation Conference

E.C.A.F.E. Economic Commission for Asia and the Far East (U.N.O.)

E.C.A.S. Electrical Contractors' Association of Scotland

117

E.C.B. electronic components board

ecc. It. *eccetera*, et cetera

Ecc. It. *Eccellenze*, Excellency

E.C.C. European Cultural Centre

Ecc. Hom. L. *Ecce Homo*, Behold the Man

eccl. ecclesiastic; ecclesiastical

Eccl., Eccles. Ecclesiastes (Bible)

Ecclus. Ecclesiasticus (Apocrypha; R.C. canonical)

ECCM electronic counter-counter-measures

E.C.C.P. East Coast Coal Port; European Committee on Crime Problems

E.C.C.U. English Cross Country Union

E.C.D. early closing day; estimated completion date

E.C.E. Economic Commission for Europe (U.N.O.)

ECFI Eastern Caribbean Farm Institute

E.C.F.M.S. Educational Council for Foreign Medical Students

ECFTUC European Confederation of Free Trade Unions in the Community

E.C.G. electrocardiogram; electrocardiograph; Export Credit Guarantee

E.C.G.B. East Coast of Great Britain

E.C.G.C. Empire Cotton Growing Corporation

E.C.G.D. Export Credit Guarantee Department

Ech. echelon

E.C.I. East Coast of Ireland

E.C.I.T.O. European Central Inland Transport Organization

Eck, Eckie Hector

écl. Fr. *éclairage*, lighting

E.C.L.A. Economic Commission for Latin America (U.N.O.)

eclec. eclectic; eclecticism

ecli. eclipse; ecliptic

ECLO emitter-coupled logic operator

ECLOF Ecumenical Church Loan Fund

ECM electric coding machine; electrochemical machining

E.C.M. electronic counter-measures; European Common Market

E.C.M.A. European Computer Manufacturers' Association

E.C.M.B.R. European Committee on Milk-Butterfat Recording

E.C.M.E. Economic Commission for the Middle East (U.N.O.)

E.C.M.F. Electric Cable Makers' Federation

E.C.M.R.A. European Chemical Market Research Association

E.C.M.T. European Conference of Ministers of Transport

E.C.O. English Chamber Orchestra

ecol. ecology

Ecol. Soc. Am. Ecological Society of America

econ. economical; economics; economist; economy

e. con. L. *e contrarie*, on the contrary

Econ. J. *Economic Journal*

Econ. R. *Economic Review*

Ecopetrol. *Expresa Colombiana de Petroleos*, Columbia

E.C.O.R. Engineering Committee on Ocean Resources (U.S.A.)

ECOSOC Economic and Social Council, one of the principal organs of U.N.O. which promotes economic and social co-operation and co-ordinates work of the specialized agencies

ECP engineering change proposal

E.C.P. European Committee of Crop Protection; L. *Evangelii Christi Praedicatur*, Preacher of the Gospel of Christ

ECPD Engineers' Council for Professional Development (U.S.A.)

E.C.P.S. Eastern Counties Poultry Society; European Centre for Population Studies

E.C.Q.A.C. Electronic Components Quality Assurance Committee

E.C.R.L. Eastern Caribbean Regional Library

ECS environmental control system

E.C.S. European Components Service

E.C.S.C. European Coal and Steel Community, estab. 1952 to increase efficiency in coal and steel industries by removing trade restrictions and introducing fair rules of competition

E.C.T. electro-convulsant therapy

E.C.T.A. Electrical Contractors' Trading Association

ECU European currency unit, equiv. to US $

E.C.U. English Church Union; environmental control unit; European Chiropractic Union; extreme close-up (photo.)

Ecua. Ecuador

E.C.U.K. East Coast of United Kingdom

E.C.Y. European Conservation Year

Ed, Eddie, Eddy Edgar; Edmund; Edward; Edwin

ED *s* Warrington (B.V.R.)

ed. Sp. *edición*, edition; It. *edile, edilizia*, building; edited; edition; editor *also* edit.; It. *edizione*, edition; educated; education

éd. Fr. *édition*, edition

Ed. Edinburgh; Education, *also* Edu., Educn.

e.d. edge distance; effective dose;

118

enemy dead; error detecting; excused/extra duty

E.D. Doctor of Engineering; education department; Efficiency Decoration; election district; electron device; employment department; entertainments duty; estate duty (tax.); ex dividend (fin.); existence doubtful; extra dividend (fin.)

EDA Electrical Development Association; *Eniea Dimokratiki Aristera*, United Democratic Left party of Greece

e.d.a. early departure authorized

E.D.A. British Electrical Development Association, *also* B.E.D.A.; Economic Development Association (U.S.A.); Education Development Association; electronic design automation

EDB ethene dibromide, chemical used as soil fumigant

Ed. B. Bachelor of Education

e.d.c. error detection and correction; extra dark colour

E.D.C. Economic Development Committee; European Defence Community; expected date of confinement; Express Dairy Company

edd. L. *ediderunt*, published by; L. *editiones*, editions

Ed. D. Doctor of Education

E.D.D. *English Dialect Dictionary*; expected date of delivery

Edg. Edgar

EDHE experimental data handling equipment

Edie Edith

Edin. Edinburgh

Ed. in Ch. editor in chief

EDIS Engineering Data Information System

edit. edited; edition; editor; It. *editore*, publisher; editorial

E.D.I.T., EDITH Estate Duties Investment Trust

e.d.l. edition de luxe

EDM electro-discharge machining

Edm. Edmund

Ed. M. Master of Education

Edm. and Ipswich Eng. episcopal title, in signature of Bp. of St. Edmundsbury and Ipswich

Edmn. Edmonton (Can.)

Edn. edition

Ednbgh. Edinburgh

e.d.o.c. effective date of change

E.D.O.N. *Eniaia Demokratiki Organosis Neolaias*, United Democratic Youth Organisation, Cyprus

E.D.P. electronic data processing; Emergency Defence Plan

E.D.P.S. electronic data processing system

EDR electronic decoy rocket

E.D.R. European Depositary Receipts

E.D.S. English Dialect Society

E.D. & S. *English Dance and Song*, qtrly. publication of English Folk Dance and Song Society

E.D.S.A.C. electronic delayed storage automatic computer

EDSAT Educational Television Satellite

E.D.T. eastern daylight time

EDTA European Dialysis and Transplant Association

E.D.U. European Democratic Union

Edw. Edward

EE *s* Grimsby (B.V.R.)

e.e. errors excepted; eye and ear

E.E. Early English; electrical engineer/engineering; electronic engineer/engineering; employment exchange; envoy-extra-ordinary; *Estado Español*, the Spanish State; Ger. *Euer Ehrwürden*, your Reverence

E.E.A. Ecurie Ecosse Association; Educational/Equipment Exhibitors' Association; Electronic Engineering Association

EEAIE Electrical, Electronic and Allied Industries, Europe

E.E.B. Eastern Electricity Board

E.E.C. English Electric Company; European Economic Community, estab. 1958 by members of E.C.S.C. to promote harmonious development of economic and political activities and to raise standard of living by establishing a customs union (Common Market)

E.E.D.C. Economic Development Committee for the Electronics Industry

E.E.F. Egyptian Expeditionary Force; Engineering Employers' Federation

E.E.G. electroencephalograph (biol.); Essence Export Group

EEI Environmental Equipment Institute (U.S.A.)

E.E.I.B.A. Electrical and Electronic Industries Benevolent Association

E.E.M.J.E.B. Electrical & Electronic Manufacturers' Joint Education Board

E.E. & M.P. Envoy Extraordinary and Minister Plenipotentiary

e'en even, evening

E. Eng. Early English

E.E.N.T. eye, ear, nose and throat

e.e.o. equal employment opportunity

E.E.O.C. Equal Employment Opportunity Commission, applies to race, colour, religion, sex and national origin

e'er ever

E.E.R.I. Earthquake Engineering Research Institute (U.S.A.)

E.E.S. European Exchange System

E.E.T. Eastern European Time

E.E.T.S. Early English Text Society

EETU/PTU Electrical Electronic Telecommunication Union/Plumbing Trades Union

E.E.U.A. Electronic/Engineering Equipment Users Association

E.E.V.C. English Electric Valve Company

EF s West Hartlepool (B.V.R.)

E.F. education/educational foundation; elevation finder; emergency fleet; expectant father; expeditionary force; experimental flight; extra fine

E.F.A. Empire Forestry Association; Eton Fives Association

E.F.C. European Federation of Corrosion; European Forestry Commission

E.F.D.S.S. English Folk Dance and Song Society

eff. It. *effetto*, bill/promissory note; efficiency; effigy

E.F.F. European Furniture Federation

Effie Euphemia

E.F.M. European Federalist Movement

E.F.N.S. Educational Foundation for Nuclear Science

E.F.P.M.B. Employers' Federation of Papermakers and Boardmakers

E.F.P.W. European Federation for the Protection of Waters

EFRC Edwards Flight Research Center (U.S.A.)

EFSA European Federation of Sea Anglers

E.F.S.C. European Federation of Soroptimist Clubs

EFTA, Efta, E.F.T.A. European Free Trade Association, estab. 1960 to promote economic development and expansion of trade by progressive reduction of trade restrictions. An earlier proposal was for a European Free Trade Area

E.F.T.C. Electrical Fair Trading Council

E.F.T.S. elementary flying training school

EFU energetic feed unit

E.F.U. Ger. *Europäische Frauenunion*, European Union of Women; European Football Union

E.F.V.A. Education Foundation for Visual Aids

EG s Huntingdon (B.V.R.)

Eg., Egy. Egypt; Egyptian

e.g. L. *ejusdem generis*, of a like kind; L. *exempli gratia*, for example

E.G. Engineers' Guild

E.G.A. European Golf Association

EGAS Educational Grants Advisory Service; Eley Game Advisory Service

E.G.C.I. Export Group for the Construction Industries

E.G.C.S. English Guernsey Cattle Society

e.g.é. Fr. *eau, gaz, électricité*, water, gas, electricity

E. Ger. East Germany

EGIFO Edward Grey Institute of Field Ornithology

E.G.L. Engineers' Guild Limited

E.G.M. Empire Gallantry Medal (*now* G.C. is awarded); European Glass Container Manufacturers' Committee; extraordinary general meeting

e.G.m.b.H. Ger. *eingetragene Gesellschaft mit beschränkter Haftung*, registered co. with limited liability

E.G.O. eccentric (orbit) geophysical observatories

E.G.S.P. electronics glossary and symbol panel

e.g.t. exhaust gas temperature

E.G.T. *Empresa Geral de Transportes*, General Transport Co., door-to-door rail freight delivery service (Port.)

E.G.U. English Golf Union, formed 1924 as union of all County Golf Unions in England

Egyptol. Egyptologist; Egyptology

EH s Stoke-on-Trent (B.V.R.)

2EH s Edinburgh (radio call-sign)

e.h. Ger. *ehrenhalber*, for the sake of honour

E.H. English Horn, cor anglais (mus.)

E.H.C. European Hotel Corporation, jointly owned by European banks and airlines

E.H.C.C. European Hops Culture Committee

EHF experimental husbandry farm; extra/extremely high frequency

E.H.F. European Hockey Federation

E.H.L. effective half-life

e.h.m. eggs per hen a month

e.h.p. effective/electric horsepower

E.H.W.S. extreme high water-level spring-tides

e.h.yr. eggs per hen a year

EI earth (atmosphere) interface; s Rep. of Ireland (I.C.A.M.); s Sligo (Rep. of Ireland V.R.)

E.I. East India/Indian/Indies; electrical insulation; endorsement irregular (fin.)

E.I.A. East Indian Association; Electronic Industries Association (U.S.A.); Engineering Industries Association

E.I.B. *Economisch Instituut voor de Bouwuijverheid*, Building Industry Economics Institute (Neth.); European Investment Bank; Export-Import Bank

E.I.B.A. Electrical Industries' Benevolent Association

E.I.C. East India Company; Electrical Industries' Club; Engineering Institute of Canada

EICM employer's inventory of critical manpower

E.I.C.S. East India Company's Service

E.I.D. East India Dock; Electrical Inspection Directorate for electrical, electronic, instruments, photographic and optical equipment for R.A.F., Army and Naval Air Arm and atomic weapons

EIF Elderly Invalids Fund

E.I.F.A.C. European Inland Fisheries Advisory Committee (FAO)

E.I.J.C. Engineering Institutions' Joint Council

EIL Electronic Instruments Limited

E.-in-C. Engineer-in-Chief

E. Ind. East Indies

einschl. Ger. *einschliesslich*, including/inclusive

Einw. Ger. *Einwohner*, population

E.I.P.C. European Institute of Printed Circuits

E.I.R. earned income relief (tax.)

EIRMA European Industrial Research Management Association

E.I.S. economic information system; Educational Institute of Scotland; epidemic intelligence service

E.I.T.B. Engineering Industry Training Board

E.I.U. Economist Intelligence Unit

E.I.V.T. European Institute for Vocational Training

EJ *s* Cardiganshire (B.V.R.); Rep. of Ireland (I.C.A.M.)

ej. Sp. *ejemplo*, example

E.J.C. Engineers' Joint Council (U.S.A.)

E.J.M.A. English Joinery Manufacturers' Association

ejusd. L. *ejusdem*, of the same

eK Nor. *etter Kristi*, after Christ

EK East Kilbride; *Enosis Kentron*, Centre Union party of Greece; *s* Wigan (B.V.R.)

EKCO E. K. Cole, Limited

EKD Ger. *Evangelische Kirche in Deutschland*, Protestant Ch. in Germany

EKG electrocardiogram; electrocardiograph; Ger. *Elektrokardiogramm*, electrocardiogram

eks Dan. *eksempel*, example

E.K.S. *Etaireia Kypriakon Spoudon*, Society of Cyprus Studies

EL *s* Bournemouth (B.V.R.); Everyman's Library; *s* Liberia (I.C.A.M.)

el. elect; elected; electric; electricity; element; elevated; elevated railway; elevation; elongation

E.L. electrical/electronics laboratory; engineer lieutenant

ELA Eritrean Liberation Army (Ethiopia)

EL AL Israeli airline

E.L.A.N.E. Electronics Association for the North East

elas. elasticity

E.L.B. Bachelor of English Literature

E.L.B.S. English Language Book Society

E.L.Cr. engineer lieutenant-commander

eld. elder; eldest

E.L.D.O. European Launcher Development Organization

Elean. Eleanor

elec., elect. election; elector; electoral; electric; electrical; electrically; electrician; electricity; electron; electuary

E.L.E.C. European League for Economic Co-operation

ELECO Engineering and Lighting Equipment Company

Electra. Electrical, Electronics and Communications Trades Association

ELECTRA London Electricity Board (trade mark)

Electr. Engin. electrical engineering

electro electrotype

electron. electronics

Elekt. Ger. *Elektrizität*, electricity

elem. element; elementary

elev. elevation; elevator

ELF Eritrean Liberation Front (Ethiopia)

e.l.f. early lunar flare; extra low frequency

E.L.F. European Landworkers' Federation

E.L.F.A. Electric Light Fittings Association

ELFC electro-luminescent ferro-electric cell

Eli Elias; Elijah

E.L.I.C. Electric Lamp Industry Council

Elien. L. *Eliensis*, of Ely, Eng. episcopal title, in bishop's signature

ELINT electromagnetic intelligence

Elis. Elisabeth

elix. elixir

Eliz. Elizabeth; Elizabethan

Eliza Elisabeth; Elizabeth

ell. Swed. *eller*, or

El. L. electrical lieutenant

Ella Eleanor; Elinor; Isabella

E.L.L.A. European Long Lines Agency

El. L. Cr. electrical lieutenant-commander

Ellie Alice
ellipt. elliptical
Elma Wilhelmina
ELMA electro-mechanical aid
E.L.M.A. Electrical Lamp Manufacturers' Association
ELMINT electromagnetic intelligence
E.L.M.O. European Laundry and Dry-cleaning Machinery Manufacturers' Organisation
ELN *Ejército de Liberación Nacional*, Communist Nat. Liberation Army (Col.)
elo. elocution; eloquence
ELOISE European Large Orbiting Instrumentation for Solar Experiments
elong. elongate; elongation
E. Long. east longitude
E.L.R. export licensing regulations
elsewh. elsewhere
Elsie Alice; Elisabeth; Eliza; Elizabeth
El. S.L. electrical sub-lieutenant
E.L.T. European letter telegram
E.L.U. English Lacrosse Union
e.l.v. extra low voltage (elec.)
E.L.W.S. extreme low water-level spring-tides
Ely. easterly
Elz. Elzevir (pub.)
'em them
Em Emily; Emma; Emmanuel
EM *s* Bootle (B.V.R.)
em. emanation; embargo, *also* emb.; eminent
Em. Eminence
e.m. electro-magnetic; emergency maintenance; expanded metal; external memorandum
E.M. Earl Marshal, a chief officer of state in Eng. and head of the Heralds' College. Since 1672 office has been held by the Howard family; Edward/Efficiency Medal; electrical and mechanical; electron microscope; engineer manager; enlisted man; European Movement
E.M. L. *Equitum Magister*, Master of the Horse
E.M.A. European Monetary Agreement; Evangelical Missionary Alliance
E.M.A.I.A. Electrical Meter and Allied Industries' Association (Aust.)
emb. embargo; embossed
Emb. Embankment; Embassy
EMBO European Centre for Molecular Biology
embr. embroider; embroidery
Embry., Embryol. embryology
E.M.C. Einstein Medical Center (U.S.A.); Engineering Manpower Commission (U.S.A.)

E.M.C.C. European Municipal Credit Community
E.M.C.C.C. European Military Communications Co-ordinating Committee
emcee master of ceremonies, M.C.
E.M.D.P. electromotive difference of potential
E.M.E.B. East Midlands Electricity Board
EMELEC East Midlands Electricity Board (trade mark)
emer. emergency
Emer. Emeritus
EMEU East Midlands Educational Union
e.m.f., EMF electromotive force
E.M.F. European Motel Federation
E.M.G. electromyogram
E.M.I. Electric and Musical Industries
E.M.I.C. emergency maternity and infant care
E. Midl. East Midland
E.M.K. Ger. *elektro-motorische Kraft*, electromotive force
E.M.L. Everyman's Library, initiated in 1906 and pub. by Joseph Malaby Dent
Emm. Emmanuel College, Cambridge, founded 1584
Emmie Emma
E.M.M.S.A. Envelope Makers' and Manufacturing Stationers' Association
E. Mn. E. Early Modern English
emol. Port. *emolumentos*, official fee
e.m.o.s. earth's mean orbital speed
emp. L. *emplastrum*, a plaster (med.)
Emp. Emperor; Empire; Empress
E.M.P. Everyman Paperback
emp. agcy. employment agency
empld. employed
E.M.R. Eastern Mediterranean Region
EMRIC Educational Media Research Information Center (U.S.A.)
E.M.R.S. East Malling Research Station
E.M.S. emergency medical service
E.M.S.A. Electron Microscope Society of America (U.S.A.)
E.M.S.C. Electrical Manufacturers' Standards Council (U.S.A.)
E.M.T.A. Electro-Medical Trade Association
EMU European Monetary Unit
e.m.u. electromagnetic unit
EN *s* Bury (B.V.R.)
en. enemy
En. engineer; English
E.N. Port. *Emissora Nacional*, Nat. Broadcasting Station; Port. *Estrada Nacional*, nat. highway; *Evening News*; exceptions noted

E.N.A. English Newspaper Association

E.N.A.B. Evening Newspaper Advertising Bureau

enam. enamel; enamelled

enc., encl. enclosed; enclosure

E.N.C.A. European Naval Communications Agency

ency., encyc. encyclopaedia; encyclopaediac; encyclopaediacal; encyclopaedial; encyclopaedian; encyclopaedic; encyclopaedical; encyclopaedism; encyclopaedist; encyclopaedize; and the above with *e* substituted for *ae*, as encyclopedia

Ency. Brit., Encyc. Brit. *Encyclopaedia Britannica*

endow. endowment

Endp. endpaper

ENDS EURATOM Nuclear Documentation System

End. Tel. Port. *endereço telegráfico*, cable address

ENE east-north-east

E.N.E.A. European Nuclear Energy Agency

ENEL *Ente Nazionale per l'Energia Elettrica*, Italian Nat. Electric Energy Agency

E.N.F. European Nuclear Force

eng. engine; engineer; engineering; engrave; engraver; engraving

Eng. *Engineering*; England; English

Eng. D. Doctor of Engineering

engg. engineering

Eng. Hist. English History

engin. engineer; engineering

Engl. England; English

Eng.° *Engenheiro*, engineer, graduate of engineering college (Port.)

engr. engineer; engrave; engraver; engraving

Engr. *The Engineer*; engraver

Eng. Sc. D. Doctor of Engineering Science

ENI *Ente Nazionale Idrocarburi*, Nat. Hydrocarbon Corporation of Italy

E.N.I.A.C. Electronic Numerical Integrator and Calculator/Computer, machine for solving mathematical problems of extreme complexity with speed

ENIT *Ente Nazionale Industrie Turistiche*, Italian State Tourist Office

enl. enlarge; enlargement; enlisted

En. L. engineer lieutenant

En. L. Cr. engineer lieutenant-commander

Ens. ensign

E.N.S.A. Entertainments National Service Association

En. S. L. engineer sub-lieutenant

ent. entomology

Ent. enter (theatre); entertainment; entomology; entrance

E.N.T., E.N. & T. ear, nose and throat

entom., entomol. entomological; entomology

Ent. Sta. Hall entered at Stationers' Hall. Until 31 Dec. 1923, in order to secure copyright, all books had to be 'entered', i.e. registered at Stationers' Hall, London

env. envelope; environs

Env. Envoy; — **Ext.,** — **Extra.** Envoy Extraordinary

e.n.z. Dutch *en zoo voort*, and so forth

EO *s* Barrow-in-Furness (B.V.R.)

e.o. L. *ex officio*, by virtue of office

E.o. Easter offerings

E.O. Eastern Orthodox (rel.); education officer; emergency operation; employers' organisation; engineer / entertainments / executive / experimental / officer; executive order

E.O.A. Essential Oil Association (U.S.A.); examination, opinion and advice

E.O.A.R.D.C. European Office of the Air Research and Development Command (U.S.A.)

EOD explosive ordnance demolition/disposal

e.o.d. entry on duty; every other day

EOE enemy occupied Europe

E. & O.E., E.O.E. errors and omissions excepted

e.o.h.p. except otherwise herein provided

Eoka, EOKA *Ethniki Organosis Kypriakou Agonos*, Nat. Organization of Cypriot Struggle for union with Greece

EOLM electro-optical light modulator

e.o.m. end of month; every other month

E.O.M. Egyptian Order of Merit

E.O.N.R. European Organisation for Nuclear Research

e.o.o.e. Fr. *erreur ou omission exceptée*, error or omission excepted

E.O.Q.C. European Organization for Quality Control

EOR earth orbit rendezvous (space)

EORTC European Organization for Research on Treatment of Cancer

E.O.S. European Orthodontic Society

e.o.t. end of transmission; enemy occupied territory

E.O.T.P. European Organisation for Trade Promotion

E. over N. E. of REGINA over N, 1843 ½-farthing (numis.)

EP *s* Iran (I.C.A.M.); *s* Montgomeryshire (B.V.R.)

Ep. electro-plate; electro-plated

Ep. L. *Episcopus*, Bishop; L. *Epistola*, Epistle/letter

e.p. easy projection; electrically polarized; end paper; engineering personnel; Fr. *en passant*, in passing; environmental protection; epoxide resin/epoxy; estimated position (nav.); expanded polystyrene; extended play (records); extreme pressure

e.p. L. *editio princeps*, first edition

E.P. European plan, no meals (travel); Extraordinary and Plenipotentiary (diplo.)

E.P.A. educational priority area; Educational Puppetry Association; Emergency Powers Act; Environmental Protection Administration (U.S.A.); European Productivity Agency

E.P.A.C. Electronic Parts Advisory Committee

E.P.A.C.C.I. Economic Planning and Advisory Council for the Construction Industries

E.P.A.Q. electronic parts of assessed quality

E.P.C. Economic and Planning Council; Educational Publishers' Council

E.P.C.A. European Petro-Chemical Association

EPC black easy-processing channel black, filler in rubber compounding

E.P.D. earliest practicable date; excess profits duty

E.P.D.A. Emergency Powers Defence Act

E.P.D.M. ethylene propylene diene monomer, synthetic rubber manufacture

E.P.E.A. Electrical Power Engineers' Association

E.P.F. European Packaging Federation

EPFZ Fr. *École polytechnique fédérale, Zürich* (Switz.)

E.P.G. eggs per gramme; Electronic Proving Ground (U.S.A.)

Eph. Epistle to the Ephesians, Bible (*also* Ephes.); Ephraim

E.P.I. electronic position indicator

E.P.I.C. End Poverty in California, Upton Sinclair's Campaign; Engineering and Production Information Control

Epict. Epictetus (*c.* A.D. 55–*c.* 135), Gk. Stoic philosopher

epid. epidemic

E.P.I.D.C. East Pakistan Industrial Development Corporation, *now* Bangladesh

Epil. epilogue

Epiph. Epiphany

Epis., Episc. Episcopal; Episcopalian

Epist. Epistle, *also* Epis.

epit. epitaph; epitome

E.P.N.S. electro-plated nickel silver; English Place-Name Society

EPOC Eastern Pacific Oceanic Conference

E.P.P.O. European and Mediterranean Plant Protection Organization

e.p.s. earnings per share (fin.)

E.P.T. ethylene/propylene terpolymer, synthetic rubber; excess profits tax

E.P.T.A. Expanded Programme of Technical Assistance (U.N.O.)

Ep. tm. Epiphany term (leg.)

E.P.U. Empire Press Union; European Payments Union

EPUL *École Polytechnique d'Université de Lausanne*, Institute of Technology of the Univ. of Lausanne (Switz.)

Epus. L. *Episcopus*, Bishop

eq. equal; equate; equation; equator; equatorial; equipment; equitable; equity; equivalent

Eq. equerry

E.Q. educational quotient

E.Q.D. Electrical Quality Assurance Directorate

eqn. equation

eqpt. equipment

equil. equilibrium

equip. equipment

E.Q.U.I.P. equipment usage information programme

equiv. equivalent

Er *s* erbium (chem.)

ER *s* Cambridgeshire (B.V.R.)

er. elder

e.r. echo ranging; effectiveness report; electronic reconnaissance; emergency request/rescue; established reliability; external resistance

E.R. Eastern Region (British Rail); East Riding, Yorks.; engine room

E.R. L. *Edwardus Rex*, King Edward; L. *Elizabetha Regina*, Queen Elizabeth

E.R.A. Electrical Research Association; electronic reading automation; Electronic Rentals Association; engine-room artificer; Evangelical Radio Alliance

Eras. Desiderius Erasmus (1466–1536), Dutch scholar and theologian

Erb. Ger. *Erbitten*, request

ERBM extended-range ballistic missile

E.R.C. Economic Research Council; Electronics Research Center (U.S.A.); Empire Rheumatism Council

E.R.C. & I. Economic Reform Club and Institute

ERCO Electric Reduction Company of Canada

E.R.D. Emergency Reserve Decoration; emergency return device; equivalent residual dose

E.R.D.A. Electrical and Radio Development Association (Aust.)

124

E.R.D.E. Engineering/Explosives Research and Development Establishment

ERDL Engineering Research and Development Laboratory

ERE *Ethniki Rizospastiki Enosis*, Nat. Radical Union of Greece

erec. erection

E.R. et I., E.R.I. L. *Edwardus Rex et Imperator*, Edward King and Emperor

E.R.F.A. European Radio Frequency Agency

E.R.G. electrical resistance gauge

ERGOM European Research Group on Management

Ergon. ergonomics

ERIC Educational Resources Information Center (U.S.A.); energy rate input controller

Erit. Eritrea

Erl. Ger. *Erläuterung*, explanatory note

erm. ermine

Ern, Ernie Ernest; Ernst

E.R.N.I.E. electronic random number indicator equipment (computer)

E.R.O. European Regional Organization of the International Confederation of Free Trade Unions

E.R.O.P.A. Eastern Regional Organization for Public Administration

EROS earth's resources observation satellite; experimental reflection orbital shot (space)

e.r.p. effective radiated power

E.R.P. European Recovery Programme

erron. erroneous; erroneously

E.R.S. earth resources satellite; engine repair section; Ergonomics Research Society; Experimental Research Society (U.S.A.)

E.R.T.S. European Rapid Train System

E.R.U. English Rugby Union

E.R.V. English Revised Version (Bible)

erw., erweit. Ger. *erweiterte*, enlarged

e.r.w. electric resistance welding

Es *s* einsteinium (chem.)

ES *s* Perthshire (B.V.R.)

es. It. *esempio*, example

e.s. eldest son; electrical sounding; electric starting

E.S. Econometric Society; electrostatic; engine-sized (paper); Entomological Society

E.S.A. Ecological/Entomological/ Epiphyllum/Euthanasia Society of America; Educational Settlements Association; Educational Supply Association; Engineer Surveyors' Association; English Scottish and Australian Bank; European Schoolmagazine Association

E.S.A.N.Z. Economic Society of Australia and New Zealand

ESAR electronically steerable array radar

E.S.B. electrical stimulation of the brain; electric storage battery; Empire State Building; English Speaking Board

E.S.B.A. English Schools' Badminton Association

E.S.B.B.A. English Schools' Basket Ball Association

esc. Fr. *escompte*, discount; escutcheon

Esc. *escudo*, Portuguese currency

E.S.C. Economic and Social Council (U.N.O.); electronic structural correlator; English Stage Company; English Steel Corporation; Entomological Society of Canada; European Space Conference; extended core storage

E.S.C.A. English Schools' Cricket/ Cycling Association

eschat. eschatology

E.S.C.M.A. Electric Steel Conduit Manufacturers' Association

Esco. Sp. *Escocia*, Scotland

E.S.C.O. Educational, Scientific and Cultural Organisation (U.N.O.)

ESCOM Electricity Supply Commission of South Africa

Esd. Books of Esdras (Bible and Apocrypha)

E.S.D. echo sounding device

ESDAC European Space Data Centre

E.S.E. east-south-east; engineers stores establishment

E.S.E.F. Electrotyping and Stereotyping Employers' Federation

E.S.G. English Standard Gauge

E.S.H. equivalent standard hours; European Society of Haematology

E.S.I.T.B. Electricity Supply Industry Training Board

Esk. eskimo

e.s.l. expected significance level

E.S.M.A. Electrical Sign Manufacturers' Association

esn., esntl. essential

E.S.N. educationally subnormal

E.S.N.Z. Entomological Society of New Zealand

ESOMAR European Society for Opinion Surveys and Market Research

esp., espec. especially

Esp. Fr. *Espagne*, Spain; Sp. *España*, Spain; Sp. *Español*, Spanish; esparto; Esperanto; It. *Espressivo*, expressive, *also* Espress., Espr.

E.S.P. extra-sensory perception

espg. espionage

Esq., Esqr. Esquire

E.S.Q.A. English Slate Quarries Association

esqº. Port. *esquerdo*, left
ESRO, Esro European Space Research Organisation
E.S.R.S. European Society for Rural Sociology
ess. essence; essential
ess. L. *essentia*, essence
Ess. Essex
ESSA Environmental Science Services Administration, of Dept. of Commerce (U.S.A.)
E.S.S.A. English Schools' Swimming Association
ESSO Standard Oil
est., estab. establish; establishment
est. estate; estimate; estimation; estimator; estuary
Est. Estonia; Estonian
E.S.T. earliest start time; Eastern Standard/Summer Time (U.S.A.)
estab., estb. establish
ESTEC European Space Technology Centre
estg. estimating
Esth. Esther (Bible)
E.S.T.I. European Space Technology Institute
estn. estimation
e.s.u. electrostatic unit
E.S.U. English-Speaking Union
E.S.V. earth satellite vehicle
et ethyl (chem.)
ET *s* Arab Republic of Egypt (I.V.R.); *s* Ethiopia (I.C.A.M.); *s* Rotherham (B.V.R.)
e.t. Fr. *en titre*, in title
E.T. Eastern Time (U.S.A.); educational therapy; electric telegraph; engineering time; English text/translation; entertainment tax; Ephemeris time; equation of time; Exchange Telegraph
e.t.a. estimated time of arrival
E.T.A. European Teachers' Association; *Euzkadi ta Azka Asuna*, Basque Separatist Organisation (Spain)
Etab. Fr. *Établissement*, business house
et al. L. *et alibi*, and elsewhere; L. *et alii*, and others
etc L. *et cetera*, and so forth, &c.
e.t.c. Fr. *en tout cas*, in any case/in emergency
E.T.C. Eastern Telegraph Company; European Translation Centre
ETCG elapsed-time code generator
E.T.C.T.A. Electrical Trades Commercial Travellers' Association
e.t.d. estimated time of departure; extension trunk dialling
e.t.e. estimated time en route
E.T.E. Experimental Tunnelling Establishment
eth. ether; ethical; ethics

Eth., Ethiop. Ethiopia; Ethiopian; Ethiopic
E.T.H. Ger. *Eidgenössische Technische Hochschule*, Swiss Federal Institute of Technology
ethnog. ethnography
ethnol. ethnological; ethnology
e.t.i. elapsed time indicator; estimated time of interception
E.T.J.C. Engineering Trades Joint Council
e.t.k.m. every test known to man
E.T.L. Ericsson Telephones Limited
E.T.M.A. English Timber Merchants' Association
ETMWG Electronic Trajectory Measurements Working Group
e.t.o. estimated time off
E.T.O. European Theatre of Operations; European Transport Organization
e.t.p. estimated turnaround/turning point
E.T.P.S. Empire Test Pilots' School
Etr. Sp. *entrada*, entrance; Etruscan
e.t.r. estimated time of return
e.t.s. estimated time of sailing; expiration of time of service
E.T.S. Electrodepositors' Technical Society
E.T.S.A. Electricity Trust of South Australia
et seq. L. *et sequens*, and the following
e.t.s.p. entitled to severance pay
et sqq. L. *et sequentes*, and the following
E.T.T.A. English Table Tennis Association
E.T.T.U. European Table Tennis Union
E.T.U. Electrical Trades Union
E.T.U.C. European Trade Union Confederation, *founded* 1973
et ux. L. *et uxor*, and wife
E.T.V. educational television; engine test vehicle
etw. Ger. *etwas*, something
ety., etym., etymol. etymological; etymologist; etymology
Eu *s* europium (chem.)
EU *s* Breconshire (B.V.R.)
E.U. Sp. *Estados Unidos*, United States; Fr. *États-Unis*, United States; Evangelical Union; experimental unit
E.U.A. Port. *Estados Unidos da América*, United States of America; Sp. *Estados Unidos de América*, United States of America; Fr. *États-Unis d' Amérique*, United States of America; European unit of account (fin.)
E.U.B. Port. *Estados Unidos do Brasil*, Brazil
Euc., Eucl. Euclid (*c* 330–*c* 275 B.C.) Greek mathematician

126

EUCEPA Fr. *Comité européen de liaison pour la cellulose et le papier*, European Liaison Committee for Cellulose and Paper

EUCOM European Command (U.S.A.)

EUFTT European Union of Film and Television Technicians

Eug. Eugene

Eugen. Eugenics

E.U.L. Everyman's University Library

E.U.M. Sp. *Estados Unidos Mexicanos*, Mexico

E.U.P. English Universities Press

Eupad mixture of calcium chloride and boric acid used as an antiseptic dry dressing, from initials of Edinburgh Univ. Pathological Department, where mixture invented

euph., euphem. euphemia

euphem. euphemism; euphemistic

Eur. Europe; European

E.U.R. It. *Esposizione Universale di Roma*, Roman Universal Exhibition, now a residential suburb of Rome

EURATOM, EURATOM European Atomic Energy Community, estab. 1958 to co-ordinate nuclear industries and develop nuclear research

Eurip. Euripides (*c* 484–407 B.C.), last of the great Greek tragedians

EURO. European Regional Office of FAO

EUROCAE European Organization for Civil Aviation Electronics

EUROCEAN European Oceanographic Association

EUROCHEMIC European Company for the Chemical Processing of Irradiated Fuels

EUROCOM European Coal Merchants' Union

Euro$ Eurodollar

EUROFIMA Fr. *Société européenne pour le financement de matériel farroviair*, European Co. for the Financing of Railway Rolling Stock

EUROFINAS Association of European Finance Houses

EUROMAISIERS Fr. *Groupement des associations des maisiers des pays de la C.E.E.*, Maize Industry Assn. Group for the E.E.C. Countries

EUROMALT Fr. *Comité de travail des malteries de la C.E.E.*, Working Committee of the Malt-Houses of the E.E.C.

EUROP European Railway Wagon Pool

EUROPECHE Fr. *Association des organisations nationales d'entreprises de pêche de la C.E.E.*, Assn. of Nat. Organizations of Fishing Enterprises of the E.E.C.

EUROPHOT Fr. *Association européenne des photographes professionnels*, Committee of the Professional Photographers of Europe

EUROSAC Fr. *Fédération européenne des fabricants de sacs en papier à grande contenance*, European Fed. of Manufacturers of Multiwall Paper Sacks

EUROSPACE European Industrial Space Study Group

EUROTOX European Standing Committee for the Protection of Populations against the Long-Term Risks of Intoxication

Eurovision television of European range

Eus., Euseb. Eusebius Pamphili of Caesarea (A.D. *c* 264–*c* 349), 'father' of eccles. history

E.U.S.E.C. Engineering Societies of Western Europe and the U.S.A.

E.U.V. extreme ultra violet

E.U.W. European Union of Women

eV, e.v. electron volt

EV *s* Essex (B.V.R.)

ev. Ger. *evangelisch*, Protestant (rel.)

e.v. efficient vulcanization; Fr. *en ville*, local

e.V. Ger. *eingetragener Verein*, registered association

E.V.A. Electric Vehicle Association of Great Britain; engineer vice-admiral; ethylene/vinyl acetate (plastic); extravehicular activity (space)

evac. evacuate; evacuation

eval. evaluate; evaluation

evan., evang. evangelical; evangelist

evap. evaporate; evaporation; evaporator

evce. evidence

EVCS extravehicular communications system (space)

evg., evng. evening

E.V.G. Ger. *Europäische Verteidigungsgemeinschaft*, European Defence Community

evid. evidence

E.V.L., EVOE E. V. Lucas (1868–1938), Eng. author and editor

evol. evolution; evolutionary; evolutionist

E.V.R. electronics video broadcasting system

E.V.T. Educational and Vocational Training; equi-viscous temperature (chem.); Ger. *Europäische Vereinigung für Tierzucht*, European Assn. for Animal Production

evtl. Ger. *eventuell*, perhaps/possibly

E.V.W. European Voluntary Workers

evy. every
EW *s* Huntingdonshire (B.V.R.)
Ew. Ger. *Euer*, your
e.w. each way (betting); early warning; electron warfare
E.W. England and Wales
E.W.A. Education Writers' Association (U.S.A.)
E.W.F. Electrical Wholesalers' Federation
E.W.O. essential work order
E.W.P. emergency war plan
E.W.R. early-warning radar
EWRC European Weed Research Association
E.W.S. emergency water supply; emergency welfare service
E.W.S.F. European Work Study Federation
EX *s* Great Yarmouth (B.V.R.)
ex. examination (*also*, exam.); examine; examiner; example; excellent; except; exception; excess; exchange; exclude; exclusive (*also*, excl.); excursion; excursus; execute; executive; executor; exempt; exercise; export; express; extension (*also*, extn.); extra; extract
Ex. excluded, without (fin.); Exeter; Exodus (Bible)
exag. exaggerate; exaggeration
exam. examination; examine; examiner
examd. examined
examg. examining
examn. examination
ex. aq. L. *ex aqua*, out of water
exc. excellent; except; exception; exchange; excommunication
exc. L. *excudit*, he/she engraved it
Exc. Excellency
exch. exchange; exchequer
excl., exclam. exclamation; exclamatory
excl. exclude; exclusive
ex cp. excluding coupon (fin.)
exd. examined
ex d., ex div. ex dividend, excluding next dividend (fin.)
exec. execute; execution; executive; executor
execx., exix., exx. executrix
exes. expenses
Exet. Exeter College, Oxford, founded 1314
ex. g., ex. gr. L *exempli gratia*, for example
exh. exhaust; exhibition, *also* exhbn., exhib.
exhib. exhibit; exhibitioner
Ex. Im., Eximbank Export-Import Bank (U.S.A.)
ex in., ex int. excluding interest (fin.)

ex-l. L. *ex libris*, from the library of
Ex.maSr.aD. Port. *Excelentissima Senhora Dona*, Mrs., followed by full name
Ex-Mer. ex-meridian
Ex.moSr. Port. *Excelentissimo Senhor*, Mr., followed by full name
ex n., ex new excluding new issue of shares (fin.)
Exod. Exodus (Bible)
ex off. L. *ex officio*, by virtue of office
Exon. L. *Exonia*, Exeter; L. *Exoniensis*, of Exeter, Eng. episcopal title, in bishop's signature
exor. executor
exp exponential (math.)
EXP Exchange of Persons Office (UNESCO)
exp. expand; expansion; expedition; expense; experience; experiment; experimental; expiration; expire; export; exportation; exporter; express (*also* expr.); expression
ex p. L. *ex parte*, on one side only
expdn. expedition
exper. experimental
expl. explain; explanation; explanatory; explosion; explosive
exploit. exploitation
expn. exposition
EXPO exposition, exhibition such as held in Canada (1967), Japan (1970)
exp. o. experimental order
expr. express
ex-Pres. ex-President
expt. experiment
exptl. experimental
exptr. exporter
expurg. expurgate
exr. executor
exs. expenses
ext. extend; extension (*also* extn.); extent; exterior; external; extinct; extra; extract; extraction; extreme
ext. L. *extractum*, extract (med.)
EXTEL Exchange Telegraph, news agency
ext. liq. L. *extractum liquidum*, liquid extract (med.)
extr. extraordinary
extrad. extradition
exx. examples
Exz. Ger. *Exzellenz*, Excellency
EY *s* Anglesey (B.V.R.)
E.Y.C. European Youth Campaign
E.Y.R. East Yorkshire Regiment (mil.)
EY & T Eaton, Yale and Towne
EZ *s* Belfast (B.V.R.)
Ez., Ezr. Ezra (Bible)
Eze., Ezek. Ezekiel (Bible)
E.Z.U. Ger. *Europäische Zahlungsunion*, European Payments Union

F

f   face value (numis.); fa, subdominant note in any key in Tonic Sol-fa, pron. Fah; femto, 10^{-15}; s fog, visibility 220–1,100 yards (met.)

f   *forte*, loud (mus.)

F   s Essex (B.V.R.); failing grade; farad, unit of electric capacitance (F = As/V); fast, on clock/watch regulator; s Faversham (B.F.P.); fine (pencils); s fluorine (chem.); s France, including overseas departments and territories (I.V.R.); s function (math.); s thick fog, visibility less than 200 yards (met.)

F_1 first filial offspring resulting from crossing the animals/plants of parental generation (biol.)

F_2 second filial generation (biol.)

F-28   short haul airliner

F27   Fokker Friendship (aircraft)

f.   facing, engine (rail.); fair; farthing; father; fathom; feet; fell; felon; female; feminine; filly (horse racing); fine; flat; fluid; focal length (photo.); Ger. *folgende Seite*, next page; folio; following; foot; for; Port. *fora*, out; force (phys.); forecastle; formed on; form of, in cross-references; formula; foul (sport); founded; frank; freehold; frequency; from; function; Ger. *für*, for; furlong; furlough

F.   Fahrenheit, thermometer; family; fast; Father; February; Fellow; It. *Ferrovia*, rail; fiction; fighter; finance; fine; firm; fleet; Foreign Member; founded; Swed. *Framkomst*, arrival; franc, currency; France; Ger. *Frauen*, women; It. *freddo*, cold; French; Port. *frente*, middle flat, when there are three on same floor; frequency; Fr. *frère*, brother; Friday. Port./Sp. *frio*, cold; Sp. *fuera*, out; Port; *Fulano*, so-and-so; It. *fuori*, out

F.   L. *fiat*, let it be made (med.)

°F.   degrees Fahrenheit

FA   s Burton-on-Trent (B.V.R.); frequency agility

f.a.   fatty acid; fire alarm; first aid/attack; folic acid; free alongside/aperture; friendly aircraft; fuel air (ratio)

Fa.   Faeroes; Ger. *firma*, firm; Florida (U.S.A.)

f. & a.   fore and aft

F.A.   Factory Act; family allowance; Fanny Adams, nothing at all; farm adviser; field activities/ambulance/allowance/artillery; Finance Act, followed by year; financial adviser; fine art; fluorescent antibody; Football Association, supreme authority from 1863 of assn. football clubs (GB and N. Ireland)

f.a.a.   free of all average, insce. term meaning that total losses only will be paid

F.A.A.   Federal Aviation Administration (U.S.A.); Fellow of the American Association for the Advancement of Science; Fellow of the Australian Academy of Science; Film Artists' Association; Fleet Air Arm

F.A.A.A.S.   Fellow of the American Academy of Arts and Sciences; Fellow of the American Association for the Advancement of Science

FAAC   Food Additives and Contaminants Committee

F.A.A.O.S.   Fellow of the American Academy of Orthopaedic Surgeons

FAAP Federal Aid to Airport Program (U.S.A.)

fab. fabric; fabricate; fabulous

f.a.b. first aid box

FABAS Farm Amalgamations and Boundary Adjustment Schemes

fabbr. It. *fabbrica*, factory, works

FABMDS field army ballistic missile defense system

fabr. fabricate; fabrication

Fab. Soc. Fabian Society

F.A.B.S.S. Fellow of the Architectural and Building Surveyors' Society

fabx. fire alarm box

fac. façade; facial; facility; facsimile; factor; factory; faculty

fac. L. *factum similie*, facsimile

f.a.c. fast as can

F.A.C. Federation of Agricultural Co-operatives

F.A.C.A. Fellow of the American College of Allergists/Anaesthetists/Anaesthesiologists/Angiology

F.A.C.C. Fellow of the American College of Cardiology

F.A.C.C.A. Fellow of the Association of Certified and Corporate Accountants

F.A.C.D. Fellow of the American College of Dentistry/Dentists

F.A.C.D.S. Fellow of the Australian College of Dental Surgeons

FACE field artillery computer equipments

F.A.C.E. Fellow of the Australian College of Education

F.A.C.E.M. Federation of Associations of Colliery Equipment Manufacturers

facet. facetious

F.A.C.F.O. Fellow of the American College of Foot Orthopedics

F.A.C.G.O. Fellow of the American College of Gastroenterology

F.A.C.I.A.A. Fellow of the Australian Commercial and Industrial Artists' Association

facil. facility

F.A.C.O.G. Fellow of the American College of Obstetricians and Gynaecologists

FACMTA Federal Advisory Council on Medical Training (U.S.A.)

F.A.C.P. Fellow of the American College of Physicians

F.A.C.P.M. Fellow of the American College of Preventive Medicine

F.A.C.R. Fellow of the American College of Radiology

Facs. facsimile

F.A.C.S. Fellow of the American College of Surgeons; Fellow of the Association of Certified Secretaries of South Africa

facsim. facsimile

F.A.C.T. flanagan aptitude classification test; fully automatic compiler-translator

fact., factᵃ Sp. *factura*, invoice

f.a.d. free air delivered

F.A.D.O. Fellow of the Association of Dispensing Opticians

Faer. Faeroe Islands

FAF free at field, quotation for delivery of aircraft

fag. It. *fagotto*, bassoon (mus.)

F.A.G.O. Fellow of American Guild of Organists

F.A.G.S. Federation of Astronomical and Geophysical Services; Fellow of the American Geographical Society

Fahr. fahrenheit (thermometer)

F.A.I. Fr. *Fédération abolitionniste internationale*, Intern. Abolitionist Fed.; Fr. *Fédération aéronautique internationale*, Intern. Aeronautical Fed.; Fellow of the Chartered Auctioneers' and Estate Agents' Institute; Fertilizer Association of India: fresh air inlet

F.A.I.A. Fellow of the American Institute of Architects; Fellow of the Association of International Accountants; Fellow of the Australian Institute of Advertising

F.A.I.A.S. Fellow of the Australian Institute of Agricultural Science

F.A.I.B. Fr. *Fédération des associations internationales établies en Belgique*, Fed. of Intern. Assns. Estab. in Belgium; Fellow of the Australian Institute of Builders

F.A.I.C. Fellow of the American Institute of Chemists

F.A.I.Ex. Fellow of the Australian Institute of Export

F.A.I.H.A. Fellow of the Australian Institute of Hospital Administration

F.A.I.I. Fellow of the Australian Insurance Institute

F.A.I.M. Fellow of the Australian Institute of Management

F.A.I.P. Fellow of the Australian Institute of Physics

F.A.I.P.M. Fellow of the Australian Institute of Personnel Management

F.A.I.S. Fellow of the Amalgamated Institute of Secretaries

FAK freights all kinds (ship.)

Fak. Ger. *Faktura*, invoice

Falk I., Falk. Is. Falkland Islands

F.A.L.P.A. Fellow of the Incorporated Society of Auctioneers and Landed Property Agents

FAM family allowance (tax.)

fam. familiar; family

f.a.m. foreign airmail; free at mill

F.A.M., F. & A.M. Free and Accepted Masons

F.A.M.A. Fellow of the American Medical Association; Foundation for Mutual Assistance in Africa

F.A.M.E.M. Federation of Associations of Mining Equipment Manufacturers

F.A.M.E.M.E. Fellow of the Association of Mining, Electrical & Mechanical Engineers

F.A.M.H.E.M. Federation of Associations of Materials Handling Equipment Manfuacturers

F.A.M.N.Z. Fellow of the Arts Galleries and Museums Association of New Zealand

F.A.M.S. Fellow of the Ancient Monuments Society; Fellow of the Indian Academy of Medical Sciences

fan fanatic

Fan, Fanny Frances

F.A.N.Y.S., Fanny First Aid Nursing Yeomanry Service

F.A.N.Z.A.A.S. Fellow of Australian and New Zealand Association for Advancement of Science

FAO Food and Agriculture Organization of the United Nations, specialized agency estab. 1945 to advise on conservation of natural resources and methods of food processing and distribution

f.a.o. finish all over

F.A.O. Fleet Accountant Officer

FAP Family Assistance Programme (U.S.A.); *Fuerzas Armadas Peronistas,* Peronists with Castroite tendencies (Argen.)

F.A.P. first aid post; *Forca Aérea Portuguesa,* Portuguese Air Force

F.A.P.H.A. Fellow of the American Public Health Association

F.A.P.H.I. Fellow of the Association of Public Health Inspectors

F.A.P.I. Fellow of the Australian Planning Institute

F.A.P.S. Fellow of the American Physical Society

F.A.P.T. Fellow of the Association of Photographic Technicians

f.a.q. fair average quality; free alongside/at quay

f.a.q.s. fair average quality of season

far. farriery; farthing

Far. Faraday; faradic

F.A.R. false alarm rate; Federal Aviation Regulations (U.S.A.)

FARELF Far East Land Forces

FAS Foreign Agricultural Service (U.S.A.)

f.a.s. firsts and seconds; free alongside ship, seller is responsible for expenses of delivering the goods alongside the loading vessel

F.A.S. Faculty of Architects and Surveyors; Federation of American Scientists (U.S.A.); Fellow of the Anthropological Society; Fellow of the Antiquarian Society

F.A.S.A. Fellow of the Acoustical Society of America; Fellow of the Australian Society of Accountants; First Auditor of Sheriff's Accounts (U.S.A.)

F.A.S.A.P. Fellow of the Australian Society of Animal Production

fasc. L. *fasciculus,* bundle

F.A.S.C.E. Fellow of the American Society of Civil Engineers

F.A.S.E. Fellow of the Antiquarian Society, Edinburgh

FASEB Federation of American Societies for Experimental Biology

F.A.S.S. Federation of Associations of Specialists and Sub-Contractors

FAST factor analysis system; fast automatic shuttle transfer

F.A.S.T. first atomic ship transport; formulae for assessing the specification of trains

F & T fire and theft (insce.)

fastnr. fastener

fath. fathom

F.A.T.I.P.E.C. Fr. *Fédération d'associations de techniciens des industries des peintures, vernis, émaux et encres d'imprimerie de l'Europe continentale,* Fed. of Assns. of Technicians in the Paint, Varnishes, Enamels and Printing-Ink Industries of Continental Europe

F.A.T.I.S. Food and Agriculture Technical Information Service (OEEC)

F.A.U. Friends' Ambulance Unit

fav. favor/favour; favorite/favourite

F.A.V.O. fleet aviation officer

F.A.W.A. Federation of Asian Women's Associations

FAX facsimile; facts; fuel air explosion

FB *s* Bath (B.V.R.)

F-B. full-bore, for rifles it signifies calibre greater than ·22″

f.b. flat bar; fog bell; freight bill; fullback (sport)

F.B. Fenian Brotherhood; fire brigade; fisheries/fishery board; flat bottom (rails); flying boat; Forth Bridge (Scot.); Free Baptist

FBA Farm Buildings Association

F.B.A. Federal Bar Association (U.S.A.); Federation of British Astrologers; Federation of British Audio; Fellow of the British Academy; fluorescent brightening agent; Freshwater Biological Association

F.B.A.A. Fellow of the British Association of Accountants and Auditors

F'ball football

F.B.B.D.O. Fibre Building Board Development Organization

f.b.c. fallen building clause

F.B.C. Farm Buildings Centre (Warwickshire)

F.B.C.M. Federation of British Carpet Manufacturers

F.B.C.P. Fellow of the British College of Physiotherapists

F.B.C.S. Fellow of the British Computer Society

f.b.c.w. fallen building clause waiver

fbd. freeboard

F.B.E.A. Fellow of the British Esperanto Association

F.B.F.M. Federation of British Film Makers

F.B.G. Federation of British Growers

F.B.H. fire brigade hydrant

F.B.H.I. Fellow of the British Horological Institute

F.B.H.T.M. Federation of British Hand Tool Manufacturers

F.B.I. Federal Bureau of Investigation (U.S.A.); Federation of British Industries, *now* C.B.I.

F.B.I.A. Fellow of the Bankers' Institute of Australasia

F.B.I.M. Fellow of the British Institute of Management

F.B.I.S. Fellow of the British Interplanetary Society

F.B.K.S. Fellow of the British Kinematograph Society

F.B.M. fleet ballistic missile

F.B.O.A. Fellow of the British Optical Association

F.B.O.U. Fellow of the British Ornithologists' Union

FBP final boiling point

F.B.P.M.C. Federation of British Police Motor Clubs

F.B.P.S. Fellow of the British Phrenological Society; Forest and Bird Protection Society of New Zealand

F.B.Ps.S. Fellow of the British Psychological Society

F.B.R.A.M. Federation of British Rubber and Allied Manufacturers

fbr. fiber/fibre

F.Brit.I.R.E. Fellow of the British Institution of Radio Engineers, *now* **F.I.E.R.E.**

fbro. Sp. *febrero*, February

FBRS Farm Business Recording Scheme

F.B.S. Fellow of the Botanical Society; Fellow of the Building Societies Institute

F.B.S.C. Fellow of the British Society of Commerce

F.B.S.E. Fellow of the Botanical Society, Edinburgh

F.B.S.I. Fellow of the National Institution of the Boot and Shoe Industry

F.B.S.M. Fellow of Birmingham & Midland Institute School of Music

F.B.S.M.G.P. Fellow of the British Society of Master Glass-Painters

F.B.U. Federation of Bone Users and Allied Trades; Fire Brigades Union

f.b.y. future budget year

FC *s* Oxford (B.V.R.)

f.c. file cabinet; fire clay; follow copy; foot candle; for cash; fuel cell

F.C. Federal Cabinet; fellow craft (freem.); fencing club; Sp. *Ferrocarril*, railway; Fifth Column, term that had its origin in Sp. Civil war, being credited to General Mola who said, when besieging Madrid, 'I have 4 columns operating against Madrid and a fifth inside composed of my sympathisers'; fighter command; fire cock/control; Fisheries' Convention; Fishmongers' Company; football club; Forestry Commission, first formed 1919 to promote forestry, afforestation and the timber trade, and to advise private owners; Free Church (Scot.)

F.C. L. *Fidei Commissum*, bequeathed in trust; L. *Fieri curavit*, the donor directed this to be done. Generally placed at end of monumental stone

F. & C. full and change (tides)

F.C.A. Farm Credit Administration (U.S.A.); Federation of Canadian Artists; Fellow of the Institute of Chartered Accountants in England and Wales

F.C.A.A. Fellow of the Australasian Institute of Cost Accountants

FCAATSI Federal Council for the Advancement of Aborigines and Torres Strait Islanders (Aust.)

F.C.A.(Aust.) Fellow of the Institute of Chartered Accountants in Australia

fcap. foolscap

F.C.A.P. Fellow of the College of American Pathologists

F.C.B. frequency co-ordinating body

F.C.B.A. Federation Communications Bar Association; Fellow of the Canadian Bankers' Association

F.C.B.I. Fellow Institute of Bookkeepers

FCC fluid catalytic cracking

F.C.C. Federal Communications Commission (U.S.A.); Federal Council of Churches; first class certificate

F.C.C.A. Floor Covering Contractors' Association

F.C.C.O. Fellow of Canadian College of Organists

F.C.C.S. Fellow of Corporation of Certified Secretaries

F.C.D.A. Federal Civil Defense Administration (U.S.A.)

F.C.E.C. Federation of Civil Engineering Contractors

F.C.E.C.A. Fishery Committee for the Eastern Central Atlantic

F.C.F.C. Free Church Federal Council

fcg. facing

FCGB Forestry Committee of Great Britain

F.C.G.I. Fellow of the City and Guilds London Institute

F.C.G.P. Fellow of the College of General Practitioners

F.Ch.S. Fellow of the Society of Chiropodists

F.C.I. Fr. *Fédération cynologique internationale*, Intern. Fed. of Kennel Clubs; Fellow of the Clothing Institute; Fellow of the Institute of Commerce; Finance Corporation for Industry; Fluid Control Institute (U.S.A.)

F.C.I.A. Fellow of Corporation of Insurance Agents; Foreign Credit Insurance Association

F.C.I.B. Fellow of Corporation of Insurance Brokers

F.C.I.C. Fellow of the Chemical Institute of Canada

F.C.I.I. Fellow of Chartered Insurance Institute

F.C.I.P.A. Fellow of the Chartered Institute of Patent Agents

F.C.I.S. Fellow of Chartered Institute of Secretaries

F.C.I.T. Four Countries International Tournament (basketball)

F.C.I.V. Fellow of the Commonwealth Institute of Valuers

F clef. the bass clef (mus.)

F.C.M.A. Fellow of the Institute of Cost and Management Accountants, *formerly* **F.C.W.A.**; Flushing Cistern Makers' Association

F.C.M.I. Federation of Coated Macadam Industries

F.C.M.I.E. Fellow of the Colleges of Management and Industrial Engineering

F.C.N.A. Fellow of the College of Nursing (Aust.)

Fco It. *Franco abord Franco*, free (com.)

FCO Foreign and Commonwealth Office

f.co It. *Franco*, free (com.)

f.co. fair copy, transcript free from corrections (typ.)

F.C.O. Farmers' Central Organisation; Fellow of the College of Organists, *now* F.R.C.O.; fire-control officer

F.C.O.G. Fellow of the College of Obstetricians and Gynaecologists, *now* F.R.C.O.G.

F.Comm.A. Fellow of the Society of Commercial Accountants

fcp. foolscap

F.C.P. Federation of Calico Printers; Fellow of the College of Preceptors; Port. *Futebol Clube do Pôrto*, Oporto Football Club

F.C.P.A. Fellow of the Canadian Psychological Association

F.C.P.O. fleet chief petty officer

F.C.R.A. Fellow of the College of Radiologists of Australasia; Fellow of the Corporation of Registered Accountants

F.C.R.O.A. Fellow of the Civic Recreation Officers' Association

fcs. francs

f.c.s., f.c. & s. warranted free of capture, seizure, arrest, detainment and the consequences thereof (insce.)

F.C.S. Fellow of the Chemical Society; Fellow of the Corporation of Secretaries

f.c.s.r.c.c. warranted free of capture, seizure, arrest, detainment and the consequences thereof, and damage caused by riots and civil commotions (insce.)

F.C.S.T. Federal Council for Science and Technology (U.S.A.); Fellow of the College of Speech Therapists

F.C.T. Federal Capital Territory (Aust.)

F.C.T.B. Fellow of the College of Teachers of the Blind

F.C.T.U. Federation of Associations of Catholic Trade Unionists

fcty. factory

F.C.U. fighter control unit

F.C.W.A. Fellow of the Institute of Cost and Works Accountants, *now* F.C.M.A.

F/d free docks

FD *s* Dudley (B.V.R.); *s* Fleetwood (B.F.P.); Ger. *Fernschnell*, long-distance; frequency diversity

fd. field; fiord; ford; forward; found; founded; fund

f.d. flight deck; focal distance; free delivery; free discharge; free dispatch

f. & d. fill and drain; freight and demurrage

F.D. finite difference; fire department; fleet duties; Free Democrat

F.D., fid. def. L. *fidei defensor*, de-

134

fender of the faith. Title granted to Henry VIII by Pope Leo X, 11 Oct. 1523, for pamphlet *Assertio Septem Sacramentorum* attacking Luther's doctrines; F.D. appeared on British coinage in the reign of George I

F.D.A. Food and Drug Administration (U.S.A.)

FDC Fire Direction Center (U.S.A.); first day cover, envelope posted on the day of issue of a stamp or stamp series

f.d.c. Fr. *fleur de coin*, mint condition (numis.)

F.D.C. Furniture Development Council

F.D. & C. Food, Drug and Colour Regulations (U.S.A.)

F.D.D. Fr. *francs de droit*, free of charge

FDDL frequency division data link (USAF)

F.D.F. Footwear Distributors' Federation

fdg. funding

F.D.H.O. Factory Department, Home Office

F.D.I. Fr. *Fédération dentaire internationale*, Intern. Dental Fed.

FDIC Federal Deposit Insurance Corporation (U.S.A.)

F.D.I.F. Fr. *Fédération démocratique internationale des femmes*, Women's Intern. Democratic Fed.

FDK *Fileleftheron Dimokratikon Kendron*, Liberal Democratic Centre (Greece)

FDM frequency division multiplex

F.D.O. fleet dental officer

FDP *Freie Demokratische Partei*, Free Democratic Party (W. Ger.); *Fuerza Democrática Popular*, Popular Democratic Force (Ven.)

Fdr. founder

F.D.R. Franklin Delano Roosevelt (1882–1945), Pres. of U.S.A.

Fdry. foundry

F.D.S. Fellow in Dental Surgery

F.D.S.R.C.S. Fellow in Dental Surgery of the Royal College of Surgeons of England

F.D.S.R.C.S.Ed. Fellow in Dental Surgery of the Royal College of Surgeons of Edinburgh

FD Zug Ger. *Fernschnellzug*, long-distance express

Fe *s* L. *ferrum*, iron (chem. and med.)

FE *s* Folkestone (B.F.P.); *s* Lincoln (B.V.R.)

f.e. first edition; for example

F.E. Far East; finite element; fish eye (buttons); foreign editor; further education

F.E.A. Federal Executive Association

(U.S.A.); Federation of European Aerosol Associations; Fr. *Fédération internationale pour l'éducation artistique*, Intern. Fed. for Art Education

F.E.A.F. Far East Air Force

F.E.A.I.C.S. Fr. *Fédération européenne des associations d'ingénieurs de sécurité et de chefs de services de sécurité*, European Fed. of Assns. of Engineers and Heads of Industrial Safety Services

F.E.A.N.I. Fr. *Fédération européenne d'associations nationales d'ingénieurs*, European Fed. of Nat. Assns. of Engineers

FEB functional electronic block

feb., febb. It. *febbraio*, February

Feb., Feby. February

fec. L. *fecerunt*, they made

F.E.C. First Edition Club; Fr. *Fondation européenne de la culture*, European Cultural Foundation

F.E.C.B. Foreign Exchange Control Board

F.E.C.E.P. Fr. *Fédération européenne des constructeurs d'équipement pétrolier*, Fed. of European Petroleum Equipment Manufacturers

FECESITLIH *Federación Central de Sindicatos de Trabajadores Libres de Honduras*, Central Fed. of Free Workers' Union of Honduras

F.E.C.M. Fellowship of the Elder Conservatorium of Music

F.E.C.S. Fr. *Fédération européenne des fabricants de céramiques sanitaires*, European Fed. of Sanitary Ceramic Manufacturers

Fed Federal Reserve (U.S.A.)

fed. federal; federated; federation, *also* fedn.

Fed. federalist

F.E.D.C. Federation of Engineering Design Consultants

FEDECAME Sp. *Féderación Cafetalera de America*, Fed. of Coffee Growers of America

FEDIOL Fr. *Fédération de l'industrie de l'huilerie de la C.E.E.*, Fed. of the Oil Industry of the E.E.C.

F.E.F.A.C. Fr. *Fédération européenne des fabricants d'aliments composés pour animaux*, European Fed. of Manufacturers of Composite Foodstuffs for Animals

F.E.F.C. Far Eastern Freight Conference

F.E.F.C.E.B. Fr. *Fédération européenne des fabricants de caisses et emballages en bois*, European Fed. of Packing Case and Wooden Crate Manufacturers

F.E.F.C.O. Fr. *Fédération européenne*

des fabricants de carton ondulé, European Fed. of Corrugated Container Manufacturers

F.E.G.R.O. Fr. *Fédération européenne du commerce de l'horlogerie en gros*, European Fed. for the Wholesale Watch Trade

F.E.I. Fr. *Fédération équestre internationale*, Intern. Equestrian Fed.; Financial Executive Institute (U.S.A.)

F.E.I.E.A. Federation of European Industrial Editors' Associations

F.E.I.S. Fellow of the Educational Institute of Scotland

Fel.A.I.E.E. Fellow of American Institution of Electrical Engineers

F.E.L.F. Far East Land Forces

Fell. Fellow

fem. female; feminine; It. *forza elettromotrice*, electromotive force

F.E.M. Fr. *Fédération européenne des motels*, European Motel Fed.; Fr. *Fédération européenne de la manutention*, European Mechanical Handling Confed.

fenc. fencing

F.E.N.S.A. Film Entertainments National Service Association

F.E.O. fleet engineer officer

FEPC Fair Employment Practices Committee

F.E.P.E. Fr. *Fédération européenne pour la protection des eaux*, European Fed. for the Protection of Waters

F.E.P.E.M. Federation of European Petroleum Equipment Manufacturers

F.E.P.F. Fr. *Fédération européenne des industries de porcelaine et de faïence de table et d'ornementation*, European Fed. of the Industries of Earthenware and China Tableware and Ornamental Ware

Fepow Far East Prisoner of War

Fer., Ferm. Fermanagh County (N. Ireland)

Ferd. Ferdinand

FERES Fr. *Fédération internationale des instituts catholiques de recherches socio-religieuses*, Intern. Fed. of Catholic Institutes for Social Research

Fergie Fergus

ferr. It. *ferrovia*, railway

ferv. L. *fervens*, boiling

F.E.S. Federation of Engineering Societies; Fellow of the Entomological/Ethnological Society; F. E. Smith (1872–1930), *later* Earl of Birkenhead, Brit. statesman and lawyer; foil, épée and sabre

F.E.S.F.P. Fr. *Fédération européenne des syndicats de fabricants de parquets*, European Fed. of Parquet Manufacturers

FESITRANH *Federación Sindical de Trabajadores Norteños de Honduras*, North

Coast Fed. of Workers' Unions of Honduras

Fest. festival

F.E.T. federal excise tax (U.S.A.)

FETS field effect transistors

feud. feudal; feudalism

fev. Port. *fevereiro*, February

fév. Fr. *février*, February

FEX fleet exercise (USN)

F.E.Z. Fr. *Fédération européenne de zoötechnie*, European Assn. for Animal Production

FF *s* Merionethshire (B.V.R.)

ff. Ger. *folgende Seiten*, following pages; folios; following/*et seq.*; forms; thick fog (naut.)

ff. L. *fecerunt*, they made; *fortissimo*, very loud (mus.)

f.f. fixed focus

f. & f. fittings and fixtures

F.f. Ger. *Fortsetzung folgt*, to be continued

F.F. Fellows; Fianna Fail, Warriors of Ireland, political party of Rep. of Ireland, founded 1927 and apart from short periods (1948–51 and 1954–9) has held office since 1932; field force; Ford Foundation; French fried; frontier force

F.F. L. *Felicissimi Fratres*, Most Fortunate Brothers

f.f.a. free fatty acid; free foreign agency; free from alongside, seller pays for lighterage if incurred at port of discharge

F.F.A. Fellow of the Faculty of Actuaries (Scot.); Future Families/Farmers of America

F.F.A.R.A.C.S. Fellow of the Faculty of Anaesthetists, Royal Australasian College of Surgeons

F.F.A.R.C.S. Fellow of the Faculty of Anaesthetists of the Royal College of Surgeons of England

F.F.A.S. Fellow Incorporated Architect of the Faculty of Architects and Surveyors

F.F.B. faradic foot-bath; Fellow of the Faculty of Building

FF black fine furnace black, filler in rubber compounding

F.F.D.R.C.S.Irel. Fellow of the Faculty of Dentistry of the Royal College of Surgeons in Ireland

fff *fortissimo plus*, as loudly as possible (mus.)

F.F.H.C. Freedom from Hunger Campaign

F.F.Hom. Fellow of the Faculty of Homoeopathy

f.f.i. free from infection

F.F.I. Fellow of the Faculty of Insurance; French Forces of the Interior

F.F.J. Franciscan Familiar of Saint Joseph

ffly. faithfully

F.F.P.S. Fellow of the Faculty of Physicians and Surgeons

F.F.P.S.G. Fellow of the Faculty of Physicians and Surgeons, Glasgow (Scot.)

F.F.R. Fellow of the Faculty of Radiologists

FF.R.I.B.A. Fellows of the Royal Institute of British Architects

F.F.S. Fellow Incorporated Surveyor of the Faculty of Architects and Surveyors; Fellow of the Franklin Society

ffss full frequency stereophonic sound

FF.SS. *Ferrovie dello Stato*, Italian State Railways

F.F.V. first families of Virginia

F.F.W.M. free floating wave meter

ffy. faithfully

F.F.Y. Fife and Forfar Yeomanry

fg *s* low fog over land, inland stations only (met.)

f.g. field goal (sports); fine grain (leather)

Fg. It. *Fagotto*, bassoon (mus.)

F.G. Federal Government; Fine Gael (Rep. of Ireland); fire guard; foot-guards; friction glazed (paper); full gilt

f.g.a. free of general average (insce.)

F.g.a. foreign general average

F.G.A. Fellow of the Gemmological Association; Flat Glass Association

F.G.A.J. Fellow of the Guild of Agricultural Journalists

F.G.C.M. field general court martial

FGDS Fr. *Fédération de la Gauche Démocrate et Socialiste*, Fed. of the Democratic and Socialist Left (France)

f.g.f. fully good, fair

F.G.I. Fr. *Fédération graphique internationale*, Intern. Graphical Fed.; Fellow of the Institute of Certified Grocers

Fgn. foreign; foreigner

F.G.O. Fellow of the Guild of Organists; fleet gunnery officer

FGS Fatstock Guarantee Scheme

F.G.S. Fellow of the Geological Society

F.G.S.A. Fellow of the Geological Society of America

F.G.S.M. Fellow of Guildhall School of Music

fgt. freight

FGTB Fr. *Fédération Générale du Travail de Belgique*, Belg. General Fed. of Labor

FH *s* Falmouth (B.F.P.); *s* Gloucester (B.V.R.)

F/H freehold

f.h. fog horn; fore hatch

f.h. L. *fiat haustus*, make a draught (med.)

F.H. field hospital; fire hydrant; fly-half (rugby football)

F.H.A. Federal Housing Administration (U.S.A.); Fellow of the Australian Institute of Hospital Administration; Fellow of the Institute of Hospital Administrators; Finance Houses Association

F.H.A.S. Fellow of the Highland and Agricultural Society of Scotland

f.h.b. family hold back

F.H.C.I. Fellow of the Hotel and Catering Institute

F.H.F. Federation of Hardware Factors

F.H.H. foetal heart heard

Fhld., f'hold. freehold

FHLBB Federal Home Loan Bank Board (U.S.A.)

f.h.p. friction horsepower

F.H.R. Federal House of Representatives (Aust.)

F.H.S. Forces Help Society and Lord Roberts Workshops

F.H.T.A. Federated Home Timber Association

F.H.W.C. Fellow of the Heriot-Watt College, Edinburgh

FI *s* Tipperary (Rep. of Ireland V.R.)

f.i. for instance; free in

F.I. Falkland/Faeroe/Fiji Islands; fire insurance

FIA Fellow of the Institute of Actuaries

f.i.a. full interest admitted

F.I.A. Fr. *Fédération internationale des acteurs*, Intern. Fed. of Actors; Fr. *Fédération internationale de l'automobile*, Intern. Automobile Fed.; Fellow of the Institute of Actuaries

F.I.A.A. Fr. *Fédération internationale athlétique d'amateur*, Intern. Amateur Athletic Fed.; Fellow Architect Member of the Incorporated Association of Architects and Surveyors

F.I.A.B. Fr. *Fédération internationale des associations de bibliothécaires*, Intern. Fed. of Library Assns.

F.I.A.B.C.I. Fr. *Fédération internationale des administrateurs de biens conseils immobiliers*, Intern. Real Estate Fed.

F.I.A.C. Fr. *Fédération interaméricaine des automobile-clubs*, Inter-American Fed. of Automobile Clubs; Fellow of the Institute of Company Accountants

F.I.A.F. Fr. *Fédération internationale des archives du film*, Intern. Fed. of Film Archives

F.I.A.I. Fr. *Fédération internationale des associations d'instituteurs*, Intern. Fed. of Teachers' Assns.

F.I.A.I.I. Fellow of the Incorporated Australian Insurance Institute

F.I.A.J. Fr. *Fédération internationale des auberges de la jeunesse*, Intern. Youth Hostel Fed.

F.I.A.L. Fellow of the International Institute of Arts and Letters

F.I.A.M. Fellow of the International Academy of Management

F.I.A.M.A. Fellow of the Incorporated Advertising Managers' Association

F.I.A.M.C. Fr. *Fédération internationale des associations des médecins catholiques*, Intern. Fed. of Catholic Physicians

F.I.A.N.E.I. Fr. *Fédération internationale d'associations nationales d'élèves ingénieurs*, Intern. Fed. of National Assns. of Engineering Students

F.I.A.N.Z. Fellow of the Institute of Actuaries of New Zealand

F.I.A.P. Fr. *Fédération internationale de l'art photographique*, Intern. Fed. of Photographic Art

F.I.A.P.F. Fr. *Fédération internationale des associations de producteurs de films*, Intern. Fed. of Film Producers' Assns.

F.I.Arb. Fellow of the Institute of Arbitrators

F.I.A.R.P. Sp. *Federación interamericana des Asociaciones de Relaciones Publicas*, Inter-American Fed. of Public Relations Assns.

F.I.A.S. Fellow of the Institute of the Aerospace Sciences (U.S.A.); Fellow Surveyor Member of the Incorporated Association of Architects and Surveyors

F.I.A.T., Fiat *Fabbrica Italiana Automobili Torino*, Italian Motor Works in Turin

F.I.A.T.A. Fr. *Fédération internationale des associations transitaires et assimilés*, Intern. Fed. of Forwarding Agents' Assns.

F.I.A.T.C. Fr. *Fédération internationale des associations touristiques de cheminots*, Intern. Fed. of Railwaymen's Travel Assns.

F.I.A.V. Fr. *Fédération internationale des agences de voyages*, Intern. Fed. of Travel Agencies

f.i.b. free into barge/bond/bunkers

F.I.B. Fr. *Fédération internationale de boules*, Intern. Bowling Fed.; Fellow of the Institute of Bankers/Building

F.I.B.M. Fellow of the Institute of Baths Management

F.I.B.P. Fellow of the Institute of British Photographers

F.I.B.S.T. Fellow of the Institute of British Surgical Technicians

F.I.B.T. Fr. *Fédération internationale de bobsleigh et de tobogganing*, Intern. Bobsleighing and Tobogganing Fed.

F.I.B.T.P. Fr. *Fédération internationale du bâtiment et des travaux publics*, Intern. Fed. of Building and Public Works

fic., fict. fiction; fictional; fictitious

FIC frequency interference control

F.I.C. Fellow of the Institute of Chemistry

FICA Federal Insurance Contributions Act (U.S.A.); Food Industries Credit Association

F.I.C.A. Fr. *Fédération internationale des cheminots antialcooliques*, Intern. Railway Temperance Union; Fellow of the Commonwealth Institute of Accountants

F.I.C.C. Fr. *Fédération internationale de camping et de caravanning*, Intern. Fed. of Camping and Caravanning; Fr. *Fédération internationale des ciné-clubs*, Intern. Fed. of Film Societies

F.I.C.C.I. Federation of Indian Chambers of Commerce and Industry

F.I.C.D. Fellow of the Institute of Civil Defence

F.I.C.E. Fr. *Fédération internationale des communautés d'enfants*, Intern. Fed. of Children's Communities

F.I.C.E.A. Fellow of the Association of Industrial and Commercial Executive Accountants

F.I.C.E.P. *Fédération internationale catholique d'éducation physique et sportive*, Catholic Intern. Fed. for Physical and Sports Education

F.I.Ceram. Fellow of the Institute of Ceramics

F.I.Chem.E. Fellow of the Institution of Chemical Engineers

F.I.C.I. Fellow of the Institute of Chemistry of Ireland

F.I.C.I.C. Fr. *Fédération internationale du commerce et des industrie. du camping*, Intern. Fed. for the Camping Trade and Industry

F.I.C.J.F. Fr. *Fédération internationale des conseils juridiques et fiscaux*, Intern. Fed. of Legal and Fiscal Consultants

F.I.C.M. Fellow of the Institute of Credit Management

F.I.C.P. *Fédération internationale des clubs de publicité*, Intern. Fed. of Advertising Clubs

F.I.C.S. Fr. *Fédération internationale des chasseurs de sons*, Intern. Fed. of Sound Hunters; Fellow of the Institute of Chartered Shipbrokers; Fellow of the International College of Surgeons

F.I.C.S.A. Federation of International Civil Servants' Associations

138

fict. L. *fictilis*, made of pottery

F.I.C.T. *Fédération internationale de centres touristiques*, Intern. Fed. of Tourist Centres

F.I.C.W.A. Fellow of the Institute of Cost and Works Accountants

fid. fidelity; fiduciary

F.I.D. Falkland Island Dependencies; Fr. *Fédération Internationale de Documentation*, Intern. Fed. for Documentation; Fr. *Fédération internationale du diabète*, Intern. Diabetes Fed.; Fellow of the Institute of Directors; field intelligence department

F.I.D.A.F. Sp. *Federación Internacional de Asociaciones de Ferreteros y Almacenistas de Hierros*, Intern. Fed. of Ironmongers' and Iron Merchants' Assns.

F.I.D.A.S.E. Falkland Islands and Dependencies Aerial Survey Expedition

F.I.D.A.Q. Fr. *Fédération internationale des associations de quincailliers et marchands de fer*, Intern. Fed. of Ironmongers' and Iron Merchants' Assns.

F.I.D.E. Fr. *Fédération de l'industrie dentaire en Europe*, Fed. of the European Dental Industry; Fr. *Fédération internationale des échecs*, World Chess Fed.

FIDEL Sp. *Frente Izquierda de Liberación*, Leftist Liberation Front (Uru.)

F.I.D.E.M. Fr. *Fédération internationale des éditeurs de médailles*, Intern. Fed. of Medal Producers

F.I.D.H. Fr. *Fédération internationale des droits de l'homme*, Intern. Fed. for the Rights of Man

F.I.D.I. Fr. *Fédération internationale des déménageurs internationaux*, Fed. of Intern. Furniture Removers

F.I.D.I.C. Fr. *Fédération internationale des ingénieurs-conseils*, Intern. Fed. of Consulting Engineers

F.I.D.J.C. Fr. *Fédération internationale des directeurs de journaux catholiques*, Intern. Fed. of Directors of Catholic Publications

F.I.D.O. Film Industry Defence Organisation; fog, intensive, dispersal of, device to clear fog from airfield by burning petrol; fog investigation dispersal operation

FIDOR Fibre Building Board Development Organisation Ltd

F.I.D.P. Fellow of the Institute of Data Processing

F.I.D.S. Falkland Islands Dependencies Survey

FIDUROP Fr. *Commission du marché commun de la Fédération européenne des utilisateurs de fibres durés*, Common Market Committee of the European Fed. of Hard Fibre Users

F.I.E. Fr. *Fédération Internationa.e d'Escrime*, International Fencing Fed.

F.I.E.D. Fellow of the Institution of Engineering Designers

F.I.E.E. Fellow of the Institution of Electrical Engineers

F.I.E.J. Fr. *Fédération internationale des éditeurs de journaux et publications*, Intern. Fed. of Newspaper Publishers

F.I.E.M. *Fédération internationale de l'enseignement ménager*, Intern. Fed. of Home Economics

F.I.E.P. Fr. *Fédération internationale d'éducation physique*, Intern. Fed. for Physical Education

F.I.E.R.E. Fellow of the Institute of Electronic and Radio Engineers, *formerly* F.Brit.I.R.E.

F.I.E.S. Fellow of the Illuminating Engineering Society

F.I.E.T. Fr. *Fédération internationale des employés et des techniciens*, Intern. Fed. of Commercial, Clerical and Technical Employees

F.I.F. Fellow of the Institute of Fuel

fi.fa. L. *fieri facias*, have it done (kind of writ)

F.I.F.A. Fr. *Fédération Internationale de Football Association*, Intern. Assn. Football Fed.; Fr. *Fédération internationale du film d'art*, Intern. Fed. of Art Films; Fellow of the International Faculty of Arts

F.I.F.C.L.C. Fr. *Fédération internationale des femmes de carrières libérales et commerciales*, Intern. Fed. of Business and Professional Women

F.I.F.D.U. Fr. *Fédération internationale des femmes diplômées des universités*, Intern. Fed. of Univ. Women

F.I.F.E. Fellow of the Institution of Fire Engineers

FIFO first in, first out (inventory)

F.I.F.S.P. Fr. *Fédération internationale des fonctionnaires supérieurs de police*, Intern. Fed. of Senior Police Officers

fig. figurative; figure

F.I.G. Fr. *Fédération internationale des géomètres*, Intern. Fed. of Surveyors; Fr. *Fédération internationale de gymnastique*, Intern. Gymnastic Fed.

F.I.G.C.M. Fellow of the Incorporated Guild of Church Musicians

F.I.G.E.D. Fr. *Fédération internationale des grandes entreprises de distribution*, Intern. Fed. of Distributors

F.I.G.M. Fellow of the Institute of General Managers

F.I.G.O. Fr. *Fédération internationale de gynécologie et d'obstétrique*, Intern. Fed. of Gynaecology and Obstetrics

F.I.G.R.S. Fellow of the Irish Genealogical Research Society

F.I.H. Fr. *Fédération Internationale de Hockey*, Intern. Hockey Fed.; Fr. *Fédération internationale de hockey sur gazon*, Intern. Lawn Hockey Fed.; Fr. *Fédération internationale des hôpitaux*, Intern. Hospital Fed.; Fellow of the Institute of Hygiene

F.I.H.C. Fr. *Fédération internationale haltérophile et culturiste*, Intern. Weightlifting and Physical Culture Fed.

F.I.Hsg. Fellow of the Institute of Housing

F.I.H.U.A.T. Fr. *Fédération internationale pour l'habitation, l'urbanisme et l'aménagement des territoires*, Intern. Fed. for Housing and Town Planning

F.I.H.V.E. Fellow of the Institution of Heating and Ventilating Engineers

F.I.I. Fellow of the Imperial Institute, *also*, F.I.Inst.

F.I.I.A. Fellow of the Indian Institute of Architects; Fellow of the Institute of Industrial Administration

F.I.I.G. Fr. *Fédération des institutions internationales semi-officielles et privées établiés à Genève*, Fed. of Semi-Official and Intern. Private Institutions Established in Geneva

F.I.I.M. Fellow of the Institute of Industrial Managers

F.I.I.P. Fellow of the Institute of Incorporated Photographers

F.I.I.Tech. Fellow of the Institute of Industrial Technicians

F.I.J. Fr. *Fédération internationale des journalistes*, Intern. Fed. of Journalists; Fr. *Fédération internationale de judo*, Intern. Judo Fed.

F.I.J.C. Fr. *Fédération internationale de la jeunesse catholique*, Intern. Catholic Youth Fed.

F.I.J.E.T. Fr. *Fédération internationale des journalistes et écrivains du tourisme*, Intern. Fed. of Travel Journalists and Writers

F.I.J.L. Fr. *Fédération internationale des journalistes libres de l'Europe centrale et orientale et des pays baltes et balkaniques*, Intern. Fed. of Free Journalists of Central and Eastern Europe and Baltic and Balkan Countries

FIL *Feira Internacional de Lisboa*, Intern. Fair of Lisbon

fil. filament; fillet; filter; filtrate

F.I.L. Fr. *Fédération internationale de laiterie*, Intern. Dairy Fed.; Fellow of the Institute of Linguists

F.I.L.A. Fr. *Fédération internationale de lutte amateur*, Intern. Amateur Wrestling Fed.; Fellow of the Institute of Landscape Architects

F.I.L.D.I.R. Fr. *Fédération internationale libre des déportés et internés de la résistance*, Intern. (Free) Fed. of Deportees and Resistance Internees

F.I.L.E. Fellow of the Institute of Legal Executives

F.I.L.O. first in, last out

filos. It. *filosofia*, philosophy

F.I.L.T. Fr. *Fédération internationale de lawn tennis*, Intern. Lawn Tennis Fed.

F.I.M. Fr. *Fédération internationale des musiciens*, Intern. Fed. of Musicians; *Fédération Internationale Motocycliste*, Intern. Motorcycle Fed.; Fellow of the Institute of Mining; Fellow of the Institution of Metallurgists

F.I.M.A. Fellow of the Institute of Municipal Administration (Aust.); Forging Ingot Makers' Association

F.I.M.Ent. Fellow of the Institute of Municipal Entertainment

F.I.M.F. Sp. *Federación Internacional de Medicine Física*, Intern. Fed. of Physical Medicine

F.I.M.I. Fellow of the Institute of the Motor Industry

F.I.M.I.T. Fellow of the Institute of Musical Instrument Technology

F.I.M.I.T.I.C. Fr. *Fédération internationale des mutilés et invalides du travail et des invalides civils*, Intern. Fed. of Disabled Workmen and Civilian Cripples

F.I.M.L.T. Fellow of the Institute of Medical Laboratory Technology

F.I.M.O.C. Fr. *Fédération internationale des mouvements ouvriers chrétiens*, Intern. Fed. of Christian Workers' Movements

F.I.M.P. Fr. *Fédération internationale de médecine physique*, Intern. Fed. of Physical Medicine

F.I.M.S. Fr. *Fédération internationale de médecine sportive*, Intern. Fed. of Sporting Medicine

F.I.M.T. Fellow of the Institute of the Motor Trade

F.I.M.T.A. Fellow of the Institute of Municipal Treasurers and Accountants

F.I.M.Wood T. Fellow of the Institute of Machine Woodworking Technology

fin. final; finance; financial; financier; finish

fin. L. *ad finem*, at (or near) the end; L. *finis*, the end

Fin. Finland; Finnish (*also* Finn.)

F.I.N. Fellow of the Institute of Navigation

f.i.n.a. following items not available

F.I.N.A. Fr. *Fédération internationale de natation amateur*, Intern. Amateur Swimming Fed.

F.I.N.A.T. Fr. *Fédération internation-*

ale des fabricants et transformateurs d'adhésifs et thermo-collants sur papiers et autres supports, Intern. Fed. of Manufacturers and Converters of Pressure-Sensitive and Heatseal Materials on Paper and Other Base Materials

F.Inc.S.T. Fellow of the Incorporated Society of Shorthand Teachers

Fine. fine champagne, old liqueur brandy

Finnair *Finnair Aero O/Y*, Finnish Airlines

Fin. Sec. financial secretary

FIN. SIDER It. *Societa Finanziaria Siderurgica*, Iron & Steel Financial Group

F. Inst. Fellow of the Institute/Institution; — **Arb.** F. of the Institute of Arbitrators; — **Ch.** F. of the Institute of Chiropodists; — **D.** F. of the Institute of Directors; — **F.** F. of the Institute of Fuel; — **H.E.** F. of the Institution of Highway Engineers; — **L.Ex.** F. of the Institute of Legal Executives; — **Met.** F. of the Institute of Metals; — **M.S.M.** F. of the Institute of Marketing and Sales Management; — **Nuc.E.** F. of the Institution of Nuclear Engineers; — **O.** F. of the Institute of Ophthalmic Opticians/Ophthalmology; — **O.B.** F. of the Institute of Builders; — **O.M.** F. of the Institute of Office Management; — **O.P.** F. of the Institute of Plumbing/Printing; — **O.Q.** F. of the Institute of Optometrists of Queensland (Aust.); — **O.Sc.** F. of the Institute of Optical Science; — **P.** F. of the Institute of Physics; — **P.A.** F. of the Institute of Park Administration/Practitioners in Advertising; — **P.A.Aust.** F. of the Institute of Park Administration, Australia; — **P.C.** F. of the Institute of Public Cleansing; — **Pet.** F. of the Institute of Petroleum/Petrology; — **P.H.E.** F. of the Institution of Public Health Engineers; — **P.I.** F. of the Institute of Patentees and Inventors; — **Pkg.** F. of the Institute of Packaging; — **Plant E.** F. of the Institution of Plant Engineers; — **P.M.** F. of the Institute of Personnel Management; — **P.R.** F. of the Institute of Public Relations; — **P.S.** F. of the Incorporated Phonographic Society; F. of the Institute of Private Secretaries; F. of the Photographic Society; — **Ptg.M.** F. of the Institute of Printing Management; — **Q.S.** F. of the Institute of Quantity Surveyors; — **R.E.** F. of the Institute of Radio Engineers (U.S.A.); — **R.E. (Aust.)** F. of the Institution of Radio Engineers, Australia; — **R.I.** F. of the Institution of the Rubber Industry; — **R.T.** F. of the Institute of Reprographic Technicians; — **S.** F. of the Institute of Statisticians; — **S.A.** F. of the Institute of Shops Acts Administration; — **San.E.** F. of the Institution of Sanitary Engineers, *also* F.I.S.E. *now* F.I.P.H.E.; — **S.C.** F. of the Incorporated Staff Sight-Singing College; — **S.P.** F. of the Institute of Sewage Purification; — **Struct.E.** F. of the Institution of Structural Engineers; — **S.W.** F. of the Institute of Social Welfare; — **T.** F. of the Institute of Transport; — **W.** F. of the Institute of Welding; — **W.E.** F. of the Institution of Water Engineers; — **W.M.** F. of the Institution of Works Managers; — **W.M.A.** F. of the Institute of Weights and Measures Administration; — **W.T.** F. of the Institute of Wireless Technology

f.i.o. for information only

F.I.O. Fr. *Fédération internationale d'oléi-culture*, Intern. Olive Growers' Fed.; fleet information office; food investigation organisation; free in and out, chartering term meaning that the charterer pays for cost of loading and discharging cargo. This does not include stowing/trimming, these must be expressed F.I.O. and trimmed/F.I.O. and stowed

F.I.O.C.C. Fr. *Fédération internationale des ouvriers de la chaussure et du cuir*, Intern. Shoe and Leather Workers' Fed.

F.I.O.C.E.S. Fr. *Fédération internationale des organisations de correspondances et d'échanges scolaires*, Intern. Fed. of Organizations for School Correspondence and Exchange

F.I.O.M. Fr. *Fédération internationale des ouvriers sur métaux*, Intern. Metalworkers' Fed.

F.I.O.P.P. Sp. *Federación Interamericana de Organizaciones de Periodistas Profesionales*, Inter-American Fed. of Working Newspapermen's Organisations

F.I.P. Fr. *Fédération internationale de la précontrainte*, Intern. Fed. of Prestressing; Fr. *Fédération internationale de philatélie*, Intern. Philatelic Fed.; Fr. *Fédération internationale pharmaceutique*, Intern. Pharmaceutical Fed.

F.I.P.A. Fr. *Fédération internationale des producteurs agricoles*, Intern. Fed. of Agricultural Producers

F.I.P.A.C.E. Fr. *Fédération internationale des producteurs auto-consommateurs industriels d'éléctricité*, Intern. Fed. of Industrial Producers of Electricity for Own Consumption

FIPAGO Fr. *Fédération internationale des fabricants de papiers gommés*, Intern. Fed. of Gummed Paper Manufacturers

F.I.P.E.S.O. Fr. *Fédération internationale des professeurs de l'enseignement*

secondaire officiel, Intern. Fed. of Secondary Teachers

F.I.P.J.F. Fr. *Fédération internationale des producteurs de jus de fruits*, Intern. Fed. of Fruit Juice Producers

F.I.P.M. Fr. *Fédération internationale de psychothérapie médicale*, Intern. Fed. for Medical Psychotherapy

F.I.P.P. Fr. *Fédération internationale de la presse périodique*, Intern. Periodical Press Fed.; Fr. *Fondation internationale pénale et pénitentiaire*, Intern. Penal and Penitentiary Foundation

FIPRESCI Fr. *Fédération internationale de la presse cinématographique*, Intern. Cinematographic Press Fed.

fir. firkin

f.i.r. flight information region; floating-in rate; fuel indicator reading

F.I.R. Fr. *Fédération internationale des résistants*, Intern. Fed. of Resistance Movements

F.I.R.A. Fr. *Fédération internationale de rugby amateur*, Intern. Amateur Rugby Fed.; Furniture Industry Research Association

FIRFLT First Fleet, Pacific (USN)

F.I.R.S. Fr. *Fédération Internationale de Patinage à Roulettes*, Intern. Fed. of Roller Skating, founded 1924

FIS family incomes supplement; farm improvement scheme; flight information service

fis. It. *fisica*, physics

F.I.S. Fr. *Fédération internationale de sauvetage*, Intern. Life Saving Fed.; Fr. *Fédération internationale des centres sociaux et communautaires*, Intern. Fed. of Settlements and Neighbourhood Centres; Fr. *Fédération Internationale de Ski*, Intern. Ski Fed.

F.I.S.A. Fr. *Fédération internationale des semaines d'art*, Intern. Art Weeks Fed.; Fr. *Fédération internationale des sociétés d'aviron*, Intern. Rowing Fed.; Fellow of the Incorporated Secretaries Association

F.I.S.A.I.C. Fr. *Fédération internationale des sociétés artistiques et intellectuelles de cheminots*, Intern. Fed. of Railwaymen's Art and Intellectual Socs.

F.I.S.C.C. Fruit Industry Sugar Concession Committee (Aust.)

F.I.S.C.E.T.C.V. Fr. *Fédération internationale des syndicats chrétiens d'employés, techniciens, cadres et voyageurs de commerce*, Intern. Fed. of Christian Trade Unions of Salaried Employees, Technicians, Managerial Staff and Commercial Travellers

F.I.S.C.M. Fr. *Fédération internationale des syndicats chrétiens de la métallurgie*,

Intern. Fed. of Christian Metalworkers' Unions

F.I.S.C.O.A. Fr. *Fédération internationale des syndicats chrétiens d'ouvriers agricoles*, Intern. Fed. of Christian Agricultural Workers' Unions

F.I.S.C.O.B.B. Fr. *Fédération internationale des syndicats chrétiens d'ouvriers du bâtiment et du bois*, Intern. Fed. of Christian Trade Unions of Building and Wood Workers

F.I.S.C.T.T.H. Fr. *Fédération internationale des syndicats chrétiens des travailleurs du textile et de l'habillement*, Intern. Fed. of Christian Trade Unions of Textile and Garment Workers

F.I.S.D. Fr. *Fédération internationale de sténographie et de dactylographie*, Intern. Fed. of Shorthand and Typewriting

F.I.S.E. Fr. *Fédération internationale syndicale de l'enseignement*, World Fed. of Teachers' Unions; Fr. *Fonds des Nations Unies pour l'enfance*, United Nations Children's Fund

F.I.S.E.M. Fr. *Fédération internationale des sociétés d'écrivains médecins*, Intern. Fed. of Doctor-Authors

fish. fishery; fishes; fishing

F.I.S.I.T.A. Fr. *Fédération internationale des sociétés d'ingénieurs des techniques de l'automobile*, Intern. Fed. of Automobile Engineers' and Technicians' Assns.

F.I.S.P. Fr. *Fédération internationale des sociétés de philosophie*, Intern. Fed. of Philosophical Socs.

F.I.S.U. Fr. *Fédération internationale du sport universitaire*, Intern. Univ. Sports Fed.

f.i.t. fabrication in transit; free in truck; free of tax

F.I.T. Federal Income Tax (U.S.A.); Fr. *Fédération Internationale des Traducteurs*, Intern. Fed. of Translators

F.I.T.A. Fr. *Fédération internationale de tir à l'arc*, Intern. Fed. for Archery

F.I.T.B.B. Fr. *Fédération internationale des travailleurs du bâtiment et du bois*, Intern. Fed. of Building and Woodworkers

F.I.T.C.E. Fr. *Fédération des ingénieurs des télécommunications de la communauté européenne*, Fed. of Telecommunications Engineers in the European Community

F.I.T.E.C. Fr. *Fédération internationale du thermalisme et du climatisme*, Intern. Fed. of Thermalism and Climatism

F.I.T.I.M. Sp. *Federación Internacional de Trabajadores de las Industrias Metalurgicas*, Intern. Metalworkers' Fed.

F.I.T.P. Fr. *Fédération internationale des travailleurs du pétrole*, Intern. Fed. of Petroleum Workers

F.I.T.P.A.S.C. Fr. *Fédération internationale des travailleurs des plantations, de l'agriculture et des secteurs connexes*, Intern. Fed. of Plantation, Agricultural and Allied Workers

F.I.T.T. Fr. *Fédération internationale de tennis de table*, Intern. Table Tennis Fed.

f.i.t.w. federal income tax withholding (U.S.A.)

Fitzw. Fitzwilliam College, Cambridge, founded 1966

F.I.V.B. Fr. *Fédération internationale de volley-ball*, Intern. Volley-Ball Fed.

F.I.V.Z. Fr. *Fédération internationale vétérinaire de zootechnie*, Intern. Veterinary Fed. of Zootechnics

f.i.w. free in wagon

FIWC Fiji Industrial Workers' Congress

fix. fixture

FJ *s* Exeter (B.V.R.)

Fj., Fjd. fjord

F.J.A. Future Journalists of America

F.J.I. Fellow of the Institute of Journalists

FK *s* Worcester (B.V.R.)

fk. fork

f.k. flat keel

Fk. Frank

F.K.C. Fellow of King's College, London

Fkn. Franklin

F.K.Q.C.P.I. Fellow of the King's and Queen's College of Physicians, Ireland, *now* F.R.C.P.I.

FKTU Federation of Korean Trade Unions, *Tai-Han No-Tong Cho-Hap Ch'ong-Yon Hap Maeng*

fL foot-lambert

FL Florida, U.S.A. (*also* Fla., Flor.); *s* Huntingdon (B.V.R.); *s* Liechtenstein (I.V.R.); *s* pressure loss due to friction, water pumping

fl. floor; florin; flourish; fluid; Port. *folha*, sheet; gulden

fl. It. *flauto*, flute (mus.); L. *flores*, flowers; L. *floruit*, flourished (*also flor.*)

Fl. Flanders; Flemish (*also* Flem.); Fr. *fleuve*, river

Fl. flute (mus.)

f.l. L. *falsa lectio*, false reading

F.L. flag/flight lieutenant; football league; *Furstentum Liechtenstein*, Principality of Liechtenstein

F.L.A. Fellow of the Library Association; Film Laboratory Association

F.L.A. L. *fiat lege artis*, let it be done by rules of the art

F.L.A.A. Fellow of Library Association of Australia

flag. *flageolet*, small flute (mus.)

flak Ger. *flugzeugabwehrkanone*, anti-aircraft gunfire

Flan blank, unminted coin (numis.)

F.L.A.S. Fellow of the Land Agents' Society

F.L.C.M. Fellow of London College of Music

F.L.C.O. Fellow of the London College of Osteopathy

fld. field

F.L.D. Friends of the Lake District

fldg. folding

FLEA flux logic element array

flex. flexible

flexo. flexographic

flg. flagging; flooring; flying; following

F.L.G.A. Fellow of the Local Government Association

F.L.I. Fr. *Fédération lainière internationale*, Intern. Wool Textile Organization

FLING Fr. *Front de Lutte pour l'Indépendance de la Guinée*, Nat. Independence Front (Port. Guinea)

Flint. Flintshire

FLIP floating instrument platform (USN)

Flli. It. *fratelli*, brothers

F.L.M. Fr. *Fédération luthérienne mondiale*, Lutheran World Fed.

f.l.n. following landing numbers

F.L.N. Fr. *Front de Libération Nationale*, Nat. Liberation Front, Algeria. Founded 1 November 1954, and dedicated to socialism, nonalignment, and pan-Arabism, the F.L.N. successfully conducted the war of independence against France

Flo Flora (*also* Florrie, Floss, Flossie); Florence

F.L.O.A.G. Front for the Liberation of the Occupied Arabian Gulf

FLOOD fleet observation of oceanographic data (U.S.A.)

Flor. Florence; Florentine; Florida (U.S.A.)

FLOSY Front for the Liberation of Occupied South of Yemen, Southern Yemen

Fl.oz. fluid ounce

f.l.p. fault location panel

fl.pl. L. *flore pleno*, with double flowers (hort.)

flr. florin

F.L.R. *Fiji Law Reports*

flrg. flooring

fl.rt. flow rate

F.L.S. *Fraternitatis Linnaei Socius*, Fellow of the Linnean Soc.

FLSA Fair Labor Standards Act (U.S.A.)

Flst. *flautist* (mus.)

Flt. flight

F/Lt., F. Lt., Flt. Lt., Ft.-Lieut. Flight Lieutenant

Flt. Comdr. Flight Commander

fltg. floating

FLTPR Sp. *Federación Libre de los Trabajadores de Puerto Rico*, Free Fed. of Workers of Puerto Rico

Flt. Sgt. Flight Sergeant

flu influenza

fluc. fluctuant; fluctuate; fluctuation

FLUG *Flugfelag Islands*, Icelandic Airways

fluor. fluorescent; fluoridation; fluoride; fluorspar

fly. flyweight (boxing)

Fm *s* fermium (chem.)

F/m *s* unit of permittivity

FM *s* Chester (B.V.R.)

F & M, F.M.D. foot and mouth disease

fm. farm; farmer; fathom; from

f.m. face/facial measurement; fine measure/measurement; frequency modulation; Fr. *femmes mariées*, married women

f.m. L. *fiat mistura*, let a mixture be made (med.)

F.m. facing matter (advert.)

F.M. field magnet (elec.); Field-Marshal; flight mechanic; foreign mission; Fr. *fraternité mondiale*, world brotherhood; free mason; Friars Minor

F.M. L. *Fraternitas Medicorum*, Fraternity of Physicians

F.M.A. Fan/Fertilizer/File/Forging Manufacturers' Association; Farm Management Association; Fellow of the Museums Association; Food Machinery Association

F.M.A.C. Fr. *Fédération mondiale des anciens combattants*, World Veterans' Fed.

fman. foreman

F.M.A.N.U. Fr. *Fédération mondiale des associations pour les Nations Unies*, World Fed. of United Nations Assns.

F.M.A.O. Farm Machinery Advisory Officer

FMAS Foreign Marriage Advisory Service

FMB Farmers' Marketing Board (Malawi); Federal Maritime Board (U.S.A.)

F.M.B. Federation of Master Builders

F.M.B.R.A. Flour Milling and Baking Research Association

F.M.C. Fatstock Marketing Corporation; Federal Maritime Commission (U.S.A.); Forces Motoring Club; Ford

Motor Company; Fr. *Section des fleuristes du marché commun de la fédération européenne des unions professionelles de fleuristes*, Common Market Florists' Section of the Fed. of European Professional Florists

F.M.C.E. Sp. *Federación Mundial Cristiana de Estudiantes*, World Student Christian Fed.; Federation of Manufacturers of Construction Equipment

F.M.C.P. Federation of Manufacturers of Contractors' Plant

F.M.C.S. Federal Mediation and Conciliation Services (U.S.A.)

FMCW frequency modulated continuous wave

fmd. formed

FMF fleet marine force

F.M.F. Food Manufacturers' Federation

FMFPAC Fleet Marine Forces, Pacific (U.S.A.)

FMG Malagasy franc (currency)

F.M.G. Federal Military Government (Nigeria)

F.M.I. Fellow of the Motor Industry

F.M.I. L. *Filii Mariae Immaculatae*, Sons of Mary Immaculate

F.M.I.G. Food Manufacturers' Industrial Group

F.M.J.D. Fr. *Fédération mondiale de la jeunesse démocratique*, World Fed. of Democratic Youth

F.M.J.F.C. Fr. *Fédération mondiale des jeunesses féminines catholiques*, World Fed. of Youth Catholic Women and Girls

Fmk. Finnmark (Nor.); Finnish Markka (currency)

fmn. formation

F.M.N. Fr. *Fédération Motocycliste Nationale*, a national organization recognized as the sole governing body for motorcycling in its own territory

F.M.O. fleet/flight medical officer

F.M.P.A. Fr. *Fédération mondiale pour la protection des animaux*, World Fed. for the Protection of Animals; Fellow of the Master Photographers Association

F.M.P.E. Federation of Master Process Engravers, now Graphic Reproduction Federation

fmr. former

fmrly. formerly

F.M.R.S. Foreign Member of the Royal Society

F.M.S. Federated Malay States, formed 1895, joined the Union of Malaya 1946; Fr. *Fédération mondiale des sourds*, World Fed. of the Deaf; Fellow of the Medical Society

F.M.S.M. Fr. *Fédération mondiale*

pour la santé mentale, World Fed. for Mental Health

F.M.T.A. Farm Machinery and Tractor Trade Association of New South Wales

FMTS field maintenance test station

F.M.T.S. Fr. *Fédération mondiale des travailleurs scientifiques*, World Fed. of Scientific Workers

F.M.V.J. Fr. *Fédération mondiale des villes jumelées*, United Towns Organization

FMVSS Federal Motor Vehicle Safety Standards (U.S.A.)

FN *s* Canterbury (B.V.R.)

f.n. footnote

f.n.a. for necessary action

F.N.A. French North Africa

F.N.A.A. Fellow of the National Association of Auctioneers, Rating Surveyors and Valuers (S. Afr.)

F.N.A.F.U. Fr. *Fonds National d'Aménagement Foncier et d'Urbanisme*, National Land Development and Town Planning Fund

F.N.C.B. First National City Bank (U.S.A.)

fnd. found; foundered

fndr. founder

fndry. foundry

fne. fine

F.N.E.C.Inst. Fellow of the North East Coast Institution of Engineers and Shipbuilders

F.N.F. flying needle frame

F.N.F.H.F.T.M. Federation of Needle, Fish Hook and Fishing Tackle Makers

F.N.I. Fr. *Fédération naturiste internationale*, Intern. Naturist Fed.; Fellow of the National Institute of Sciences in India

F.N.I.E. *Fédération Nationale des Industries Électriques*, Nat. Fed. of Electrical Industries (France)

F.N.I.L.P. Fellow of the National Institute of Licensing Practitioners

F.N.L. Friends of the National Libraries

FNMA Federal National Mortgage Association (U.S.A.)

F.N.O. fleet navigation officer

F.N.U. Fr. *Fonds des Nations Unies pour les réfugiés*, United Nations Refugee Fund; Fr. *Forces des Nations Unies*, United Nations Forces

F.N.W.C. Fleet Numerical Weather Center (U.S.A.)

F.N.Z.I.A. Fellow of the New Zealand Institute of Architects

F.N.Z.I.C. Fellow of the New Zealand Institute of Chemistry

F.N.Z.I.E. Fellow of the New Zealand Institution of Engineers

F.N.Z.I.M. Fellow of the New Zealand Institute of Management

F.N.Z.L.A. Fellow of the New Zealand Library Association

F.N.Z.S.A. Fellow of the New Zealand Society of Accountants

F/o full out terms (grain trade)

F/O, F.O. Flying Officer

FO *s* Radnorshire (B.V.R.)

fo. It. *firmato*, signed; folio

f/o. for orders; full out

f.o. fast operating; firm offer; for orders; free overside; fuel oil

F.O. federal official; field/first/flag officer; Foreign Office, *now* F.C.O.; formal offer, to shareholders in business mergers

F.O., F. Org. *full organ* (mus.)

f.o.b. free on board, (1.) tramp trade, charterers pay for cost of loading cargo but not trimming/stowing (F.O.B. and trimmed/stowed); (2.) contract of sale, seller of goods is responsible for charges on the goods until they are placed on board the exporting vessel; fuel on board

F.O.B.F.O. Federation of British Fire Organisations

FOBS fractional orbital ballistic/bombardment system

FOBTSU forward observer target survey unit

FOC Fire Offices Committee (insce.)

f.o.c. free of charge

F.O.C. Father of the Chapel (printing trade union local body)

F.O.C.A.P. Sp. *Federación Odontológica Centro América Panama*, Odontological Fed. of Central America and Panama

F.O.C.O.L. Federation of Coin-Operated Launderettes

fo'c's'le forecastle (naut.)

F.O.C.T. flag officer carrier training

f.o.d. free of damage

F.O.E. Fraternal Order of Eagles

F.O.F.A.T.U.S.A. Federation of Free African Trade Unions of South Africa

F. of F. Firth of Forth (Scot.)

F.O.H. front of house

F.O.I.C. flag officer in charge

fol. folio; follow; following

F.O.O. forward observation officer

F.O.P. forward observation post

f.o.q. free on quay

FOR flying objects research

for. foreign; foreigner; forensic; forest; forester; forestry

For. forint, Hungarian currency

For. *forte*, loud (mus.)

f.o.r. free on rail, selling term which includes all costs of transporting the goods to railway station named up to loading into rail wagons

F.O.R. Fellowship of Reconciliation

'fore before

FORATOM Fr. *Forum atomique euro-péen*, European Atomic Forum

formn. foreman; formation

for.rts. foreign rights

for's'l. foresail (naut.)

fort. fortification; fortify

f.o.r.t. full out rye terms

FORTRAN formula translation, computer programming algebraic language; formula translator

Forts. Ger. *Fortsetzung*, continuation

fort. tn. fortified town

forz. forzando (mus.)

f.o.s. free of stamp (fin.); free on station/steamer

F.O.S. Fisheries Organization Society

FOSDIC film optical sensing device (computer)

f.o.t. free of tax (fin.); free on trucks, selling term which includes all costs of transporting the goods to railway station named up to loading into rail wagons

Found. foundation; foundry

f.o.w. first open water, usually refers to ice bound ports and abbrev. appears in timber freight quotations; free on wagon

FP *s* Rutland (B.V.R.)

F/P fire policy (insce.)

fp. fireplace; foolscap

Fp. frontispiece

f.p. fine paper; fixed price; flame-proof; flash-point; footpath; foot pound; forward pass; freezing-point; full point

f.p. L. *fiat pilula*, let a pill be made (med.); *forte piano*, loud and then immediately soft (mus.)

F.p. fully paid (fin.)

F.P. Federal Parliament; field punishment; fire-plug; floating/open policy (insce.); former pupil; fowl pest; Free Presbyterian; fresh paragraph

f.p.a. free of particular average, insurers/underwriters are not responsible for partial loss claims (insce.)

F.P.A. Family Planning Association; Film Production Association of Great Britain; Fire Protection Association; first point of Aries; Foreign Press Association

F.P.A.N.Z. Fellow Public Accountant Member of the New Zealand Society of Accountants

F.P.A.S. Fellow of the Pakistan Academy of Sciences

F.P.B.A.I. Federation of Publishers' and Booksellers' Associations in India

FPC fish protein concentrate

f.p.c. for private circulation

F.P.C. Federal Power Commission (U.S.A.); Federation of Painting Contractors; Flowers Publicity Council

F.P.C.E.A. Fibreboard Packing Case Employers' Association

F.P.C.M.A. Fibreboard Packing Case Manufacturers' Association

F.P.D.A. Finnish Plywood Development Association

F.P.F. *Federação Portuguesa de Futebol*, Portuguese Football Fed.

F.Pharm.S. Fellow of the Pharmaceutical Society of Great Britain

F.Ph.S. Fellow of the Philosophical Society of England

F.Phy.S. Fellow of the Physical Society

F.P.I. Federal Prison Industries (U.S.A.); Fr. *Fédération prohibitionniste internationale*, World Prohibition Fed.; Fellow of the Plastics Institute

F.P.I.S. forward propagation ionosphere scatter

FPL Forest Products Laboratory (U.S.A.)

f.p.m. feet per minute

FPMR Federal Property Management Regulation (U.S.A.)

F.P.O. field post office; fire prevention officer; fleet post office (USN)

F.P.R.C. Flying Personnel Research Committee

F.P.R.L. Forest Products Research Laboratory

f.p.s. feet/foot/frames per second; foot-pound-second

F.P.S. Fauna Preservation Society; Fellow of the Pharmaceutical/Philharmonic/Philological/Philosophical/Physical Society; Fluid Power Society (U.S.A.)

F.P.S.L. Fellow of the Physical Society, London

f.p.s.p.s. feet per second per second

F.P.T. fixed price tenders; fore peak tank

FPTS forward propagation tropospheric scatter

F.P.T.S. forward propagation troposphere scatter

f.q. fiscal quarter

F.Q. *Faerie Queene* by Edmund Spencer (*c* 1552–1599), Eng. poet

F.Q.O. Federation Quarry Owners of Great Britain

FQS Federal Quarantine Service (U.S.A.)

Fr *s* francium (chem.)

FR *s* Blackpool (B.V.R.); *s* Fraserburgh, Scot. (B.F.P.); frequency rate, number of lost-time injury accidents per 100,000 man/hours worked

fr. fragments; frame; franc; free; Ger. *frei*, free; frequent; from; front

Fr. Father; France; It. *fratelli*, brothers; Ger. *Frau*, Mrs./wife; French; Friar; Friday

f.r. L. *folio recto*, right hand page

F.R. Federal Republic; fine rim (buttons); freight release

F.R. L. *Forum Romanum*, the Roman Forum

Fra It. *frate*, brother, title given to friar/monk

F.R. Fellow of the Royal; — **A.C.I.** F. of the Royal Australian Chemical Institute; — **A.C.P.** F. of the Royal Australasian College of Physicians; — **A.C.S.** F. of the Royal Australasian College of Surgeons; — **A.D.** F. of the Royal Academy of Dancing; — **Ae.S.** F. of the Royal Aeronautical Society;—**Ag. S.** F. of the Royal Agricultural Societies;—**A.H.S.** F. of the Royal Australian Historical Society; — **A.I.** F. of the Royal Anthropological Institute; — **A.I.A.** F. of the Royal Australian Institute of Architects; — **A.I.C.** F. of the Royal Architectural Institute of Canada; — **A.M.** F. of the Royal Academy of Music; — **A.S.** F. of the Royal Asiatic/Astronomical Society; — **B.S.** F. of the Royal Botanic Society; F. of the Royal Society of British Sculptors; — **C.A.** F. of the Royal College of Art; — **C.I.** F. of the Royal Colonial Institute (*now* R.C.S.); — **C.M.** F. of the Royal College of Music; — **C.O.** F. of the Royal College of Organists; **F.R.C.O. (Ch.M.)** F. of the Royal College of Organists with Diploma of Choir Mastership); — **C.O.G.** F. of the Royal College of Obstetricians and Gynaecologists (*formerly* F.C.O.G.); — **C.P.** F. of the Royal College of Physicians, London; — **C.Path.** F. of the Royal College of Pathologists; — **C.P.Can.** F. of the Royal College of Physicians of Canada; — **C.P.E.** F. of the Royal College of Physicians of Edinburgh; — **C.P.Ed.** F. of the Royal College of Physicians, Edinburgh; — **C.P.Glas.** F. of the Royal College of Physicians and Surgeons of Glasgow; — **C.P.I.** F. of the Royal College of Physicians of Ireland; — **C.S.** F. of the Royal College of Surgeons, England; F. of the Royal Commonwealth Society; — **C.S.Can.** F. of the Royal College of Surgeons of Canada; — **C.Sc.I.** F. of the Royal College of Science, Ireland; — **C.S.E., C.S.Ed.** F. of the Royal College of Surgeons of Edinburgh; — **C.S.Glas.** F. of the Royal College of Physicians and Surgeons of Glasgow; — **C.S.I.** F. of the Royal College of Surgeons of Ireland; — **C.S.L.** F. of the Royal College of Surgeons of London; — **C.V.S.** F. of the Royal College of Veterinary Surgeons; — **Econ.S.** F. of the Royal Economic Society (*now* ceased); — **Ent.S.** F. of the Royal Entomological Society; — **E.S.** F. of the Royal Empire Society (*now* R.C.S.); — **E.S.** F. of the Royal Entomological Society of London; — **F.P.S.G., F.P.S.Glas.** F. of the Royal Faculty of Physicians and Surgeons of Glasgow; — **G.S.** F. of the Royal Geographical Society; — **Hist.S.** F. of the Royal Historical Society; — **H.S.** F. of the Royal Horticultural Society; — **I.** F. of the Royal Institution; — **I.A.** F. of the Royal Irish Academy; — **I.A.I.** F. of the Royal Institute of Architects of Ireland; — **I.A.S.** F. of the Royal Institute of Architects in Scotland; — **I.B.A.** F. of the Royal Institute of British Architects; — **I.C.** F. of the Royal Institute of Chemistry; — **I.C.S.** F. of the Royal Institution of Chartered Surveyors; — **I.I.A.** F. of the Royal Institute of International Affairs; — **I.N.A.** F. of the Royal Institution of Naval Architects; — **I.P.A.** F. of the Royal Institute of Public Administration; — **I.P.H.H.** F. of the Royal Institute of Public Health and Hygiene; — **M.C.M.** F. of the Royal Manchester College of Music; — **M.C.S.** F. of the Royal Medical and Chirurgical Society; — **Met.S.** F. of the Royal Meteorological Society; — **M.I.T.** F. of the Royal Melbourne Institute of Technology (Aust.); — **M.S.** F. of the Royal Microscopical Society; — **N.S.** F. of the Royal Numismatic Society; — **N.S.A.** F. of the Royal Navy School of Architects; — **N.Z.I.H.** F. of the Royal New Zealand Institute of Horticulture; — **P.S.** F. of the Royal Photographic Society; — **P.S.L.** F. of the Royal Philatelic Society, London; — **S.** F. of the Royal Society, Royal Society of Lond. for Promoting Natural Knowledge, the oldest scientific soc. in Britain; — **S.A.** F. of the Royal Society for the Encouragement of the Arts, Manufs. and Commerce, founded 1754; — **S.A.I.** F. of the Royal Society of Antiquaries of Ireland; — **San.I.** F. of the Royal Sanitary Institute, *now* F.R.S.H.; — **S.C., S.Can.** F. of the Royal Society of Canada; — **S.E.** F. of the Royal Society of Edinburgh; — **S.G.S.** F. of the Royal Scottish Geographical Society; — **S.H.** F. of the Royal Society for the Promotion of Health; — **S.L.** F. of the Royal Society of Literature; — **S.M.** F. of the Royal Society of Medicine; — **S.N.A.** F. of the Royal School of

Naval Architecture; — **S.N.Z.** F. of the Royal Society of New Zealand; — **S.S.** F. of the Royal Statistical Society (*also* F.S.S.); — **S.S.A.** F. of the Royal Scottish Society of Arts; F. of the Royal Society South Africa; — **S.(S.A.)** F. of the Royal Society of South Africa; — **S.S.I.** F. of the Royal Statistical Society of Ireland; — **S.S.S.** F. of the Royal Statistical Society of Scotland; — **S.T.M. & H.** F. of the Royal Society of Tropical Medicine and Hygiene; — **V.I.A.** F. of the Royal Victorian Institute of Architects; — **Z.S.(N.S.W.)** F. of the Royal Zoological Society of New South Wales; — **Z.S.(Scot.)** F. of the Royal Zoological Society of Scotland

FRAM fleet rehabilitation and modernisation program (USN)

FRAME Fund for the Replacement of Animals in Medical Experiments

Fran Frances

Franc. Franciscan (rel. order)

Frank Francis

Frank. Frankish

F.R.A.N.Z. Fellow Registered Accountant Member of the New Zealand Society of Accountants

FRAP *Frente de Acción Popular*, Popular Action Front (Chile)

frat college fraternity

F.R.A.T.E. formulae for routes and technical equipment (rail.)

fratting fraternizing

fraud. fraudulent

FRB Sp. *Frente de la Revolución Boliviana*, Bolivian Revolutionary Front

F.R.B. Federal Reserve Bank/Board (U.S.A.); Fisheries Research Board of Canada

FRC flight research center (U.S.A.)

F.R.C. Federal Radiation Council (U.S.A.); Federal Radio Commission (U.S.A.); Flight Research Center (NASA)

F.R.C.A.B. Felt Roofing Contractors' Advisory Board

Fr.-Can. French-Canadian

f.r. & c.c. free of riots and civil commotions (insce.)

FRCS Federation of Rabbit Clearance Societies

frd. friend

F.R.Dist. Federal Reserve District (U.S.A.)

fre. Fr. *fracture*, invoice

Fre. Ger. *Freitag*, Friday; French

Fred, Freddie, Freddy Alfred; Frederic; Frederick; Frederik; Wilfred

F.R.E.D. Fast Reactor Experiment, Dounreay; figure reading electronic device

Freda Winifred

Fredk. Frederick; Frederik

Free. freeway

F.R.E.I. Fellow of the Real Estate and Stock Institute of Australia

FRELIMO *Frente de Libertação de Mozambique*, Mozambique Liberation Front

freq. frequency; frequent; frequentative; frequently

Fr.Eq.A. French Equatorial Africa

FRESH foil research hydrofoil

Fr.G. French Guiana

F.R.G. Federal Republic of Germany (W. Ger.)

frgt. freight

F.R.H.B. Federation of Registered House Builders

Frhr. Ger. *Freiherr*, Baron

Fri. Fribourg (Switz.); Friday

F.R.I. Fellow of the Institute of Realtors (Can.); Food Research Institute

fric., frict. friction; frictional

fridge refrigerator

Fris. Friesland; Frisia; Frisian

'Frisco San Francisco

frk. Swed. *fröken*, Miss

Frk. Dan./Nor. *Frøken*, Miss

Frl. Ger. *Fräulein*, Miss

frld. foreland; freehold

frm. from

F.R.M.A. Floor Rug Manufacturers' Association

F.R.O. Fellow of the Register of Osteopaths; Fire Research Organisation

f.r.o.f. fire risk on freight (insce.)

FROLINAT *Front de Libération Nationale Tchadienne*, Chad National Liberation Front

Frolizi Front for the Liberation of Zimbabwe

front., frontis. frontispiece

frpf. fireproof

Frs. Frisian

F.R.S. Federal Reserve System (U.S.A.); Festiniog Railway Society; fuel research station

Fr.S. French Somaliland, *now* French Territory of the Afars and the Issas

frt. freight; —/**fwd.** freight forward; —/**ppd.** freight prepaid

FRUCOM Fr. *Fédération européenne des importateurs de fruits sec, conserves, épices et miels*, European Fed. of Importers of Dried Fruits, Preserves, Spices and Honey

frum. L. *fratrum*, of the brothers

frust. L. *frustillatim*, in small portions

F.R.V.A. Fellow of the Incorporated Association of Rating and Valuation Officers

frwk. framework

frwy., fry. freeway

fs *s* low fog over sea, coast stations only (met.)

FS *s* Edinburgh (B.V.R.); Forest Service (U.S.A.)

fs. facsimile

f.s. factor of safety; Fr. *faire suivre*, please forward; far side; film strip; fire station; flight service; flying saucer/status; foot-second

F.S. Fabian Society, Eng. socialist society founded 1883 and named from E. Fabius Maximus (dictator 217 B.C.); Faraday Society; feasibility study; *Ferrovie dello Stato*, Italian State Railway (*also* F.de.S.); field security; financial secretary/statement; fleet surgeon; flight-sergeant; foreign service; Friendly Society (insce.)

FSA Federal Security Agency (U.S.A.); foreign service allowance

f.s.a. fuel storage area

F.S.A. Farm/Federal Security Administration (U.S.A.); Fellow of the Society of Antiquaries; Field Survey Association; Flax Spinners' Association; Friendly Societies Act

F.S.A.A. Fellow of the Society of Incorporated Accountants and Auditors, *now* amal. with Chartered Accountants

F.S.A.G. Fellow of the Society of Australian Genealogists

F.S.A.L. Fellow of the Society of Antiquaries of London, *usually* F.S.A.

F.S.A.L.A. Fellow of the South African Library Association

F.S.A.O. Fellowship Diploma of the Scottish Association of Opticians

F.S.Arc. Fellow of the Society of Architects, *now* F.R.I.B.A.

F.S.A.S., F.S.A.Scot. Fellow of the Society of Antiquaries of Scotland

F.S.A.Scot. Fellow of the Society of Arts of Scotland

F.S.A.S.M. Fellow of the South Australian School of Mines

F.S.C. Federal Supreme Court (U.S.A.); Fellow of the Society of Chiropodists; Field Studies Council; Friends Service Council

F.S.C. L. *Fratres Scholarum Christianorum*, Brothers of the Christian Schools (Christian Brothers)

F.S.C.G. It. *Figli del Sacro Cuore de Gesù*, Sons of the Sacred Heart of Jesus (Verona Fathers)

FSCT Floyd satellite communications terminal

F.S.D.C. Fellow of the Society of Dyers and Colourists

FSE field support equipment

F.S.E. Fellow of the Society of Engineers

F.S.F. Fellow of the Institute of Shipping and Forwarding Agents

F.S.F.A. Federation of Specialised Film Associations

F.S.G. Fellow of the Society of Genealogists

F.Sgt. flight sergeant

F.S.G.T. Fellow of the Society of Glass Technology

F.S.H. follicle-stimulating hormone (biol.)

F.S.H.M. Fellow of the Society of Housing Managers

FSI federal stock item

F.S.I. Federation of Sussex Industries; Fr. *Fédération spirite internationale*, Intern. Spiritualist Fed.; Fellow of the Surveyors' Institution; Free Sons of Israel

F.S.I.A. Fellow of the Society of Industrial Artists

F.S.K. frequency-shift keying

F.S.L. First Sea Lord

F.S.M. Fr. *Fédération syndicale mondiale*, World Fed. of Trade Unions; flying spot microscope; Free Speech Movement (U.S.A.)

F.S.M.C. Diploma in Ophthalmic Optics of the Worshipful Company of Spectacle-Makers; Freeman of the Worshipful Company of Spectacle-makers

FS Method Federal Standard Method

FSN federal stock number

F.S.N.A. Fellow of the Society of Naval Architects

F.S.O. field security officer; fleet signals officers

F.S.P. field security police; foreign service pay

F.S.P.B. field service pocket book

F.S.P.T. Federation of Societies for Paint Technology

FSR *Fleet Street Patent Law Reports*

F.S.R. field service regulations

FSS Fr. *Front des Forces Socialistes*, Socialist Forces Front, Algeria

F.S.S. Fellow of the Royal Statistical Society

F.S.S.I. Fellow of the Statistical Society of Ireland

F.S.S.U. Federated Superannuation Scheme for Universities

F.S.T.D. Fellow of the Society of Typographic Designers

F.S.U. family service unit

F.S.U.C. Federal Statistics Unit Conference

FSUEO Fr. *Fédération des Syndicats Unis des Employés et Ouvriers du Liban*, United Unions for Employees and Workers, Lebanon (*alt.* UUEW)

F.S.V.A. Fellow of the Incorporated Society of Valuers and Auctioneers

f.s.w. completed satisfactorily a short war course at R.A.F. Staff College

FT *s* Tynemouth (B.V.R.)

ft. feet (ft.^{2} square feet/ft.^{3} cubic feet); feint; flat (paper); foot (ft.^{2} square foot/ft.^{3} cubic foot); fort; fortification; fortify

ft. L. *fiat*, let there be made (med.)

f.t. formal training; full terms

f. & t. fire and theft (insce.)

F.T. *Financial Times*

F.T.A. Freight Transport Association; Future Teachers of America

F.T.A. (Index) Financial Times Actuaries Index

F.T.B. fleet torpedo bomber

FT black fine thermal black, filler in rubber compounding

ftbrg. footbridge

FTC fast time constant; Federal Trade Commission (U.S.A.); flight test center (U.S.A.)

ft.-c. foot-candle

F.T.C. flying training command; Full Technological Certificate of City & Guilds of London Institute

F.T.C.D. Fellow of Trinity College, Dublin

F.T.C.L. Fellow of Trinity College of Music, London

FTD foreign technology division

F.T.D.A. Fellow of the Theatrical Designers' and Craftsmen's Association

F.T.D.C. Fellow of the Society of Typographic Designers of Canada

F.T.E.S.A. Foundry Trades Equipment and Supplies Association

FTG Fuji Texaco Gas

ftg. fitting

fth., fthm. fathom

ft./hr. foot per hour

F.T.I. Fellow of the Textile Institute

F.T.I.I. Fellow of the Taxation Institute Incorporated

F.T. (Index) Financial Times Industrial Ordinary Share Index

F.T.I.T. Fellow of the Institute of Taxation

ft.lb. foot-pound

ft.lb.f. foot-pound-force

F.T.M. flying training manual

ft.mist. L. *fiat mistura*, let a mixture be made (med.)

F.T.O. Fleet Torpedo Officer

f. to f. face to face

F.T.P.A. Fellow of the Town and Country Planning Association

FTPR Sp. *Féderación del Trabajo de Puerto Rico*, Fed. of Labor of Puerto Rico

ft.pulv. L. *fiat pulvis*, let a powder be made (med.)

ft./s. feet/foot per second

ft./s.^{2} feet/foot per second squared

ft.^{3}/s. cubic feet per second

F.T.S. Fellow of the Television Society; flying training school

F.T.S.C. Fellow of Tonic Sol-Fa College

ft. sec. foot second

fttr. fitter

F.T.U. Federation of Trade Unions (Hong Kong)

FTUC The Trade Union Congress of the Federation of Rhodesia and Nyasaland

F.T.W. free trade wharf

FU feed unit; *Freie Universität*, Free Univ., Berlin; *s* Lincolnshire, Lindsey (B.V.R.)

F.U. Farmers' Union; Freeman time-unit, *also* F.T.U. (photo.)

F.U.A.C.E. Fr. *Fédération universelle des associations chrétiennes d'étudiants*, World Student Christian Fed.

F.U.E.N. Federal Union of European Nationalities

F.U.E.V. Ger. *Föderalistische Union Europäischer Volksgruppen*, Federal Union of European Nationalities

FUGE Federation of Unions of Government Employees (Guyana)

fund. fundamental

FUNDWI Fund of the United Nations for the Development of West Irian

FUNK Fr. *Front Uni National du Kampuchea*, Khmer Nat. United Front (Cambodia/Khmer)

F.U.N.U. Fr. *Force d'urgence de Nations Unies*, United Nations Emergency Force

fur. furlong; further

furn. furnace; furnish; furniture

FUS *Frontul Unităţii Socialiste*, Front of Socialist Unity, Romania

fus. fuselage; fusilier

F.u.S.f. Ger. *Fortsezung und Schluss folgen*, to be continued and concluded

fut. future

F.U.W. Farmers' Union of Wales

FV *s* Blackpool (B.V.R.)

f.v. fire vent; flush valve

f.v. L. *folio verso*, on the back of the sheet

F.V.A. Fellow of the Valuers' Association

F.V.C.Q.F.R.A. Fruit and Vegetable Canning and Quick Freezing Research Association

F.V.D.E. Fighting Vehicles Design Establishment

F.V.I. Fellow of the Valuers' Institution

F.V.P.R.A. Fruit and Vegetable Preservation Research Association

FVRDE Fighting Vehicles Research and Development Establishment

FW *s* Lincolnshire, Lindsey (B.V.R.)

F.W. fresh water

FWA Federal Works Agency (U.S.A.)

F.W.A. Factories and Workshops Act; Family Welfare Association; Free Wales Army

f.w.b. four wheel brake/braking; free/front wheel bicycle

F.W.B. Free Will Baptists

F.W.C.C. Friends' World Committee for Consultation

fwd. forward

f.w.d. four-wheel drive; free/fresh water damage

fwdg. forwarding

F.Weld.I. Fellow of the Welding Institute

F.W.F.M. Federation of Wholesale Fish Merchants

F.W.I. Federation of West Indies; Fellow of the Institute of Welfare Officers; French West Indies

F.W.L. Foundation of World Literacy

F.W.O. Federation of Wholesale Organisations; fleet wireless officer

F.W.P.C.A. Federal Water Pollution Control Administration (U.S.A.)

F.W.R.M. Federation of Wire Rope Manufacturers of Great Britain

F.W.S. fighter weapons school; fleet work study

FWSG farm water supply grant

fwt. featherweight

F.W.T. fair wear and tear

FX *s* Dorset (B.V.R.)

f.x. foreign exchange

F.X. Francis Xavier

fxd. fixed; foxed

fxg. fixing

fxle. forecastle (naut.)

FY fiscal year; *s* Fowey (B.F.P.); *s* Southport (B.V.R.)

f.y.i. for your information

FYM farmyard manure

F.Y.P. five-year plan; four-year plan

FZ *s* Belfast (B.V.R.)

fz. It. *forzando*, to be strongly accentuated (mus.); *forzato* (mus.)

Fz. Fernández; Franz

F.Z. Franc/Free/French Zone

F.Z.A. Fellow of the Zoological Academy (U.S.A.)

F.Z.G.B. Federation of Zoological Gardens of Great Britain and Ireland

F.Z.S. Fellow of the Zoological Society of London; — **Scot.** Fellow of the Zoological Society of Scotland

G

g *s* gloom (met.)

2g, 3g, etc. multiples of acceleration of gravity at earth's surface wind is 32·2 ft per sec. per sec.

G Dan. *Gade,* / Ger. *Gasse,* / Swed. *Gata,* / Nor. *Gate,* street; *s* Galway (Rep. of Ireland F.P.); gauss (phy.); giga, 10^9; *s* Glasgow (B.V.R.); grand, 1,000 dollars; gravitation constant (phys.); *s* specific gravity; *s* U.K. (I.C.A.M.)

g. garage; Fr. *gauche,* left; gauge; gelding; gender; general; general factor; general intelligence; genitive; gilt; goal (keeper); gold; good; *gourde,* Haitian currency; government; grain; gramme; grand; gravity; great; green; grey; Fr. *gros, grosse,* large; ground colour; guardian; guide; guilder; guinea; gunnery (naval)

G. conductance (elec.); German; Germany; grid direction; Guernsey; guinea; gulf

Ga *s* gallium (chem.)

GA *s* Glasgow (B.V.R.)

G/A, g/a, G/a., G.A. general average (insce.); ground to air

Ga. Gallic; Georgia, *also* GA (U.S.A.)

G.A. Gamblers Anonymous; garrison artillery; general agent; general assembly; general assignment; Geologists' Association; Geographical Association; gibberellic acid; goal attack (netball); government actuary; graphic arts; greenhouse annual

G.A.A. Gaelic Athletic Association

GAB general arrangements to borrower (IMF)

gab. gabble

Gab. Gabon

Gabby, Gabr. Gabriel, Gabrielle

GAC groups advisory council (RoSPA)

Gae., Gael. Gaelic

G.A.F.L.A.C. General Accident Fire and Life Assurance Corporation

Gail. Abigail

G.A.J. Guild of Agricultural Journalists

gal., Gal., gall. gallon

Gal. Galatians, Epistle to the; Galicia; Galway

GALAXY General Automatic Luminosity and X, Y (measuring machine) for high speed scanning of direct photographs developed at the Royal Observatory, Edinburgh

gal. cap. gallon capacity

GALCIT Guggenheim Aeronautical Laboratory of California Institute of Technology

gall. gallery

GALT gut associated lymphoid tissue

galv. galvanic; galvanism; galvanized; galvanometer

GAM guided aircraft missile

gam. gamut

Gam. Gambia

gamba It. *viola da gamba,* a forerunner of the cello (mus.)

GAMM *Gesellschaft für Angewante Mathematik und Mechanik,* Assn. for Applied Mathematics and Mechanics (Ger.)

gänz. Ger. *gänzlich,* complete

GAO general accounting office (U.S.A.); *Glovaya Astronomicheskaya Ob-*

servatoriya, main astronomical observatory (U.S.S.R.)

GAP general assembly programme; government aircraft plant; Great American Public; gross agricultural product; *Groupement d'Action Populaire,* Popular Action Group (Upper Volta)

G.A.P.A.N., Gapan Guild of Air Pilots and Air Navigators

G.A.P.C.E. General Assembly of the Presbyterian Church of England

gar. garage; garrison

G.A.R. Grand Army of the Republic; guided aircraft rocket

G.A.R. L. *Gustavus Adolphus Rex,* King Gustav II, Sweden

GARD gamma atomic radiation detector

gard. garden

G.A.R.I.O.A. government aid and relief in occupied areas

G.A.R.P. Global Atmospheric Research Programme (WMO)

gas. gasoline

G.A.S. George Augustus (Henry) Sala (1828–95), Brit. journalist; group apprenticeship scheme

GASBIINDO *Gabungan Serikat Buruh Islam Indonesia,* Fed. of Indonesian Islamic Trade Unions

GASC German-American Securities Corporation

gastroent. gastroenterological

G.A.T. Greenwich Apparent Time

G.A.T.C.O. Guild of Air Traffic Control Officers

GATT General Agreement on Tariffs and Trade, signed, 1947, by 23 countries and directed towards reduction of trade barriers

G.A.U.F.C.C. General Assembly of Unitarian and Free Christian Churches

Gaul. Gaulish

G.A.V. gross annual value (tax.)

GAW guaranteed annual wage

GAWU Guyana Agricultural Workers' Union

gaz. gazette; gazetteer

GB *s* Glasgow (B.V.R.); *s* Great Britain and Northern Ireland (I.V.R.)

5GB *s* Daventry (radio call-sign)

G.B. Gas Board; the Girls' Brigade, formed 1965, an intern. girls' Christian movement; Great Britain, the largest island of the British Isles, consisting of Eng., Wales and Scot.; greenhouse biennial; guide book; gunboat

GBA *s* Alderney, Channel Is. (I.V.R.)

G.B.A. Association of Governing Bodies of Public Schools

G.B.A.D. Great Britain Allied and Dominion

G.B.C. Green Belt Council of Greater London

G.B.C.W. Governing Body of the Church in Wales

G.B.D.O. Guild of British Dispensing Opticians

g.b.d.p. gas board distance place

g.b.e. gilt bevelled edge

G.B.E. Knight or Dame Grand Cross Order of the British Empire

GBG *s* Guernsey, Channel Is. (I.V.R.)

G.B. gas odourless, colourless volatile nerve gas that can kill in minutes in dosages of 1 mg.

G.B.G.S.A. Association of Governing Bodies of Girls Public Schools

GBH gamma benzene hydrochloride; grievous bodily harm

G.B.I. Governesses' Benevolent Institution

G.B. and I. Great Britain and Ireland

GBJ *s* Jersey, Channel Is. (I.V.R.)

GBM *s* Isle of Man (I.V.R.)

G.b.o. goods in bad order

G-bomb gravitational bomb

gbr. Ger. *gebräuchlich,* usual

G.B.R.E. General Board of Religious Education

G.B.S. George Bernard Shaw (1856–1950), Irish-born Brit. dramatist and critic

G.B.S.M. Graduate of Birmingham & Midland Institute School of Music

GBZ *s* Gibraltar (I.V.R.)

GC *s* London (B.V.R.)

G.C. Gas Council; gentleman cadet; George Cross, silver cross depicting St. George and Dragon and inscribed *For Gallantry,* with dark blue ribbon, instituted 1940 for acts of conspicuous courage. It is intended mainly for civilians and ranks next to V.C.; gliding club; golf club; good conduct; Goldsmiths' College; government chemist; Grand Chancellor; Grand Chaplain; Grand Chapter; Grand Conductor; grand cross; gun carriage; gyro-compass

GCA Girls Clubs of America; ground-controlled approach; *s* Guatemala (I.V.R.)

g.cal. gramme calorie

G.Capt. Group Captain

G.C.B. good conduct badge; Knight Grand Cross of the Most Honourable Order of the Bath

G.C.C. Girton College, Cambridge, founded 1869; Gonville and Caius College, Cambridge (*see* Cai.)

GCD General Certificate in Distribution; general and complete disarmament

g.c.d. greatest common divisor (math.)

G.C.E. General Certificate of Ed. is awarded at Ordinary 'O' and Advanced

'A' level by 8 examining bodies; General College Entrance (U.S.A.)

g.c.f. greatest common factor (math.)

G.C.F.I. Gulf and Caribbean Fisheries Institute

G.C.H. Guild Certificate of Hairdressing; Knight Grand Cross of the Hanoverian Order

G.C.H.Q. Government Communications Headquarters (FCO)

GCI ground-controlled interception

G.C.I.E. Knight Grand Commander of the Order of the Indian Empire

G.C.L. Guild of Cleaners and Launderers

G clef *the treble clef* (mus.)

G.C.L.H. Grand Cross of the Legion of Honour

g.c.m. greatest common measure/multiple (math.)

G.C.M. general court martial; Good Conduct Medal

GCMG Knight Grand Cross of the Most Distinguished Order of St. Michael and St. George

G.C.M.I. Glass Container Manufacturers Institute (U.S.A.)

G.C.N. Greenwich civil noon

G.C.O. gun control officer (naval)

G.C.R. ground controlled radar

G.C.R.I. Glasshouse Crops Research Institute

G.C.R.O. General Council and Register of Osteopaths

GCSI Knight Grand Commander of the Most Exalted Order of the Star of India

G.C.St.J. Bailiff/Dame Grand Cross of the Order of Saint John of Jerusalem

G.C.T. Greenwich Civil Time

G.C.U. Glasgow Choral Union

G.C.V.O. Dame Grand Cross of the Royal Victorian Order

Gd *s* gadolinium (chem.)

GD *s* Glasgow (B.V.R.)

gd. good; grand-daughter; ground

g.d. general duties; good delivery

g.-d. gravimetric density

G.D. goal defence (netball); graduate in divinity; Grand duchess/duchy/duke; gunnery division

G.D.B.A. Guide Dogs for the Blind Association

G.D.C. General Dynamics Corporation

Gd. Ch. Fr. *Grand Chœur*, full choir or full organ (mus.)

gde. gourde; gilt deckled edge

Gdk. Gdansk, formerly Danzig

gdn. garden; guardian

g.d.p. gross domestic product

GDR German Democratic Republic (East Ger.), *estab.* 7 Oct. 1949

gds. goods

Gds. guards

Gdsm. guardsman

Ge *s* germanium (chem.)

GE General Electric; *s* Glasgow (B.V.R.); gross energy; *s* Goole (B.F.P.)

g.e. gilt edges (binding)

G.E. garrison engineer; general election

geb. Ger. *geboren*, born; Ger. *gebunden*, bound

GEBCO general bathymetric chart of the oceans

Gebr. Ger. *Gebrüder*, brothers

G.E.C. General Electric Company

GECOMIN General Congolese Ore Company, Zaïre *formerly* Congo (K.)

ged. Ger. *gedämpft*, muted

G.E.D.A. Goodyear electronic differential analyser

GEEIA Ground Electronics Engineering Installation Agency

GEFAB Fr. *Groupement européen des associations nationales des fabricants de pesticides*, European Group of Nat. Pesticide Manufacturers' Assns.

gegr. Ger. *gegründet*, founded

Geh.Rat. Ger. *Geheimrat*, privy councillor

G. & E.I.C. Gilbert and Ellice Islands Colony

gel. gelatin

GEM ground effect machine; guidance evaluation missile

G.E.M.A. Gymnastic Equipment Manufacturers' Association

GEMMWU, GEM General, Electrical, Mechanical and Municipal Workers' Union, proposed merger of General and Municipal Workers' Union with Electrical, Electronic, Telecommunications and Plumbing Union

gen. gender; genealogy (*also* geneal.); general; generator; generic; genetic; genital; genitive (*also* genit.); genuine; genus

Gen. General (*also* Genl., Genrl.); Genesis; Geneva; Genoa

Gen. av. general average (insce.)

Gend. Fr. *Gendarme*, police

Gene Eugene; Eugenia

genn. It. *gennaio*, January

gent. gentleman

gents. gentlemen; gentlemen's

Geo. George; Georgia

geod. geodesy; geodetic

Geoff Geoffrey, Jeffray, Jeffrey

geog. geographer; geographic; geography

geol. geologic; geologist; geology

geom. geometer; geometric; geometry

geon, GEON gyro-erected optical navigation

geophy., geophys. geophysics

geopol. geopolitics

Geordie, Georgie, Georgy George

GECREF World Geographic Reference System

ger. gerund

Ger. German, Germany

Gert, Gertie Gertrude

ges. Ger. *gesetzlich geschützt*, registered trade mark; Ger. *Gesellschaft*, a company or society

G.E.S.A.M.P. Group of Experts on the Scientific Aspects of Marine Pollution

gesch. Ger. *Geschichte*, history (*also* ges.); Ger. *geschützt*, registered

GESCO General Electric Supply Corporation

gest. Ger. *gestorben*, deceased

Gestapo Ger. *Ge*heime *Sta*ats-*po*lizei, German secret police

gev, GeV, G.e.v. Giga electron volt 10⁹ electron v.

gez. Ger. *gezeichnet*, signed

GF *s* London (B.V.R.)

G.F. General Foods; government form; Guggenheim Foundation, estab. by Daniel Guggenheim (1856–1930), Amer. industrialist and benefactor

g.f.a. good fair average; good freight agent

g. factor general factor

G.F.C.M. General Fisheries Council for the Mediterranean (FAO)

GFE government-furnished equipment

GFG *Good Food Guide*, published by Consumers' Assn.

G.F.H. George Frideric Handel (1685–1759), Eng. composer of Ger. birth

G.F.R. German Federal Republic, West Ger.

G.F.S. Girls' Friendly Society

G.F.T.U. General Federation of Trade Unions

G.F.W.C. General Federation of Women's Clubs

GG *s* Glasgow (B.V.R.)

g.g. gamma globulin; gas generator

G.G. Georgian Group; Girl Guides; Grenadier Guards

G.G.A. The Girl Guides Association

g.gd. great grand-daughter

gge. garage

g.gr. a great gross, or 144 doz.

g.gs. great grandson

G.G.S.M. Graduate of Guildhall School of Music

GH *s* Ghana (I.V.R.); *s* Grangemouth (B.F.P.); *s* London (B.V.R.)

g.h., G.H. said to be the initials of George Horne, a specialist in retailing out-of-date news, a compositor's term (typ.)

G.H. general hospital; Green Howards; Greenwich Hospital

ghe ground handling equipment

G.H.I. Good Housekeeping Institute

G.H.M.S. Graduate in Homoeopathic Medicine and Surgery

Gh.N. Ghana Navy

GHOST global horizontal sounding technique

G.H.Q. general headquarters

G.H.S. Girls' High School

gi. gill

g.i. galvanised iron; gastro-intestinal

G.I. general/government issue, *also* U.S. soldier; Government of India; Royal Glasgow Institute of the Fine Arts

GIA Garuda Indonesian Airways

Gib Gibraltar

Gib, Gibbie Gilbert

Gibair Gibraltar Airways

G.I. bride Foreign-born wife of U.S. soldier; — **Joe** enlisted man U.S. army. See G.I.

Gib-TV Gibraltar television

G.I.C. Fr. *Guilde internationale des coopératrices*, Intern. Co-operative Women's Guild

G.I.E.E. Graduate of the Institution of Electrical Engineers

GIGO garbage in, garbage out, applied to computers: when input data is inaccurate, the feedout will also be inaccurate

G.I.I.P. Fr. *Groupement international de l'industrie pharmaceutique des pays de la C.E.E.*, Intern. Pharmaceutical Industry Group for the EEC countries

Gil, Gib, Gibbie Gilbert

Gill, Gilly Gillian; Jillian

G.I.Mech.E. Graduate of the Institution of Mechanical Engineers

GIMRADA Geodesy, Intelligence and Mapping Research and Development Agency (U.S.A.)

Ginny Virginia

G.Inst.T. Graduate of the Institute of Transport

G.I.Nuc.E. Graduate of the Institution of Nuclear Engineers

gio., giov. It. *giovedì*, Thursday

G.I.O. Guild of Insurance Officials

giorn. It. *giornaliero*, daily; It. *giornalista*, newspaperman

G.I.P. get/getting into publishing; Great Indian Peninsular Railway

GIRLS generalized information retrieval and listing system

gin. It. *giugno*, June

GIUK Greenland, Iceland, United Kingdom

GJ *s* London (B.V.R.)

G.J.A.B. groups joint administration board

G.J.A.C. groups joint administration committee

G.J.C. grand junction canal

G.J.D. grand junior deacon (freem.)

GK *s* Greenock (B.F.P.); *s* London (B.V.R.)

Gk., Gk Greek

G.K. goalkeeper

G.K.A. Garter King of Arms

G.K.C. Gilbert Keith Chesterton (1874–1936), Brit. journalist and author

G.K.D. Gordon-Kendall-Davison Notation

G.K.N. Guest, Keen and Nettlefolds

Gl glucinum (chem.)

GL *s* Bath (B.V.R.)

gl. gill; glass; gloss

gl. L. *gloria* (liturgy)

g/l. grams per litre

G.L. gothic letter; government laboratories; grand lodge (freem.); ground level; gun layer; gun licence

glab. glabrous

glad. gladiolus

Glam. Glamorganshire

Glas. Glasgow

glau. glaucous

glav. red. Russ. *glavnyi redaktor*, editor-in-chief

G.L.B. Girls' Life Brigade

G.L.C. gas/liquid chromatography (chem.); Greater London Council/Councillor, constituted under Lond. Govt. Act 1963 for area of 610 sq. m.; Guild of Lettering Craftsmen

G.L.C.M. Graduate of the London College of Music

gld., gldr guilder, Dutch currency

G.L.D.P. Greater London Development Plan

G.L.E.E.P. graphite low energy experimental pile (phys.)

G.L.F.C. Great Lakes Fisheries Commission

G.L.I.S. Greater London Information Service

GLOBECOM Global Communications System (USAF)

GLOMEX Global Oceanographic and Meteorological Experiment, 1975–80

Glos., Gloc., Glouc., Glr. Gloucester; Gloucestershire

gloss. glossary

G.L.P. Gibraltar Labour Party; Greater London Plan

G.L.S. Grand Lodge of Scotland; Gypsy Lore Society

glt. gilt

G.L.T. greetings letter telegram

GLU Guyana Labour Union

GM *s* Motherwell and Wishaw (B.V.R.)

gm. gram/gramme

GM Gyro-Magnetic Compass equipment using a gyroscope to smooth indications of direction derived from magnetic detectors (nav.)

G.M. general manager/merchandise/ mortgage; General Motors Corporation; Geological Museum; George Medal, instituted 1940 for acts of greatest heroism or of conspicuous courage in extreme danger; gold medal; grand master; guided missile

GMA Guyana Manufacturers' Association

G-man a Federal criminal investigation officer (U.S.A.)

G.M.A.T. Greenwich Mean Astronomical Time

g.m.b. good merchantable brand

G.M.B. Grand Master of the Order of the Bath

G.M.B.E. Grand Master of the Order of the British Empire

G.m.b.H., GmbH Ger. *Gesellschaft mit beschränkter Haftung*, limited liability co.

Gmc. Germanic

G.M.C. general management committee; General Medical Council; Guild of Memorial Craftsmen

GM counter geiger counter

G.M.F. Glass Manufacturers' Federation

G.M.I.E. Grand Master of the Order of the Indian Empire

G.M.K.P. Grand Master of the Knights of St. Patrick

G.M.M.G. Grand Master of the Order of St. Michael and St. George

gm.mol., g.mol. gram-molecule, molecular weight in grams (phys.)

G.M.P. Grand Master of the Order of St. Patrick; Gurkha Military Police

g.m.q. good merchantable quality

GMR ground mapping radar

G.M.S.I. Grand Master of the Order of the Star of India

G.M.T. Greenwich mean/meridian time

GM tube geiger tube

GMWU National Union of General and Municipal Workers, *also* NUGMW

GN *s* Granton (B.F.P.); *s* London (B.V.R.)

gn. guinea, *formerly* 21*s.* now £1.05

g.n. grandnephew; grandniece

G.N.A.S. Grant National Archery Society

G.N.C.(E.W.) General Nursing Council for England and Wales

gnd. ground

G.N.P., g.n.p. gross national product defined as income of labour and property in the form of wages, profits, interest, rent, etc., earned from the production of goods and services

gnr. gunner (mil.)

G.N.R. Port. *Guarda Nacional Republicana*, Nat. Republican Guard

G.N.S.R.A. Great North of Scotland Railway Association

G.N.T.C. Girls' Nautical Training Corps

GO *s* London (B.V.R.)

G.O. gas operated; general office/officer/order; Group Officer

G.O. Grand Organ *also* *G.Org.*; *Great Organ*, the chief division of the organ containing foundation stops, controlled by one of the keyboards (mus.)

g.o.b. good ordinary brand

G.O.C. General Officer Commanding; General Optical Council; Greek Orthodox Church

G.O.C. in C. General Officer Commanding in Chief

G.O.E. General Ordination Examination

GOFAR Global Geological and Geophysical Ocean Floor Analysis and Research

G.O.M. Grand Old Man, orig. used of William Ewart Gladstone (1809–98), Brit. statesman

GOMAC Fr. *Groupement des opticiens du marché commun*, Common Market Opticians' Group

GOOF General On-Line Oriented Function (Computers)

G.O.P. Grand Old Party, Republican party (U.S.A.)

GORA government oil refineries administration (Iraq)

G.O.S. Global Observation Station

Gosplan State Planning Commission (U.S.S.R.)

Gosud., Gos. Russ. *Gosudarstvo*, State

Goth. gothic

Gou. *Gourde*, Haitian currency

Gouv. Fr. *gouverneur*, governor

gov. government; governor

Gov.-Gen. Governor-General

govt. government

gox, GOX gaseous oxygen

GP *s* London (B.V.R.)

Gp. Group

g.p. galley proofs; geometrical progression, i.e. 2, 4, 8, 16, 32; great primer (typ.)

G.P. Gallup Poll, public opinion investigations founded by G. H. Gallup (1901–), founder of Amer. Institute of Public Opinion; general paralysis; general practitioner; general purpose; Graduate in Pharmacy; grand prix; greenhouse perennial

G.P. general pause (mus.); L. *Gloria Patri*, glory be to the Father

G.P.A. General Practitioners' Association

GPATS General-Purpose Automatic Test System

G.P.C. general purposes committee

Gp.Capt., Gp.C. Group Captain (R.A.F.)

Gp. Comdr. Group Commander

gpd, g.p.d. gallons per day

GPD *Groupement Patriotique et Démocratique*, Democratic Party (Lux.)

G.P.D.A. Gypsum Plasterboard Development Association

G.P.D.S.T. Girls' Public Day School Trust

G.P.E. guided projectile establishment

g.p.h. gallons per hour

G.Ph. Graduate in Pharmacy

G.P.H.I. Guild of Public Health Inspectors

G.P.I. general paralysis of the insane

G.P.K.T. Grand Priory of the Knights of the Temple

g.p.l. grams per litre

G.P.L.C. Guild of Professional Launderers and Cleaners

g.p.m. gallons per minute

G.P.M. Grand Past Master (freem.)

G.P.O. General Post Office; Government Printing Office (U.S.A.)

G.P.R. Glider Pilot Regiment

G.P.R. L. *Genio Populi Romani*, to the genius of the Roman people; Fr. *Grand-Positif-Récit*, great, choir and swell coupled (organ mus.)

g.p.s. gallons per second

G.P.S. Graduated Pension Scheme

G.P.T. Guild of Professional Toastmasters

G.P.U. Russ. *Gosudarstvennoye Politicheskoe Upravleniye*, State Political Admin. of U.S.S.R. 1922–4, when changed to O.G.P.U.

GPV *Gereformeerd Politiek Verbond*, Reformed Political Union, a small Calvinist party in Neth.

G.P.W. gross plated weight

G.Q. general quarters

GR *s* Gloucester (B.F.P.); *s* Greece (I.V.R.); *s* Sunderland (B.V.R.)

gr. grade; grain; grammar; gramme; grand; gravity; great; greater; grind; gross; ground; group; gunner

Gr. Grecian; Greece; Greek

G.R. general reconnaissance; general reserve; grand recorder; ground rent; Gurkha Rifles

G.R. L. *Georgius/Gulielmus, Rex,* King George/William; Fr. *Grand Récit,* great and swell organs coupled (mus.)

G.R.A. Game Research Association; Greyhound Racing Association

G.R.A.C.E. group routing and charging equipment

grad a graduate of a school or college (U.S.A.)

grad. gradient; grading; graduate

Grad.I.A.E. Graduate of the Institution of Automobile Engineers

Grad.I.M. Graduate of the Institution of Metallurgists

Grad.Inst.B.E. Graduate Member of the Institution of British Engineers

Grad.Inst.P. Graduate of the Institute of Physics

Grad.Inst.R. Graduate of the Institute of Refrigeration

Grad.I.P.M. Graduate of the Institute of Personnel Management

Grad.I.R.I. Graduate of the Institution of the Rubber Industry

Grad.S.E. Graduate of the Society of Engineers

gram. grammar; grammarian; grammatical

'gram telegram

gran. grandmother; granulated sugar

Graz., Grazo. It. *grazioso,* gracious

G.R.B.I. Gardeners' Royal Benevolent Institution

Gr. Br., Gr. Brit. Fr. *Grande Bretagne,* Great Britain; Great Britain

G.R.B.S. Gardeners' Royal Benevolent Society

Gr.Capt. Group Captain (R.A.F.)

G.R.C.M. Graduate of the Royal College of Music

GRE Guardian Royal Exchange Assurance Group

Greg. Gregorian; Gregory

Greta Margaret

G.R.F. The Graphic Reproduction Federation

gr.f. grey filly (horse racing

Gr.Fl. Ger. *Grosse Flöte,* the normal flute (mus.)

G.R.I. Glasshouse/Grassland Research Institute

G.R.I., G.R.et.I. L. *Georgius Rex et Imperator,* George, King and Emperor

griff griffin, a tip, a hint (slang)

Gr.L. gunner lieutenant

Gr.-L. Graeco-Latin

grm. gramme

grn. green

G.R.N. goods received note

gro. gross

G.R.O. General Register Office; Greenwich Royal Observatory

G.R.O.B.D.M. General Register Office for Births, Deaths and Marriages

Grove Grove's *Dictionary of Music and Musicians,* first published 1879–89

GRP glass/glassfibre reinforced plastics/polyester

Grp. group

grs. grandson

G.R.S.E. Guild of Radio Service Engineers

Gr.S.L. gunner sub-lieutenant

G.R.S.M. Graduate of the Royal Schools of Music

Grs.t. gross tons

g.r.t. gross registered tonnage/tons

gr.t.m. gross ton-mile

gr. tons gross tons

Gr.Tr. Ger. *Grosse Trommel,* bass drum (mus.)

gr.wt. gross weight

g.r.y. gross redemption yield (fin.)

Gs *guaranis,* currency of Paraguay

GS German silver; *s* Perthshire (B.V.R.)

gs. grandson, *also* g.s.; ground speed, speed of a craft relative to the solid surface of the planet below it (nav.); guineas

G.S. general secretary/service (mil.)/staff; geographical/geological survey; goal shooter (netball); gold standard, monetary unit in which the currency unit is a fixed weight of gold or is equivalent to the value of gold, on which there are no trading restrictions. Britain returned to the G.S. in 1925, a contributory factor in the economic depression, and finally left it in 1931; grammar school; grand scribe/secretary/sentinel/sentry/steward

G.S.A. Girl Scouts of America; Glasgow School of Art

G.S.B. Government Savings Bank

G.S.C. general service corps; general staff corps (U.S.A.)

G.S.D. general supply depot

GSE ground service/support equipment

GSEE *Geniki Synomospondia Ergaton Hellados,* Greek General Confed. of Labour

G.S.F. General Scientific Framework, for world oceanographic study

GSFC Goddard Space Flight Center (NASA)

GSFG Group of Soviet Forces in Germany

G.S.G.B. Geological Survey of Great Britain

G.S.G.S. Geographical Section, General Staff

G.S.I. Geological Survey of India

G.S.L. Geological Society of London; Geological Survey of London; group scout leader

g.s.m. good sound merchantable; grammes per square metre

G.S.M. garrison sergeant-major; general sales manager; grammes per square metre

G.S.M.D. Guildhall School of Music and Drama, *also* G.S.M.

GSMS Graduate Student Management Society

G.S.N.C. General Steam Navigation Company

G.S.O. General Staff Officer

G.S.P. good service pension (naval)

G.S.R. galvanic skin reflex/response

GSS geo-stationary satellite; global surveillance system

G.-st. garter-stitch (knit.)

G.S.T. Greenwich Sidereal Time

G.S.W. gunshot wound

G.S. & W.R. Great Southern and Western Railway (Ireland)

GT *s* London (B.V.R.)

gt. gilt; great

g.t. gas tight; gilt top (binding); gross tonnage

G.T. Good Templar; Grand Tiler; grand tourer/touring/treasurer; greetings telegram

G.T.A. Gun Trade Association

G.T.B.C. Guild of Teachers of Backward Children

Gt. Br., Gr. Brit. Great Britain

G.T.C. Girls' Training Corps; good till cancelled; Government Training Centre

G.T.C.L. Graduate of Trinity College of Music, London

gtd. guaranteed

g.t.e. gilt top edge

Gtee. guarantee

g.t.m. good this month

G.T.M. general traffic manager

G.T.M.A. Galvanized Tank Manufacturers' Association; Gauge and Tool Makers' Association

G.T.P.D. Guild of Television Producers and Directors, *now* S.F.T.A.

gtr. greater

GTS gas turbine ship

G.T.S. global telecommunication system; Greenwich time signal; Guinean Trawling Survey

gtt. L. *guttatim*, drop by drop (med.)

GTUC Grenada Trade Union Council; Guyana Trades Union Council

g.t.w. good this week

GU Guam; *s* Guernsey (B.F.P.); *s* London (B.V.R.)

Gu. Guinea; gules

G.U. gastric ulcer; genito-urinary

guar. guarantee

Guat. Guatemala

Gui. Guiana

G.U.I. Golfing Union of Ireland

Guil. guilder

guin. guinea (fin.)

GUM Russ. *Gosudarstvenni Universalni Magazin*, Universal State Store (U.S.S.R.)

gun. gunnery

Gus, Gussie Augustus; Gustav

G.U.S. Great Universal Stores

gutt., gt. L. *gutta* or *guttae*, drop *or* drops (med.)

guttat. L. *guttatim*, drop by drop (med.)

guv., guv'nor governor

g.u.v. Ger. *gerecht und vollkommen*, correct and complete

GV *s* Suffolk, West (B.V.R.)

g.v. gravimetric volume; gross valuation

G.V. Fr. *Grande Vitesse*, fast goods train

gvt. government

G.V.W. gross vehicle weight

GW *s* Glasgow (B.F.P.); *s* London (B.V.R.)

G.W. George Washington, President of U.S.A. 1789–97; guided weapons

GWDU General Workers' Development Union, Br. Honduras

Gwen, Gwenda, Gweny Gwendolen; Gwendolene

G.W.P. Government White Paper

G.W.R. Great Western Railway, *now* Western Reg. British Rail

GWU Gambia Workers' Union; General Workers' Union, Malta

GX *s* London (B.V.R.)

GY *s* Grimsby (B.F.P.); *s* London (B.V.R.)

gym. gymnasium; gymnastics

gyn., gynae., gynaecol. gynaecological; gynaecology

G.Y.P. Guild of Young Printers

GZ *s* Belfast (B.V.R.); ground zero, atomic detonation

H

h *s* hail (met.); hecto, 10^2; *s* measure of precision in psychophysical experiments; *s* Planck's constant

h small increment (math.)

H *s* Hamiltonian (phys.); hard (pencils); Heaton, mintmark, Birmingham (numis.); henry, unit of inductance (H = Vs/A); Hibernia, Ireland, in Brit. bot. records; *s* horizontal force of earth's magnetism; *Høyre*, Conservative Party (Norway); *s* Hull (B.F.P.); *s* Hungary (I.V.R.); *s* hydrogen (chem.); *s* London (B.V.R.); *s* total energy (anal. mech.)

2H, 3H hard pencil
4H very hard pencil

h. habitants; harbour; hard; hardness; has; hatch; have; hearts (cards); heat; heavy; height; high; hip, hit; horizontal; horse; hot; hour; house; hull; hundred; husband; It. *hora*, hour

h. *horn* (mus.)

H. half-page, type area (advert.); hard (pencils); Ger. *Heft*, number, part; herbaceous; Ger. *Herren*, gentlemen; Holy; Fr. *Hommes*, men; hydrant; hydraulics

HA *s* Hungary (I.C.A.M.); *s* Warley (B.V.R.)

ha. hectare; Ger. *Hektar*, hectare

Ha. Haiti; Haitian; Hawaii; Hawaiian

h.a., h. app. heir apparent

h.a. L. *hoc anno*, this year; L. *hujus anni*, this year's

H.A. hardy annual (hort.); Hautes-Alpes (France); heavy artillery; high angle; Highway(s) Act; Historical/Hockey Association; horse artillery; hostile air-

craft; hour angle; human adaptability; Hydraulic Association of Great Britain

H.A.A. heavy anti-aircraft; Helicopter Association of America; Hotel Accountants' Association (U.S.A.)

HAAC Harper Adams Agricultural College (U.S.A.)

HAAW heavy anti-tank assault weapon

hab. habitat; habitation

Hab. Habakkuk (Bible); *Habana*, Havana (Cuba); Halbert, *also* Habbie (Scot.)

H.A.B. high altitude bombing

H.A.B.A. Hardwood Agents' and Brokers' Association

hab. corp. L. *habeas corpus*, may you have the body, in law, that a prisoner be brought before court to decide on legality of his detention

habt. L. *habeat*, let him have

H.A.C. Honourable Artillery Company, oldest regiment in British Army

hack. hackney, taxicab

h.a.d. head acceleration device; hereinafter described

hadn't had not

HADS hypersonic air data sensor

H.A.F. high abrasion furnace; high altitude fluorescence

H.A.F. black high abrasive furnace black, filler in rubber compounding

HAFMED Headquarters Allied Forces Mediterranean

HAFO home accounting and finance office (USAF)

H.A.F.R.A. British Hat and Allied Feltmakers' Research Association

160

HAG Hardware Analysis Group (computer)

Hag. Haggai (Bible)

H.A.G.B. Helicopter Association of Great Britain, *now* incorporated with Royal Aeronautical Society

hagiol. hagiology

H.A.I.A. Hearing Aid Industry Association

Hak. Hakka

Hak. Soc. Hakluyt Society

Hal Harold; Harry

hal. halogen

Halle a/S. Ger. *Halle an der Saale*

Hal. Orch. Hallé Orchestra

H.A.L.T.A.T.A. high and low temperature accuracy testing apparatus

HAM hardware associative memory (computer)

Ham. Hamburg (Ger.); *Hamlet* (Shake.)

H.A. & M. *Hymns Ancient and Modern*

hamletom ham, lettuce and tomato sandwich

Han. Hanover; Hanoverian

Hank Henry

hankie, hanky handkerchief

Hans Ger. *Johann*, John

Hants Hampshire

H.A.O. horticultural advisory officer

H/A. or D. Havre, Antwerp or Dunkirk (grain trade)

HAP high altitude platform

hapdec hard-point decoy

ha'penny halfpenny

ha'p'orth halfpennyworth

Har. harbour; Harold

hard. hardware

harm. harmonic; harmony

HARP high altitude relay point

harp. *harpsichord* (mus.)

HARTRAN Hartwell Atlas Fortran (computer)

Harv. Harvard University (U.S.A.)

HAS Helicopter Air Service; high altitude sample; hospital advisory service

H.A.S. Headmasters' Association of Scotland; Hellenic Astronautical Society (Greece); hydrographic automated system

hash. hashish

hasn't has not

HASP hardware assisted software polling (computer); high altitude sampling programme; high altitude space platform

H.A.T.R.A. Hosiery and Allied Trades Research Association

H.A.T.S. helicopter advanced tactical system; hour angle of the true sun

Hattie Harriet

Hauptw. Ger. *Hauptwerk*, great organ (mus.)

haust. L. *haustus*, draught

Haut. *hautboy*, old English name for oboe (mus.)

hav. haversine

haven't have not

HAW heavy anti-tank assault weapon

HAWK homing-all-the-way killer

haz. hazard; hazardous

Hb haemoglobin

HB Brinell hardness; hard black (pencils); *s* Merthyr Tydfil (B.V.R.); *s* Switzerland (I.C.A.M.)

Hb. haemoglobin; hardy biennial (bot.)

Hb. Ger. *Hoboe*, oboe (mus.) ·

h.b. half back; half bound; hand book; hard back (pub.); homing beacon; human being

H.B. hard black (pencils); hardy biennial (hort.); House of Bishops, part of the C. of E. Assembly

H. & B. Humboldt and Bonpland (bot.)

Hba. Sp. *Habana*, Havana (Cuba)

H.B.C. high breaking capacity; Historic Buildings Council; Hudson's Bay Company, granted royal charter 1670 and controlled all land draining into Hudson Bay (named after Henry Hudson who explored the region 1610). The company eventually surrendered the land to the government in 1869

H.B.D. had/has been drinking

Hbf. Ger. *Hauptbahnhof*, central/main station

hbk. hollow back

H.B. & K. Humboldt, Bonpland and Kunth (bot.)

H.B.M. Her/His Britannic Majesty; — S. Her/His Britannic Majesty's Service/ Ship

H.B.O.G. Hudson's Bay Oil and Gas

H-bomb hydrogen bomb

hbr. harbour

H.B.R. *Harvard Business Review*; Hudson's Bay Railway

H.B.S. Harvard Business School

Hbt. Hobart (Aust.)

HBWR Halden boiling heavy water reactor

hby. hereby

HC *s* Eastbourne (B.V.R.); *s* Ecuador (I.C.A.M.)

h.c. habitual criminal; hand control; heating cabinet; high capacity; high carbon; hot and cold, *also* h. & c.

h.c. L. *honoris causa*, for the sake of the honour; honorary

H.C. Hague Convention, agreement on settlement of international disputes, etc., resulting from Hague Conferences 1899, 1907; Headmasters' Conference; health certificate; held covered (insce.);

Heralds' College; high church; High Commission/Commissioner, diplomatic representative of a Commonwealth country undertaking duties of, and equivalent in rank to, an Ambassador; High Court; higher certificate; highly commended; *Highway Code*; hockey club; Holy Communion; home counties; Fr. *hors concours*, not for competition; house correction; House of Clergy/Commons (*also* H. of C.); house of correction; housing centre

H.C. Fr. *haute-contre*, alto (mus.)

H.C.A. High Conductivity Copper Association; High Court of Admiralty; Horder Centre for Arthritics; Hospital Caterers' Association; Hunting Clan Air Transport

H.C.A.A.S. Homeless Children's Aid and Adoption Society

H'cap., Hcap., Hcp. handicap

H.C.B. House of Commons Bill

hcc hydraulic cement concrete

hcd high current density

H. C. Deb. *House of Commons Debates* from 1909

h.c.e. human-caused error

H.C. & E.S. Hull Chemical and Engineering Society

h.c.f. highest common factor (math.); hundred cubic feet

H.C.F. Honorary Chaplain to the Forces

h.c.g. horizontal location of centre of gravity

HCH hexachlorocyclohexane, used as an insecticide

H.C.H. Herbert Clark Hoover, pres. of U.S.A., 1929–33

H. Ch. D. Diploma in High Chiropody

H.C.I. Hotel and Catering Institute

HCIL Hague Conference on International Law

HCITB Hotel and Catering Industry Training Board

H.C.J. High Court of Justice; Holy Child Jesus

HCl *s* hydrochloric acid (chem.)

h.c.l. high cost of living; horizontal centre line

H.C.M. Her/His Catholic Majesty; High Court Master

H.C.M.P.A. Home Counties Master Printers' Alliance

H.C.O. Harvard College Observatory; higher clerical officer

HCP *House of Commons Paper*

H.C.p. heat of combustion of an element under constant pressure (chem.)

H.C.P.T. Historic Churches Preservation Trust

hcptr. helicopter

H.C.R. High Chief Ranger

h.c.s. high carbon steel

H.C.S. Hallé Concerts Society; Home Civil Service

hcsht. high carbon steel heat-treated

H.C.T. High Commission Territories

HCTBA Hotel and Catering Trades Benevolent Association

h.c.u. hydraulic cycling unit

H.C.v. heat of combustion of an element under constant volume

H.C.V.C. Historic Commercial Vehicle Club

HD *s* Dewsbury (B.V.R.); 51st Highland Division (mil.); horizontal distillation, an obsolete process for smelting zinc

H/D Havre–Dunkirk (ship.)

hd. hand; head; hogshead

h.d. heavy duty; Ger. *Hochdruck*, high pressure

h.d. L. *hora decubitus*, at bedtime (med.)

H.D. Hansen's disease (leprosy); high-density; home defence; honourable discharge; honorary degree (freemason.); Hoover Dam; horse-drawn; hourly difference

H.D.A. Diploma of the Hawkesbury Agricultural College, N.S.W. (Aust.); high duty alloy; Hydrographic Department (MOD)

hdatz high density air traffic zone

hdbk. handbook

HDC Helicopter Direction Center (U.S.A.); holder in due course

hd. cr. hard chromium

H.D.D. Diploma of Dairying, Hawkesbury Agricultural College, N.S.W. (Aust.); Higher Dental Diploma

hdg. heading

H.D.G.A. Hot Dip Galvanizers' Association

H. Dip. E. Higher Diploma in Education

h. dk. hurricane deck

hdkf. handkerchief

hdl. handle

H.D.L. Harry Diamond Laboratories (US Army); high density lipoproteins

hdlg. handling

h.d.m. high duty metal

HDMR high density moderated reactor

HDMS *Hizbah Destur Mustakil Somalo*, Independent Constitutional Somali Party (Somalia)

hdn. harden

hdqrs. headquarters

H.D.R.I. Hannah Dairy Research Institute

hdsp. hardship

HDST high density shock tube
H.D.V. heavy duty vehicle
hdw., hdwe hardware (computer)
Hdwbch. Ger. *Handwörterbuch*, school or pocket dictionary
He *s* helium (chem.)
HE *s* Barnsley (B.V.R.); *s* Hale (B.F.P.)
He. Hebraic; Hebrew
h.e. heat engine; heavy enamel; height of eye; high explosive; horizontal equivalent; hub end
h.e. L. *hic est*, this is
h. and e. heredity and environment
H.E. His Eminence; His Excellency; home establishment; hydraulic engineer
H.E.A. Horticultural Education Association
heat. heating
Heb., Hebr. Hebraic; Hebrew; Hebrews, Epistle to the (Bible)
hebd. hebdomadal
Hebr. Hebrides
hectog. hectogram/hectogramme, hundred grammes
hectol. hectolitre, hundred litres
hectom. hectometre, hundred metres
H.E.C.T.O.R. Heated Experimental Carbon Thermal Oscillator Reactor
he'd he had; he would
HEDCOM headquarters command (USAF)
H.E.F. high energy fuel
H.E.H. Her/His Exalted Highness
h.e.i. high explosive incendiary
H.E.I.C. Honourable East India Company
H.E.I.C.N. Honourable East India Company Navy
H.E.I.C.S. Honourable East India Company Service
Heidel. Heidelberg (Ger.)
heir app. heir apparent
heir pres. heir presumptive
hel. helicopter, *also* heli.
Hel. Helen; Helena; Helvetia (Switz.)
HELEN hydrogenous exponential liquid experiment
he'll he shall; he will
Hellen. Hellenic; Hellenism; Hellenistic
helo. heliport
H.E.L.P. haulage emergency link protection; helicopter electronic landing path; Help Establish Lasting Peace
hem. hemoglobin; hemorrhage
Hen. IV. *King Henry IV*, Pt. I pub. 1598 and Pt. II 1600 (Shake.); — **V.** *King Henry V*, pub. 1600, imperfect text corrected 1623 (Shake.); — **VI.** *King Henry VI* (ascrib. Shake.); — **VIII.** *King Henry VIII*, perf. 1613 (Shake.)

H.E.O. higher executive officer
HEOS high excentricity orbit satellite
HEPC hydro-electric power commission (U.S.A.)
HEPCAT helicopter pilot control and training
H.E.P.C.C. Heavy Electrical Plant Consultative Council
HEPL high energy physics laboratory, Stanford Univ. (U.S.A.)
her. heraldry
her. L. *heres*, heir
Her. Herefordshire
hera high explosive rocket assisted
HERALD highly enriched reactor Aldermaston
herb herbalist; herbarium
Herb herbaceous; Herbert
HERC Humber Estuarial Research Committee, British Transport Docks Board
herd.º Port. *herdeiro*, heir
hered. heredity
here's here is
h.e.r.f. high energy rate forming
HERMES heavy element and radioactive material electromagnetic separator
HERO Sp. *Hidroelétrica Industria & Comercio* (Braz.)
H.E.R.O. hot experimental reactor of 0 (i.e. zero) power
Herod. Herodotus (*c* 484–*c* 424 B.C.), Gk. historian
Herp., herpet. herpetologist; herpetology
herst. Ger. *herstellung*, manufacture
HERTIS Hertfordshire Technical Information Service
Herts. Hertfordshire
HERU Higher Education Research Unit
he's he has; he is
H'est Highest (cricket)
Hesych. Hesychius (fifth cent. A.D.), Gk. grammarian of Alexandria
HET heavy equipment transporter
HETP hexaethyl tetraphosphate
HETS hyper-environmental test system (USAF)
Hetty Esther, Hester
heu hydroelectric unit
HEVAC Heating, Ventilating and Air Conditioning Manufacturers' Association
HEW Department of Health, Education and Welfare (U.S.A.)
hex. hexachord; hexagon; hexagonal
Hex. uranium hexafluoride
hexa. hexamethylene tetramine, in rubber compounding (chem.)
Hf *s* hafnium (chem.)
HF hard firm (pencils); Holiday Fellowship; *s* Wallasey (B.V.R.)

H/F *Hlutafjelagid*, limited company (Iceland)

hf. half

h.f. hageman factor; height finding; high frequency; hold fire; hook fast; horse and foot (mil.)

H.F. Holy Father; home fleet; home forces

HFA Holiday Fun Association

Hfa. Haifa (Israel)

HFAA Holstein-Friesian Association of America

H.F.A.R.A. Honorary Foreign Associate of the Royal Academy

hf. bd. half binding/bound, leather back and corners, paper/cloth sides (pub.); — **cf.** half calf, calf leather back and corners, paper/cloth sides (pub.); — **cl.** half cloth, cloth sides (pub.); — **mor.** half morocco, morocco leather back and corners, cloth sides (pub.)

hfc high frequency current

H.F.D.F. high frequency detecting and finding; high frequency direction-finder

HFFF Hungarian Freedom Fighters' Federation

HFG high frequency gas

HFM Henry Ford Museum (U.S.A.)

hfo high frequency oscillator

H.F.R.A. Honorary Fellow of the Royal Academy

Hfrz. Ger. *Halb/franzband*, half-bound calf (pub.)

hfs hyperfine structure

Hft. Ger. *Heft*, part, number

Hfx. Halifax (Can.)

Hg *s* L. *hydrargyrum*, mercury, used in defining pressures and temperatures of gases or liquids (chem.)

HG *s* Burnley (B.V.R.)

hg. hectogram; heliogram

H.G. hand generator; Haute-Garonne, dept. of France bordering on Spain.; Her/His Grace; High German (*also* H.-G.); high grade; Holy Ghost; Home Guard; Horse Guards

HGB Ger. *Handelsgesetzbuch*, commercial law code

H.G.C.A. Home Grown Cereals Authority

Hgd. hogshead

H.G.D.H. Her/His Grand Ducal Highness

H.G.H. human growth hormone

H.G.J.P. Henry George Justice Party (Aust.)

H.G.M.M. Hereditary Grand Master Mason

h.g.pt. hard gloss paint (building)

hgr. hangar; hanger

hgt. height

HGTAC Home Grown Timber Advisory Committee

H.G.V. heavy goods vehicle

H.G.W. Herbert George Wells (1866–1946), Eng. novelist and sociologist

hgy. highway

HH *s* Carlisle (B.V.R.); double hard (pencils); *s* Haiti (I.C.A.M.); *s* Harwich (B.F.P.); Ger. *Herren*, gentlemen

H/H. Havre to Hamburg (grain trade)

H.H. heavy hydrogen; Her/His Highness; His Holiness; His Honour

H.H.A. half-hardy annual (hort.)

H.H.B. half-hardy biennial (hort.)

H.H.B.S. Hereford Herd Book Society

hhd. hogshead, cask of 63 galls.

H.H.D. L. *Humanitatum Doctor*, Doctor of Humanities

H.H.D.W.S. Heavy Handy Deadweight Scrap

HHFA Housing and Home Finance Agency (U.S.A.)

HHH very hard (pencils)

H.H.I. Highland Home Industries

H-Hour the hour at which an operation is to begin

H.H.P. half-hardy perennial (hort.)

Hi Hiram

HI *s* Dominican Republic (I.C.A.M.); Hawaii; *s* hydriodic acid (chem.); *s* Tipperary (B.V.R.)

Hi. high; Hindi; humidity index

H.I. Hawaiian Islands; high intensity; horizontal interval; Hudson/Hydraulic Institute (U.S.A.)

H.I. L. *hic iacet*, here lies

H.-I. Herbert-Ingersoll

H.I.A. Horological Institute of America; Hospital Industries' Association; Housing Improvement Association

hi. ac. high accuracy

Hib. Hibernia; Hibernian

H.I.B. Herring Industry Board

HIBEX high-acceleration booster experiment

HICAPCOM high capacity communication system

hicat high altitude clear air turbulence

Hi. Com. high command; High Commission/Commissioner

H.I.D.B. Highlands and Islands Development Board, created 1965 (Scot.)

H.I.E. Hibernation Information Exchange

Hier. hieroglyphics; Hierosolyma (Jerusalem)

HIFAR High Flux Australian Reactor

hi. fi. high fidelity

Hi-Flex combination of hydraulic high working pressures, exceeding 1,000 psi, and flexibility of rubber hoses as against rigid metal pipes

hifor. high level forecast
H.I.H. Her/His Imperial Highness
Hil Hilary
H.I.M. Her/His Imperial Majesty
HIMet process for converting iron ore to metallized agglomerates of high iron content, which may be fed direct to electric arc furnace
Hind. Hindi; Hindu; Hindustan; Hindustani
H-ion. hydrogen ion
HIPAR high-power acquisition radar
HIPERNAS high-performance navigation system
HIPOE high pressure oceanographic equipment
hipot. high potential
Hipp. Hippocrates (*c* 460–*c* 375 B.C.), Gk. physician, the 'father' of medicine
hippo. hippopotamus
H.I.P.S. high-impact polystyrene (plastic)
hirel. high reliability
H.I.S. Horticulture Improvement Scheme
H.I.S. L. *hic iacet sepultus*, here lies buried
HISSBI Federation of Indonesian Trade Unions
hist. historian (*also* histn.); historic; historical; history
HISTADRUT *Histadrut Haovdim*, General Fed. of Jewish Labor in Israel
Histol. histology
Hit. Holzman inkblot technique (psy.)
hi-T. high torque
hi temp. high temperature
Hitt. Hittite. The Hs. were early inhab. of Turkey and N. Syria. Powerful *c* 1460–1190 B.C.
HIUS Hispanic Institute of the United States
hiv. Fr. *hiver*, winter
HIVOS high-vacuum orbital simulator
HJ *s* Southend (B.V.R.)
H.J. high jump (ath.); Ger. *Hitler Jugend*, Hitler Youth; Honest John (missile)
H.J. L. *hic jacet*, here lies
H.J.S. L. *hic jacet sepultus*, here lies buried
HK *s* Colombia (I.C.A.M.); *s* Essex (B.V.R.); *s* Hong Kong (I.V.R.)
H.K. Ger. *Handelskammer*, Chamber of Commerce; Hong Kong (*also* H. Kg., Hg. Kg.); housekeeper allowance (tax); House of Keys, Isle of Man
hkf. handkerchief
HKJ *s* Jordan (I.V.R.)
H.K.J. Hashemite Kingdom of Jordan

HKMA Hong Kong Management Association
HL *s* Hartlepool (B.F.P.); *s* Korea (I.C.A.M.); *s* Wakefield (B.V.R.)
hl. hectolitre; Ger. *heilig*, holy; Ger. *Hektoliter*, 22 galls.; holiday
h.l. L. *hoc loco*, in this place
H.L. hard labour; Haute-Loire (France); honours list; House of Laity/Lords, *also* H. of L.
HLCC Home Laundering Consultative Council
HLHS heavy lift helicopter system
H.L.I. Highland Light Infantry
HLIS Hill Land Improvement Scheme
hlpr. helper
H.L.P.R. Howard League for Penal Reform
H.L.R.S. Homosexual Law Reform Society
hl. S. Ger. *heilige Schrift*, Holy Scripture
H.L.S. Harvard Law School; heavy logistics support
Hlw. Ger. *halbleinwand*, half-bound cloth (pub.)
H.L.W.N. highest low water of neaptides
Hlzbl. Ger. *Holzbläser*, 'woodblowers', i.e. wood-wind dept. (mus.)
H/m *s* unit of magnetic permeability
HM *s* London (B.V.R.)
hm. hectometre
h.m. hallmark; hand made (paper); headmaster; headmistress
h.m. L. *hoc mense*, in this month; L. *huius mensis*, this month's
H.M. harbour master; harmonic mean; Haute-Marne (France); Her/His Majesty; home mission
H.M.A. Head Masters' Association
H.M.A.C. Her/His Majesty's Aircraft Carrier
H.M.A.S. Her/His Majesty's Australian Ship
H.M.B. Hops Marketing Board
H.M.B.D.V. Her/His Majesty's Boom Defence Vessel
H.M.B.I. Her/His Majesty's Borstal Institution
H.M.C. Headmasters' Conference, *estab.* by Edward Thring, h.m. Uppingham School, 1869; Her/His Majesty's Customs; Historical Manuscripts Commission, first appointed 1869 to list and abstract important historical documents in private collections. One of its most important catalogues was of the Cecil papers at Hatfield House; Horticultural Marketing Council; hospital management committee
HMCIF Her/His Majesty's Chief Inspector of Factories

H.M.C.N. Her/His Majesty's Canadian Navy

H.M.C.S. Her/His Majesty's Canadian Ship

H.M.C.S.C. Her/His Majesty's Civil Service Commissioners

hmd. humid; hydraulic mean depth

H.M.D. Her/His Majesty's Destroyer

H.M.F. Haslemere Music Festival; Her/His Majesty's Forces

H.M.F. black high modulus furnace black, filler in rubber compounding

HMFI Her/His Majesty's Factory Inspectorate

H.M.G. heavy machine gun; Her/His Majesty's Government; Higher Middle German

H.M.H.S. Her/His Majesty's Hospital Ship

H.M.I. Her/His Majesty's Inspector

H.M.I.S., H.M.I.(S.) Her/His Majesty's Inspector of Schools

H.M.I.T. Her/His Majesty's Inspector of Taxes

H.M.L. Her/His Majesty's Lieutenant

H.M.L.R. Her/His Majesty's Land Registry

H.M.M.L. Her/His Majesty's Motor Launch

H.M.M.S. Her/His Majesty's Motor Mine Sweeper

H.M.O.C.S. Her/His Majesty's Overseas Civil Service

H.M.O.W. Her/His Majesty's Office of Works

h.m.p. handmade paper

H.M.P. L. *hoc monumentum posuit*, he/she erected this monument

H.M.R.T. Her/His Majesty's Rescue Tug

HMS Hind Mazdoor Sabha (India)

h.m.s. hours, minutes, seconds

H.M.S. Her/His Majesty's Service/Ship

H.M.S.O. Her/His Majesty's Stationery Office, publisher for H.M.G. estab. 1786

hmstd. homestead

H.M.T. Her/His Majesty's Trawler/Treasury/Tug

H.M.V. His Master's Voice

H.M.W.A. Hairdressing Manufacturers' and Wholesalers' Association

HN *s* Darlington (B.V.R.)

Hn. horn (mus.)

h.n. L. *hac nocte*, tonight (med.)

H.N.C. higher national certificate

H.N.D. higher national diploma

hndbk. handbook

hnos. Sp. *hermanos*, brothers

Hnrs. Honours

Ho *s* holmium (chem.)

HO *s* Hampshire (B.V.R.)

ho. house

h.o. hold over

H.O. Ger. *Handelsorganisation*, trade organ.; head office; Home Office; hostilities only; Hydrographic Office

hob height of burst

HOBS high orbital bombardment system

h.o.c. held on charge

H.O.C. heavy organic chemical

hock. Ger. *Hochheimer*, Rhine wine

H.o.D. head of department

H. of C., H.O.C. House of Commons

H. of K. House of Keys

H. of L. House of Lords

H. of R. House of Representatives

H. of sp. hybrid of species

HOJ home on jamming

Hol., Holl. Holland

H.O.L.C. Home Owners' Loan Corporation (U.S.A.)

holl. Fr. *hollandais*, Dutch

hols. holidays

Hom. Homer

HOME Home Ownership Made Easy Plan (Can.)

home ec. home economics

homeo. homeopathic

homo. homeopath; homeopathic; homeopathy; homosexual

hon. honor; honorary; honour; honourable; Fr. *honoré*, honoured

Hon. A.R.C.M. Honorary Associate of the Royal College of Music

Honble., Hon'ble. Honourable (former Indian title)

Hond. Honduras, *also* Hon.

Hon. F. Inst. P. Honorary Fellow of the Institute of Physics; — **F.I. Plant E.** Honorary Fellow of the Institution of Plant Engineers; — **F.I.S.P.** Honorary Fellow of the Institute of Sewage Purification; — **F.R.I.N.A.** Honorary Fellow of the Royal Institution of Naval Architects; — **F.S.E.** Honorary Fellow of the Society of Engineers; — **F.S.G.T.** Honorary Fellow of the Society of Glass Technology; — **F.T.C.L.** Honorary Fellow of Trinity College of Music, London; — **F. Weld. I.** Honorary Fellow of the Welding Institute; — **G.S.M.** Honorary Member of the Guildhall School of Music; — **Life M. Inst. Gas. E.** Honorary Life Member of the Institute of Gas Engineers; — **M.I.A.E.** Honorary Member of the Institution of Automobile Engineers; — **M.I.E.I.** Honorary Member of the Institution of Engineering Inspection; — **M. Inst. Gas. E.** Honorary Member of the Institute of Gas Engineers; — **M. I. Plant E.** Honorary Member of the Institution of Plant Engineers; — **R.A.M.** Honorary Member of the Royal Academy of Music; — **R.C.M.** Honorary Member of the Royal College of Music

Hono. Honolulu

hons. honours

Hon. Sec. Honorary Secretary

Hon. T.C.L. Honorary Member of Trinity College of Music

Hook. Sir W. Hooker (bot.)

Hook. fil. Sir J. D. Hooker (bot.)

HOPBEG Hotel and Public Building Equipment Group

H.O.P.E. Health Opportunity for People Everywhere; Help Organize Peace Everywhere

hor. horizon; horizontal; horology

Hor. Horace, Quintus Horatius Flaccus (65–8 B.C.), L. poet

HORACE H_2O Reactor Aldermaston Critical Experiment

hor. decub. L. *hora decubitus*, at bedtime (med.)

HoReCa International Union of National Associations of Hotel, Restaurant and Café Keepers

horol. horological; horology

H.O.R.S.A. Hut Operation Raising School-leaving Age

hort., hortic. horticulture

H.O.R.U. Home Office Research Unit

Hos. Hosea (Bible)

hosp. hospital

HOTAC Hotel Accommodation Service (Lond.)

how. howitzer (mil.)

How. *Howard*, Supreme Court reports (U.S.A.)

howe'er however

HP *s* Coventry (B.V.R.)

Hp. *harp* (mus.)

h.p. half pay; heir presumptive; high power/pressure; hire purchase; horizontal parallax; horizontally polarized; horse power

H.P. Handley Page (aircraft); hardy perennial (hort.); Hautes-Pyrénées (France); high priest; Himachal Pradesh (India); hot-pressed (paper); house physician; Houses of Parliament; hybrid perpetual (rose)

H.P.A. Hospital Physicists' Association; Hurlingham Polo Association

H.P.C. history of present complaint

H.P.C. black hard processing channel black, filler in rubber compounding

Hpchd. *harpsichord* (mus.)

Hpchdst. *harpsichordist* (mus.)

hp. cyl. high pressure cylinder

H.P.F. highest possible frequency; Horace Plunkett Foundation

hp.-hr. horsepower-hour

h.p.n. horse power nominal

H.P.P.A. Horses' and Ponies' Protection Association

H.P.R. House of Pacific Relations; Hungarian People's Republic

h.p.s. high pressure steam; high protein supplement; hot pressed sheet

Hpst. *harpist* (mus.)

hpt. high point; high pressure test

H.P.T.A. Hire Purchase Trade Association

Hptw. Ger. *Hauptwerk*, great organ (mus.)

hpu. hydraulic pumping unit

h.q., H.Q. headquarters

h.q. L. *hoc quaere*, look for this

H.Q.B.A. Headquarters Base Area

HQMC Headquarters, Marine Corps (U.S.A.)

h(r) *s* rain and hail (met.)

HR holiday routes; *s* Wiltshire (B.V.R.)

hr. hour; hussar

Hr. Ger. *Herr, Herren*, Mr., Sir

Hr. Ger. *Hörner*, horns (mus.)

h.r. home run

H.R. Highland Regiment; Home Rule; Home Ruler; House of Representatives (U.S.A.); house record

Hra. Fin. *Herra*, Mr.

H.R.A. *Historical Records of Australia*

HRB Highways Research Board/Bureau (U.S.A.)

H.R.C. Holy Roman Church; Hop Research Centre

H.R.C.A. Honorary Member of the Royal Cambrian Academy of Art

hrd. hard

H.R.E. Holy Roman Emperor/Empire

Hrf. Ger. *Harfe*, harp (mus.)

H.R.H. Her/His Royal Highness

H.R.H.A. Honorary Member of the Royal Hibernian Academy of Arts

H.R.I. Honorary Member of the Royal Institute of Painters in Water Colours

H.R.I.P. L. *hic requiescit in pace*, here rests in peace

HRMA Hampton Roads Maritime Association

Hrn. Ger. *Herrn*, gentlemen

Hrn. Ger. *Hörner*, horns (mus.)

H.R.O.I. Honorary Member of the Royal Institute of Oil Painters

HRP Hampton Roads Ports

H.R.R. higher reduced rate (tax.)

H.R.S. Hydraulics Research Station

H.R.S.A. Honorary Member of the Royal Scottish Academy

hrsg. Ger. *herausgegeben*, edited published

H.R.S.W. Honorary Member of the Royal Scottish Society of Painters in Water Colours

HRT Honolulu Rapid Transit

HRWMC House of Representatives Ways and Means Committee (U.S.A.)

HS *s* Renfrewshire (B.V.R.); *s* sesterce, silver coin equivalent to quarter of denarius (numis.); *s* Thailand (I.C.A.M.)

Hs. Ger. *Handschrift*, manuscript

h.s. highest score; high school

h.s. L. *hoc sensu*, in this sense; L. *hora somni*, at bedtime (med.)

H.S. Hakluyt / Hansard / Harleian / Society; Haute-Saône (France); Hawker Siddeley (aircraft); Home Secretary/ Service; hospital ship; house surgeon

H.S. L. *hic sepultus* or *situs*, here is buried

H.S.A. Hospital Saving(s) Association

HSAA Health Sciences Advancement Award (U.S.A.)

H.S.A.C. Hebridean Spinners' Advisory Committee

HSBR high-speed bombing radar

H.S.C. Higher School Certificate *now* G.C.E. Advanced level; Honourable Society of Cymmrodorion

H. Sch. High School

hse. house

H.S.E. L. *hic sepultus/situs est*, here lies buried

hsekpr. housekeeper

H.S.F. Hospital Saturday Fund

hsg. housing

HSG. *Hochschule St. Gallen für Wirtschaft und Sozialwissenschaft*, St. Gall School of Economics (Switz.)

H.S.H. Her/His Serene Highness

H.S.L. Huguenot Society of London

H.S.M. Her/His Serene Majesty

HSNP Hot Springs National Park (U.S.A.)

H.S.O. Hamburg Symphony Orchestra

h.s.p. high speed printer (computer)

H.S.P.G. Hansard Society for Parliamentary Government

H.S.Q. Historical Society of Queensland (Aust.)

h.s.r. high speed reader (computer)

H.S.S. high speed steel; History of Science Society (U.S.A.)

H.S.S. L. *Historicae Societatis Socius*, Fellow of the Historical Society

H.S.S.A. High Speed Steel Association

H.S.T. Harry S. Truman, pres. of U.S.A. 1945–1953; highest spring tide; hypersonic transport

HT *s* Bristol (B.V.R.)

H-T, H.T. high-temperature

ht. heat; height

h.t. half time; halftone; heat treated/ treatment; heavy tank; high tension (elec.)

h.t. L. *hoc tempore*, at this time; L. *hoc titulo*, in/under this title

h. & t. hardened and tempered

H.T. high tide; high treason; hybrid tea rose

h.t.a. heavier than air

H.T.A. Harris Tweed Association Limited; Horticultural Traders' Association; Household Textile Association

Htb. *hautboy*, oboe (mus.)

h.t.b. high tension battery (elec.)

htd. heated; — **pl.** heated pool; — **rm.** heated room

Hte. Gar. Haute-Garonne; — **L.** Haute-Loire; — **M.** Haute Marne; — **Saô.** Haute-Saône; — **Sav.** Haute-Savoie; **Htes. Pyr.** Hautes-Pyrénées (France)

H.T.G.C.R., H.T.G.R. high temperature gas-cooled reactor

H.T.M. heat transfer medium

Htn. Hamilton (Bermuda)

HTOL horizontal take off and landing

htr. heater

H.T.R. high temperature reactor

H. Trin. Holy Trinity

Hts. heights, in place names

h.t.s. half time survey; high-tensile steel

HTSUP height supervisor

HTT heavy tactical transport

HTU heat transfer unit

H.T.V. Harlech Television; hypersonic test vehicle

HTW high temperature water

ht. wkt. hit wicket (cricket)

HU *s* Bristol (B.V.R.)

H.U. Harvard University, at Cambridge, Mass., U.S.A.

hubby husband

HUCR highest useful compression ratio

H.U.D. head-up display system; Housing and Urban Development (U.S.A.)

HUFF-DUFF high-frequency direction finder

H.U.G.O. highly unusual geophysical operations

HUJ Hebrew University of Jerusalem

HUKFORLANT hunter-killer forces, Atlantic (USN)

Huks *Hukbong Mapgapalayang Bayan*, military arm of banned Communist Party of the Philippines

HUKS hunter-killer submarine (USN)

HUL Harvard/Helsinki University Library

HULTIS Hull Technical Interloan Scheme

hum. human; humane; humanities; humanity; humble; humorous

Hum. L. *Humaniora*, the humanities

humi. humidity

Humph Humphrey

HUMRRO Human Resources Research Office

Hun., Hung. Hungarian; Hungary

hund. hundred

Hunts. Huntingdonshire

H.U.P. Harvard University Press

hur., hurr. hurricane

husb. husbandry

HUSTLE helium underwater speech translating equipment

HV *s* London (B.V.R.); Vickers hardness

h.v. high vacuum/velocity/voltage

H.V. L. *hoc verbum*, this word

H.V.A. Health Visitors' Association

H.V.A.R. high-velocity aircraft rocket

H.V.C.A. Heating and Ventilating Contractors' Association

HVEC High Voltage Engineering Association (U.S.A.)

HVI Howe Ventilating Institute (U.S.A.)

H.V.R.A. Hawaii Volcano Research Association; Heating and Ventilating Research Association

hvsa high voltage slow activity

hvss horizontal volute spring suspension

hvy. heavy

h/w husband and wife

HW *s* Bristol (B.V.R.)

H & W Harland and Wolff, Belfast shipbuilders

h/w herewith

h.w. hit wicket (cricket)

H.W. high water

H.W. Ger. *Hauptwerk*, great organ (mus.)

Hwb. Ger. *Handwörterbuch*, school *or* pocket dictionary

h.w.c. hot water circulating

H.W.C. Heriot-Watt College, *now* Univ.

h.w.i. high water interval

h.w.l. high water line

H.W.L. Henry Wadsworth Longfellow (1807–82), Amer. poet

H.W.L.B. high water, London Bridge

HWM high-wet-modulus (tex.)

H.W.M. high water mark; — **N.T.** high water, neap tide; — **O.N.T.** high water, ordinary neap tide; — **O.S.T.** high water, ordinary spring tide; — **S.T.** high water, spring tide

HWS hot water soluble; hurricane warning system

HWWW *Hochschule für Welthandel, Wien,* School for World Trade, Vienna (Austria)

hwy. highway

HX *s* London (B.V.R.)

hx. hexode

HY *s* Bristol (B.V.R.); *Helsingin Yliopisto,* Helsinki Univ. (Finland)

hy. heavy

Hy. Henry; highway

hyb. hybrid

hyd. hydrate; hydraulic; hydrographic; hydrostatics

Hyd. Hyderabad

HYDAC hybrid digital-analog computer

Hydr. hydrographer

HYDRA hydrographic digital positioning and depth recording system

hydro. hydropathic; hydrostatics

hydrog. hydrographic

hydros sodium hydrosulphite, vat dyeing

hydt. hydrant

hyg. hygiene

H.Y.M.A. Hebrew Young Men's Association

hyp. hypodermic; hypotenuse; hypothesis; hypothetical

hypo. hypochondriac; hypodermic syringe; hyposulphite, *now* thiosulphate of soda

hypoth. hypothesis

Hz hertz, unit of frequency (Hz = s^{-1})

HZ *s* Saudi Arabia (I.C.A.M.); *s* Tyrone (B.V.R.)

Hzk. Hezekiah

hzy. hazy

I

i *s* current (elec.); *s* imaginary unit (math.); *s* intermittent precipitation (met.); one (Roman)

i' in

I *s* current (elec.); *s* iodine (chem. and med.); *s* Italy (I.C.A.M. and I.V.R.); *s* moment of inertia (mech.); one (Roman)

i. indicate; interest; intransitive; island; isle

i. L. *id*, that

I. Idaho; Iesus; Ger. *Ihr*, your; Imperial; incisor (dent.); incumbent; Independent; inspector; institute; instructor; intelligence; interceptor; interpreter; Ireland; Irish; island; isle; isospin; issue; Italian; Italy; single column inch (advert.)

Î. Fr. *Î le*, isle

I. L. *imperator*, emperor; L. *imperatrix*, express; L. *Imperium*, Empire; L. *Infidelis*, unbeliever, infidel

IA *s* Antrim (B.V.R.); Iowa, *also* Ia.

I/A Isle of Anglesey

Ia. Indiana

i.a. immediately available; indicated altitude; initial appearance

i.a. L. *in absentia*, in absence

i.A. Ger. *im Auftrage*, by order of

I.A. Incorporated Accountant; Indian Army; infected area; initial allowance (tax.); Institute of Actuaries

I.A.A. International Academy of Astronautics; International Advertising Association; *International Aerospace Abstracts*; International Association of Allergology

I.A.A.A. Irish Amateur Athletic Association; Irish Association of Advertising Agencies

I.A.A.B. Inter-American Association of Broadcasters

I.A.A.C. International Agricultural Aviation Centre; International Antarctic Analysis Centre

I.A.A.C.C. Inter-Allied Aeronautical Commission of Control

I.A.A.E. Institution of Automotive and Aeronautical Engineers (U.S.A.)

I.A.A.F. International Amateur Athletic Federation

I.A.A.L.D. International Association of Agricultural Librarians and Documentalists

I.A.A.M. Incorporated Association of Assistant Masters in Secondary Schools

I.A.A.P. International Association of Applied Psychology

I.A.A.S. Incorporated Association of Architects and Surveyors

I.A.B. Imperial Agricultural Bureaux, *now* Commonwealth A.B.; Industrial Advisers to the Blind; Industrial Advisory Board; Inter-American Bank

I.A.B.A. International Association of Aircraft Brokers and Agents

I.A.B.L.A. Inter-American Bibliographical and Library Association

I.A.B.O. International Association of Biological Oceanography

I.A.B.S.E. International Association for Bridge and Structural Engineering

i.a.c. integration, assembly and checkout

I.A.C. Industrial Advisory Council (U.S.A.); Institute of Amateur Cinematographers

I.A.C.A. Independent Air Carriers' Association

I.A.C.B. International Advisory Committee on Bibliography (UNESCO)

I.A.C.C.P. Inter-American Council of Commerce and Production

I.A.C.E.S. International Air Cushion Engineering Society

I.A.C.M.E. International Association of Crafts and Small and Medium-sized Enterprises

I.A.C.O.M.S. International Advisory Committee on Marine Sciences (FAO)

I.A.C.P. International Association for Child Psychiatry and Allied Professions; International Association of Computer Programmers (U.S.A.)

I.A.C.S. International Annealed Copper Standard

IAD initiation area discriminator; International Astrophysical Decade, 1965–1975

I.A.D.B. Inter-American Defense Board; Inter-American Development Bank

I.A.D.F. Inter-American Association for Democracy and Freedom

I.A.D.L. International Association of Democratic Lawyers

IADPC Inter-Agency Data Processing Committee

I.A.D.R. International Association for Dental Research

I.A.D.S. International Association of Dental Students; International Association of Department Stores

I.A.E. *Institut Atomnoi Energii*, Atomic Energy Institute (U.S.S.R.); Institute of Automobile/Automotive Engineers

I.Ae.A. Institution of Aeronautical Engineers

I.A.E.A. Indian Adult Education Association; International Atomic Energy Agency (U.N.O.)

I.A.E.C. Israel Atomic Energy Commission

IAECOSOC Inter-American Economic and Social Council

I.Ae.E. Institution of Aeronautical Engineers, *now* incorporated with Royal Aeronautical Soc.

I.A.E.E. International Association of Earthquake Engineers

I.A.E.S.T.E. International Association for the Exchange of Students for Technical Experience

i.a.f. interview after flight

I.A.F. Indian Air/Auxiliary Force; International Abolitionist (of Prostitution) Federation; International Astronautical Federation

I.A.F.D. International Association on Food Distribution

I.A.F.M.M. International Association of Fish Meal Manufacturers

I.A.F.W.N.O. Inter-American Federation of Working Newspapermen's Organizations

I.A.G. International Association of Geodesy/Geology/Gerontology

I.A.G.A. International Association of Geomagnetism and Aeronomy

I.A.G.B. & I. Ileostomy Association of Great Britain and Ireland

I.A.G.C. International Association for Geochemistry and Cosmochemistry

I. Agr. E. Institution of Agricultural Engineers

I.A.H. International Association of Hydrogeologists/Hydrology

I.A.H.A. Inter-American Hotel Association

I.A.H.M. Incorporated Association o Head Masters

I.A.H.P. International Association of Horticultural Producers

I.A.H.R. International Association for Hydraulic Research; International Association for the History of Religions

I.A.I. International African Institute

I.A.I.A.S. Inter-American Institute of Agricultural Sciences

I.A.L. Imperial Airways Ltd; Imperial Arts League; International Algebraic Language; International Association of (Theoretical and Applied) Limnology; Irish Academy of Letters

I.A.L.A. International African Law Association; International Association of Lighthouse Authorities

I.A.L.L. International Association of Law Libraries

I.A.L.P. International Association o Logopedics and Phoniatrics

I.A.L.S. International Association of Legal Science

I.A.M. Institute of Administrative Management;—**(Cert.)** Certificate of Institute of Administrative Management;— **(Cert. O. & M.)** Certificate in Organization and Method of the Institute of Administrative Management; Institute of Advanced Motorists: Institute of Aviation Medicine; International Association of Meteorology/ Microbiologists

I.A.M.A. Incorporated Advertising Managers' Association; International Abstaining Motorists' Association; Irish Association of Municipal Authorities

I.A.M.A.P. International Association of Meteorology and Atmospheric Physics

I.A.M.B. Irish Association of Master Bakers

I.A.M.C. Indian Army Medical Corps;

Institute for Advancement of Medical Communication (U.S.A.)

I.A.M.C.R. International Association for Mass Communication Research

I.A.M.L. International Association of Music Libraries

I.A.M.M. International Association of Medical Museums

I.A.M.S. International Association of Microbiological Societies/Studies

I.A.M.W.F. Inter-American Mine Workers Federation

I.A.N.C. International Airline Navigators' Council

I.A.N.E.C. Inter-American Nuclear Energy Commission

I.A.O. Incorporated Association of Organists

I.A.O.C. Indian Army Ordnance Corps

I.A.O.S. Irish Agricultural Organization Society

I.A.P. Institute of Animal Physiology (A.R.C.); International Academy of Pathology

I.A.P.A. Industrial Accident Prevention Association (U.S.A.); Inter-American Press Association

I.A.P.B. International Association for the Prevention of Blindness

I.A.P.G. International Association of Physical Geography

I.A.P.H. International Association of Ports and Harbours

I.A.P.I.P. International Association for the Protection of Industrial Property

I.A.P.N. International Association of Professional Numismatists

I.A.P.O. International Association of Physical Oceanography

I.A.P.S. Incorporated Association of Preparatory Schools

I.A.P.S.O. International Association for the Physical Sciences of the Oceans

I.A.P.T. International Association for Plant Taxonomy

I.A.R.A. Inter-Allied Reparations Agency

I. Arb. Institute of Arbitrators

IARC International Agency for Research on Cancer

I.A.R.C. Indian Agricultural Research Council

I.A.R.F. International Association for Liberal Christianity and Religious Freedom

I.A.R.I. Indian Agricultural Research Institute

I.A.R.I.W. International Association for Research into Income and Wealth

I.A.R.O. Indian Army Reserve of Officers

I.A.R.U. International Amateur Radio Union

i.a.s. immediate access storage (computer); indicated air speed (nav.); instrument approach system

I.A.S. Indian Administrative Service; Institute of the Aerospace Sciences (U.S.A.)

I.A.S.A. International Air Safety Association

I.A.S.C. Indian Army Service Corps; International Association of Seed Crushers

I.A.S.H. International Association of Scientific Hydrology

I.A.S.I. Inter-American Statistical Institute

I.A.S.L.I.C. Indian Association of Special Libraries and Information Centres

IASM It. *Istituto per l'Assistenza allo Sviluppo del Mezzogiorno*, Institute for Assistance to the Development of Southern Italy

i.a.s.o.r. ice and snow on runway

I.A.S.P. International Association for Social Progress

I.A.S.P.E.I. International Association of Seismology and Physics of the Earth's Interior

I.A.S.S. International Association for Shell Structures; International Association of Soil Science

I.A.S.S.W. International Association of Schools of Social Work

I.A.S.Y. International Active Sun Years

i.a.t. inside air temperature

I.A.T.A. International Air Transport Association; International Amateur Theatre Association

I.A.T.E. International Association for Temperance Education

I.A.T.T.C. Inter-American Tropical Tuna Commission

I.A.T.U.L. International Association of Technical University Libraries

I.A.U. International Association of Universities; International Astronomical Union

I.A.U.P.L. International Association of University Professors and Lecturers

I.A.V. International Association of Volcanology

I.A.V.F.H. International Association of Veterinary Food Hygienists

I.A.V.G. International Association for Vocational Guidance

i.a.w. in accordance with

I.A.W. International Alliance of Women

I.A.W.A. International Association of Wood Anatomists

I.A.W.M.C. International Association of Workers for Maladjusted Children

I.A.W.P.R. International Association on Water Pollution Research

I.A.W.S. Irish Agricultural Wholesale Society

IB *s* Armagh (B.V.R.); *Iberia*, Spanish airlines

ib. L. *ibidem*, in the same place

I.B. in bond; incendiary bomb; infectious bronchitis; information bureau; Institute of Bankers/Building; instruction book; intelligence branch; international bank; International Rugby Football Board; invoice book

I.B.A. Independent/Industrial/Investment/Bankers' Association; Independent Broadcasting Authority, formerly **I.T.A.**; industrial buildings allowances (tax); Institute of British Architects; International Bar Association

I.B.A.A. Investment Bankers' Association of America

I.B.A.E. Institution of British Agricultural Engineers

I.B.A.M. Institute of Business Administration and Management (Jap.)

I.B.B. Institute of British Bakers; International Bowling Board

I.B.C. International Biotoxicological Centre; International Broadcasting Corporation

I.B.C.A. Institute of Burial and Cremation Administration

I.B.D. Incorporated Institute of British Decorators and Interior Designers

I.B.E. Institute of British Engineers; International Bureau of Education

IBEG International Book Export Group

I.B.E.N. incendiary bomb with explosive nose

I.B.F. Institute of British Foundrymen; International Badminton Federation

I.B.F.M.P. International Bureau of the Federations of Master Printers

I.B.F.O. International Brotherhood of Firemen and Oilers

I.B.G. Incorporated Brewers Guild; Institute of British Geographers

I.B.H.A. Insulation, Building and Hardboard Association

i.b.i. invoice book inwards

IBID international bibliographical description

ibid. L. *ibidem*, in the same place

I.B.I.E. International Brewing Industries Exposition

I. Biol. Institute of Biology

I.B.K. Institute of Book-Keepers

I.B.L. Institute of British Launderers

I.B.M. Institute of Baths Management; intercontinental ballistic missile; International Business Machines

I.B.M.R. International Bureau for Mechanical Reproduction

I.B.N. Fr. *Institut Belge de Normalisation*, Belg. Standards Institute

i.b.o. invoice book outwards

i.b.p. initial boiling point

I.B.P. Institute of British Photographers; International Biological Programme

I.B.R.D. International Bank for Reconstruction and Development (World Bank), estab. after Bretton Woods Conference 1946. It guides international investment and provides loans for development purposes, mainly in underdeveloped countries (U.N.O.)

I.B.R.O. International Bank/Brain Research Organization

I.B.S., I.B. (Scot.) Institute of Bankers in Scotland

I.B.S.A. Inanimate Bird Shooting Association

I.B.S.S. International Banking Summer School

I.B.S.T. Institute of British Surgical Technicians

i. b. test ink blot test (psy.)

i. bu. imperial bushel

I.B.W.M. International Bureau of Weights and Measures

IBY International Book Year

IC *s* Carlow (Rep. of Ireland V.R.)

i/c. in charge/command

2 i/c. second in command

i.c. index/instrument correction; integrated circuit; internal combustion/communication/connection

I.C. identity card; Imperial College of Science and Technology, Lond.; Imperial Conference; industrial court; information centre; Institute of Charity (Rosminians); Intelligence Corps; *Investors Chronicle*

I.C. L. *Iesus Christus*, Jesus Christ

I.-C. Indo-China

ICA ignition control additive (tricresyl phosphate) added to motor fuel to diminish spark plug fouling; Industrial Catering Association; International Co-operation Administration

I.C.A. Fr. *Fédération internationale chrétienne des travailleurs de l'alimentation, du tabac et de l'hôtellerie*, Intern. Christian Fed. of Food, Drink, Tobacco and Hotel-workers; Ice Cream Alliance; Institute of Chartered Accountants in England and Wales; Institute of Company Accountants; Institute of Contemporary Arts; International Cartographic/Chef's/Chiropractors' Association; International Colour Authority; International Commission on Acoustics; International Co-operative Alliance; International Council on Archives; Irish Cyclists' Association

I.C.A.A. Invalid Children's Aid Association; Investment Counsel Association of America

I.C.A.C. International Cotton Advisory Committee

I.C.A.E. International Commission on Agricultural Engineering; International Conference of Agricultural Economists

I.C.A.I. International Commission for Agricultural Industries

I.C.A.M. Institute of Corn and Agricultural Merchants

I.C.A.N. International Commission for Air Navigation

I.C.A.O. International Civil Aviation Organization, specialized agency *estab.* 1947 to promote safe and orderly development of civil aviation

Icap. Inter-American Committee for the Alliance for Progress

I.C.A.P. Institute of Certified Ambulance Personnel; International Congress of Applied Psychology

I.C.A.R. Indian Council of Agricultural Research

I.C.A.S. Institute of Chartered Accountants of Scotland; International Council of Aeronautical/Aerospace Sciences

I.C.B. Indian Coffee Board; Institute of Comparative Biology; International Container Bureau

I.C.B.A. International Community of Booksellers' Associations

I.C.B.D. International Council of Ballroom Dancing

I.C.B.H.I. Industrial Craft (Member) of the British Horological Institute

I.C.B.M. intercontinental ballistic missile, *also* I.B.M.

I.C.B.P. International Committee for Bird Preservation/Protection

I.C.B.S. Incorporated Church Building Society

ICC Indian Claims Commission (U.S.A.)

I.C.C. Imperial Cricket Conference; inter-county championship; International Association for Cereal Chemistry; International Chamber of Commerce; International Children's Centre; International Congregational Council; International Correspondence Colleges; Interstate Commerce Commission (U.S.A.)

I.C.C.A. Intercontinental Corrugated Case Association

I.C.C.A.T. International Commission for the Conservation of Atlantic Tunas

I.C.C.B. International Catholic Child Bureau

I.C.C.C. International Conference of Catholic Charities

I.C.C.E. International Council of Commerce Employers

I.C.C.F. International Correspondence Chess Federation

I.C.C.J. International Committee for Co-operation of Journalists

I.C.C.P. International Council for Children's Play

I.C.C.S. International Centre of Criminological Studies

I.C. & C.Y. Inns of Court and City Yeomanry

ICDC Industrial & Commercial Development Corporation (Kenya)

I.C.D.O. International Civil Defence Organization

Ice., Icel. Iceland; Icelandic

I.C.E. Institution of Chemical/Civil Engineers; internal combustion engine; International Cultural Exchange

I.C.E.F. International Council for Educational Films

I.C.E.G. Insulated Conductors' Export Group

I.C.E.I. Institution of Civil Engineers of Ireland

ICEL International Committee on English in the Liturgy

ICEM inverted coaxial magnetron

I.C.E.M. Inter-governmental Committee for European Migration

I.C.E.R. Information Centre of the European Railways

I. Ceram. Institute of Ceramics

I.C.E.S. International Council for the Exploration of the Sea

ICETT Industrial Council for Educational and Training Technology

I.C.F. Ice Cream Federation; Industrial Christian Fellowship; International Canoe Federation

I.C.F.C. Industrial and Commercial Finance Corporation; International Centre of Films for Children

I.C.F.P.W. International Confederation of Former Prisoners of War

I.C.F.T.A. International Committee of Foundry Technical Associations

I.C.F.T.U. International Confederation of Free Trade Unions

I.C.F.W. International Christian Federation of Food, Drink, Tobacco and Hotel-workers

icg. icing

I.C.G. International Commission on Glass; International Congress of Genetics

I.C.G.S. International Catholic Girls' Society

174

ich., ichth. ichthyology

I.C.H.C. International Committee for Horticultural Congresses

I.C.H.C.A. International Cargo Handling Co-ordination Association

I. Chem. E. Institution of Chemical Engineers

I.C.H.E.O. Inter-University Council for Higher Education Overseas

I.C.H.P.E.R. International Council for Health, Physical Education and Recreation

I.C.H.S. International Committee of Historical Sciences

I.C.I. Imperial Chemical Industries; Investment Costing Institute (U.S.A.)

I.C.I.A. International Credit Insurance Association

I.C.I.A.N.Z. Imperial Chemical Industries, Australia and New Zealand

I.C.I.D. International Commission on Irrigation and Drainage

I.C.I.E. International Council of Industrial Editors

I.C.I.T.A. International Co-operative Investigation of the Tropical Atlantic (UNESCO)

I.C.J. International Commission of Jurists; International Court of Justice, all members of U.N.O. are parties to the statute of the Court, binding themselves to comply with its decisions in cases to which they are parties

I.C.J.W. International Council of Jewish Women

I.C.L. International Computers Limited; International Confederation of Labour

I.C.L.A. International Committee on Laboratory Animals; International Comparative Literature Association

Iclnd. Iceland

I. & C.L.Q. *International and Comparative Law Quarterly*

I.C.L.S. Irish Central Library for Students

I.C.M. Institute of Computer/Credit Management; International Confederation of Midwives; Irish Church Missions

I.C.M.A. Independent Cable Makers' Association

I.C.M.C. International Catholic Migration Commission

I.C.M.L.T. International Congress of Medical Laboratory Technologists

I.C.M.M.P. International Committee of Military Medicine and Pharmacy

I.C.M.R.E.F. Interagency Committee on Marine Science, Research, Engineering and Facilities (U.S.A.)

I.C.N. International Council of Nurses

I.C.N. L. *In Christi nomine*, in Christ's name

I.C.N.A.F. International Commission for Northwest Atlantic Fisheries

I.C.O. Interagency Committee on Oceanography (U.S.A.); International Coffee Organization; International Commission for Optics

I.C.O.M. International Council of Museums

icon. iconographical; iconography

I.C.O.R. Intergovernmental Conference on Oceanic Research (UNESCO)

I. Corr. T. Institution of Corrosion Technology

I.C.O.S. International Committee of Onomastic Sciences

I.C.O.T. Institute of Coastal Oceanography and Tides

I.C.O.U. Fr. *Office international des unions de consommateurs*, Intern. Office of Consumers' Unions

I.C.P.A. International Commission for the Prevention of Alcoholism; International Co-operative Petroleum Association

I.C.P.H.S. International Council for Philosophy and Humanistic Studies

I.C.P.I.G.P. Fr. *Internationale chrétienne professionnelle pour les industries graphiques et papetières*, Intern. Fed. of Christian Trade Unions of the Graphic and Paper Industries

I.C.P.O. International Criminal Police Organization (Interpol)

I.C.P.U. International Catholic Press Union

I.C.R.C. International Committee of the Red Cross

I.C.R.F. Imperial Cancer Research Fund

I.C.R.I.C.E. International Centre of Research and Information on Collective Economy

I.C.R.O. International Cell Research Organization

I.C.R.P. International Commission on Radiological Protection

I.C.R.S.C. International Council for Research in the Sociology of Co-operation

I.C.R.V. Inns of Court Rifle Volunteers

ICS instalment credit selling; international consultancy service

I.C.S. Imperial College of Science and Technology, Lond.; Indian Chemical Society; Indian Civil Service; Institute of Chartered Shipbrokers; International Chamber of Shipping; International Correspondence Schools

I.C.S.B. International Centre of School-Building

I.C.S.C.H.M. International Commission for a History of the Scientific and Cultural Development of Mankind

I.C.S.E. intermediate current stability experiment

I.C.S.E.M.S. International Commission for the Scientific Exploration of the Mediterranean Sea

I.C.S.H.B. International Committee for Standardization in Human Biology

I.C.S.I.D. International Council of Societies of Industrial Design

I.C.S.L.S. International Convention for Saving of Life at Sea

I.C.S.P.E. International Council of Sport and Physical Education

ICSPRO International Calcium Silicate Products Research Organisation

I.C.S.P.R.O. Inter-secretariat Committee on Scientific Programmes Relating to Oceanography

I.C.S.S.D. International Committee for Social Sciences Documentation

I.C.S.T. Imperial College of Science and Technology, Lond.

I.C.S.T.A. International Co-operative Study of the Tropical Atlantic

I.C.S.U. International Council of Scientific Unions (UNESCO)

I.C.S.W. International Conference of Social Work

I.C.T. Institute of Clay Technology; International Computers and Tabulators; International Council of Tanners

I.C.T. L. *Iesu Christo Tutore,* Jesus Christ being our protector

I.C.T.A. Imperial College of Tropical Agriculture, Trinidad; International Council of Travel Agents

I.C.T.A. 1970 Income and Corporation Taxes Act 1970

I.C.T.M.M. International Congresses on Tropical Medicine and Malaria

Ictus. L. *Iurisconsultus,* counsellor-at-law

I.C.U. international code use

I.C.U.A.E. International Congress of University Adult Education

I.C.U.M.S.A. International Commission for Unified Methods of Sugar Analysis

I.C.V.A. International Council of Voluntary Agencies

I.C.V.D. Inns of Court Volunteer Decoration

i.c.w. in connection with; interrupted continuous wave

I.C.W. Institute of Clerks of Works of Great Britain; Inter-American Commission of Women; International Council of Women

I.C.W.A. Indian Council of World Affairs; Institute of Cost and Works Accountants

I.C.W.G. International Co-operative Women's Guild

I.C.W.P. International Council of Women Psychologists

I.C.Y. International Co-operation Year, 1965

I.C.Y.F. International Catholic Youth Federation

I.C.Z.N. International Commission on Zoological Nomenclature

I'd I had; I should; I would

ID s Cavan (Rep. of Ireland V.R.); Idaho, *also* Id., Ida.

id. L. *idem,* the same

i.d. inside diameter

I.D. identification; induced draft/draught; industrial dynamics; infectious diseases; information/intelligence department; Institute of Directors; Iraqi dinar, currency

I.D.A. Industrial Diamond Association; Institute for Defense Analysis (U.S.A.); International Development Association (U.N.O.); Irish Dental Association

I.D.A. L. *Immortalis Dei Auspicio,* with the guidance of Immortal God

I.D.A.C. Import Duties Advisory Committee

IDACE Fr. *Association des industries des aliments diététiques de la C.E.E.,* Assn. of Dietetic Foodstuff Industries of the E.E.C.

IDB internal drainage board

I.D.B. illicit diamond buyer/buying (S. Afr.); Inter-American Development Bank

I.D.B.T. Industrial Development Bank of Turkey

i.d.c. has completed course at/served for a year on the staff of, the Imperial Defence College

I.D.C. Imperial Defence Committee; International Dermatological Committee

Id. card identification card

iden., ident. identification; identify

I.D.F. International Dairy Federation; International Democratic Fellowship; International Dental/Diabetes Federation

I.D.F.F. Ger. *Internationale Demokratische Frauenföderation,* Women's Intern. Democratic Fed.

I.D.I. Fr. *Institut de droit international,* Institute of Intern. Law

I.D.I.A. Industrial Design Institute of Australia

I.D.I.B. Industrial Diamond Information Bureau

I.D.L. international date line

I.D.L.I.S. International Desert Locust Information Service

I.D.L.S.G. International Drycleaners and Launderers Study Group

id. lt. identification light

I.D.M.A. International Dancing Masters' Association

I.D.N. L. *In Dei nomine*, in God's name

I.D.O.E. International Decade of Ocean Exploration, 1970–1980

I.D.P. Institute of Data Processing; integrated data processing; International Driving Permit

idr. It. *idraulica*, hydraulics

I.D.R. infantry drill regulations

I.D.R.C. International Drycleaning Research Committee

I.D.S. Institute of Dental Surgery

I.D.S.A. Indian Dairy Science Association

I.D.S.M. Indian Distinguished Service Medal

I.D.S.O. International Diamond Security Organization

IDT Industrial Detergents Trade

I.D.T. Industrial Design Technology

I.D.T.A. International Dance Teachers' Association

I.D.V. International Distillers and Vintners

IE *s* Clare (Rep. of Ireland V.R.); *s* Irvine (B.F.P.)

i.e. L. *id est*, that is; inside edge

I.E. index error; Indian Empire; Indo-European; initial equipment; Institution of Electronics/Engineers

I.E.A. Institute of Economic Affairs; Institution of Engineers, Australia; International Economic/Electrical/Ergonomics Association

I.E.C. Imperial Economic Committee, *now* C.E.C.; International Electrotechnical Commission

I.E.D. Institution of Engineering Designers

I.E.E. Institution of Electrical/Environmental Engineers

I.E.E.E. Institute of Electrical & Electronics Engineers, *now* I.R.E. (U.S.A.)

I.E.E.T.E. Institute of Electrical & Electronics Technician Engineers

I.E.F. Indian Expeditionary Force

i.e.i. indeterminate engineering items

I.E.I. Industrial Education/Engineering Institute; Institution of Engineering Inspection

I.E.(I). Institution of Engineers (India)

I.E.I.C. Institution of Engineers-in-Charge

I.E.K.V. Ger. *Internationale Eisenbahn-Kongress-Vereinigung*, Intern. Railway Congress Assn.

I.E.M.E. Inspectorate of Electrical & Mechanical Engineering

I.E.N. Imperial Ethiopian Navy

I.E.R. Institute of Environmental Research

I.E.R.E. Institution of Electronic and Radio Engineers

I.E.S. Illuminating Engineering Society; Indian Educational Service; Institution of Engineers and Shipbuilders in Scotland, *also* I.E.S.S.

i.e.t. initial engine test

I-et-L Indre-et-Loire (France)

I-et-V Ille-et-Vilaine (France)

IF *s* Cork (Rep. of Ireland V.R.); *s* grid current (elec.)

i.f. information feedback; intermediate frequency

i.f. L. *ipse fecit*, he did it himself

I.F. Imperial Father, senior chairman of associated printing trade local bodies known as chapels; Fr. *Ingénieur forestier*, Forest Engineer; inside forward (sport); Institute of Fuel, *also* I.o.F.

I.F.A. Incorporated Faculty of Arts; instrumented fuel assembly; International Federation of Actors; International Fertility/Fiscal Association; Irish Football Association

I.F.A.C. International Federation of Automatic Control

I.F.A.L.P.A. International Federation of Air Line Pilots' Associations

I.F.A.P. International Federation of Agricultural Producers

I.F.A.T.C.A. International Federation of Air Traffic Controllers' Associations

I.F.A.T.C.C. International Federation of Associations of Textile Chemists and Colourists

IFB Independent Forward Bloc (Mauritius); invitation for bid (fin.)

I.F.B.P.W. International Federation of Business and Professional Women

I.F.B.W.W. International Federation of Building and Woodworkers

I.F.C. International Finance Corporation, specialized agency to further economic development in underdeveloped countries by investing in productive private enterprise (U.N.O.); International Fisheries Convention

I.F.C.A.T.I. International Federation of Cotton and Allied Textile Industries

I.F.C.A.W.U. International Federation of Christian Agricultural Workers' Unions

I.F.C.C. International Federation of Camping and Caravanning; International Federation of Children's Communities

I.F.C.C.A. International Federation of Community Centre Associations

I.F.C.C.T.E. International Federation of Commercial, Clerical and Technical Employees

I.F.C.J. International Federation of Catholic Journalists

I.F.C.L. International Faculty of Comparative Law

I.F.C.M. International Federation of Christian Metalworkers' Unions

I.F.C.M.U. International Federation of Christian Miners' Unions

I.F.C.O. International Fisheries Cooperative Organisation

I.F.C.P. International Federation of Catholic Pharmacists

I.F.C.T.U. International Federation of Christian Trade Unions

I.F.C.T.U.B.W.W. International Federation of Christian Trade Unions of Building and Wood Workers

I.F.C.T.U.G.P.I. International Federation of Christian Trade Unions of the Graphical and Paper Industries

I.F.C.T.U.S.E.T.M.S.C.T. International Federation of Christian Trade Unions of Salaried Employees, Technicians, Managerial Staff and Commercial Travellers

I.F.C.T.U.T.G.W. International Federation of Christian Trade Unions of Textile and Garment Workers

I.F.C.U.A.W. International Federation of Christian Unions of Agricultural Workers

I.F.E. Institution of Fire Engineers

I.F.E.M.S. International Federation of Electron Microscope Societies

IFEP Dan. *Instituttet for Elektronikmateriels Pålidelighed*, Electronics Reliability Institute

I.F.F. identification / indicator friend or foe; Institute for the Future (U.S.A.); International Federation of Industrial Organisations and General Workers' Unions

I.F.F.A. International Federation of Film Archives

I.F.F.J. International Federation of Free Journalists of Central and Eastern Europe, Baltic and Balkan Countries

I.F.F.J.P. International Federation of Fruit Juice Producers

I.F.F.P.A. International Federation of Film Producers' Associations

I.F.F.S. International Federation of Film Societies

I.F.F.S.G. International Fellowship of Former Scouts and Guides

I.F.F.T.U. International Federation of Free Teachers' Unions

I.F.G.A. International Federation of Grocers' Associations

I.F.G.O. International Federation of Gynaecology and Obstetrics

I.F.H.E. International Federation of Home Economics

I.F.H.P. International Federation for Housing and Planning

I.F.I.A. International Federation of Ironmongers' and Iron Merchants' Associations

I.F.I.F. Ger. *Internationale Föderation von Industriegewerkschaften und Fabrikarbeiterverbänden*, Intern. Fed. of Industrial Organisations and General Workers' Unions

I.F.I.P. International Federation for Information Processing

I.F.I.W.A. International Federation of Importers' and Wholesale Grocers' Associations

I.F.J. International Federation of Journalists

I.F.K.A.B. Dutch *Internationale Federatie van Katholieke Arbeiders Bewegingen*, Intern. Fed. of Christian Workers' Movements

I.F.K.M. Ger. *Internationale Föderation für Kurzschrift und Maschinenschreiben*, Intern. Fed. of Shorthand and Typewriting

IFL Icelandic Federation of Labour

I.F.L. Institute of Fluorescent Lighting; International Friendship League

I.F.L.A. International Federation of Landscape Architects; International Federation of Library Associations

I.F.L.F.F. Ger. *Internationale Frauenliga für Frieden und Freiheit*, Women's Intern. League for Peace and Freedom

I.F.M. International Falcon Movement

I.F.M.C. International Folk Music Council

I.F.M.P. International Federation for Medical Psychotherapy

I.F.M.S.A. International Federation of Medical Students' Associations

I.F.N.E. International Federation for Narcotic Education

I.F.O.F.S.A.G. International Fellowship of Former Scouts and Guides

I.F.O.R. International Fellowship of Reconciliation

I.F.O.R.S. International Federation of Operational Research Societies

I.F.O.S.A. International Federation of Stationers' Associations

I.F.P. imperial and foreign post; *Institut Français du Pétrole*, French Petroleum Institute

I.F.P.A. Industrial Film Producers' Association

I.F.P.A.A.W. International Federation of Plantation, Agricultural and Allied Workers

I.F.P.C.S. International Federation of Unions of Employees in Public and Civil Services

I.F.P.I. International Federation of the Phonographic Industry

I.F.P.L.V.B. Ger. *Internationale Föderation der Plantagen und Landarbeiter und verwandter Berufsgruppen,* Intern. Fed. of Plantation, Agricultural and Allied Workers

I.F.P.M. International Federation of Physical Medicine

I.F.P.W. International Federation of Petroleum (and Chemical) Workers

I.F.R. instrument flight rules; Ger. *Internationaler Frauenrat,* Intern. Council of Women

I.F.R.B. International Frequency Registration Board

I.F.R.U. *Institut Français du Royaume-Uni,* French Institute of the U.K.

IFS *International Financial Statistics* (IMF)

I.F.S. Indian Forest Service; International Federation of Settlements and Neighbourhood Centres; International Federation of Surveyors; Irish Free State

I.F.S.C.C. International Federation of Societies of Cosmetic Chemists

I.F.S.D.A. International Federation of Stamp Dealers' Associations

I.F.S.D.P. International Federation of the Socialist and Democratic Press

I.F.S.P. International Federation of Societies of Philosophy

I.F.S.P.O. International Federation of Senior Police Officers

I.F.S.T. International Federation of Shorthand and Typewriting

I.F.S.W. International Federation of Social Workers

I.F.T. Institute of Food Technologists; international frequency tables (radio)

I.F.T.A. International Federation of Teachers' Associations; International Federation of Travel Agencies

I.F.T.C. International Film and Television Council

I.F.T.I. International Fur Trade Federation

I.F.T.U. International Federation of Trade Unions, *now* World Federation of Trade Unions

I.F.T.W.A. International Federation of Textile Workers' Associations

I.F.U.W. International Federation of University Women

I.F.W.E.A. International Federation of Workers' Educational Associations

I.F.W.L. International Federation of Women Lawyers

I.F.W.R.I. Institute of the Furniture Warehousing and Removing Industry

I.F.W.T.A. International Federation of Workers' Travel Associations

I.F.Y.C. International Federation of Young Co-operators

IG imperial gallon, *also* i. gal.

ig., ign. ignition

I.G. Indo-Germanic; industrial group; inertial guidance; inner guard; inside guardian; inspector-general; instructor of gunnery; Ger. *Interessengemeinschaft,* Combine; Irish Guards

I.G.A. International Geographical/ Golf Association

I.G.A.P. Ger. *Internationale Gesellschaft für Ärtzliche Psychotherapie,* Intern. Fed. for Medical Psychotherapy

I. Gas. E. Institution of Gas Engineers, *also* I.G.E.

I.G.B. *International Geophysics Bulletin*; International Gravimetric Bureau

I.G.C. International Geophysical Committee/Co-operation

I.G.C.C. Inter-Governmental Copyright Committee

I.G.C.M. Incorporated Guild of Church Musicians

i.g.d. illicit gold dealer

I.G.E. It. *Imposta Generale sull' Entrata,* turnover tax

I.G.F. inspector-general of fortifications (mil.); International Graphical/ Gymnastic Federation

I.G.H. Incorporated Guild of Hairdressers

I.G.M. Ger. *Internationale Gesellschaft für Moorforschung,* Intern. Soc. for Research on Moors

ign. ignition

ign. L. *ignotus,* unknown

Ign. Ignatius

Ignº Sp. *Ignacio,* Ignatius

I.G.O. Inter-Governmental Organisation

IGOR injection oil-gas ratio; intercept ground optical recorder (space)

IGORTT intercept ground optical recorder tracking telescope (space)

I.G.O.S.S. integrated global ocean station system (UNESCO)

igr. L. *igitur,* therefore

I.G.R.O.F. Ger. *Internationale Rorschach-Gesellschaft,* Intern. Rorschach Soc.

I.G.R.S. Irish Genealogical Research Society

I.G.S. Imperial General Staff; Institute of General Semantics; International Geranium Society

I.G.T. Institute of Gas Technology

I.G.U. Ger. *Internationale Gewerbeunion*, Intern. Assn. of Crafts and Small and Medium-Sized Enterprises; International Gas/Geographical Union

I.G.V. Ger. *Internationaler Gemeindeverband*, Intern. Union of Local Authorities

I.G.W.F. International Garment Workers' Federaton

I.G.Y. International Geophysical Year (1 July 1957–31 Dec. 1958) during which 11 nations operated research stations in Antarctica and approx. 200–300 scientists and technical personnel participated in Antarctic projects in the fields of geology, terrestrial and upper atmosphere physics, biology, glaciology, oceanography, meteorology, and cartography

IH *s* Donegal (Rep. of Ireland V.R.); *s* Ipswich (B.F.P.)

i.h. L. *iacet hic*, here lies

I.H. Fr. *Diplôme d'infirmière hygiéniste*, Diploma in Public Health Nursing; industrial house (Poor Law); industrialized housing; infective hepatitis; International Harvester (agric.)

I.H.A. Imperial Highway Authority (Ethiopia); Institute of Hospital Administrators; International Hotel/House Association; Issuing Houses' Association

IHAB International Horticultural Advisory Bureau

I.H.A.T.I.S. International Hide and Allied Trades' Improvement Society

I.H.B. International Hydrographic Bureau

I.H.C. Intercontinental Hotels Corporation; International Help for Children

I.H.C.A. International Hebrew Christian Alliance

I.H.D. International Hydrological Decade, 1965–1974

I.H.E. Institution of Highway Engineers

I.H.E.U. International Humanist and Ethical Union

I.H.F. Industrial Hygiene Foundation; Institute of High Fidelity (U.S.A.); International Hockey/Hospital Federation; International Lawn Hockey Federation

I.H.F.A. Industrial Hygiene Foundation of America

I.H.K. Ger. *Internationale Handelskammer*, Intern. Chamber of Commerce

I.H.L. International Homeopathic League

I.H.M. L. *Iesus Mundi Salvator*, Jesus, Saviour of the World

I.H.O.U. Institute of Home Office Underwriters

i.h.p. indicated horse-power (mech.)

I.H.R. Institute of Historical Research

I.H.R.B. International Hockey Rules Board

I.H.S. L. *Iesus Hominum Salvator*, Jesus, Saviour of Mankind; L. *In hoc signo*, in this sign

IHSBR improved high-speed bombing radar

I.H.T. Institute of Handicraft Teachers

I.H.T.U. Interservice Hovercraft Trials Unit, *now* I.H.U.

I.H.U. Interservice Hovercraft Unit; Irish Hockey Union

I.H.V.E. Institution of Heating and Ventilating Engineers

II two (Roman)

I.I.A. Information Industry Association (U.S.A.); Institute of Industrial Administration

I.I.A.I. Indian Institution of Art in Industry

I.I.A.L. International Institute of Arts and Letters

I.I.A.S. International Institute of Administrative Sciences

I.I.B. Fr. *Institut international des brevets*, Intern. Patent Institute

I.I.B.D. & I.D. Incorporated Institute of British Decorators and Interior Designers

I.I.C. International Institute for the Conservation of Museum Objects

I.I.C.C. International Institute for Study and Research in the Field of Commercial Competition

IICY International Investment Corporation for Yugoslavia

I.I.E. Institute for International Education; Fr. *Institut international de l'épargne*, Intern. Thrift Institute; International Institute of Embryology

I.I.E.I.C. International Institute Examinations Inquiry Committee

I.I.E.L. Fr. *Institut international d'études ligures*, Intern. Institute for Ligurian Studies

I.I.E.P. International Institute of Educational Planning

I.I.E.T. Inspection Instructions for Electron Tubes

I.I.F. Fr. *Institut international du froid*, Intern. Institute of Refrigeration

I.I.F.A. International Institute of Films on Art

I.I.H.F. International Ice Hockey Federation

III three (Roman)

I.I.I. Inter-American Indian Institute;

International Institute of Interpreters; International Isostatic Institute

IIII four (Roman); IV generally used, except sometimes on clock-face

I.I.L.S. International Institute of Labour Studies (ILO)

I.I.M. Institute of Industrial Managers

I. Inf. Sc. Institute of Information Scientists

I.I.O.E. International Indian Ocean Expedition

I.I.P. Fr. *Institut international de la presse*, Intern. Press Institute; International Ice Patrol; International Institute of Philosophy

I.I.P.E.R. International Institution of Production Engineering Research

IIR isobutylene isoprene rubber (butyl rubber)

I.I.R. International Institute of Refrigeration

I.I.R.B. Fr. *Institut international de recherches betteravières*, Intern. Institute of Sugar-Beet Researches

I.I.R.S. Institute for Industrial Research and Standards (Rep. of Ireland)

I.I.S. Institute of Industrial Supervisors; Fr. *Institut international de la soudure*, Intern. Institute of Welding; Fr. *Institut international de statistique*, Intern. Statistical Institute; Ger. *Internationales Institut des Sparwesens*, Intern. Thrift Institute; International Institute of Sociology

I.I.S.A. Fr. *Institut international des sciences administratives*, Intern. Institute of Admin. Sciences

I.I.S.L. International Institute of Space Law; It. *Istituto Internazionale di Studi Liguri*, Intern. Institute for Ligurian Studies

I.I.S.O. Institution of Industrial Safety Officers

I.I.S.R.P. International Institute of Synthetic Rubber Producers

I.I.S.S. International Institute for Strategic Studies, *formerly* I.S.S., founded 1958 as centre for the provision of information on and research into problems of international security, defence and arms control in the nuclear age

I.I.S.W.M. Institute of Iron and Steel Wire Manufacturers

I.I.T. Indian/Israel Institute of Technology; Institute of Industrial Technicians; Fr. *Institut international du théâtre*, Intern. Theatre Institute

I.I.W. International Institute of Welding

IJ *s* Down (B.V.R.)

i.J. Ger. *im Jahre*, in the year

I.J. Irish Jurist

IJAC Industrial Injuries Advisory Council

i.J.d.W. Ger. *im Jahre der Welt*, in the year of the World

I.J.K. Ger. *Internationale Juristen-Kommission*, Intern. Commission of Jurists

Ik, Ike, Ikey, Iky Isaac; Izaak

IK *s* Dublin (Rep. of Ireland V.R.)

I.K.G. Ger. *Internationale Kommission für Glas*, Intern. Commission on Glass

I.K.H. Ger. *Ihre königliche Hoheit*, Her Royal Highness

I.K.I. Fr. *Internationales Kali-Institut*, Intern. Potash Institute

I.K.M.B. Ger. *Internationale Katholische Mittelstands-bewegung*, Intern. Catholic Union of the Middle Classes

I.K.N. Ger. *Internationale Kommission für Numismatik*, Intern. Numismatic Commission

Ikr. Icelandic króna, currency

I.K.R.K. Ger. *Internationales Komitee vom Roten Kreuz*, Intern. Committee of the Red Cross

I.K.U.E. *Internacia Katolika Unuigo Esperantista*, Intern. Union of Catholic Esperantists

I.K.V. Ger. *Internationaler Krankenhausverband*, Intern. Hospital Fed.

I.K.V.S.A. Ger. *International Katholische Vereinigung für Soziale Arbeit*, Catholic Intern. Union for Social Service

Il *s* illinium (chem.)

IL *s* Fermanagh (B.V.R.); Illinois; Israel (I.V.R.)

IL18 Ilyushin 18; — 62 (aircraft)

Il. Iliad, Greek epic

i.l. inside leg

I/L import licence

I.L. including loading; inside left (sport); instrument landing; Fr. *L'Internationale libérale* (*Union libérale mondiale*), Liberal Intern. (World Liberal Union)

I.L.A. Institute of Landscape Architects; instrument landing approach; International Laundry/Law/Leprosy/Longshoremen's Association

I.L.A.A. International Legal Aid Association

I.L.A.B. International League of Antiquarian Booksellers

I.L.A.R. Institute of Laboratory Animal Resources (U.S.A.)

I.L.C. International Labelling Centre; International Law Commission (U.N.O.)

I.L.C.O.P. International Liaison Committee of Organisations for Peace

I.L.E. Institution of Locomotive Engineers

I.L.E.A. Inner London Education Authority

I.L.E.I. *Internacia Ligo de Esperantistaj Instruistoj*, Intern. League of Esperantist Teachers

Ilf Ilya Arnoldovich Feisilber (1897–1937), Russian novelist

I.L.F. International Landworkers' Federation

I.L.F.I. International Labour Film Institute

I.L.G.A. Institute of Local Government Administration

I.L.G.W.U. International Ladies' Garment Workers' Union

I.L.I. Inter-African Labour Institute

I'll I shall; I will

ill., ills., illus., illust. illustrate; illustration; illustrator

ill. L. *illustrissimus*, most distinguished

Ill. Illinois

I.L.L.A. Irish Ladies Lacrosse Association

illegit. illegitimate

illit. illiterate

illum. illuminate

I.L.M. International Literary Management

I.L.N. *llustrated London News*, the first (1842) illustrated newspaper

i.l.o. in lieu of

I.L.O. industrial liaison officer; International Labour Office/Organization, *estab.* at Geneva in 1919 by the League of Nations, aiming to improve working conditions (U.N.O.)

I.L.O.A. Industrial Life Officers' Association

I. Loco. E. Institution of Locomotive Engineers

ILP Israel Labour Party, *Mifleget Ha'avoda Hayisre'elit*

I.L.P. Independent Labour Party

I.L.R.I. Indian Lac Research Institute

I.L.R.M. International League for the Rights of Man

I.L.S. Incorporated Law Society; Industrial Locomotive Society; instrument landing system, provides pilot with vertical and lateral guidance landing at an airport under adverse weather conditions; International Latitude Service; International Lunar Society

I.L.S.C. International Learning Systems Corporation

i.l.t. in lieu thereof

I.L.T. infectious laryngo-tracheitis

I.L.T.F. International Lawn Tennis Federation

I.L.U. Institute of London Underwriters

I'm I am

IM *s* Galway (Rep. of Ireland V.R.)

im. Ger. *in dem*, in the

Im. Imperial

I.M. Ger. *Ihre Majestät*, Your Majesty; impulse/intermediate modulation; Institute of Metals; Institution of Metallurgists; interceptor missile

Ima It. *prima*, first

I.M.A. Indian Military Academy; Industrial Marketing/Medical Association; Institutional Management Association; International Management/Mineralogical/Music Association; Irish Medical Association

IMACE Fr. *Association des industries margarinières des pays de la C.E.E.*, Assn. of Margarine Industries of the E.E.C.

imag. imaginary; imagination; imagine

I. Mar. E. Institute of Marine Engineers, *also* I.O.M.E.

IMAS International Marine and Shipping Conference

I.M.A.U. International Movement for Atlantic Union

I.M.B. Institute of Marine Biology; Ger. *Internationaler Metallarbeiterbund*, Intern. Metalworkers' Fed.

I.M.C. image motion compensation; Institute of Management Consultants; Institute of Measurement Control; Instrument Meteorological Conditions; International Maritime Committee; International Missionary/Music Council

IMCC integrated mission control center (U.S.A.)

I.M.C.O. Intergovernmental Maritime Consultative Organisation, *estab.* 1959 to promote co-operation on intern. maritime questions

IMCOS International Meteorological Consultant Service

I.M.C.S. International Movement of Catholic Students

I.M.D. Indian Medical Department

I.M.E. Institution of Mechanical/Mining/Municipal Engineers

I. Mech. E. Institution of Mechanical Engineers

IMEG International Management and Engineering Group of Britain

IMEG (Benevolent) Institute of Marine Engineers Guild of Benevolence

I. Met. Institute of Metals

I. Meth. Independent Methodist

IMF International Monetary Fund, promotes foreign exchange stability to stimulate world trade and operates as central banker for major exchange transactions

I.M.F. Institute of Metal Finishing; International Marketing/Metalworkers'/Motorcycle Federation

I.M.H. Institute of Materials Handling

IMI Imperial Metal Industries; improved/intermediate manned interceptor

I.M.I. Imperial Mycological Institute, now C.M.I.; Institute of the Motor Industry; Irish Management Institute

I. Min. E. Institution of Mining Engineers

imit. imitate; imitation; imitative

I.M.L.T. Institute of Medical Laboratory Technology

I.M.M. Institute of Mining and Metallurgy; International Mercantile Marine

IMMAC inventory management and material control applied systems (computer)

immed. immediate

I.M.M.T.S. Indian Mercantile Marine Training Ship

immun. immunity; immunization; immunology

I.M.N.S. Imperial Military Nursing Service

I.M.O. Inter-American Municipal Organization; International Meteorological Organization

IMP inflatable micrometeoroid paraglide

imp. imperative; imperfect; imperial; impersonal; implement; import; important; importer; impression; Fr. *imprimé*, printed; Fr. *imprimeur*, printer; imprint

imp. L. *imprimatur*, let it be printed

Imp. L. *Imperator*, Emperor

I.M.P. International Match Point; interplanetary monitoring platform

IMPACT implementation planning and control technique

impce. importance

imper. imperative

imperf. imperfect; imperforate (stamps)

impers. impersonal

impf., impft. imperfect

imposs. impossible

impreg. impregnate

improp. improper; improperly

Imps Imperial Tobacco Company (fin.)

IMPS interplanetary measurement probes

impt. important

imptr. importer

I.M.R. individual medical report; Institute of Medical/Mortuary/Motivational /Muscle Research (U.S.A.); International Medical Research

I.M.R.A. Industrial Marketing Research Association

IMRAN international marine radio aids to navigation

I.M.R.C. International Marine Radio Company

I.M.S. Indian Medical Service; Industrial Management/Mathematical Society; industrial methylated spirit; International Musical/Musicological/Mythological Society

I.M.S.M. Institute of Marketing and Sales Management

I.M.S.O. Institute of Municipal Safety Officers

I.M.S.Tech. Institution of Metallurgists Senior Technician

I.M.T. International Military Tribunal

I.M.T.A. Imported Meat Trade Association; Institute of Municipal Treasurers and Accountants

I.M.T.D. Inspectors of the Military Training Directorate

I.M.Tech. Institution of Metallurgists Technician

I.M.U. inertial measurement unit; International Mathematical Union

I. Mun. E. Institution of Municipal Engineers

I.M.V.S. Institute of Medical and Veterinary Science (Aust.)

I.M.W. Institute of Masters of Wine

In *s* indium (chem.)

IN Indiana; *s* Kerry (Rep. of Ireland V.R.)

in. inch; — **in.**^{2} square inch; — **in.**^{3} cubic inch

In. India; Indian; Instructor

I.N. Indian Navy

I.N.A. Indian National Army; Institution of Naval Architects; International Newsreel Association

inaug. inaugurate

inbd. inboard

Inbucon International Business Consultants

inc. include; inclusive; income; incorporated; increase; incumbent

Inc., Incorp. Incorporated

In. C. Instructor Captain

I.N.C. Indian National Congress; International Nickel Company; International Numismatic Commission

I.N.C. L. *in nomine Christi*, in the name of Christ

I.N.C.A. International Newspaper Colour Association

Incalz. It. *Incalzando*, increasing or working up speed and tone (mus.)

I.N.C.A.P. Institute of Nutrition of Central America and Panama

incho. inchoate

incid. incidental

INCIDI Fr. *Institut international des civilisations différentes*, Intern. Institute of Differing Civilizations

Incid. m. *Incidental music* (mus.)

incl. incline; include; includes; inclusive; Fr. *inclusivement*, inclusive

incog. incognito
incor. incorporated
Incorp. Incorporated; Incorporation
incorr. incorrect
incr. increase; increment
In. Cr. Instructor Commander
INCRA International Copper Research Association
INCREF International Children's Rescue Fund
incun. incunabula
IND *s* India (I.V.R.); interceptor director
ind. independence; independent; index; indicate; indication; indicative; indigo; indirect; indirectly; industrial; industry
ind. L. *indies*, daily (med.)
Ind. India; Indian; Indiana; Indies
I.N.D. L. *in nomine Dei*, in the name of God
I.N.D.E.C. Independent Nuclear Disarmament Election Committee
indecl. indeclinable
INDECO Industrial Development Corporation (Zamb.)
indef. indefinite
Ind.-et-L. Indre-et-Loire (France)
indic. indicative; indicator
Ind. Imp. L. *Indiae Imperator*, Emperor of India
indiv. individual
Ind. L. Independent Liberal
Ind. Meth. Independent Methodist
Indo.-Eur. Indo-European
Indo.-Ger. Indo-German; Indo-Germanic
Indo.-Pak. India-Pakistan
indre. indenture
Ind. T., Ind. Ter., Ind. Terr. Indian Territory (U.S.A.)
induc. induction
indust. industrial; industrious; industry
I.N.E. *Instituto Nacional de Estatística*, Nat. Statistics Institution (Port.)
ined. L. *ineditus*, unpublished
in ex. L. *in extenso*, at length
inf. infantry; inferior; infinitive; influence; information
inf. L. *infra*, below; L. *infusum,* an infusion (med.)
Inf. Fr. *Inférieure*, lower (geog.)
I.N.F. International Naturist Federation
infin. infinitive
infirm. infirmary
infl. inflammable; inflated; inflect; influence
infm. information
info. information
INFORFILM International Information Film Service

infra dig. L. *infra dignitatem*, undignified
ing. It. *ingegnere*, engineer; It. *ingegneria*, engineering
Ing. Ger. *Ingenieur*, engineer
Ingl. It. *Inghilterra*, England
I.N.G.O. International Non-Governmental Organization
Inh. Ger. *Inhaber*, proprietor; Ger. *Inhalt*, contents
inhab. inhabitant
I.N.I. L. *in nomine Iesu*, in the name of Jesus
in./in. inch per inch
in init. L. *in initio*, in the beginning
init. initial; initially
init. L. *initio*, at the beginning
inj. injection; injury
inj. L. *injectio*, an injection (med.)
I.N.J. L. *in nomine Jesu*, in the name of Jesus
inkl. Ger. *inklusiv*, inclusive
In. L. Instructor Lieutenant
In.L.Cr. Instructor Lieutenant-Commander
in lim. L. *in limine*, at the outset
in loc. L. *in loco*, in place of
in loc. cit. L. *in loco citato*, in the place cited
INM Imbokodvo National Movement (Swaziland)
inn. innings (cricket)
I.N.O. inspectorate of naval ordnance
inorg. inorganic
I.N.O.R.G.A. Institute for Industrial Management and Automation (Czech.)
in partibus. L. *in partibus infidelium*, in the regions of unbelievers
I.N.P.F.C. International North Pacific Fisheries Commission
in pr. L. *in principio*, in the beginning
in pro. in proportion
inq. inquiry; inquisition
INQUA International Association on Union for Quaternary Research
I.N.R.I. L. *Iesus Nazarenus Rex Iudaeorum*, Jesus of Nazareth, King of the Jews; L. *Imperator Napoleon Rex Italiae*, Emperor Napoleon, King of Italy
INS *s* Inverness (B.F.P.)
ins. Ger. *in das*, into the; inscribe; inscription; inspector; insular; insulate; insulation; insurance
in s. L. *in situ*, in original place
I.N.S. Indian Naval Ship; International News Service (U.S.A.)
INSCAIRS instrumentation calibration incident repair service
insce. insurance
inscr. inscribe; inscription
INSDOC Indian National Scientific Documentation Centre

I.N.S.E.A. International Society for Education through Art

in./sec. inches per second

insep. inseparable

In. S. L. Instructor Sub-Lieutenant

INSMAT Inspector of Naval Materiel (U.S.A.)

insol. insoluble

insolv. insolvent

insoly. insolubility

insp. inspect; inspection; inspector

INSPEC Information Services in Physics, Electrotechnology, Computers and Control of the Institution of Elect. Engineers

Insp. Gen. Inspector General

inst. instance; instant; instantaneous; institute; institution; instruct; instruction; instructor; instrument; instrumental

I.N.S.T. L. *in nomine Sanctae Trinitatis*, in the name of the Holy Trinity

INSTAB Information Service on Toxicity and Biodegradability (water pollution)

Inst. Institute; Institution; — **Act.** Institute of Actuaries; — **C.E.** Institution of Civil Engineers; — **D.** Institute of Directors; — **E.E.** Institution of Electrical Engineers; — **F.** Institute of Fuel; — **Gas.E.** Institution of Gas Engineers; — **H.E.** Institution of Highway Engineers; — **M.E.** Institute of Marine Engineers; — **Mech.E.** Institution of Mechanical Engineers; — **Met.** Institute of Metals; — **M.M.** Institution of Mining and Metallurgy; — **P.** Institution of Physics; — **Pckg.** Institute of Packing; — **Pet.** Institute of Petroleum; — **P.I.** Institute of Patentees and Inventors; — **R.** Institute of Refrigeration; — **T.M.A.** Institute of Trade Mark Agents; — **W.** Institute of Welding; — **W.E.** Institution of Water Engineers

instl. installation

Instn. institution

instr. instruction; instructor; instrument; instrumental

in sum. in the summary

int. intelligence; intercept; interest; Fr. *intérêt*, interest; interim; interior; interjection; intermediate; internal; international; interpret; interpretation; interpreter; interval; intransitive

int. al. L. *inter alia*, amongst other things

I.N.T.A.L. Institute for Latin American Integration, Buenos Aires

intcl. intercoastal

int. comb. internal combustion

INTELSAT communications satellite

intens. intensive; intensify; intensive

inter. intermediate; interrogation mark (typ.)

INTERASMA International Association of Asthmology

intercom. intercommunication

INTEREXPO Fr. *Comité des organisateurs de participations collectives nationales aux manifestations économiques internationales*, Committee of Collective Nat. Participation in Intern. Fairs

INTERFILM International Inter-Church Film Centre

interj. interjection

INTERLAINE Fr. *Comité des industries lainières de la C.E.E.*, Committee for the Wool Industries of the E.E.C.

Internat. International

interp. interpreter

INTERPHOTO Fr. *Fédération internationale des négociants en photo et cinéma*, Intern. Fed. of Photograph and Cinema Dealers

Interpol International Criminal Police Commission

interrog. interrogation; interrogative

INTERSTENO International Federation of Shorthand and Typewriting

intl. international

I.N.T.O. Irish National (Primary) Teachers' Organization

intr., intrans. intransitive

in trans. in transit

in trans. L. *in transitu*, on the way

Int. Rev. internal revenue

intro. introduce; introduction; introductory

Int. Std. D. International Standard Depth

I.N.T.U.C. Indian National Trade Union Congress

I. Nuc. E. Institution of Nuclear Engineers

inv. invent; invention; inventor; inversion; invert; invoice

inv. L. *invenit*, designed it

Inv. Inverness; Investment

Invar trade-mark of nickel-steel alloy with coefficient of expansion negligible or invariable

inv. et del. L. *invenit et delineavit*, designed and drew

Io ionium (chem.)

IO *s* Kildare (Rep. of Ireland V.R.)

I/O inspecting order

Io. Iowa

I.O. India Office; inspecting/intelligence officer

I.O.A.T. International Organisation Against Trachoma

I.o.B. Institute of Bankers/Builders

I.O.B. Institute of Bookkeepers/Brewing

I.O.B.C. Indian Ocean Biological Centre (India)

I.O.B.I. Institute of Bankers in Ireland

I.O.B.S. Institute of Bankers in Scotland

I.O.C. initial/interim operational capability; Intergovernmental Oceanographic Commission; International Olympic Committee

I.O.C.U. International Office of Consumers' Unions

I.O.C.V. International Organisation of Citrus Virologists

I.O.D.E. Imperial Order of Daughters of the Empire (Can.)

I.O.E. Indian Ocean Expedition; International Organization of Employers

I.o.F. Institute of Fuel

I.O.F. Independent Order of Foresters; International Oceanographic Foundation; International Orienteering Federation

I. of A. instructor of artillery

I. of Arb. Institute of Arbitrators

I. of E. Institute of Export

I. of M. Isle of Man

I.O.F.S.I. Independent Order of the Free Sons of Israel

I.O.G.T. Independent/International Order of Good Templars

I.o.J. Institute of Journalists

I.O.J. International Organisation of Journalists

I.O.M. Indian Order of Merit; Institute of Metals; Institute of Office Management; Institution of Metallurgists; Isle of Man

I.O.M.E. Institute of Marine Engineers

I.O.M.T.R. International Office for Motor Trades and Repairs

Ion. Ionic

I.O.O. inspecting ordnance officer

I.O.O.F. Independent Order of Odd Fellows

I.O.O.T.S. International Organisation of Old Testament Scholars

I.O.P. Institute of Packaging/Painters in Oil Colours/Petroleum/Physics/Plumbing/Printing

I.O.P.A.B. International Organisation for Pure and Applied Biophysics

I.O.Q. Institute of Quarrying

I.O.R. Independent Order of Rechabites, a Friendly Soc. of total abstainers, *estab.* 1835

I.O.R.S. International Orders' Research Society

I.O.S.A. Incorporated Oil Seed Association

I.O.S.M. Independent Order of the Sons of Malta

I.o.T. Institute of Transport

I.o.T.A. Institute of Traffic Administration

I.O.U. Industrial Operations Unit; I owe you

I.O.V.P.T. Ger. *Internationale Organisation für Vakuum-Physik und Technik*, Intern. Organisation for Vacuum Science and Technology

I.O.V.S.T. International Organisation for Vacuum Science and Technology

I.O.W. Institute of Welding; Isle of Wight, *also* I.o.W.

I.O.Z.V. Ger. *Internationale Organisation für Zivilverteidigung*, Intern. Civil Defence Organisation

IP *s* Kilkenny (Rep. of Ireland V.R.)

i.p. identification point; incentive pay; indexed and paged; initial phase; input primary

I.P. Imperial Preference; India Paper; instalment plan; Institute of Petroleum, organization primarily responsible for advancement of study of petroleum and its allied products

IPA isopropanol, isopropyl alcohol

I.P.A. India Pale Ale; Institute of Park Administration; Institute of Practitioners in Advertising; Institute of Public Administration; Institute of Public Affairs (Aust.); International Phonetic Alphabet/Association; International Poetry Archives (Manchester); International Police Academy/Association; International Processing Association (Israel); International Publishers' Association

I.P.A.A. International Petroleum Asciation of America; International Prisoners' Aid Association

I.P.A.R.S. International Programmed Airline Reservation System

i.p.b.m. interplanetary ballistic missile

I.P.B.M.M. International Permanent Bureau of Motor Manufacturers

IPC International Petroleum Company (Peru); Iraq Petroleum Company

I.P.C. Institute of Printed Circuits (U.S.A.); Institute of Public Cleansing; Inter-African Phytosanitary Commission; International Polar/Poplar Commission; International Publishing Corporation

I.P.C.A. Industrial Pest Control Association

I.P.C.C.I.O.S. Indo-Pacific Council of the International Committee of Scientific Management

I.P.C.L. *Institut du pétrole, des carburants et lubrifiants*, French Fuel Research Institute

I.P.C.S. Institution of Professional Civil Servants

I.P.D. individual package delivery

I.P.D. L. *in praesentia dominorum*, in

the presence of the Lords of Session (Scot.)

I.P.E. Institution of Plant/Production Engineers; *Instituto Português de Embalagem*, Portuguese Packaging Institute

Ipecac. Ipecacuanha

IPEX International Printing Machinery and Allied Trades' Exhibition, *estab.* 1955

I.P.F. Irish Printing Federation

I.P.F.C. Indo-Pacific Fisheries Council (FAO)

I.P.G. Independent Publishers' Group; Industrial Painters' Group

i.p.h. impressions per hour

I.P.H.C. International Pacific Halibut Commission

I.P.H.E. Institution of Public Health Engineers

i.p.i. L. *in partibus infidelium*, in the regions of unbelievers

I.P.I. Institute of Patentees and Inventors; International Press Institute

IPKI *Ikatan Pendukung Kemerdekaan Indonesia*, Upholders of Indonesia's Independence

IPKO International Information Centre on Peacekeeping Operations

IPL information processing language

I. Plant E. Institution of Plant Engineers

I.P.M. immediate past master; inches per minute/month; Institute of Personnel/Printing Management

I.P.M.S. International Polar Motion Service

I.P.O. Israel Philharmonic Orchestra

I.P.O.E.E. Institution of Post Office Electrical Engineers

I.P.P.D. isopropylamino-diphenylamine, antioxidant for rubber

I.P.P.F. International Penal and Penitentiary Foundation; International Planned Parenthood Federation

I.P.R. Institute of Pacific/Public Relations

I.P.R.A. Indian Paint Research Association; International Public Relations Association

I. Prod. E. Institution of Production Engineers

IPS, ips inches per second; interceptor pilot simulator; interpretative programming system

Ips. Ipswich

I.P.S. Incorporated Phonographic Society; Indian Police Service; Institute of Public Supplies; International Confederation for Plastic Surgery

I.P.S.A. International Political Science Association

I.P.S.C. International Pacific Salmon Committee

I.P.S.F. International Pharmaceutical Students' Federation

I.P.S.F.C. International Pacific Salmon Fisheries Commission

I.P.T.P.A. International Professional Tennis Players' Association

i.p.t.s. international practical temperature scale

I.P.T.T. Fr. *Internationale du personnel des postes, télégraphes et téléphones*, Postal, Telegraph and Telephone Intern.

IPU input preparation unit (computer)

I.P.U. International Peasant Union; Inter-Parliamentary Union

i.p.y. inches per year

i.q. L. *idem quod*, the same as

I.Q. Institute of Quarrying; intelligence quotient, being the percentage ratio of the mental age to the chronological age (psy.); international quota

I.Q.C.A. Irish Quality Control Association

i.q.e.d. L. *id quod erat demonstrandum*, that which was to be proved

I.Q.S. Institute of Quantity Surveyors

I.Q.S.Y. International Quiet Solar Year, International Years of the Quiet Sun (1964–5)

Ir *s* iridium (chem.)

IR incidence rate; index register; *s* Iran (I.V.R.); *s* Offaly (Rep. of Ireland V.R.); synthetic cis-polyisoprene, isoprene rubber

Ir. Ireland; Irish

i.r. information retrieval; infra-red; inside radius; instrument reading

i.R. Ger. *im Ruhestand*, retired

I.R. informal report; Inland Revenue; inside right (sport); inspector's report; Institute of Refrigeration; international registration; *Irish Reports*

I.R.A. Institute of Registered Architects; International Reading/Recreation Association; Irish Republican Army

I.R.A.D. Institute for Research on Animal Diseases

IRAN inspect and repair as necessary

Iran. Iranian; Iranic

IRANAIR Iran National Airlines

I.R.A.S.A. International Radio Air Safety Association

IRASER infra-red amplification by stimulated emission of radiation

I.R.B. Irish Republican Brotherhood

I.R.B.M. intermediate range ballistic missile

I.R.C. Indian Road Congress; Industrial Reorganisation Corporation; infantry

187

reserve corps; International Rainwear Council; International Red Cross; International Research Council; International Rice Commission

I.R.C.A. International Railway Congress Association

IRD International Research and Development Company

I.R.D.A. Industrial Research and Development Authority

I.R.D.C. International Rubber Development Committee

Ire., Irel. Ireland

I.R.E. Institute of Radio Engineers (U.S.A.)

I.R.E.C. Irrigation Research and Extension Advisory Committee (Aust.)

I.R.E.R. infra-red extra rapid

I.R.F. International Road/Rowing Federation

I.R.F.A.A. International Rescue and First Aid Association

I.R.F.U. Irish Rugby Football Union

I.R.F.V. Ger. *Internationaler Regenmantelfabrikantenverband*, Intern. Rainwear Council

I.R.G. Fr. *Internationale des résistants à la guerre*, War Resisters' Intern.

I.R.I. Institution of the Rubber Industry; It. *Istituto per la Ricostruzione Industriale*, Institute for the Reconstruction of Industry

irid. iridescent

IRIG inter-range instrumentation group

I.R.I.S. Industrial Research and Information Service

IRL *s* Republic of Ireland (I.V.R.)

I.R.L. Ger. *Internationaler Ring für Landarbeit*, Intern. Agric. Labour Science Group

I.R.L.C.S. International Red Locust Control Service

I.R.L.S. interrogation recording location system (nav.)

I.R.M. Islamic Republic of Mauritania

I.R.M.C. Inter-Services Radio Measurements Committee

I.R.M.R.A. Indian Rubber Manufacturers' Research Association

IRO International Refugee/Relief Organization

I.R.O. industrial relations officer; inland revenue office/officer

iron. ironic; ironical

IRQ *s* Iraq (I.V.R.)

irr. irredeemable (fin.); irregular

I.R.R. infra-red rays (physiotherapy); infra-red reflectance, of dyed shades for camouflage purposes; Institute of Race Relations

I.R.R.D.B. International Rubber Research and Development Board

I.R.L.C.S. International Red Locust Control Service

I.R.L.S. interrogation recording location system (nav.)

I.R.M. Islamic Republic of Mauritania

I.R.M.C. Inter-Services Radio Measurements Committee

I.R.M.R.A. Indian Rubber Manufacturers' Research Association

IRO International Refugee/Relief Organization

I.R.O. industrial relations officer; inland revenue office/officer

iron. ironic; ironical

IRQ *s* Iraq (I.V.R.)

irr. irredeemable (fin.); irregular

I.R.R. infra-red rays (physiotherapy); infra-red reflectance, of dyed shades for camouflage purposes; Institute of Race Relations

I.R.R.D.B. International Rubber Research and Development Board

irreg. irregular; irregularly

IRS Internal Revenue Service (U.S.A.)

I.R.S. information retrieval system; International Rorschach Society; irrigation research station

I.R.S.E. Institution of Railway Signal Engineers

I.R.S.F. Inland Revenue Staff Federation

I.R.S.F.C. International Rayon and Synthetic Fibres Committee

I.R.S.G. International Rubber Study Group

I.R.T. Institute of Reprographic Technology

I.R.T.E. Institute of Road Transport Engineers

I.R.T.U. International Railway Temperance Union

I.R.U. industrial rehabilitation unit; International Relief Union; International Road Transport Union

I.R.W.C. International Registry of World Citizens

IS *s* Iceland (I.V.R.)

is. island; isle

Is. Isabella (*also* Isa., Isab.); Isaiah, Book of the Prophet, Bible (*also* Isa.); Islam; Islamic; Israel; Israeli

i.s. ingot steel; input secondary

I.S. Industrial Society; information science/service/system; International Society of Sculptors, Painters and Gravers; Irish Society

i.s.a. international standard atmosphere

I.S.A. Incorporated Society of Authors, Playwrights and Composers; Independent Showmen of America; Instrument Society of America; International Schools' / Silk / Sociological / Standards Association; International Scientific/Security Affairs

I.S.A.B. Institute for the Study of Animal Behaviour

ISAC Industrial Safety Advisory Council (D.E.P.); International Security Affairs Committee

I.S.A.E. *Internacia Scienca Asocio Esperantista*, Intern. Esperantist Scientific Assn.

ISAF black intermediate super abrasion furnace black, filler in rubber compounding

I.S.A.L.P.A. Incorporated Society of Auctioneers and Landed Property Agents

I.S.A.P.C. Incorporated Society of Authors, Playwrights and Composers

I.S.A.W. International Society of Aviation Writers

i.s.b. independent sideband

I.S.B. Ger. *Internationaler Studentenbund*, Intern. Union of Students; International Society of Bio-meteorology

I.S.B.A. Incorporated Society of British Advertisers

I.S.B.B. International Society for Bioclimatology and Biometeorology

I.S.B.N. International Standard Book Number

ISC Imperial Smelting Corporation

I.S.C. Imperial Service/Staff College; Indian School Certificate; Indian Staff Corps; Inter-American Society of Cardiology; International Sericultural Commission; International Society of Cardiology; International Sports Company; International Statistical Classification; International Student Conference; International Sugar Council; International Supreme Council (freem.)

ISCA International Sailing Craft Association

I.S.C.A.Y. International Solidarity Committee with Algerian Youth

I.S.C.B. International Society for Cell Biology

ISCC Iron and Steel Consumers' Council

I.S.C.E. International Society of Christian Endeavour

I.S.C.E.H. International Society for Clinical and Experimental Hypnosis

ISCERG International Society for Clinical Electroretinography

I.S.C.M. International Society for Contemporary Music

I.S.C.P. International Society of Clinical Pathology

I.S.D. induction system deposit; international standard depth; international subscriber dialling

I.S.D.S. International Sheepdog Society

I.S.E. Indian Service of Engineers; Institute of Space Engineering (Can.); Institution of Sanitary Engineers, *now* I.P.H.E.; Institution of Structural Engineers

I.S.E.A. Industrial Safety Equipment Association (U.S.A.)

I.S.E.C.W. Incorporated Society of Estate Clerks of Works

ISETU International Secretariat of Entertainment Trade Unions

ISF International Solidarity Fund

I.S.F. International Shipping Federation; International Society for Fat Research; International Spiritualist Federation

I.S.F.A. Institute of Shipping and Forwarding Agents; International Scientific Film Association

I.S.G.E. International Society of Gastroenterology

I.S.G.S. International Society for General Semantics

Ish. Ishmael

I.S.H. International Society of Haematology

I.S.H.A.M. International Society for Human and Animal Mycology

I.S.H.R.A. Iron and Steel Holding and Realisation Agency

I.S.H.S. International Society for Horticultural Science

I.S.I. Indian Standards Institution; International Statistical Institute; Iron and Steel Institute

I.S.I.B. Inter-Services Ionospheric Bureau

I.S.I.M. International Society of Internal Medicine

ISIP Iron and Steel Industry Profile Service

ISIS Independent Schools Information Service; International Shipping Information Services

isl. island; isle

I.S.L.F.D. Incorporated Society of London Fashion Designers

I.S.L.I.C. Israel Society of Special Libraries and Information Centres

I.S.L.W. Indian spring low water

I.S.L.W.F. International Shoe and Leather Workers' Federation

I.S.M. Imperial Service Medal: Incorporated Society of Musicians; Institute of Supervisory Management; International Society for Musicology

I.S.M. L. *Iesus Salvator Mundi*, Jesus, Saviour of the World

I.S.M.A. Incorporated Sales Managers' Association, *now* I.M.S.M.; International Superphosphate Manufacturers' Association

I.S.M.E. International Society for Musical Education

I.S.M.H. International Society of Medical Hydrology

I.S.M.I. Institute for the Study of Mental Images

I.S.M.R.C. Inter-Services Metallurgical Research Council

I.S.M.U.N. International Student Movement for the United Nations

I.S.N.P. International Society of Naturopathic Physicians

isn't is not

I.S.O. Imperial Service Order; International Standardization/Standards/Sugar Organization

isol. isolate; isolation

iso. wd. isolation ward (med.)

ISP Imperial Smelting Process, a process for smelting zinc and lead simultaneously by means of a blast furnace

I.S.P. Interamerican Society of Psychology; Fr. *Internationale des services publics*, Public Services Intern.

I.S.P.A. International Screen Publicity Association; International Small Printers' Association; International Sporting Press Association

I.S.P.C.A. Ironmaking & Steelmaking Plant Contractors' Association

I.S.P.E. Institute and Society of Practitioners in Electrolysis

I.S.P.E.M.A. Industrial Safety (Personal Equipment) Manufacturers' Association

I.S.P.O. International Statistical Programs Office (U.S.A.)

I.S.P.P. inter-services plastic panel

I.S.R. Institute of Social Research; International Society for Radiology

I.S.R.B. inter-services research bureau

I.S.R.C. International Synthetic Rubber Company

I.S.R.C.S.C. Inter-Service Radio Components Standardisation Committee

I.S.R.D. International Society for Rehabilitation of the Disabled

I.S.R.F.C.T.C. Inter-Services Radio-Frequency Cables Technical Committee

iss. issue

I.S.S. Institute of Space Sciences/Studies; Institute for Strategic Studies, *see* I.I.S.S.; International Seismological Summary; International Social Service

I.S.S.A. International Social Security Association

I.S.S.B. Inter-Service Security Board

I.S.S.C. International Social Science Council

I.S.S.C.B. International Society for Sandwich Construction and Bonding

I.S.S.C.T. International Society of Sugar Cane Technologists

I.S.S.M.F.E. International Society of Soil Mechanics and Foundation Engineering

I.S.S.S. International Society of Soil Science

Is't is it

ist. It. *istituto*, institute

I.S.T. Indian Standard Time; Information Sciences Technology; Institute of Science Technology

I.S.T.A. International Seed Testing Association

I.S.T.C. Iron and Steel Trades' Confederation

I.S.T.D. Imperial Society of Teachers of Dancing; Institute for the Study and Treatment of Delinquency; International Society of Tropical Dermatology; inter-services topographical department

I.S.T.E.A. Iron and Steel Trades Employers' Association

isth. isthmus

I. Struct. E. Institution of Structural Engineers

I.S.U. International Seamen's/Shooting/Skating Union; International Society of Urology

Isum intelligence summary

I.S.U.S.E. International Secretariat for the University Study of Education

I.S.V. International Scientific Vocabulary

I.S.W.C. International Society for the Welfare of Cripples, *now* I.S.R.D.

I.S.W.G. imperial standard wire gauge

It Italian vermouth, *hence* Gin and It

IT Industrial Tribunal 1971, to deal with 'unfair industrial practices'; *s* Leitrim (Rep. of Ireland V.R.)

5IT *s* Birmingham (radio call-sign)

It. Italian; italic; Italy

i.t. information theory; inspection tag; internal thread; international tolerance; in transit

I.T. Idaho Territory (U.S.A.); immunity test; Port. *Imposto de transacções*, purchase tax; income tax; Indian Territory (*also* Ind. T.); infantry training; Inner Temple

ITA Industrial Training Act, 1964

i.t.a. initial teaching alphabet

I.T.A. Independent Television Authority *now* I.B.A.; Industrial Transport Association; Fr. *Institut du transport aérien*, Institute of Air Transport; Institute of Travel Agents; International Temperance/Typographic Association

I.T.A. **1952** Income Tax Act 1952

I.T.A.C. Imperial Three Arts Club; Industrial Training Atlantic Convention

I.T.A.I. Institution of Technical Authors and Illustrators; — **(Aust.)** Institution of Technical Authors and Illustrators of Australia

ital. italic

Ital. Italian; Italy

ITB Industrial Training Board; Industry Training Board prefixed by name of industry, *e.g.* **CITB,** Construction Industry Training Board

I.T.B. Ger. *Internationaler Turnerbund,* Intern. Gymnastic Fed.; International Time Bureau; Irish Tourist Board

ITC Intertropical Confluence (ocean./met.)

i.t.c. installation time and cost

I.T.C. Imperial Tobacco Company; Industrial Training Council; Infantry Training Centre; International Tea/Tin Council; ionic thermoconductivity/thermocurrent

I.T.C.A. Independent Television Companies' Association; Inter-American Technical Council of Archives; International Typographic Composition Association

I.T.C.R.M. Infantry Training Centre, Royal Marines

it'd it had/would

I.T.D.A. Indirect Target Damage Assessment

I.T.E. Institute of Traffic Engineers (U.S.A.); Institution of Telecommunication Engineers (India)

ITEX Industrial Training Exhibition and Symposium

I.T.F. Ger. *Internationale Transportarbeiter-Föderation,* Intern. Transport Workers' Fed.

I.T.G.W.F. International Textile and Garment Workers' Federation

I.T.I. International Technical Institute of Flight Engineers; International Theatre/Thrift Institute

I.T.I.C. International Tsunami Information Centre

itin. itinerary

Itl. Italian

it'll it shall/will

I.T.M. Institute of Travel Managers

ITMA *It's That Man Again,* Tommy Handley B.B.C. series, WW2

I.T.M.A. Institute of Trade Mark Agents

I.T.M.A. **1964** Income Tax Management Act 1964

I.T.M.R.C. International Travel Market Research Council

I.T.N. Independent Television News

I.T.O. India Tourist Office; Industrial Therapy Organization; International Trade Organization (U.N.O.)

I.T.P.P. Institute of Technical Publicity and Publications

I.T.P.S. Income Tax Payers' Society

it's it has/is

ITS Industrial Training Service

I.T.S. International Technogeographical Society; International Tracing Service; International Trade Secretariat

ITT, I.T. & T. International Telephone and Telegraph Corporation

I.T.T.F. International Table Tennis Federation

I.T.T.T.A. International Technical Tropical Timber Association

ITU Inter-American Telecommunications Unions; International Typographical Union

I.T.U. International Telecommunication Union (U.N.O.); International Temperance Union

I.T.V. Independent Television

I.T.W. initial training wing

I.T.W.F. International Transport Workers' Federation

IU *s* Limerick (Rep. of Ireland V.R.)

I.Ü. *Istanbul Üniversitesi,* Univ. of Istanbul (Turkey)

I.U.A. International Union Against Alcoholism; International Union of Architects

I.U.A.A. International Union of Advertisers' Associations; International Union of Alpine Associations

I.U.A.D.M. International Union of Associations of Doctor-Motorists

IUAES International Union of Anthropological and Ethnological Sciences

I.U.A.I. International Union of Aviation Insurers

I.U.A.J. International Union of Agricultural Journalists

I.U.A.O. International Union for Applied Ornithology

IUAPPA International Union of Air Pollution Prevention Associations

I.U.A.T. International Union Against Tuberculosis

I.U.B. International Union of Biochemistry; International Universities Bureau

I.U.B.S. International Union of Biological Sciences

I.U.C. International University Contact for Management Education

I.U.C.D. intra-uterine contraceptive device

I.U.C.N. International Union for the

Conservation of Nature and Natural Resources

I.U.Cr. International Union of Crystallography

I.U.C.S.T.P. Inter-Union Commission on Solar and Terrestrial Physics

I.U.C.S.T.R. Inter-Union Commission on Solar and Terrestrial Relationships

I.U.C.W. International Union for Child Welfare

I.U.D. intra-uterine device

I.U.D.W. & C. Irish Union of Distributive Workers and Clerks

I.U.E.F. International University Exchange Fund

I.U.F. International Union of Food and Allied Workers' Associations

I.U.F.D.T. International Union of Food, Drink and Tobacco Workers' Associations

I.U.F.O. International Union of Family Organisations

I.U.F.R.O. International Union of Forest Research Organizations

I.U.G.G. International Union of Geodesy and Geophysics

I.U.G.S. International Union of Geological Sciences

I.U.H.P.S. International Union of the History and Philosophy of Science

I.U.H.R. International Union of Hotel, Restaurant and Bar Workers, *now* merged with I.U.F.

I.U.K.P. Ger. *International Union der Katholischen Presse*, Intern. Catholic Press Union

I.U.L.A. International Union of Local Authorities

I.U.L.C.S. International Union of Leather Chemists' Societies

I.U.L.C.W. International Union of Liberal Christian Women

I.U.M.I. International Union of Marine Insurance

I.U.N.S. International Union of Nutritional Sciences

I.U.O.T.O. International Union of Official Travel Organisations

I.U.P.A. International Union of Practitioners in Advertising

I.U.P.A.B. International Union of Pure and Applied Biophysics

I.U.P.A.C. International Union of Pure and Applied Chemistry

I.U.P.A.P. International Union of Pure and Applied Physics

I.U.P.P.M. International Union for Protecting Public Morality

I.U.P.S. International Union of Physiological Sciences

I.U.R.N. Fr. *Institut unifié de recherches nucléaires*, Joint Institute for Nuclear Research

I.U.S. International Union of Students

I.U.S.D.T. International Union of Social Democratic Teachers

I.U.S.P. International Union of Scientific Psychology

I.U.S.S.I. International Union for the Study of Social Insects

I.U.S.Y. International Union of Socialist Youth

I.U.T.A.M. International Union of Theoretical and Applied Mechanics

I.U.V.D.T. International Union Against the Venereal Diseases and the Treponematoses

I.U.W.D.S. International Ursigram and World Days Service

IV four (Roman); intravenous

i.v. increased value; initial velocity; invoice value

i.v. L. *in verbo*, under the word

i.V. Ger. *in Vertretung*, acting for by proxy/as a substitute

I.V.A. Ger. *Internationale Vereinigung de Anschlussgeleise-Benützer*, Intern. Assn. of Users of Private Sidings

I.V.A.K.V. Ger. *International Vereinigung Aertzlicher Kraftfahrer-Verbänd*, Intern. Union of Assns. of Doctor-Motorists

I.V.B.F. International Volley-Ball Federation

I.V.B.H. Ger. *Internationale Vereinigung für Brückenbau und Hochbau*, Intern. Assn. for Bridge and Structural Engineering

I.V.C. International Vacuum/Veterinary Congress

Ive Ivan

I've I have

I.V.E. Institute of Vitreous Enamellers; Ger. *Internationale Vereinigung der Eisenwaren und Eisenhändlerverbänd*, Intern. Fed. of Ironmongers' and Iron Merchants' Assns.

I.V.F.Z. International Veterinary Federation of Zootechnics

I.V.J.H. Ger. *Internationale Vereinigung für Jugendhilfe*, Intern. Union for Child Welfare

I.V.K.M. Ger. *Internationaler Verband der Katholischen Mädchenschutzvereine*, Intern. Catholic Girls' Soc.

I.V.L. Ger. *International Vereinigung für theoretische und angewandte Limnologie*, Intern. Assn. of Theoretical and Applied Limnology

I.V.L.D. Ger. *Internationale Vereinigung der Organisationen von Lebensmittel-Detaillisten*, Intern. Fed. of Grocers' Associations

I.V.M.B. Ger. *Internationale Vereinigung der Musikbibliotheken*, Intern. Assn. of Music Libraries

I.V.R. Ger. *Internationale Vereinigung des Rheinschiffsregisters*, Intern. Assn. for the Rhine Ships Register

I.V.S. Ger. *Internationale Verbindung für Schalentragwerke*, Intern. Assn. for Shell Structures; International Voluntary Service

I.V.S.S. Ger. *Internationale Vereinigung für Soziale Sicherheit*, Intern. Social Security Assn.

I.V.S.U. International Veterinary Students' Union

IVT intravehicular transfer

I.V.T. Ger. *Internationale Vereinigung der Textileinkaufsverbände*, Intern. Assn. of Textile Purchasing Socs.

I.V.U. International Vegetarian Union

IVW Ger. *Informationsstelle zur Feststellung der Verbreitung von Werbetragern*, alt. forms ABC in English, O.J.D. in French, IAD in Italian (advert.)

I.V.W.S.R. Ger. *Internationale Verband für Wohnungswesen, Städtebau und Raumordnung*, Intern. Fed. for Housing and Planning

IW *s* Londonderry (B.V.R.)

i.w. indirect waste; inside width; isotopic weight

i.W. Ger. *innere Weite*, inside diameter

I.W. Inspector of Works; Isle of Wight

I.W.A. Indian Workers' Association; Inland Waterways Association; Institute of World Affairs; International Wheat Agreement; International Women's Auxiliary to the Veterinary Profession

IWBP Integration with Britain Party (Gib.)

I.W.C. International Whaling Commission; International Wheat Council

I.W.C.A. International World Calendar Association

I.W.C.C. International Wrought Copper Council

I.W.D., I.W. & D. Inland Waterways and Docks

I.W.D.S. International World Days Service

I.W.E. Institution of Water Engineers

I.W.G. imperial wire gauge

I.W.G.C. Imperial War Graves Commission

I.W.H.S. Institute of Works and Highway Superintendents

I.W.M. Imperial War Museum; Institution of Works Managers

I.W.O. International Vine and Wine Office

I.W.P. Indicative World Plan for Agricultural Development (FAO)

I.W.P.C. Institute of Water Pollution Control

I.W.R.M.A. Independent Wire Rope Manufacturers' Association

I.W.S. Industrial Welfare Society, *now* Industrial Society; International Wool Secretariat

I.W.S.A. International Water Supply Association; International Workers' Sport Association

I.W.Sc. Institute of Wood Science

I.W.S.G. International Wool Study Group

I.W.T. inland water transport

I.W.T.A. Inland Water Transport Authority

I.W.T.D. Inland Water Transport Department

I.W.T.O. International Wool Textile Organization

I.W.V. Ger. *Internationale Warenhaus-Vereinigung*, Intern. Assn. of Department Stores

I.W.W. Industrial Workers of the World (U.S.A.); International Workers of the World

IX *s* Longford (Rep. of Ireland V.R.)

I.X. L. *Iesus Christus*, Jesus Christ

IY *s* Louth (Rep. of Ireland V.R.)

I.Y. Imperial Yeomanry

I.Y.C.S. International Young Christian Students

I.Y.E.O. Institute of Youth Employment Officers

IYF International Youth Federation for Environmental Studies and Conservation

I.Y.H.F. International Youth Hostels Federation

I.Y.R.U. International Yacht Racing Union

i.y.s.w.i.m. if you see what I mean

i.y.v. Sp. *ida y vuelta*, there and back/ return journey

IZ *s* Mayo (Rep. of Ireland V.R.)

I.Z. I Zingari

izd. Russ. *izdanie*, edition

I.Z.D. Ger. *Internationaler Zivildienst*, Intern. Voluntary Service

Izdat. Russ. *izdatel'*, publisher

Izzy Isidore

J

j *s* one (med.); *s* square of minus one
J *s* action variable; advance ratio; *s* current density; *s* Durham (B.V.R.); *s* Jacobean determinant (math.); *s* Japan (I.V.R.); *s* Jersey (B.F.P.); *s* joule, unit of work, energy, quantity of heat (J = Nm)
j. Fr. *jour*, day; journal (*also* J.); Fr. *journal*, newspaper
j. L. *juris*, of law; L. *jus.* law
J. Jack (playing cards); Jacobean; Ger. *Jahr*, year; Jalliard; January; Jesus; jet; Jew; Jewish; *Johnsons's Dictionary*; joint; Fr. *Journal*, journal; Judaic; Judaism; Judge; June; July; Jupiter, God/planet; Justice
J. L. *judex*, judge
JA *s* Jamaica (I.V.R.); *s* Japan (I.C.A.M.); *s* Stockport (B.V.R.)
Ja. January
J/A., J.A. joint account
J.A. Judge-Advocate (*also* J. Adv.); Justice of Appeal
J.A.A. Japan Aeronautic Association; Jewish Athletic Association, formed 1899, since 1926 Association for Jewish Youth
Jab. Jabal; Jabalpur; Jabez; Jabreel
Jac. Jacobean
Jac. L. *Jacobus*, James
J.A.C. Joint Advisory Airworthiness Committee; Joint Apprenticeship Committee (U.S.A.)
J.A.C.A.R.I. Joint Action Committee Against Racial Interference
Jackie, Jacky Jacqueline
JACOB Junior Achievement Corporation of Business (U.S.A.)

Jacq. J. F. Jacquin (1766–1839)/N. J. Jacquin (1727–1817), both Fr. botanists
J.A.C.T. Joint Association of Classical Teachers
JAD Julian Astronomical Day
JADB Joint Air Defense Board (U.S.A.)
JADE Japanese Air Defence Environment
J.A.E.C. Japan Atomic Energy Commission; Joint Atomic Energy Committee, of U.S. Congress
J.A.F. Judge Advocate of the Fleet
J.A.F.C. Japan Atomic Fuel Corporation
Jag. Jaguar
J.A.G., J. Adv. G. Judge Advocate General
Jahrb., Jb. Ger. *Jahrbuch*, yearbook
Jahrg. Ger. *Jahrgang*, annual publication
JAIEG Joint Atomic Information Exchange Group
Jake Jacob
JAL Japan Air Lines; jet approach and landing chart (aircraft)
Jam James
Jam. Epistle of Saint James (Bible); Jamaica; *Jamieson's Scottish Dictionary*
JAMA *Journal of the American Medical Association*
JAMI'AT Arabic *Jami'at Niqabat al Ummal wal Mustakhdamin Fil Joumhouriya Loubnaniya*, League of Trade Unions of Workers and Employees in the Lebanese Rep.
Jamie James

195

jan. janitor
Jan., Jany. January
Janie Jane; Jean
janv. Fr. *janvier*, January
JAP J. A. Prestwich and Company (engines)
jap. japanned
Jap. Japan; Japanese
JAPC Joint Air Proto Center (U.S.A.)
Jap. Cur. Japan current
jar. jargon
J.A.R.E. Japanese Antarctic Research Expedition
Jas. James
J.A.S. Jamaica/Jewish Agricultural Society; Junior Astronomical Society
Jaspr. Jasper
jastop jet assisted stop (aircraft)
JAT *Jugoslovenski Aero-Transport*, Yugoslav Airlines
J.A.T.C.C. Joint Aviation Telecommunications Co-ordination Committee
JATCRU joint air traffic control radar unit
j.a.t.o. jet assisted take-off (aircraft)
JATS joint air transportation service
jaund. jaundice
Jav. Java; Javanese; javelin (ath.)
Jax. Jacksonville, Florida (U.S.A.)
JB *s* Berkshire (B.V.R.)
j.b. jet bomb; joint board; junction box
J.B. John Bull, popular term for typical Englishman, originated from Arbuthnot's *History of John Bull* (1712), in which the C. of E. figures as his mother; junior beadle; Stetson hat, inventor J. B. Stetson
J.B. L. *Jurum Baccalaureus*, Bachelor of Laws
J.-B. Fr. Jean-Baptiste
J.B.A.A. *Journal of the British Archaeological Association*
J.B.C. Jamaica/Japan Broadcasting Corporation; Joint Publishers' Committee, estab. by P.A. and B.A.
J.B. & Co. John Brown and Company (shipbuilders, *now* U.C.S.)
JBCSA Joint British Committee for Stress Analysis
Jber. Ger. *Jahresbericht*, annual report
J.B.E.S. Jodrell Bank Experimental Station
J.B.G. Jewish Board of Guardians
J.B.L. *Journal of Business Law*
J.B.S. John Birch Society (U.S.A.)
JC *s* Caernarvonshire (B.V.R.)
Jc. junction
j.c. joint compound
J.C. Jesus Christ; *Jewish Chronicle*; Jockey Club; Julius Caesar; justice-clerk; justiciary case; juvenile court

J.-C. Fr. *Jésus-Christ*, Jesus Christ
J.C. L. *Juris-consultus*, jurisconsult
JCAE Joint Committee on Atomic Energy (U.S.A.)
J.C.A.R. Joint Commission on Applied Radioactivity
J.C.B. L. *Juris Canonici Baccalaureus*, Bachelor of Canon Law; L. *Juris Civilis Baccalaureus*, Bachelor of Civil Law
J.C.C. Jesus College, Cambridge, founded 1496; Joint Computer Conference; Joint Consultative Committee; Junior Carlton Club (Lond.), founded 1864; Junior Chamber of Commerce, *also* J.C. of C.
J.C.D. John Chard Decoration; *Juris Canonici Doctor*, Doctor of Canon Law; *Juris Civilis Doctor*, Doctor of Civil Law
JCEC Joint Communication-Electronics Committee
JCFA Japan Chemical Fibres Association
J.C.I. Junior Chamber International
J.C.L. *Juris Canonici/Civilis Licentiatus*, Licentiate in Canon/Civil Law
JCLA Joint Council of Language Associations
JCNAAF Joint Canadian Navy-Army-Air Force
J.C.P. Japan Communist Party, *Nihon Kyosanto*; Joint Committee on Printing (U.S.A.)
J.C.R. junior common room
J.C.R.F.D. Joint Commission for Regulation of Fishing on the Danube
J.C.S. Jersey Cattle Society of the United Kingdom; Joint Chiefs of Staff; Joint Commonwealth Societies; *Journal of the Chemical Society*
J.C.S.T.R. Joint Commission on Solar and Terrestrial Relationships
JCT Joint Tribunal on the Standard Form of Building Contract
jct. junction; — **pt.** junction point
JD *s* London (B.V.R.)
jd. joined
J.d. Jordan dinar, currency
J.D. Diploma in Journalism; Julian Day; junior deacon; junior dean; *Jurum Doctor*, Doctor of Jurisprudence Laws; jury duty; Justice Department (U.S.A.); juvenile delinquent
JDA Japan Defence Agency; Japan Domestic Airlines
JDB Japan Development Bank
J/deg. joule per degree
JDM Jersey Democratic Movement (Channel Is.)
J.D.R.E.M.C. Joint Departmental Radio and Electronics Measurements Committee

j.d.s. job data sheet
JE *s* Cambridge (B.V.R.)
Je. June
j.e.a. joint export agent
J.E.A. Jesuit Educational Association; Joint Engineering Association
Jeannie Jane; Jean
J.E.C. Joint Economic Committee, of U.S. Congress
J.E.C.C. Joint Egyptian Cotton Committee
J.E.C.I. Fr. *Jeunesse étudiante catholique internationale*, Intern. Young Catholic Students
J. Ed., J. of E. *Journal of Education*
J.E.D.E.C. Joint Electron Device Engineering Council (U.S.A.)
Jeep general purpose, G.P. (vehicle)
J.E.F. Fr. *Jeunesses européennes fédéralistes*, Young European Federalists
Jeff Geoffrey; Jeffray; Jeffrey
Jeho Jehosaphat
J.E.L. Fr. *Jeunesses européennes libérales*, Young European Liberals
Jem. Jemima
J.E.M. Jerusalem and the East Mission
JEMC Joint Engineering Management Conference (U.S.A.)
J.E.N. Sp. *Junta de Energia Nuclear*, Nuclear Energy Authority
Jennie, Jenny Jane; Jean; Jennifer
Jer. Jeremiah (Bible); Jeremias; Jersey; Jerusalem
JERC Joint Electronic Research Committee
J.E.R.I. Japan Economic Research Institute
jerob. jeroboam
JERS Japanese Ergonomics Research Society
Jerry Gerald; Gerard; Gerome; Jeremiah; Jeremy, which is an abbrev. of Jeremiah
Jes. Jesus
JESA Japanese Engineering Standards Association
Jes. Coll. Jesus College, Oxford (founded 1571)/Cambridge (founded 1496)
jet. jet-engine (aircraft); jetsam; jettison (*also* jett.)
jet.-p. jet propelled/propulsion
JETP *Journal of Experimental and Theoretical Physics* (U.S.S.R.)
jeu. Fr. *jeudi*, Thursday
Jew. Jewish; — **Q.** *Jewish Quarterly*
jf *s* fog at a distance, but not at station (met.)
JF *s* Leicester (B.V.R.)
J/F journal folio (accy.)
j.f.b. jet flying belt
J.F.K. John Fitzgerald Kennedy, pres. of U.S.A. 1961–3

J.F.M. Fr. *Jeunesses fédéralistes mondiales*, Young World Federalists
J.F.P.S. Japan Fire Prevention Society
J.F.R.C.A. Japanese Fisheries Resources Conservation Association
J.F.R.O. Joint Fire Research Organization; Joint Fisheries Research Organisation (Central Africa)
J.F.S. Japan Fishery Society
J.F.T.C. Joint Fur Trade Committee
J.F.U. Jersey Farmers' Union
JG *s* Canterbury (B.V.R.)
j.g. junior grade
J.G.R. Jamaica Government Railway
J.G.T.C. Junior Girls' Training Corps, estab. 1942
J.G.W. Junior Grand Warden (freem.)
JH *s* Hertfordshire (B.V.R.); Jubilee head-Victoria (numis.)
Jh. Ger. *Jahresheft*, annual publication or volume
j.h. juvenile hormone
j.h.a. job hazard analysis
J.H.D.A. Junior Hospital Doctors' Association
J.H.M.O. junior hospital medical officer
J.H.O.S. Johns Hopkins Oceanographic Studies (U.S.A.)
J.H.S. junior high school
J.H.S. L. *Jesus Hominum Salvator*, Jesus Saviour of Men
J.H.U. Johns Hopkins University (U.S.A.)
J.H.V.H. Jehovah, probably the oldest abbreviation
JI *s* Tyrone (B.V.R.)
J.I. John Innes compost (hort.); Journalists' Institute
J.I.B. joint intelligence bureau
J.I.C. Joint Industrial/Iron Council; joint intelligence center (U.S.A.) committee
J.I.C.T.A.R. Joint Industry Committee for Television Advertising Research
J.I.E., J. Inst. E. Junior Institution of Engineers
Jill, Jilly Gillian; Jillian
Jim, Jimmie, Jimmy James
JIM Japan Institute of Metals
JIMA Japan Industrial Management Association
J.I.N.R. Joint Institute for Nuclear Research (U.S.S.R.)
J.I.Nuc.E. Junior member of the Institution of Nuclear Engineers
J.I.O.A. joint intelligence objectives agency
J.I.S. Jamaica Information Service; Japan Industrial Standard; Jewish Information Society; joint intelligence staff

JJ *s* London (B.V.R.)
JJ. justices
J.-J. Fr. Jean-Jacques
JK *s* Eastbourne (B.V.R.)
J. & K. Jammu and Kashmir
J/kg unit of enthalpy, *also* kilogramme-mole
J/kg°K unit of entropy, heat capacity
jkt. jacket
j.k.t. job knowledge test
JL *s* Lincolnshire, Holland (B.V.R.)
jl., jnl. journal
Jl. July
Jla. Julia
J.L.A. Jewish Librarians' Association
J.L.B. Jewish Lads' Brigade
J.L.C. Jewish Labor Committee (U.S.A.)
J.L.P. Jamaica Labour Party, founded in 1943 by Alexander Bustamente
JM *s* Westmorland (B.V.R.)
J.M.A. Japanese Meteorological Agency; Japan Management Association
J.M.B. J. M. Barrie (1860–1937), Brit. novelist and playwright; Joint Matriculation Board
J.M.B.A. *Journal of the Marine Biological Association*
J.M.C.S. Junior Mountaineering Club of Scotland
J.M.D. Joseph Malaby Dent (1849–1926), Brit. publisher
J.M.J. Jesus, Mary and Joseph
J.M.P. People's Bank's Dollar (China)
J.M.R.P. Joint Meteorological Radio Propagation Sub-Committee
J.M.S.A.C. Joint Meteorological Satellite Advisory Committee
J.M.S.D.F. Japan Maritime Self Defence Force
J.M.S.O. Joint Meetings of Seafarers' Organisations
JN *s* Southend (B.V.R.)
jn. join
Jn. John; June; junction; junior
J.N.C. joint negotiating committee
J.N.D. just noticeable difference (psy. tests)
J.N.F. Jewish National Fund
jnl. journal
jnlst. journalist
Jno. John
jnr. junior
j.n.s. just noticeable shift
jnt. joint
JNTA Japan National Tourist Association
JNTO Japan National Tourist Organization
jnt. stk. joint stock

J.N.V. *Junta Nacional do Vinho*, Nat. Wine Board (Port.)
Jo Joel; Joseph (*also* Joe); Josephine
JO *s* Oxford (B.V.R.)
J.O. Fr. *Journal Officiel*, Official Gazette
Jo. Bapt. John the Baptist
JOBMAN job management
Joburg, Jo'burg Johannesburg (S. Afr.)
joc. jocose; jocular
J.O.C. Fr. *Jeunesse ouvrière chrétienne internationale*, Intern. Young Christian Workers; joint operations center (U.S.A.)
J.O.C.C.A. *Journal of the Oil and Colour Chemists' Association*
j.o.d. joint occupancy date
J.O.D.C. Japanese Oceanographic Data Centre
Jo. Div. John the Divine
Joe Joel; Joseph; Josephine
joe. Port. *johannes*, coin (numis.)
Jo. Evang. John the Evangelist
JOG junior offshore group (yachting)
Joh. Ger. *Johann*, John
Johan. Johannesburg (S. Afr.)
Johnnie, Johnny John; Jonathan
join. joinery
Joint Four Joint Executive Committee of Associations of Head Masters, Head Mistresses, Assistant Masters and Assistant Mistresses
Jolyon *Joseph Lyons* & Co., acronym developed, 1969, at the time of TV presentation of Galsworthy's *Forsyte Saga* in which Jolyon Forsyte was a leading character
Jon. Book of Jonah (Bible); Jonathan, *also* Jona
Jos Joseph; Josephine; Josiah
Josh Joshua; Book of Joshua (Bible)
Josie, Josy Josephine
J.O.T. joint observer team
jour. journal; journalist; journey; journeyman
jp *s* precipitation within sight of meteorological station
JP *s* Wigan (B.V.R.)
j.p. jet pilot/propellant/propelled/propulsion; Junior Principal (freem.)
J.P. Justice of the Peace; **— & D.L.** Justice of the Peace and Deputy Lieutenant
J.P.A. Jamaica Press Association; Joint Passover Association
J.P.C. Jet Propulsion Center (U.S.A.); joint planning/production council; Judge of the Prize Court
J.P.C.A.C. joint production, consultative and advisory committee

J.P. Econ., J. Pol. Econ. *Journal of Political Economy*

j.p. fuel jet propulsion fuel

J.P.L. Jet Propulsion Laboratory (NASA); *Journal of Planning Law*

Jpn. Japan

J.P.R.S. Joint Publications Research Service (U.S.A.)

J.P.S. jet propulsion systems; Jewish Publications Society (U.S.A.); Joint Parliamentary Secretary; joint planning staff; Junior Philatelic Society

j.p.t.o. jet propelled take-off

JR *s* Northumberland (B.V.R.)

jr. Ger. *der Jüngere*, junior; Fr. *jour*, day; junior, *also* jun., junr

Jr. journal; juror

J.R. joint resolution; Judges' Rules; Jurist Reports

J.R. L. *Jacobus Rex*, King James

J.R.A.I. *Journal of the Royal Anthropological Institute*

J.R.C. Junior Red Cross

Jr. Gr. junior grade

JS *s* Ross and Cromarty (B.V.R.).

J.S. Japan Society (U.S.A.); Johnson Society; judgment summons (leg.); judicial separation (leg.); junior secondary

J.S.A.W.C. Joint Services Amphibious Warfare Centre

j.s.c. junior staff course

J.S.D., J. Sc. D. *Jurum Scientiae Doctor*, Doctor of Juristic Science

J.S.D.C. *Journal of the Society of Dyers and Colourists*

Jsey. Jersey (Channel Is.)

J.S.L.S. Joint services liaison staff

J.S.L.T.C. *Journal of the Society of Leather Trade Chemists*

J. Soc. Arts *Journal of the Society of Arts*

JSME Japan Society of Mechanical Engineers

J.S.P. Japanese Socialist Party, *Shakaito*

J.S.S. joint services standard

j.s.s.c. joint services staff college, signifies that officers have completed course

JT *s* Dorset (B.V.R.)

jt. joint

j.t. joint tenancy

J.T.A. Jewish Telegraphic Agency, news service

jt. agt. joint agent

J.T.C. Junior Training Corps

Jt.-Ed. joint-editor

J.T.I., J. Text. Inst. *Journal of the Textile Institute*; *Jydsk Teknologisk Institut*, Jutland Technological Institute (Den.)

jtly. jointly

j.t.o. jump take-off (aircraft)

jt. r. joint rate

J.T.S. job training standards; joint tactical school

J.T.U.A.C. Joint Trade Union Advisory Committee

Ju Junkers (aircraft)

JU *s* Leicestershire (B.V.R.

Ju. June

j.u. joint use

J.U. Fr. *Jeunesse universelle*, World Youth

jud. judgment; judicial; judo

Jud, Judy Judith

Jud. Judah; Judaism; Judea; Judge

J.U.D. L. *Juris utriusque Doctor*, Doctor of Canon and Civil Law

Judg. Book of Judges (Bible)

judgt. judgment

juev. Sp. *jueves*, Thursday

juil. Fr. *juillet*, July

Jul Julia; Julian (*also* Jule); Juliet; Julius

jul. Port. *julho*, July; Sp. *julio*, July

Jul. July

Jul. Caes. *Julius Caesar* (Shake.)

Ju/n. Sp. *Julián*, Julius

jun. Sp. *jun*, June; junior (*also* junr.); Ger. *junior*, *der Jüngere*, junior

Jun. June; Juneau, Alaska (U.S.A.)

junc. junction

Jun. Opt. Junior Optime, Cambridge University

jun. part., j.p. junior partner

Jup. Jupiter, god/planet

Jur.D. *Juris Doctor*, Doctor of Law

Juris., jurisp. Jurisprudence

jurisd. jurisdiction

jus. justice

JUSE Union of Japanese Scientists and Engineers

J.U.S.M.A.G. Joint United States Military Advisory Group

J.U.S.M.A.P. Joint United States Military Advisory and Planning Group

juss. jussive

Juss. Jussieu, name of a Fr. family of botanists spanning 17th–19th cent.

Just. Justinian

juv. juvenile

Juv. Juvenal, Decimus Junius Juvenalis (*c* A.D. 50–*c* 130), Roman poet

JUWTFA Joint Unconventional Warfare Task Force, Atlantic

jux. juxtaposition

JV *s* Grimsby (B.V.R.)

Jv. Java; Javanese

J.V. junior varsity (U.S.A.)

JVP *Jatika Vimukthi Peramuna*, political party Ceylon

JW *s* Wolverhampton (B.V.R.)

J.W. Jehovah's Witness; junior warden

J.W.B. Jewish Welfare Board; joint wages board

J.W.E.F. Joinery and Woodwork Employers' Federation

jwlr. jeweller

j.w.o., j. & w.o. jettisoning and washing overboard, term meaning a policy will/will not include this risk (insce.)

J.W.S. Japan Welding Society; joint warfare staff

J.W.T. J. Walter Thompson (advert.)

JX *s* Halifax (B.V.R.)

J.X. Jesus Christ

JY *s* Jordan (I.C.A.M.); *s* Plymouth (B.V.R.)

Jy. July; jury

JZ *s* Down (B.V.R.)

JZS *Jugoslovenski Zavod za Standardizacija*, Yugoslavian Standards Institute

K

k *s* constant (math.); *s* curvature

K *s* Cambodia (I.V.R.); *s* centuple calorie; *s* L. *kalium*, potassium (chem.); *s* kaon, either of two mesons (phys.); king (chess); *s* Kirkwall (B.F.P.); *s* Liverpool (B.V.R.); solar constant (astron.)

°K *s* degree Kelvin, unit of thermodynamic temperature

k. *s* cumulus (met.); keel; killed; kilogram; king; knight; knot; *kopeck*, Russian currency; *koruna*, Czechoslovakian currency; kosher; *krona*, Swedish currency; *krone*, Danish/Norwegian currency

K. capacity; carat (assay); joint services specification; Dutch *Kade*, quay; Norw. *Kald*, cold; Swed. *Kall* cold; Ger. *Kalt*, cold; Kandahar Ski Club, formed 1924, based at Murren in Switzerland. Premier British Ski Club for Alpine Racing; Kelvin; *Keskustapuolue*, Centre Party (Finland); king; King's (College, Cambridge); Kinshasa (Zaire) *formerly* Léopoldville (Congo); *kip*, unit of currency (Laos); knit; Dutch *koel*, cold; Dan. *Kold*, cold; Dan. *Krinda*, women; Norw. *Krinne*, women; Swed. *Krinnor*, women; Fin. *Kylmä*, cold

K. *Köchel*, compiler of thematic catalogue of Mozart's works (mus.)

KA *s* Liverpool (B.V.R.)

Ka. Fin. *Komppania*, company

K.A. King of Arms; Knight of the Order of St. Andrew (Russia)

K.A.D.U., Kadu Kenya African Democratic Union, absorbed by K.A.N.U.

KAIIN *Zen Nihon Kaain Kumiai*, All Japan Seamen's Union

KAK *Kungl Automobil Klubben*, Royal Swedish Automobile Club

Kal. L. *Kalendae*, calends, first day of month

Kan., Kans. Kansas

K.A.N. Knight of St. Alexander Nevskoi (Russia)

KANKORO *Okinawa Kenkocho Rodo Kumiai Rengokai*, Okinawa Government and Public Workers' Labor Union

K.A.N.T.A.F.U. Kenya African National Traders' and Farmers' Union

K.A.N.U. Kenya African National Union

KANUPP Karachi Nuclear Power Plant (Pak.)

kao. kaolin

kap. Dan., Swed. *kapitel*, chapter

Kap. Ger. *Kapital*, capital (fin.); Ger. *Kapitel*, chapter

Kar. Karachi

K.A.R. King's African Rifles

Karel. Karelia; Karelian

Kash Kashmir

K.A.S.S.R. Karakalpak Autonomous Soviet Socialist Republic

Kate, Kath, Katie, Katy, Kay Catherine; Katharine; Katherine

kath. Ger. *katholisch*, catholic

KB *s* Liverpool (B.V.R.)

Kb. Ger. *Kontrabass*, Double-bass (mus.)

k. & b. kitchen and bathroom

K.B. King's Bench (leg.); king's bishop (chess); Knight Bachelor; Knight of the Order of the Bath; knit into back of stitch (knit.); *Kommanditbolaget*, limited partnership (Norwegian); Flem. *Koninkrijk Belgie*, Kingdom of Belgium

K.B.A. Knight of the Order of St. Benedict of Aviz (Port.)

k. bar kilobar

K.B.A.S.S.R. Kabardian-Balkar Autonomous Soviet Socialist Republic

K.B.C. King's Bench Court (leg.)

K.B.D. King's Bench Division (leg.)

K.B.E. Knight Commander of the Black Eagle (Russia); Knight Commander of the Order of the British Empire

Kbhvn. *København*, Copenhagen (Den.)

KBIM *Kongres Buruh Islamic Merdeka*, Free Islamic Trade Union Congress (Indonesia)

KBKI Indonesian Democratic Labour Organization

Kbl. Kabul, Afghanistan

K. Bon. Klein Bonaire (Neth. Antilles)

K.B.P. king's bishop's pawn (chess)

KBSI *Kongres Buruh Seluruh Indonesia*, Rep. of Indonesia—Trade Union

K.B.W. King's Bench Walk, Temple (Lond.)

KC *s* Liverpool (B.V.R.)

kc. kilocycle

Kc. *koruna*, Czechoslovakian currency

K.C. Kansas City; kennel club; King's College/Counsel/Cross; Knight Commander; Knight of Columbus (*also* K. of C.); Knight of the Crescent (Turk.)

kcal. kilocalorie

K.C.B. Knight Commander of the Most Honourable Order of the Bath

K.C.C. kathodic closure contraction; King's College, Cambridge; Knight Commander of the Order of the Crown, Belgium and the Congo Free State

K.C.H. King's College Hospital; Knight Commander of the Hanoverian Guelphic Order

K.C.H.S. Knight Commander of the Order of the Holy Sepulchre

K.C.I.E. Knight Commander of the Most Eminent Order of the Indian Empire

K.C.L. King's College, London

K.C.L.S. Knight Commander of the Lion and the Sun (Iran)

K.C.L.Y. Kent and County of London Yeomanry

K.C.M.G. Knight Commander of the Most Distinguished Order of St. Michael and St. George

K.C.N.S. King's College, Nova Scotia

K.C.P. Knight Commander of the Order of Pius IX

kcs, kc/s kilocycles per second

Kčs *koruna*, Czechoslovakian currency

K.C.S. Knight of Charles III of Spain

K.C.S.G. Knight Commander of the Order of Saint Gregory the Great

K.C.S.I. Knight Commander of the Most Exalted Order of the Star of India

K. Cur. Klein Curaçao (Neth. Antilles)

K.C.V.O. Knight Commander of the Royal Victorian Order

KD *s* Liverpool (B.V.R.)

kd. killed

K.d. Kuwait dinar, currency of Kuwait

K.D. kiln dried; knocked down; *Kongeriget Danmark*, Kingdom of Denmark; Ger. *Kriegsdekoration*, war decoration

K.D.F. Ger. *Kraft durch Freude*, 'Strength through Joy', Nazi political holiday and recreational assn.

K.D.G. King's Dragoon Guards

K.D.I. Dutch *Stichting Kwaliteitsdienst voor de Industrie*, Soc. for Industrial Quality Control

k.d.l.c.l. knocked down in less than carloads

K.D.M. *Kongelige Danske Marine*, Royal Dan. Navy

KDP potassium dihydrogen phosphate

KE *s* Kent (B.V.R.)

K.E. kinetic energy; Knight of the Eagle (Prussia); Knight of the Elephant (Den.)

k.e.a.s. knots equivalent air speed

Keb. Coll. Keble College, Oxford, founded 1868

Kef. Keflavik (Iceland)

K.E.H. King Edward's Horse

K.E.H.F. King Edward's Hospital Fund

K.E.L.I. *Kristana Esperantista Ligo Internacia*, Christian Esperanto Intern. Assn.

KEMA *Keuring van Electrotechnische Materialen*, Testing Institute for Electrotechnical Materials (Neth.); Kitchen Equipment Manufacturers' Association (U.S.A.)

Ken, Kennie, Kenny Kenelm; Kenneth

Ken. Kensington (Lond.); Kentucky, *also* Kent. (U.S.A.); Kenya

KESP Courtauld's Edible Spun Protein, synthetic meat spun from protein fibre

Kester Christopher

keV, K.E.V. kiloelectron volt (elec.)

Kev Kevin

Kew Obs. Kew Observatory

KF *s* Liverpool (B.V.R.)

K.F. Knight of Ferdinand (Sp.)

K.F.A. Kenya Farmers' Association

K.F.A.S.S.R. Karelo-Finnish Autonomous Soviet Socialist Republic

KFL Kenya Federation of Labour

Kfm. Ger. *Kaufmann*, merchant

KFP *Kristelig Folkeparti*, Christian

People's Party, created 1933 with aim of maintaining principles of Christianity in public life (Norway)

Kfz. Ger. *Kraftfahrzeug*, motor vehicle

kg, kg. kilogramme, unit of mass

KG *s* Cardiff (B.V.R.)

kg. keg

K.G. Knight of the Most Noble Order of the Garter, order founded *c* 1348; Ger. *Kommanditgesellschaft*, limited partnership

K. Ga. A. Ger. *Kommanditgesellschaft auf Aktien*, limited partnership on share basis

K.G.B. *Komitet Gosudarstvdnnoi Bezopasnosti*, Committee of State Security (U.S.S.R.)

K.G.C. Knight of the Golden Circle, Amer. anti-federal pro-slavery secret society and political organization, flourished in the N. (1855–64) and sympathized with the Secessionists; Knight of the Grand Cross

kg. cal. kilogram calorie

K.G.C.B. Knight of the Grand Cross of the Bath

K.G.C.S.G. Knight Grand Cross of the Order of Saint Gregory the Great

kg. cum. kilograms per cubic metre

K.G.E. Knight of the Order of the Golden Eagle (Ger.)

kgf. kilogram force

Kgf. Ger. *Kriegsgefangener*, prisoner of war

K.G.F. Knight of the Order of the Golden Fleece (Austria, Spain)

K.G.K. *Kabuskiki Goshi Kaisha*, Japanese joint stock limited partnership

Kgl. Ger. *Königlich*, Royal

kg/m² kilogramme per square metre, unit of density

kg/m³ kilogramme per cubic metre, unit of density

kg. m. kilogrammetre

Kgn. Kingston (Jamaica)

K.G.St.J. Knight of Grace of the Order of Saint John of Jerusalem, *now* K.St.J.

K.G.V. Knight of Gustavus Vasa (Swed.)

KH *s* Kingston-upon-Hull (B.V.R.)

kH. kilohertz

Kh. Khmer, *formerly* Cambodia

K.H. kennel huntsman; King's Hussars; Knight of the Royal Guelphic Order of Hanover

K.H.C. Honorary Chaplain to the King

K.H.D.S. Honorary Dental Surgeon to the King

K.H.M. King's Harbour Master

K.H.N.S. Honorary Nursing Sister to the King

K.H.P. Honorary Physician to the King

K.H.S. Honorary Surgeon to the King; Knight of the Holy Sepulchre (freem.)

khz., kHz. kiloherz

KI *s* Waterford (B.V.R.)

ki. kitchen

K.I.A. killed in action

kias knots indicated air speed

kid. kidney

K.i.H. *Kaisar-i-Hind*, Emperor of India, medal

kil. kilderkin (*also* kild.); kilometre

Kild. Kildare

Kilk. Kilkenny

kilo., kilog. kilogram; kilogramme

kilohm. kilo-ohm

kilovar. kilovolt-ampère

kin. kinematic; — **visc.** kinematic viscosity

Kinc. Kincardine

kind. kindergarten

kingd. kingdom

Kinr. Kinross

Kirk. Kirkcudbright

Kirsty Christina; Christine

KISZ Communist Youth Association (Hungary)

Kit Catherine; Christopher; Katharine; Katherine

kit. kitchen; kitten, *also* kitty

Kittie, Kitty Catherine; Katherine

K.I.V.I. *Koninklijk Instituut van Ingenieurs*, Royal Institution of Engineers (Neth.)

K.I.W.A. *Keurings Instituut voor Waterleiding-Artikelen*, Institute for Testing Waterworks Equipment (Neth.)

KJ *s* Kent (B.V.R.)

kJ. kilojoule

K.J. kneejerk; Knight of St. Joachim

K.J.St.J. Knight of Justice of the Order of Saint John of Jerusalem, *now* K.St.J.

K.J.V. King James version (Bible)

KK *s* Kent (B.V.R.

K.K. *Kabushiki Kaisha*, Japanese joint stock company with limited liability; Ger. *Kaiserlich Königlich*, Imperial Royal Majesty; *Kolonialgross istenes Kundeservice*, body of 61 independent wholesalers serving most of the independent retailers (Nor.)

K.K.K., KKK Ku Klux Klan, secret organization opposed to various races and religions, *also* Klan (U.S.A.)

K. Kt. king's knight (chess)

KL *s* Kent (B.V.R.)

kl. kilolitre

Kl. Ger. *Klasse*, class

Kl. Ger. *Klarinette*, clarinet (mus.)

K.L. *King Lear* (Shake.); Knight of Leopold, Austria/Belgium; Kuala Lumpur (Malaysia)

K.L.A. Karachi Library Association (Pak.); Kingdom of Libya Airlines, *see* L.A.A.; Knight of Leopold of Austria

klax. klaxon

K.L.B. Knight of Leopold of Belgium

klepto. kleptomaniac

Kl. Fl. Ger. *Kleine Flöte*, piccolo (mus.)

K.L.H. Knight of the Legion of Honour (France)

klim dried milk, 'milk' in reverse

K.L.J. Knight of Justice of the Order of Saint Lazarus of Jerusalem

K.L.M. *Koninklijke Luchtvaart Maatschappij*, Royal Dutch Air Lines

Kluᴠer member of Ku Klux Klan

KM *s* Kent (B.V.R.)

km. kilometre

km.² square kilometre

km.³ cubic kilometre

Km. Kingdom

K.M. King's Medal; King's Messenger (*also* K. Mess.); Knight of Malta

K. & M. King and Martyr, sometimes used of Charles I

K.M.A. Incorporated Association of Kinematograph Manufacturers

kmc. kilomegacycle

km./h., kmph. kilometres per hour

K.M.H. Knight of Merit of Holstein

km/hr, kph kilometres per hour

K.M.J. Knight of the Military Order of Maximilian Joseph (Bavaria)

K.M.O. Kobe Marine Observatory (Jap.)

K.M.O.M. Knight Magistral of the Order of Malta

km.p.h., kmps kilometres per hour

KMT *Kuo-min Tang*, Nationalist Party (Taiwan)

K.M.T. Knight of Maria Theresa (Austria)

K.M.U.L. Karl Marx Universität, Leipzig (East Ger.)

kmw. kilomegawatt

kmwhr. kilomegawatt hour

KN *s* Kent (B.V.R.); King's Norton Mint-mark, Birmingham (numis.)

kn. knot; *krona*, Swedish currency; *krone*, Danish/Norwegian currency

KNAK *Kongelik Norsk Automobilklubb*, Royal Norwegian Automobile Club

K.N.A.N. *Koninklijke Nederlandse Akademie voor Naturwetenschappen*, Royal Neth. Academy of Sciences

KNDP Kamerun National Democratic Party (Cameroun)

K.N.G.R. Kruger National Game Reserve (S. Afr.)

knickers knickerbockers

KNK *Kita Nippon Koku*, Northern Japanese Airlines

K.N.L. Knight of the Order of the Netherlands Lion

K.N.M. *Kongelige Norske Marine*, Royal Norwegian Navy

K.N.M.I. *Koninklijk Nederlands Meteorologisch Instituut*, Royal Neth. Meteorological Institute

K.N.S. Knight of the Order of the Royal Northern Star (Swed.)

KNSM *Koninklijke Nederlandsche Stoomboot Maatschappij*, Royal Neth. Steamship Company

kn. sw. knife switch

Knt. Knight

knu. knuckle

K.N.V.L. *Koninklijke Nederlandse Vereniging voor Luchtvaart*, Royal Neth. Aero Club

Knxv. Knoxville

KO *s* Kent (B.V.R.)

k.o. keep off; keep out; kick off; knock-out (boxing)

K.O. King's Own

K.O.C. Knight of the Order of the Oak Crown; Kuwait Oil Company

KOD kick-off drift, *also* decrab, removal of crab/drift prior to landing by introduction of slideslip (nav.)

K. of C. Knights of Columbus (U.S.A. and Canada) (R.C. fraternal order)

KOFF *Kjobmennenes Okonomiske Fellesforetagende*, a co-operative organization owned by over 5,000 retailers (Nor.)

K. of K. Kitchener of Khartoum

K. of L. Knight of Labor, trade union (U.S.A.)

K. of P. Knights of Pythias (U.S.A.)

KOK *Kansallinen Kokoomus*, National Coalition Party (Finland)

K.O.M. Knight of the Order of Malta

Komp. Ger. *Kompanie*, company

Kon. Dan. *Kongeriget Danmark*, Kingdom of Denmark

Kon. Nor. *Kongerikat Norge*, Kingdom of Norway

Konr. Konrad

Kon. Sver. *Konungariket Sverige*, Kingdom of Sweden

Konz. Ger. *Konzentriert*, concentrated

kop. *kopeck*, Russian currency

Kor. Koran; Korea

K.O.R.R. King's Own Royal Regiment

K.O.S.B. King's Own Scottish Borderers

KOTRA Korea Trade Promotion Corporation

K.O.Y.L.I. King's Own Yorkshire Light Infantry

KP *s* Kent (B.V.R.)

Kp. Ger. *Kochpunkt*, boiling point

k.p. key personnel; kick plate; knotty pine

K.P. King's Parade; king's pawn (chess); kitchen police (U.S.A., mil.); Knight of the Most Illustrious Order of St. Patrick

K.P.D. *Kommunistische Partei Deutschlands*, German Communist Party

K.P.D.R. Korean People's Democratic Republic

K.P.F.S.M. King's Police and Fire Service Medal

k.p.h. kilometres per hour

K.P.M. King's Police Medal

Kpmtr. Ger. *Kapellmeister*, conductor (mus.)

K.P.P. Kamerun People's Party (Cameroun); Keeper of the Privy Purse

kpr. keeper

Kpt. Dutch *Kaptajn*, captain

K.P.U. Kenya People's Union

KQ *s* line squall (met.)

Kr *s* krypton (chem.)

KR *s* Kent (B.V.R.)

kr. *krona*, Swedish currency; *krone*, Danish, Norwegian currency

K.R. King's Regiment; *King's Regulations* (mil.); king's rook (chess); Knight of the Order of the Redeemer (Greece)

K.R. & A.I. *King's Regulations and Admiralty Instructions*

K.R.C. Knight of the Red Cross

K.R.E. Knight of the Order of the Red Eagle

Kripo Ger. *Kriminalpolizei*, Criminal Investigation Department

K.R.P. king's rook's pawn (chess)

K.R.R. King's Royal Rifles; — **C.** King's Royal Rifle Corps

K.R.S. Kinematograph Renters' Society

k.r.t. cathode ray tube

ks *s* storm of drifting snow (met.)

k/so. *s* slight storm of drifting snow generally low (met.)

k/S *s* heavy storm of drifting snow, generally low (met.)

KS *s* Roxburghshire (B.V.R.)

Ks., KS Kansas

K.S. keep type standing, *also* Ks. (typ.); King's Scholar/School; Kipling Society; Kitchener Scholar; Knight of the Sword (Swed.)

K.S.A. Knight of St. Anne (Russia)

KSC *Komunistická Strana Československa*, Communist Party of Czechoslovakia, formed 1921

K.S.C. King's School, Canterbury

K.S.E. Knight of the Order of Saint-Esprit (France)

K.S.F. Knight of San Fernando (Sp.)

K.S.F.M., K.F.M. Knight of the Order of Saint Ferdinand and Merit (Sicily)

K.S.G. Knight of the Order of Saint George (Russia); Knight of the Order of Saint Gregory the Great

K.S.H. Knight of the Order of Saint Hubert (Bavaria)

K.S.I. Knight of the Order of the Star of India

k.i.s.a. thousand square inches absolute

K.S.J. Knight of St. Januarius (Naples)

K.S.K. ethyl iodoacetate, tear gas

k.s.l. kidney, spleen, liver

K.S.L. Knight of the Order of the Sun and Lion (Iran)

K.S.L.I. King's Shropshire Light Infantry

K.S.M. Korean Service Medal; *Kungliga Svenska Marinen*, Royal Swed. Navy

K. Soc. Kamashastra Society

K.S.P. Knight of the Order of Saint Stanislaus of Poland

KSS *Komunisticka Strana Slovenska*, Communist Party of Slovakia (Czech.)

K.S.S. Knight of the Southern Star (Braz.); Knight of the Sword of Sweden

K.S.S.R. Kazakh Soviet Socialist Republic

KSSU Kiev I.G. Strevchenko State University; KLM, SAS, Swissair, UTA (airlines)

K. St. J. Knight Commander of the Order of Saint John of Jerusalem

K.S.V. Knight of the Order of Saint Vladimir (Russia)

KT *s* Kent (B.V.R.)

kt. karat; kiloton, thousand tons of high explosives (nuclear); knot

Kt. Knight

K.T. Knight of the Most Ancient and Most Noble Order of the Thistle, founded in 1687; Knight Templar

Ktb. Ger. *Kriegstagebuch*, war diary

Kt. Bach. Knight Bachelor

K.T.H. *Kungliga Tekniska Högskolan*, Royal Institute of Technology, Stockholm (Swed.)

KTIBF *Kibris Turk Ischi Birlikleri Federasyonu*, Cyprus Turkish Trade Union Federation

K.t.l., KTΛ Gr. *kai ta leipomena*, and the rest, and so forth

Kto. Ger. *Konto*, account

K.T.S. Knight of the Order of the Tower and Sword (Port.)

KU *s* Bradford (B.V.R.)

K.U. *Københavns Universitet*, Univ. of Copenhagen (Den.); Kuwaiti Airways

KUNC Kamerun United National Congress (Cameroun)

KURRI Kyoto University Research Reactor Institute (Jap.)

KUSS KLM, UTA, Swissair, SAS (airlines)

k.u.t.d. keep up to date

Kuw. Kuwait

KV *s* Coventry (B.V.R.)

kv., kV., k.V. kilovolt (elec.)

kVA., k.V.A. kilovolt-ampère

K.V.A. *Kungliga Vetenscaps Akademien*, Royal Swed. Academy of Sciences

k.V.A.h. kilovolt ampère hour

K.–value measure of thermal conductivity

K.v.K. Ger. *Kriegsverdienstkrauz*, War Merit Cross

KVP *Katholieke Volkspartij*, Catholic People's Party (Neth.)

kvp. kilovolt peak

kW, KW, kw., kW., K.W. kilowatt (elec.)

KW *s* Bradford (B.V.R.)

K.W. Knight of the Order of William (Neth.)

k.w.a.c. key word and context

K.W.E. Knight of the Order of the White Eagle (Pol.)

kWh, kwh., kWh., K.W.H., Kwhr. kilowatt hour (elec.)

k.w.i.c. key word in context

k.w.o.c. key word out of context

k.w.o.t. key word out of title

KWP Korean Workers' Party, *Chosun No-Dong Dang*, formed in 1949

KWT *s* Kuwait (I.V.R.)

k.w.t. key word in title

KX *s* Buckinghamshire (B.V.R.)

KY *s* Bradford (B.V.R.); Kentucky, *also* Ky.; *s* Kirkcaldy (B.F.P.)

ky., K. *kyat*, Burmese currency

K.Y. *Kol Yisrael*, Israel Broadcasting Service

kybd. keyboard

Kyo. Kyoto (Japan)

Kyr., Kyrie Gk. *Kyrie eleison*, Lord, have mercy

kz *s* dust/sand storm (met.)

KZ *s* Antrim (B.V.R.); Ger. *Konzentrationslager*, concentration camp

206

L

l   *s* azimuthal/orbital quantum number; *s* lightning (met.); la, subdominant note in any key in Tonic Sol-fa pron. Lah

L   fifty (Roman); *s* Glamorgan (B.V.R.); *s* inductance (elec.); *s* latent heat per molecule; Learner, on card affixed to motor vehicle; *s* Limerick (Rep. of Ireland F.P.); *s* Luxembourg (I.V.R.); *s* tabular logarithm (math.)

l.   *s* elbow; lady; lake; lambda; land; large; late; lateral; latitude; law; leaf; league; leasehold; left, or port; legitimate; length; Ger. *lies*, read; light; line; link; Ger. *links*, left; literate; litre; little; Fr. *livre*, book; loch; long; lost; lough; low; pound, early typ. for £

L.   Labour; Finn. *läheä*, departure; Lambert; Lancers (mil.); Latin; left, in stage directions (theatre); lethal; Liberal; licentiate; lieutenant; *s* lift; light colour; Linnaeus, after the Lat. name of a plant, indicates that he was responsible for giving its name. Most Brit. plants were named by him; *lira*, Italian currency; lithium (chem.); litre; Fr. *livre*, pound; Lodge; London; Lord; lost (sport); Luxembourg; pound sterling, *earlier* l, *also* £

£   L. *libra*, pound sterling

L.   L. *liber*, book; L. *locus*, place

La   *s* lanthanum (chem.)

LA   *s* Llanelly (B.F.P.); *s* London (B.V.R.); Louisiana, *also* La.

L/A, L.A.   ledger account; letter of authority

la.   last

l/a.   Fr. *lettre d'avis*, letter of advice

La.   Lancastrian; lane

l.a.   landing account; leading article; lighter than air; local agent

l.a.   L. *lege artis*, as directed

L.A.   large apertures (photo.); Latin America/American; law agent; leave allowance; legal adviser; Legislative Assembly; Library Association; licensing act/authority; Lieutenant-at-Arms; light alloy; Literate in Arts; Liverpool Academy; Lloyd's/local agent; local association/authority; long acting; Los Angeles; low altitude

L.A.A.   Lancashire Authors' Association; League of Advertising Agencies (U.S.A.); Library Association of Australia; Libyan Arab Airlines, *formerly* KLA; Lieutenant-at-Arms; Life Assurance Advertisers (U.S.A.); light anti-aircraft

LAADS   Los Angeles Air Defense Sector (U.S.A.)

L.A.A.O.H.   Ladies' Auxiliary, Ancient Order of Hibernians

LAAR   liquid air accumulator rocket

L.A.A.S.   Lincolnshire Architectural and Archaeological Society

LAB   linear alkyl benzenes

lab.   label; laboratory; labour; labourer

Lab.   Laborite (U.S.A.); Labour (pol.); Labrador; — **Cur.** Labrador Current

L.A.B.   Laboratory Animals Bureau; Licentiate of the Associated Board, *now* L.R.S.M. Lond.; low altitude bombing

LABA   Laboratory Animal Breeders' Association (U.S.A.)

lac.   lacquer; lactation

L.A.C.   Laboratory Animals Centre; leading aircraftman; — **W.** leading aircraftwoman; Licentiate of the Apothecaries' Company; London Athletic Club

LACBW La Crosse boiling water reactor

LACE liquid air cycle engine

LACES London airport cargo electronic processing scheme; Los Angeles Council of Engineering Societies (U.S.A.)

Lachie, Lachy Lachlan

LACONIQ laboratory computer online inquiry

L.A.C.P. London Association of Correctors of the Press

LACSA *Líneas Aéreas Costarricenses*, Costa Rican Airlines

lad. ladder

L.A.D. light aid detachment

LADAR laser detection and ranging

LADE *Líneas Aéreas del Estado*, Argentine Airlines

ladp. ladyship

L.A.D.S.I.R.L.A.C. Liverpool and District Scientific, Industrial and Research Library Advisory Council

L.Adv. Lord Advocate (leg.)

laev. L. *laevus*, left

LAF *L'Académie Française*, the French Academy

La.F. Louisiana French

L.A.F.C. Latin-American Forestry Commission

L.A.F.D. London Association of Funeral Directors

LAFE *Laboratorio de Física Espacial*, Space Physics Laboratory (Braz.)

La Font. Jean de La Fontaine (1621–1695), Fr. poet

LAFTA, LAFTA, L.A.F.T.A. Latin American Free Trade Association

lag. lagoon

LAGS laser activated geodetic satellite (AFCRL)

Lah. Lahore (Pak.)

L.A.H. Licentiate of Apothecaries' Hall (Dublin)

LAHS low altitude, high speed

L.A.I. leaf area index; Library Association of Ireland

L.A.L. *Laboratoire de l'Accelerateur Linéaire*, Linear Accelerator Laboratory (France)

l.a.l.i. lonely aged, low income

lam. laminate

Lam. Lamarck (bot.); Lamentations (Bible)

L.A.M. *Liberalium Artium Magister*, Master of the Liberal Arts; London Academy of Music

L.A.M.A. Locomotive and Allied Manufacturers' Association of Great Britain

Lamb. Lambeth, degree granted by Archbishop of Canterbury

LAMCO Liberian-American-Swedish Mineral Corporation

L.A.M.D.A. London Academy of Music and Dramatic Art

L.A.M.I.D.A. Lancashire and Merseyside Industrial Development Association

LAMP Library Additions and Maintenance Program (U.S.A.); low altitude manned penetration; Lunar Analysis and Mapping Program (U.S.A.)

Lamp. Lampeter (Wales)

LAMS launch acoustic measuring system

L.A.M.S. London Association of Master Stonemasons

L.A.M.T.P.I. Legal Associate Member of the Town Planning Institute

L. An. Los Angeles

L.A.N. *Línea Aérea Nacional de Chile*, national airlines, Chile; local apparent noon

Lanc. Lancaster; lancer (mil.)

Lance Lancelot

Lancs. Lancashire

Landw. Ger. *Landwirtschaft*, agriculture

Lan. Fus. Lancashire Fusiliers (mil.)

lang. language

Lang. Languedoc (France)

LANICA *Líneas Aéreas de Nicaragua*, national airlines, Nicaragua

LANRAC, Lanrac Land Army Reunion Association Committee

Lan.R.(P.W.V.) Lancashire Regiment (Prince of Wales' Volunteers)

LANSA *Líneas Aéreas Nacionales*, national airlines, Peru

LANY Linseed Association of New York (U.S.A.)

LAO *s* Laos (I.V.R.)

L.A.O. Licentiate in Obstetric Science

LAOAR Latin American Office of Aerospace Research (USAF)

Lap., Lapp. Lapland; Lappish

La.P. La Paz (Bolivia)

L.A.P. Laboratory of Aviation Psychology (U.S.A.); *Líneas Aéreas Paraguayas*, national airlines, Paraguay; London Airport

LAPES low altitude parachute extraction system

L.A.P.O. Los Angeles Philharmonic Orchestra

L.A.P.T. London Association for Protection of Trade

L.A.R. life assurance relief (tax.); limit address register

LARA light armed reconnaissance aircraft

L.A.R.C. Libyan-American Reconstruction Commission

larg. Fr. *largeur*, width

larg. It. *largamente*, broadly (mus.); It. *largo*, very slow (mus.)

largo. It. *larghetto*, medium slow (mus.)

LARO Latin American Regional Office (FAO)

Larry Laura; Laurence; Lawrence

laryngol. laryngology

LAS large astronomical satellite; low altitude satellite; lower airspace

L.A.S. Land Agents' Society; League of Arab States; Legal Aid Society; Licentiate of the Society of Apothecaries; Lord-Advocate of Scotland (leg.)

L.A.S.A. Licentiate of the Art of Speech (Aust.)

LASCO Latin American Unesco Science Co-operation Office

L.A.S.E.R. light amplification by stimulated emission of radiation (*also* laser); London and South Eastern Library System, *formerly* South Eastern Regional Library System

LASH lighter aboard ship

LASL Los Alamos Scientific Laboratory (U.S.A.)

LASMEC Local Authorities School Meals Equipment Consortium

LASP low altitude space platform

L.A.S.R.A. Leather and Shoe Research Association (N.Z.)

LASS lighter than air submarine simulator

lat. lateral; latitude, *also* latd.

lat. L. *latus*, wide

Lat. Latin; Latvia (*also* Latv.); Latvian, *also* Latvn.

L.A.T. local apparent time; *Los Angeles Times*

L.A.T.C.C. London air traffic control centre

L.A.T.C.R.S. London air traffic control radar station

lat. dol. L. *lateri dolenti*, to the side which is painful (med.)

lat. ht. latent heat

lau. laundry

L.A.U.A. Lloyd's Aviation Underwriters' Association

L.A.U.K. Library Association of United Kingdom

laun. launched

Launce Lancelot

Laurie Laurence

LAV *Lineas Aéreas Venezolanas*, Venezuelan Airlines

lav. lavatory

LAW light anti-tank weapon

law. lawyer

L.A.W. League of American Wheelmen/Writers

Law-L. Law-Latin

Law Rept., Law Rpts. *Law Reports*

Lawrie Lawrence

LAWRS limited airport weather reporting system

lax. laxative

Laz. Lazarus

LB *s* Liberia (I.V.R.); *s* London (B.V.R.)

lb. L. *libra*, pound (weight); — in² pounds per square inch; — in³ pounds per cubic inch

l.b. landing barge; left back (sport); leg bye (cricket); letter box; link belt

L.B. L. *Baccalaureus Litterarum*, Bachelor of Letters; lavatory basin; light bomber; local board

L.B. L. *Lectori benevolo*, to the kind reader

L.B. & A. Lever Brothers & Associates Limited

lb. ap. pound, apothecaries'

lb. av., lb. avoir. pound, avoirdupois

L.B.B.A. London Beer Bottlers' Association

Lbc. Lübeck (Ger.)

L.B.C. Land Bank Commission; London Builders' Conference

L.B.C.H. London Bankers' Clearing House

lb. chu pound centigrade heat unit

L.B.C.M. Licentiate of Bandsmen's College of Music; London Board of Congregational Ministers

L.B.D. League of British Dramatists

L/Bdr., L.Bdr., Lbr. lance-bombardier

lb.f. pound force

lb.-ft. pound-foot

L.B.H. length, breadth, height

LBI Lloyds & Bolsa International Bank Limited

L.B.J. Lyndon Baines Johnson, Pres. of U.S.A. (1963–9)

L.B.M.S. London Boroughs Management Services

L.B.P. length between perpendiculars

lbr. labor; labour; lumber

LBS Libyan Broadcasting Service; life boat station; London Botanical Society

L.b.s. L. *Lectori benevolo salutem*, to the kind reader, greeting

L.B.S. London Graduate School of Business Studies

L.B. & S.C.R. London, Brighton and South Coast Railway, *included in* S. Railway, *later* S. Region of B.R.

L.B.S.M. Licentiate of Birmingham & Midland Institute School of Music

lb.t. pound troy

L.B.V. landing barge vehicle; late bottled vintage

l.b.w. leg before wicket (cricket)

lc little change (met.)

LC latent crimp, bi-component acrylic fibre; *s* London (B.V.R.)

L/C, L.C. letter of credit

l.c. label clause; law courts; lead covered; leading cases; legal currency; letter card; low calorie/carbon; lower case, *not* caps. (typ.)

l.c., loc. cit. L. *loco citato*, in the place cited

L.C. landing craft; Leander Club; left centre (theatre); Legislative Council; level crossing; Library of Congress (U.S.A.); Lieutenant Commander; livestock commissioner; London cheque/clause; Lord Chamberlain/Chancellor; *A Lover's Complaint* (Shake.); Lower Canada; *Scottish Land Court Reports*

L.C.A. Library Club of America; Licensed Company Auditor; Liverpool Cotton Association; low cost automation

l.c.b. longitudinal centre of buoyancy

L.C.B. Liquor Control Board; Lord Chief Baron

L.C.C. life cycle cost/costing; London Chamber of Commerce; London County Council, *now* G.L.C.; London County Councillor

L.C.C.C. Library of Congress Catalog Card

l.c.d. lowest common denominator

L.C.D. London College of Divinity; Lord Chamberlain's/Chancellor's Department; lower court decisions

lcdo. Sp. *licenciado*, licensed

lce. lance

L.C.E. Licentiate in Civil Engineering

l.c.f. local cycle fatigue; longitudinal centre of flotation; lowest common factor (math.)

L.C.F.T.A. London Cattle Food Trade Association

l.c.g. longitudinal centre of gravity

L.C.G.B. Locomotive Club of Great Britain

LCGIL *Liberia Confederazione Generale Italiana dei Lavoratori*, Confed. of Italian Workers

L.Ch. L. *Licentiatus Chirurgiae*, Licentiate in Surgery; Lord Chancellor

L.C.I.G.B. Locomotive and Carriage Institution of Great Britain and Ireland

L.C.I.S.C. Laundry and Cleaning Industry Sports Club

L.C.J. Lord Chief Justice

l.c.l. less than carload/lots; lower control limit

L.C.L. Fr. *Licencié en Droit canonique*, Licentiate in Canon Law

LCLS Livestock Commission Levy Scheme

l.c.m. least/lowest common multiple; liquid curing media

L.C.M. landing craft mechanized; London College of Music

Lcn. Lincoln

L.C.N. Local Civil Noon

L.C.O. landing craft officer; launch control officer

L.Col., L.-Col., Lieut.-Col. lieutenant-colonel

L.Corp., L.-Corp., L.Cpl. lance-corporal

LCP Lebanese Communist Party; London College of Printing

L.C.P. last complete programme; Licentiate of the College of Preceptors; low cost production

L.C.P. & S.A. Licentiate of the College of Physicians and Surgeons of America

L.C.P. & S.O. Licentiate of the College of Physicians and Surgeons of Ontario (Can.)

l/cr. Fr. *lettre de crédit*, letter of credit

L.C.T. landing craft tank; local civil time

lcty. locality

L.C.U. large close up (photo.)

L.C.V. Licentiate of the College of Violinists

LCY League of Communists of Yugoslavia, *Saves Komunista Jugoslavije*

LD *s* London (B.V.R.)

L/D Letter of Deposit

ld. land; lead; load

Ld. limited; lord

l.d. legal/lethal dose; light difference; line of departure/duty

L.D. Lady Day; Licentiate in Divinity; Light Dragoons; L. *Litterarum Doctor*, Doctor of Letters; London Docks; low density; Low Dutch

L.D. L. *Laus Deo*, Praise be to God; L. *lepide dictum*, wittily said; L. *Litera Dominicalis*, Dominical letter

L. & D. loans and discounts; loss and damage

lda., Ld^a Port. *limitada*, limited

L.D.A. Lead Development Association

l.d.b. light distribution box

l.d.c. less developed countries; long distance call; lower dead centre

L.D.E.G. L. *Laus Deo et Gloria*, Praise and Glory be to God

L.Dent.Sc. Licentiate in Dental Science

Lderry., Ldy. Londonderry

ldg. landing; leading; loading; lodging

Ldg. leading

ldg. and dely. landing and delivery

Ldge. lodge
L.d'H. *Légion d'Honneur*, Belgian/French award
L.Div. Licentiate in Divinity
ldk. lower deck
L.D.M.A. London Discount Market Association
Ld. May. Lord Mayor
LDMK. landmark
Ldn. London
L.D.O.S. Lord's Day Observance Society
Ldp. Ladyship; Lordship
L.D.P. Liberal-Democratic Party, *Jiyu-Minsuto* (Jap.); London daily price
LDPD *Liberal-Demokratische Partei Deutschlands*, Liberal Democratic Party of Germany (E. Ger.)
ldr. leader; ledger; lodger
ldry. laundry
LDS Latter Day Saints
L.D.S. Licentiate in Dental Surgery; — I. Licentiate in Dental Surgery, Ireland
L.D.S. L. *Laus Deo semper*, Praise be to God always
L.D.Sc. Licentiate in Dental Science
L.D.V. Local Defence Volunteers, *later* Home Guard, formed 1940, *also* Look, Duck and Vanish Brigade, *also* Long-Dentured Veterans
L.D.X. long distance xerography
L.D.Y. Leicestershire and Derbyshire Yeomanry
LE *s* London (B.V.R.); *s* Lyme (B.F.P.)
Le., Leb. Lebanese; Lebanon
l.e. leading edge; left eye; library/limited edition; light equipment; low explosive
L.E. Labour Exchange
lea. league; leather; leave
L.E.A. Local Education Authorities/Authority
LEAA Lace and Embroidery Association of America
LEAJ Law Enforcement and Administration of Justice (U.S.A.)
LEAP Lift-off Elevation and Azimuth Programmer
L.E.A.P. Loan and Educational Aid Programme
L.E.A.P.S. London Electronic Agency for Pay and Statistics
Lear *The Tragedy of King Lear* (Shake.)
L.E.B. London Electricity Board
L.E.C. Local Employment Committee
L.E.C.E. Fr. *Ligue européenne de coopération économique*, European League for Economic Co-operation
lect. lecture
lect. L. *lectio*, lesson
lectr. lecturer

LED Library Association Division of American Library Assn.
led. ledger
l.e.d. light emitting diode
L.E.D.C. Lighting Equipment Development Council
l.e.f. Fr. *liberté, égalité, fraternité*, liberty, equality, fraternity
leg. legal; legate; legation; legislation; legislative; legislature
leg. It. *legato*, smooth, sustained (mus.)
Leg. Ger. *Legierung*, alloy
legg. It. *leggiero*, light, rapid (mus.)
legis. legislation; legislative, *also* legisl.; legislature
legit. legitimate; legitimate theatre/drama
Leg.wt. legal weight
leichtl. Ger. *leichtlöslich*, easily soluble
Leics. Leicester; Leicestershire
Leip. Leipzig (E. Ger.)
Le.Is. Leeward Islands
Leit. Leitrim
L.E.L. Laureate in English Literature
lem, LEM lunar excursion module
Lem Lemuel
Lem. Lempira
LEMA Lifting Equipment Manufacturers' Association
Len Leonard
Lena Helena; Magdalen; Magdalene
LENA *Labatorio Energia Nucleare Applicata*, Applied Nuclear Energy Laboratory (Italy)
L. en D. Fr. *Licencié en droit*, Licentiate of Law
L.E.N.D. It. *Linguia e Nuova Didattica*, Italian Organization of Teachers of English
Len. Lib. Lenin Library, Moscow
L.Ens. Fr. *Licencié en enseignement*, Licentiate in Teaching
lento It. *lentando*, with increasing slowness (mus.)
Leo Leonard; Leonora
L.E.O. Lyons Electronic Office
LEPORE long-term and expanded programme of oceanic research and exploration
LEPMA Lithographic Engravers' and Plate Makers' Association (U.S.A.)
LEPRA Leprosy Relief Association
LEPT long-endurance patrolling torpedo
Les Lesley; Leslie; Lester
les. lesbian
L.E.S. launch escape system; Liverpool Engineering Society
L. ès L. Fr. *Licencié ès Lettres*, Licentiate in/of Letters
LESS least cost estimating and scheduling

211

L. ès Sc. Fr. *Licencié ès sciences*, Licentiate in Science
let. letter
let's let us
lett. It. *letteratura*, literature; It. *letterario*, literary
Lett. Lettish
Lettie, Letty Letitia
lev, LEV lunar excursion vehicle
Lev. Levant; Leviticus, *also* Levit. (Bible)
Lew, Lewie Ludovic; Ludovick
LEX land exercise
lex. lexicon
lexicog. lexicographer; lexicographical; lexicography
L.E.Y. Liberal European Youth
Leyd. Leiden/Leyden (Neth.)
LF *s* London (B.V.R.)
lf. leaf
l.f. ledger folio; life float; light face (typ.); low frequency
L.F. Lancashire Fusiliers
l.f.a. local freight agent
L.F.B. London Fire Brigade
L.F.B.C. London Federation of Boys' Clubs
l.f.c. low frequency current
L.F.C. Lutheran Free Church
Lfd. Ger. *Laufend*, current; Longford
L.F.D. least fatal dose; low fat diet
L.F.E. laboratory for electronics; London fur exchange
Lfg. Ger. *Lieferung*, delivery
L.F.M. London and South Eastern Furniture Manufacturers' Associaton
L.F.O. Licentiate of the Faculty of Osteopathy; low frequency oscillator
L.F.P.S. Licentiate of the Faculty of Physicians and Surgeons; — G. Licentiate of the Faculty of Physicians and Surgeons, Glasgow
LFRD lot fraction reliability deviation
L.F.S. Licentiate Surveyor of the Faculty of Architects and Surveyors
L/ft² lumens per square foot (elec.)
lft. leaflet
l.ft. linear feet/foot
LFTU landing force training unit
LG *s* Cheshire (B.V.R.)
lg. lagoon; large; long
L.G. landing ground; large grain, gunpowder, leather and wheat trade; Lewis gun; Lieutenant-General; Life Guards; David Lloyd George (1863–1945), Brit. statesman; London Gazette; Low German, *also* L. Ger., L-Ger.
L.G.A.R. Ladies of the Grand Army of the Republic (U.S.A.)
L.G.B. Local Government Board
LGC Laboratory of the Government Chemist; lunar module guidance computer
L.G.C.C. Letchworth Garden City Corporation (1963), successor of First Garden City Ltd. formed in 1903 to build the world's first garden city, setting a pattern for Welwyn Garden City and Canberra, etc.
lge. large; league
L.G.E.B. Local Government Examination Board
L.-Gen. Lieutenant-General
LGIO Local Government Information Office
L.G.M. *Laboratorium voor Grondmechanica*, Soil Mechanics Laboratory (Neth.); Lloyd's Gold Medal
Lgn. Leghorn (Italy)
L.G.O. Lamont Geological Observatory (U.S.A.)
L.G.O.C. London General Omnibus Company, *now* L.T.E.
L.Gr. Late/Low Greek
L.G.R. leasehold ground rent; local government reports
L.G.S.M. Licentiate of Guildhall School of Music
LGTA Fr. *Ligue Générale des Travailleurs de l'Angola*, General League of Angolan Workers in Exile
LGTB Local Government Trair ing Board
lgth. length
lg. tn. long ton
L.G.U. Ladies' Golf Union
LH *s* Leith (B.F.P.); *s* London (B.V.R.)
LH 1889 large head (numis.)
l.h. left hand/hand
L.H. licensing hours; Licentiate of Hygiene; light horse; Ger. *Linke Hand*, left hand; luteinizing hormone
L.H.A. landing helicopter assault; Licentiate of the Australian Institute of Hospital Administration; local health authority; local hour angle; Lord High Admiral; lower hour angle
L.H.A.R. London, Hull, Antwerp, Rotterdam, grain trade
l.h.b. left halfback (sport)
L.H.C. Lord High Chancellor
L.H.D. L. *Litterarum Humanorum Doctor*, Doctor of Human Letters; L. *Litterarum Humanioribus Doctor*, Doctor of Humane Letters
LHDC lateral homing depth charge
L.Heb. late Hebrew
L.H.I. Fr. *Ligue homéopathique internationale*, Intern. Homeopathic League
L.H.M.C. London Hospital Medical College
L.H.O. livestock husbandry officer

l.hr. lumen hour (phys.)

L.H.S. left hand side

LHSV liquid hourly space velocity (phys.)

L.H.T. Lord High Treasurer

L.H.W.N. lowest high water neaptides

Li s lithium (chem.)

LI s Littlehampton (B.F.P.); s Westmeath (Rep. of Ireland V. R.)

li. link; lira, It. currency

l.i. letter of introduction; longitudinal interval

L.I. Leeward Islands; Liberal International; Licentiate of Instruction (U.S.A.); Light Infantry (mil.); Fr. *Ligue internationale de la représentation commerciale*, Intern. League of Commercial Travellers and Agents; Lincoln's Inn, Lond. (leg.); Long Island (U.S.A.)

LIA Laser Industry Association (U.S.A.); Lead Industries Association (U.S.A.); Leather Industries of America; Lebanese International Airways

lib. liberal; liberation; liberty; librarian; library; libretto

lib. L. *liber*, book

Lib. Liberal Party; Liberation, Women's; Liberia

Lib. It. *Libretto*, text of opera/musical work (mus.)

lib. cat. library catalogue

Lib. Cong. Library of Congress (U.S.A.)

L.I.B.E. *Ligo Internacia de Blindaj Esperantistoj*, Intern. League of Blind Esperantists

Lib-Lab Liberal-Labour, denoting a member of the Labour party who has affiliations with Liberals, 1906

Libst. It. *librettist*, author of libretto (mus.)

LIC Lands Improvement Company

Lic. Sp. *Licenciado*, lawyer

Lic.D. Licentiate in Theology, Malta

L.I.C.D. Fr. *Ligue internationale contre la concurrence déloyale*, Intern. League Against Unfair Competition

L.I.Ceram. Licentiate of the Institute of Ceramics

Lic.Med. Licentiate in Medicine

Lic.Theol. Licentiate in Theology

L. & I.D. London and India Docks

LIDAR light detection and ranging

L.I.D.A.S.E. Lecturer in Design and Analysis of Scientific Experiments

L.I.D.C. Lead Industries Development Council

L.I.D.H. Fr. *Ligue internationale des droits de l'homme*, Intern. League for the Rights of Man

L.I.D.I.A. Fr. *Liaison internationale des industries de l'alimentation*, Intern. Liaison for the Food Industries

L.I.E.N. Fr. *Ligue internationale pour l'éducation nouvelle*, New Education Fellowship (Intern.)

Lieut. Lieutenant; — **Cdr., Com.** Lieutenant-Commander; — **Col.** Lieutenant-Colonel; — **Gen.** Lieutenant-General; — **Gov.** Lieutenant Governor

L.I.Fire E. Licentiate of the Institution of Fire Engineers

LIFMOP linearly frequency-modulated pulse

L.I.F.O. last in, first out

L.I.F.P.L. Fr. *Ligue internationale de femmes pour la paix et la liberté*, Women's Intern. League for Peace and Freedom

Lig. Liguria; Limoges

L.I.H.G. Fr. *Ligue internationale de hockey sur glace*, Intern. Ice Hockey Fed.

Lil, Lilly, Lily Lilian; Lillian

L.I.L. Laporte Industries Limited

L.I.L.A. Fr. *Ligue internationale de la librairie ancienne*, Intern. League of Antiquarian Booksellers

L.I.L.O. last in, last out

L.I.L.S. lead in light system (aircraft)

lim. limit

Lim. Limerick

L.I.M. Licentiate of the Institution of Metallurgists

limo. limousine

limp limp cloth binding

L.I.M.P.L. Sp. *Liga Internacional de Mujeres pro Paz y Libertad*, Women's Intern. League for Peace and Freedom

lin. lineal; linear; — **ac.** linear accelerator; lines; liniment

Lina Angelina; Caroline

Linc. Coll. Lincoln College, Oxford, founded 1427

Lincs. Lincolnshire

Lindl. John Lindley (1799–1865), Eng. botanist

L.Infre. Loire-Inférieure (France)

lin.ft. linear feet/foot

ling. linguistics

Linn. Carolus Linnaeus (1707–78), Swed. botanist

Lino Linotype

lino. linoleum

L.Inst.P. Licentiate of the Institute of Physics

Lintas Lever's International Advertising Service

L.I.O.B. Licentiate of the Institute of Building

L.I.P. life insurance policy

L.I.P.M. Lister Institute of Preventative Medicine

liq. liquid; liquor

L.I.R.A. Linen Industry Research Association

L.I.R.I. Leather Industries Research Institute (S. Afr.); Licentiate of the Institution of the Rubber Industry

L.I.R.R. Long Island Railroad Company (U.S.A.)

Lis. Lisbon (Port.)

Lisbeth Elisabeth; Eliza; Elizabeth

L.I.S.M. Licentiate of Incorporated Society of Musicians

LIST Library and Information Services, Tees-side

lit. literal; literally; literary; literature; litter; little

Lit. *Lire*, It. currency; litre

Lit. L. *Litterae*, Letters

Lit.D., Litt.D. *Litterarum Doctor*, Doctor of Letters/Literature

Lith. Lithuania; Lithuanian

litho., litho lithograph; lithographic; lithography

Lit. Hum. L. *Literae Humaniores*, classical honours course at Oxford Univ.

Lit. Sup. *Times Literary Supplement*

Litt.B. *Litterarum Baccalaureus*, Bachelor of Letters/Literature

Litt.D.(Econ.) Doctor of Letters/Literature in Economic Studies

Litt.M. *Litterarum Magister*, Master of Letters/Literature

liturg. liturgical; liturgy

liv. Fr. *livre*, m. book, f. pound

Liv. Liverpool (*also* Liver.); Titus Lavius, called in Eng. Livy (59 B.C.–A.D. 17), Rom. historian; pound

liv.st. Fr. *livre sterling*, pound sterling

Liz, Liza, Lizzie, Lizzy Elisabeth; Eliza; Elizabeth

Liz. lizard; lizzie, an early Ford car, *also* Tin Lizzie

LJ *s* Bournemouth (B.V.R.)

l.j. life jacket

l.J. Ger. *laufen Jahre*, current year

L.J. Library Journal; long jump (ath.); Lord Justice

L.J.C. London Juvenile Courts

L.JJ. Lords Justices

LK *s* Lerwick (B.F.P.); *s* London (B.V.R.)

Lk. Luke

lkd. locked

lkg. locking

lkg. & bkg. leakage and breakage

LKP *Liberaalinen Kansanpuolue*, Liberal People's Party (Finland)

L.K.Q.C.P.I. Licentiate of the King and Queen's College of Physicians, Ireland, *now* L.R.C.P.I.

lkr. locker

Lkw., LKW Ger. *Lastkraftwagen*, lorry/truck

'll contraction of will/shall

LL *s* Liverpool (B.F.P.); *s* London (B.V.R.)

ll. leaves; lines

ll. L. *leges*, laws

l.l. live load; lower left/limit

l.l. L. *loco laudato*, in the place quoted

Ll. Llewellyn; Lloyd

LL. laws; Lords

L.L. late/law latin; *Law List*; lending library; Lend-Lease, Act passed by U.S. Congress, March 1941, to lend/lease supplies to Britain and other countries in WW2. Britain received over £5,000 m. worth of supplies. The Act was passed when Brit. and Commonwealth reserves were almost exhausted; limited liability; London Library; Lord-Lieutenant, Brit. sovereign's personal representative in a county. 'Her/His Majesty's lieutenant of and in the county of . . .'; lower limb; low latin; Loyalist League of Rights

L./L. Norw. *Lutlang*, limited company

L.L.A. Lady Literate in Arts

LL.AA.II. Fr. *Leurs Altesses Impériales*, Their Imperial Highnesses

LL.AA.RR. Fr. *Leurs Altesses Royales*, Their Royal Highnesses

LL.B. L. *Legum Baccalaureus*, Bachelor of Laws

l.l.c. lower left centre

L.L.C.M. Licentiate of London College of Music

L.L.C.O. Licentiate of the London College of Osteopathy

LL.D. L. *Legum Doctor*, Doctor of Laws

LL.EE. Fr. *Leurs Éminences*, Their Eminences; F. *Leurs Excellences*, Their Excellencies

L.Lett. Licentiate of Letters

l.l.i. latitude and longitude indicator

L.L.I. Lord-Lieutenant of Ireland

LLL low-level logic

LL.LL. Licentiate in Laws

L.L.L. loose leaf ledger; *Love's Labour's Lost* (Shake.)

L.L.L.T.V. low light level television

LL.M. L. *Legum Magister*, Master of Laws

LL.M.Com. Master of Laws, in Commercial Law

LL.MM. Fr. *Leurs Majestés*, Their Majesties

LLN League for Less Noise (U.S.A.)

LLS lunar logistics system (space)

LLSV lunar logistics system vehicle (space)

L.L.U. lending library unit

LLV lunar logistics vehicle (space)

l.l.w. low level waste

lm lumen, unit of luminous flux (phys.)

LM *s* London (B.V.R.)

l.m. land mine; light/liquid metal; It. *livello del mare*, sea level

l.m. L. *locus monumenti*, place of the monument

l.M. Ger. *laufenden Monats*, of the current month

L.M. Legion of Merit; Licentiate in Medicine / Midwifery / Music; Lindley Medal (R.H.S.) for exceptional service to hort.; London Museum; Lord Marquis (Scot.); Lord Mayor; lunar module (space)

L.M. *long metre* (mus.)

L.M.A. Lebanese Management Association; Linoleum Manufacturers' Association; low moisture avidity

L.M.A.G.B. Locomotive and Allied Manufacturers' Association of Great Britain

L.M.B.A. London Master Builders' Association

L.M.B.C. Lady Margaret Boat Club (St. John's College), Cambridge; Liverpool Marine Biological Committee

l.m.c. low middling clause

L.M.C. Lloyd's Machinery Certificate

LMCA Lorry Mounted Crane Association

L.M.C.C. Licentiate of the Medical Council of Canada

lmd. leafmould

L.M.D. local medical doctor

L.M.D. *long metre double* (mus.)

L.M.E. London Metal Exchange

L. Med. Licentiate in Medicine

L.M.G. light machine gun

L.M.H. Lady Margaret Hall (Oxford), founded 1878

lm.hr. lumen hour (phys.)

L.M.I. Logistics Management Institute (U.S.A.)

LMO lens-modulated oscillator; light machine oil

LMP lunar module pilot

L.M.P. last menstrual period; *Literary Market Place*

L.M.P.A. London Master Plasterers' Association; London Master Printers' Alliance

L.Mq. Lourenço Marques

L.M.R. London Midland Region, British Rail

L.M.R.C.P. Licentiate in Midwifery of the Royal College of Physicians

L.M.R.S.H. Licentiate Member of the Royal Society for the Promotion of Health

LMS London Medical Schools

L.M.S. Licentiate in Medicine and Surgery; London, Midland and Scottish Railway, before nationalization; London Mathematical/Missionary/Municipal Society

L.M.S.S.A. Licentiate in Medicine and Surgery of the Society of Apothecaries

L.M.T. length, mass, time (phys.); local mean time

L.M.T.A. London Master Typefounders' Association

L.M.T.P.I. Legal Member of the Town Planning Institute

L.Mus. Licentiate of Music; — **L.C.M.** Licentiate in Music, London College of Music; — **T.C.L.** Licentiate in Music, Trinity College of Music, London

ln *s* Napierian logarithm

LN *s* King's Lynn (B.F.P.); *s* London (B.V.R.); *s* Norway (I.C.A.M.)

Ln. Lane

L.N. It. *Lira Nuova*, Genoa coin (numis.)

L.Nat. Liberal National

L.N.C. League of Nations Covenant

L.N.E.R. London and North Eastern Railway, before nationalization

LNG liquefied natural gas

L.N.H.S. London Natural History Society

Lnrk. Lanark (Scot.)

L. & N.R.R. Louisville and Nashville Railroad (U.S.A.)

L.N.S. land navigation system

L.N.U. League of Nations Union

L.N.W.R., L. & N.W.R. London & North-Western Railway, before nationalization

LO *Landsorganisasjon i Norge*, Norwegian Fed. of Trade Unions; *Landsorganisationen i Sverige*, General Fed. of Swed. Trade Unions; *s* London (B.F.P. and B.V.R.)

2LO *s* London (radio call-sign)

Lo. loam (bot.); local; Lord; low

Lo. It. *Loco*, an indication that notes are to be played at normal pitch following 8va (mus.)

l.o. Fr. *leur ordre*, their order; longitudinal optical; lubricating oil/order

L.O. launch operator; liaison officer; local oscillator; London office

l.o.a. length over all (shipping)

L.O.A. leave of absence; Life Officers'/Offices Association; light observation aircraft

loadg. & dischg. loading and discharging

LOB line of balance; Location of Offices Bureau

LOBAL long base line buoy

LOBAR long base line radar

LOC launch operations centre/complex

loc. local; location; locative
l.o.c. letter of credit; lines of communication
loc.cit. L. *loco citato*, in the place cited
loc.laud. L. *loco laudato*, in the place cited with approval
locn. location
loco. locomotion; locomotive
loc.primo cit. L. *loco primo citato*, in the place first cited
locum L. *locum tenens*, holding temporary position (med., eccles.)
L.O.D. *Little Oxford Dictionary*
L. of C. Library of Congress, *also* L.O.C. (U.S.A.)
L. of N. League of Nations
LOFTI low-frequency trans-ionosphere satellite
log. logarithm; logic; logical; logistic
LOH light observation helicopter
loi, LOI lunar orbit insertion
Lola Dolores
LOLA library on-line acquisition; lunar orbit landing approach
lolly lollipop
LOM Loyal Order of Moose
LOMA Life Office Management Association (U.S.A.)
Lomb. Lombard; Lombardian; Lombardy
lon., long. longitude
Lond. London; Londonderry
Londin. L. *Londoninensis*, of London, Eng. episcopal title, in bishop's signature
Long. Longford
Longl. longitudinal
Lonrho London Rhodesian (fin.)
L.O.O.M. Loyal Order of Moose
l.o.p. line of position
LOPAR low-power acquisition radar
loq. L. *loquitur*, he/she speaks
LOR light output ratio; lunar orbit rendezvous
L. Or. Fr. *Licencié en orientation*, Licentiate in Orientation
LORAC long-range accuracy
LORAD long-range active detection
LORAN long-range navigation
LORAPH long-range passive homing system
LORV low observable re-entry vehicle
L.O.S. Latin Old Style; line of sight; loss of signal (space)
lösl. Ger. *löslich*, soluble
L.O.S.S. large object salvage system
LOT large orbital telescope; load on top (oil tanker system); *Polskie Linie Lotnicze*, Polish Air Lines
lot. lotion
Lot-et-Gar. Lot-et-Garonne (France)
Lottie, Lotty Charlotte

Lou Louisa; Louise; Ludovic; Ludovick
Lou. Louisiana; Louth (Lincs.)
Louie Louisa; Louise; Ludovic; Ludovick
LOX liquid oxygen
loy. loyal; loyalty
LOYA League of Young Adventurers, founded 1962, an offshoot of National Assn. of Boys' Clubs
Loz. Lozère
LP *s* London (B.V.R.)
L/P life policy
lp. limp
Lp. Ladyship; Lordship
l.p. large paper; last paid; latent period; launch platform; linear programming; long primer (typ.); low pressure
L.P. Labor/Labour Party; large post (paper); last post; legal procurator; *Legião Portuguesa*, Portuguese Legion; Liberal Party; life policy; liquid petroleum; long play/player/playing record; Lord Provost
L./P. letterpress
LPA Local Productivity Association
L.P.A. Leather Producers' Association for England
L.P.A.A. London Poster Advertising Association
l.p.c. low pressure chamber
L.P.C. Lord President of the Council
L.P.C.M. London Police Court Mission
L.P.E. London Press Exchange (advert.)
L. Ped. Licentiate of Pedagogy
L.P.F.S. London Playing Fields Society; London Public Fur Sales
LPG liquefied petroleum gas
L. Ph. Licentiate of Philosophy
l.p.i. lines per inch
L.P. & K.T.F. London Printing and Kindred Trades' Federation
L. Plms. Las Palmas
L.P.M. long particular/peculiar metre; lines per millimetre/minute
L.P.N. Licensed Practical Nurse
L.P.N. L. *Legio Patria Nostra*, The Legion is our Fatherland
L.P.N.A. Lithographers' and Printers' National Association (U.S.A.)
L.P.O. local posts/purchasing officer; London Philharmonic Orchestra
L'pool Liverpool
LPP Laotian People's Party, clandestine communist party
L.P.P.T.F.S. London and Provincial Printing Trades' Friendly Society
L.P.S. London Philharmonic Society; Lord Privy Seal

L.Ps.Ped. Fr. *Licencié en psycho-pédagogie de l'enfance inadaptée*, Licentiate in Psychoeducation of Handicapped Children

L.Ps.Sc. Fr. *Licencié en psychologie scolaire*, Licentiate in Psycho-education Counselling

L.P.T.B. London Passenger Transport Board, *now* L.T.E.

l.p.w. lumens per watt (elec.)

Lpz. Leipzig, E. Ger.

l.q. L. *lege quaeso*, please read

lqdr. liquidator

L.Q.R. *Law Quarterly Review*

L.Q.T. Liverpool quay terms (shipping)

Lr Lawrencium (chem.)

LR *s* Lancaster (B.F.P.); *s* London (B.V.R.)

L/R left to right

Lr. Lancer; ledger; *Lira*, It. currency

l.r. landing report; log/long run; long range

l.R. Ger. *laufen Rechnung*, current account

L.R. Land Registry; *Law Report*; liquor/liquor-to-goods ratio (dyeing): *Lloyd's Register* (shipping); Lowland/Loyal Regiment

L.R.A. Lace Research Association

L.R.A.C. *Law Reports, Appeal Cases*

L.R.A.D. Licentiate of the Royal Academy of Dancing

L.R.A.M. Licentiate of the Royal Academy of Music

L.R.B. London Rifle Brigade

LRC Langley/Lewis Research Center (NASA)

L.R.C. Labour Representation Committee; Leander/London Rowing Club

L.R.C.A. London Retail Credit Association

L.R.Ch. *Law Reports, Chancery Division*

L.R.C.M. Licentiate of the Royal Academy of Music

L.R.C.P. Licentiate of the Royal College of Physicians

L.R.C.P.E. Licentiate of the Royal College of Physicians of Edinburgh

L.R.C.P.Ed. Licentiate of the Royal College of Physicians of Edinburgh

L.R.C.P.I. Licentiate of the Royal College of Physicians, Ireland

L.R.C.S. League of Red Cross Societies; Licentiate of the Royal College of Surgeons

L.R.C.S.Ed. Licentiate of the Royal College of Surgeons of Edinburgh

L.R.C.S.I. Licentiate of the Royal College of Surgeons of Ireland

L.R.C.V.S. Licentiate of the Royal College of Veterinary Surgeons

L.R.F.P.S. Licentiate of the Royal Faculty of Physicians and Surgeons

L.R.F.P.S.G. Licentiate of the Royal Faculty of Physicians and Surgeons of Glasgow (Scot.)

L.R.H.L. *Law Reports, House of Lords*

L.R.I.B.A. Licentiate of the Royal Institute of British Architects

L.R.I.C. Licentiate of the Royal Institute of Chemistry

L.R.Ind.App. *Law Reports, Indian Appeals*

L.R.K.B. *Law Reports, King's Bench*

LRLS London Regional Library System, *formerly* S.E.R.L.S., South Eastern Regional Library System

L.R.P. *Law Reports, Probate Division*; long range planning

L.R.Q.B. *Law Reports, Queen's Bench*

L.R.R. lower reduced rate (tax.)

Lrs. Lancers (mil.)

L.R.S. Land Registry Stamp; *Lloyd's Register of Shipping*

L.R.S.M. Licentiate of the Royal Schools of Music

L.R.T.L. Light Railway Transport League

LRU least recently used; line replaceable unit

LRV lunar roving vehicle (space)

L.R.W.E.S. long range weapons experimental station

LS *s* Lesotho, *formerly* Basutoland (I.V.R.); liminal sensitivity (psy.); *s* Selkirkshire (B.V.R.)

2LS *s* Leeds/Bradford (radio call-sign)

l.s. landing ship; Fr. *latitude sud*, south latitude; left side; letter signed; litres per second; local sunset; long sight; low speed

l.s. L. *locus sigilli*, place of the seal (leg.)

L.s. Letter signed

L.S. Law Society; leading seaman; letter service; licensed surveyor; Licentiate in Surgery; Linnean Society; London Scottish; Long Shot, shot from distance of an actor, showing whole person (photo.); loud speaker

L.S.A. Land Settlement Association; leading supply assistant; Licentiate of Science in Agriculture; Licentiate of the Society of Apothecaries

L.S.A.A. Linen Supply Association of America

L.S.A.C. London Small Arms Company

L.S.B. London School Board

L.S.B.A. leading sick-bay attendant

217

l.s.c. L. *loco supra citato*, in the place before cited

L.S.C. Licentiate of Sciences; London Salvage Corps; Lower School Certificate

L.Sc.Act. Licentiate of Actuarial Science

L.Sc.Com. Fr. *Licencié en sciences commerciales*, Licentiate of Commercial Sciences

L.Sc.Comptables Fr. *Licencié en Sciences comptables*, Licentiate of Accountancy

L.Sc.O. Fr. *Licencié en sciences-optométrie*, Licentiate of Optometry

L.Sc.Pol. Fr. *Licencié ès sciences politiques*, Licentiate in Political Sciences

LSD lysergic acid diethylamide, consciousness expanding drug

L.S.D. League of Safe Drivers; Lightermen, Stevedores and Dockers

L.s.d. L. *Librae, solidi, denarii*, Pounds, Shillings, Pence

lsd.li. leased line

l.s.e. limited signed edition

L.S.E. London School of Economics and Political Science; London Stock Exchange

Lsg. Ger. *Lösung*, solution

L.S. & G.C.M. Long Service and Good Conduct Medal

L.Sgt. Lance Sergeant

L.S.H.T.M. London School of Hygiene and Tropical Medicine

L.S.I. Labour and Socialist International

L.S.J.M. L. *Laus sit Jesu et Mariae*, Praise be to Jesus and Mary

LSL landing ship logistic; low speed logic

l.s.m. L. *litera scripta- manet*, the written word remains

L.S.O. London Symphony Orchestra

L.S.P.C. Lead Sheet and Pipe Council, *now* B.L.M.A.

L.S.P.G.A. London School of Printing and Graphic Arts *now* College of Printing

LSS life saving service/station

L.S.S. Licentiate of Sacred Scripture

L.S.Sc. Licentiate in Sanitary Science

l.s.t. local standard time

L.S.T. landing ship tank/transport; Licentiate in Sacred Theology; local standard time

L.S.W. licensed shorthand writer

L. & S.W.R. London and South-Western Railway, became S.R. until nationalization

LT *s* London (B.V.R.); *s* Lowestoft (B.F.P.)

lt. Ger. *laut*, according to

Lt. lieutenant; light

l.t. landed terms; landing team; large tug; local time; loop test; low tension (elec.)

l.t. L. *locum tenens*, substitute

L.t. long ton

L.T. lawn tennis; leading telegraphist; letter telegram; Licentiate in Teaching/Theology; *Lira Turca*, Turkish pound, *also* £T

L.T.A. Lawn Tennis Association; lighter than air; London Teachers' Association

L.T.A.A. Lawn Tennis Association of Australia

l.t.b. low tension battery (elec.)

L.T.B. London Transport Board

L.T.B.C. Lawn Tennis Ball Convention

L.T.C. Lawn Tennis Club

L.T.C.L. Licentiate of Trinity College of Music, London

Lt.Col., Lt.-Col., Lieut.-Col. lieutenant colonel

Ltd. Limited

L.T.E. London Transport Executive

L.T.F. Lithographic Technical Foundation

ltg. lettering; lighting

ltge. lighterage

Lt.Gen., Lieut.-Gen. lieutenant general

Lt.Gov., Lieut.-Gov. lieutenant governor

L.Th. Licentiate in Theology

L.T.H. light training helicopter

L.T.I. Licentiate of the Textile Institute

L.T.I.B. Lead Technical Information Bureau

Lt.Inf. Light Infantry

l.t.l. less than truckload

LTM London Terminal Market

L.T.M. Licentiate in Tropical Medicine; Little Theatre Movement

ltn. lightning

ltng.arr. lightning arrester

L.T.O. leading torpedo operator

L.T.O.S. *Law Times*, Old Series

L.T.P.D. lot tolerance percent defective

ltr. letter; lighter

L.T.R.A. Lands Tribunal Rating Appeals

Lt.R.N. Lieutenant, Royal Navy

L.T.R.S. Low Temperature Research Station

L.T.S. London Typographical Society

L.T.S.B. London Trustee Savings Bank

L.T.S.C. Licentiate of Tonic Sol-Fa College

L.T. & S.R. London, Tilbury and Southend Railway, became part of L.M.S. until nationalization

218

LTV long tube vertical
Lu *s* lutetium (chem.)
LU *s* London (B.V.R.)
lu., lug. It. *luglio*, July
Lu. Lucerne (Switz.)
L.U. Liberal Unionist; *Ligue universelle* (*esperantiste*), Universal Esperantist League
L.U.A. Linotype Users' Association; Liverpool Underwriters' Association
LUAR League of Union and Revolutionary Action (Port.)
lub., lubr. lubricant; lubricate; lubrication
LUCOM lunar communication system (space)
Lucr. *The Rape of Lucrece* (Shake.)
l.u.e. left upper entrance (theatre)
LUG light utility glider
lug. luggage; lugger
lu.h. lumen hour (phys.)
L.U.H.F. lowest useful high frequency (elec.)
Luke Lucanus; Lucas; Lucilius
L.U.L.O.P. *London Union List of Periodicals*
lum. lumbago; lumber; luminous
LUM lunar excursion module (space)
LUMAS lunar mapping system (space)
lun. Fr. *lundi*, Monday; It. *lunedì*, Monday; Sp. *lunes*, Monday
L.U.O.T.C. London University Officers' Training Corps
L.U.S. Land Utilization Survey
LUSI lunar surface inspection (space)
Lusing. It. *Lusingando*, coaxing, caressing (mus.)
LUT launch umbilical tower
Luth. Lutheran
lux. luxurious
Lux. Luxembourg
LV *s* Argentine Republic (I.C.A.M.); *s* Liverpool (B.V.R.)
6LV *s* Liverpool (radio call-sign)
LVI, LVII, LVIII regnal years, on edge legend of crowns (numis.)
lv. leave; Fr. *livre*, book
l.v. low voltage
L.V. largest vessel; licensed victualler; luncheon voucher
L.V.A. Licensed Victuallers' Association
LVI low viscosity index
L.V.I. L. *Laus Verbo Incarnato*, Praise to the Incarnate Word
L.V.N.D.L. Licensed Victuallers' National Defence League

L.V.S. Licentiate in Veterinary Science
L.V.T. landing vehicle tracked
Lw *s* lawrencium (chem.)
LW *s* London (B.V.R.)
l.w. lumens per watt (elec.)
l.W. Ger. *lichte Weite*, internal diameter
L.W. left wing; light weight; long wave; low water
L. & W. living and well
L.W.A. London Welsh Association
l.w.b. long wheel base
L.W.C.A. London Wholesale Confectioners' Association
L.W.E.S.T. low water equinoctial spring tide
L.W.F. Lutheran World Federation
L.W.L. length on water line; load water line (ship.)
L.W.M. low water mark
L.W.M.M.A. London Wholesale Millinery Manufacturers' Association
L.W.O.N.T. low water ordinary neap tide
L.W.O.S.T. low water ordinary spring tide
LWR light water reactor
L.W.T. London Weekend Television
L.W.T.M.A. London Wood Terminal Market Association
lx lux, unit of illumination (lx = lm/m^2)
LX *s* London (B.V.R.); *s* Luxembourg (I.C.A.M.)
lx. L. *lux*, light
Lxa Port. *Lisboa*, Lisbon
Lxmbrg. Luxembourg
LXX Septuagint, version of the Old Testament in Greek
LY *s* London (B.V.R.); *s* Londonderry (B.F.P.)
Ly. Lyon (France)
L.Y. Queen's Own Lowland Yeomanry
Lylis Lilian
L.Y. & L.T. lastex yarn & lactron thread
lyr. lyric; lyrical
L. & Y.R. Lancashire and Yorkshire Railway, became part of L.M.S.R. until nationalization
LZ *s* Armagh (B.V.R.); *s* Bulgaria (I.C.A.M.)
L.Zug. Ger. *Luxus-Zug*, luxury railway train
lzy. lazy

219

M

m em (typ.); *s* mass (phys.); milli, 10^{-3}; *s* mist (met.); *s* modulus (phys.)

m meta (chem.)

'm madam

m/ Fr. *mois*, month

M *s* Cheshire (B.V.R.); *s* gram-molecule; *s* mean, intermediate value between extremes (math.); *s* Mach number (phys.); *s* Malta (I.V.R.); mass (phys.); mega, 10^6; metal (chem.); *s* middle term of a syllogism (logic); Milford (B.F.P.); *s* modulus (phys.); *s* molar (chem.); moment (phys.); *s* mutual inductance (phys.); 1,000 (Roman)

ᴟ name for the mediant note in any key in Tonic Sol-fa pron. Me

3M Minnesota Mining and Manufacturing Company

m. maiden over (cricket); male; manual; mark; married; masculine; mass (mech.); master; mate; measure; medical; medicine; medium; memorandum; meridian; metre; — **m.²** square metre, unit of area; — **m.³** cubic metre, unit of volume; midday; middle; mile; mill (currency); Fr. *mille*, thousand; million; minim; minimum; minor; minute; missing; mix; mixture; moderate; molar (dental); month; moon; morning; Fr. *mort*, dead; It. *morto*, dead; mountain

m. L. *manipulus*, handful; L. *meridies*, noon; L. *misce*, mix

M. *s* Mach number, speed through air compared to speed of sound (nav.); magistrate; magnetic direction, direction measured clockwise through 360° from magnetic meridian (nav.); Fr. *main*, hand; Majesty; Manitoba (Can.); It. *mano*,

hand; mark (Ger. currency); marquess; marquis; martyr; medal; medieval; member; Methodist; metropolitan; It. *mezzo*, *mezza*, half; militia; mine-sweeper; minim (liquid measure); Monday; Fr. *Monsieur*, Mr./Sir; It. *Monte*, mount (*also* Mt.); mother; motorway

M. L. *magister*, master; L. *medicinae*, of medicine; *metronome* (mus.); L. *mitte*, send

M' Gaelic *Mac*, son of

ma mamma

m/a my account

Ma *s* masurium (chem.)

MA *s* Cheshire (B.V.R.); Massachusetts (U.S.A.); mental age, measurement of mental level of an individual (psy.); *s* Morocco (I.V.R.)

mA milliampère (elec.)

Ma. L. *Mater*, mother

Mᵃ Port. *Maria*, Mary

m.a. manufacturing assembly; map analysis; menstrual age

M.A. L. *Magister Artium*, Master of Arts; Magistrates'/Magnesium/Mahogany /Mathematical Association; Manpower/ Maritime Administration (U.S.A.); medieval archaeology; Metric Association; middle ages; military academy/attaché/ aviation; Mountaineering Association

M.A. L. *Missionarius Apostolicus*, Apostolic Missionary

MAA methacrylic acid

M.A.A. Manufacturers' Agents' Association of Great Britain; Manufacturers' Aircraft Association (U.S.A.); master army aviator; master-at-arms; Mathematical Association of America; Medieval

Academy of America; Member of the Architectural Association; Motor Agents' Association; Mutual Aid/Assurance Association (U.S.A.)

M.A.A.C. Mastic Asphalt Advisory Council

M.A.A.F. Mediterranean Allied Air Force/Forces

M.A.A.G. Military Assistance Advisory Group

M.A.A.G.B. Medical Artists' Association of Great Britain

ma'am madam

M.A.A.S. Member of the American Academy of Arts and Sciences

Mab Mabel

M.A.B. Metropolitan Asylums Board

m.a.b.p. mean arterial blood pressure (med.)

MABS marine air base squadron (U.S.A.)

M.A.B.Y.S. Metropolitan Association for Befriending Young Servants

mac mackintosh, raincoat

Mac shortened name used for surname beginning with this syllable

MAC Manchester auto-code (Manchester Univ.); maximum allowable concentration; Mineralogical Association of Canada; multiple access computer

mac. macadam

Mac. Macao; Maccabees, The Books of Maccabees, books of the Apocrypha. Protestant churches consider all books apocryphal but for R.C. the first two are canonical (*also* Macc.)

Macb. *Macbeth* (Shake.)

M.Acc. Master of Accountancy

M.A.C.C. military aid to the civilian community

M.A.C.D. Member of the Australasian College of Dermatologists; Member of the Australian College of Dentistry

MACE Metropolitan Architectural Consortium for Education

M.A.C.E. Master of Air Conditioning Engineering; Member of the Australian College of Education

Maced. Macedonia; Macedonian

mach. machine; machinery; machinist

M.A.C.I. Member of the American Concrete Institute

macroeco. macro-economics

M.A.C.S. Member of the American Chemical Society

MACSS medium-altitude communication satellite system

MAD magnetic anomaly detection; maintenance, assembly and disassembly; mathematical analysis of downtime (computer); mean absolute deviation; Michigan algorithm decoder (computer)

Mad. madam/madame

Madag. Madagascar

MADAM Manchester automatic digital machine; moderately advanced data management

Madge Margaret

Mad. Is. Madeira Islands

M.Admin., M.Ad. Master of Administration

Madr. Madras; Madrid

MADRE magnetic drum receiving equipment (computer)

Ma.E. Master in Engineering

m.a.e. mean absolute error

M.A.E. Master of Aeronautical Engineering; Master of Art Education; Master of Arts in Education/Elocution

MAECON Mid-America Electronics Conference

M.A.(Econ.) Master of Arts in Economic and Social Studies/Economic Studies

M.A.(Ed.) Master of Arts in Education

M.A.E.E. Marine Aircraft Experimental Establishment

M.A.E.F. Master Asphalt Employers' Federation

Maesto. It. *Maestoso*, majestic, stately (mus.)

m.a.f. major academic field

M.A. & F. Ministry of Agriculture and Fisheries

M.A.F.A. Manchester Academy of Fine Arts

M.A.F.F. Ministry of Agriculture, Fisheries and Food

mag. magazine; It. *maggio*, May; magnesia; magnesium; magnet; magnetic; magnetism; magneto; magnitude; magnum

mag., magn. L. *magnus*, great

Mag. Magyar (Hungarian)

M.Ag. Master of Agriculture

Maga William Blackwood presented his wife with the first issue of *Blackwood's Magazine* with the words 'There's ma maga-zine'. His Doric pronunciation of the first syllable appealed to his associates and the pub. became *Maga*

MAGB Microfilm Association of Great Britain

Magd. Magdalen College, Oxford, founded 1458; Magdalene College, Cambridge, founded 1542

M.Ag.Ec. Master of Agricultural Economics

Magg. It. *Maggio*, May

Magg. It. *Maggiore*, Major (mus.)

Maggie, Maggy Margaret

MAGLOC magnetic logic computer

magnalium magnesium and aluminium (alloy)

M.Agr. Master of Agriculture; — **Sc.** M. of Agricultural Science; — **Sc. (Dairy Tech.)** M. of Agricultural Science (Dairy Technology); — **Sc. (Hort.)** M. of Agricultural Science (Horticulture)

mah., mahog. mahogany

M.A.H. Fr. *Maître en administration hospitalière*, Master of Hospital Admin.

MAI *Moskovskiy Aviatsionny Institut*, Moscow Aviation Institute (U.S.S.R.)

M.A.I. L. *Magister in Arte Ingeniaria*, Master of Engineering; Member of the Anthropological Institute

M.A.I.A.S. Member of the Australian Institute of Agricultural Science

MAIBL Midland and International Banks Limited

M.A.I.Ch.E. Member of the American Institute of Chemical Engineers

M-aid financial aid given to European countries by U.S.A. under Marshall Plan. Plan originally proposed by Gen. George Marshall (1880–1959) 5 June 1947, and Interim Aid Bill signed by Pres. Truman 17 Dec. 1947

M.A.I.E.E. Member of the American Institute of Electrical Engineers

MAIG Matsushita Atomic Industrial Group (Jap.)

M.A.I.H.R. Member of the Australian Institute of Human Relations

MAILLEUROP Fr. *Secrétariat des industries de la maille des pays de la C.E.E.*, Secretariat of the Knitting and Weaving Industries of the EEC Countries

M.A.I.M.E. Member of the American Institute of Mining and Metallurgical Engineers

maint. maintenance

M.A.I.S.E. Member of the Association of Iron and Steel Engineers

Maisie Maria; Marie; Mary

maj. major; — **gen.** major-general; majority

MAJAC maintenance anti-jam console (USAF)

Mak Movement for Autonomy in Kurdistan

Mal. Malay; Malayan; Malaysia; Malaysian; Malta; Fr. *Maréchal*, Marshal; The Book of Malachi (Bible)

malac. malacology

M.A.L.D. Master of Arts in Law and Diplomacy

mall. malleable

m. à m. Fr. *mot à mot*, word for word

M.A.M.B.O. Mediterranean Association for Marine Biology and Oceanography

M.Am.Conc.Inst. Member of the American Concrete Institute

M.A.M.E.M.E. Member of the Association of Mining, Electrical & Mechanical Engineers

Mamie Maria; Marie; Mary

M.Am.Soc.C.E. Member of the Amalgamated/American Society of Civil Engineers

M.Am.Soc.H.R.A.E. Member of the American Society of Heating, Refrigeration and Air Conditioning Engineers

M.Am.Soc.Mech.E. Member of American Society of Mechanical Engineers

man. management; manager; manual; manufacture; manufacturer

Man. Manchester (*also* Manch., Manestr.); manila (paper); Manitoba, *also* Manit. (Can.); It. *Mano*, hand

M.A.N. Ger. *Maschinenfabrik Augsburg-Nürnberg A.G.*

M.Anaes. Master of Anaesthesiology

manc. It. *mancando*, gradually softer (mus.)

Manch. Manchuria

mand. L. *mandamus*, we command

Mand.ap. L. *mandatum apostolicum*, apostolic mandate

Man.Dir. managing director

Man.Ed. managing editor

manf. manufacturer

M.A.N.F. May, August, November, February

Mang.B. manganese bronze

Man.L.R. *Manitoba Law Reports*

Man.op. manually operated

man.pr. L. *mane primo*, early in the morning (med.)

Mans. mansion

M.A.N.S. Member of the Academy of Natural Science (U.S.A.)

Mansf. Mansfield College, Oxford, founded 1886

Manuel, Manny Emmanuel

manuf. manufacture; manufacturer

M.A.N.W.E.B. Merseyside and North Wales Electricity Board

M.A.N.Z.C.P. Member Australian and New Zealand College of Psychiatrists

m.a.o. Swed. *med andra ord*, in other words

M.A.O.T. Member of the Association of Occupational Therapists

M.A.O.U. Member of the American Ornithologists' Union

M.A.P. maximum average price; medical aid post; minimum association price; Ministry of Aircraft Production; modified American plan

M.A.(Ph.) Fr. *Maître ès arts* (*philosophie*), Master of Arts (Philosophy)

M.A.P.H. manned ambient-pressure habitat (underwater)

MAPHI Member of Association of Public Health Inspectors

M.A.P.I. Member of the Australian Planning Institute

M.App.Sc. Master of Applied Science

MAPU *Moviemiento Acción Popular Unitario*, Unitary Popular Action Movement (Chile)

mar. marine; maritime; married; It. *martedì*, Tuesday; It. *marzo*, March

Mar. March

M.Ar., M.Arch. Master of Architecture

M.A.R. marginal age relief (tax.)

MARAD Maritime Administration (U.S.A.)

marc. It. *marcato*, marked (mus.)

March. marchioness

marg. margin; marginal

Marg., Margie, Margot, Mrgt. Margaret

marge margarine

marg.trans. marginal translation

Marion Mary

marit. maritime

mar.lic. marriage licence

marm madam

mar. merc. It. *marina mercantile*, merchant marine

mar. mil. It. *marina militare*, navy

Marq. marquess; marquis

MARS master agents research system; meteorological automatic reporting station/system; military affiliate radio system; mobile atlantic range station

mar.settl. marriage settlement

mart. market; martyr

Mart. Marcus Valerius Martialis (*c* A.D. 40–*c* 104), Roman poet; Martin (*also* Marty)

MAS middle airspace

mas., masc. masculine

M.a.S. milliampère-second (elec.)

M.A.S. Master of Applied Science (*also* M.A.Sc.); military agency for standardization; It. *motoscafo antisommergibile*, motor torpedo boat

M.A.S.C.E. Member of the American/Australian Society of Civil Engineers

mascons mass concentrations, heavy matter beneath lunar maria (astron.)

MASER microwave amplification by stimulated emission of radiation

M.A.S.H.A.E. Member of the American Society of Heating & Air Conditioning Engineers

M.A.S.H.V.E. Member of the Australian Society of Heating & Ventilating Engineers

M.A.S.M.E. Member of the American /Australian Society of Mechanical Engineers

Mass. Massachusetts (U.S.A.)

M.A.(S.S.) Master of Arts in Social Science

MAST missile automatic supply technique

Mat Martha; Matilda; matrix (*i*) the papier-mâché or other mould which is used in making stereos of type or blocks (typ.); (*ii*) a mould from which type is cast; Matthew

mat. maternity; matins; maturity (fin.)

M.A.T. Master of Arts in Teaching

MATA multiple answering teaching aid

M.A.T.A. Museums Association of Tropical Africa

MATCON microwave aerospace terminal control (USAF)

math. mathematical; mathematically; mathematician; mathematics (*also* maths.)

MATI *Moskovskiy Aviatsionnyy Teknologicheskiy Institut*, Moscow Aviation Technology Institute

matr. L. *matrimonium*, marriage

matric. matriculate; matriculation

MATS Military Air Transport Service (USAF)

Matt. The Gospel according to St. Matthew (Bible)

MATTS multiple airborne target trajectory system

Matty Martha; Matilda; Matthew

matut. L. *matutinus*, in the morning

Maur. Mauritius

M.Aus.I.M.M. Member of the Australasian Institute of Mining and Metallurgy

MAV maleic anhydride value (med.)

MAW marine air wing (USMC); medium assault weapon

Max Maximilian

max. maxim; maxima; maximum;—**cap.** maximum capacity

May Maria; Marie; Mary

MAYDAY Fr. *m'aidez*, help me (intern. distress call)

mayn't may not

MB *s* Cheshire (B.V.R.); methyl bromide, used for fire fighting

mb. millibar

m.b. magnetic bearing; main battery; medium bomber; motor barge/boat

m.b. L. *misce bene*, mix well (med.)

M.B. maritime / marketing / medical board; Fr. *Médaille de la Bravoure*, Medal of Bravery (Can.); metropolitan/municipal Borough; L. *Medicinae Baccalaureus*, Bachelor of Medicine; L. *Musicae Baccalaureus*, Bachelor of Music

M. & B. initials of May and Baker

Limited, makers of M & B 693 (etc.) a sulphonamide drug; mild and bitter (beer); Mitchells and Butlers Limited, brewers

Mba. Mombasa

M.B.A. Marine Biological Association; Master of Business Administration; Mountain Bothies Association

M.B.A.A. Master Brewers' Association of America

M.B.A.C. Member of the British Association of Chemists

M.B.A.L. Master Bookbinders' Alliance of London

MBALE 1,000 bales (U.S.A.)

MBBL 1,000 barrels (U.S.A.)

MBC Mauritius Broadcasting Corporation

m.b.c. maximum breathing capacity

M.B.C. metropolitan/municipal borough council

M.B.C.P.E. Member of the British College of Physical Education

MBCS Member British Computer Society

M.Bdg.Sc. Master of Building Science

M.B.E. Member of the Order of the British Empire

M.B.F. Musicians' Benevolent Fund

M.B.F.et H. L. *Magna Britannia, Francia et Hibernia*, Great Britain, France and Ireland

MBFR mutual and balanced force reductions. Item on agenda of negotiations between NATO and Warsaw Powers, 1971

m.b.H. Ger. *mit beschränkter Haftung*, limited liability

M.B.H.I. Member of the British Horological Institute

MBI mercaptobenzimidazole, antioxidant for rubber

M.B.I.M. Member of the British Institute of Management

M.B.K. missing, believed killed (mil.)

M.B.L. Marine Biological Laboratory

M.B.M. Master of Business Management

MBO management by objectives, *also* M.b.O., used by Institute of Personnel Management

M.B.O.U. Member of the British Ornithologists' Union

m.b.p. mean blood pressure

mbr. member

M.Bret. Middle Breton

M.Brit.I.R.E. Member of the British Institution of Radio Engineers

M.B.S. Manchester Business School; Mutual Broadcasting System (U.S.A.)

M.B.Sc. Master of Business Science

M.B.S.I. Member of the British Boot and Shoe Institution

m.b.t. mean body temperature; mechanical bathythermograph; mercaptobenzthiazole, vulcanization accelerator; mobile boarding team

M.B.T.A. Metropolitan Board Teachers' Association

MBU 1,000 bushels (U.S.A.)

M.Build. Master of Building

M.B.W. Metropolitan Board of Works, *later* L.C.C. *now* G.L.C.

m/c, m.c. machine; motor cycle

Mc megacycle

MC *s* London (B.V.R.); *s* Monaco (I.V.R.)

mc. megacycle; millicuries, measurement for radium

m.c. Fr. *mois courant*, current month

M/C Manchester; marginal credit (fin.); metalling clause (marine insce.)

M.C. machinery certificate; L. *Magister Chirurgiae*, Master of Surgery; Magistrates' Court; magnetic course (nav.); Marine/Medical Corps (U.S.A.); Maritime Commission (U.S.A.); marked capacity; marriage certificate; master commandant; master of ceremonies/congress; medical certificate/college/corps; Member of Congress (U.S.A.); Member of Council; Mennonite/Methodist Church; mess committee; military college/committee; Military Cross; millicurie; Monday Club (pol.); morse code; motor contact

M.-C. medico-chirurgical

MCA Malayan-Chinese Association (Malaysia); Muslim Committee of Action (Mauritius)

M.C.A. Malaysian Commercial Association; Management Consultants' Association; Manufacturing Chemists' Association; Master of Commerce and Administration; Matrimonial Causes Act 1937; Ministry of Civil Aviation

MCAA Mechanical Contractors' Association of America

M.C.A.A.A. Midland Counties Amateur Athletic Association

MCAB marine corps air base

MCAF marine corps air field

MCAR 1,000 carats (U.S.A.)

MCAS marine corps air station

MCB marine corps base

m.c.b. miniature circuit breaker

MCC midcourse correction (nav.)

M.C.C. Mains Cable Council; Marylebone Cricket Club formed 1787 and moved to present Lord's Ground in 1814; Melbourne Cricket Club; Member of the County Council; meteorological communications centre; Middlesex County Council

M.C.C.C. Middlesex County Cricket Club

MCC - H mission control center, Houston (NASA)

m.c.d. It. *minimo comune denominatore*, lowest common denominator

M.C.D. Doctor of Comparative Medicine; Master of Civic Design

MCDS management control data system

M.C.E. Master of Civil Engineering

Mcf 1,000 cubic feet

Mcfd 1,000 cubic feet per day

Mcfh 1,000 cubic feet per hour

Mcfm 1,000 cubic feet per month

MCFTU Mauritius Confederation of Free Trade Unions

MC & G mapping, charting and geodesy

McG. U. McGill University (Can.)

Mch. Manchester (*also*, M'chter.); March

M.Ch., M.Chir. L. *Magister Chirurgiae*, Master of Surgery

M.Ch.D. L. *Magister Chirurgiae Dentalis*, Master of Dental Surgery

M.Ch.E. Master of Chemical Engineering

M.Ch.Orth. L. *Magister Chirurgiae Orthopaedicae*, Master of Orthopaedic Surgery

M.Ch.Otol. Master of Oto-Rhino-Laryngological Surgery

M.Chrom. Master of Chromatics

mcht. merchant

m.c.i. malleable cast iron

M.C.I.E. Midland Counties Institution of Engineers

M.C.L. Manchester Central Library; Master of Civil Law

M.Clin.Psychol. Master of Clinical Psychology

M.C.L.O.S.A. Member of the Continental Law Office Society of America

M.Cl.Sc. Master of Clinical Science

m.c.m. It. *minimo comune multiple*, lowest common multiple

M.C.M.A. Mains Cable Manufacturers' Association

M.C.M.E.S. Member of Civil and Mechanical Engineers' Society (U.S.A.)

Mco. Morocco

M.C.O. motor contact officer; movement control officer

M.C.O.D.A. Motor Cab Owner-Drivers' Association

Mcol. musicological; musicologist (*also* mcolst.); musicology

M.Coll.H. Member of the College of Handicrafts

M.Com., M.Comm. Master of Commerce; Minister of Commerce

M.Cons.E. Member of the Association of Consulting Engineers; — (C.A.) Member of the Assn. of Consulting Engineers of Central Africa

MCP Malawi Congress Party

M.C.P. Malayan Communist Party; Master of City Planning; Member of the College of Preceptors

M.C.P.A. Member of the College of Pathologists of Australia

m.c.p.s., mc/s megacycles per second

M.C.P.S. Mechanical Copyright Protection Society; Member of the College of Physicians and Surgeons

M.C.Q.S. Member of the Chapter of Quantity Surveyors of the South African Institute of Architects

MCR mass communications research; mobile control room

M.C.R.A. Member of the College of Radiologists of Australia

MCRD Marine Corps Recruit Depot

MCS Management Computing Services

M.C.S. Madras/Malayan Civil Service; Master of Commercial Science; medium close shot; Military College of Science

MCSIB Management Consulting Information Bureau

M.C.S.P. Member of the Chartered Society of Physiotherapy

MCT mechanical comprehension test

M.C.T. Member of the College of Technologists

M.C. & T.S. Monotype Casters' and Typefounders' Society

M.C.U. Modern Churchmen's Union

m.c.w. modulated continuous wave

M.C.W. maternity and child welfare

MCWT 1,000 hundred weight (U.S.A.)

Md *s* mendelivium (chem.)

MD *s* London (B.V.R.); Maryland, *also* Md. (U.S.A.)

M/D memorandum of deposit (*also*, M.D.); months after date

md. Fr. *marchand*, dealer; milliard (1,000 million)

m.d. It. *mano destra*, right hand

M.D. Fr. *main droite*, right hand; managing director; map distance; market day; medical department; L. *Medicinae Doctor*, Doctor of Medicine; mentally deficient; message-dropping; mess deck; meteorology department; Middle Dutch (*also*, M.Du.); military district; Millwall Docks; Monroe Doctrine (1823) declared that the U.S.A. had no interest in European wars, but warned European powers that any attempt to interfere in the W. Hemisphere would be considered dangerous to the safety of U.S.A.; musical director

M. and D. medicine and duty
M.D.A. Muscular Dystrophy Association
M.D.A.P. Mutual Defense Assistance Program (U.S.A.)
M-day mobilization day, on which national prep. for war is ordered (U.S.A.)
MDB *Movimento Democrático Brasileiro*, Brazilian Democratic Movement
M.d.B. Ger. *Mitglied des Bundestages*, Member of the Bundestag
MDC Malawi Development Corporation
Mddx. Middlesex
M.D.E. Master of Domestic Economy
M.Dent.Sc. Master in Dental Science
M.Des. Master of Design
MDF Manitoba Development Fund
M.D.G. medical director-general
M.D.H.B. Mersey Docks and Harbour Board
M.Di. Master of Didactics
m.dict. L. *more dicto*, in the manner directed (med.)
M.Dip. Master of Diplomacy
M.Div. Master of Divinity
mdl. model
Mdlle., Mlle. Fr. *Mademoiselle*, Miss
Mdm. Madam
Mdme. Fr. *Madame*, Mrs.
MDN Mark of the German Bank of Issue (E. Ger.)
Mdn. median
mdnt. midnight
MDPMA Member Data Processing Managers Association
m.d.r. minimum daily requirement
MDRA *Mouvement Démocratique du Renouveau Algérien*, Democratic Movement for Algerian Renewal
Mds. Fr. *Mesdames*
M.D.S. main dressing station; Master of Dental Surgery
M.D.S.A. Multiple Disc Sampling Apparatus
M.D.Sc. Master of Dental Science
mdse. merchandise
M.D.S.T. mountain daylight saving time
MDT mean time down
MDTS modular data transaction system
M.D.U. Medical Defence Union
M.D.V. Doctor of Veterinary Medicine
M.D.W. Military Defence Works
Mdx. Middlesex
ME *s* London (B.V.R.); Maine (U.S.A.); memory error; metabolizable energy; modified effigy, new portrait of monarch (numis.); Montrose (B.F.P.)
Me. Maine (U.S.A.); Fr. *maître*, French advocate's title, *also* Mᵉ· (leg.); *Messerschmitt*, Ger. aircraft manufacturer
m.e. maximum effort; mobility equipment
m.E. Ger. *meines Erachtens*, in my opinion
M.E. managing editor; marbled edges (bookbinding); marine engineer; Master of Education/Engineering; mechanical engineer/engineering (*also*, Mech.E.); Methodist Episcopal; Middle East/Eastern; Middle English; military engineer; milled edge; mining engineer/engineering; Most Excellent; mottled edges; Fr. *Movement européen*, European Movement
M.E.A. Medical Exhibitors' Association (U.S.A.); Middle East Airlines; Music Education/Educators' Association (U.S.A.)
M.E.A.F. Middle East Air Force
Meanie, Meany ungenerous-minded person
MEAR maintenance engineering analysis record (USN)
meas. measurable; measure; measurement
M.E.(Auto.) Master of Automobile Engineering
M.E.B. Midlands Electricity Board
M.Ec. Master of Economics
M.E.C. Master of Engineering Chemistry; Member of Executive Council; It. *Mercato Comune Europeo*, European Common Market
M.E.C.A.S. Middle East Centre for Arab Studies
mecc. It. *meccanica*, mechanic
mech. mechanic; mechanical; mechanically; mechanics; mechanism; mechanize
M.E.Ch., M.E.C. Methodist Episcopal Church
M.E.(Chem.) Master of Engineering (Chemical)
MECO main engine cut-off
M.Econ. Master of Economics; — S. Master of Economic Science
med. medallist; median; medical; medicine; medieval; medium
Med., Medit. Mediterranean
M.Ed. Master in/of Education; — (Agr.) Master of Education (Agriculture)
M.E.D. Master of Elementary Didactics (U.S.A.); minimal effective dose
MEDAL micro-mechanized engineering data for automated logistics
Med.Gr. Medieval Greek
medic. medical practitioner/student
MEDICO Medical International Cooperation; model experiment in drug indexing by computer
med. jur. medical jurisprudence

med. lab. medical laboratory
Med.Lat. medieval latin
M.Ed.L.Sc. Master of Education in Library Science
Med.R.C. medical reserve corps
Medresco. Medical Research Council
M.Ed.S., M.Ed.San. Fr. *Maître en éducation sanitaire*, Master of Health Education
Med.Sc.D. Doctor of Medical Science
Med.Sch. medical school
Med.Tech. medical technician/technologizer/technology
M.E.E. Master of Electrical Engineering
M.E.(Elec.) Master of Engineering (Electrical)
M.E.E.S. *Middle East Economic Survey*
M.E.F. Mediterranean Expeditionary Force; Middle East Forces
meg. megacycle; megaton (million tons of TNT); megawatt; megohm (million ohms)
Meg, Meggie Margaret
M.E.G.H.P. Most Excellent Grand High Priest
MEI Mathematics in Education & Industry
M.E.I.C. Member of the Engineering Institute of Canada
MEIU Management Education Information Unit
Mej. Dutch *Mejuffrouw*, Miss
MEK methyl ethyl ketone, solvent widely used in vinylite lacquers, nitrocellulose lacquers and thinners, artificial leather dopes, as a solvent for resins and waxes and in dewaxing process
M.E.L. Master/Mistress of English Literature
Melan. Melanesia; Melanesian
Melb. Melbourne (Aust.)
M.E.L.F. Middle East Land Forces
mem. member; memoirs; memorandum; memorial
Mem. L. *Memento*, remember
M.E.M.A. Marine Engine Manufacturers' Association
M.E.(Mech.) Master of Engineering (Mechanical)
memo. memorandum
Men. It. *Meno*, less (mus.)
M.E.N.A. mixed manned element in Nato's armament
M.Eng. Master of Engineering; — **and P.A.** M. in Engineering and Public Administration; — **(Min.)** M. of Engineering (Mining); — **(Sc.)** M. of Engineering Science
M.Ens. Fr. *Maître en enseignement*, Master of Teaching

mensur. mensuration
mentd. mentioned
MEP *Movimiento Electoral del Pueblo*, People's Electoral Movement (Ven.); *Mahajana Eksath Peramuna*, People's United Front (Ceylon)
m.e.p. mean effective pressure
M.E.(P.H.) Master of Engineering (Public Health)
meq. milliequivalent
mer. mercantile (*also*, merc.); merchandise; meridian; meridional; It. *mercoledì*, Wednesday (*also*, merc.); Fr. *mercredi*, Wednesday
Mer. Vickers/BEA Merchantman (aircraft); mercurial; mercury (*also*, merc.); Merioneth; Merionethshire
M.E.R.B. Mechanical Engineering Research Board
Merc. Mercedes (car)
Merch.V. *Merchant of Venice* (Shake.)
M.E.R.L. Mechanical Engineering Research Laboratory, *now* National Engineering Laboratory
MERLIN medium energy reactor light water industrial neutron source
Merry W. *Merry Wives of Windsor* (Shake.)
Mert. Merton College, Oxford, founded 1264
M.E.R.U. Mechanical Engineering Research Unit (S. Afr.)
MES Michigan Engineering Society (U.S.A.)
Mes., Mesd. Fr. *Mesdames*, ladies
MESA modularized equipment storage assembly
M. ès A. Fr. *Maître ès arts*, Master of Arts
MESAN *Mouvement d'Évolution Sociale en Afrique Noire*, Social Evolution Movement of Black Africa (Central African Republic)
M.E.Sc. Master of Engineering Science
MESCO Middle East UNESCO Science Co-operation Office
meson particle with mass between that of proton and electron
Messrs. Fr. *Messieurs*, gentlemen
met. metallurgical; metaphor; metaphysical; metaphysics; meteorological; meteorology; metropolitan (*also* metro.)
met. *metronome* (mus.)
M.E.T. Fr. *Maître en enseignement technique*, Master in Technical Teaching
Meta Margaret
M.E.T.A. Model Engineering Trade Association
metal., metall. metallurgical; metallurgy
metaph. metaphor; metaphorical;

227

metaphorically; metaphysics; metaphysical; metaphysically; metaphysician
metath. metathesis; metathetic
met.bor. metropolitan borough
Met.E. metallurgical engineer
meteor. meteorological; meteorology
Meth. Methodist; — **Epis.** Methodist Episcopal
meths. methylated spirits
M.-et-L. Maine-et-Loire (France)
M.-et-M. Meurthe-et-Moselle (France)
M.et n. L. *mane et nocte*, morning and night (med.)
Met.O. meteorological office/officer
M.E.T.O. Middle East Treaty Organisation, *now* CENTO
meton. metonymy
Met.R. Metropolitan Railway (Lond.)
métro. Fr. *chemin de fer métropolitain*, underground-train system, Paris
Metro. Convair 440 Metropolitan (aircraft)
metrol. metrological; metrology
metrop., metropol. metropolis; metropolitan
metsat meteorological satellite
METSO sodium metasilicate (chem.)
Met.-Vic. Metropolitan-Vickers
M.E.U. *Modern English Usage*
MEV mega/million electron volts
Mev. Dutch *Mevrouw*, Mrs.
M.E.W. microwave early warning; Ministry of Economic Warfare
MEX *s* Mexico (I.V.R.)
Mex. Mexican; Mexico; — **C.** Mexico City; — **Sp.** Mexican Spanish
mez. It. *mezzo*, half, medium (mus.)
M.E.Z. Ger. *Mitteleuropäische Zeit*, time of the Middle European zone, one hour in advance of Greenwich
mezzo. mezzotint
mF millifarad
MF *s* London (B.V.R.)
m/f. Sp. *mi favor*, my favour
m.f. machine/mill finish; medium frequency, 300–3,000 Kc; Fr. *moyenne fréquence*, intermediate frequency
m.f. It. *mezzo-forte*, moderately loud (mus.)
MF., M.F., M.Fr. Middle French
M.F. machine finished, paper with medium smooth surface given while it is still on the paper-making machine; Malvern Festival; Master of Forestry; Minister of Food
M.F.A. Master of Fine Arts; Metal Finishing Association; Motor Factors' Association
M.F.A.B.I. Metal Fixing Association for Building Insulation
M.F.A.Mus. Master of Fine Arts in Music

M.F.A.R.C.S. Member of the Faculty of Anaesthetists of the Royal College of Surgeons
M.F.B. Metropolitan Fire Brigade
M.F.C. Fr. *Mouvement familial chrétien*, Christian Family Movement
M.F.C.M. Member of the Faculty of Community Medicine
mfd. manufactured; microfarad
M.F.D. Ger. *Mennonitischer Freiwilligen Dienst*, Mennonite Voluntary Service; minimum fatal dose
M.F.E. Fr. *Mouvement fédéraliste européen*, European Federalist Movement
M.Fed. Miners' Federation
mfg. manufacturing
M.F.H. Master of Foxhounds; mobile field hospital
M.F.H.A. Masters of Foxhounds Association
M.F.Hom. Member of the Faculty of Homoeopathy
M.F.I. melt flow index (polymers)
m.fl. Dan. *med flere*, and others
M.Flem. Middle Flemish
M.F.N. most favoured nation, in trade agreements
M.F.N.O. Midland Federation of Newspaper Owners
M. for M. *Measure for Measure* (Shake.)
MFP Marematlou Freedom Party (Lesotho)
mfr., mfre. manufacture; manufacturer
MFS magnetic flux sensor; Malleable Founders' Society; manned flying system; multiple frequency shift
M.F.S. Master of Food Science; Master of Foreign Study
mfst. manifest
m.f.t. motor freight tariff
M.ft. L. *Mistura fiat*, let a mixture be made (med.)
m.ft.m. L. *misce fiat mistura*, mix to make a mixture
M.F.V. motor fleet vessel
M.F.W. Maritime Federation of the World
Mg *s* magnesium (chem.); Ger. *Molekulargewicht*, molecular weight
MG *s* London (B.V.R.); Morris Garage (*also* M.G.), Morris sports car
mg. milligram; morning
m.g. machine gun; Fr. *main gauche*, left hand; milligram; mixed grain; motor generator
m.G. Fr. *méridien de Greenwich*, Greenwich Meridian
M.G. machine glazed, paper which has glazed surface on one side only; Major-General; — **A.** Major-General

228

Administration; — **G.S.** Major-General, General Staff; — **R.A.** Major-General Royal Artillery; medical gymnast

M.-G. Middle German

M.G.A. Mushroom Growers' Association

m.g.a.w.d. make good all works disturbed

M.G.B. *Ministerstvo Gosudarstvennoi Bezopasnosti,* Ministry of State Security (U.S.S.R.); motor gunboat

M.G.C. machine gun corps; Marriage Guidance Council/Counsellor

mg. cu. m. milligrammes per cubic metre

MGD million gallons a day

mge. message

MGI Mapping and Geography Institute (Ethiopia)

M.G.I. Member of the Institute of Certificated/Certified Grocers; Mining and Geological Institute of India

M.Gk. Middle/Modern Greek

MGM mobile guided missile

M.G.M. Metro-Goldwyn-Mayer, film studio

M.G.M.S. Manchester Geological and Mining Society

M.G.O. Master-General of Ordnance; Master of Gynaecology and Obstetrics

M.Goth. meso-gothic

mgr. manager

Mgr. Fr. *Monseigneur,* My Lord; Monsignor, title of R.C. protonotaries apostolic and (unofficially) bishops

M.Gr. medieval/middle Greek

m.g.s. metre-gram-second

mgt. management

MGU *Moskoviskiy Gosudarstvennyy Universitet,* Moscow State Univ.

MH *s* London (B.V.R.); Master of Hounds; Middlesborough (B.F.P.)

mh. millihenry

MH. megahertz

M.H. magnetic heading; main hatch; marital history; Master of Horse; Master of Horticulture; Master of Hygiene; Medal of Honour; mental health; military hospital; Ministry of Health

M.H.A. Master of Hospital Administration; Member of House of Assembly; Mental Health Administration (U.S.A.)

M.H.C.I. Member of the Hotel and Catering Institute

m.h.cp. mean horizontal candle-power

MHD magnetohydrodynamics

M.H.E.A. Mechanical Handling Engineers Association

M.Heb. Middle Hebrew

MHEDA Material Handling Equipment Distributors' Association (U.S.A.)

m.h.f. medium high frequency

M.H.G. Middle High German

M.H.H.W. mean higher high water

M.H.K. Member of the House of Keys (Isle of Man)

MHLG Ministry of Housing and Local Government

mho unit of conductance (elec.)

M.Hon. Most Honourable

M.Hort.Sc. Master of Horticultural Science

M.H.R. Member of the House of Representatives

M.H.R.A. Modern Humanities Research Association

M.H.R.F. Mental Health Research Fund

M.H.R.I. Mental Health Research Institute

M.H.S. medical history sheet; Member of the Historical Society

M.H.Sc. Master of Home Science

MHT mild heat treatment

M.Hum. Master of Humanities

M.H.W. mean high water

M.H.W.I. mean high water lunitidal interval

M.H.W.N.T. mean high water neap tide

M.H.W.S.T. mean high water spring tide

M.Hy. Master of Hygiene

MHz MegaHertz

MI Michigan (U.S.A.); *s* Wexford (B.V.R.)

mi. mile; — **mi.**2 square mile; — **mi.**3 cubic mile; mill; minute

Mi. minor; Mississippi (U.S.A.)

m.i. monumental inscription; mutual induction

M.I. malleable iron; metal industries; military intelligence; Minister of Information; mounted infantry

M.I.A. Malleable Ironfounders' Association; Manitoba Institute of Agrologists; Member of the South African Institute of Architects; missing in action

M.I. Member of the Institute/Institution; — **A.E.** M. of the Institution of Automobile Engineers; — **Ae.E.** M. of the Institute of Aeronautical Engineers; — **A.M.A.** M. of the Incorporated Advertising Managers' Association; — **B.E.** M. of the Institution of British Engineers; — **B.F.** M. of the Institute of British Foundrymen; — **Biol.** M. of the Institute of Biology

M.I.B. Metal Information Bureau

M.I.B.K. methyl isobutyl ketone (solvent)

M.I.Brit.E. Member of the Institution of British Engineers

Mic. Micah (Bible)

M.I.C. Malayan Indian Congress

M.I.C.A. Maternity and Infant Care Association

M.I.C.E. Member of the Institution of Civil Engineers; — **I. M.** of the Institution of Civil Engineers India/Ireland

Mich. Michaelmas (also, Michs.); Michigan (U.S.A.)

M.I.Chem.E. Member of the Institution of Chemical Engineers

Mick Michael

Micky, Mickey Michael

M.I.C.M. Associate Member of the Institute of Credit Management

mic.pan. L. *mica panis*, crumb of bread

M.I.C.R. magnetic ink character recognition

micro., micros. microscope

micros. microscopist; microscopy

Micro. Micronesia

mid. middle; midnight

Mid. Midlands, *also* Midl.; midshipman, *also* middy

MIDAC Michigan digital automatic computer

MIDAS missile defence alarm system

M.I.D.A.S. measurement information and data analysis system; media investment decisions analysis systems

Middx., Middlx. Middlesex

MIDEASTFOR Middle East Force (USN)

M.I.D.E.C. Middle East Industrial Development Projects Corporation

M.I.D.E.(S.A.) Member of the Institute of Diesel Engineers (S. Afr.)

MIDELEC Midlands Electricity Board

Midl. Midlothian (Scot.)

Mid.Lat. Middle Latin

Mids.N.D. *Midsummer Night's Dream* (Shake.)

midw. mid-western

M.I. Member of the Institute/Institution; — E. M. of the Institute of Engineers (S. Afr.); — **E.Aust.** M. of the Institution of Engineers, Australia; — **E.C.** Fr. *Pax Romana, mouvement international des étudiants catholiques*, Pax Romana, Intern. Movement of Catholic Students;—**E.D.** M. of the Institution of Engineering Designers; — **E.E.** M. of the Institution of Electrical Engineers; — **E.I.** M. of the Institution of Engineering Inspection;—**E. (India)** M. of the Institution of Engineers (India); — **E.R.E.** M. of the British Institute of Electronic and Radio Engineers; — **E.S.** M. of the Institution of Engineers & Shipbuilders in Scotland; — **Ex.** M. of the Institute of Export; — **F.A.** M. of the Institute of Foresters of Australia; — **Fire E.** M. of the Institute of Fire Engineers

M.I.F. Miners' International Federation; modulus irregularity factor

MIFI *Moskovskiy Inzhenerno Fizicheskiy Institut*, Moscow Engineering Physics Institute

M.I.5. Brit. military intelligence division which deals with matters of state security

m.i.g. magnesium-inert/metallic-inert gas

M.I.G., MiG Mikhail Ivanovich Glinka, jet fighter designed by Mikoyan and Gurevich (Russian aircraft)

M.I.Gas.E. Member Institution of Gas Engineers

M.I.G.B. Millinery Institute of Great Britain

mightn't might not

m.i.h. miles an hour

M.I.H.V.E. Member of the Institution of Heating & Ventilating Engineers

M.I.I.A. Member of the Institute of Industrial Administration, *now* B.I.M.

M.I.I.C. Fr. *Pax Romana, mouvement international des intellectuels catholiques*, Pax Romana, Intern. Catholic Movement for Intellectual and Cultural Affairs

M.I.I.E. Member of the Institution of Industrial Engineers

M.I.I.S. Member of the Institute of Industrial Supervisors

Mij. *Maatschapij*, joint stock company (Neth.)

M.I.J. Member of the Institute of Journalists, *correctly* M.J.I.

M.I.J.A.R.C. Fr. *Mouvement international de la jeunesse agricole et rurale catholique*, Intern. Movement of Catholic Agricultural and Rural Youth

Mike Michael; microphone

MIL 1,000,000 (U.S.A.)

mil. mileage; military; militia (also, milit.); millilitre

Mil. Milan (Italy)

M.I.L. Member of The Institute of Linguists

Mil.Att. military attaché

MILCOMSAT military communication satellite

M.I.L.E. Member of the Institution of Locomotive Engineers

mill. million; Ger. *millionen*, million

MIL-LB 1,000,000 pounds (U.S.A.)

Millie, Milly Amelia; Mildred; Millicent

M.Illum.E.S. Member of the Illuminating Engineers' Society

M.I.Loco.E. Member of the Institution of Locomotive Engineers

MILS missile impact location system

MILSPEC military specification

Milt. John Milton (1608–74), Eng. poet

Milw. Milwaukee (U.S.A.)

Mima Jemima

M.I. Member of the Institute/Institution; — **Mar.E.** M. of the Institute of Marine Engineers; — **M.E.** M. of the Institution of Mining Engineers; — **Mech. E.** M. of the Institution of Mechanical Engineers; — **M. & G.E.** M. of the Institute of Mechanical & General Engineers; — **M.I.** M. of the Institute of the Motor Industry; — **Min.E.** M. of the Institution of Mining Engineers; — **M.M.** M. of the Institution of Mining and Metallurgy; — **M.T.** M. of the Institute of the Motor Trade; — **Mun.E.** M. of the Institution of Municipal Engineers

M.I.M.E. Midland Institute of Mining Engineers

mi./min. miles per minute

min. mineralogical; mineralogy; minim; minima; minimum; mining; ministry; minor; minute, time unit

Min. minister; ministerial

M.I.N. Member of the Institute of Navigation

Mina Wilhelmina

MinAgric. Ministry of Agriculture, Fisheries and Food

Min.B/L. minimum bill of lading

Min.Can. minor canon

Min.Counc. mining councillor

MinDef., M.O.D. Ministry of Defence

mineral. mineralogical; mineralogy

MinFuel. Ministry of Fuel and Power

MinHous. Ministry of Housing and Local Government

Minn. Minnesota (U.S.A.)

Minnie Maria; Marie; Mary; Ger.
Minenwerfer, a mine-thrower; Wilhelmina

mino. Sp. *ministro*, minister; ministry

MINPAC Mine Warfare Forces, Pacific (USN)

MinPBW. Ministry of Public Building and Works

min.pen. minimum premium

Min.Plen. Minister Plenipotentiary

Min.Res. Minister Resident/Residentiary

M. Inst. Member of the Institute/Institution; — **A.M.** Member of the Institute of Administrative Management; — **B.E.** M. of the Institution of British Engineers; — **C.E.** M. of the Institution of Civil Engineers; — **F.** M. of the Institute of Fuel; — **Gas. E.** M. of the Institution of Gas Engineers; — **H.E.** M. of the Institution of Highway Engineers; — **M.** M. of the Institute of Metals; — **M.E.** M. of the Institution of Mining Engineers; — **Met.** M. of the Institute of Metals; — **M.M.** M. of the Institution of Mining and

Metallurgy; — **M.S.M.** M. of Institute of Marketing and Sales Management; — **P.C.** M. of the Institute of Public Cleansing; — **P.I.** M. of the Institute of Patentees and Inventors; — **Pkg.** M. of the Institute of Packaging; — **P.T.** M. of the Institute of Petroleum Technologists; — **R.** M. of the Institute of Refrigeration; — **R.A.** M. of the Institute of Registered Architects; — **S.P.** M. of the Institution of Sewage Purification; — **T.** M. of the Institute of Technology/Transport; — **W.** M. of the Institute of Welding; — **W.E.** M. of the Institution of Water Engineers

MinTech. Ministry of Technology

M.I.Nuc.E. Member of the Institution of Nuclear Engineers

min.wt. minimum weight

M.I.O.B. Member of the Institute of Building

MIOM Member, Institute of Office Management

m.i.p. malleable iron pipe; marine insurance policy; mean indicated pressure; monthly investment plan

M.I. Member of the Institute/Institution; — **Pet.** M. of the Institute of Petroleum; — **P.H.E.** M. of the Institution of Public Health Engineers; — **Plant E.** M. of the Institution of Plant Engineers; — **P.M.** M. of the Institute of Personnel Management; — **P.R.** M. of the Institute of Public Relations; — **Prod.E.** M. of the Institution of Production Engineers; — **Ptg.M.** M. of the Institute of Printing Management; — **Q.** M. of the Institute of Quarrying

M.Ir. Middle Irish

M.I.R.A. Member of the Institute of Registered Architects; Motor Industry's Research Association

M.I.R.D. med. internal radiation dose

M.I.R.E. Member of the British Institution of Radio Engineers; Member of the Institution of Railway Signal Engineers

MIRROS modulation inducing reactive retrodirective optical system (NASA)

M.I.R.T. Member, Institute of Reprographic Technicians

M.I.R.T.E. Member of Institute of Road Transport Engineers

M.I.R.V. multiple independently-targeted re-entry vehicle

Mis. Mississippi (U.S.A.) *also* Miss.; Missouri (U.S.A.)

Mis. L. *Miserere*, have mercy

M.I.S. Mining Institute of Scotland

M.I.(S.A.)C.E. Member of South African Institution of Civil Engineers

misc. miscellaneous; miscellany; — **doc.** miscellaneous documents

231

miscend. L. *miscendus*, to be mixed

M.I.S.E. Member of the Institution of Sanitary Engineers

M.I.S.I., M.I. and S.Inst. Member of the Iron and Steel Institute

M.I.S.(India) Member of the Institution of Surveyors (India)

MISLIC Mid-Staffordshire Libraries in Co-operation

miss. miscarriage

Miss. mission; missionary; missioner

M.I.S.S. Member of the Institute of Industrial Supervisors

mist. L. *mistura*, mixture

mistrans. mistranslation

M.I.Struct.E. Member of the Institution of Structural Engineers

M.I.S.W. Member of the Institute of Shorthand Writers, practising in High Court of Justice

mit., mitt. L. *mitte*, send (med.)

Mit. Ger. *Mittwoch*, Wednesday

M.It. Middle Italian

M.I.T. Massachusetts Institute of Technology (U.S.A.)

M.I.T.I. Ministry of International Trade and Industry (Jap.)

M.I.T.M.A. Member Institute of Trade Mark Agents

mitt. mitten; It. *mittente*, sender

Mitt. Ger. *Mitteilung*, report

M.I.W.E. Member of the Institution of Water Engineers

M.I.W.M. Member of the Institution of Works Managers

M.I.W.M.A. Member of the Institute of Weights and Measures Administration

M.I.W.T. Member of the Institute of Wireless Technology

mixt. mixture

MJ *s* Bedfordshire (B.V.R.)

M.J. Ministry of Justice; monkey jacket

M.J.D. management job description

M.J.G. management job guide

M.J.I. Member of the Institute of Journalists

M.J.Inst.E. Member of the Junior Institution of Engineers

M.J.S. Member of the Japan Society

M.J.S.D. March, June, September, December

MK *s* London (B.V.R.)

mk. mark

Mk. mark (German currency); markka (Finnish currency)

M.K. Multy-Kontact. This trade mark M.K. was name given to one of the earliest designs of the M.K. Electric Ltd., when the co. first began to manufacture electrical accessories in the early 1920s

M.K. Ger. *Manualkoppel*, manual coupler (mus.)

mkd. marked

m.kg. metre kilogramme

MKK *Mitsubishi Kakoki Kaishi* (Jap.)

mkr. Ger. *mikroskopisch*, microscopic

m.k.s. metre-kilogramme-second, basis of metric system

mksA metre-kilogramme-second-ampère (elec.)

mkt. market

M.K.W. Military Knight of Windsor

ML *s* London (B.V.R.), Methil (B.F.P.)

ml. mail; millilitre

mL., ml. millilambert

Ml. matmazel

m.l. machine language; maintained load; mean level; middle left; mine layer

M.L. Licentiate in Midwifery; Master of Law/Laws/Letters; L. *Medicinae Licentiatus*, Licentiate in Medicine; Medieval/Middle Latin; Ministry of Labour; motor-launch; muzzle-loading

M.L.A. Master in Landscape Architecture; Master of the Liberal Arts; Medical Library Association; Member of the Legislative Assembly; Modern Language Association

m'lady my lady

MLB 1,000 pounds (U.S.A.)

MLC Mauritius Labour Congress; Meat & Livestock Commission (*also*, M & LC); Mutual Life and Citizens' Company (insce.)

M.L.C. Member of the Legislative Council

MLD minimum lethal dose; minimum line of detection

mld. moulded

M.L.D. Master of Landscape Design

mldg. moulding

mldr. moulder

mle. Fr. *modèle*, pattern

m.l.e. maximum loss expectancy

M.L.E.U. Fr. *Mouvement libéral pour l'Europe unie*, Liberal Movement for a United Europe

M.L.F. multilateral nuclear force

M.L.G. Middle Low German; *Ministry of Labour Gazette*

M.Lib. Master of Librarianship/Library Science

M.Lib.Sc. Master of Library Science

M.Litt. Master of Letters/Literature

M.L.J. *Madras Law Journal*

M.L.L. manned lunar landing

Mlle. Fr. *Mademoiselle*, Miss

M.L.L.W. mean lower low water (tides)

M.L.M.A. Miners' Lamp Manufacturers' Association

M.L.N.S. Ministry of Labour and National Service

M.L.O. Midland Light Orchestra; military liaison officer

MLP Malta/Mauritius Labour Party

m.l.r. muzzle-loading rifle

M.L.R. *Modern Law Review*

M.L.R.G. muzzle-loading rifled gun

MLS mixed language system; multi-language system

M.L.S. Master of Library Science; medium long shot; Member of the Linnean Society

M.L.S.A. Ministry of Labour Staff Association

M.L.S.C. Member London Society of Compositors

MLTN 1,000 long tons (U.S.A.)

M.L.W. Master of Labour Welfare; mean low water (tides)

M.L.W.N.T. mean low water neap tide

M.L.W.S.T. mean low water spring tide

m'm madam

MM *s* London (B.V.R.); maintenance manual; Mariner Mars project (of NASA); materials measurement; memory module

mm. millimetre

mm.² square millimetre

mm.³ cubic millimetre

M/m., m.m. made merchantable

m.m. L. *mutatis mutandis*, with the necessary changes

MM. Fr. *Messieurs*, Gentlemen

M.M. Majesties; Martyrs; Master Mason (freem.); Medal of Merit; medical man (U.S.A.); mercantile marine; military medal; Minister of Mines; Ministry of Munitions; music master

M.M. *Maelzel's Metronome*, invented by Maelzel in 1814 (mus.)

M.M.A. Manitoba Medical Association; Merchandise Marks Act; Meter Manufacturers' Association; Music Masters' Association

M.Math. Master of Mathematics

M.M.B. Milk Marketing Board

MMC maximum metal condition

M.Mde. Fr. *Marine Marchande*, Merchant Marine

MME midlands mathematical experiment

Mme. Fr. *Madame*, Mrs.

M.M.E. Master of Mechanical/Mining Engineering

M.Mech.E. Master of Mechanical Engineering

M.Med. Master of Medicine; — **Sc.** Master of Medical Science

M.M.E.G. Meter Manufacturers' Export Group

Mmes. Fr. *Mesdames*, ladies

M.Met. Master of Metallurgy; — **E.** Master of Metallurgical Engineering

m.m.f. magnetomotive force

M.M.F. Member of the Medical Faculty

mmfd. micromicrofarad

M.M.G. medium machine gun

M.M.G.I. Member of the Mining, Geological and Metallurgical Institute of India

m.mk. material mark

MMM *Mouvement Militant Mauricien* (Mauritius)

mmm. millimicron

M.M.M. Fr. *Membre de l'Ordre du Mérite Militaire*, Member of the Order of Military Merit (Can.); Fr. *Mouvement mondial des mères*, World Movement of Mothers

MMO medium machine oil

M.M.P. Military Mounted Police

M.M.P.A. Midland Master Printers' Alliance

M.M.R. mass miniature radiography

M.M.R.A. Maritime Marshland Rehabilitation Administration (Can.)

M.M.R.B.M. mobile medium range ballistic missile

M.M.S. Master of Management Studies; Methodist/Moravian Missionary Society; motor mine sweeper

M.M.S.A. Master of Midwifery of the Society of Apothecaries; Mercantile Marine Service Association

M.M.S.C. Mediterranean marine sorting centre

MMU million monetary units

M.Mus. Master of Music; — **R.C.M.** Master of Music of the Royal College of Music

Mn *s* manganese (chem.)

MN *s* Isle of Man (B.V.R.); Maldon (B.F.P.); Minnesota (U.S.A.)

mn. Fr. *maison*, house; million

m/n. Sp. *moneda nacional*, nat. money

Mn. midnight; Montenegro

m.n. L. *mutato nomine*, the name being changed

M.N. magnetic north; Master of Nursing; Merchant Navy

MNAOA Merchant Navy & Airline Officers' Association

M.N.A.S. Member of the National Academy of Sciences (U.S.A.)

MNB Moscow Narodny Bank Limited

M.N.D. *Midsummer Night's Dream* (Shake.); Ministry of National Defence

M.N.E.C.Inst. of E. & S. Member of North East Coast Institution of Engineers & Shipbuilders

mng. managing

mngmt. management
mngr. manager
M.N.I. Madras Native Infantry; Ministry of National Insurance
Mnl. Manila (Philippines)
MNLOA Merchant Navy and Air Line Officers' Association
mnm. minimum
M.N.P. Malay Nationalist Party
M.N.P.T. meta-nitro-para-toluidine, dye component
Mnr. Dutch *Mijnheer*
M.N.R. mean neap rise (tides)
M.N.S. Member of the Numismatical Society (U.S.A.)
M.N.T. mean neap tide
M.Nurs. Master of Nursing
MNWEB Midlands & North Western Electricity Board
M.N.Z.I.E. Member New Zealand Institution of Engineers
Mo *s* molybdenum (chem.)
MO *s* Berkshire (B.V.R.); Missouri *also* Mo. (U.S.A.)
mo. moment; month; mouth
12mo. twelvemo/duodecimo, a book each sheet of which forms 12 leaves/24 pages (typ.)
16mo. sextodecimo, book each sheet of which forms 16 leaves/32 pages (typ.)
18mo. eighteenmo/decimo-octavo, book each sheet of which forms 18 leaves/36 pages (typ.)
20mo. twentymo/vigesimo, book each sheet of which forms 20 leaves/40 pages (typ.)
24mo. twenty-fourmo/vigesimo-quarto, book each sheet of which forms 24 leaves/48 pages (typ.)
32mo. thirty-twomo/trigesimo-secundo, book in which each sheet forms 32 leaves/64 pages (typ.)
64mo. sixty-fourmo/sexagesimo-quarto, book each sheet of which forms 64 leaves/128 pages (typ.)
Mo. Monday
Mo. It. *Moderato*, moderate (mus.)
m.o. mail/money/monthly order
m.o. L. *modus operandi*, way of operating
m.-o. months old
M.O. manually operated; mass observation; Master of Obstetrics/Oratory; master oscillator; medical officer; Meteorological Office; method of operating/operation; motor operated; municipal officer
M.o.A. Ministry of Aviation
mob. mobile; mobilization (*also*, mobizn.); mobilize
möbl. Ger. *möbliert*, furnished

M.O.C. Mother of the Chapel (printing union)
MOD Ministry of Overseas Development
mod. moderate; modern; modification; modified; modulus (math.)
mod. It. *moderato*, moderate (mus.)
M.O.D. mail order department; Ministry of Defence
MODAP Modified *Apollo*
mod.con. modern convenience
mod.dict. L. *modo dicto*, as prescribed (med.)
Mod.E. Modern English
MODEM modulator/demodulator
Mod.Gr. Modern Greek
modif. modification
Mod.L. Modern Latin
MOD(N) Ministry of Defence (Navy Department)
mod.praes. L. *modo praescripto*, in the manner directed (med.)
MODS manned orbital development system (NASA/USAF)
Mods. Moderations, the First Public Examination, Oxford University
Mod.S. Modern Secondary
*Mod*to. It. *Moderato*, moderate (mus.)
M. of A. Ministry of Agriculture, Fisheries and Food
M. of E. Ministry of Education
M. of F. Ministry of Food
M. of P. Ministry of Pensions and National Insurance; Ministry of Power
M. of R.A.F. Marshal of the Royal Air Force
M. of V. *The Merchant of Venice* (Shake.)
M. of W. Ministry of Works
M.O.G., M.O. & G. Master of Obstetrics and Gynaecology
Moh., Moham. Mohammedan; Mohammedanism
M.o.H. Ministry of Housing and Local Government
M.O.H. Master of Otter Hounds; Medical Officer of Health; Ministry of Health
M.O.H.L.G. Ministry of Housing and Local Government
MOHO mohorovicic discontinuity
M.O.I. military operations and intelligence; Ministry of Information; Ministry of the Interior
m.o.i.v. mechanically operated inlet valve
M.O.J.M.R.P. Meteorological Office, Joint Meteorological Radio Propagation Sub-Committee
mol gram-molecule
MOL manned orbital laboratory
mol. molecular; molecule

234

M.o.L. Ministry of Labour

M.O.L. Master of Oriental Learning

Mold., Moldv. Moldavia; Moldavian

Moll, Molly Maria; Marie; Mary

M.O.L.N.S. Ministry of Labour and National Service

mol.wt. molecular weight

mom mother

m.o.m. middle of month

M.O.M. milk of magnesia

MON motor octane number

mon. Fr. *maison*, house; monastery; monastic; monetary; monitor; monsoon

Mon. Monaco; Monaghan; Monday; Monmouthshire (*also*, Monm.); Ger. *Montag*, Monday; Montana, *also* Mont. (U.S.A.)

Mong., Mongol. Mongol; Mongolia; Mongolian

Mono Monotype (typ.)

monog. monograph

Mons. Fr. *Monsieur*, Mr. *preferably* M.

Mont., Montgom. Montgomeryshire

Monte Monte Carlo

Montford Report. *Montagu-Chelmsford Report* (India)

Montr. Montreal (Can.)

Monty Montagu; Montague

M.O.O. money order office

Moore's Adj. *Moore's International Adjudications*

Moore's Arb. *Moore's International Arbitrations*

Moore's Dig. *Moore's Digest of International Law*

m.o.p. mother-of-pearl

M.o.P. Member of Parliament; Ministry of Pensions; Ministry of Power; Ministry of Production

M.O.P. Port. *Ministério das Obras Públicas*, Ministry of Public Works

MOPAR master oscillator-power amplifier radar

moped motorized pedal cycle

M.O.P.H. Military Order of the Purple Heart (U.S.A.)

mor. morocco (leather)

Mor. Moroccan; Morocco

Mor. It. *Morendo*, dying away (mus.)

M.O.R. Ministry of Reconstruction

Morb. Morbihan

M.O.R.C. medical officers reserve corps

mor.dict. L. *more dicto*, in the manner directed

morn. morning

morph. morphological; morphology

mor.sol. L. *more solito*, in the usual manner (med.)

Mort Mortimer; Morton

mort. mortal; mortality; mortar; mortgage; mortuary

Mos. Moscow; Moselle

M.O.S. Ministry of Supply

M.O.S.A. medical officers of schools association

M.O.S.I.D. Ministry of Supply Inspection Department

MOSS manned orbital space system (NASA/USAF)

MOST metal oxide silicon transistors

mot. motor; motorized

M.O.T. Ministry of Transport

M.O.T.C.P. Ministry of Town and Country Planning

motel hotel for motor-car tourists

mot.op. motor-operated

Mounty member of the Royal Canadian Mounted Police

M.O.U.S.E., mouse minimum orbital unmanned satellite of the earth, miniature artificial satellite for gathering data

Mov. It. *Movimento*, movement (mus.)

M.O.W. Ministry of Works

M.O.W.T. Ministry of War Transport

moy. money

Moz. Mozambique

MP s London (B.V.R.); main/minimum phase; miscellaneous paper/publication; Mitsubishi Plastics (Jap.); *Millet Partisi*, Nation Party (Turk.); *Mouvement Populaire*, Popular Movement (Morocco)

m.p. medium pattern/pressure; meeting point; melting point/pot; mile post, *also* MP (cartog.); months after payment; mooring post

m.p. It. *mezzo piano*, moderately soft (mus.); L. *mille passuum*, thousand paces

M/P. memorandum of partnership

M.P. Madhya Pradesh (India); Master of Painting/Planning; Member of Parliament; Mercator's projection; Methodist Protestant; Metropolitan Police; military police/policeman; Minister-Plenipotentiary; mounted/municipal police; motion picture

M.P. L. *mille passus*, 1,000 paces of five feet/the Roman mile

M.P.A. Master of Public Accounting/Administration; Master Photographers' Association of Great Britain; Metropolitan Pensions Association; Music Publishers' Association

M.P.A.A. Motion Picture Association of America

M.P.A.G.B. Modern Pentathlon Association of Great Britain

M.P.B. Missing Persons Bureau (U.S.A.)

M.P.B. and W. Ministry of Public Building and Works

MPC maximum permissible concentration; *Movimiento Popular Cristiano*, Popular Christian Movement (Bolivia)

m.p.c. mathematics, physics, chemistry; maximum possible concentration

M.P.C. Member of Parliament, Canada; Member of Provincial Council (S. Afr.); Metropolitan Police College/Commissioner

MPCA Manpower Citizens' Association (Guyana)

MPC black medium processing channel black, filler in rubber compounding

M.Pd. Master of Pedagogy

M.P.D. maximum permissible dose; meta-phenylene diamine

MPE maximum permissible exposure (radiation)

M.P.E. Master of Physical Education

M.Pen. Ministry of Pensions

M.Per. Middle Persian

m.p.f. multi-purpose food

M.P.F. Metallurgical Plantmakers' Federation

MPFG 1,000 proof gallons (U.S.A.)

mpg miles per gallon

MPG Ger. *Max-Planck-Gesellschaft zur Foerderung der Wissenschaften*, Max Planck Soc. for the Promotion of Science

m.p.g. miles per gallon

M.P.G.A. Metropolitan Public Gardens Association

m.p.h. miles per hour

M.Ph. Master of Philosophy

M.P.H. Master in Public Health

M.Pharm. Fr. *Maître en pharmacie*, Master of Pharmacy

M.Phil. Master of Philosophy

M.Phty. Master of Physiotherapy

m.p.i. mean point of impact

M.P.L. Master of Patent Law; Master of Polite Literature; maximum permissible level

MPLA *Movimento Popular de Libertacão de Angola*, Angola Popular Liberation Movement

m.p.m. metres per minute; multi-purpose meal

M.P.N.I. Ministry of Pensions and National Insurance

M.P.O. Metropolitan Police Office, Scotland Yard (Lond.); military post office; milk production officer; mobile printing/publishing office

M.Pol.Econ. Master of Political Economy

m.p.p. most probable position

M.P.P. Master of Physical Planning; Member of Provincial Parliament

M.P.P.A. Music Publishers' Protective Association

MPR 1,000 pair (U.S.A.)

M.P.R. *Maritime Provinces Reports* (Can.); Mongolian People's Republic

M.Prof.Acc. Master of Professional Accountancy

MPRP Mongolian People's Revolutionary Party, *Mongol Ardyn Khuv'sgalt Nam*

MPRS *Madjelis Permusjawaratan Ratjat Sementara*, Provisional People's Consultative Congress (Indonesia)

m.p.s. megacycles/metres per second

M.Ps. Master in Psychology; — **Sc.** Master of Psychological Science

M.P.S. manufacturer's part specification; Medical Protection Society; Member of the Pharmaceutical Society of Great Britain; Member of the Philological/Physical Society

MPSA Military Petroleum Supply Agency

M.P.S.C. military provost staff corps

M.Ps.O. Master of Psychology-Orientation

M.P.S.W. Master of Psychiatric Social Work

M.Psych. Master of Psychology

m. pt. melting point

M.P.T.A. Municipal Passenger Transport Association

M.P.U. Medical Practitioners' Union

Mpy. *Maatschappij*, company (Neth.)

M.Q. metol-quinol, a photographic developer

mq. mosque

Mqe. Martinique

MQF mobile quarantine facility (NASA)

MR *s* Manchester (B.F.P.); *s* Wiltshire (B.V.R.)

Mr. Master (*also* Mastr.); Mister

m.r. memorandum receipt; mill run; moment of resistance

M/R. mate's receipt

M.R. map reference; Master of the Rolls (leg.); match rifle, category of long-barrelled rifle, normally ·303″/7·62 mm. calibre; Middlesex Regiment; Minister-Residentiary; Ministry of Reconstruction; motorways traffic regulations; municipal reform

M. & R. maintenance and repairs

MRA, M.R.A. Moral Re-Armament *also* Buchmanism

M.R.A. Maritime Royal Artillery

M.R.A.C. Member of the Royal Agricultural College

M.R.A.C.P. Member of the Royal Australasian College of Physicians

M.Rad. Master of Radiology

M.R.Ae.S. Member of the Royal Aeronautical Society

M.R.A.F. Marshal of the Royal Air Force

M.R.A.I.C. Member of the Royal Architectural Institute of Canada

M.R.A.S. Member of the Royal Academy of Science; Member of the Royal Asiatic/Astronomical Society

M.R.B. Mersey River Board

M.R.B.M. medium range ballistic missile

M.R.C. Medical Registration/Research Council; medical reserve corps; Melbourne Racing Club (Aust.); model railway club

MRCA multi-role combat aircraft

M.R.C.C. Member of the Royal College of Chemistry

M.R.C.I. Medical Registration Council of Ireland

M.R.C.O. Member of the Royal College of Organists

M.R.C.O.G. Member of the Royal College of Obstetricians and Gynaecologists

M.R.C.P. Member of the Royal College of Physicians

M.R.C.Path. Member of the Royal College of Pathologists

M.R.C.P.E., M.R.C.P.Ed. Member of the Royal College of Physicians of Edinburgh

M.R.C.P.Glas. Member of the Royal College of Physicians and Surgeons of Glasgow

M.R.C.P.I. Member of the Royal College of Physicians of Ireland

M.R.C.S. Member of the Royal College of Surgeons

M.R.C.S.E. Member of the Royal College of Surgeons of Edinburgh

M.R.C.S.I. Member of the Royal College of Surgeons of Ireland

M.R.C.V.S. Member of the Royal College of Veterinary Surgeons

M.R.D. Microbiological Research Department

MR & DF Malleable Research and Development Foundation (U.S.A.)

M.R.E. Master of Religious Education; Microbiological Research Establishment; Mining Research Establishment

M.R.Emp.S. Member of the Royal Empire Society, *now* R.C.S.

MRFB Malayan Rubber Fund Board

M.R.Flight meteorological research flight

M.R.G.S. Member of the Royal Geographical Society

M.R.H. Member of the Royal Household

M.Rh.I.E. Member of Rhodesian Institution of Engineers

M.R.I. Fr. *Maître en relations industrielles*, Master of Industrial Relations; Meat Research Institute; Member of the Royal Institution

M.R.I.A. Member of the Royal Irish Academy

M.R.I.A.I. Member of the Royal Institute of the Architects of Ireland

M.R.I.C.S. Member of the Royal Institution of Chartered Surveyors

M.R.Inst.N.A. Member of the Royal Institution of Naval Architects

M.R.I.P.H.H. Member of the Royal Institute of Public Health and Hygiene

mrkr. marker

m.r.m. mail readership measure; miles of relative movement

mrng. morning

M.R.O. Member of the Register of Osteopaths

M.R.P. Master in/of Regional Planning

MRR material rejection report; medical research reactor

MRRC materiel requirements review committee (U.S.A.)

Mrs. Missis; Missus; Mistress

M.R.S. Market Research Society

M.R.San.A.S. Member of the Royal Sanitary Association of Scotland

M.R.Sc., M.Rur.Sc. Master of Rural Science

M.R.S.H. Member of the Royal Society for the Promotion of Health, *formerly* M.R.San.I.

M.R.S.L. Member of the Royal Society of Literature

M.R.S.M. Member of the Royal Society of Medicine; Member of the Royal Society of Musicians of Great Britain

M.R.S.M.P. Member of the Royal Society of Miniature Painters, Sculptors and Gravers

M.R.S.P.E. Member of the Royal Society of Painter-Etchers and Engravers

M.R.S.P.P. Member of the Royal Society of Portrait Painters

M.R.S.T. Member of the Royal Society of Teachers

M.R.S.W. Member of the Royal Society of Scottish Painters and Watercolours

MRU manpower research unit; mobile repair unit

M.R.U.A. Mobile Radio Users' Association

M.R.U.S.I. Member of the Royal United Service Institution

m/s metre per second, unit of mass velocity coefficient

m²/s unit of kinematic viscosity, diffusivity

m/s² metre per second squared, unit of acceleration

MS *s* Mauritius (I.V.R.); mile stone (cartog.); Mississippi (U.S.A.); modal sensitivity; *s* Stirlingshire (B.V.R.)

M/S metal shank (buttons); month after sight (fin.)

ms. manuscript; millisecond, *also* m.sec.

Ms. Miss/Mrs.

m.s. machinery survey; machine selection; mail steamer; margin of safety; mass spectrometry; material specification; maximum stress; medium/mild steel

M.S. maiden surname; Master of Science/Surgery; medical staff; medium/mid shot, of an actor, approximately from the waist upwards (photo.); mess sergeant; Metallurgical Society (U.S.A.); metric system; military secretary; mine sweeper; minister for science; Ministry of Supply; motor ship; multiple sclerosis; municipal surveyor

M.S. It. *Mano sinistra*, left hand (mus.); L. *memoriae sacrum*, sacred to the memory of

M. & S. maintenance and supply; Marks & Spencer Limited

MSA Malaysia–Singapore Airways

m.s.a. L. *misce secundum artem*, mix skilfully

M.S.A. Maritime Safety Agency; Master of Science and Arts; Master of Science in Agriculture (*also*, M.S.Agr.); Master of Scientific Agriculture; Member of the Society of Apothecaries of London; Member of the Society of Architects/ Arts; Merchant Shipping Act; Motor Schools' Association of Great Britain; Mutual Security Agency (U.S.A.)

M.S.A.E., M.S.Aut.E. Member of the Society of Automotive Engineers (U.S.A.)

M.S.Agr.Eng. Master of Science in Agricultural Engineering

M.S.Agr.Ex. Master of Science in Agricultural Extension

M.(S.A.)I.C.E. Member of the South African Institution of Civil Engineers

M.(S.A.)I.E.E. Member of the South African Institution of Electrical Engineers

M.(S.A.)I.M.E. Member of the South African Institution of Mechanical Engineers

M.S.A.Inst.M.M. Member South African Institute of Mining and Metallurgy

M.S.A.I.T. Member of the South African Institute of Translators

M.S.A.I.V. Member of the South African Institute of Valuers

M.S.A.P.S. Member of the South African Pharmaceutical Society

M.S.Arch. Master of Science in Architecture

M.S.A.Soc.C.E. Member of the South African Society of Civil Engineers

MSB Metropolitan Society for the Blind

M.S.B. Maritime Safety Board

M.S.B.A. Master of Science in Business Administration

M.S.B.E. Member of Belgian Society of Engineers

M.S.Bus. Master of Science in Business

MSC Manned Spacecraft Center (NASA)

msc. miscellaneous

m.s.c. moved, seconded and carried

m.s.c. L. *mandatum sine clausula*, authority without restriction

M.Sc. Master of Science; — **A., App.** Master of Applied Science; — **(Ag.)**, **(Agr.), (Agri.), (Agric.)** Master of Science in Agriculture; — **(Ag.Econ.)** Master of Science in Agricultural Economics; — **(Agr. & A.H.)** Master of Science in Agriculture and Animal Husbandry; — **(Agric.Eng.)** Master of Science in Agricultural Engineering; — **(Arch.)** Master of Science in Architecture; — **C.E.** Master of Science in Civil Engineering; — **(Cer.)** Master of Science in Ceramics; — **(Ch.E.), (Chem.Eng.)** Master of Science in Chemical Engineering; — **(Chem.Tech.)** Master of Science in Chemical Technology; — **Clin.** Master of Clinical Science; — **Com.** Master of Commercial Science; — **(C.P.)** Master of Science (Community Planning); — **D.** Master of Dental Science; Master of Science in Dentistry (*also*, **M.Sc.(Dent.)**); — **(Econ.)** Master of Science in Economics; — **(Ed.)** Master of Science in Education; — **(Elec.)** Master of Science (Electronics); — **(Eng.), (Engg.), (Engin.)** Master of Science in Engineering; — **(Est.Man.)** Master of Science in Estate Management; — **F.** Master of Science in/of Forestry; — **(Hort.)** Master of Science in Horticulture; — **(Med.)** Master of Science in Medicine; — **(Med.Sc.)** Master of Science in Medical Science; — **(Met.Eng.)** Master of Science (Metallurgical Engineering); — **(Min.)** Master of Science in Mining; — **N.** Master of Science in Nursing; — **(Nutr.)** Master of Science (Nutrition); — **(Pharm.)** Master of Science in Pharmacy; — **(Pl.)** Master of Science in Urban and Regional Planning; — **(Soc.)** Master of Science in the Social Sciences; — **Sur.** Master of Science in Land Surveying; — **Tech.** Master of Technical Science; — **(Tech.)** Master of

Science (Technology); — **(V. of Sc.)** Master of Veterinary Science

M.Sc., M.Scot. Middle Scottish

M.S.C. Madras Staff Corps; Manchester Ship Canal; medical staff corps; Mediterranean Sub-Commission (FAO); Meteorological Service of Canada; metropolitan special constabulary

M.S.C. L. Missionarii Sacratissimi Cordis Jesu, Missionaries of the Most Sacred Heart of Jesus

M.Scand. Middle Scandinavian

M.S.C.P. mean spherical candlepower

M.S.D. Doctor of Medical Science; Master of Scientific Didactics; Master Surgeon Dentist

M.S.Dent. Master of Science in Dentistry

M.S.(Dent.) Master of Surgery (Dental Surgery)

m.s.e. mean square error

M.S.E. Master of Science in Engineering; Member of the Society of Engineers

M.S.Ed. Master of Science in Education

M.S.E.E. Master of Science in Electrical Engineering

M.S.E.M. Master of Science in Engineering Mechanics

mses. Fr. *marchandises*, goods

M.S.E.U.E. Fr. *Mouvement socialiste pour les États Unis d'Europe*, Socialist Movement for the United States of Europe

M.S.F. Master of Science in Forestry; mine-sweeping flotilla; Multiple Shops Federation

MSFC Marshall Space Flight Center (NASA)

MSG monosodium glutamate

msg. message

msgr. messenger

M.Sgt. master sergeant

M.S.H. Master of Staghounds

M.S.H.Ec. Master of Science in Home Economics

Mshl. marshal

M.S.Hyg. Master of Science in Hygiene

MSI manned satellite inspector; *Movimento Sociale Italiano*, Italian Social Movement

M.S.I. Member of the Chartered Surveyors' Institution

M.S.I.A. Member of the Society of Industrial Artists and Designers

m'sieur Fr. *monsieur*, Mr., Sir

M.S.Ind.E. Master of Science in Industrial Engineering

M.S.I.T. Member of the Society of Instrument Technology

M.S.J. Master of Science in Journalism

MSL Management Selection Limited

m.s.l. mean sea-level

M.S.L.S. Master of Science in Library Science

M.S.M. Master of Medical Science; Master of Sacred Music; Meritorious Service Medal

M.S.M.A. Master Sign Makers' Association; Member of the Sales Managers' Association of Southern Africa

M.S.M.E. Master of Science in Mechanical Engineering

M.S.Med. Master of Medical Science

M.S.Mus. Master of Science in Music

M.S.N., M.S.Nurs. Master of Science in Nursing

M.S.N.E. Master of Science in Nursing Education

M.Soc.C.E.(France) Member of the French Society of Civil Engineers

M.Soc.Sc., M.Soc.Sci. Master of Social Science

M.Soc.St. Master of Social Studies

M.Soc.(S.W.) Master of Social Science (Social Welfare)

M.Soc.Wk. Master of Social Work

M.sop. It. *Mezzo-soprano* (mus.)

M.S.(Ophthal.) Master of Surgery (Ophthalmology)

M.S.(Ortho.) Master of Orthopaedic Surgery

M.S.P. Master of Science in Pharmacy; Mutual Security Program (U.S.A.)

M.S.P.E. Master of Science in Physical Education

M.S.P.H. Master of Science in Public Health

M.S.Phar. Master of Science in Pharmacy

M.S.P.H.E. Master of Science in Public Health Engineering

MSR missile site radar

m.s.r. main supply route

M.S.R. mean spring rise (tides); Member of the Society of Radiographers

M.S. & R. Merchant Shipbuilding and Repairs

M.S.R.A. Multiple Shoe Retailers' Association

M.S.Ret. Master of Science in Retailing

M.S.R.G. Member of the Society for Remedial Gymnasts

mss. manuscripts

M.S.S. Medical Superintendents' Society; Member of the Statistical Society

MSSCS manned space station communications system

M.S.S.E. Master of Science in Sanitary Engineering

M.S.S.G.B. Motion Study Society of Great Britain

M.S.S.I.G. Manchester Statistical Society Industrial Group

M.S.S.R.C. Mediterranean Social Sciences Research Council

M.S.S.S. Master of Science in Social Service

M.S.S.U. mid-stream specimen of urine

M.S.S.V.D. Medical Society for the Study of Venereal Diseases

M.S.S.W. Master of Science in Social Work

mst. measurement

M.S.T. Master of Sacred Theology; mean spring tide; mountain standard time (U.S.A.)

M.Stat. Master of Statistics

M.S.T.D. Member of the Society of Typographic Designers

MSTN 1,000 short tons (U.S.A.)

mstr. master

M.S.T.S. military sea transport/transportation service (U.S.A.)

M.S.Trans. Master of Science in Transportation; — **E.** Master of Science in Transportation Engineering

Mstr.Mech. master mechanic

MSU main storage unit

M.S.U.L. Medical Schools of the University of London

M.Surgery Master in Surgery

M.Surv. Master of Surveying; — **Sc.** Master of Surveying Science

M.Sw. Middle Swedish

M.S.W. Master of Social Work

M.S.Wales I.E. Member of South Wales Institute of Engineers

MSYD 1,000 square yards (U.S.A.)

MT s London (B.V.R.); Maryport (B.F.P.); Montana (U.S.A.)

M/T mail transfer

Mt. mount; mountain

m.t. machine translation; maximum torque; metric ton; missile test; mountain time (U.S.A.)

M.T. empty; mail transfer; mandated territory; masoretic text; Master of Teaching; mean time; mechanical transport; Middle Temple (leg.); motor tanker; motor transport

m.ta Port. *muita*, much

M.T.A. Mica Trade Association; Motor Traders' Association, *now* B.M.T.A.; Multiple Tailors' Association; Music Teachers'/Trades' Association

M.T.B. motor torpedo boat

MTBF mean time between failures

M.T.C. Marcus Tullius Cicero (106–43 B.C.), Roman orator; Master of Textile Chemistry; Mechanical Transport Corps; Music Teacher's Certificate

M.T.C.A. Ministry of Transport and Civil Aviation

M.T.C.P. Ministry of Town and Country Planning

Mtd. mounted

M.T.D. Master of Transport Design; mean temperature difference; meta-tolylene diamine; Midwife Teacher's Diploma

M.T.D.E. maintenance technique development establishment

MTDS marine corps tactical data system

M.Tech. Master in Technology

M.Tel.E. Master of Telecommunications Engineering

M.Text. Master of Textiles

mtg. meeting; mortgage (*also*, mtge.); mounting

mtgee. mortgagee

mtgor. mortgagor

mth. month

M.Th. Master of Theology

M.T.H. Master of Trinity House

MTI *Magyar Távirati Iroda*, Hungarian Press Agency; moving target indicator/information

mtl. material; Ger. *monatlich*, monthly

m.t.l. mean tidal level

MTLU Montserrat Trades and Labour Union

M.T.M. methods-time measurement

mtn. motion; mountain

M.T.N.A. Music Teachers' National Association

MTO Mediterranean theatre of operations

m.to Port. *muito*, much

M.T.O. mechanical transport officer

M.T.P. Master of Town Planning

M.T.P.I. Member of the Town Planning Institute

MTR mean time to restore (USAF)

mtr. meter

Mt.Rev. Most Reverend, title of Archbishop

M.T.R.P. Master of Town and Regional Planning

MTS mercurized turf sand

M.T.S. machine tractor station; Marine Technology Society (U.S.A.); Member of the Television Society; Merchant Taylors' School; motor transport service

M.T.T.A. Machine Tools Trades' Association

MTTF mean time to failure

MTTFF mean time to first failure

MTTI *Muszaki Tudomanyos Tajekoztato Intezetben*, Hungarian Institute of Scientific and Technical Information

MTTR maximum/mean time to repair; mean time to restore

MTU missile training unit (USAF)
MTUC Malayan Trades Union Congress; Mauritius Trades Union Congress
M.T.V. motor torpedo vessel
MU *s* London (B.V.R.)
mu. micron; millimicron
M.U. maintenance/mass/monetary unit; Mothers'/Musicians' Union
M.U.A. Machinery/Monotype Users' Association
M.U.C. Missionary Union of the Clergy
M.U.F. maximum usable frequency
M.U.F.M. Fr. *Mouvement universel pour une fédération mondiale*, World Assn. of World Federalists
mum chrysanthemum; madam; mother
mun., munic. municipal; municipality
MURA Midwestern University Research Association (U.S.A.)
mus. museum; music; musical; musician (*also*, musn.)
M.U.S. manned underwater station
M.U.S.A. multiple-unit steerable antenna
Mus.B., Mus.Bac. L. *Musicae Baccalaureus*, Bachelor of Music
Mus.D., Mus.Doc. L. *Musicae Doctor*, Doctor of Music
Mus.M. L. *Musicae Magister*, Master of Music
mustn't must not
mut. mutilated; mutual
MUX multiplexing equipment
mV millivolt
Mv mendelivium (chem.)
MV *s* London (B.V.R.); megavolt; motor vessel
mv. micro-volt (elec.)
m.v. market value; mean variation; medium voltage; muzzle velocity
M.V. merchant/motor vessel; *The Merchant of Venice* (Shake.)
M.V. It. *Mezza voce*, half the power of voice (mus.)
M. & V. meat and vegetable
MVA Mississippi/Missouri Valley Authority (U.S.A.)
M.V.D. Doctor of Veterinary Medicine; *Ministersvo Vnutrennykli Del*, Ministry of Internal Affairs, secret police of U.S.S.R., *formerly* O.G.P.U.
M.V.D.A. Motor Vehicle Dismantlers' Association of Great Britain
M.Vet.Med. Master of Veterinary Medicine
M.Vet.Sc. Master of Veterinary Science
M.V.G. Medal for Victory over Germany
M.V.M. Motor Vehicle Mechanic of City & Guilds

M.V.O. Member of the Royal Victorian Order
M.V.S. Master of Veterinary Science, *also* M.V.Sc.; Mennonite Voluntary Service
mvt. movement
M.V.T. Motor Vehicle Technician of City & Guilds
mW milliwatt
MW *s* Malawi *formerly* Nyasaland (I.V.R.); megawatt; *s* Wiltshire (B.V.R.)
M/W. midwife
M.W. medium wave; Ger. *Meines Wissens*, to my knowledge; Middle Welsh; molecular weight; Most Worshipful; Most Worthy
M.W.A. Metal Window Association; Modern Woodmen of America
M.W.B. Metropolitan Water Board; Ministry of Works and Buildings
M.W.D. Military Works Department
M.Weld.I. Member of the Welding Institute
M.W.F. Medical Women's Federation
m.w.g. music wire gauge
M.W.G.C.P. Most Worthy Grand Chief Patriarch
M.W.G.M. Most Worshipful/Worthy Grand Master (freem.)
mWh megawatt hour
M.W.I. Member of the Institute of Welfare Officers
M.W.I.A. Medical Women's International Association
M.W.L.A. Midlands Women's Lacrosse Association
M.W.N. *Madras Weekly Notes*
M.W.N.T. mean water neap tide
M.W.P. mechanical wood pulp; Most Worthy Patriarch
MWPA Married Women's Property Act
M.W.W. *The Merry Wives of Windsor* (Shake.)
Mx maxwell (phys.)
MX *s* London (B.V.R.)
Mx. Middlesex
mxd. mixed
mxm. maximum
MY *s* London (B.V.R.)
my. myopia
M.Y. motor yacht
myc., mycol. mycological; mycology
myg. myriagram
myl. myrialitre
mym. myriametre
M.Y.O.B. mind your own business
myst. mysteries; mystery
myth., mythol. mythological; mythology
MZ *s* Belfast (B.V.R.)
M.Z. Ger. *Mangels Zahlung*, for nonpayment

N

n *s* indefinite number (math.); *s* load factor; *s* notative speed; *s* revolutions per second

n L. *natus*, born

n/ Port. *nosso*, ours; Fr. *nous*, us/we

'n' and, as in fish 'n' chips

N *s* avogadro number; *s* knight (chess); *s* magnetic flux; *s* Manchester (B.V.R.); *s'* near (optics); *s* Newport (B.F.P.); *s* Newry (B.F.P.); *s* newton, unit of force; *s* nitrogen (chem.); *s* Norway (I.V.R.); *s* U.S.A. (I.C.A.M.)

Nº It. *numero*, number

n. en (typ.); nail, of 2¼ inches; name; nasal; It. *nato*, born; nautical; naval; navy; neap; near; negative; nephew; nerve; net; neuter; neutral; It. *neutro*, neuter; neutron; new; night; nominative; noon; norm; normal; north; northern; It. *nostro*, our/ours; note; Fr. *notre*, our; noun; Fr. *nous*, us/we; number

n. L. *natus*, born; L. *nocte*, at night (med.)

N. national; nationalist; navigation; Dutch *neer*, down; nitrogen (med.); Dutch *noord*, north; Dan./Fr./It./Nor./ Swed. *nord*, north; Ger. *Nord*, north; Norse; north; northern; Northern postal district (Lond.); Norway; November; nullity (leg.); nurse; nursing

N. L. *nocte*, at night (med.); L. *nomen*, *nomina*, name(s); L. *noster*, our

n/a no account (fin.); no advice

Na *s* natrium, sodium (chem.)

NA *s* Manchester (B.V.R.); *s* Netherlands Antilles (I.V.R.); next address

N/A, N/a non-acceptance

Na. Nebraska (U.S.A.); *Nature*

N.A. Narcotics Anonymous (U.S.A.); National Academician/Academy/Airlines/ Archives/Army/Assembly; native administration; *Nautical Almanac*; naval architect/attaché/auxiliary/aviator; Netherlands Antilles; Neurotics Anonymous; new account; North America/American; not above, used in fixing loading positions, River Plate; nursing auxiliary

N.A.A. National Academy of Arbitrators (U.S.A.); National Aeronautic Association (U.S.A.); National Artillery Association; National Association of Accountants (U.S.A.); National Assistance Act, 1948; National Automobile Association (U.S.A.); not always afloat, referring to loading/discharging of vessel

N.A.A.A. National Alliance of Athletic Associations

N.A.A.B.C. National Association of American Business Clubs

N.A.A.B.S.A. not always afloat but safe aground, loading and/or discharging a vessel

N.A.A.C. National Association of Agricultural Contractors

NAACIE National Association of Agricultural, Commercial and Industrial Employees (Guyana)

N.A.A.C.P. National Association for the Advancement of Coloured People (U.S.A.)

N.A.A.F. North-African Air Force

N.A.A.F.I. Navy Army and Air Force Institutes

N.A.A.S. National Agricultural Advisory Service; Naval Auxiliary Air Station (U.S.A.)

NAATS National Association of Air Traffic Specialists (U.S.A.)

N.A.A.U.S. National Archery Association of the United States

N.A.B. National Alliance of Businessmen; National Assistance Board; National Association of Broadcasters/Businessmen (U.S.A.); naval advanced/air/amphibious base; News Agency of Burma; novarsenobenzol, an arsenic preparation (med.)

N.A.B.B.C. National Association of Brass Band Conductors

N.A.B.C. National Association of Bingo Clubs; National Association of Boys' Clubs

N.A.B.E. National Association for Business Education, *now* part of B.A.C.I.E.

N.A.B.M. National Association of British Manufacturers, *now* C.B.I.

N.A.B.M.A. National Association of British Market Authorities

N.A.B.S. National Advertising Benevolent Society; nuclear-armed bombardment satellite

N.A.C. National Advisory Council; National Agriculture Centre; National Air Council; National Amusements Council; National Anglers'/Archives Council; National Association of Cemeteries/Chiropodists/Choirs/Coroners; naval aircraftman; National Airways Corporation (U.S.A.); National Aviation Club/Corporation (U.S.A.); north Atlantic coast/Council; Nyasaland African Congress, *now* Malawi Congress Party

N.A.C.A. National Advisory Commitee for Aeronautics, *now* N.A.S.A. (U.S.A.); National Agricultural Chemicals Association (U.S.A.); National Air Carrier Association (U.S.A.); National Association of Cost Accountants (U.S.A.)

NACAE National Advisory Council for Art Education

N.A.C.A.M. National Association of Corn and Agricultural Merchants

NACCAM National Co-ordinating Committee for Aviation Meteorology

N.A.C.C.G. National Association of Crankshaft and Cylinder Grinders

NACE National Association of Corrosion/Corrosive Engineers (U.S.A.)

NACEIC National Advisory Council on Education for Industry & Commerce

N.A.C.F. National Art Collections Fund

Nachf. Ger. *Nachfolger*, successor

nachm. Ger. *nachmittags*, afternoon

NaCl sodium chloride, salt (chem.)

N.A.C.M. National Association of Chain/Charcoal Manufacturers; National Association of Colliery Managers

N.A.C.O.D.S. National Association of Colliery Overmen, Deputies and Shotfirers

NACRO, NACRO National Association for the Care and Resettlement of Offenders

N.A.C.T. National Association of Careers Teachers; National Association of Craftsman Tailors; National Association of Cycle Traders

N.A.C.T.S.T. National Advisory Council on the Training and Supply of Teachers

nad. nadir, lowest point

n.a.d. no appreciable difference/disease; nothing abnormal detected/discovered; not on active duty

N.A.D. National Academy of Design (U.S.A.); naval aircraft department; naval air division

N.A.D.A. National Association of Drama Advisers; National Association of Dealers in Antiques (U.S.A.)

NADC Naval Air Development Center (USN)

N.A.D.C. naval aide-de-camp

N.A.D.E.E. National Association of Divisional Executives for Education

N.A.D.F.S. National Association of Drop Forgers and Stampers

N.A.D.G.E. NATO Air Defence Ground Environment

NADOP North American Defense Operational Plan (U.S.A.)

N.A.D.P.A.S. National Association of Discharged Prisoners' Aid Societies

NADWARN Natural Disaster Warning System (U.S.A.)

N.A.E. National Academy of Engineering (U.S.A.); National Aeronautical Establishment (Can.); naval aircraft establishment

N.A.E.A. National Association of Estate Agents

N.A.E.C. National Aeronautical Establishment (Can.); National Aerospace Education Council (U.S.A.)

N.A.E.D.S. National Association of Engravers and Diestampers

N.A.F.A.S. National Association of Flower Arrangement Societies

N.A.F.D. National Association of Funeral Directors

NAFEC National Aviation Facilities Experimental Center (U.S.A.)

N.A.F.F.P. National Association of Frozen Food Producers

Naffy canteen organized by N.A.A.F.I.

N.A.F.O. National Association of Fire Officers

N.Afr. North Africa

NAFTA North Atlantic Free Trade Area

N.A.F.W.R. National Association of Furniture Warehousemen and Removers

Nag. Nagasaki (Jap.)

n.a.g. net annual gain

N.A.G. National Association of Goldsmiths/Groundsmen; Northern Army Group

NAGARD NATO Advisory Group for Aeronautical Research and Development

N.A.G.C. National Association for Gifted Children

N.A.G.M. National Association of Glove Manufacturers

N.A.G.S. National Allotments and Gardens Society

Nah. Nahum (Bible)

N.A.H.B. National Association of Home Builders (U.S.A.)

N.A.H.T. National Association of Head Teachers

N.A.I.C. National Association of Investment Clubs

NAIG Nippon Atomic Industry Group (Jap.)

N.A.I.S.S. National Association of Iron and Steel Stockholders

NAL National Airlines; National Alliance of Liberals (Ghana); National Astronomical League

N.A.L.C.C. National Automatic Laundry and Cleaning Council

N.A.L.G.O., NALGO National and Local Government Officers' Association

N.A.L.M. National Association of Lift Makers

N.A.L.S.A.T. National Association of Land Settlement Association Tenants

N.Am. North America

N.A.M. National Association of Manufacturers (U.S.A.)

N.A.M.B. National Association of Master Bakers

NAMC Naval Air Materiel Center (U.S.A.)

NAMDI National Marine Data Inventory (U.S.A.)

N.A.M.E. National Association of Marine Engine Builders; National Association of Marine Engineers of Canada

NAMFI NATO Missile Firing Installation

N.A.M.H. National Association for Mental Health

N.A.M.M.C. Natural Asphalt Mineowners' and Manufacturers' Council

Nan Ann; Anna; Anne

Nancy Agnes; Ann; Anna; Anne

Nanty Anthony

N.A.O. National Accordion Organization of Great Britain; National Association of Outfitters

N.A.O.P. National Association of Operative Plasterers

Nap Napoleon

Nap. Naples; Napoleonic

N.A.P. National Association for the Paralysed; Niger Agricultural Project

N.A.P.O. National Association of Performing Artists (U.S.A.); National Association of Purchasing Agents (U.S.A.)

N.A.P.E. National Association of Port Employers

NAPF National Association of Pension Funds

Naph. naphtha

N.A.P.M. National Association of Paper Merchants; National Association of Purchasing Management (U.S.A.)

NAPO National Association of Property Owners

N.A.P.O. National Association of Probation Officers

nappy napkin

N.A.P.T. National Association for the Prevention of Tuberculosis, *now* C.H.A.

NAPUS nuclear auxiliary power unit system

nar. narrow

n.a.r. net assimilation rate

narc. narcotic

N.A.R.F. National Association of Retail Furnishers

N.A.R.I. Natal Agricultural Research Institute

NARL National Aero Research Laboratory (Can.); Naval Arctic Research Laboratory

NARO North American Regional Office (FAO)

N.A.R.S.I.S. National Association for Road Safety Instruction in Schools

NARTEL North Atlantic Radio Telephone Committee

N.A.R.T.M. National Association of Rope and Twine Merchants

NARTU naval air reserve training unit

NAS Noise Abatement Society

N.A.S. National Academy of Sciences (U.S.A.); National Adoption Society; National Association of Schoolmasters/Shopfitters; naval air station; nursing auxiliary service

N^{a}S^a Port. *Nossa Senhora*, Our Lady

N.A.S.A., NASA National Aeronautics and Space Administration (U.S.A.)

NASCO National Academy of Sciences Committee on Oceanography (U.S.A.)

N.A.S.D. National Amalgamated Stevedores and Dockers

N.A.S.E. National Academy of Stationary Engineers (U.S.A.)

Nasees National Association for Soviet and East European Studies

NASH National Association of Specimen Hunters

Nash. Nashville (U.S.A.)

N.A.S.M. National Air and Space Museum (U.S.A.); National Association of School Magazines

N.A.S.P.M. National Association of Seed Potato Merchants

Nass. Nassau (Bahamas)

N.A.S.S. naval air signals school

N.A.S.U. National Adult School Union

Nat Natalie; Nathan; Nathaniel

nat. national; nationalist; native; natural; naturalize; naturist

Nat. Natal (S. Afr.)

N. At. North Atlantic

n.a.t. normal allowed time

N.A.T. National Arbitration Tribunal

N.A.T.A. National Association of Testing Authorities (Aust.); National Aviation Trades Association (U.S.A.)

Nat. Absten. National Abstentionalist

natat. natation

N.A.T.B. National Automobile Theft Bureau (U.S.A.)

N.A.T.C.G. National Association of Training Corps for Girls

natch. naturally

NATCOM National Communications Symposium

N.A.T.C.S. National Air Traffic Control Service

N.A.T.D. National Association of Teachers of Dancing

Nat.Dem. National Democrats

Nat.Fed. National Federation

Nat.Gal. National Gallery

Nat.Hist. natural history

Nativ. Nativity

N.A.T.K.E. National Association of Theatrical & Kine Employees

natl. national

Nat.Lib. National Liberal

NATMC National Advanced Technology Management Conference

NATO, N.A.T.O., NATO North Atlantic Treaty Organization, founded in 1949 to unite efforts for collective defence

nat.ord. natural order

N.A.T.O.U.S.A. Northern African Theater of Operations (U.S.A.)

nat.phil. natural philosophy

NATPRO, Nat.Prov. National Provincial Bank, *now* National Westminster Bank

NATS Naval Air Transport Service (U.S.A.)

Nat.Sc., Nat.Sci. natural science

Nat.Sc.D. Doctor of Natural Science

N.A.T.S.O.P.A NATSOPA National Society of Operative Printers and Assistants. Acronym retained although proper title *now* National Society of Operative Printers, Graphical and Media Personnel

NATSPG North Atlantic Systems Planning Group (I.C.A.O.)

N.Att. naval attaché

NATTS National Association of Trade and Technical Schools

natur. naturalist

Nat West National Westminster Bank

N.A.U.A. National Automobile Underwriters' Association (U.S.A.)

naut. nautical

nav. naval; navigable; navigate; navigation; navigator

n.a.v. net asset value (fin.)

NAVA National Audiovisual Association (U.S.A.)

Navaids navigation aids

NAVAIR Naval Air Systems Command (U.S.A.)

NAVAIRLANT Naval Air Forces, Atlantic

NAVAIRPAC Naval Air Forces, Pacific

Nav.Const., Nav.Constr. naval constructor

NAVFORJAP Naval Forces, Japan

NAVFORKOR Naval Forces, Korea

N.A.V.H. National Association of Voluntary Hostels

NAVIC Navy Information Center (USN)

navig. navigation; navigator

NAVMAR Naval Forces, Marianas

NAVOCEANO Naval Oceanographic Office (U.S.A.)

NAVOCS Naval Officer Candidate School (USN)

NAVPHIL Naval Forces, Philippines

NAVROM mercantile marine (Romania)

N.A.V.S. National Anti-Vivisection Society

NAVSAT navigational satellite

NAVSEC Naval Ship Engineering Center (USN)

NAVSUPFORANT Naval Support Forces, Antarctica

NAWAPA North American Water and Power Alliance

N.A.W.B. National Association of Workshops for the Blind Incorporated

N.A.W.C.H. National Association for the Welfare of Children in Hospital

N.A.W.N.D. National Association of Wholesale Newspaper Distributors

N.A.Y.C. National Association of Youth Clubs

naz. It. *nazionale*, national

Nazi *Nationale Sozialisten,* German National Socialist party/member

Nb nimbus; *s* niobium (chem.)

NB *s* Manchester (B.V.R.); Nebraska (U.S.A.)

n.b. no ball (cricket)

n.b. L. *nota bene*, note well

N.B. narrow-bore; naval base; New Brunswick; North Borneo; North Britain, *inaccurately* Scotland

N.B.A. National Basketball/Boxing Association (U.S.A.); National Brassfoundry Association; National Building Agency; Net Book Agreement; North British Academy

N.B.A.A. National Business Aircraft Association

N.B.B.C. National Brass Band Club

NBBS New British Broadcasting Station

NBC National Boys' Club

N.B.C. National Book Council, *now* N.B.L.; National Broadcasting Company (U.S.A.); National Broadcasting Corporation/Council

N.b.E. north by east

N.B.E.R. National Bureau of Economic Research (U.S.A.); National Bureau of Engineering Registration

n.b.g. no bloody good

NBHC New Broken Hill Consolidated, associated company of RTZ

N.B.I. National Benevolent Institution

n.b.l. not bloody likely

N.B.L. National Book League

N.B.O. National Buildings Association (India)

NBPI National Board for Prices and Incomes, *alternative* PIB

n.br. naval brass

n.Br. Ger. *nördliche Breite*, north latitude

N.B.R. acrylonitrile/butadiene rubber; National Buildings Record

nbre. Sp. *noviembre*, November

N.B.R.I. National Building Research Institute (S. Afr.)

N.B.S. National Broadcasting Service (N.Z.); National Bureau of Standards (U.S.A.)

nb.st. nimbo-stratus

nbv net book value

NBW National Book Week, *successor* to National Library Week

N.b.W. north by west

NC *s* Manchester (B.V.R.); North Carolina (U.S.A.); numerically controlled (machine tools)

N/C nitrocellulose

n.c. new charter/crop; no charge; north country; numerical control/controlled; nurse corps

N.C. national certificate; national congress/council; Nature Conservancy; New Caledonia; new church; nitro-cellulose; normally closed; North Carolina (U.S.A.); northern command

NCA National Cricket Association

N.C.A. no copies available

N.C.A.A. National Collegiate Athletic Association (U.S.A.); Northern Counties Athletic Association

N.C.A.C.C. National Civil Aviation Consultative Committee

N.C.A.I. National Congress of American Indians

N.C.A.P.C. National Center for Air Pollution Control (U.S.A.)

N.C.A.R. National Center for Atmospheric Research (U.S.A.)

NCARB National Council of Architectural Registration Boards (U.S.A.)

NCAVAE National Council for Audio-Visual Aids in Education

N.C.A.W. National Council for Animal Welfare

NCB no claim bonus; — AE, no claim bonus as earned (insce.)

N.C.B. National Coal Board; National Conservation Bureau

N.C.B.A. National Cattle Breeders' Association

N.C.B.M.P. National Council of Building Material Producers

NCC National Computing Centre; National Cotton Council (U.S.A.)

N.C.C. non-combatant corps; Northern Counties Committee (N.I.)

NCCAT National Committee for Clear Air Turbulence (U.S.A.)

N.C.C.E.E. Netherlands Committee for the Common Market

NCCI National Committee for Commonwealth Immigrants

N.C.C.L. National Council for Civil Liberties; National Council of Canadian Labor

N.C.C.M. National Council of Catholic Men

NCCS national command and control system; National Council for Civic Responsibility

N.C.C.V.D. National Council for Combating Venereal Diseases

N.C.C.W. National Council of Catholic Women

n.c.d. no can do

N.C.D. naval construction department

N.C.D.A.D. National Council for Diplomas in Art and Design

N.C.D.L. National Canine Defence League

N.C.E.L. Naval Civil Engineering Laboratory (U.S.A.)

N.C.E.R.T. National Council for Educational Research and Training

NCET National Council for Educational Technology

NCFT National College of Food Technology

N.C.G.G. National Committee for Geodesy and Geophysics (Pak.)

N.C.H. National Children's Home; National Clearing House

N.Chem.L. National Chemical Laboratory

n.Chr. Ger. *nach Christi Geburt*, after Christ, A.D.

N.C.H.S. National Center for Health Statistics (U.S.A.)

N.C.H.S.O. National Committee of Hungarian Student Organisation

NCHVRFE National College for Heating, Ventilating, Refrigeration and Fan Engineering

n.c.i. no common interest

N.C.I.C. National Cancer Institute of Canada; National Crime Information Center (U.S.A.)

N.C.I.T. National Council on Inland Transport

N.C.L. National Carriers Limited; National Central Library; National Chemical Laboratory; National Church League

N.C.L.C. National Council of Labour Colleges

N.C.M.H. *New Cambridge Modern History*

N.C.M.U.A. National Committee of Monotype Users' Associations

N.C.N. National Council of Nurses

NCNA New China News Agency, *Hsinhua She* (China)

N.C.N.C. National Council of Nigerian Citizens

N.C.N.E. National Campaign for Nursery Education

N.C.O. non-commissioned officer

NCOIC non-commissioned officer in charge

n.c.p. normal circular pitch

N.C.P. national cycling proficiency

N.C.P.L. National Centre for Programmed Learning

N.C.P.P.L. National Committee on Prisons and Prison Labour

N.C.P.S. non-contributory pension scheme

N.C.P.T. National Congress of Parents and Teachers

NCr new cruzeiro, Brazilian currency

N.C.R. National Cash Register Company; no carbon required

N.C.R.D. National Council for Research and Development (Israel)

N.C.R.E. Naval Construction Research Establishment

N.C.R.L. National Chemical Research Laboratory (S. Afr.)

NCR paper no carbon required paper

NCS National Chrysanthemum Society; National Communications System; Numerical Control Society

N.C.S.S. National Council of Social Service, founded in 1919, a voluntary organisation which is the principal agency for voluntary social service in Britain

N.C.T. National Chamber of Trade

N.C.T.A. National Community Television Association (U.S.A.); National Council for Technological Awards

NCTAEP National Committee on Technology, Automation and Economic Progress

NCTEC Northern Counties Technical Examinations Council

NCTJ National Council for the Training of Journalists

n.c.u. nitrogen control unit

N.C.U. National Cyclists' Union

N.C.U.M.C. National Council for the Unmarried Mother and her Child

n.c.u.p. no commission until paid

n.c.v. no commercial value

N.C.W. National Council of Women; — **G.B.** National Council of Women of Great Britain

2nd second; — **Lieut.** second lieutenant

Nd *s* neodymium (chem.)

ND *s* Manchester (B.V.R.); North Dakota (U.S.A.)

nd. Ger. *niederdruck*, low pressure

n.d. next day; no date; no decision; no deed; no delay; no drawing; not dated; not deeded; not drawn; nothing doing; nuclear detonation

N.D. Doctor of Naturopathy; National Debt; National Diploma; North Dakota (U.S.A.); Fr. *Notre Dame*, Our Lady

n.d.a. not dated at all

N.d.A. It. *Nota dell'autore*, author's note

N.D.A. National Dairymens' Association Inc.; National Diploma in Agriculture (U.S.A.)

N.D.A.C. Nuclear Defence Affairs Committee (NATO)

N. Dak. North Dakota (U.S.A.)

N. da R. Port. *Nota da Redacção*, editor's note

N.D.B.I. National Dairymen's Benevolent Institution

N.D.C. Natural Distribution Certificate; Nato Defence College
N.D.C.S. National Deaf Children's Society
N.D.D. National Diploma in Dairying/Design; navigation and direction division
N.D.D.T. National Diploma in Dairy Technology
NDEA National Defence Education Act
NDEI National Defense Education Institute (U.S.A.)
N.D.F. National Diploma in Forestry
N.D.H. National Diploma in Horticulture
Ndl. Nederland, The Netherlands
N.D.M.B. National Defense Mediation Board (U.S.A.)
N.D.O. Northern Dance Orchestra (B.B.C.)
N. do A. Port. *Nota do Autor*, author's note
N. do E. Port. *Nota do Editor*, publisher's note
N. do T. Port. *Nota do Tradutor*, translator's note
NDP New Democratic Party (Can.)
n.d.p. normal diametric pitch
N.D.P. National Diploma in Poultry Husbandry
NDPD *National-Demokratische Partei Deutschlands*, Nat. Democratic Party of Germany (E. Ger.)
N.D.P.S. National Data Processing Service (Post Office)
N.d.R. It. *Nota della Redazione*, editor's note
N.D.R.C. National Defence Research Committee
N.D.S.B. Narcotic Drugs Supervisory Body (U.N.O.)
NDT non-distributive trade
n.d.t. Fr. *note du traducteur*, translator's note
N.d.T. It. *Nota del Traduttore*, translator's note
N.D.T. non-destructive testing
N.D.T.A. National Defense Transportation Association (U.S.A.)
N.D.U. Notre-Dame University
NDUF National Democratic Front (Burma)
ne Fr. *né*; *née*, born
n/e no effects (fin.)
Ne *s* neon (chem.)
NE *s* Manchester (B.V.R.); *s* Newcastle (B.F.P.)
Ne. Nepal; Nepalese; Netherlands
n.e. not essential/exceeding
NE. Fr. *nord-est*, north-east
N.E. national emergency/executive;

naval engineer/engineering; new edition; New England/Englander; news editor; north-east/easterly/eastern; nuclear explosion/explosive
NEA North-east Airlines (U.S.A.)
N.E.A. National Education Association (U.S.A.)
N.E.A.C. New English Art Club
N.E.A.F. near-east air force
N.E.A.F.C. North-East Atlantic Fisheries Commission, includes Britain, Iceland, Norway, Sweden, Denmark, W. Germany, Rep. of Ireland, Portugal, Spain, France, Belgium and the Netherlands
N.E.A.H.I. Near East Animal Health Institute
Neapol. Neapolitan
N.E.A.R. National Emergency Alarm Repeater (U.S.A.)
'neath beneath
NEB *New English Bible*
Neb., Nebr. Nebraska (U.S.A.)
NEBSS National Examinations Board for Supervisory Studies
N.E. by E. north-east by east
N.E. by N. north-east by north
NEC National Economic/Egg Council (U.S.A.); National Electrical Code (U.S.A.); National Electronics Conference/Council; national executive committee; National Extension College; Nippon Electric Company (Japan)
n.e.c. not elsewhere classified
N.E.C. Netherlands Electrotechnical Committee
N.E.C.I.E.S. North-East Coast Institution of Engineers and Shipbuilders
NECM New England Conservatory of Music
necr. necrosis
necrol. necrology
NECS National Electrical Code Standards (U.S.A.)
necy. necessary; necessity
Ned Edgar; Edmund; Edward; Edwin
N.E.D. *New English Dictionary on Historical Principles*, original abbrev. of O.E.D.
NEDC North East Development Council
N.E.D.C. National Economic Development Council, *also* Neddy
Neddy Edgar; Edmund; Edward; Edwin; National Economic Development Council, *alt.* N.E.D.C.
N.E.D.O. National Economic Development Office
N.E.E.B. North-East Engineering Bureau; North Eastern Electricity Board (trade mark)
ne'er never

NEES naval engineering experimental station (U.S.A.)

NEF net energy for fattening

n.e.f. noise exposure forecast

N.E.F. New Education Fellowship

N.E.F.A. North East Frontier Agency

N.E.F.C. Near East Forestry Commission

neg. negation; negative; negotiate

nég. Fr. *négation*, negation

Neg. Negro

negt. Fr. *négociant*, merchant

Neh. Nehemiah (Bible)

n.e.i. not elsewhere indicated

n.e.i. L. *non est inventus*, it is not found

N.E.I. Netherlands East Indies

N.E.L. National Electronics/Engineering Laboratory (U.S.A.)

NELA National Electric Light Association

NELINET New England Library Information Network (U.S.A.)

Nell, Nellie, Nelly Eleanor; Elinor; Ellen

Nell Helen; Helena

NEM net energy for milk

N.E.M.A. National Electrical Manufacturers'/Motor Association (U.S.A.)

nem. con. L. *nemine contradicente*, no one opposing/unanimously

nem. dis. L. *nemine dissentiente*, nobody dissenting

N.E.M.P.A. North-Eastern Master Printers' Alliance

ne/nd new edition, no date given (pub.)

N.Eng. New/North England

neol. neologism

N.E.O.P.A.C. North East Overseas Publicity Advisory Committee

Nep. Nepal; Neptune

n.e.p. new edition pending

N.E.P. New Economic Policy, adopted U.S.S.R. 1922–7

NEPA nuclear energy for propulsion of aircraft

N.E.P.A.L. National Egg Packers' Association Limited

NEPCON National Electronic Packaging Conference (U.S.A.)

N.E.P.P. National Egg and Poultry Promotion

N.E.P.R. Nato Electronic Parts Recommendation

N.E.R.A. National Emergency Relief Administration (U.S.A.)

N.E.R.C. Natural Environment Research Council

NEREM Northeast Electronics Research and Engineering Meeting

ne rep. L. *ne repetatur*, do not repeat (med.)

NERO Na Experimental Reactor of Zero power; Near East Regional Office (FAO)

N.E.R.V.A. nuclear engine for rocket vehicle application

NES News Election Service (U.S.A.)

n.e.s. not elsewhere specified

N.E.S. National Extension Service (India); naval education service

N.E.S.C. National Electric Safety Code (U.S.A.); Nuclear Engineering and Science Conference

Nessie Agnes

NEST naval experimental satellite terminal; node execution selection table (computer)

NESTOR neutron source thermal reactor

net netto, lowest

Net, Nettie, Netty Antonia

NET National Education Television (U.S.A.)

n.e.t. not earlier than

N.E.T.A.C. Nuclear Energy Trade Associations' Conference

Neth. Netherlands; — **Ant.** Netherlands Antilles

n. et m. L. *nocte et mane*, night and morning (med.)

NETS network techniques

neubearb. Ger. *neubearbeitet*, revised

neur., neurol. neurological; neurology

neuro. neurotic

neut. neuter; neutral; neutralize; neutralizer

Nev. Nevada (U.S.A.)

Newf. Newfoundland (Can.)

New. L. Newberry Library (U.S.A.)

New M. New Mexico (U.S.A.)

new par. new paragraph

news. newsagency; newsagent

New Test. *New Testament* (Bible)

NF *s* Manchester (B.V.R.); noise factor/figure; *nouveau franc*, new franc (France)

N/f. no funds

n.f. near face; no fool/funds; noun feminine

n.F. Ger. *neue Folge*, new series

N.F. national formula; Newfoundland (*also*, Nfld.); *Newfoundland Law Reports*; New Forest; New French; Norman-French; Northumberland Fusiliers

NFA National Federation of Anglers

n.f.a. no further action

N.F.A. National Farmers' Association; National Food Administration (U.S.A.)

NFAL National Foundation of Arts and Letters

NFB, N.F.B.Ca. National Film Board (Can.)

N.F.B.P.M. National Federation of Builders' and Plumbers' Merchants

N.F.B.T.E. National Federation of Building Trades' Employers

N.F.B.T.O. National Federation of Building Trades' Operatives

NFC National Freight Corporation

n.f.c. not favourably considered

N.F.C.A. National Federation of Community Associations

N.F.C.T.A. National Federation of Corn Trade Associations

NFCU Navy Federal Credit Union

Nfd. Newfoundland (Can.)

NFDA National Food Distributors' Association (U.S.A.)

N.F.E.A. National Federated Electrical Association

N.F.E.R. National Foundation for Education Research in England and Wales

N.F.F. National Froebel Foundation

N.F.F.C. National Film Finance Corporation

N.F.F.E. National Federation of Federal Employees (U.S.A.)

N.F.F.F. National Federation of Fish Friers

N.F.F.P.T. National Federation of Fruit and Potato Trades

NFFTR National Federation of Fishing Tackle Retailers

Nfg. Ger. *Nachfolger*, successor

N.F.H.S. National Federation of Housing Societies

N.F.I. National Federation of Ironmongers; National Fisheries Institute (U.S.A.)

NFL National Football League (U.S.A.)

Nfld. Newfoundland (Can.)

NFLSV National Front for the Liberation of South Vietnam

n.f.m. nearest/next full moon (freem.)

N.F.M.P.S. National Federation of Master Printers in Scotland

N.F.M.T.A. National Federation of Meat Traders' Associations

N.F.O. National Freight Organization

N.F.O.O. naval forward observing officer

NFPA National Fire Protection Association (U.S.A.); National Flexible Packaging Association (U.S.A.); National Fluid Power Association (U.S.A.); National Forest Products Association (U.S.A.)

N.F.P.W. National Federation of Professional Workers

n.f.r. no further requirements

N.F.R.N. National Federation of Retail Newsagents, Booksellers and Stationers

NFS not for sale

N.F.S. National Fire/Forest Service; National Flying Services

NFSA National Fertiliser Solutions Association (.A.S.U)

N.F.S.A. National Fire Services' Associations

NFSAIS National Federation of Science Abstracting and Indexing Services (U.S.A.)

N.F.T. National Film Theatre

NFTU National Federation of Trade Unions (Libya)

N.F.U. National Farmers'/Froebel Union

NFUW National Farmers' Union of Wales

N.F.W.I. National Federation of Women's Institutes

N.F.Y.F.C. National Federation of Young Farmers' Clubs, movement began 1923 in Devon

NG *s* Norfolk (B.V.R.)

5NG *s* Nottingham (radio call-sign)

Ng. Norwegian

n.g. narrow gauge; new genus; no go/good; not given/good; nitroglycerine

N.G. National Gallery/Government/Guard/Guardsman; New Granada; New Guinea; Noble Grand/Guard (freem.); North German

N.G.A. National Glider/Graphical Association

N.G.A.A. National Gasoline Association of America

N.G.A.C. National Guard Air Corps (U.S.A.)

N.G.C. *New General Catalogue* (astronomy)

N.gen. new genus

N.Gk., N Gr. New Greek

N.Gmc. North Germanic

N.G.O. non-governmental organizations

NGPA Natural Gas Processors Association

N.G.R.I. National Geophysical Research Institute (India)

N.G.R.S. Narrow Gauge Railway Society; National Greyhound Racing Society of Great Britain Limited

N.G.S. National Geographic Society

ngt. Fr. *négociant*, merchant

N.G.T. National Guild of Telephonists

N.G.T.E. National Gas Turbine Establishment

N.G.U.T. National Group of Unit Trusts

N.G.V. *Nederlands Genootschap van Vertalers*, The Netherlands Assn.

NH New Hampshire (U.S.A.); *s* Northampton (B.V.R.)

N.H. National Hunt; naval hospital; New Hampshire (U.S.A.); Northumberland Hussars

N.H.A. National Horse Association of Great Britain

N.H.B.R.C. National House-Builders' Registration Council

N.H.C. National Hunt Committee

N.H.D. Doctor of Natural History

NHDC Naval Historical Display Center (U.S.A.)

N.Heb. New Hebrew; New Hebrides

N.H.F. National Hairdressers' Federation

N.H.G. New High German

N.H.I. National Health Insurance

NHK *Nippon Hoso Kyokai*, Japan Broadcasting Corporation

NHL National Hockey League (U.S.A.)

N.H.L.A. National Hardwood Lumber Association (U.S.A.)

N.H.M.R.C.A. National Health and Medical Research Council of Australia

NHO Navy Hydrographic Office

n.h.p. nominal horse-power

NHR National Housewives Register

N.H.R. National Hunt Rules

N.H.R.P. National Hurricane Research Project

N.H.R.U. National Home Reading Union

N.H.S. National Health Service

NHSB National Highway Safety Bureau (U.S.A.)

N.H.S.R. National Hospital Service Reserve

N.H.T.P.C. National Housing and Town Planning Council

Ni *s* nickel (chem.)

NI *s* Wicklow (B.V.R.)

N.I. national insurance; native infantry; naval instructor/intelligence; Northern Ireland; *Northern Ireland Law Reports*; nuclear institute

N.I.A.A.A. Northern Ireland Amateur Athletic Association

N.I.A.B. National Institute of Agricultural Botany

N.I.A.B.C. Northern Ireland Association of Boys' Clubs

NIAE National Institute of Agricultural Engineering

N.I.A.E. National Institute of Adult Education; National Institute of Agricultural Engineering

N.I.B. National Institute for the Blind, *now* R.N.I.B.

Nic, Nick, Nicky Nicholas; Nicola; Nicolas

NIC *s* Nicaragua (I.V.R.)

Nic., Nicar. Nicaragua

n.i.c. not in contact

N.I.C. National Incomes Commission

Nica. Nicaragua

N.I.C.B. National Industrial Conference Board (U.S.A.)

N.I.C.E.I.C. National Inspection Council for Electrical Installation Contracting

N.I.C.F. Northern Ireland Cycling Federation

N.I.C.H.A. Northern Ireland Chest and Heart Association

N.I.C.I.A. Northern Ireland Coal Importers' Association

NICP national inventory control point

N.I.C.S.S. Northern Ireland Council of Social Science

N.I.D. National Institute for the Deaf, *now* R.N.I.D.; National Institute of Drycleaning (U.S.A.); naval intelligence directorate/division; *New International Dictionary* (Webster's); Northern Ireland District

NIDB Nigerian Industrial Development Bank

N.I.D.C. Northern Ireland Development Council

N.I.D.F.A. National Independent Drama Festivals Association

N.I.E. National Institute of Education

niedr. Ger. *niedrig*, low

N.I.E.F. National Ironfounding Employers' Federation

N.I.E.S.R. National Institute of Economic and Social Research

NIEU Negro Industrial Economic Union

N.I.F.E.S. National Industrial Fuel Efficiency Service

NIG *s* Niger (I.V.R.)

Nig. Nigeria; Nigerian

nightie nightdress

N.I.H. National Institute of Hardware; National Institutes of Health (U.S.A.); North Irish Horse

NIHT Northern Ireland Housing Trust

N.I.I. Netherlands Industrial Institute

N.I.I.P. National Institute of Industrial Psychology

N.I.M.A. National Insulation Manufacturers' Association

n.imp. new impression

N.I.M.R. National Institute for Medical Research

NIN national information network

N.I.N.B. National Institute of Neurology and Blindness

Nina Ann; Anna; Anne

N.I.O. National Institute of Oceanography/Oceanology

N.I.O.C. National Iranian Oil Company

nip. nipple

Nip. Nippon; Nipponese

NIPPORO *Nihon Hoso Rodo Kumiai*, Japan Broadcasting Workers' Union

N.I.P.R. National Institute of Personnel Research (S. Afr.)

ni.pri. L. *nisi prius*, unless before (leg. and med.)

N. Ir., N. Ire. Northern Ireland

N.(I).R.A.A. National (Industrial) Recovery Act (U.S.A.)

N.I.R.C. National Industrial Relations Court, set up under Industrial Relations Act 1971, has status of a high court and deals with 'unfair industrial practices'

N.I.R.D. National Institute for Research in Dairying

N.I.R.N.S. National Institute for Research in Nuclear Science

N.I.R.R.A. Northern Ireland Radio Retailers' Association

NIS national insurance scheme

n.i.s. not in stock

NISC National Industrial Safety/Space Committee

NISCON National Industrial Safety Conference (RoSPA)

N.I.S.E.R. Nigerian Institute for Social and Economic Research

NISSC National Industrial Safety Study Conference (RoSPA)

NISTEX National Industrial Safety Trade Exhibition (RoSPA)

Nisuco Nigerian Sugar Company

nit *s* unit of luminance

N.I.T. national intelligence test; none in town

Nita Anita; Juanita

NITV National Iranian Television (Iran)

NIVE *Nederland Instituut voor Efficiency*, Neth. Efficiency Institute

N.I.W.A.A.A. Northern Ireland Women's Amateur Athletic Association

NJ New Jersey (U.S.A.); *s* Sussex, East (B.V.R.)

n.J. Ger. *nächsten Jahres*, of next year

N.J. New Jersey (U.S.A.)

N.J.A. National Jewellers' Association

N.J.A.C. National Joint Advisory Council

N.J.C. National Joint Council

N.J.C.C. National Joint Consultative Committee

NJE New Jersey Experiment

N.J.F. *Nordiske Jordbrugsforskeres Forening*, Scandinavian Agricultural Research Workers' Assn.

N.J.N.C. National Joint Negotiating Committee

NK *s* Hertfordshire (B.V.R.)

N.K. not known

NKG Swed. *Nordiska Kommissionen for Geodesi*, Scandinavian Commission for Geodesy

N.K.G.B. *Norodny Komitet Gosudarstvennoi Bezopasnosti*, People's Commissariat of State Security (U.S.S.R.)

NKL *Norges Kooperative Landsforening*, Norwegian Consumer Co-operative

NKOA National Knitted Outerwear Association (U.S.A.)

NKP *Norges Kommunistiske Parti*, Communist Party of Norway

N.Kr. Norwegian Krone (currency)

N.K.V.D. *Narodny Komitet Vnutrennih Del*, People's Commissariat of Internal Affairs (U.S.S.R.)

NL *s* Netherlands (I.V.R.); *s* Northumberland (B.V.R.)

Nl. national

n.l. new line (typ.); Ger. *nicht löslich*, not soluble; Fr. *non longue*, not far

n.l. L. *non licet*, it is not permitted; L. *non liquet*, it is not clear

NL. New Latin

N.L. National Labour; National Liberal; Navy League/List; New Latin; north latitude

N.L. L. *non liquet*, it is not clear

N.L.A. National Lumbermen's Association (U.S.A.); Nigerian Library Association

N.lat. north latitude

N.L.B. National Labor Board (U.S.A.); National Library for the Blind

N.L.C. National Liberal Club; National Library of Canada

N.L.C.A. Norwegian Lutheran Church of America

N.L.C.I.F. National Light Castings Ironfounders' Federation

NLF National Liberation Front (Southern Yemen)

n.l.f. nearest landing field

N.L.F. National Labour/Liberal Federation; National Liberation Front (South Vietnam)

NLGI National Lubricating Grease Institute

NLHS *Neo Lao Hak Sat*, Lao Patriotic Front, *sometimes Neo Laottak Xat*, NLHX (Laos)

N.L.I. National Library of Ireland; National Lifeboat Institution, *now* R.N.L.I.

N.L.L. National Lending Library for Science and Technology
N.L.M. National Library of Medicine
N.L.M.C. National Labour Management Council
N.L.N. National League for Nursing
N.L.O. naval liaison officer
N.L.O.G.F. National Lubricating Oil and Grease Federation
N.L.R. *Nationaal Lucht en Ruimtevaartlaboratorium*, Nat. Aeronautics and Astronautics Laboratory (Neth.); *Newfoundland/Nigeria Law Reports*
N.L.R.B. National Labor Relations Board (U.S.A.)
N.L.S. National Library of Scotland
n.l.t. not later/less than
NLW National Library Week, *now* NBW
N.L.W. National Library of Wales
Nly. northerly
N.L.Y.L. National League of Young Liberals
N/m newton per metre, unit of surface tension
N/m² newton per square metre, unit of pressure
NM *s* Bedfordshire (B.V.R.); New Mexico (U.S.A.)
nm. nutmeg
n/m. no mark
Nm. Ger. *Nachmittag*, afternoon
n.m. nautical mile; new moon; noun masculine; nuclear magneton
n.m. L. *nocte et mane*, night and morning (med.)
N.m. next matter (advert.)
N.M. national marketing; New Mexico (U.S.A.)
N.M.A. National Management/Medical/Microfilm Association; Needle Makers' Association
N.M.B. National Maritime/Mediation Board
n.m.c. no more credit
N.M.C. National Marketing Council; National Meteorological Center (U.S.A.)
NMCS National Military Command/Center System (U.S.A.)
N.M.E. National Military Establishment (U.S.A.)
NMEA National Marine Electronics Association (U.S.A.)
N. Mex. New Mexican/Mexico
N.M.G.C. National Marriage Guidance Council
N.M.H.A. National Mental Health Association
N.M.H.C. National Material Handling Centre
N.M.P.A. National Marine Paint Association

N.M.P.C. National Milk Publicity Council
NMR normal mode rejection; nuclear magnetic resonance
N.M.R. National Milk Records, Milk Marketing Board
N.M.S.S.A. NATO Maintenance Supply Services Agency
N.M.S.U. naval motion study unit; New Mexico State University (U.S.A.)
n.m.t. not more than
N.M.T.F. National Market Traders' Federation
N.M.T.F.A. National Master Tile Fixers' Association
N.M.T.S. National Milk Testing Service
N.M.U. National Maritime Union
NN *s* Newhaven (B.F.P.); *s* Nottinghamshire (B.V.R.)
N/N not to be noted
nn. names; notes; nouns
n.n. neutralization number; no name
NNDP Nigerian National Democratic Party
N.N.E. north-north-east
NNEB National Nursery Examination Board
N.N.F. Northern Nurses' Federation
N.NG Netherlands New Guinea
N.N.I. *Nederlands Normalisatie Instituut*, Neth. Standards Institute; noise and number index; noise nuisance index; Norwegian Nobel Institute
NNLC Ngwame National Liberatory Congress (Swaziland)
n.n.m. nearest/next new moon (freem.)
N.N.R.C. Neutral Nations Repatriation Commission
N.N.R.O. *Norske Nasjonalkomite for Rasjonell Organisasjon*, Norwegian Nat. Committee for Scientific Management
N.N.S.C. Neutral Nations Supervisory Commission
N.N.W. north-north-west
No *s* nobelium (chem.); *s* Norium
NO *s* Essex (B.V.R.); Ger. *Nordosten*, north-east
5NO *s* Newcastle-upon-Tyne (radio call-sign)
no. north; northern; number
No. Norway; Norwegian; It. *numero*, number
No. 10 10 Downing St. (Lond.), prime minister's official residence
n.o. natural order (bot.); normally open; not out (cricket)
N/O no orders (banking)
No. L. *numero*, in number, number
N.O. natural order (bot.); naval officer/operations; navigation officer; New Orleans (U.S.A.); Fr. *nord-ouest*, north-

west; It. *Nord-Ovest*, north-west; Nuffield Observatory, Jodrell Bank

NOA new obligational authority; not otherwise authorized

N.O.A. National Onion/Opera/Optical/Orchestral Association

N.O.A.A. National Oceanographic and Atmospheric Administration (U.S.A.)

NOALA noise-operated automatic level adjustment

NOB naval operating base

nob. noble

nob. L. *nobis*, for/on our part

N.O.B.E.V. *The New Oxford Book of English Verse*, 1250–1950

n.o.c. notation of content; not otherwise classified

NOCIL National Organic Chemical Industries (India)

No. Co. northern counties

noct. L. *nocte*, at night (med.)

N.O.D. naval ordnance department; night observation device

N.O.D.A. National Operatic and Dramatic Association

NODAC Naval Ordnance Data Automation Center (U.S.A.)

N.O.D.C. National Oceanographic Data Centre

n.o.e. notice of exception; not otherwise enumerated

NOFI National Oil Fuel Institute (U.S.A.)

n.o.h.p. not otherwise herein provided

n.o.i.b.n. not otherwise indexed by name

N.O.I.C. National Oceanographic Instrumentation Center (U.S.A.); naval officer in charge

n.o.k. next of kin

NOL Naval Ordnance Laboratory (U.S.A.)

nol. con. L. *nolo contendere*, I do not wish to contend

Noll, Nolly Oliver

Noll Oliver Cromwell (1599–1658), Lord Protector of England

nol. pros. L. *nolle prosequi*, do not continue (leg.)

nom. nomenclature; nominal; nomination; nominative

NOMA National Office Management Association (U.S.A.)

NOMAD navy oceanographic meteorological automatic device (USN)

nom. cap. nominal capital (fin.)

nomen. nomenclature

nomin. nominative

Nomm. nomination

nom. nov. L. *nomen novum*, new name

NOMSS National Operational Meteorological Satellite System (U.S.A.)

nonce-wd. nonce-word

Non-Coll. non-collegiate

non-com. non-commissioned

Noncon. nonconformist

non cul. L. *non culpabilis*, not guilty

non-cum non-cumulative (fin.)

non obs., non obst. L. *non obstante*, notwithstanding

non pros. L. *non prosequitur*, he does not prosecute

non repetat. L. *non repetatur*, do not repeat

non res. non resident

non seq. L. *non sequitur*, it does not follow logically

nonstand., nonstd. nonstandard

non-U not upper-class, especially in spoken English

NOO Navy Oceanographic Office (USN)

Noo. numbers

NOP National Opinion Poll; numerical oceanographic office (USN)

n.o.p. not otherwise provided for

NOPA National Office Products Association (U.S.A.)

no par. matter to run on and have no break (typ.)

N.O.P.W.C. National Old People's Welfare Council

nor' north, *generally* as in nor'-western

nor. normal; north; northern

Nor. Norman; Norway; Norwegian; Norwich

Nora, Norah Eleanor; Elinor; Honor; Honora; Leonora

NORAD North American Air Defense Command (Can/U.S.A.)

Nor. Ant. Norwegian Antarctica

Nor. Arc. Norwegian Arctic

Nor'ard northward

NORC National Opinion Research Center (U.S.A.); naval ordnance research computer

Nor. Cur. Norwegian current

Nor'd northward

NORDCHURCHAID Scandinavian Churches Relief Organisation

NORDFORSK *Nordiska Samarbetsorganisationen för Teknisk-Naturvetenskaplig Forening*, Scandinavian Council for Applied Research

Norf. Norfolk

Norm Norma; Norman

NORM not operationally ready maintenance

norm. normal; normalized

NORS not operationally ready supplies/supply

north. northern

NORTHAG North European Army Group (NATO)

Northants. Northamptonshire

Northmb., **Northumb.** Northumberland; Northumbrian

Norvic. L. *Norvicensis*, of Norwich, Eng. episcopal title, in bishop's signature

Norw. Norway; Norwegian

NORWEB North Western Electricity Board (trade mark)

NOS *Nederlandse Omroep Stichting*, Neth. Broadcasting Corporation

nos. numbers

n.o.s. not otherwise specified

NOSA National Occupational Safety Association (S. Afr.)

NOSC Naval Ordnance Systems Command (USN)

No SIG no engraver's signature (numis.)

not. notice

Not. notary

NOTAM notice to airmen

N.O.T.B. National Ophthalmic Treatment Board

NOTS naval ordnance test station (USN)

Nottm. Nottingham

Notts. Nottinghamshire

notwg. notwithstanding

nouv. Fr. *nouvelle*, new

nov. novel; novelist; It. *novembre*, November; novice; novitiate

Nov. November

NOW National Organisation of Women (U.S.A.)

N.o.W. *News of the World*

N.O.W.C. National Association of Women's Clubs

n.o.y. not out yet

noz. nozzle

np new pence, introduced in Britain 1971

Np *s* Napalm, incendiary petrol mixture; *s* neptunium (chem.)

NP Nationalist Party (Malta); *Nasionale Party*, Nat. Party (S. Afr.); National Party (Namibia/South West Africa); neuropsychiatric; neuropsychiatry; *s* Worcestershire (B.V.R.)

n/p. net proceeds

n.p. near point; net proceeds; new paragraph; new pattern; nickel-plated; non participating; no place of publication given; no printer; no publisher; normal pitch/pressure; nursing procedure

N.P. New Providence (Bahamas); nitro proof, firearm proved for modern ammunition at an official proof establishment; Nobel Prize, prizes are awarded from income of £1.75 m. left in trust by Swed. scientist Alfred Nobel; Norwegian patent; notary public

NPA New People's Army, military arm of Maoist Communist Party (Philippines)

N.P.A. National Pigeon Association; National Packaging Association (Aust.); National Parenthood/Parking/Parks/Pet/Petroleum/Planning Association (U.S.A.); National Production Authority; Newspaper Proprietors' Association; Nigerian Ports Authority; numerical production analysis

NPAC National Program for Acquisition and Cataloging of Library of Congress (U.S.A.)

N. Pac. Cur. North Pacific current

N.P.A.C.I. National Production Advisory Council on Industry

N.P.B. National Provincial Bank, *now* Nat West

N.P.B.A. National Paper Box Association (U.S.A.); National Pig Breeders' Association

N.P.C. National Patents/Petroleum Council (U.S.A.); National Peace/Ports Council; National Press Club (U.S.A.); NATO Parliamentarians' Conference; naval personnel committee; Northern People's Congress (Nigeria)

NPCCE National Pollution Control Conference and Exposition (U.S.A.)

NPD *Nationaldemokratische Partei Deutschlands*, Nat. Democratic Party, neo-Nazi (W. Ger.)

N.P.D. north polar distance (nav.)

n.p.f. not provided for

N.P.F. Newspaper Press Fund

N.P.F.A. National Playing Fields Association, founded 1925 to encourage the provision of playing fields and recreational facilities for the whole population

N.P.F.C. Northwest Pacific Fisheries Commission

N.P.F.S.C. North Pacific Fur Seal Commission

NPG Nile Provisional Government, rebel organization Sudan

N.P.G. National Portrait Gallery

N.Ph. nuclear physics

N.P.I.P.F. Newspaper and Printing Industries' Pension Fund

NPIS National Physics Information System (U.S.A.)

n.pl. noun plural

N.P.L. National Physical Laboratory

NPN negative-positive-negative (elec.); nonprotein nitrogen

n.p.n.a. no protest for nonacceptance

NP/ND not published, no date given

NPO navy purchasing office

256

n.p.o. L. *ne per oris*, not by mouth (med.)

N.P.O. navy post/purchasing office (U.S.A.); New Philharmonia Orchestra

n.p. or d. no place or date (pub.)

n.p.p. no passed proof

NPPO Navy Publications and Printing Office (USN)

N.P.P.T.B. National Pig Progeny Testing Board

n.p.r. noise power ratio

NPRA National Petroleum Refiners Association; naval personnel research activity (USN)

NPS naval postgraduate school (USN); non-professorial staff (univ.)

n.p.s. nominal pipe size; no prior service

N.P.S. National Portrait Society

n.p.s.h. net positive suction head

NPT non-proliferation treaty

n.p.t. normal pressure and temperature

N.P.T.A. National Paper Trade Association (U.S.A.)

n.p.u. L. *ne plus ultra*, nothing beyond

N.P.U. National Pharmaceutical/ Postal Union

n.p.v. net present value (fin.); no par value (fin.)

N.P.Y. National Productivity Year

N. & Q. *Notes and Queries*, jnl. founded 1849 and devoted to Eng. studies, literary, historical, linguistical and bibliographical

n.q.a. net quick assets (fin.)

NR *s* Leicestershire (B.V.R.); Nepalese rupee

nr. near; number

Nr. Dan./Ger. *Nummer*, number

n.r. narrow resonance; net register; no risk (insce.)

n.r. L. *non repetatur*, not to be repeated (med.)

N.R. National Register; natural rubber; naval rating; navy regulations; Northern Rhodesia, *now* Zambia (*also* N.Rh.); North Riding, Yorkshire

n.r.a. never refuse anything

N.R.A. National Reclamation Association; National Recovery Act/Administration (U.S.A.); National Rifle Association founded 1860, estab. at Wimbledon, moving to Bisley 1890. Governs full-bore shooting within the U.K.

NRAA National Rifle Association of America

n.r.a.d. no risk after discharge

N.R.B. National Roads Board (N.Z.); National Rubber Bureau (U.S.A.)

NRC National Reformation Council (Sierra Leone)

N.R.C. National Redemption Council (Ghana); National Research Corporation/ Council; Netherlands Red Cross; Nuclear Research Council

N.R.C.A. National Retail Credit Association

N.R.C.C. National Republican Congressional Committee (U.S.A.); National Research Council of Canada

N.R.D. national recruiting department; National Register of Designers; naval recruiting department

N.R.D.B. Natural Rubber Development Board

N.R.D.C. National Research Development Corporation/Council; National Retail Distributive Certificate

NRDO National Research and Development Organisation

NRDS nuclear rocket development station

NREC National Resource Evaluation Center (U.S.A.)

N.R.F. National Relief Fund

N.R.F.L. Northern Rugby Football League

N.R.H.A. National Roller Hockey Association

N.R.I.A.D. National Register of Industrial Art Designers

NRK *Norsk Rikskringkasting*, Norwegian State Broadcasting Co.

NRL naval research laboratory

N.R.L. National Reference Library of Science and Invention; Nelson Research Laboratory

N.R.L.R. *Northern Rhodesia Law Reports*

N.R.L.S.I. National Reference Library of Science and Invention

N.R.M.A. National Retail Merchants' Association (U.S.A.); National Roads and Motorists' Association of New South Wales

N.R.M.C.A. National Ready Mixed Concrete Association (U.S.A.)

nrml. normal

N.R.N.L.R. *Northern Region of Nigeria Law Reports*

N.R.O. non-returnable outer

NRP Nevis Reformation Party

N.R.P.R.A. Natural Rubber Producers' Research Association

N.R.R. Northern Rhodesia Regiment

N.R.S. National Rose Society; naval recruiting service

N.R.S.A. National Rural Studies Association

NRT, n.r.t. net registered tonnage

N.R.V. non-return valve

Nrw. Norwegian

NRZ   non return to zero
n/s   not sufficient (banking)
NS   Ger. *Nachschrift*, postscript; *s*
New Ross (B.F.P.); *s* Sutherland (B.V.R.)
ns.   It. *Nostro*, our/ours
Ns.   nimbostratus (met.)
n.s.   Graduate of the Royal Naval
Staff College, Greenwich; near side; new
series; nickel steel; not specified
N.S.   National Service/Society; natural
science; naval service; *Nederlandsche
Spoorwegen*, Netherlands Railway; new
school/series/side; Newspaper Society;
New Style Calendar since 1752; Port.
Nosso Senhor, Our Lord; Fr. *Notre-
Seigneur*, Our Lord; Nova Scotia; nuclear
science; Numismatic Society
N.-S.   Fr. *Notre-Seigneur*, Our Lord
NSA   National Shipping Authority
(U.S.A.)
N.S.A.   National Sawmilling Asso-
ciation; National Service Act, 1947;
National Skating Association, founded
1879; New Society of Artists; non-
sterling area; Nursery School Association
N.S.A.A.   National Sulphuric Acid
Association
N.S.A.C.S.   National Society for the
Abolition of Cruel Sports
N.S.A.E.   National Society of Art
Education
N.S.A.F.A.   National Service Armed
Forces Act
N.S.A.S.   National Smoke Abatement
Society
N.S.B.   National   Science   Board
(U.S.A.)
N.S.B.A.   National Sheep Breeders'
Association; National Silica Brickmakers'
Association; National Small Business
Association
N.S.C.   National Safety Council; Na-
tional Savings Committee; National
Security Council (U.S.A.); National
Sporting Club; National Steel Corpora-
tion; Nutrition Society of Canada
N.S.C.A.   National Safety Council of
Australia; National Society for Clean
Air
N.S.C.R.   National Society for Cancer
Relief
NSD   naval supply depot; non-soapy
detergent
N.S.D.   naval stores department
N.S.D.A.P.   *Nationalsozialistische Deut-
schlands Arbeiterpartei*, Nat. Socialist
German Workers' Party, founded 1919,
brought to power by Hitler, 1933
NSDF   National Social Democratic
Front (South Vietnam)
NSDO   National Seed Development
Organisation

NSEC   nanosecond (phys.)
N.S.E.C.   National Service Entertain-
ments Council
N.S.E.S.   National Society of Electro-
typers and Stereotypers
n.s.f.   not sufficient funds (fin.)
N.S.F.   National   Sanitation/Science
Foundation (U.S.A.); *Norges Standard-
iserings-Forbund*, Norwegian Standards
Institute
N.S.F.G.B.   National Ski Federation
of Great Britain, formed 1964 to ad-
minister nat. and intern. ski racing and
develop skiing in Britain
N.S.G.T.   non-self-governing   terri-
tories
N.S.H.E.B.   North of Scotland Hydro-
Electric Board
NSIA   National Security Industrial
Association (U.S.A.)
n.sing.   noun singular
N.S.I.S.   National Softwood Impor-
ters' Section of the Timber Trade Federa-
tion
N.S.J.   Sp. *Nuestro Señor Jesucristo*,
Our Lord Jesus Christ
N.-S.J.-C.   Fr. *Notre-Seigneur Jésus-
Christ*, Our Lord Jesus Christ
N.S.K.K.   *Nazionalistisches   Sozialis-
tische Kraftfahrkorps*, Nat. Socialist Auto-
mobile Corps (Nazi Ger.)
N.S.L.   National   Service/Sporting/
Sunday League
Ns/m²   newton second per square
metre, unit of dynamic viscosity
N.S.M.   National   Savings/Socialist
Movement
N.S.M.H.C.   National Society for
Mentally Handicapped Children
N.S.M.M.   National Society of Metal
Mechanics
N.S.M.P.   National Society of Master
Patternmakers
N.S.O.   naval staff officer
N.S.O.P.A.   National   Society   of
Operative Printers and Assistants, *now*
S.O.G.A.T.
n.sp.   new species
N.S.P.A.   Nova Scotia Pharmaceutical
Association
N.S.P.C.A.   National Society for the
Prevention of Cruelty to Animals, *now*
R.S.P.C.A.
N.S.P.C.C.   National Society for the
Prevention of Cruelty to Children
NSPE   National Society of Profes-
sional Engineers (U.S.A.)
n.s.p.f.   not specially provided for
N.S.P.S.   National   Sweet   Pea
Society
N.S.P.S.E.   National Society of Paint-
ers, Sculptors and Engravers

n.s.r. natural/normal sinus rhythm (med.)

N.S.R.A. National Small-bore Rifle Association, governs small-bore shooting in U.K.

NSRB National Security Resources Board

N.S.R.F. Nova Scotia Research Foundation

NSS national sample survey; National Staff Side of the Whitley Council; normal saline solution

N.S.S. New Shakespeare Society

N.S.S.A. National School Sailing Association

N.S.S.U. National Sunday School Union

NST Newfoundland standard time

n.s.t. nonslip thread

N.S.T.C. Nova Scotia Technical College

N.S.T.I.C. Naval Scientific and Technical Information (MOD *formerly* A.C.S.I.L.)

NSTP Nuffield Science Teaching Project

N.S.Trip., N.S.Tripos Natural Science Tripos

N.S.W. New South Wales (Aust.)

N.S.W.L.V.R. *New South Wales Land Valuation Reports*

N.S.W.S.R. *New South Wales State Reports*

N.S.Y. New Scotland Yard

n't not

Nt nitron

NT *s* Salop (B.V.R.)

n.t. net tonnage; normal temperature

N.t. new terms (grain trade)

N.T. National Trust; neap tide; New Testament/Translation; Northern Territory (Aust.); not titled; no trumps

N.T.A. National Tax/Technical/Tuberculosis Association (U.S.A.); National Therapeutics Association; Northern Textile/Trade Association (U.S.A.)

NTC National Trading Company (Malawi); National Trading Corporation (Uganda)

n.t.c. negative temperature coefficient

N.T.C. Nigerian Tobacco Company

N.T.D.A. National Trade Development Association; National Tyre Distributors' Association

N.T.D.S. naval tactical data system

N.T.E.T.A. National Traction Engine and Traction Association

ntfy. notify

N.T.G.B. North Thames Gas Board

N.T.Gk. New Testament Greek

Nthb. Northumberland

nthn. northern

n.t.l. no time lost

n.t.m. net ton mile

n.t.o. not taken out

N.T.O. naval transport officer

n.t.p. normal temperature and blood pressure; normal temperature and pressure/progress; no title page

N.T.R.L. National Telecommunications Research Laboratory (S. Afr.)

NTS National Labour Alliance, Russian emigré anti-Communist organization based Frankfurt; National Trust for Scotland; naval torpedo station (USN)

n.t.s. not to scale

N.T.S. naval transport service (U.S.A.); Nevada Test Site

NTSA National Traffic Safety Agency

NTSC National Television Systems Committee (U.S.A.)

NTUC Nyasaland Trade Union Congress

NTV Nippon Television

nt.wt. net weight

NU *s* Derbyshire (B.V.R.); *Nahdatul Ulama*, Muslim Scholars' Party (Indonesia)

n.u. name unknown; naval unit; number unobtainable

N.U. Sp. *Naciones Unidas*, United Nations; National Union; Fr. *Nations Unies*, United Nations; Northern Union

NUAAW National Union of Agricultural and Allied Workers

N.U.A.T. *Nordisk Union for Alkoholfri Trafik*, Scandinavian Union for Non-Alcoholic Traffic

NUAW National Union of Agricultural Workers

NUB National Union of Blastfurnacemen, Ore Miners, Coke Workers, and Kindred Trades

N.U.B.E. National Union of Bank Employees

N.U.B.S.O. National Union of Boot and Shoe Operatives

nuc. nuclear

N.U.C.O. National Union of Co-operative Officials

N.U.C.U.A. National Union of Conservative and Unionist Associations

nud. nudism; nudist

NUDBTW National Union of Dyers, Bleachers and Textile Workers

NUDETS nuclear detection system

Nufcor Nuclear Fuels Corporation (S. Afr.)

N.U.F.C.W. National Union of Funeral and Cemetery Workers

NUFLAT National Union of Footwear, Leather and Allied Trades

N.U.F.T.O. National Union of Furniture Trade Operatives

N.U.G.M.W. National Union of General and Municipal Workers, *alt.* G.M.W.U.

N.U.H.W. National Union of Hosiery Workers

N.U.I., N.U.Irel. National University of Ireland

NUIW National Union of Insurance Workers

N.U.J. National Union of Journalists

N.U.J.M.B. Northern Universities Joint Matriculation Board

N.U.L.I.S. Norwich Union Life Insurance Society

N.U.L.W. & A.T. National Union of Leather Workers and Allied Trades

num. number; numeral; numeration; numerical; numerologist; numerology

Num., Numb. Numbers (Bible)

N.U.M. National Union of Manufacturers, *now* C.B.I.; National Union of Mineworkers; New Ulster Movement

num. adj. numeral adjective

NUMEC Nuclear Materials and Equipment Corporation

numis., numism. numismatic; numismatics; numismatology

NUOS naval underwater ordnance station

NUP National Unionist Party (Sudan)

N.U.P. National Union of Protestants

N.U.P.B.P.W., N.U.P.B. & P.W. National Union of Printing, Bookbinding and Paper Workers

N.U.P.E. National Union of Public Employees

NUPSE National Union of Public Services Employees (Guyana)

N.U.P.T. National Union of Press Telegraphists

N.U.R. National Union of Railwaymen

N.U.R.A. National Union of Ratepayers' Associations

N.U.R.C. National Union of Retail Confectioners

Nurs.R. nursery rhyme

N.U.R.T. National Union of Retail Tobacconists

N.U.S. National Union of Seamen/ Students

N.U.S.A.S. National Union of South African Students

N.U.S.E.C. National Union of Societies for Equal Citizenship

NUSMWCHDE National Union of Sheet Metal Workers, Coppersmiths, Heating and Domestic Engineers

N.U.S.S. National Union of Small Shopkeepers

N.-u.-T. Newcastle-upon-Tyne

N.U.T. National Union of Teachers

NUTAW National Union of Textile and Allied Workers

NUTGW, N.U.T. & G.W. National Union of Tailors and Garment Workers

N.U.T.N. National Union of Trained Nurses

nutr. nutrition

N.U.V.B. National Union of Vehicle Builders

N.U.W.A. National Unemployed Workers' Association

N.U.W.C. Naval Undersea Warfare Center (U.S.A.)

N.U.W.T. National Union of Women Teachers

N.U.W.W. National Union of Women Workers

NV Nevada (U.S.A.); *s* Northamptonshire (B.V.R.)

Nv., n.v. nonvoting (fin.)

n.v. needle valve; new version

N.V. *naamloze vennootschap*, limited company (Neth.); new version

nva. Sp. *nueva*, new

N.V.A. North Vietnam Army

N.V.B. National Volunteer Brigade

N.V.G.A. National Vocational Guidance Association (U.S.A.)

n.v.m. non-volatile matter

N.V.M. Nativity of the Virgin Mary

N.V.M.A. National Veterinary Medical Association

N.V.O. Northern Variety Orchestra (B.B.C.)

NVPO Nuclear Vehicle Projects Office (NASA)

n.v.r. no voltage release

N.V.R.S. National Vegetable Research Station

NVV *Nederlands Verbond van Vakverenigingen*, Neth. Trade Union Fed.

NW *s* Leeds (B.V.R.)

n.w. nanowatt; net weight; no wind

N.W. North Wales; north-west/westerly/western; North-Western postal district (Lond.)

NWA North west Orient Airlines

N.W.A. North-West Africa/African

N.W. by N. north-west by north

N.W. by W. north-west by west

NWDR *Nordwestdeutscher Rundfunk*, North-Western German Broadcasting Station

N.W.E.B. North Western Electricity Board

N.W.F. National Wildlife Federation

Nwfld. Newfoundland (Can.)

N.W.F.P. North-West Frontier Province (Pak.)

n.w.g. national wire gauge

N.W.G.A. National Wool Growers' Association

N.W.I. Netherlands West Indies
N.W.I.D.A. North West Industrial Development Association
NWL naval weapons laboratory
n.w.l. natural wave-length
N.W.L.A. North Women's Lacrosse Association
N.W.M.P. North-West Mounted Police, *now* R.C.M.P.
N.W.M.P.A. North Wales Master Printers' Alliance; North-Western Master Printers' Alliance
NWNT North Wales Naturalists' Trust
N.W.P. North West Provinces (India)
n.w.s. normal water surface
N.W.S.A. National Welding Supply Association (U.S.A.); National Women's Suffrage Association
N.W.S.C. National Weather Satellite Center (U.S.A.)
n.wt. net weight
n.w.t. non watertight
N.W.T. North West Territories (Can.)
n.w.t.d. non watertight door
NWTEC National Wool Textile Export Corporation
NWU National Worker Union (Jamaica)
NX *s* Warwickshire (B.V.R.)
NY *s* Glamorgan (B.V.R.); New York, *also* N.Y. (U.S.A.)
N.Y. new/no year
N.Y.A. National Youth Administration (U.S.A.)
N.Y.C. New York Central Railway; New York City (U.S.A.)
n.y.d. not yet diagnosed
Nye Aneurin
N.Y.H.S. New York Historical Society
nyl. nylon
Ny.L.R. *Nyasaland Law Reports*
NYO not yet out (pub.)
n.y.p. not yet published
n.y.r. not yet returned
N.Y.S. New York State (U.S.A.)
N.Y.S.A. New York State Assembly
N.Y.S.A.C. New York State Athletic Commission
N.Y.S.B.B. New York State Banking Board
NYSE New York Stock Exchange
N.Y.T. National Youth Theatre; *New York Times*
NYU New York University

NZ *s* Londonderry (B.V.R.); *s* New Zealand (I.V.R.)
N.Z. neutrality zone; New Zealand
N.Z.A.B. New Zealand Association of Bacteriologists
N.Z.A.Sc. New Zealand Association of Scientists
NZBC New Zealand Broadcasting Corporation
N.Z.B.S. New Zealand Broadcasting Service
N.Z.C.E.R. New Zealand Council for Educational Research
N.Z.D. New Zealand Division
N.Z.D.A. New Zealand Department of Agriculture; New Zealand Dietetic Association
N.Z.D.C.S. New Zealand Department of Census and Statistics
N.Z.D.L.S. New Zealand Department of Lands and Survey
N.Z.D.S.I.R. New Zealand Department of Scientific and Industrial Research
N.Zeal. New Zealand
N.Z.E.F. New Zealand Expeditionary Force
N.Z.E.I. New Zealand Electronics Institute
NZFL New Zealand Federation of Labor
N.Z.F.R.I. New Zealand Forest Research Institute
N.Z.F.S. New Zealand Forest Service
N.Z.G.A. New Zealand Golf Association
N.Z.Gen.S. New Zealand Genetical Society
N.Z.G.S. New Zealand Geographical Society
N.Z.I.C. New Zealand Institute of Chemistry
N.Z.I.E. New Zealand Institution of Engineers
N.Z.I.M. New Zealand Institute of Management
N.Z.J.C.B. New Zealand Joint Communications Board
N.Z.L.A. New Zealand Library Association
N.Z.L.R. *New Zealand Law Reports*
N.Z.M.S. New Zealand Meteorological Service
N.Z.S.A. New Zealand Statistical Association
N.Z.V.A. New Zealand Veterinary Association

O

o   *s* overcast sky (met.)
4o   quarto
o'   of; descendant of, used in Irish names
ö   Sw. *öst*, east
ø   Dan./Nor. *øst*, east
O   *s* centre of earth; *s* Birmingham (B.V.R.); *s* human blood type of ABO group; *s* oxygen (chem.)
Ø   *s* shortage
o.   occasional; octavo; Sp./Port. *oeste*, west; off; ohm (elec.); old; only; Dutch *ooste*, west; order; organ; ortho; Fr. *ouest*, west; over; overseer; It. *ovest*, west
o.   L. *optimus*, best
O.   observe; observer; occiput, back of head presented in labour (med.); occupation; ocean; October; Odd Fellows; Office; officer; Ohio (U.S.A.); Ontario; operation; orange; order (knighthood); ordinary; Orient; Ger. *Osten*, east; Fr. *ouest*, west; over (cricket); overseer (typ.); owner
O.   L. *octarius*, a pint (med.); L. *Oculus*, eye; It. *Ottava*, octave (mus.)
OA   *s* Birmingham (B.V.R.); Office of Applications (NASA); Olympic Airways
O/A   on account; on or about
o.a.   Ger. *onder andere*, among others
O.A.   Fr. *Océan Atlantique*, Atlantic Ocean; office address; officers' association; oil absorption; old account; operation analysis; ordnance artificer; over all
O. & A.   October and April
O.A.A.   old age assistance; Fr. *Organisation des Nations Unies pour l'alimentation et l'agriculture*, United Nations Food and Agriculture Organisation

O.A.B.E.T.A.   Office Appliance and Business Equipment Trades' Association, now B.E.T.A.
O.A.C.I.   Fr. *Organisation de l'aviation civile internationale*, Intern. Civil Aviation Organisation
o.a.d.   over all depth
O.A.G.   *Official Airline Guide* (U.S.A.)
O.A.G.B.   Osteopathic Association of Great Britain
o.a.h.   over all height
O.A.H.   Organization of American Historians
O.A.I.A.   Fr. *Organisation des agences d'information d'Asie*, Organisation of Asian News Agencies
o. alt. hor.   L. *omnibus alternis horis*, every other hour (med.)
O.A.M.D.G.   L. *Omnia ad Majorem Dei Gloriam*, All to the Greater Glory of God
O.A.N.A.   Organisation of Asian News Agencies
o.a.o.   off and on
O.A.O.   Orbiting Astronomical Observatory
O.A.P.   old age pension/pensioner
O.A.P.C.   Office of Alien Property Custodian (U.S.A.)
OAR   Office of Aerospace Research (USAF)
O. Ar.   Old Arabic
OART   Office of Advanced Research and Technology (NASA)
O.A.S.   old age security; on active service; Fr. *Organisation de l'Armée Secrète*, organ. pledged to keep Algeria French; Organization of American States

263

O.A.S.I. Old Age and Survivors' Insurance

OASP organic acid soluble phosphorus

o.a.t. outside air temperature

O.A.T.C. Oceanic Air Traffic Control

O.A.U. Organization for African Unity

O.A.U.L.C. Organization for African Unity Liberation Committee

Ob, Obad Obadiah

OB *s* Birmingham (B.V.R.); *s* Oban (B.F.P.); *s* Peru (I.C.A.M.)

ob. obligation; obsolete; obstetric

ob. L. *obiit*, he/she/it died; L. *obiter*, incidentally; *oboe* (mus.)

O.B. observed bearing; official board; oil bomb; Old Bailey; old bonded (whisky); old boy; order of battle; ordnance board; outside broadcast

O.B., Oberw., Obw. Ger. *Oberwerk*, swell organ (mus.)

OBA optical bleaching agent

O.B.A.A. Oil Burning Apparatus Association

ÖBB Ger. *Österreichische Bundesbahnen*, Federal Railways of Austria

obb., obbl. It. *obbligato*, instrumental part in a work that is 'essential' in the sense that it performs an important soloistic function (mus.)

O.B.C. old boys' club; outdoor boating club

ob. dk. observation deck

obdt. obedient

O.B.E. Officer of the Order of the British Empire

O.B.E.V. *Oxford Book of English Verse*

Obgᵒ. Port. *Obrigado*, thank you

obit. obituary

obj. object; objection; objective

objn. objection

obl. obligation; oblige; oblique; oblong

O.B.L.I. Oxford and Buckinghamshire Light Infantry (mil.)

OBO ore-bulk-oil carrier (ship.)

Ob. Ph. oblique photography

O.B.R.A. Overseas Broadcasting Representatives' Association

Obre. Fr. *Octobre*, October

obs. obscure; observation; observatory; observe; observer; obsolete; obstetric; obstetrician; obstetrics

obs. oboes (mus.)

Obs. *The Observer*

obsc. obscure

obsol. obsolescent; obsolete

ob.s.p. L. *obiit sine prole*, died without issue

O.B.S.P. *Old Bailey Sessions Papers*

Obst. Oboist (mus.)

obstet. obstetric; obstetrical; obstetrician; obstetrics

obt. obedient

O.B.T.A. Oak Bark Tanners' Association

obtd. obtained

O.B.U. Oriental Boxing Union

O. Bul. Old Bulgarian

obv. obverse

O.B.V. ocean boarding vessel

o'c o'clock, of the clock

o/c, o.c. overcharge

OC *s* Birmingham (B.V.R.); operating characteristic

oc. ocean

O/c. old charter/crop

o.c. odour control; office copy; official classification; on centre; only child; open charter/cover; over the counter

o.c. L. *opere citato*, in the work cited

O.C. Observer Corps; Office of Censorship (U.S.A.); officer commanding; officer of the Order of Canada; Old Carthusian / Catholic / Cheltonian / Comrade; Order in Council, proclaimed by Brit. monarch on advice of Privy Council. With transfer of power to Parliament from the Crown their scope has been reduced; Order of Carmelites; Order of the Coif; Orienteering Club; Oslo/Ottawa Convention; overseas command

O.C. L. *Ordo Charitatis*, Order of Charity; L. *Ordo Cisterciensis*, Cistercian Order; It. *Organo corale*, Choir Organ (mus.)

O. & C. onset and course, of a disease (med.)

oca. *ocarina* (mus.)

O.C.A. Old Comrades Association

OCAM. *Organisation commune africaine et malgache*, Joint African and Malagasy Organization

OCAMA Oklahoma City Air Materiel Area

O. Carm. Order of Carmelites

O. Cart. Order of Carthusians

O.C.A.S. Organization of Central American States

O. Catal. Old Catalan

Oc. B/L. ocean bill of lading

occ. occasion (*also* occn.); occasional; occident; occidental; occupation; occurrence

O.C.C.A. Oil and Colour Chemists' Association

occas. occasion; occasional

OCCC Oil Control Co-ordination Committee (U.S.A.)

OCD on line communications driver (computer)

264

O.C.D. Office of Civil Defense (U.S.A.); L. *Ordinis Carmelitarum Discalceatorum*, Order of Discalced Carmelites

O.C.D.E. Fr. *Organisation de coopération et de développement économiques*, Organisation for Economic Co-operation and Development

OCDM Office of Civil Defense Mobilization (U.S.A.)

O/Cdt. officer-cadet

OCE Office of the Chief of Engineers (U.S.A.)

oceanog. oceanography

O.C.E.L. *Oxford Companion to English Literature*

O. Celt. Old Celtic

O.C.F. Officiating Chaplain to the Forces

O.C.F.R. Oxford Committee for Famine Relief

och. ochre

O.C.I.C. Fr. *Office catholique international du cinéma*, Intern. Catholic Film Office

O. Cist. L. *Ordinis Cisterciensis*, (of the) Cistercian Order

O.C.M. *Oxford Companion to Music*

OCMA Oil Companies' Material Association

O.C.M.I. Fr. *Organisation consultative maritime inter-gouvernementale*, Inter-Governmental Maritime Consultative Organisation

OCONUS Outside Continental United States

OCORA *Office de Coöpération Radiophonique* (Dahomey/Mali)

O. Corn. Old Cornish

OCR optical character reader (computer)

O.C.R. Office for Civilian Requirements (U.S.A.); Officer of the Order of the Crown of Romania; Order of Corporate Reunion

O.C.R. L. *Ordinis Cisterciensium Reformatorum*, (of the) Order of Reformed Cistercians (Trappists), *also* O.C.S.O.

OCRA *Organisation Clandestine de la Révolution Algérienne*, Secret Organization of the Algerian Revolution

OCRD Office, Chief of Research and Development (U.S.A.)

OCS Officer Candidate School (U.S.A.)

O.C.S. Fr. *Organe de contrôle des stupéfiants*, Drug Supervisory Body

OCSA Office, Chief of Staff, Army (U.S.A.)

OCSigO Office, Chief Signal Officer (U.S.A.)

O.C.S.O. *Ordinis Cisterciensium Stric-* *tionis Observantiae*, (of the) Order of Cistercians of the Strict Observance (Trappists), *also* O.C.R.

ocst. overcast

oct. octavo

oct. octave (mus.)

Oct. Octavius; October

O.C.T. Associated Overseas Countries and Territories (EEC)

O.C.T.I. Fr. *Office central des transports internationaux par chemins de fer*, Central Office for Intern. Railway Transport

oct. pars. L. *octava pars*, an eighth part (med.)

O.C.T.U. Officer Cadet Training Unit

octupl. octuplicate

O.C.U.C. Oxford and Cambridge Universities' Club

ocul. L. *oculis*, to the eyes

OD *s* Devon (B.V.R.); *s* Lebanon (I.C.A.M.)

O/D on demand; overdraft; overdrawn

od. Ger. *oder*, or

Od. Odyssey

o.d. olive drab; on demand; optical density; outside diameter

O.D. Doctor of Ophthalmology/Optometry/Osteopathy; officer of the day; Old Danish (*also* O. Dan.); Old Dutch; operations division; ordnance data/department/depot

ODA Overseas Development Administration

O.D.Ch. chaplain for other denominations

O.D.E.C.A. Sp. *Organización de Estados Centroamericanos*, Organisation of Central American States

ODECO Ocean Drilling and Exploration Company

O.D.E.E. *Oxford Dictionary of English Etymology*

O.D.E.P. *Oxford Dictionary of English Proverbs*

O.D.E.S.S.A. Ocean Data Environmental Sciences Services Acquisition

O.d.G. It. *Ordine del giorno*, order of the day

O.D.I. Open Door International (for the Economic Emancipation of the Woman Worker)

ODM Office of Defense Mobilization (U.S.A.)

O.D.O. outdoor officer (customs)

O.D.P. office development permit; official development planning; open door policy; orbit determination programme (space); overall development planning

O. Ds. other denominations

O.D.S. Ocean Data Station

O.D.V. Fr. *Eau de Vie*, cognac

Oe *s* oersted, unit of magnetic force named after Hans Christian Oersted (1777–1851), Dan. physicist

OE *s* Austria (I.C.A.M.); *s* Birmingham (B.V.R.)

o.e. open end

O.E. Office of Education (U.S.A.); Old English; Old Etonian; omissions excepted; original equipment/error; other essays

O.E. It. *Organo espressivo*, swell organ (mus.)

O. & E. operations and engineering

O.E.A. Fr. *Organisation des états américains*, Organisation of American States; Outdoor/Overseas Education Association

Ö.E.C. *Österreichischer Aero Club*, Austrian Aero Club

O.E.C.D. Organization for Economic Co-operation and Development, *formerly* **O.E.E.C.**

O.E.C.E. Fr. *Organisation européenne de coopération économique*, Organisation for European Economic Co-operation

o.e.c.o. outboard engine cut off

OECON Offshore Exploration Conference (U.S.A.)

O.E.C.Q. Fr. *Organisation européenne pour le contrôle de la qualité*, European Organisation for Quality Control

O.E.D. *Oxford English Dictionary*

O.E.E.C. Organization for European Economic Co-operation, *now* O.E.C.D.

O.E.F. Organisation of Employers' Federations and Employers in Developing Countries; Osteopathic Educational Foundation

O.E.G. Operations Evaluation Group

O.E.I. Sp. *Oficina de Educación Iberoamericana*, Ibero-American Bureau of Education

O.E.I.U. Office Employees International Union

OEM original equipment manufacturer

OEO Office of Economic Opportunity (U.S.A.)

O.E.O. Ordnance Engineer Overseer

OEP Office of Emergency Planning

O.E.P.P. Fr. *Organisation européenne et méditerranéenne pour la protection des plantes*, European and Mediterranean Plant Protection Organisation

o'er over

O.E.R. Officers' Emergency Reserve; Organization for European Research

OERC optimum earth re-entry corridor (space)

OERS Organization of Senegal River States, Guinea, Mali, Mauritania and Senegal

O.E.R.S. Fr. *Organisation européenne de recherches spatiales*, European Space Research Organisation

O.E.S. Order of the Eastern Star; Organization of European States

OESBR oil-extended styrene/butadiene rubber

OET Office of Education and Training

OEW Office of Economic Warfare

OEX Office of Educational Exchange

OEZ Ger. *osteuropäische Zeit*, East German Time

OF *s* Birmingham (B.V.R.)

o.f. oil fired; optional form; outside face; oxidizing flame

O.F. oceanographic facility; Odd Fellows; old-face type (typ.); Old French; operating/operational forces

O Factor oscillation factor (psy.)

O.F.C. Overseas Food Corporation

OFCA Ontario Federation of Construction Associations (Can.)

O.F.E.M.A. Fr. *Office Français d'Exportation de Matériel Aéronautique*, French Office for the Export of Aeronautical Material

off. offer; office; officer (*also* offr.); official (*also* offcl.); It. *officina*, workshop/shop

offg. offering; officiating

offic. official; officially

Oflag Ger. *Offizierelager*, officers' camp, prisoners-of-war

O. Flem. Old Flemish

O.F.M. Order of Friars Minor; — **Cap.** Order of Friars Minor Capuchin; — **Conv.** Order of Friars Minor Conventual (Franciscans)

O. Fr. Old French

O. Fris. Old Frisian

O. Frk. Old Frankish

O.F.S. Orange Free State

OFST Office of the Secretary of the Air Force (U.S.A.)

OG *s* Birmingham (B.V.R.)

O.G. Officer of the Guard; ogee, a moulding (arch.); Olympic Games; original gum (philately); outside guard

O. Gael. Old Gaelic

ÖGB Ger. *Österreichischer Gewerkschaftsbund*, Austrian Fed. of Trade Unions

o.g.e. operational ground equipment

OGG Orchard Grubbing Grant

ogg. It. *oggetto*, object

O.G.M. ordinary general meeting

O.G.O. Orbiting Geophysical Observatory

Ogpu., O.G.P.U. *Obedinénnoe Gosud-*

árstvennoe Politicheskoe Upravlyénie, United State Political Admin. (U.S.S.R.)

O.G.S. Oratory of the Good Shepherd

OH *s* Birmingham (B.V.R.); *s* Finland (I.C.A.M.); Ohio (U.S.A.); old head, Victoria (numis.)

o.h. observation helicopter; office hours; on hand; open hearth

o.h. L. *omni hora*, hourly (med.)

O/H. Dutch *Overzuche Handelsmaatschappij*, foreign trade co.

O.H.B.M.S. On Her/His Britannic Majesty's Service

OHC overhead cam/camshaft

O.H.D. organic heart disease

OHDETS over-horizon detection system

O.H.E. Office of Health Economics

OHG *Offene Handelsgesellschaft*, ordinary partnership (Ger.)

O.H.G. Old High German

ohm. ohmmeter; — **cm.** ohm centimetre

O.H.M.S. On Her/His Majesty's Service

O.H.S. open hearth steel; Oxford Historical Society

OHV overhead valve/vent

OI *s* Belfast (B.V.R.)

O.I. office/operating instruction; Old Irish

O.I.A. Oceanic Industries Association (U.S.A.); Oil Import Association (U.S.A.)

O.I.A.B. Oil Import Appeals Board (U.S.A.)

O.i/c. officer in charge

O.I.C. Fr. *Organisation interafricaine du café*, Inter-African Coffee Organization; Fr. *Organisation internationale du commerce*, Intern. Trade Organization

O. Icel. Old Icelandic

O.I.C.I. Sp. *Organizaçión Interamericana de Cooperación Intermunicipal*, Inter-American Municipal Organization

O.I.E. Fr. *Office international des épizooties*, Intern. Office of Epizootics; Fr. *Organisation internationale des employeurs*, Intern. Organization of Employers

O.I.E.C. Fr. *Office international de l'enseignement catholique*, Catholic Intern. Education Office

O.I.G. Fr. *Organisation intergouvernementale*, Inter-Governmental Organization

O.I.J. Fr. *Organisation internationale des journalistes*, Intern. Organization of Journalists

OIL Orbiting International Laboratory

oilies oilskin coats

O.I.N.G. Fr. *Organisation internationale non gouvernementale*, Intern. Non-Governmental Organisation

OIP operations improvement programme

O.I.P. Oxford India Paper

O.I.P.C. Fr. *Organisation internationale de police criminelle*, Intern. Criminal Police Organisation (Interpol); Fr. *Organisation internationale de protection civile*, Intern. Civil Defence Organisation

O.I.P.H. Office of International Public Health

O. Ir. Old Irish

O.I.R.T. Fr. *Organisation internationale de radiodiffusion et télévision*, Intern. Radio and Television Organisation

O.I.S. organiser industrial safety

O.I.S.S. Fr. *Organisation ibéro-américaine de sécurité sociale*, Ibero-American Social Security Organisation

O.I.S.T.V. Fr. *Organisation internationale pour la science et la technique du vide*, Intern. Organisation for Vacuum Science and Technology

O. It. Old Italian

O.I.T. Fr. *Organisation internationale du travail*, Intern. Labour Organisation

O.I.V.V. Fr. *Office international de la vigne et du vin*, Intern. Vine and Wine Office

OJ *s* Birmingham (B.V.R.)

o.j. open joint/joist; orange juice

O.J.A.J. October, January, April, July

O.J.R. old Jamaica rum

o.j.t. on job training

OK *s* Birmingham (B.V.R.); *s* Czechoslovakia (I.C.A.M.); Oklahoma (U.S.A.)

o.K. Ger. *ohne Kosten*, without cost

O.K. all correct/orl k'rect/okay

o.k.a. otherwise known as

Okla. Oklahoma (U.S.A.)

Okt. Ger. *Oktober*, October

OKW *Oberkommando der Wehrmacht*, German Military High Command, WW2

OL *s* Birmingham (B.V.R.)

ol. oil; olive

Ol. Olympiad, period of 4 years between celebrations of the Olympic Games, beginning 776 B.C.; Olympic

o.l. overflow level; overhead line

O.L. Officer of the Order of Leopold; oil lighter; Old Latin; ordnance lieutenant; outside left (sport)

OLAS Organisation of Latin American Solidarity (Cuba)

OLBM orbital launched ballistic missile

OLC oak leaf cluster (mil. award); on-line computer

O.L.Cr. Ordnance Lieutenant-Commander

old-fash. old-fashioned

Old Test. Old Testament (Bible)

oleo. oleomargarine; oleum

O-level Ordinary level examinations of General Certificate of Education

O.L.G. Old Low German

O-licence operators' licence

OLIVER on-line instrumentation via energetic radioisotopes

Ollie, Olly Oliver

O.L.M.R. organic liquid moderated reactor

O.L.Q. officer-like qualities

OLRT on-line real time (computer)

Olym. Olympia, in the Peloponnese, scene of quadrennial Olympic Games

OM s Birmingham (B.V.R.); Order of Merit, founded 1902

O & M organization and method

Om. Sultanate of Oman

o.m. old measurement

o.m. L. *omni mane*, every morning (med.)

O.M. old man; old measurement; Order of Merit; ordnance map

O.M. L. *Optimus Maximus*, greatest and best, title given by Romans to Jupiter as king of gods

O.M.A. Overall Manufacturers' Association of Great Britain

O.M.A.I. Fr. *Organisation mondiale Agudas Israel*, Agudas Israel World Organization

omarb. Swed. *omarbetad*, revised

O.M.C.I. Fr. *Organisation intergouvernementale consultative de la navigation maritime*, Inter-Governmental Maritime Consultative Organization

O.M.E. ordnance mechanical engineer

O.M.E.P. Fr. *Organisation mondiale pour l'éducation préscolaire*, World Organization for Early Childhood Education

O.M.G.E. Fr. *Organisation mondiale de gastroentérologie*, World Organization of Gastroenterology

O.M.I. Oblates of Mary Immaculate

O.M.M. Fr. *Officier de l'Ordre du Mérite Militaire*, Officer of the Order of Military Merit (Can.); Fr. *Organisation météorologique mondiale*, World Meteorological Organisation

omn. bid. L. *omnibus bidendis*, every two days (med.)

omn. bih. L. *omni bihora*, every two hours (med.)

omn. hor. L. *omni hora*, every hour (med.)

omn. noct. L. *omni nocte*, every night (med.)

omn. quad. hor. L. *omni quadrante hora*, every quarter of an hour (med.)

OMPA octamethyl pyrophosphoramide

O.M.P.S.A. Fr. *Organisation mondiale pour la protection sociale des aveugles*, World Council for the Welfare of the Blind

o.m.s. output per man shift

O.M.S. Fr. *Organisation mondiale de la santé*, World Health Organization

OMSF office of manned space flight (NASA)

O.M.T. Old Merchant Taylors'

OMTS Organizational Maintenance Test Station (U.S.A.)

ON s Birmingham (B.V.R.)

On. It. *Onorevole*, Honorable

o.n. L. *omni nocte*, every night (med.)

O.N. octane number; Old Norse; orthopaedic nurse

Ö.N. *Österreichische Nationalbibliotek*, Austrian Nat. Library

ONA optical navigation attachment

on appro on approval

O.N.C. Ordinary National Certificate; Orthopaedic Nursing Certificate

O.N.D. Ophthalmic Nursing Diploma; Ordinary National Diploma

O.N.F. Old Northern French

o.n.f.m. on/nearest full moon (freem.)

O.N.G. Fr. *Organisation non-gouvernementale*, Non-Governmental Organization

ONI Office of Naval Intelligence

ONM Office of Naval Material

o.n.n.m. on/nearest new moon (freem.)

o.n.o. or near offer

onomat. onomatopoeia; onomatopoeical; onomatopoeian; onomatopoeic

O. Norm. Fr. Old Norman French

O. North. Old Northumbrian

O. Norw. Old Norwegian

O.N.R. Office of Naval Research (U.S.A.); Official Naval Reporter

ONSS Central National Office of Social Security (Belg.)

Ont. Ontario (Can.)

o.n.t. ordinary neap tide

O.N.U. Fr. *Organisation des Nations Unies*, United Nations Organization; Port. *Organização das Nacões Unidas*, United Nations Organization

O.N.U.C. Fr. *Opération des Nations Unies au Congo*, United Nations Operation in the Congo

ONWARD Organization of the North Western Authorities Rationalized Design

% per cent; percentage

OO s Belgium (I.C.A.M.); s Essex (B.V.R.)

o/o. on order; order of

O.O. observation officer; Office of Oceanography (UNESCO); operation order; orderly officer; Order of Owls; own occupation

O.O.D. officer of the day/deck

O.O.G. officer of the guard

O/OO, %° per mille

o/o/o out of order

O.O.Q. officer of the quarters

OOR Office of Ordnance Research (U.S.A.)

007, oh-oh-seven code name of James Bond in Ian Fleming's novels

Ooty. Ootacamund, Madras (India)

OO/USA Out of stock but on order from (e.g.) U.S.A.

O.O.W. officer of the watch

OP *s* Birmingham (B.V.R.)

op. opaque; opera; operation; operator; opinion; opposite; optime, one next in merit to wranglers (Cambridge Univ.)

op. L. *opera*, works; L. *optimus*, excellent; L. *opus*, work

o.p. observation post; old/open pattern; opposite prompter's side/actor's right (theatre); order/original policy

O.P. Old Persian; Old Playgoers; old prices; open policy (insce.); other people's; out of print, title discontinued and as far as is known will not be reprinted; over proof, in industrial alcohol strength figures

O.P. L. *Ordinis Praedicatorum*, of the Order of Preachers (Dominicans)

OPA optical plotting attachment

O.P.A. Office of Price Administration (U.S.A.)

OPAL optical platform alignment linkage

O.P.C. ordinary Portland cement; outpatients' clinic; Overseas Press Club of America

op. cit. L. *opere citato*, in the work cited

O.P.D. outpatients' department

OPDAR optical detection and ranging

OPEC, O.P.E.C. Organization of Petroleum Exporting Countries

O.P.E.G. O.E.E.C. Petroleum Emergency Group

O.P.E.P. Fr. *Organisations des pays exportateurs de pétrole*, Organization of Petroleum Exporting Countries

O. Per. Old Persian

OPEX operational, executive and administrative personnel (U.N.O.)

opg. opening

O. Pg. Old Portuguese

O.P.G. Overseas Project Group (BoT)

ophth., ophthal. ophthalmic; ophthalmologist; ophthalmology

O. Pip. observation post

opl. operational; Dan. *oplag*, edition

O.P.M. office of production management (U.S.A.)

O.P.M.A.C. operation for military aid to the community

O.P.M.A.C.C. operation military aid to the civilian community

opn. operation; opinion; option

o.p.n. L. *ora pro nobis*, pray for us

O. Pol. Old Polish

opp. opportunity; oppose; opposite; opposition

O.P.P. out of print at present

oppy. opportunity

opr. operate; operator

O.P. Riots Old Prices Riots (1809) against raising prices at theatres

O. Prov. Old Provençal

O. Pruss. Old Prussian

ops. operations

O.P.S. Fr. *Organisation panaméricaine de la santé*, Pan-American Health Organization

opt. optative; optical; optician; optics; optimal; optimum; option; optional

Opt. D. Doctor of Optometry

OPTEVFOR operational test and evaluation force (USN)

OPUR objective program utility routines (computer)

OR *s* Hampshire (B.V.R.); Oregon (U.S.A.)

or. other

or. *oratorio*, a vocal work with some kind of instrumental accompaniment, usually founded on a Biblical subject (mus.)

Or. Oregon (U.S.A.); Oriel College, Oxford Univ., founded 1326; orient; oriental; orientalist; original

o.r. operational requirement; operationally risky; operations requirement/room; out of range; overhaul and repair; owner's risk

O.R. official receiver; official referee; Old Roman; operational/operations research; orderly room; other ranks (mil.); outside right (sport)

Ö.R. Ger. *Österreichischer Rundfunk*, Austrian Radio and Television

O.R.A.P. Fr. *Organisation régionale de l'Orient pour l'administration publique*, Eastern Regional Organization for Public Admin.

orat. oration; orator; oratorical; oratory

Orat. *Oratorio*, a vocal work with some kind of instrumental accompaniment, usually founded on a Biblical subject (mus.)

o.r.b. owner's risk of breakage

O.R.B. oceanographic research buoy
ORBIS orbiting radio beacon ionospheric satellite
ORBIT on-line retrieval of bibliographic information
O.R.C. Orange River Colony, *now* O.F.S.; Order of the Red Cross; Overseas Research Council; owner's risk of chafing
O.R.C.A. Ocean Resources Conservation Association
orch. orchestra; *orchestral*; *orchestrate*; *orchestration* (mus.)
orcon. organic control
ORD once-run distillate
ord. ordain; order; ordinal; ordinance; ordinary; ordnance
o.r.d. owner's risk of damage
Ord. Bd. Ordnance Board
Ord. Dept. ordnance department (U.S.A.)
ordn. ordnance
Ord. Sgt. ordnance sergeant
Ore., Oreg. Oregon (U.S.A.)
O.R.E. Office for Research and Experiments of the International Union of Railways; Fr. *Organisation régionale européenne de la Confédération internationale des syndicats libres*, European Regional Organisation of the Intern. Confed. of Free Trade Unions
O.R.E.A.M. Fr. *Organisation d'Études d'Aires Métropolitaines*, Organization for Studies of Metropolitan Areas
ORESCO Overseas Research Council
o.r.f. owner's risk of fire
Or. F.S. Orange Free State (S. Afr.)
org. organ; organic; organism; organization; organize
org. organ; *organist* (mus.)
O.R.G. Operations Research Group
ORGALIME Fr. *Organisme de liaison des industries métalliques européennes*, Liaison Group for the European Metal Industries
organ. organic; organization, *also* orgzn.
Orgst. Organist (mus.)
ORI Ocean Research Institute (Jap.)
Orient. oriental; orientalist
orig. origin; original; originally; originate
O.R.I.T. Sp. *Organización Regional Inter-americana de Trabajadores*, Inter-American Regional Organization of Workers of the Intern. Confed. of Free Trade Unions
Ork., Orkn. Orkney Islands
o.r.l. owner's risk of leakage
orn. ornament; ornithology, *also* ornith.
ORNL Oak Ridge National Laboratory (U.S.A.)
orph. orphan; orphanage

o.r.r. owner's risk rates
O-RS organizer road safety
ors. others
ORSA Operations Research Society of America
orse. otherwise
O.R.S.T.O.M. Fr. *Office de la Recherche Scientifique et Technique d'Outre-Mer*, Overseas Office of Scientific and Technical Research
O.R.T. Organization for Rehabilitation by Training
ORTF *Office de Radiodiffusion et Télévision Française*, French Radio and Television Office
orth. orthography; orthopaedic; orthopaedics
O.R.T.P.A. Oven-Ready Turkey Producers' Association
O.R.T.U. other ranks training unit
O. Russ. Old Russian
o/s on sale; out of service/stock; outsize; outstanding
Os *s* osmium (chem.)
OS *s* Wigtownshire (B.V.R.)
o.s. ocean station; oil switch; only son; on spot; on station; outside (measurement)
o.s. L. *oculus sinister*, left eye
O.S. Old Saxon; old school/series/ side; Old Style, before 1752; ordinary seaman; Ordnance Survey; output secondary
OSA Office of the Secretary of the Army (U.S.A.)
O.S.A. Official Secrets Act; old style antique; Optical Society of America; Overseas Sterling Area
O.S.A. L. *Ordinis Sancti Augustini*, (of the) Order of St. Augustine
OSAF Office of the Secretary of the Air Force (U.S.A.)
O.S.A.S. Overseas Service Aid Scheme
O. Sax. Old Saxon
OSB *Occupational Safety Bulletin*, RoSPA
O.S.B. L. *Ordinis Sancti Benedicti*, (of the) Order of St. Benedict
O.S.B.M. L. *Ordo Sancti Basilii Magni*, Order of Saint Basil the Great
osc. oscillate; oscillator
O.S.C. Old Water Colour Society's Club; Order of Saint Charles
O.S.Cam. Order of Saint Camillus
O. Scan., O. Scand. Old Scandinavian
O.S.C.A.R. Orbital Satellite Carrying Amateur Radio; Oxygen Steel-making Computer and Recorder
OSD Office of the Secretary of Defense (U.S.A.); on-line systems driver (computer)

O.S.D. Order of St. Dominic; Ordnance Survey Department

o'seas overseas

O. Serb. Old Serbian

O.S.F. L. *Ordinis Sancti Francisci*, (of the) Order of St. Francis

O.S.F.S. Oblates of Saint Francis of Sales

o/sg. outstanding

o.s.h. L. *omni singula hora*, every hour

OSI Office of Special Investigation (USAF)

O.S.J. Oblates of Saint Joseph; Order of Saint Jerome (Hieronymites)

O.S.J.D. L. *Ordo Hospitalarius Sancti Joannis de Deo*, Order of Brothers Hospitallers of Saint John of God

Osl. Oslo (Nor.)

O. Sl., O. Slav. Old Slavonic

O.S.L. Old Style Latin; ordnance sub-lieutenant

O.S.M. Order of the Servants of Mary (Servites)

OSN Office of the Secretary of the Navy (U.S.A.)

O.S.N.C. Orient Steam Navigation Company

OSO orbiting solar observatory

osp outside purchase

O. Sp. Old Spanish

o.s.p. L. *obiit sine prole*, died without issue

O.S.P. Order of Saint Paul

O.S.P.A. Fr. *Organisation de la Santé Panaméricaine*, Pan-American Health Organisation; Overseas Service Pensioners' Association

OSR Office of Scientific Research (U.S.A.); Office of Security Review (U.S.A.)

O.S.R. Old Style Roman; *Orchestre de la Suisse Romande*, Orchestra of French Switzerland

O.S.R.B. Overseas Service Resettlement Bureau

O.S.R.D. Office of Scientific Research and Development (U.S.A.)

OSRP Offices, Shops and Railway Premises Act 1963

OSS Office of Space Sciences (NASA)

o.s.s. orbiting space station

O.S.S. Office of Strategic Services (U.S.A.)

O.SS.T. L. *Ordo Sanctissimae Trinitatis Redemptionis Captivorum*, Order of the Most Holy Trinity for the Ransom of Prisoners (Trinitarians)

Öst. Ger. *Österreich*, Austria

o.s.t. ordinary spring tides

osteo. osteopath; osteopathic; osteopathy

O.S.T.I. Office/Organization for Scientific and Technical Information; Organization for Social and Technological Innovation (U.S.A.)

O.S.T.I.V. Fr. *Organisation scientifique et technique internationale du vol à voile*, Intern. Technical and Scientific Organisation for Soaring Flight

O. St. J. Officer of the Order of Saint John of Jerusalem

O.S.T.S. official seed testing station

O.S.U. Order of St. Ursula

O.S.U.K. Ophthalmological Society of the United Kingdom

o.s.v. Swed. *och sa vidare*, and so forth

O.S.V. ocean station vessel

Osv. Rom. *Osservatore Romano*, semi-official newspaper of Vatican City State, founded 1860

Osw. Oswald

O. Sw. Old Swedish

OT *s* Hampshire (B.V.R.)

O/t. Old term

O.T. occupational therapist/therapy; ocean transportation; off time; Old Testament (Bible); Old Teutonic; Olympic Trench, form of competitive clay pigeon shooting; overseas trade; overtime

O.T.A. Fr. *Organisation mondiale du tourisme et de l'automobile*, World Touring and Automobile Organisation

OTAC ordnance tank and automotive command

O.T.A.N. Fr. *Organisation du traité de l'Atlantique nord*, North Atlantic Treaty Organisation; Port. *Organização do Tratado do Atlântico Norte*, North Atlantic Treaty Organisation

O.T.A.S.E. Fr. *Organisation du traité de défense collective pour l'Asie du sud-est*, South-East Asia Treaty Organisation

otbd. outboard

o.t.c. over the counter

O.T.C. officer in tactical command (U.S.A.); Officers' Training Corps; Officers' Transit Camp

O. Teut. Old Teutonic

Oth. *Othello* (Shake.)

OTK Co-operative Wholesale Society (Finland)

O.T.M. Old Turkey Mill (paper)

otol. otological; otology

OTO/Lux only to order from (e.g.) Luxembourg

O.T.S. Office of Technical Services; Officers' Training School

Ott. Ottawa (Can.); It. *ottobre*, October

Ott. It. *Ottava*, octave (mus.)

O.T.U. Office of Technology Utilization (NASA); operational training unit

O. Turk. Old Turkish

OU s Hampshire (B.V.R.); oat unit
O.U. official use; Open/Oxford University
O.U. Oxford University; — **A.C.** Appointments Committee; Athletic Club; — **A.F.C.** Association Football Club; — **A.S.** Air Squadron; — **B.C.** Boat Club; — **C.C.** Cricket Club; — **D.S.** Dramatic Society; — **G.C.** Golf Club; — **H.C.** Hockey Club; — **H.S.** Historical Society; — **L.C.** Lacrosse Club; — **L.T.C** Lawn Tennis Club; — **M.** Mission; — **P.** Press; — **R.C.** Rifle Club; — **R.F.C.** Rugby Football Club; — **S.C.** Swimming Club
O.U.A. Order of United Americans
O.U.A.M. Order of United American Mechanics
out. outlet
outbd. outboard
OV s Birmingham (B.V.R.)
ov. ovary; over; overture
Ov. P. Ovidius Naso, Ovid (43 B.C.– A.D. 17), Lat. poet
o.v. observed velocity; orbiting vehicle
Ova It. *Ottava*, octave (mus.)
O.V.A.C. Overseas Visual Aids Centre
ovbd. overboard
ovc other valuable consideration; overcast, *also* ovct.
ovfl. overflow
OVH overhead projector
ovhd. overhead
ovld. overload
Ö.V.P. Ger. *Österreichische Volkspartei*, Austrian People's Party
ovpd. overpaid
Ovra *Opera di vigilanza e di repressione dell'anti-fascismo*, secret police of the Fascist regime (Italy)
ovrd. override
ovsp. overspeed
OW s Southampton (B.V.R.)
o.w. old woman; one way; ordinary warfare; out of wedlock
o.W. Ger. *ohne Wert*, without value

ö.W. Ger. *österreichische Währung*, Austrian currency
O/W. Oil in Water
O.W. Office of Works; Old Welsh
O.W. Ger. *Oberwerk*, swell organ (mus.)
O.W.A.E.C. Organization for West African Economic Co-operation
OWC ordnance weapons command
o.w.f. on fibre weight
O.W.F. optimum working frequency
O.W.I. Office of War Information (U.S.A.)
O.W.R.R. Office of Water Resources Research (U.S.A.)
O.W.S. ocean weather service/ship/ station; Old Water-colour Society
OX s Birmingham (B.V.R.)
Ox., Oxf., Oxon. Oxford
Oxbridge from Oxford-Cambridge, expression used to describe the classical type of university; newer univs. described as 'Redbrick' and recent univs. as 'Plateglass'
oxer ox-fence
Oxf., Oxon. Oxfordshire
OXFAM, OxFAM Oxford Committee for Famine Relief
Oxf. & Bucks. Oxfordshire and Buckinghamshire Light Infantry
Oxon. *Oxonia*, signature of Bp. of Oxford
Oxon. L. *Oxonia*, Oxford; L. *Oxoniensis*, of Oxford/Oxford Univ.
OY s Denmark (I.C.A.M.); s London (B.V.R.)
O/Y *Osakeytio*, Finnish limited company
oys. oysters
OZ s Belfast (B.V.R.)
Oz., oz. ounce
oz. ap. apothecaries' ounce
oz. av., oz. avdp. avoirdupois ounce
OZONE International Bureau of Atmospheric Ozone
oz. t. troy ounce

P

p *s* absolute humidity; *s* fluid density; *s* momentum (phys.); pico, 10^{-12} (phys.)

p- *s* para- (chem.)

P medieval Roman numeral for 400; *s* parity (phys.); park (car); pawn (chess); pedestrian (crossing); *s* phosphorus (chem.); *s* Portsmouth (B.F.P.); Portugal, including Angola, Cape Verde Islands, Mozambique, Portuguese Guinea, Portuguese Timor, São Tomé, and Princípe (I.V.R.); Post Office (cartog.); *s* pressure (phys.); Surrey (B.V.R.)

P₁ parental generation (biol.)

p. page; pamphlet; paragraph; park; parking; part; particle; participle; pass; Fr. *passé*, past; passed; passing showers (naut.); past; pawn; peak; pectoral (ichth.); penny; per; perch; percussion; peseta (Sp. currency); peso (currency); piastre (currency); Fr. *pied*, foot; pint; pipe; pitcher; plaster; Sp./It. *poco*, little; polar; pole; population; port; Fr. *pouce*, inch; Fr. *pour*, for; power; president; pressure (mech.); pro; professional (*also* pro.); proton; purl; squalls (met.)

p. L. *partim*, in part; L. *per*, by/for; It. *piano*, soft (mus.); L. *pius*, holy; L. *pondere*, by weight; L. *post*, after; L. *primus*, first; L. *pro*, for

P. pale; Paris (France); park; parson; pastor; Fr. *Père*, Father, if member of a rel. order or congregation; perennial; period; person; personnel; pipe; pitch; Portugal; positive; post; postage; posterior, baby's head facing backwards in labour (med.); Presbyterian; priest; prince; privy, lavatory; probate; probation; pro-

consul; progressive; protestant; public; pupil

P. L. *Papa*, Pope; L. *Pater*, Father; *Pedal* (mus.); *Percussion* (mus.); L. *pontifex*, a bishop; L. *populus*, people; Fr. *Positif*, choir organ (mus.)

¶ fifth reference mark for footnotes in math. works; reversed/blind P, paragraph mark to indicate commencement of new paragraph (typ.)

⅌ per, by/for

pa papa

p/a personal account

Pa *s* protoactinium (chem.)

PA *s* Panama (I.V.R.); Pennsylvania, *also* Pa. (U.S.A.); personal accident (insce.); polyamide (nylon); *s* Surrey (B.V.R.)

P/A power of attorney

p/a. put away

p.a. Fr. *par amitié*, by favour; Fr. *par avion*, by air; participial adjective; permanent address; personal appearance; Fr. *poids atomique*, atomic weight; power amplifier; Fr. *progression arithmétique*, arithmetical progression

p.a. L. *per abdomen*, by abdomen (med.); L. *per annum*, yearly

p.A. Ger. *per Adresse*, care of; Sp. *por autorización*, by authority of

P/A. private account (book-keeping)

P.A. Paintmakers' Association of Great Britain; Pakistan Army; particular average, *also* P/Av. (insce.); Patients' Association, represents interests of patients both in and out of hospital; Personal Allowance (tax.); personal assistant; please apply (med.); post adjutant; Prefect Apostolic; Press Agent/Association/ Attaché; product analysis; prosecuting attorney; provisional allowance; public accountant/analyst; public address system; Publishers' Association; purchasing agent

P. & A. Pastoral and Agricultural Society

p.a.a. L. *parti affectae applicetur*, let it be applied to the affected region (med.)

P.A.A. Pan American Airways Inc.; Paper Agents' Association; per acetic acid (chem.); Phonetic Alphabet Association; polyacrylic acid (chem.); Purchasing Agents' Association

PAAA Premium Advertising Association of America

PAAC program analysis adaptable control (U.S.A.)

P.A.A.D.C. principal air aide-de-camp

P.A.B.X. Private Automatic Branch Exchange (telephone)

PAC Pacific Air Command (USAF); Pan-Africanist Congress (S. Afr.); public accounts committee

Pac. Pacific

p.a.c. passed final examination of the advanced class (mil.)

P.A.C. Pan-African Congress; Pan-American Congress; Political Action Committee (U.S.A.); Public Assistance Committee

PACAF Pacific Air Forces (USAF)

PACB Pan-American Coffee Bureau

PACCS Post Attack Command and Control System (ESD)

PACE performance and cost evaluation

P.A.C.E. Precision Analogue Computing Equipment

Pacif. Pacific

PACOM Pacific Command (U.S.A./ USN/USAF)

PACS Pacific area communications system

PACT Production Analysis Control Technique (USN)

pad. padding; padlock

P.A.D. passive air defence; payable after death

PADAR passive detection and ranging

Paddy Patricia; Patrick

PADLOC passive detection and location of countermeasures (USAF)

p. Adr. Ger. *per Adresse*, care of

p.ae. L. *partes aequales*, equal parts

P.A.E.C. Pakistan/Philippines Atomic Energy Commission

PAF peripheral address field

p.a.f. Fr. *puissance au frein*, brake-horsepower

PAFMECA Pan-American Freedom Movement of East and Central Africa

pag. It. *pagina*, page

pág. Port./Sp. *página*, page

PAGB Proprietary Association of Great Britain

P.A.G.C. port area grain committee

P.A.H.O. Pan-American Health Organisation (OAS)

P.A.I.G.H. Pan-American Institute of Geography and History of OAS (Mex.)

paint. painter; painting

PAK Pakistan (I.V.R.); *Panellinion Apeleftherotikon Kinima*, Panhellenic Liberation Movement, formed in Feb. 1968 by Andreas Papandreou, and based Stockholm. PAK purports to 'co-ordinate resistance activities' within Greece as well as campaigning abroad for restoration of genuinely democratic government (Greece)

Pak. Pakistan; Pakistani

Pakistan Name originated in the 1930s based on first letters of the western provinces in former British India with Muslim majority, Punjab, *A*fghania (N. W. Frontier), and *K*ashmir, with suffix taken from Baluch*istan*

PAL peripheral availability list (computer); phase alternation line (T.V.); Philippine Air Lines

Pal. Palace; palaeology (*also* palaeo.); palaeontology (*also* palaeo.); Palestine

palaeob. palaeobotanical; palaeobotany

palaeog. palaeographical; palaeography

palaeont. palaeontology

Palm. palmistry

PALS permissive action link systems

Pam Pamela

pam., pamph. pamphlet

p.a.m. pulse amplitude modulation

P.A.M.A. Pan-American Medical Association; Press Advertisement Managers' Association

P.A.M.C. Pakistan Army Medical Corps

P.A.M.E.T.R.A.D.A. Parsons and Marine Engineering Turbine Research and Development Association, organ. to centralize turbine research and design on *Queen Elizabeth 2*

PAN *Partido Acción Nacional*, Nat. Action Party (Mex.)

pan. panchromatic; panoramic; pantomime; pantry

Pan. Panama; Panamanian

PANAIR *Panair do Brasil*, Brazilian Airways, *now* VRG

Pan-Am Pan-American World Airways

Pan. Can. Panama Canal

P.A.N.S. procedures for air navigation services

PANSDOC Pakistan National Scientific and Technical Documentation Centre

panto. pantomime

pants. pantaloons

P.A.O. poultry advisory officer; public affairs officer

P.A.O.A. Pan-American Odontological Association

PAP People's Action Party (Singapore); *Polska Agencja Prasowa*, Polish Press Agency

Pap. Papua

pa. p. past participle

P.A.P. Fr. *Prêt à Porter*, ready to wear

P.A.P.C. Poster Advertising Planning Committee

Papermac paperback published by Macmillan

p. app. Fr. *puissance apparente*, apparent power

pa. pple. passive/past participle

Pap. Ter., Pap. Terr. Territory of Papua

par planed all round (woodworking)

PAR *Partido de Acción Renovadora*, Renovating Action Party (El Salvador); perimeter acquisition radar; precision approach radar, rapid-scanning radar at airports that tells air traffic controller whether aircraft is making a normal angle of descent and is lined up with runway; program appraisal and review (U.S.A.), pulse acquisition radar

par. paragraph (*also* para.); parallax (*also* para.); parallel (*also* para.); paraphrase; parenthesis; parish; parochial

Para., Parag. Paraguay

parab. parabola

paradrop. parachute air drop

Paras. parachute troops

parch. parchment

Par. Ch. Parish Church

paren., parens. parenthesis

Parl. Parliament (*also* Parlt.); Parliamentary

Parl. Agt. Parliamentary Agent

Parl. S. Parliamentary Secretary

PARM *Partido Auténtico de la Revolución Mexicana*, Authentic Party of the Mexican Revolution (Mex.); program analysis for resource management

PARMEHUTU *Parti de l'Emancipation Hutu*, Party for Hutu Emancipation (Rwanda)

PARSYN parametric synthesis

part. partial; participate; participle; particle; particular; partition; partner; partnership

part. adj. participle adjective

part. aeq. L. *partes aequales*, equal parts (med.)

pas., pass. passive

Pas. L. *Terminus Paschae*, Easter Term

p.a.s. power assisted steering

P.A.S. public address system

P.A.S.B. Pan-American Sanitary Bureau, *now* P.A.H.O.

PASC Palestine Armed Struggle Command, embraces most of main guerrilla movements, controlled by El Fatah

P.A.S.I. Professional Associate of the Chartered Surveyors' Institution, *now* A.R.I.C.S.

PASLIB Pakistan Association of Special Libraries

P.A.S.O. Pan-American Sanitary Organisation, *now* P.A.H.O.

pass. passage; passenger; — **tr.** passenger train; passive

pass. L. *passim*, here and there, throughout

Pass. Passover

PASSIM Presidential Advisory Staff on Scientific Management (U.S.A.)

PA system public address system

Pat Patricia; Patrick

pat. patent; pattern, *also* patt.

pa. t. past tense

p.-à.-t. Fr. *pied-à-terre*, an occasional lodging

Pata. Patagonia

P.A.T.A. Pacific Area Travel Association; Proprietary Articles Trade Association

patd. patented

path., pathol. pathological; pathology

Pat. Off. patents office

pat. pend. patent pending

P.A.T.R.A. Printing, Packaging, and Allied Trades' Research Association, *now* P.I.R.A.

P.A.T.W.A. Professional and Technical Workers' Aliyah

P.A.U. Pan-American Union; programmes analysis unit

P/Av particular average (insce.)

Pav. pavilion

PAW powered all the way

P.A.W.A. Pan-American Women's Association; Pan-American World Airways Inc.

pax L. *pax vobiscum*, peace be with you

P.A.X. private automatic exchange (telephone)

P.A.Y.E. pay as you earn, system by which income tax is deducted from remuneration before it is paid. Onus of deduction lies with employer rather than with government; pay as you enter

275

paymr. paymaster
payt., pay't. payment
Pb *s* L. *plumbum*, lead (chem.)
PB *s* Surrey (B.V.R.)
P.B. pass book; permanent base; Port. *peso bruto*, gross weight; picket boat; Sp. *planta baja*, ground floor; Plymouth Brethren, Christian sect founded in 19th cent., fundamentalist in doctrine; pocket/prayer book; premium bond; Primitive Baptists; provisional battalion; Publications Board (U.S.A.); purl into back of stitch (knit.); push button
P.B. L. *Philosophiae Baccalaureus*, Bachelor of Philosophy
P.B.A. poor bloody assistant; Public Buildings Administration (U.S.A.)
P.B.C. power boat club
p.b.i. poor bloody infantry
P.B.I. plant breeding institute; protein-bound iodine
P.B.K.T.O.A. Printing, Bookbinding and Kindred Trades Overseers' Association
P.B.M. permanent bench mark; principal beach master
P. boat. patrol boat
P. Bor. L. *Pharmacopoeia Borussica*, Prussian Pharmacopoeia
P.b.P. person before place
PBR payment by results
P.b.S. place before subject
P.B.S. Pacific Biological Station (Can.)
P.B. & S.C. power boat and ski club
p.b.t. profit before tax (fin.)
P.B.T. President of the Board of Trade
P.B.T.B. Paper Bag/Box Trade Board (U.S.A.)
p.b.wt. parts by weight
P.B.X. private branch exchange (telephone)
PC Parliamentary Commissioner, *also* known as Ombudsman; Fr. *Parti Communiste*, Communist Party (Lux.); Sp. *Partido Colorado*, Colorado Party (Uru.); Sp. *Partido Comunista*, Communist Party (Chile/Ecu.); Sp. *Partido Conservador*, Conservative Party (Col./Ecu.); polycarbonate; public convenience, in rural areas (cartog.); *s* Surrey (B.V.R.)
P/C, p.c. petty cash; price current
pc. pica (typ.); piece
p.c. per cent; percentage; Fr. *point de congélation*, freezing point; postcard
p.c. L. *post cibum*, after meals (med.)
P.C. Panama Canal; parish council/councillor; past commander; paymaster captain; Peace Commissioner; perpetual curate; pioneer corps (mil.); pistol club; pitch circle; *Plaid Cymru*, Party of Wales, founded 1925 with the aim of obtaining

dominion status for Wales; point of curve; police constable (*also* P.c.); polo club; port of call; post commander; Fr. *Première classe*, First Class; preparatory commission; press club/council; printing cylinder; prison commission; Privy Council/Councillor; publicity club; *The Publishers Circular*
P.C. L. *Patres Conscripti*, senators; L. *per centum*, by the hundred
PCA *Parti Communiste Algérien*, Algerian Communist Party
P.C.A. Permanent Court of Arbitration; Portland Cement Association (U.S.A.); Printers' Costing Association; Proprietary Cremation Association
P.C.A.C. Professional Classes Aid Council
PCB *Partido Comunista Boliviano*, Communist Party of Bolivia; private car benefits (insce.)
P.C.B. petty cash book
PCB-BKP *Parti Communiste Belge/Belgische Kommunistischem Partij*, Belgian Communist Party
PCB's polychlorinated biphenyls
pcc precipitated calcium carbonate
PCC *Partido Comunista Cubano*, Communist Party of Cuba
P.C.C. parochial church council; Prerogative Court of Canterbury; Print Collectors' Club; Privy Council Cases
P.C.C.C. Pakistan Central Cotton Committee
P.C.C.E.M.R.S.P. Permanent Commission for the Conservation and Exploitation of the Maritime Resources of the South Pacific
P.C.D.G. Prestressed Concrete Development Group
P.C.E.M. Parliamentary Council of the European Movement
PCF *Parti Communiste Français*, French Communist Party
p.c.f. pounds/power per cubic foot
P.C.F. pistol, centre fire, pistol of calibre greater than .22″
P.C.G.N. Permanent Committee on Geographical Names
P. Ch. parish church
P.C.I. It. *Partito Comunista Italiano*, Italian Communist Party
P.C.I.F.C. Permanent Commission of the 1946 International Fisheries Convention
Pcl. parcel
p. clk. pay clerk
PCM *Partido Comunista Mexicano*, Mexican Communist Party
p.c.m. pulse code modulation
P.C.M.A. Plaited Cordage Manufacturers' Association; Professional Con-

ventional Management Association (U.S.A.)

PCMI photochromic micro image

P.C.M.O. principal colonial medical officer

PCN *Partido de Conciliación Nacional*, Nat. Conciliation Party (El Salvador)

p.c.n. part/procurement control number

P.C.O.B. Permanent Central Opium Board

PCP *Partido Comunista Paraguayo*, Paraguayan Communist Party, proscribed since 1936; *Partido Comunista Peruviano*, Peruvian Communist Party; polychloroprene rubber

P.C.P. Past Chief Patriarch; Progressive Constitutional Party (Malta)

PC(PBC)R Pedestrian Crossings (Push Button Control) Regulations and General Directions

P.C.P.V. prestressed concrete pressure vessel

PCR Pedestrian Crossings Regulations

P. Cr. paymaster commander

P. & C.R. *Planning and Compensation Reports*

P.C.R.S. Poor Clergy Relief Society

P.C.R.V. Prestressed concrete reactor vessel (U.S.A.)

PCS *Parti Chrétien Social*, Christian Social Party (Lux.); *Partito Comunista Sammarinese*, San Marino Communist Party

P.C.S. parcels clearing service; Principal Clerk of Session (Scot.)

P.C.S.I.R. Pakistan Council of Scientific and Industrial Research

P.C.S.P. Permanent Commission for the South Pacific

pct. per cent

P.C.T.A. Provisional Collection of Taxes Act

PCTFE polychlorotrifluoroethylene

p.c.u. power/pressurization control unit

P.C.V. passenger controlled vehicle; Peace Corps Volunteers

P. Cyc. *Penny Cyclopedia*

PCZ Panama Canal Zone

PCZST Panama Canal Zone Standard Time

Pd *s* palladium (chem.)

PD *s* Peterhead (B.F.P.); pulse duration; *s* Surrey (B.V.R.)

pd. paid; passed; Fr. *pied*, foot; pound

p/d. post dated

p.d. pitch diameter; poop deck; port dues; position doubtful; postage due; post dated; potential difference (elec.); preliminary design; printer's devil

p.d. L. *per diem*, by the day

P.D. pepper adulterant; L. *Pharmaciae Doctor*, Doctor of Pharmacy; L. *Philosophiae Doctor*, Doctor of Philosophy; plans division; Polar distance; police department; Sp. *posdata*, postscript; postal district; preventive detention; Ger. *Privatdozent*, univ. teacher; production department

P.D. L. *Pharmacopoeia Dublinensis*, Dublin Pharmacopoeia

p.d.a. Fr. *pour dire adieu*, to say goodbye

P.D.A. Photographic Dealers' Association; predicted drift angle

P.D.A.D. Probate, Divorce, and Admiralty Division (leg.)

P.D.A.E.S. *Proceedings of the Devon Archaeological Exploration Society*

Pd. B. L. *Pedagogiae Baccalaureus*, Bachelor of Pedagogy

PDC *Parti Démocratique Chrétien*, Christian Democratic Party (Burundi); *Partido Demócrata Cristiano*, Christian Democratic Party, political parties of this name found in most S. American countries

P.D.C. personnel despatch/dispersal centre

PDCI *Parti Démocratique de la Côte d'Ivoire*, Democratic Party of Ivory Coast

PDCS *Partito Democratico Cristiano Sammarinese*, San Marino Christian Democratic Party

Pd. D. L. *Pedagogiae Doctor*, Doctor of Pedagogy

P.D.E. projectile development establishment

P. de C. Pas de Calais (France)

P.-de-D. Puy-de-Dôme (France)

PDFLP Popular (Democratic) Front for the Liberation of Palestine

PDG *Parti Démocratique de Guinée*, Democratic Party of Guinea; *Parti Démocratique Gabonais*, Gabon Democratic Party

P.D.G. paymaster director-general

P.D.G.W. Principal Director of Guided Weapons

PDI *Parti Démocrate de l'Indépendance*, Democratic Independence Party (Morocco); powered descent initiation

p.d.i. pre-delivery inspection

PDIUM *Partito Democratico Italiano di Unità Monarchica*, Italian Democratic Party of Monarchical Unity

PDM *Progrès et Démocratie Moderne*, Democracy and Progress (France)

Pd. M. L. *Pedagogiae Magister*, Master of Pedagogy

p.d.m. pulse duration modulation

pdn. production

PDO Petroleum Development (Oman) Limited

p./doz. per dozen

PDP People's Democratic Party (Sudan); program development plan (NASA); programmed data processor

p.d.q. pretty damned quick

pdr. pounder

P.D.R.Y. People's Democratic Republic of Yemen, *formerly* Aden

PDS programming documentation standards (computer)

P.D.S.A. People's Dispensary for Sick Animals

P.D.S.C. Performers and Teachers' Diploma, Sydney Conservatorium (Aust.)

P.D.S.R. principal director of scientific research

P.D.S.T. Pacific daylight saving time

P.D.T. Pacific daylight time

PdUP Party of Proletarian Unity formed 1972 from Socialist Party of Proletarian Unity and *Movimento Politico dei Lavoratori* (Italy)

PE personal effects (insce.); *s* Peru (I.V.R.); polyethylene; polythene; *s* Poole (B.F.P.); *s* Surrey (B.V.R.)

P/E price-earnings ratio (fin.)

Pe. Port. *Padre*, Father

p.e. Fr. *par exemple*, for example; It. *per esempio*, for example; personal estate; Fr. *point d'ébullition*, boiling point; Sp. *por ejemplo*, for example; printer's error

P/E. port of embarkation

P.E. permissible error; physical education; pocket edition; Port Elizabeth (S. Afr.); presiding elder; probable error (math.); Protestant Episcopal

P.E. L. *Pharmacopoeia Edinburgensis*, Edinburgh Pharmacopoeia

P.E.A. Physical Education Association of Great Britain and Northern Ireland; Portuguese East Africa

P.E.A.B. Professional Engineers' Appointments Bureau

PEAL Professional Engineers Association Limited

P.E.A.S. Production Engineering Advisory Service

P.E.A.T. Fr. *Programme élargi d'assistance technique des Nations Unies*, United Nations Expanded Programme of Technical Assistance

Pe. B., Ped. B. L. *Pediatriae Baccalaureus*, Bachelor of Pediatrics

P.E.C. photo electric cell; Protestant Episcopal Church

ped. pedal; pedestrian

Ped. pedal (mus.)

Ped. D. L. *Pedagogiae Doctor*, Doctor of Pedagogy

pediat. pediatrics

Peeb., Peebles. Peeblesshire (Scot.)

P.E.E.P. pilot's electronic eye level presentation

P.E.F. Palestine Exploration Fund

Peg, Peggie, Peggy Margaret

PEGE Program for Evaluation of Ground Environment

PEH *s* Perth (B.F.P.)

P.E.I. Prince Edward Island (Can.)

p. ej. Sp. *por ejemplo*, for example

Pek. Peking (China)

peke pekin(g)ese dog

PELNI *Pelajaran Nasional Indonesia*, national shipping company of Republic of Indonesia

PEM Production Engineering Measures (U.S.A.)

Pem., Pemb. Pembrokeshire (Wales)

Pemb. Pembroke College, Cambridge, founded 1347, and Oxford, founded 1624

Pemex *Petroleos Mexicanos*, Mexican Oils

Pem. Yeo. Pembroke Yeomanry

pen. penal; penetration; peninsula; peninsular

Pen., Penit. penitentiary

P.E.N. Club Poets, Playwrights, Essayists, Editors and Novelists, intern. assn. of writers

Pene, Penny Penelope

P. Eng. Member of the Society of Professional Engineers

Penn., Penna. Pennsylvania (U.S.A.)

Penol. Penology

pent. pentagon

Pent. Pentateuch; Pentecost

P.E.O. Programme Evaluation Organization (India)

P.E.P. Political and Economic Planning

PEPP Professional Engineers in Private Practice (U.S.A.)

P.E.P.S.U. Patiala and East Punjab States Union (India)

per. period; It. *perito*, expert; person

Per. *Pericles* (Shake.)

P.E.R.A. Production Engineering Research Association of Great Britain

per. agrim. It. *perito agrimensore*, surveyor

per an. L. *per annum*, yearly

perc. *percussion* (mus.)

per. call. It. *perito calligrafo*, handwriting expert

Perce, Percy, Perse Percival

per cent. L. *per centum*, by the hundred

Per con. L. *per contra*, on the other side

Perd. It. *Perdendosi*, dying away (mus.)

perf. perfect; perfection; perforated

278

(philately); perforation; perform; performance

perh. perhaps

peri., perig. perigee

perjy. perjury (leg.)

perk percolate; perquisite

PERK perchlorethylene

perm. permanent; permission; permutation; unit of water vapour transmission, 1 grain water/hour/sq. ft./inch mercury pressure

Pern. Pernettiana (rose)

PERO President's Emergency Relief Organization

perp. perpendicular; perpetual

per pro L. *per procurationem*, on behalf of, alt. form p.p.

pers. person; personal; personally; perspective (*also* persp.)

Pers. Persia; Persian

PERT performance/programme evaluation review technique

pert. pertain

per. tecn. comm. It. *perito tecnico commerciale*, estimator

Peru., Peruv. Peruvian

P.E.S.C. Public Expenditure Survey Committee

Pesh. Peshawar (Pak.)

PEST Pressure for Economic and Social Toryism, left wing Conservative group

pet. petroleum; petrological; petrologist; petrology

Pet. Gaius Petronius; Peterhouse, Cambridge, founded 1284; The Epistles General of Peter (Bible)

P.E.T. paper equilibrium tester

Pete Peter

petn. petition

PETP polyethylene terephthalate (polyester)

petr. petrification; petrify; petrology

Petriburg. L. *Petriburgensis*, of Peterborough, Eng. episcopal title, in bishop's signature

petro. petrochemical

petrog. petrography

petrol. petrology

PETS Pacific Electronics Trade Show; posting and enquiry terminal system (computer)

p. ex. Fr. *par exemple*, for instance

Pf Ger. *pfennig*, German currency

PF phenol-formaldehyde resin (phenolic); *s* Surrey (B.V.R.)

pf. perfect; prefer; proof

p.f. pneumatic float; Fr. *pour féliciter*, to congratulate; Port. *próximo futuro*, in the future; pulverised fuel

p.f. It. *piano e forte*, soft and then loud (mus.); It. *più forte*, louder (mus.);

L. *pro forma*, for the sake of form, a provisional invoice

P.F. panchromatic film; power factor; Procurator-fiscal; public funding (fin.)

P.F. *pianoforte* (mus.)

P.F.A. Private Fliers' Association (U.S.A.); Professional Footballers' Association; Pulverised Fuel Ash

P. factor preservation factor (psy.)

P.F.A.S. President of the Faculty of Architects and Surveyors

PFB pre-formed beams

Pfc private first class (U.S.A.)

p.f.c. passed flying college

pfce. performance

pfd. preferred (fin.)

Pfd. Ger. *Pfund*, pound

P.F.D. position fixing device

pfd. sp. preferred spelling

P.F.F. pathfinder force

P.F.L.O.A.G. People's Front for the Liberation of Occupied Arab Gulf, group opposed to Sultan of Oman

PFLP Popular Front for the Liberation of Palestine, proponent of hi-jacking and terrorism against targets in West and against Israelis

p.f.m. power factor meter; pulse frequency modulation

P.F.M.A. Pressed Felt Manufacturers' Association

PFN *Partido Frente Nacional*, National Front Party (Costa Rica); pulse forming network

PFR prototype fast reactor

PFRT preliminary flight rating test

p.f.s.a. Fr. *pour faire ses adieux*, to say goodbye

Pfst. pianist; *pianoforte player* (mus.)

Pft. Acct. pianoforte accompaniment (mus.)

Pfte. *pianoforte* (mus.)

p.f.v. Fr. *pour faire visite*, to make a call

pfx. prefix

PG *s* Surrey (B.V.R.)

pg. page; Port. *pago*, paid

Pg. Portugal; Portuguese

p.g. pay group; paying guest; proof gallons; proving ground

p.g. L. *persona grata*, acceptable person

P.G. plate-glazed (paper); post graduate; Preacher General; Fr. *prisonnier de guerre*, prisoner of war; It. *Procuratore Generale*, Attorney-General; Procurator-General

P.G. L. *Pharmacopoeia Germanica*, German Pharmacopoeia

P. & G. Procter and Gamble

P.G.A. Professional Golfers' Association; Public General Acts

P.G.A.D. Past Grand Arch Druidess
p.g.c. per gyro compass
P.G.C. Patent Glazing Conference
P.G.C.E. Post Graduate Certificate of Education
P.G.D. Past Grand Deacon (freem.)
P.G.J.D. Past Grand Junior Deacon
P.G.L. Provincial Grand Lodge (freem.)
P.G.M. Past Grand Master (freem.)
P.G.M.A. Private Grocers' Merchandising Association
Pgn. pigeon
P.G.P.R. Provincial Guild of Printers' Readers
P.G.R. population growth rate; psychogalvanic response, reflex (psy.)
P.G.R.O. Pea Growing Research Organization
P.G.S.D. Past Grand Senior Deacon
P.G.S.W. Past Grand Senior Warden
p.g.t. per gross ton
P. & G.W.A. Pottery and Glass Wholesalers' Association
pH *s* measure of acidity/alkalinity of a liquid, hydrogen-ion concentration. With numeral indicates degree, e.g. pH8.5 very alkaline, pH5 very acid, pH7 neutral
PH Plymouth (B.F.P.); public house (cartog.); *s* Surrey (B.V.R.)
ph. phase
Ph. Philosophy
p.h. past history (med.); precipitation/previous hardening
P.H. Purple Heart (U.S.A. mil. award)
P.H.A. Public Health Act; Public Housing Administration (U.S.A.)
phal. phalange; phalanx
phar., pharm. pharmaceutical; pharmacist; pharmacology (*also* pharmac.); pharmacopoeia; pharmacy
Phar. B. L. *Pharmaciae Baccalaureus*, Bachelor of Pharmacy
Phar. D., Pharm. D., Ph. D. L. *Pharmaciae Doctor*, Doctor of Pharmacy
Phar. M. L. *Pharmaciae Magister*, Master of Pharmacy
Pharm. Chem. Pharmaceutical Chemistry
Ph. B. L. *Philosophiae Baccalaureus*, Bachelor of Philosophy
Ph. B. J. Bachelor of Philosophy in Journalism (U.S.A.)
ph. brz. phosphor bronze
Ph. B. Sp. Bachelor of Philosophy in Speech (U.S.A.)
Ph. C., Phar. C. Pharmaceutical Chemist (U.S.A.)
Ph. D. L. *Philosophiae Doctor*, Doctor of Philosophy
P.H.D. Doctor of Public Health

Ph. D. Ed. Doctor of Philosophy in Education
P.H.F.C. *Proceedings of the Hampshire Field Club*
Ph. G. Graduate in Pharmacy (U.S.A.)
Ph. G. L. *Pharmacopoeia Germanica*, German Pharmacopoeia
P.H.G. postman higher grade
Ph. I. L. *Pharmacopoeia Internationalis*, Intern. Pharmacopoeia
PHIBLANT Amphibious Forces, Atlantic (USN)
PHIBPAC Amphibious Forces, Pacific (USN)
Phil Philip; Philippa; Phillipa; Phillis; Phyllis
phil. philosopher; philosophical; philosophy
Phil. Philadelphia, *also* Phila. (U.S.A.); philharmonic; Philippians; Philippine; philological; philology (*also* philol.); philosophical (*also* Philos.); philosophy; The Epistle of Paul the Apostle to Philippians
Philem. The Epistle of Paul the Apostle to Philemon
Phil. I., Phil. Is. Philippine Islands
Phil. Soc. Philharmonic Society
Phil. Sp. Philippine Spanish
Phil. Trans. *Philosophical Transactions of the Royal Society of London*
Ph. L. Licentiate of Pharmacy/Philosophy
P.H.L.S. Public Health Laboratory Service
Ph. M. L. *Philosophiae Magister*, Master of Philosophy
P.H.N. Public Health Nursing
Phoen. Phoenician; Phoenix
PHOENIX Plasma Heating Obtained by Energetic Neutral Injection Experiment
phon. phonetic; phonetics; phonology, *also*, phonol.
phone telephone
phonet. phonetic; phonetics
phot., photo., photog., photogr. photograph; photographer; photographic; photography
phot. photostat
photo photo-finish, used to verify winners of a race, particularly horseracing; photograph
photom. photometrical; photometry
Phot. R. photographic reconnaissance
p'house steak porterhouse steak
p.h.p. pounds per horsepower; pump horsepower
phr. phrase; phraseology
Ph. R. photographic reconnaissance
p.h.r. parts per 100 parts of rubber, in rubber compounding

phren. phrenic; phrenological; phrenology

P.H.S. Pennsylvania Historical Society; Printing House Square, H.Q. of *The Times* (Lond.); Public Health Service (U.S.A.)

P.H.T.S. Psychiatric Home Treatment Service (U.S.A.)

phys. physical; physically; physician; physicist; physics; physiological; physiology

Phys. Ed. physical education

Physiog. physiography

physiol. physiological; physiologist; physiology

physog. physiognomy, the face

Phys. Sc. physical science

PI Philippine Islands (I.V.R.)

P.I. Pasteur Institute; petrol injected; Philippine Islands; photographic interpretation/interpreter; Plastics Institute; programmed instruction; Fr. *Protocol International*, Intern. protocol

P.I. L. *Pharmacopoeia Internationalis*, Intern. Pharmacopoeia

P.I.A. Pakistan International Airlines Corporation; Photographic Importers' Association

P.I.A.N.C. Permanent International Association of Navigation Congresses

Piang. It. *Piangendo*, plaintive, mournful (mus.)

Pianiss. It. *Pianissimo*, very soft (mus.)

P.I.A.R.C. Permanent International Association of Road Congresses

P.I.A.T. projector infantry anti-tank, portable weapon (mil.)

PIAWA Printing Industry and Allied Workers' Union (Guyana)

PIB polyisobutylene; Prices and Incomes Board

P.I.B. Petroleum Information Bureau

P.I.B.A.C. Permanent International Bureau of Analytical Chemistry of Human and Animal Food

Pic., Pict. pictorial

P.I.C.A.O. Provisional International Civil Aviation Organization, *now* ICAO

P.I.C.G.C. Permanent International Committee on Genetic Congresses

P.I.C.I.C. Pakistan Industrial Credit and Investment Corporation

P.I.C.M. Permanent International Committee of Mothers

P.I.C.S. Publishers' Information Card Services

P.I.C.U.T.P. Permanent and International Committee of Underground Town Planning

PID *Partido Institucional Democrático*, Institutional Democratic Party (Guatemala)

P.I.D.A. Pig Industry Development Authority

P.I.D.E. *policía internacional e de defesa do estado*, political police in Portugal, abol. by Dr. Caetano 1969

P.I.E. Pulmonary Infiltration associated with blood Eosinophilia

P.I.E.A. Petroleum Industry Electrical Association (U.S.A.)

Piffer member of the Punjab Irregular Frontier Force

pigmt. pigment

pigmtn. pigmentation

pil. L. *pilula*, pellet/pill

P.I.L. Pest Infestation Laboratory

PIM pulse interval modulation

p. in² parts per square inch

p. in³ parts per cubic inch

PINAC Permanent International Association of Navigation Congresses

P.-in-C. Priest-in-Charge

Pind. Pindar (518–438 B.C.), Greek lyric poet

PINRO *Polyarnyï Nauchno-issledovatel'skiï Institut Morskogo Rybnogo Khozyaïstva i Okeanografii*, Polar Scientific Research Institute of Marine Fisheries and Oceanography (U.S.S.R.)

pinta pint of (advert.)

pinx. L. *pinxit*, he/she painted it

PINZ Plastics Institute of New Zealand

P.I.O. photographic interpretation officer; public information officer

P.I.O.S.A. Pan-Indian Ocean Science Association

Pip Philip; Philippa; Phillipa

pip. pippin

PIPER pulsed intense plasma for exploratory research

Pippa Philippa; Phillipa

PIPS pulsed integrating pendulums

PIQSY Probes for the International Quiet Solar Year

PIRA Paper Industries Research Association

Pis. pisces

Pit. Pittsburgh (U.S.A.)

P.I.T.A.C. Pakistan Industrial Technical Assistance Centre

pix motion pictures; — sec. pictures per second

pizz. It. *pizzicato*, a direction to pluck stringed instruments which are normally bowed (mus.)

PJ *s* Surrey (B.V.R.)

p.j. physical jerks

P.J. police justice; Presiding/Probate Judge

PK *s* Surrey (B.V.R.)

pk. pack; park; peak; peck

Pk. Ger. *Pauken*, kettle-drums (mus.)

P.K. psychokinesis
P.K. Ger. *Pedalkoppel*, pedal coupler (mus.)
pkg. package (*also*, pkge.); packing
PKN *Polski Kometet Normalizacyjny*, Polish Standards Commission
pkt. packet; pocket
P.K.T.F. Printing and Kindred Trades' Federation of Great Britain and Ireland, now Printing Trade Unions Co-ordinating Bureau
PKW Ger. *Personenkraftwagen*, motor car
Pkwy. Parkway
PL *Partido Liberal*, Liberal Party (Col., Hond., Para.); passenger liability (insce.); *s* Peel (B.F.P.); *s* perception of light; *s* Poland (I.V.R.); *s* Surrey (B.V.R.)
pl. place (*also* pla.); Fr. *place*, place; plain; plate; platoon; Ger. *Platz*, place; Dutch *plein*, place; plural
P.l. partial loss (insce.)
P.L. *Paradise Lost*; patrol leader (scouting); paymaster lieutenant; Port. *peso liquido*, net weight; Plimsoll line, sign showing max. loading level in salt water of a merchant ship, mark invented by Samuel Plimsoll (1824–98); Poet Laureate; position line; Primrose League; public law/library
P.L. L. *Pharmacopoeia Londinensis*, Pharmacopoeia of London
P. & L. profit and loss
PLA Palestine Liberation Army, offshoot of Palestine Liberation Organisation; Pedestrians' League of America
Pla. plaza
P.L.A. People's Liberation Army (China); Port of London Authority; Private Libraries' Association; Pulverized Limestone Association
plan. planet; planetarium
'plane aeroplane; airplane
plas. plaster; plastic
plat. platform (*also* platf.); platinum; platonic; platoon
PLATO programmed logic for automated learning operation
Plaut. Titus Maccius Plautus (*c* 254–184 B.C.) Roman comic poet
P.L.B. Poor Law Board
P.L.C. Poor Law Commissioners
P.L.C. L. *Poeta Laureatus Caesareus*, Imperial Poet Laureate
plcy. policy
pld. payload
pleb., plebe plebian
Plen. plenipotentiary
plf. plaintiff
P.L.G. Poor Law Guardian
plgl. plateglass

PLGS *Partito Liberale dei Giovani Somali*, Liberal Somali Youth Party (Somalia)
PLI *Partido Liberal Independiente*, Independent Liberal Party, advocates restoration of civil and political freedom (Nicaragua)
P.L.I. *Partito Liberale Italiano*, Italian Liberal Party
plk. plank
p.l.m. pulse length modulation
P.L.M. Paris–Lyons–Mediterranean Railway
plmb. plumber; plumbing
PLN *Partido Liberacion Nacional*, National Liberation Party (Costa Rica); *Partido Liberal Nacionalista*, Nationalist Liberal Party (Nicaragua)
pl.-n. place name
plng. planning
PLO Pacific launch operations (NASA); Palestine Liberation Organization, *Munazamat Tahrir Falastin* (Jordan)
PL/1. Programme Language number one, symbolic language designed for programming computers and having a structure closely analogous to English
PLP Progressive Labour Party (Bermuda); Progressive Liberal Party (Bahamas)
P.L.P. Parliamentary Labour Party
PLP-PVV *Parti pour la Liberté et le Progrès/Partij voom Vrijheid en Vooruitgang*, Party of Freedom and Progress (Belg.)
PLR *Partido Liberal Radical*, Radical Liberal Party (Para.); Public Lending Right, scheme advocated by Brit. authors and publishers for payment of royalties on books loaned by public libraries
P.L.R.A. Photo Litho Reproducers' Association
PLRE *Partido Liberal Radical Ecuatoriano*, Ecuadorian Radical Liberal Party
plry. poultry
pls. plates
Pl. Sgt. platoon sergeant
plshr. polisher
P.L.S.S. personal/portable life support system (Space)
plstc. plastic
plstr. plasterer
plt. pilot
pltc. political
pltf. plaintiff
plu. plural
Plum Sir Pelham Warner, Eng. cricketer (1873–1963)
PLUNA *Primeras Líneas Uruguayas de Navigacion Aérea*, Uruguayan Airlines
plup., plupf. pluperfect

Pluto pipe line under the ocean, pipe laid under North Sea to convey petrol to Allied invasion forces, WW2

Ply. Plymouth

plywd. plywood

p/m pounds per minute

Pm *s* promethium (chem.)

PM *s* Sussex, East (B.V.R.)

pm. paymaster; premium; premolar

p.m. permanent magnet; phase modulation; Fr. *poids moléculaire,* molecular weight; post mortem

p.m. L. *post meridiem,* after noon

P.M. Pacific mail; parachute mine; past master; peculiar metre; pipe major; police magistrate; Port. *Policia Militar,* military police; It. *Polizia Military,* military police; Pope and Martyr; postmaster; Prime Minister; product manager; provost-marshal

P.M. L. *Piae Memoriae,* of pious memory

PMA Petroleum Marketing Agencies (Guyana); phenylmercuric acetate

P.M.A. Pakistan Medical Association; Permanent Magnet Association; Precision Measurements Association (U.S.A.); Printers' Medical Aid and Friendship Society; Purchasing Management Association (U.S.A.)

P.M.A.F. Pharmaceutical Manufacturers' Association Foundation (U.S.A.)

P.M. & A.T.A. Paint Manufacturers' and Allied Trades Association

P.M.B. Potato Marketing Board

P.M.C. president of the mess committee

P.M.G. *Pall Mall Gazette;* pay/postmaster general

P.M.G. Tables Parlett McLaren Gordon Alpine Points Tables, method of compiling Alpine ski race results, introduced 1967

p.m.h. past medical history; per man hour

P.M.H. production per man hour

PMI *Partai Muslimin Indonesia,* Indonesian Islamic Party

PMIP Pan-Malayan Islamic Party (Malaysia)

pmk. postmark

P.M.L. Prime Minister's list

P.M.L.O. Principal Military Landing Officer

PMM pulse mode multiplex

PMMA polymethylmethacrylate, acrylic

PMMI Packaging Machinery Manufacturers' Institute (U.S.A.)

P.M.M.T.S. Printing Machine Managers' Trade Society, *now* L.T.S.

PMO phenylmercuric oleate

P.M.O. principal medical officer

P.M. & O.A. Printers' Managers and Overseers Association

p.m.p. Port. *por mão própria,* by bearer

pmr. paymaster

P.M.R. Pacific missile range; private milk records

P.M. & R. physical medicine and rehabilitation

P.M.R.A.F.N.S. Princess Mary's Royal Air Force Nursing Service

PMRM periodic maintenance requirements manual (USN)

PMSD *Parti Mauricien Social Démocrate,* Mauritian Social Democratic Party (Mauritius)

pmt. payment

PMTS predetermined motion time system

PMVI periodic motor vehicle inspection

p. mvr. prime mover

P.M.X. private manual exchange

PN performance number; *s* Preston (B.F.P.); *s* Sussex, East (B.V.R.)

P/N part number; promissory note

p.n. percussion/percussive note; please note; positive negative

P.N. Port. *Padre Nosso,* Our Father; Pakistan Navy

Pna. Panama

P.N.A. para-nitroaniline, dye component

PNB Philippine National Bank

P.N.B. Port. *Produto national bruto,* gross national product

PNC People's National Congress (Guyana)

P.N.Db., p.n.d.b. perceived noise decibels

pndg. pending

P.N.E. Preston North End Football Club

pneu., pneum. pneumatic

P.N.E.U. Parents' National Educational Union

p.n.g. L. *persona non grata,* undesirable person

P.N.G. Papua New Guinea

pnl. panel

PNM People's National Movement (Trinidad and Tobago)

PNP *Partido Nuevo Progresista,* New Progressive Party (Puerto Rico); People's National Party (Jamaica); positive-negative-positive (transistor)

Pnr. pioneer

p.n.r. prior notice required

Pnt. Pentagon (U.S.A.)

P.N.T.O. principal naval transport officer

pntr. painter

pnxt. L. *pinxit*, he/she painted it

PNYA Port of New York Authority (U.S.A.)

Pnz. Penzance, Cornwall

Po s polonium (chem.)

PO s Sussex, West (B.V.R.)

p.o. part of; petty officer; post office; power oscillator; previous orders; putout (baseball)

P.O. parcels/passport/patent office; Fr. *Par ordre*, by order; personnel/petty/pilot officer; postal order; power-operated; Province of Ontario (Can.); public office/officer; Pyrénées-Orientales (France)

P. & O. Peninsular and Oriental Steam Navigation Company (ship.)

P.O.A. Prison/Purchasing Officers' Association

POAC Post Office Advisory Council

P.O.B. post office book/box

p.o.c. port of call

P.O.D. pay on death/delivery; *Pocket Oxford Dictionary*; port of debarkation; Post Office Department (U.S.A.)

P.O.E. port of embarkation/entry

P.O.E.D. Post Office Engineering Department; provincial officer of establishment division

poet. poetic; poetical; poetry

P.O.E.U. Post Office Engineering Union

P.O.F.I. Pacific Ocean Fisheries Investigations

P.O.G.O. Polar Orbiting Geophysical Observatories

poi. poison; poisonous

POINTER Particle Orientation Interferometer (ASD)

pol. polar; polarize; police; polish

Pol., polit. political; politician; politics

Pol. Poland; Polish

P.O.L. Patent Office Library

Pol. Ad. political adviser

Pol. Econ. political economics/economy

pol. ind. pollen index

polio. poliomyelitis

Politburo *Politicheskoe Byuro*, Political Bureau of the Central Committee of Communist Party (U.S.S.R.)

poll. pollution

Polly Maria; Marie; Mary

POLP Popular Organisation for the Liberation of Palestine

Pol. Sci. Political Science

polwar. political warfare

Poly. Polynesia (*also*, Polyn.); Polynesian (*also*, Polyn.); Polytechnic; polytechnical (*also*, polytech.); polyvinyl

Polyb. Polybius (*c* 204–122 B.C.), Gk. historian of Rome

polyol. polyhydroxylic compound (plastics)

Poly.-pom. dwarf polyanthus or pompom (rose)

pom polyformaldehyde (plastic); polyoxymethylene (plastic)

pom. pomeranian dog

P.O.M.E. principal ordnance mechanical engineer

Pommy, Pome an emigrant from Britain (Aust./N.Z.); *Also* said to be *prisoner of mother England*, early convict immigrants

POMS panel on operational meteorological satellites

pont. br. pontoon bridge

Pont. Max. L. *Pontifex Maximus*, Supreme Pontiff

P.O.O. post office order

POOF peripheral on-line oriented function (computer)

Poop Nincompoop

Pop popular (mus.)

POP point of purchase; post office preferred (envelopes)

pop. popular; population

P.O.P. Perpendicular Ocean Platform (U.S.A.); plaster of paris; printing-out paper (photo.)

POPA Property Owners Protection Association

Pops popular concerts/rhythm (mus.)

POR *Partido Obrero Revolucionario*, Revolutionary Workers' Party (Bolivia)

por. porosity; porous; portion

p.o.r. pay/payable on receipt; pay on return

P.O.R. personnel occurrence report; *Policy, Organisation, and Rules*, Girl Guides and Scouts Assn.'s official rule book first pub. 1916

P.O.R.I.S. post office radio interference station

porn pornography

port. portable; portrait; portraiture

Port. Portugal; Portuguese; — **Chi.** Portuguese China (Macao); — **Ind.** Portuguese India, most important poss. was Goa under Port. rule 1505–1961; — **Tim.** Portuguese Timor

POS point of sale

pos. apostrophe; position; positive

Pos. Fr. *Positif*, choir organ (mus.); Fr. *Position*, position (mus.); It. *Posizione*, position (mus.)

P.O.s. Postal Orders

P.O.S. Port of Spain (Trinidad)

P.O.S.B. Post Office Savings Bank *now* (in U.K.) National Savings Bank

P.O.S.D. Post Office Savings Department

POSH port side out, starboard home

(of ships plying between England and India) being cooler and more expensive cabins on route Britain to India

posish position

POSL *Parti Ouvrier Socialiste Luxembourgeois,* Socialist Workers' Party (Lux.)

posn. position

pos. pro. possessive pronoun

POSS passive/prototype optical surveillance system

poss. possession (*also* possn.); possessive; possible; possibly

post-Aug. L. *post-Augustan*

post-cl. L. *post-classical*

poster. posterity

posthum. posthumous; posthumously

pot. potash; potassium; potential

pot. L. *potio,* dose

P.O.Tel. petty officer telegraphist

poul. poultry

POUNC Post Office Users' National Council

POUR President's Organization for Unemployment Relief (U.S.A.)

p.o.v. privately owned vehicle

P.O.W. please oblige with; Prince of Wales, title conferred since 15th cent. on eldest son and heir-apparent of the Eng. monarch; prisoner of war

powd. powder

P.O.W.S. pyrotechnic outside warning system

PP *s* Buckinghamshire (B.V.R.); *Parti du Peuple,* Party of the People (Burundi); polypropylene; Progressive Party (S. Afr.); Progress Party (Ghana)

pp. pages; past participle

pp. It. *pianissimo,* very soft (mus.)

p.p. It. *pacco postale,* parcel post; parcel post; parish priest; part/partial paid; passive/past participle; It. *per procura,* by proxy; physical properties; picked ports (chartering); pickpocket; It. *piera pelle,* real leather; play or pay; post paid; present position; privately printed; Port. *pronto pagamento,* immediate payment/cash down; Port. *proximo passado,* of recent date; Fr. *publié par,* published by

p.p., per. pro. L. *per procurationem,* by proxy

p. & p. post and packing

PP. L. *Patres,* Fathers

P.P. parish priest; Parliamentary papers; Past President, *sometimes* initials before abbrev. of institutions; pastures protection; permanent pass; petrol point; phenolphthalein, test paper for alkalinity; pilotless plane; port pipe; postpaid; present pupil; primary producers; proportional part; *The Passionate Pilgrim,*

anthology of poems pub. 1599 by Jaggard attributed, erroneously, to Shake.

P.P. L. *Pastor Pastorum,* Shepherd of the Shepherds; L. *Pater Patriae,* Father of his Country

ppa It. *per procura,* by proxy

PPA Progressive People's Alliance (Gambia)

p.p.a. parallel processing automata; photo-peak analysis; polyphosphoric acid

P.P.A. Pakistan Press Association; Periodical Proprietors'/Publishers' Association; Pre-school Playgroups Association; Printers' Provident Association; Produce Packers' Association

PPB parts per billion (U.S.A.); Party Political Broadcast; planning-programming-budgeting

Ppb. Ger. *Pappband,* boards

P.P.B. private posting box

PPBAS planning-programming-budgeting-accounting system

PPBS planning-programming-budgeting system

p.p.c. Fr. *pour prendre congé,* to take leave

PP.C. L. *Patres Conscripti,* Conscript Fathers, members of the Roman Senate

P.P.C.L.I. Princess Patricia's Canadian Light Infantry

PPCRGD Pelican Pedestrian Crossing Regulations and General Directions, 1969

P.P.C.S. Primary Producers' Cooperative Society (N.Z.)

PPD *Partido Popular Democrático,* Popular Democratic Party (Puerto Rico)

ppd. postpaid (*also* p. pd.); prepaid

P.P.D.A. Produce Packaging Development Association

P.P.D.S. Publishers' parcels delivery service

P.P.D.S.E. Plate Printers, Die Stampers and Engravers (U.S.A.)

P.P.E. Philosophy, Politics and Economics, degree course Oxford Univ.

P.P.F. Plumbers and Pipefitters (U.S.A.)

P.P.F.A. Planned Parenthood Federation of America

P.P.F.A.S. Past President of the Faculty of Architects and Surveyors

pph pamphlet

p.p.h.m. parts per 100 parts of mix, in rubber compounding

p.p.h.r. parts per 100 parts of rubber, in rubber compounding

p.p.i. parcel post insured; policy sufficient proof of interest (marine insce.)

P.P.I. plan position indicator (nav.)

P.P. Inst. R.A. Past President of the Institute of Registered Architects

P.P.L. private pilot's licence

ppl.a. participial adjective

P-plane explosive-carrying reaction-propelled crewless aeroplane

pple. participle

P.P.L.O. pleuropneumonia-like organisms

PPM *Parti du Peuple Mauritanien/ Hizb es Sha'b*, Mauritanian People's Party

p.p.m. parts per million; pulse position modulation

P.P.M.S. Plastic Pipe Manufacturers' Society

PPN-RDA *Parti Progressiste Nigérien*, Nigerian Progressive Party (Niger)

ppp It. *pianissimo*, very soft (mus.)

PPP People's Progressive Party (Gambia/Guyana/Malaysia)

P.P.P. private patients plan (med.)

Ppr. paper; proper

P.P.R. Polish People's Republic; printed paper rate

P.P.R.A. Past President of the Royal Academy of Arts

P.P.R.I.C.A. Pulp and Paper Research Institute of Canada

PPS *Partido Popular Salvadoreño*, Salvadoran Popular Party (El Salvador); *Partido Popular Socialista*, Popular Socialist Party (Mex./El Salvador)

p.p.s. L. *post post scriptum*, additional postscript

P.P.S. Parliamentary/principal private secretary; *Proceedings of the Prehistoric Society*

P.P.S.A. Pan-Pacific Surgical Association

P.P.S.E.A. *Proceedings of the Prehistoric Society of East Anglia*

P.P.S.E.A.W.A. Pan-Pacific and South-East Asia Women's Association

PPT *Parti Progressiste Tchadien*, Chad Progressive Party

ppt. precipitate

pptd. precipitated

pptg. precipitating

pptn. precipitation

P.P.T.P.I. Past President of the Town Planning Institute

ppty. property

P.P.U. Peace Pledge Union; Primary Producers' Union

P.Q. Parliamentary/preceding/previous question; personality quotient; Province of Quebec (Can.)

PQD *Partido Quisqueyano Demócrata*, Quisqueyano Democratic Party (Dom. Rep.)

Pr *s* praseodymium (chem.)

PR *s* Dorset (B.V.R.); *Partido Radical*, Radical Party (Chile); *Partido Reformista*, Reformist Party (Dom. Rep.); *Partido*

Republicano, Republican Party (Costa Rica); *Partido Revolucionario*, Revolutionary Party (Guatemala); purchase request

P/R payroll

pr. painter; pair; per; pounder; present; pressure; price; print; printer; printing; pronoun; proper; prove

Pr. Port. *Praça*, Plaza/square; Prayer; preferred stock (fin.); priest; Prince; Protestant; Provençal; Provincial

p.r. parcel receipt

p.r. L. *per rectum*, by the rectum (med.)

P.R. *Paradise Regained*; Pipe Rolls, most anct. and complete series of public records in Brit., beginning 1131; plotting and radar; postal regulations; preliminary / progress / project report; Pre-Raphaelite; press representative; prize ring (boxing); proportional representation; public relations; Puerto Rico

P.R. L. *Populus Romanus*, the Roman people; Fr. *Positif-Récit*, choir swell (mus.)

PRA *Partido Revolucionario Auténtico*, Authentic Revolutionary Party (Bolivia)

Pr. A. Ger. *Prachtausgabe*, édition de luxe

P.R.A. paymaster rear-admiral; People's Republic of Albania; President of the Royal Academy; Psoriasis/Psychological Research Association (U.S.A.); Puerto Rico Association

prag. pragmatic; pragmatism

pram perambulator

prand. L. *prandium*, breakfast *or* luncheon

P.R.A.T.R.A. Philippines Relief and Trade Rehabilitation Administration

PRB *Partido de la Revolución Boliviana*, Bolivian Revolutionary Party

P.R.B. People's Republic of Bulgaria; Pre-Raphaelite Brotherhood, group of artists and critics. D. G. Rossetti used the initials on a painting in 1849

P.R.C. People's Republic of China, *Chung-hua Jen-min Kung-ho Kuo*; Price Regulation Committee (U.S.A.)

P.R.C. L. *Post Romam Conditam*, after the foundation of Rome (753 B.C.)

P.R.C.A. President of the Royal Cambrian Academy

prchst. parachutist

prcht. parachute

P.R.C.P. President of the Royal College of Physicians

prcs. process

P.R.C.S. President of the Royal College of Surgeons of England

prcst. precast

PRD *Partido Revolucionario Dominicano*, Dominican Revolutionary Party

preb. prebend; prebendary
prec. preceding; precision
Prec. Precentor
pred. predicate; predicative; — **adj.** predicative adjective
predic. predicative
pref. preface; prefatory; prefer; preferably; preference; prefix
Pref. prefect (*also* pfc.); preference; preferred
prefab. prefabricated, *also* particular type of housing
prehist. prehistoric; prehistorical; prehistory
prej. prejudice
prelim. preliminaries; preliminary
prelims. preliminaries/preliminary pages (leaves) being the pages, in a book, which precede the actual text, *e.g.* half title, title, list of contents, dedication, preface
prem. premium
premed. premedical, student
prep. preparation; preparatory; prepare; preposition
Prep. preparatory; preparatory school
prepd. prepared
prepg. preparing
prepn. preparation
pres. present; presumptive
Pres. presbyter (*also* Presby.); presbyterian (*also* Presby.); presentation; presidency; president
pres. part. present participle
PRESS pacific range electromagnetic signature studies
press. pressure
PRESTO program reporting and evaluation system for total operation (U.S.A.)
presv. preservation; preserve
pret. preterite
pre-Teut. pre-Teutonic
prev. previous; previously
PRF *Partido Revolucionario Febrerista*, Febrerista Revolutionary Party (Para.)
prf. proof
prf. L. *praefatio*, preface
p.r.f. pulse recurrence/repetition frequency
P.R.F. Petroleum Research Fund; Plywood Research Foundation; Public Relations Foundation
prfnl. professional
prfr. proof reader
P.R.H. petrol railhead
P.R.H.A. President of the Royal Hibernian Academy
PRI *Partito Repubblicano Italiano*, Italian Republican Party, founded 1897, follows Giuseppe Mazzini's moderate leftist principles of social justice in a modern free society; *Partido Revolucion-*

ario Institucional, Institutional Revolutionary Party (Mex.) founded 1929 as National Revolutionary Party, and redesignated in 1938 as Mexican Revolutionary Party, the PRI took its present name 1946
pri., prim. primary; primate; primer; primitive
pri. priority; private
P.R.I. Fr. *La prévention routière internationale*, Intern. Prevention of Road Accidents; President of the Royal Institute of Painters in Water Colours
P.R.I.A. President of the Royal Irish Academy; *Proceedings of the Royal Irish Academy*
P.R.I.B.A. President of the Royal Institute of British Architects
PRIN *Partido Revolucionario de Izquierda Nacionalista*, Nat. Leftist Revolutionary Party (Bolivia)
Prin. principal; Principality
PRINCE Parts Reliability Information Center (NASA)
print. printing
Pris, Prissy Priscilla
PRISE program for integrated shipboard electronics
PRISM personnel record information system (computer); program reliability information system for management (U.S.A.)
prism. prismatic
prithee I pray thee; please
priv. private; privative
P.R.L. Prairie Research Laboratory (Can.); Price Reduction League
prm. premium
p.r.n. L. *pro re nata*, as occasion arises (med.)
pro, pro. procedure; proceed: procure; profession; professional; prostitute
Pro. provost
PR.O. press officer
P.R.O. Public Record Office; Public Relations Officer
pro-am professional-amateur (sport)
prob. probability; probable; probably; problem
Prob. Probate (leg.)
PROBCOST probabilistic budgeting and forward costing
prob. off. probation officer
proc. proceedings; process
Proc. proctor
Procop. Procopius (6th cent. A.D.), Byzantine historian
Proc. Roy. Soc. *Proceedings of the Royal Society*
Prod protestant (N. Ireland)
prod. produce; producer; product; production

287

PRODAC Production Advisers Consortium

prof. profession; professional; professor

prog. prognosis; program/programme; progressive

P.R.O.I. President of the Royal Institute of Oil Painters

proj. project; projectile; projection; projector

Prol. prologue

prole. proletarian

prom. promenade; promenade concert; promontory; promote

Prom. promoter; promotion

pron. pronominal; pronoun; pronounce; pronounceable; pronouncement; pronouncing; pronunciation

pron. a. prenominal adjective

prond. pronounced

Pro. Note promissory note (fin.)

pronunc. pronunciation

PROP planetary rocket ocean platform; Preservation of the Rights of Prisoners

prop. propeller (R.A.F. slang); proper; properly; property (theatre); proposition; proprietary; proprietor, *also* propr.

Prop. Sextus Aurelius Propertius (*c* 50–*c* 16 B.C.), Roman poet

propl. proportional

propn. proportion

props. properties (theatre)

P.R.O.R.M. Pay and Records Office, Royal Marines

pros. prosodical; prosody

Pros. prospectus rate (advert.)

Pros. Atty. prosecuting attorney

prost. prostate; prostitution

Prot. protestant

protec. protectorate, *also* prot.

pro. tem L. *pro tempore*, for the time being

prov. proverb; proverbial (*also*, provb.); proverbially (*also*, provb.); province; provincial; provisional; provost

Prov. Provençal; Provence; Provence rose; province; Ger. *Provinz*, province; provost; The Proverbs (Bible)

Prov. Eng. provincial English

Prov. G.M. Provincial Grand Master (freem.)

Provo provisional (auxiliary) member of I.R.A.

prox. L. *proximo*, in/of the next month; — *acc. proxime accessit*, he/she came nearest; — *luc. proxima luce*, the day before

PRP People's Revolutionary Party (Rep. of Vietnam)

P.R.P. petrol refilling point

pr. pple. present participle

pr. pr. L. *praeter propter*, about, nearly

PRR pulse repetition rate

PRS paint research station; Pattern Recognition Society (U.S.A.)

P.R.S. Performing Right Society; President of the Royal Society (Lond.); Protestant Reformation Society

P.R.S.A. President of the Royal Scottish Academy; Public Relations Society of America

PRSC *Partido Revolucionario Social Cristiano*, Revolutionary Social Christian Party (Dom. Rep.)

prsd. pressed; — **met.** pressed metal

P.R.S.E. President of the Royal Society of Edinburgh

Pr. S.T. Prairie Standard Time (U.S.A.)

P. & R.T. physical and recreational training

prtg. printing

PRU Pneumoconiosis Research Unit of Medical Research Council

Pru. Prudential Assurance Company

P.R.U. photographic reconnaissance units (R.A.F.)

Prue Prudence

Pruss. Prussia; Prussian

p.r.v. Fr. *pour rendre visite*, to return a call; pressure reducing valve

P.R.W.S. President of the Royal Society of Painters in Water Colours

PS *Partido Socialista*, Socialist Party (Chile); Ger. *Pferdestarke*, horse-power; polystyrene (chem.); *s* Shetland, Zetland (B.V.R.)

Ps., Psa. Psalm (Bible)

Ps. Ger. *Posaunen*, trombones (mus.)

p.s. particle size; parts shipped/shipper; passed school of instruction (mil.) passenger service/steamer; Fr. *poids spécifique*, specific weight; pull switch

p.s. L. *post scriptum*, postscript

P.S. paddle steamer; parade state; Parliamentary secretary; Pastel Society; penal servitude; permanent secretary; Pharmaceutical Society of Great Britain; Philological Society; Philosophical Society of England; Physical/Physiological Society; police sergeant; press/private secretary; Privy Seal; prompt side (theatre); provost sergeant; It. *Pubblica Sicurezza*, police; public school

p.s.a. passed staff college (R.A.F.)

P.S.A. Pacific Science Association; Photographic Society of America; pleasant Sunday afternoons; Political Studies Association of the United Kingdom; President of the Society of Antiquaries; *Proceedings of the Society of Antiquaries*

P.S.A.B. Public Schools Appointments Bureau

PSAC President's Science Advisory Committee (U.S.A.)

P. sac pericardial cavity, cavity within which heart lies (biol.)

P.S.A.I. *Proceedings of the Suffolk Archaeological Institute*

p's and q's pints and quarts, perhaps from beer consumed therefore 'minding one's p's and q's', *but* more likely warning to compositors handsetting of similar shape of letters p and q; *also* to children visiting—'mind your pleases and thank-yous' (i.e. be on your best behaviour)

P.S.A.S. *Proceedings of the Society of Antiquaries of Scotland*

P.S.B. Pacific Science Board; pistol, small-bore with calibre of up to .22″

P.S.B.A. Public Schools Bursars' Association

P.S.B.O. Premium Savings Bond Office

p.s.c. passed staff college (mil.); per standard compass

P.S.C. Pacific Science Council; Public Service Commission

PSC-CVP *Parti Social Chrétien/Christelijk Volkspartij*, Social-Christian Party (Belgium)

P.S.C.D. patrol service central depot

P.S.C.J. L. *Societas Presbyterorum Sacratissimi Cordis Jesu de Betharram*, Soc. of Priests of the Sacred Heart of Jesus of Betharram

P.S.C.T. permanent service on crustal thickness

PSD *Partido Social Demócrata*, Social Democratic Party (Bolivia); *Parti Social Démocrate*, Social Democratic Party (Madag.); *Parti Socialiste Démocratique*, Democratic Socialist Party (Morocco)

P.S.D. pay supply depot; personal services department; petty sessional division (leg.)

p. s. detn. particle size determination

PSDI *Partito Socialista Democratico Italiano*, Italian Democratic Socialist Party

PSDIS *Partito Socialista Democratico Independente Sammarinese*, San Marino Independent Social Democratic Party

p. s. distn. particle size distribution

P.S.E.T. Permanent Service on Earth Tides

pseud., psdo. pseudonym, an assumed name

p.s.f. pounds per square foot

P.S.G.I. Permanent Service for Geomagnetic Indices

PSHFA Public Servants Housing and Finance Association

PSI *Partito Socialista Italiano*, Italian Socialist Party

p.s.i. pounds per square inch, lb/in²

P.S.I. Pharmaceutical Society of Ireland; President of the Service Institute; Public Services International

p.s.i.a. pounds per square inch absolute

p.s.i.g. pounds per square inch gauge

PSII *Partai Sjarekat Islam Indonesia*, United Islamic Party of Indonesia

P.S.I.P. Poultry Stock Improvement Plan

PSIUP *Partito Socialista Italiano di Unitá Proletaria*, Italian Socialist Party of Proletarian Unity

P.S.L. paymaster sub-lieutenant

p.s.m. passed school of music, graduation from Royal Military School of Music

P.S.M. product sales manager

P.S.M.A. President of the Society of Marine Artists

P.S.M.S.L. Permanent Service for Mean Sea Level

P.S.N.C. Pacific Steam Navigation Company

P.S.O. personnel selection officer; principal scientific officer

PSP *Pacifistich Socialistische Partij*, Pacifist Socialist Party (Neth.); phenol-sulphone-phthalein (chem.)

P.S.P. *Policía de Segurança Pública*, Portuguese Police Force

PSQC Philippine Society for Quality Control

PSS *Partito Socialista Sammarinese*, San Marino Socialist Party

P.S.S. Printing and Stationery Service; Professor of Sacred Scripture

P.S.S.C. Pious Society of the Missionaries of Saint Charles

p.s.s.o. pass slipped stitch over (knit.)

P.S.T. Pacific Standard Time (U.S.A.)

pstl. postal

P.S.T.O. principal sea transport officer

PSU *Parti Socialiste Unifié*, Unified Socialist Party (France); *Partito Socialista Unitario*, Unitary Socialist Party (Italy)

P. Surg. plastic surgery

P.S.V. public service vehicle

P.S.W. psychiatric social worker

psych. psychic; psychical

psych., psychol. psychological; psychologist; psychology

psycho. psychopath

psy-op psychological operation (mil.)

Pt *s* platinum (chem.)

PT *s* Durham (B.V.R.)

pt. part; payment; pint; point (math.); port, *also* P't. (nav.); preterit

p.t. part time; past tense; physical therapy/training; point of turn/turning; primary target

p.t. L. *pro tempore*, for the time being

P.T. Pacific Time (U.S.A.); parcel ticket; postal telegraph; It. *Poste e Telegrafi*, Post & Telegraph Service; post town; preferential treatment; public trustee; pupil teacher; purchase tax; *The Phoenix and the Turtle* (attrib. to Shake.)

PTA Pet Traders' Association; plasma thromboplastin antecedent (med.); post traumatic amnesia (med.); proposed technical approach

pta. peseta (Spanish currency); Sp. *punta*, point

P.T.A. Parent-Teacher/Teachers Association; Passenger Transport Authorities; Pianoforte Tuners' Association; Printing Trades Alliance

P.T.A.S. Productivity and Technical Assistance Secretariat

ptbl. portable

PT boat patrol torpedo boat

PTBT Partial Test Ban Treaty

p.t.c. positive temperature coefficient

P.T.C. personnel transfer capsule (diving); personnel transit centre; photographic type composition; primary training centre

Ptd. painted; printed

PTE Passenger Transport Executive (rail.)

p^{te.} Sp. *parte*, part

Pte. plate; Fr. *Pointe*, Point; private (mil.)

pt. ex., pt. exch. part exchange

PTFE polytetrafluorethylene, synthetic material producing irritant vapours when heated

ptg. printing

Ptg. Portugal; Portuguese

p. tgt. primary target

P.T.I. physical training instructor; Press Trust of India

P.T.I.D.G. Presentation of Technical Information Discussion Group

p.t.l. primary target line

PTM *s* Malaysia (I.V.R.); pulse time modulation/multiplex

PTMA phospho-tungsto-molybdic acid, used in manufacture of certain pigments

ptn. partition; portion

Ptnr. partner

P.T.O. please turn over; power take off; public trustee office

PTP paper tape printer (computer)

ptpg. participating (fin.)

pt/pt point-to-point

ptr. printer

P.T.S. Philatelic Traders' Society;

preliminary training school (nursing); printing technical school

pts./hr. parts/pieces per hour

Ptsmth., Pts. Portsmouth

P.T.T. Fr. *Postes, Télégraphe, Téléphones*, Mail, Telegraphs and Telephones

P.T.T.I. Postal, Telegraph and Telephone International

pt.-tm. part-time

pttnmkr. patternmaker

P.T.U. Plumbing Trades Union

PTUC Philippine Trade Unions Council

PTV propulsion test vehicle

ptw per thousand words

pty. party; proprietary

Pu *s* plutonium (chem.)

PU *s* Essex (B.V.R.); polyurethane

p.u. paid up

p.-u. pick-up, water absorption figure in certain dyeing processes

P.U. public utilities

P.U.A.S. Postal Union of the Americas and Spain

pub public house

pub., publ. public; publican; publication; publish; published; publisher; publishing

Pub. publishers' announcement (advert.)

pubbl. It. *pubblicità*, advertisements

pub. doc. public document

pub. wks. public works

P.U.C. papers under consideration; pick-up car; Public Utilities Commission (U.S.A.)

P.U.C. L. *Post Urbem Conditam*, after the foundation of the City (Rome)

PUCR *Partido Unión Cívico Revolucionaria*, Revolutionary Civic Union Party (Costa Rica)

pud. pudding

pug. pugilist

PULHEEMS physical capacity, upper and lower limbs, hearing, eyesight, emotional capacity, mental stability (med.)

pulv. L. *pulvis*, powder (med.)

p.u.m.s. permanently unfit for military service

PUN *Partido Unión Nacional*, National Union Party (Costa Rica)

pun. puncheon; punish; punishment

punc. punctuation

Punj. Punjab

P.U.O. Pyrexia (fever) of unknown origin (med.)

pup. puppy

P.U.P. People's United Party (Brit. Honduras); Princeton University Press (U.S.A.)

pur. purchase (*also*, purch.); purchaser; purification; purify; purple (also, purp.); pursuit

P.U.R.V. powered underwater research vehicle

p.u.s. permanently unfit for service

P.U.S. Parliamentary / permanent under-secretary; Pharmacopoeia of the United States

PUVA plutonium value analysis system

PUWP Polish United Workers' Party, *Polska Zjednoczona Partia Robotnicza*

Puy-de-D. Puy-de-Dôme (France)

PV *s* Ipswich (B.V.R.)

p.v. post village; priest vicar

p.v. L. *per vaginam*, by the vagina (med.)

P.V. patrol vessel; Fr. *Petite Vitesse*, freight train; It. *Piccola Velocità*, slow train; pole vault (sport); Porte de Versailles, district of Paris (France); positive vetting; Public Vaccinator

PVA polyvinyl acetate (also, PVAC); polyvinyl alcohol, a synthetic material used for personal protective equipment (also, PVAL)

PVB, PVBr polyvinyl butyral

PVC polyvinyl chloride, synthetic material used for personal protective equipment

p.v.c. pigment volume concentration, in paint technology

PVCH polyvinylcyclohexane

PvdA *Partij van de Arbeid*, Labour Party (Neth.)

PVDC polyvinylidene chloride

PVF polyvinyl fluoride

PVG polyvinylene glycol

P.V.O. principal veterinary officer

PVP polyvinylpyrrolidone

P.V.P.M.P.C. Perpetual Vice-President and Member of the Pickwick Club (Dickens)

PVT polyvinyl toluene

pvt., pvte. private (mil.)

p.v.t. Fr. *par voie télégraphique*, by telegraph

PVTCA polyvinyl trichlororacetate

PW *s* Norfolk (B.V.R.); *s* Padstow (B.F.P.); pulse width

p.w. per week; purlwise

P.W.A. Public Works Administration (U.S.A.), New Deal Agency, estab. 1933 to create work and promote economic recovery, abol. 1943

PWC post-war credits (WW2)

P.W.C. People's World Convention

P.W.C.F.C. *Proceedings of the West Cornwall Field Club*

pwd. powered

P.W.D. Public Works Department

PWFA Petroleum Workers' Federation of Aruba

PWG *s* Port Glasgow (B.F.P.)

P.W.I.F. Plantation Workers' International Federation

P.W.L.B. Public Works Loan Board

P.W.N.D.A. Provincial Wholesale Newspaper Distributors' Association

P.W.O. Prince of Wales' Own (mil.)

pwr. power; — sup. power supply

P.W.R. police war reserve; pressurized water reactor; — -F.L.E.C.H.T. pressurized water reactor—full length emergency cooling heat transfer

pwt. pennyweight

P.W.T. Pacific War Time

PX physical examination; please/private exchange; post exchange; *s* Sussex, West (B.V.R.)

pxt., pinx., pnxt. L. *pinxit*, he/she painted it

PY *s* Paraguay (I.V.R.); *s* Yorkshire, NR (B.V.R.)

5PY *s* Plymouth (radio call-sign)

pyro. pyromaniac; pyrotechnics (also, pyrotech.)

Pyr.-Or. Pyrenées-Orientales (France)

PZ *s* Belfast (B.V.R.); *s* Penzance (B.F.P.)

P.Z.S. President of the Zoological Society

P.Z.T. photographic zenith tube

P.zza It. *Piazza*, square

Q

q *s* coefficient of association (math.); *s* dynamic pressure; *s* electrical charge; *s* quartile deviation or range altern. known as semi-quartile range and probable error (psy.); *s* stagnation pressure

Q Quarto (MS.); queen (chess); *quetzal*, currency of Guatemala

Q10 temperature coefficient (biol.)

q. It. *qualcuno*, somebody; quart; quarter; quarterly; quarto; queen; quench; query; question; quick; quintal; It. *quintale*, quintal; quire; squalls (naut.)

q. L. *quaere*, inquire; L. *quasi*, almost

Q. *s* Coulomb, unit of quality (elec.); quantity (*also* qty.); quartermaster; quarter-page (advert.); quarto; Quebec; Queensland (Aust.); *nom de plume* of Sir A. T. Quiller-Couch (1863–1944), Eng. author

Q. L. *quadrans*, farthing (also *Qa*.)

QA *s* London, for vehicles temporarily imported from abroad (B.V.R.); qualification approval (*also* Q/A); quality assurance; quarters allowance

q.a. quick assembly

Q. & A. question and answer

Q.A.B. Queen Anne's Bounty, fund estab. (1704) to give financial aid to poor Anglican clergy. In 1925 Q.A.B. became responsible for collection and distribution of Church tithes, and became part of the Church Commissioners in 1948

QAD quality assurance division

QADS quality assurance data system

Q.A.I.M.N.S. Queen Alexandra's Imperial Military Nursing Service, *now* Q.A.R.A.N.C.

qal. Fr. *quintal*

Q.A.L.A.S. Qualified Associate of the Land Agents' Society

Qantas, QANTAS, Q.A.N.T.A.S. Queensland and Northern Territory Aerial Service (Aust.)

Q.A.R.A.N.C. Queen Alexandra's Royal Army Nursing Corps

Q.A.R.N.N.S. Queen Alexandra's Royal Naval Nursing Service

Q.A.S. quaternary ammonium compound, *also* quat.

QB *s* London, for vehicles temporarily imported from abroad (B.V.R.); queen's bishop (chess)

q.b. quarterback

Q.B. Queen's Bays; Queen's Bench

Qbc. Quebec

Q.B.D. Queen's Bench Division

Q-boat anti-submarine vessels used in WW1

QBP queen's bishop's pawn (chess)

Q.B.S.M. Sp. *que besa su mano*, who kisses your hand, precedes signature in a letter

Q.B.S.P. Sp. *que besa sus pies*, who kisses your feet

QC *s* London, for vehicles temporarily imported from abroad (B.V.R.)

q.c. It. *qualcosa*, something

Q.C. quality control; quartermaster corps; Queen's College/Consort/Counsel; quit claim

Q.C.E. quality control engineering

Q.C.H. Queen Charlotte's Hospital

Q.C.I.M. *Quarterly Cumulative Index Medicus*

Q.C. Is. Queen Charlotte Islands

Q.C.L.L.R. *Queensland Crown Lands Law Reports*

Q. Co. Queen's County

Q.C.R. quality control reliability

Q.C.T. quality control technology

Q.C.W.A. Quarter Century Wireless Association (U.S.A.)

QD *s* London, for vehicles temporarily imported from abroad (B.V.R.)

q.d. L. *quater in die*, four times a day (med.); L. *quasi dicat*, as if one should say; L. *quasi dictum*, as if said

q.d.D.g. Sp. *que de Dios goce*, may he be in God's keeping

Q.d'O. Fr. *Quai d'Orsay*

QDRI Qualitative Development Requirement Information (U.S.A.)

QE *s* London, for vehicles temporarily imported from abroad (B.V.R.)

q.e. L. *quod est*, which is

Q.E. quantum electronics

Q.E.2 Queen Elizabeth the second, Cunard liner

Q.E.A. Qantas Empire Airways Limited (Aust.)

q.e.d. L. *quod erat demonstrandum*, which was to be demonstrated/proved

q.e.f. L. *quod erat faciendum*, which was to be done

QEH Queen Elizabeth Hall, South Bank, Lond.

q.e.i. L. *quod erat inveniendum*, which was to be discovered/found out

QER *Quarterly Economic Review*

QF *s* London, for vehicles temporarily imported from abroad (B.V.R.)

Q.F. quality factor (*also* Q-factor); quick-firing (gun)

Q.F.R.I. Queensland Fisheries Research Institute (Aust.)

Q.F.S.M. Queen's Fire Service Medal

QG *s* London, for vehicles temporarily imported from abroad (B.V.R.)

Q.G. quadrature grid; Port. *quartel-general*, headquarters; quartermaster general; Fr. *quartier-général*, headquarters; It. *quartier generale*, headquarters

QH *s* London, for vehicles temporarily imported from abroad (B.V.R.)

q.h. L. *quaque hora*, every hour

Q.H. Queen's Hall

Q.H.C. Queen's Honary Chaplain

QHM Queen's Harbour Master

Q.H.N.S. Queen's Honorary Nursing Sister

Q.H.P. Queen's Honorary Physician

Q.H.S. Queen's Honorary Surgeon

q.i. quality indices

q.i.d. L. *quater in die*, four times a day (med.)

Q.I.D.N. Queen's Institute of District Nursing

Q.I.P. L. *quiescat in Pace*, may he/she rest in peace

QJ *s* London, for vehicles temporarily imported from abroad (B.V.R.)

Q.J.P.R. *Queensland Justice of the Peace Reports* (Aust.)

QK *s* London, for vehicles temporarily imported from abroad (B.V.R.)

qk. quick

qkm Ger. *Quadratkilometer*, square kilometre

Q. Kt. queen's knight (chess)

Q. Kt. P. queen's knight's pawn (chess)

QL *s* London, for vehicles temporarily imported from abroad (B.V.R.)

ql. quarrel; quintal

q.l. L. *quantum libet*, as much as you please

Q.L. Queen's Lancers

Qld. Queensland (Aust.)

qlty. quality

qm Ger. *Quadratmeter*, square metre

QM *s* London, for vehicles temporarily imported from abroad (B.V.R.)

qm. L. *quomodo*, by what means

Q.M. quartermaster, *also* Qmr.; Queen's Messenger, *also* Q-Mess

Q.M.A.A.C. Queen Mary's Army Auxiliary Corps, *now* W.R.A.C.

Q.M.C. quartermaster corps; Queen Mary College, Lond.

QMDO Qualitative Materiel Development Objective (U.S.A.)

Q.M.G. quartermaster-general

Q.M.G.F. quartermaster-general to the forces

QMR qualitative material requirement

Q.M.S. quartermaster-sergeant

QN *s* London, for vehicles temporarily imported from abroad (B.V.R.)

qn. question; quotation

Qn. Queen

Q.N.S. quantity not sufficient

Qns. Coll. Queen's College

Qns/d. Queensland (Aust.)

qnty. quantity

Q.O. qualified in ordnance (naval)

Q.O.C.H. Queen's Own Cameron Highlanders

Q.O.R. qualitative operational requirement; *Quebec Official Reports*

QP *s* London, for vehicles temporarily imported from abroad (B.V.R.)

q.p. L. *quantum placet*, as much as you please/at discretion (also *q.pl.*)

Q.P. qualification pay; queen's pawn (chess)

QPC Qatar Petroleum Company

Q.P.F.C. Queen's Park Football Club (Scot.)

QPL qualified products list

Q.P.M. Queen's Police Medal

Q.P.R. *Quebec Practice Reports*; Queen's Park Rangers Football Club

QQ *s* London, for vehicles temporarily imported from abroad (B.V.R.)

qq. quartos; questions

qq.v. L. *quae vide*, which see; L. *quantum vis*, as much as you wish

qr. quarter, 28 lbs; quarterly; quire, 24 sheets of paper

qr. L. *quadrans*, farthing

Q.R. *Quarterly Review*; queen's rook (chess); quick reaction

Qr. Mr. quartermaster

Q.R.P. queen's rook's pawn (chess)

Q.R.R. Queen's Royal Rifles

Q.R.V. Qualified Valuer Real Estate Institute of New South Wales (Aust.)

QS *s* London, for vehicles temporarily imported from abroad (B.V.R.)

q.s. L. *quantum sufficit*, a sufficient quantity (also *quant. suff.*)

Q.S. quarantine station; quarter section; quarter sessions (leg.); Queen's Scholar

QSO quasi-stellar object (astron.)

Q.S.R.I.G. Research and Information Group of the Quantity Surveyors' Committee, Royal Institute of Chartered Surveyors

Q.S.R.S. quasi-stellar radio source (astron.)

QSTS quadruple screw turbine ship

qt. quantity (*also* qty.); quart

q.t., Q.T. quiet, on the

Q.T.C. Queensland Turf Club (Aust.)

qtly. quarterly

qto. quarto

qtr. quarter

qu. quart; quarter; quarterly; queen; query; question

qu. L. *quasi*, as it were

quack quacksalver, a pretended doctor

quad. quadrangle; quadrant; quadrat (typ.); quadrilateral; quadruple; quadruplet; quadruplicate, *also* quadrupl.

qual. qualification (*also* qualn.); qualitative; quality

quant. quantitative; quantity

quant. suff. L. *quantum sufficit*, a sufficient quantity, also *q.s.*, *quantum suff.*

quar. quarter; quarterly, *also* quart.

quart. pars L. *quarta pars*, a fourth part (med.)

quat. quaternary ammonium compound, class of bactericides

Q.U.B., Q.U.Belf. Queen's University, Belfast

Qué. Québec (Can.)

Queensl. Queensland (Aust.)

ques. question

questn. questionnaire

quins quintuplets

Quins. Harlequins Rugby Football Club

quint. quintuplicate

q.u.i.p. query interactive processor; questionnaire interpreter programme

quor. quorum

quot. quotation; quote

quotes quotation marks

q.v. L. *quantum vis*, as much as you will; L. *quantum volueris*, at will (med.); L. *quod vide*, which see

Q.V.C.F. Queen Victoria Clergy Fund

Q.V.R. Queen Victoria Rifles

Q.W.N. *Queensland Law Reporter and Weekly Notes* (Aust.)

qy. quay; query

qz. quartz

R

r *s* correlation coefficient (psy.); radius; *s* radius vector of co-ordinates (math.); *s* rain (met.); *s* resistance ohm (elec.); run (sports); the Supertonic note in any key in Tonic Sol-fa, pron. Ray

R *s* Derbyshire (B.V.R.); 80 (Roman); *s* gas constant (chem.); *s* heavy rain (met.); *s* radical (chem.); radioactive mineral/range; *s* Ramsgate (B.F.P.); retarder, regulator on clock/watch; *s* roentgen, unit of radiation; *s* Romania (I.V.R.); rook (chess); *s* stimulus, Ger. *Reiz* (psy.); *s* telephone, R.A.C., on ordnance maps

R′ radius of circle in minutes of arc (math.)

R″ radius of circle in seconds of arc (math.)

r. radius; railroad; railway; range; rare; ratio; recipe; recto; red; reply; reserve; residence; resides; response; retired; right; rises; river; road; rod (measurement); rood (measurement); rouble; rubber (card games); rule (leg.); rule (measurement); runs (cricket); rupee

R. rabbi; It. *Raccomandata*, registered (mail); radical; radiolocation; radiologist; radiology; radius; railroad; railway; It. *Rapido*, express train; Réaumur thermometer; Ger. *Rechnung*, bill/invoice; Ger. *Recht*, law; recommendation; rector; regiment; registered; regular; relative (nav.); reliability; reply; report; republic; republican; reserve; retard; retire; retired; reward; Rifles; right, from actor's point of view (theatre); Port. *rio*, river; Sp. *río*, river; river; road; Roman; Romania; Romanian; Rome; rosary; Rouble, Russian currency; route; royal; Port. *Rua*,

street; Fr. *Rue*, street; run, deserted; run, distance travelled from noon to noon (naut.); runic (typ.); Rupee (currency)

R. Fr. *Récit*, swell organ (mus.); L. *regina*, queen; L. *regius*, royal; L. *remotum*, far; L. *respublica*, Republic; L. *rex*, king

® *s* registered United States Patent Office. In some other countries it is used to indicate registered trade mark

℞ *s* reluctance (magnet.)

℞ *s recipe*, take, used at head of med. prescription; *s* response, to a versicle

Ra *s* radium (chem.)

RA *s* Argentine (I.V.R.); *s* Derbyshire (B.V.R.)

ra. radio

R/A. refer to acceptor (fin.); return to author

R.A. Ramblers' Association; Ratepayers' Association; Rear Admiral; Recidivists Anonymous; reduction of area; Referees' Association (Association Football); Regular Army (U.S.A.); Sp. *República Argentina*, Argentine Rep.; research association; Resettlement Administration (U.S.A.); rifle association; right arch; right ascension (astr.); Road Association; Royal Academician; Royal Academy; royal arch; Royal Artillery; Russian America

R. & A. Royal and Ancient Golf Club, St. Andrews, Fife (Scot.)

R.A.A. Rabbinical Alliance of America; Royal Academy of Arts; Royal Artillery Association; Royal Australian Artillery

295

R.A.(A). Rear-Admiral of Aircraft Carriers

R.A.A.F. Royal Afghan/Australian/Auxiliary/Air Force

R.A.A.F.N.S. Royal Australian Air Force Nursing Service

R.A.A.M.C. Royal Australian Army Medical Corps

R.A.A.N.C. Royal Australian Army Nursing Corps

R.A.A.N.S. Royal Australian Army Nursing Service

R.A.A.S. Racial Adjustment Action Society; Royal Amateur Art Society

Rab François Rabelais (*c* 1494–*c* 1553), Fr. satirist and humorist; R. A. Butler, *now* Lord Butler of Saffron Walden (1902–), Brit. statesman; Robert

Rab. Rabat (Morocco)

RABAR Raytheon advanced battery acquisition radar

Rabb. rabbinate; rabbinic; rabbinical

Rabbie Robert (Scot.)

R.A.B.D.F. Royal Association of British Dairy Farmers

R.A.B.F.M. Research Association of British Flour Millers

R.A.B.I. Royal Agricultural Benevolent Institution

RABPCVM Research Association of British Paint Colour and Varnish Manufacturers

RAC Railway Association of Canada; Regional Advisory Committee (TUC); Regional Advisory Council for Further Education; Regional Advisory Councils

R.A.C. Royal Aero Club; Royal Agricultural College, Cirencester; Royal Arch Chapter (freem.); Royal Armoured Corps; Royal Automobile Club

R.A.C.A. Royal Automobile Club of Australia

RACE radiation adaptive compression equipment; rapid automatic checkout equipment

RACEP random access and correlation for extended performance (computer)

R.A.Ch.D. Royal Army Chaplains' Department

R.A.C.I. Royal Australian Chemical Institute

RACON radar beacon

R.A.C.P. Royal Australasian College of Physicians

R.A.C.S. Royal Australasian College of Surgeons

R.A.C.V. Royal Automobile Club of Victoria (Aust.)

rad. radian, unit of plane angle; radiation (phys.); radical; radio; radius; radix

rad. L. *radix*, root

Rad. radar; Radical Left, pol. party (Den.); radio; radiologist; radiology; radiotherapist; radiotherapy; Radnorshire (Wales)

r.a.d. radiation absorbed dose; random access disc; rapid automatic drill

R.A.D. Royal Academy of Dancing; Royal Albert Docks

R.A.(D). Rear Admiral of Destroyers

rada radioactive

R.A.D.A. Royal Academy of Dramatic Art

RADAR radio detection and ranging

RADAS random access discrete address system

RADC Rome Air Development Center (USAF)

R.A.D.C. Royal Army Dental Corps

RADCM radar countermeasures

R.A.D.D. Royal Association in Aid of the Deaf and Dumb

Raddol. It. *Raddolcendo,* growing calmer and more gentle (mus.)

RADIST radar distance indicator

R.A.Dks. Royal Albert Docks

R.Adm. Rear Admiral

radmon radiological monitor/monitoring

radn. radian; radiation

RADOT real-time automatic digital optical tracker (NASA)

RADRON radar squadron (USAF)

rad/s radians per second, unit of angular velocity

rae radio astronomy explorer

Rae Rachel; Raquelle

R.A.E. Royal Aircraft Establishment; Royal Australian Engineers

R. Ae. C. Royal Aero Club

R.A.E.C. Royal Army Educational Corps

Ra. Em. radium emanation

R. Aero. C. Royal Aero Club of the United Kingdom

R. Ae. S. Royal Aeronautical Society

R.A.F. Royal Aircraft Factory; Royal Air Force

R.A.F.A. Royal Air Force Association; Royal Australian Field Artillery

R.A.F.B.F. Royal Air Force Benevolent Fund

R.A.F.E.S. Royal Air Force Educational Service

R.A.F.F.C. Royal Air Force Ferry Command, *now* R.A.F.T.C.

R.A.F.G.S.A. Royal Air Force Gliding and Soaring Association

R.A.F.M.S. Royal Air Force Medical Services

R.A.F.O. Reserve of Air Force Officers

R.A.F.R. Royal Air Force Regiment

R.A.F.R.O. Royal Air Force Reserve of Officers

R.A.F.S.A.A. Royal Air Force Small Arms Association

R.A.F.S.C. Royal Air Force Staff College

R.A.F.T.C. Royal Air Force Transport Command

R.A.F.V.R. Royal Air Force Volunteer Reserve

rag. It. *ragioniere*, accountant; ragtime

r.a.g. river assault group

R.A.G.A. Royal Australian Garrison Artillery

R.A.G.B. Refractories Association of Great Britain

R.A.G.C. Royal and Ancient Golf Club, St. Andrews (Scot.)

R.A.H. Royal Albert Hall, a large circular hall in S. Kensington (Lond.), completed 1871 and building financed from profits of Great Exhibition 1851

R.A.H.S. Royal Australian Historical Society

RAI *Radio Audizioni Italiane*, Italian Broadcasting Corporation; — TV *Radio Audizioni Italiane e Televisione*, Italian Broadcasting and Television Corporation

R.A.I. Royal Albert Institution; Royal Anthropological Institute

R.A.I.A. Royal Australian Institute of Architects

R.A.I.C. Royal Architectural Institute of Canada

rail railroad; railway

RAILS Remote Area Instrument Landing Sensor

Raj. Rajasthan (India)

RAK *Rikets Allmanna Kartverk*, Geographical Survey Office (Swed.)

rall. It. *rallentando*, gradually slackening speed (mus.)

RAM radio attenuation measurement; random access method; rocket-assisted motor; Royal Air Maroc, Moroccan airlines

R.A.M. right ascension of the meridian; Royal Academy of Music (Lond.); Royal Arch Masons (freem.)

RAMAC Radio Marine Associated Companies; random access memory accounting

Ramb. Rambler (rose)

R.A.M.C. Royal Army Medical Corps

R.A.M.N.A.C. Radio Aids to Marine Navigation Application Committee

RAMP Raytheon Airborne Microwave Platform (sky station)

RAMPART Radar Advanced Measurements Program for Analysis of Reentry Techniques

RAMPS resources allocation and multi-project scheduling

R.A.M.S. right ascension of the mean sun

R.A.N. request for authority to negotiate; Royal Australian Navy

R.A.N.C. Royal Australian Naval College

RANCOM random communication satellite

Rand Witwatersrand, Johannesburg (S. Afr.)

R.A.N.R. Royal Australian Naval Reserve

R.A.N.V.R. Royal Australian Naval Volunteer Reserve

R.A.O.B. Royal Antediluvian Order of Buffaloes

R.A.O.C. Royal Army Ordnance Corps

R.A.O.U. Royal Australasian Ornithologists' Union

RAP Radical Alternatives to Prison

rap. rapid

R.A.P. Rupees, Annas, Pies (currency)

R.A.P.C. Royal Army Pay Corps

RAPCON radar approach control center (USAF)

RAPPI random access plan position indicator (computer)

R.A.P.R.A. Rubber and Plastics Research Association of Great Britain

R.A.R.D.E. Royal Armament Research and Development Establishment

R.A.R.O. Regular Army Reserve of Officers

Ras Desiderius Erasmus (1466–1536), Dutch scholar and theologian

RAS. rectified air speed, indicated air speed corrected for installation and positioning errors (nav.)

R.A.S. Royal Aeronautical/Agricultural Society; Royal Albert School; Royal Asiatic/Astronomical Society

R.A.S.B. Royal Asiatic Society of Bengal

R.A.S.C. Royal Army Service Corps, *now* R.C.T.; Royal Astronomical Society of Canada

R.A.S.E. Royal Agricultural Society of England

RASER radio frequency amplification by stimulated emission of radiation

R.A.S.K. Royal Agricultural Society of Kenya

RAT rocket-assisted torpedo

rat. rate; rating; rations

RATAN radar and television aid to navigation

RATCC radar air traffic control center (U.S.A.)

RATO rocket-assisted take-off

R.A.T.P. Fr. *Régie autonome des transports parisiens*, Paris municipal transport control (Metro)

R. Aux. A.F. Royal Auxiliary Air Force

R.A.V.C. Royal Army Veterinary Corps

Ray Rachel; Raymond

Rb s rubidium (chem.)

RB s Botswana, *formerly* Bechuanaland (I.V.R.); s Derbyshire (B.V.R.)

R & B ring and ball

r.b. reconnaissance bomber; right bank (sport); rubber band

R.B. Sp. *República Boliviana*, Rep. of Bolivia; Rifle Brigade; river board

R. & B. rhythm and blues

R.B.A. River Boards Association; Road Bitumen Association; Roads Beautifying Association; Royal Society of British Artists

R.B.A.F. Royal Belgian Air Force

r.b.c. red blood cell/corpuscle

RBD rapid beam deflector

RBDE radar bright display equipment

RBE relative biological effectiveness/efficiency (phys.)

R. Berks. Royal Berkshire Regiment

RBF read bit feedback (computer)

R.B.G. Royal Botanic Gardens, Kew

RBI right back inside on edge of skate

r.b.i. require better information; run batted in (baseball)

R.B.K. Royal Borough of Kensington

rbl. rouble, Russian currency

R. Bn. radio beacon, medium frequency non-direction beacon

R.B.N. Registry of Business Names

R.B.N.A. Royal British Nurses' Association

RBO right back outside on edge of skate

R-boat a German motor mine-sweeper, WW2

R.B.S. Royal Society of British Sculptors

rbt. roundabout

r/c Port. *rés-do-chão*, ground floor

RC s China, Taiwan (I.V.R.); s Derby (B.V.R.); racing/road club (cycling)

R/C re-credited

r.c. radio code; radio coding; red cell/corpuscle; reinforced concrete; release clause; reverse course; right centre (sport); rotary combustion; rubber-cushioned

R.C. Red Cross; Reformed Church; Republican Convention (U.S.A.); research centre/contribution; rifle club; right of centre (theatre); Roman Catholic; Royal College/Commission

RCA s Central African Republic

(I.V.R.); Rabbinical Council of America; Radio Club of America; Rhodesian Constitutional Association

R.C.A. Racecourse Association; Radio Corporation of America; Railway Clerks' Association; Reinforced Concrete Association; Royal Cambrian/Canadian Academy; Royal College of Art; Royal Company of Archers

R.C.A.A. Royal Canadian Academy of Arts

R.C.A.F. Royal Canadian Air Force

R. Cam. A. Royal Cambrian Academy of Art

R.C.A.M.C. Royal Canadian Army Medical Corps

R.C.A.S. Royal Central Asian Society

R.C.A.S.C. Royal Canadian Army Service Corps

R.C.A.T. Royal College of Advanced Technology

RCB s Congo, Brazzaville (I.V.R.)

RCC recovery control center; rescue coordination center/centre; rough combustion cut-off

r. & c.c. riots and civil commotions

R.C.C. Radiochemical Centre at Amersham; Roman Catholic Chaplain/Church; Rubber Cable Council; Rural Community Council

RCCE Regional Congress of Construction Employers (U.S.A.)

R.C.Ch. Roman Catholic Church

RCD Regional Co-operation for Development (Iran, Pak., Turk.)

rcd. received

R.C.D.A. Retail Coin Dealers' Association (U.S.A.)

R.C.D.C. Royal Canadian Dental Corps

r.c.f. relative centrifugal force

R.C.F.C.A. Royal Canadian Flying Clubs' Association

R.C.G.A. Royal Canadian Golf Association

R.C.G.P. Royal College of General Practitioners

R.C.G.S. Royal Canadian Geographical Society

RCH s Chile (I.V.R.)

R.C.H. railway clearing house

r.c.i. radar coverage indicator

R.C.I. Royal Canadian Institute; Royal Colonial Institute, *now* R.C.S.

recirc. recirculate

R.C.J. reaction control jet; Royal Courts of Justice

RCK *Research Centrum Kalkzandsteen Industrie*, Dutch calcium silicate brick organ.

R.C.L. Royal Canadian Legion; ruling case law

R.C.M. radar counter measures; regimental corporal-major; regimental court martial; Royal College of Midwives/Music

R.C.M.P. Royal Canadian Mounted Police

R.C.N. record control number; Royal Canadian Navy; Royal College of Nursing

R.C.N.C. Royal Corps of Naval Constructors

R.C.N.R. Royal Canadian Naval Reserve

R.C.N.T. Registered Clinical Nurse Teacher

R.C.N.V.R. Royal Canadian Naval Volunteer Reserve

R.C.O. Royal College of Organists

R.C.O.C. Royal Canadian Ordnance Corps

R.C.O.G. Royal College of Obstetricians and Gynaecologists

R.C.P. *Radio Clube Português*, Port. Radio Club; Royal College of Physicians/Preceptors

R.C.P.S.Glasg. Royal College of Physicians and Surgeons of Glasgow

rcpt. receipt

R.C.R.D.C. Radio Components Research and Development Committee

R.C.S. reaction/reactor control system; Royal Choral Society; Royal College of Science/Surgeons; Royal Commonwealth Society; Royal Corps of Signals; Royal Counties Show

R.C.S.C. Radio Components Standardization Committee

R.C.S.E. Royal College of Surgeons of Edinburgh, *also*, R.C.S.Edin.

R.C.S.(I.) Royal College of Surgeons of Ireland

RCSS random communication satellite system

R.C.S.T. Royal College of Science and Technology

rct. recruit

R.C.T. regimental combat team; Royal Corps of Transport

RCU remote control unit; rocket countermeasure unit

R.C.U. road construction unit

R.C.V.S. Royal College of Veterinary Surgeons

R. Cy. N. Royal Ceylon Navy

3rd third; — **degree**, police interrogation

Rd radium (unofficial abbrev.)

RD *s* Reading (B.V.R.)

R/D refer to drawer, of a cheque

R & D research and development

rd. rod, unit of measurement; — **²** square rod; round

R.D. Sp. *Repúblic Dominicana*, Dominican Republic; research department; Fr. *Rive Droite*, right bank; Royal Dragoons; Royal Naval Research Decoration; rural dean/delivery

RDA *Rassemblement Démocratique Africain*, African Democratic Rally (Guinea); recommended daily allowance

R.D.A. Diploma of Roseworthy Agricultural College, South Australia; reliability design analysis; Retail Distributors' Association; Royal Docks Association

RDB research and development board; rural development board

R.D.B. Royal Danish Ballet

R.D.C. Royal Defence Corps; running down clause (insce.); rural district council

R.D.C.A. Rural District Councils' Association

r.d.d. required delivery date

RD & E research, development and engineering

R.D.E. research and development establishment

RDF radio direction finder/finding

R.D.F. Royal Dublin Fusiliers

rd. hd. round head

RDI Royal Designer for Industry, diploma awarded by Royal Society of Art

rdr. radar

R.D.S. Royal Drawing/Dublin Society

RDT & E research, development, test and evaluation

rdy. ready

R. Dy., R.D.Y. Royal Dockyard

RDZ radiation danger zone

Re Reynolds number; *s* rhenium (chem.); Rupee, Ceylon, India and Pakistan currency

RE *s* Staffordshire (B.V.R.)

re. with reference to

R.e. red edges (book-binding)

R.E. radium emanations; real estate (U.S.A.); Reformed Episcopal; reliability engineering; Revised Edition; Right Excellent; right eye; ring edge (buttons); Royal Engineers/Exchange; Royal Society of Painter-Etchers and Engravers

R. & E. research and engineering

R.E.A. Radar and Electronics Association; request for engineer's authorization; Rubber Export Association; Rural Electrification Administration (U.S.A.)

REAC Regional Education Advisory Committee (TUC)

reac. reactor

REACT register enforced automated control technique (computer)

REAL *Real-Aerovias do Brasil*, Brazilian Airways

Rear Adm. Rear-Admiral

reasm. reassemble

Réau., Réaum. Réaumur's thermometric scale
REB radar evaluation branch; regional examining body
Reba Rebecca
rec. receipt; receive; recent; reception; recipe; record; recorder; recreation
rec. L. *recens,* fresh
R.E.C. Railway Executive Committee
recap. recapitulate; recapitulation
recce., reccy. reconnaissance (mil.)
recd. received
recep. reception
recip. reciprocal; reciprocity
recit. recitation
Recit. It. *Recitativo,* recitative (mus.)
reclam. reclamation
recm., recom. recommend
R.E.C.M.F. Radio & Electronic Comonent Manufacturers' Federation
recog. recognition; recognize
recon. reconcentration; reconciliation; recondition (*also* recond.); reconduction; reconnaissance; reconnoitre; reconsign; reconsignment; reconstruct (*also* reconst.); reconstruction; reconvey
R. Econ. S. Royal Economic Society
recpt. receipt
recr. receiver
recryst. recrystallize
Rec. Sec. recording secretary
rect. rectangle; rectangular; rectify
rect. L. *rectificatus,* rectified (med.)
rec't., rect. receipt
Rect. Rector; Rectory
red. redeemable (fin.); reduce; reduction
réd. Fr. *rédigé,* edited/compiled
redisc. rediscount
redup., redupl. reduplicate; reduplication; reduplicative
ref. refer; referee; reference; refining; reform; reformation; reformer; refunding; refuse
refash. refashioned
Ref. Ch. Reformed Church
refd. referred; refund
refl. reflection; reflective; reflex; reflexive
Reform. reformatory
Ref. Pres. Reformed Presbyterian
Refrig. refrigerate; refrigeration; refrigerator
Reg, Reggie, Reggy Reginald
reg. regent; regiment; region; register; registered; registrar; registry; regular; regulation; regulator
Reg. L. *regina,* queen
REGAL range and elevation guidance for approach and landing
Reg. Bez. Ger. *Regierungsbezirk,* admin. district

regd. registered
Reg.-Gen. Registrar-General
Reg. Prof. Regius Professor
regr. registrar
regt. regent; regiment
Regtl. regimental
Reg. T.M. Registered Trade Mark
R.E.I. Ger. *Rat der Europäischen Industrieverbände,* Council of European Industrial Feds.
REIG rare-earth iron garnets
reinf. reinforce
reinfmt. reinforcement
reit. reiteration, the printing of the second side of a sheet (typ.)
rej. reject
rel. relate; relative; release; relic; religion (*also* relig.); religious (*also* relig.); Fr. *reliure,* binding
rel. L. *reliquiae,* relics
Rel. Pron. relative pronoun
rel. to related to
rem Roentgen equivalent in man (phys.)
rem. remarks; remittance
Rem. remit
REMAD remote magnetic anomaly detection
R.E.M.C. Radio and Electronics Measurements Committee
R.E.M.E. Royal Electrical and Mechanical Engineers; — **(T.A.)** Royal Elec. and Mech. Engineers (Territorial Army)
R.E.M.P. Research Group for European Migration Problems
REMS registered equipment management system (USAF)
REMSA Railway Engineering Maintenance Suppliers Association (U.S.A.)
rem. stgs. remaining stages
Ren. Renaissance
Rene Irene
Renf. Renfrewshire (Scot.)
Renfe, RENFE *Red Nacional de Ferrocarriles Españoles,* Spanish State Railways
renv. renovate; renovation
REO regional education officer
rep Roentgen+equivalent+physical (phys.)
REP recovery and evacuation program (U.S.A.)
rep. repair; It. *reparto,* department; repeat; repertory (theatre); report; reporter; represent; representative; reprint; republic; republican
rep. L. *repetatur,* let it be repeated (med.)
Rep. Port. *Repartição,* Government Department; Republic; Republican party (U.S.A.)
R.E.P. *Rede dós Emissores Portu-*

gueses, Portuguese Amateur Radio Network

REPC Regional Economic Planning Council

repet. L. *repetatur*, let it be repeated

repl. replace; replaced; replacement

repo. repossess

repr. represent; representative, *also* repres.

repro. reproduced; reproduction

R.E.P.S. rail express parcel service

rep. sem. L. *repetatur semel*, let it be repeated once only (med.)

rept. receipt; report

repub. republish

Repub. Republic; Republican

req. request; require; requisition

reqd. required

reqn. requisition

reqs. requires

R.E.R.O. Royal Engineers Reserve of Officers

RES reticuloendothelial system

res. rescue; research; researcher; reservation; reserve; reserved; reside; residence; resident; resign; resolution

R.E.S. Royal Empire Society, *now* R.C.S.; Royal Entomological Society

resgnd. resigned

resig. resignation

resp. respective; respiration; respondent; responsibility

Resp. Bn. responder beacon

Res. Sec. resident secretary

REST routine execution selection table (computer)

rest., restr. restaurant

Rest. restoration; restrict; restriction

ret. retain; retire; retired; return

retd. retained; retired; returned

R. et I. L. *Regina et Imperatrix*, queen and empress; L. *Rex et Imperator*, king and emperor

retnr. retainer

Ret. P. retired pay

REV re-entry vehicle (space)

rev. revenue; reverse; review; revise; revision; revolution, of an engine; revolve; revolver

Rev. Book of Revelation (Bible); Reverend; Review

Rev. a/c revenue account

rev. ed. revised edition

rev/min revolutions per minute

Rev. Stat. revised statutes

Rev. Ver. Revised Version (Bible)

rew. reward

Rex Reginald

Reykjvk. Reykjavik (Iceland)

RF Rhodesian Front, the political spearhead of the drive for independence and permanent white supremacy; *s* Staffordshire (B.V.R.)

rf. It. *Rinforzando*, reinforcing, sudden crescendo made on short phrase (mus.)

Rf. reef; rough finish (paper)

r.f. radio frequency; range finder; rapid fire; reception fair; relative flow; replacement factor; representative fraction; rheumatic fever; right field/fielder (sport)

R.F. regular forces; representative fraction (cart.); *République française*, French Republic; Rockefeller Foundation; Royal Fusiliers; Rugby football

R.F.A. Royal Field Artillery; Royal Fleet Auxiliary

R.F.A.C. Royal Fine Art Commission

R.F. black reinforcing furnace black, filler in rubber compounding

R.F.C. Radio Frequency Choke; Reconstruction Finance Corporation (U.S.A.); Royal Flying Corps (*now* R.A.F.); Rugby Football Club

R.F.C.W.A. Regional Fisheries Commission for Western Africa (FAO)

RFD radio frequency devices; reporting for duty; rural free delivery (U.S.A.)

R.F.D.S. Royal Flying Doctor Service (Aust.)

R.F.E. Radio Free Europe

R.F.H. Royal Festival Hall, South Bank (Lond.)

RFI radio-frequency interference; request for information; right forward inside on edge of skate

R.F.L. Rugby Football League

Rfn. Rifleman

R.F.N. Registered Fever Nurse

RFO right forward outside on edge of skate

RFP request for proposal

r.f.p. retired on full pay

R.F.P.S.(G.), R.F.P.S.Glasg. Royal Faculty of Physicians and Surgeons of Glasgow

RFQ request for quotation

R.F.R. Royal Fleet Reserve

rfrd. referred

R.F.S. Registry of Friendly Societies; Royal Forestry Society of England and Wales

R.F.S.U. Rugby Football Schools' Union

R.F.U. Rugby Football Union

R.F.Y.C. Royal Forth Yacht Club

rfz. It. *Rinforzando*, reinforcing, sudden crescendo made on short phrase (mus.)

RG *s* Aberdeen (B.V.R.)

R.G. reserve guard; Fr. *Rive Gauche*, Left Bank

Rga. Riga (Latvia, U.S.S.R.)

R.G.A. Royal Garrison/Guernsey Artillery; Rubber Growers' Association
R.G.A.H.S. Royal Guernsey Agricultural and Horticultural Society
rgd. registered; reigned
R.G.D. Radio Gramophone Development Company
R.G.D.A.T.A. Retail Grocery, Dairy and Allied Trades Association
rge. range
R.G.E. Ger. *Rat der Gemeinden Europas*, Council of European Municipalities
R.-Genl. Registrar-General
R.G.G. Royal Grenadier Guards
R.G.H. Royal Gloucestershire Hussars
R.G.I. Royal Glasgow Institute of Fine Arts
rgn. region
Rgn. Rangoon (Burma)
R.G.N. Registered General Nurse
R.G.S. Royal Geographical Society
R.G.S.A. Royal Geographical Society of Australasia
Rgt. regiment
R.G.T.F. Royal General Theatrical Fund
Rgtl. regimental
Rh *s* Rhesus; *s* rhodium (chem.)
RH *s* Haiti (I.V.R.); *s* Kingston-upon-Hull (B.V.R.)
r.h. relative humidity; right half/hand
R.H. Ger. *Rechte Hand*, right hand; Royal Highlanders (Black Watch); Royal Highness/Hospital
R.H.A. Road Haulage Association; Royal Hibernian Academy; Royal Horse Artillery (mil.)
RHAF Royal Hellenic Air Force (Greece)
R. Hamps. Royal Hampshire Regiment (mil.)
rhap. rhapsody
R.H.B. regional hospital board; Robin Hood's Bay (Yorks.)
rhbdr. rhombohedron
r.h.c. rubber hydrocarbon content
R.H.C. Road Haulage Cases
R.H.E. Road Haulage Executive
RHEL Rutherford High Energy Laboratory
rheo. rheostat
rheol. rheological; rheology
rhet. rhetoric; rhetorical
R.H.F. Royal Highland Fusiliers
RH Factor Rhesus Factor, substance occurring in blood corpuscles of high proportion of human beings
R.H.G. Royal Horse Guards
R.H.H.I. Royal Hospital and Home for Incurables
RHI range-height indicator

rhino. rhinoceros
R. Hist. S. Royal Historical Society
RHM Rank Hovis McDougall
R.H.M.S. Royal Hibernian Military School
R.H.N. Royal Hellenic Navy (Greece)
R.H.O. regional hospital officer
Rhod. Rhodesia
rhom., rhomb. rhombic; rhomboid; rhombus
r.h.p. rated horsepower
RHQ regimental headquarters
R.H.R. Royal Highland Regiment (The Black Watch)
r.h.(s.) right hand side; round-headed screw
R.H.S. Royal Historical/Horticultural /Humane/Society
R.H.S.I. Royal Horticultural Society of Ireland
RI *s* Dublin (B.V.R.); *s* Indonesia (I.V.R.); Rhode Island, *also* R.I. (U.S.A.)
r.i. reflective insulation; refractive index; re-insurance; rubber insulated/insulation
R.I. Regimental Institute; religious instruction; report of investigation; Rotary International; Royal Institute of Painters in Water-Colours; Royal Institution
R.I. L. *Regina et Imperatrix*, Queen and Empress; L. *Regina Imperatrix*, Queen Empress; L. *Rex Imperator*, King Emperor
R.I.A. Royal Irish Academy
R.I.A.A. Recording Industry Association of America (U.S.A.)
R.I.A.C. Royal Irish Automobile Club
R.I.A.I. Royal Institute of the Architects of Ireland
R.I.A.M. Royal Irish Academy of Music
RIAS Ger. *Rundfunk im amerikanischen Sektor von Berlin*, Radio in the American Sector of Berlin
R.I.A.S. Royal Incorporation of Architects in Scotland
RIB Racing Information Bureau; Rural Industries Bureau
R.I.B.A. Royal Institute of British Architects
R.I.B.I. Rotary International in Great Britain and Ireland
Ric, Rich, Richd., Richie, Rick, Rickie, Ricky Richard; Rick, Rickie, Ricky *also* for Roderick
ric. It. *ricevuta*, receipt
R.I.C. Radio Industry Council; Royal Institute of Chemistry; Royal Irish Constabulary
RICA Research Institute for Communist/Consumer Affairs
Rich. Richmond

Rich. II *King Richard II* (Shake.)
Rich. III *King Richard III* (Shake.)
R.I.C.M. Fr. *Registre international des citoyens du monde*, Intern. Registry of World Citizens
RICMO radar input countermeasures officer (U.S.A.F.)
R.I.C.S. Royal Institution of Chartered Surveyors
rif. It. *rifatto*, restored
R.I.F. resistance inducing factor; Royal Irish Fusiliers
Rif. Brig. Rifle Brigade
RIFT reactor in flight test
Right Revd., Rt. Revd. Right Reverend
R.I.I.A. Royal Institute of International Affairs
R.I.L.E.M. Fr. *Réunion internationale des laboratoires d'essais et de recherches sur les matériaux et les constructions*, Intern. Union of Testing and Research Laboratories for Materials and Structures
RIM *s* Mauritania (I.V.R.)
R.I.M. Royal Indian Marines, *now* Indian Marines
R.I.N. Royal Indian Navy, *now* Indian Navy
R.I.N.A., R. Inst. N.A. Royal Institution of Naval Architects
rinf. It. *Rinforzando*, reinforcing, sudden crescendo made on short phrase (mus.)
RINSMAT resident inspector of naval materiel (U.S.A.)
Rio Rio de Janeiro (Braz.)
RIO reporting in and out
R.I.O.P. Royal Institute of Oil Painters
RIP recoverable item program (U.S.A.)
rip. It. *ripieno*, filling up, synonymous with *tutti* (mus.)
R.I.P. remainder in proportion, instruction to blockmaker to reduce/enlarge all parts in same ratio as marked for specified portion (typ.)
R.I.P. L. *Requiescat in pace*, may he/she rest in peace
R.I.P.H.H. Royal Institute of Public Health and Hygiene
R.I.P.P.L.E. radioactive isotope powered pulsed light equipment
RIPS range instrumentation planning study
rip. viet. It. *riproduzione vietata*, reproduction forbidden; copyrighted
R. Ir. A.M. Royal Irish Academy of Music (Dublin)
R. Ir. F. Royal Irish Fusiliers
R.I.S. Research Information Service
R.I.S.A. L. *Romani Imperii Semper Auctor*, Continual Increaser of the Roman Empire

R.I.S.C.O. Rhodesian Iron and Steel Company
R.I.S.D. Rural Institutions and Services Division of the Food and Agriculture Organization
RISE research in supersonic environment
RISS range instrumentation and support systems
R.I.S.W. Royal Institution of South Wales
RIT Rochester Institute of Technology (U.S.A.); Rorschach ink-blot test (psy.)
rit., ritard. It. *ritardando*, gradually getting slower (mus.)
Rita Margaret; Margarita
RITA reusable interplanetary transport approach vehicle
RITE rapid information technique for evaluation
riten. It. *ritenuto*, held back (mus.)
riv. It. *riveduto*, revised; river
R.I.V. repayment issue voucher
RJ ramjet; *s* Salford (B.V.R.)
R.J.A. Royal Jersey Artillery
R.J.A.S. Royal Jersey Agricultural Society
R.J.L.I. Royal Jersey Light Infantry
R.J.M. Royal Jersey Militia
R.J.O. Fr. *Rapports Judiciares Officiels*, Official Law Reports (Quebec, Can.)
RK *s* London (B.V.R.)
Rk. *Rank*, referring to the mixture stops of an organ (mus.)
R.K.O. Radio-Keith-Orpheum (theatre)
rky. rocky
RL *s* Cornwall (B.V.R.); *s* Lebanon (I.V.R.)
Rl. Rouble, Russian currency; Royal
R.L. radiation/research laboratory; radio location; reading list; reference library; resistor logic; rocket launcher; Rugby League
R.L.D.P.A.S. Royal London Discharged Prisoners' Aid Society
rl. est. real estate
R.L.F. Royal Literary Fund
R.L.I. Rhodes-Livingstone Institute (Zambia)
R. Lincolns. Royal Lincolnshire Regiment
R.L.O. railway liaison officer; returned letter office, *formerly* dead letter office
R.L.P.A.S. Royal London Prisoners' Aid Society
RLPO Royal Liverpool Philharmonic Orchestra
R.L.S. Robert Louis Stevenson (1850–1894), Scot. poet, novelist and essayist
R.L.S.S. Royal Life Saving Society
rly. railway; relay

r/m revolutions per minute
RM *s* Cumberland (B.V.R.); *s* Malagasy Republic (I.V.R.)
rm. ream, 20 quires/480 sheets (paper); room
r.m. radio monitoring; range mark; raw material; research memorandum; ring micrometer
r. & m. reliability and marketing; reports and memoranda
R.M. Registered Midwife; Ger. *Reichs-mark*, Ger. currency; resident magistrate; riding master; Royal Mail/Marines
R.M.A. Radio Manufacturers' Association (U.S.A.); Retread Manufacturers' Association; Rice Millers' Association (U.S.A.); Royal Malta/Marine Artillery; Royal Marines Association; Royal Military Academy (Sandhurst); Royal Military Asylum; Royal Musical Association; Rubber Manufacturers' Association (U.S.A.)
RMAG Rocky Mountain Association of Geologists (U.S.A.)
R.M.A.I. Radio Manufacturers' Association of India
r. mast radio mast
RMC *Radio Monte Carlo* (Monaco); rod memory computer
R.M.C. Radio Modifications Committee; Royal Military College
R.M.C.C. Royal Military College of Canada
R.M.C.M. Royal Manchester College of Music
R.M.C.S. Royal Military College of Science
r.m.d. ready money down
RMEA Rubber Manufacturing Employers' Association
R. Met. S. Royal Meteorological Society
R.M.F.V.R. Royal Marine Forces, Volunteer Reserves
RMI radio magnetic indicator; reliability maturity index
r/min revolutions per minute
R.M.L.I. Royal Marine Light Infantry
RMM *s* Mali (I.V.R.)
R.M.N. Registered Mental Nurse; Royal Malaysian Navy
R.M.O. regimental/regional/resident/medical officer; Royal Marine Office
R.Mon.R.E.(M.) Royal Monmouthshire Royal Engineers (Militia)
R.M.P. Royal Marine/Military Police
R.M.P.A. Royal Medico-Psychological Association
R.M.R.A. Royal Marines Rifle Association

rms. root mean square value, square root of the mean of the squares of the values dealt with (psy.)
R.M.S. Railway Mail Service; Royal Mail Service / Ship / Steamer / Steamship; Royal Medical/Meteorological/Microscopical Society; Royal Society of Miniature Painters
R.M.S.A. Rural Music Schools Association
R.M.Sch. Mus. Royal Marines School of Music
R.M.S.M. Royal Military School of Music
R.M.S.P. Royal Mail Steam Packet Company
Rn *s* radon (chem.)
RN *s* Preston (B.V.R.); *s* Runcorn (B.F.P.)
Rn. region
r.n. reception nil; research note
R.N. Registered Nurse (U.S.A.); Royal Naval/Navy
R. & N. *Rhodesia and Nyasaland Law Reports*
RNA ribonucleic acid (chem.)
R.N.A. Romantic Novelists' Association
R.N.A.F. Royal Naval Air Force, *now* F.A.A.
R.N.A.S. Royal Naval Air Service/Station
R.N.A.V. Royal Naval Artillery Volunteers
R.N.A.W. Royal Naval Aircraft Workshop
R.N.A.Y. Royal Naval Aircraft Yard
R.N.B. Royal Naval Barracks
R.N.B.T. Royal Naval Benevolent Trust
R.N.C. Republican National Committee (U.S.A.); Royal Naval College, *also* R. N. Coll.
rnd. round
R.N.D. *Rijksnijverheidsdienst*, Neth. Government Industrial Advisory Service; Royal Naval Division
R.N.E.C. Royal Naval Engineering College
RNF receiver noise figure
Rnf. Renfrewshire (Scot.)
R.N.F. Royal Northumberland Fusiliers
RNFP radar not functioning properly
R.N.F.U. Rhodesia National Farmers' Union
R.N.I.B. Royal National Institute for the Blind
R.N.I.D. Royal National Institute for the Deaf
RNLAF Royal Netherlands Air Force

R.N.L.I. Royal National Life-boat Institution

R.N.L.O. Royal Naval Liaison Officer

R.N.M.D. Registered Nurse for Mental Defectives

R.N.M.D.S.F. Royal National Mission to Deep Sea Fishermen

R.N.M.S. Registered Nurse of the Mentally Subnormal; Royal Naval Medical School

R. No. N. Royal Norwegian Navy

R. Norfolk Royal Norfolk Regiment

R.N.P.F.N. Royal National Pension Fund for Nurses

R.N.P.L. Royal Naval Physiological Laboratory

RNR *s* Zambia, *formerly* Northern Rhodesia (I.V.R.)

R.N.R. Royal Naval Reserve

R.N.R.A. Royal Naval Rifle Association

R.N.R.R.A. Royal Naval Reserve Rifle Association

Rns. runs

R.N.S. Royal Numismatic Society

R.N.S.A. Royal Naval Sailing Association

R.N.S.C. Royal Naval Staff College

R.N.S.R. Royal Naval Special Reserve

R.N.S.S. Royal Naval Scientific Service

R.N.T. Registered Nurse Tutor

R.N.T.E. Royal Naval Training Establishment

R.N.T.U. Royal Naval Training Unit

R.N.V.R. Royal Naval Volunteer Reserve

R.N.V.S.R. Royal Naval Volunteer Supplementary Reserve

R.N.W.A.R. Royal Naval Wireless Auxiliary Reserve

rnwy. runway

R.N.Y.C. Royal Northern Yacht Club

R.N.Z.A.C. Royal New Zealand Aero Club

R.N.Z.A.F. Royal New Zealand Air Force

R.N.Z.A.S. Royal Astronomical Society of New Zealand

R.N.Z.N. Royal New Zealand Navy

rº recto, right hand page

ro *s* slight rain (met.)

Rº *s* radius of circle in degrees of arc (math.)

RO *s* Hertfordshire (B.V.R.); *s* Rothesay (B.F.P.)

ro. recto; rood (measurement)

r.o. right/rough opening; rowed over (rowing); run out (cricket)

R.O. radar observer/operator; radio operator; receiving office/officer/order; record/registered office; recruiting/relieving officer; reserve occupation; returning officer; routine order; Royal Observatory

R.Ö. *Republik Österreich*, Rep. of Austria

R.O.A. Reserve Officers' Association; return on assets (fin.); Roller Owners' Association

ROAD reorganized objective army division

ROAMA Rome air materiel area

R.O.A.R. right of admission reserved

Rob, Robbie, Robin, Robt. Robert

R.O.B. remaining on board (ship.)

ROBIN rocket balloon instrument

R.O.C. Royal Observer Corps

R.O.C.E. return on capital employed (fin.)

ROCP radar out of commission for parts

Roddy Roderick; Rodney

ROE reflector orbital equipment

R.O.E. Royal Observatory, Edinburgh

R.O.F. Royal Ordnance Factory

Roffen. L. *Roffensis*, of Rochester, Eng. episcopal title, in bishop's signature

R. of O. Reserve of Officers

ROGER *s* your message received and understood; phonetic alphabet for *R* (received)

R.O.I. return on investment (fin.); Royal Institute of Oil Painters

ROJ range on jamming

Rolf Rudolf; Rudolph

Rolls Rolls-Royce (engine and car)

ROM red oxide of mercury (chem.)

rom. roman type, ordinary type as distinct from italics (typ.)

Rom. Epistle to the Romans (Bible); Roman; Romance language; Romanic

R.O.M. record office memorandum; Royal Ontario Museum (Can.)

Rom. Ant. Roman antiquities

Rom. Cath. Roman Catholic

Rom. Hist. Roman history

Rom. and Jul. *Romeo and Juliet* (Shake.)

Ron, Ronnie, Ronny Ronald

RON remain overnight; research octane number

R.O.O. railhead ordnance officer

ROOST reusable one-stage orbital space truck

r.o.p. run of paper

RORC Royal Ocean Racing Club

Ro-Ro roll-on roll-off (ship.)

Ros Rosamund; Rosemary

Ros. Rosary; Roscommon (Rep. of Ireland)

Rosetta Rose

Rosie Rosa; Rosamund; Rose; Rosemary

ROSIE reconnaissance by orbiting ship-identification equipment

ROSLA raising of school leaving age

Rospa, RoSPA Royal Society for the Prevention of Accidents

rot. rotary; rotation; rotor

Rot. Rotterdam (Neth.)

R.O.T. remedial occupational therapy

R.O.T.C. Reserve Officers' Training Corps (U.S.A.)

roul roulette (philately)

rout. routine

Rov. Rovers

R.O.W. right of way

Rox. Roxburgh; Roxburghshire

Roxy Roxana

Roy. Royal

RP *s* Northamptonshire (B.V.R.); received pronunciation (BBC pronunciation) commonly used by educated people living in SE England accepted, generally understood form of speech, without regional accent; reprint, a second/new impression/edition of any printed work, a re-impression (typ.); reprinting (typ.)

Rp. Rappen, Swiss centime (currency); Rupiah, Indonesian currency

r.p. reply paid

R.P. reaction product; reception poor; recovery phase; Reformed Presbyterian; Regimental Police; Regius Professor; reinforced plastic; reply paid; *República Portuguesa*, Portuguese Rep.; research paper; Fr. *Révérend Père*, Reverend Father; rocket projectile; Royal Society of Portrait Painters; rules of procedure

R.P.A. record of personal achievement used in place of school leaving examinations (educ.); Registered Plumbers' Association; Rubber Proofers' Association

R.P.C. Reports of Patents, Designs and Trade Marks Cases; Republican Party Conference (U.S.A.); request pleasure of your company; Royal Pioneer Corps (mil.)

R.P.D. regional port director; Regius Professor of Divinity; rocket propulsion department

R.P.D. L. *Rerum Politicarum Doctor*, Doctor of Political Science

R.P.E. radio production executive; Reformed Protestant Episcopal; rocket propulsion establishment

R.P.F. Fr. *Rassemblement du Peuple Français*, Rally of the French People

R.P.F.M.A. Rubber and Plastics Footwear Manufacturers' Association

r.p.g. radiation protection guide; rounds per gun

r.p.h. revolutions per hour

R. Phil. S. Royal Philharmonic Society

RPI radar precipitation integrator; general index of retail prices

RP/June reprinting in (e.g.) June

rplca. replica

RPM reliability performance measure

r.p.m. revolutions/rotations/rounds/per minute; Port. *rotações por minuto*, revolutions per minute

R.P.M. resale price maintenance

RP/ND reprinting, no date

R.P.O. railway post office; regional personnel officer; Royal Philharmonic Orchestra

R.P.R. Romanian People's Republic

rprt. report

r.p.s. revolutions per seond

R.P.S. radiological protection service; rapid processing system; Royal Philharmonic/Photographic Society

RP/shortly reprinting, shortly

rpt. repeat; report; reprint

RP/2m reprinting in (e.g.) 2 months

RP/UC reprint under consideration

R.P.V. remotely piloted vehicle

R/Q request for quotation

R.Q., r.q. respiratory quotient, being ratio of the volume of carbon dioxide expired to volume of oxygen consumed during same period (biol.)

RQL reference quality level

R.Q.M.S. regimental quartermaster sergeant

rqmt. requirement

rqr. require; requirement

rr *s* continuous rain (met.)

RR *s* continuous heavy rain (met.); *s* Nottinghamshire (B.V.R.); road race (cycling); *s* Rochester (B.F.P.)

Rr. Rare

r.r. radiation resistance; radio ranging; ready reckoner; rendezvous radar; respiratory rate

r. & r. rest and recreation (mil.); rock 'n' roll (dancing)

R-R., RR, R.R. Rolls-Royce

R.R. railroad; Remington Rand (U.S.A.); research reactor/report; return rate; Right Reverend; rural route

R.R.A. Radiation Research Association; Road Records Association (cycling); Royal Regiment of Artillery; rubber reclaiming agent

R.R.A.F. Royal Rhodesian Air Force

RRB Railroad Retirement Board (U.S.A.)

R.R.B. Radio Research Board

RRC Road Racing Club (cycling)

R.R.C. Royal Red Cross, *also* Lady of the Royal Red Cross

R.R.E. Royal Radar Establishment

R.R.F. Refrigeration Research Foundation (U.S.A.)

RRI *Radio Republik Indonesia*, Indonesia, government-owned and operated radio station

R.R.I. Rowett Research Institute, Bucksburn; Rubber Research Institute (Malaya)

R.R.I.C. Rubber Research Institute of Ceylon

R.R.I.M. Rubber Research Institute of Malaysia

RRL Radio Research Laboratory (Jap.)

R.R.L. Registered Record Librarian; Road Research Laboratory

RRP Recommended retail price

RR.PP. Fr. *Révérends Pères*, Reverend Fathers

R.r.r. It. *raccomandata con ricevuta di ritorno*, registered/return receipt requested

R.R.S. Radiation Research Society; radio research station; Royal Research Ship

RRV rate of rise of voltage

rs *s* sleet (met.)

Rs rupees, currency of India and Pakistan

RS *s* Aberdeen (B.V.R.)

r.s. right side

R/S. rejection slip

R.S. reconnaissance squadron/strike; recording secretary; recruiting service; research station; Revised Statutes (leg.); Rolls series; Royal Scots (mil.); Royal Society

RSA Road Safety Act

R.S.A. Registered Statistical Assistant; Royal Scottish Academician/Academy; Royal Society for the Encouragement of Arts, Manufactures and Commerce; Royal Society of Antiquaries/Arts; Royal Society of Australia

R.S.A.C. Reactor Safety Advisory Committee (Can.)

R.S.A.F. Royal Small Arms Factory

R.S.A.I. Royal Society of Antiquaries of Ireland

R.S.A.M. Royal Scottish Academy of Music

R. San. I. Royal Sanitary Institute, *now* R.S.H.

R.S. Arts Royal Society of Arts

R.S.A.S. Royal Sanitary Association of Scotland; Royal Surgical Aid Society

R.S.A.S.A. Royal South Australian Society of Arts

r.s.b. range safety beacon

R.S.B. regimental stretcher-bearer

R.S.C. Royal Shakespeare Company; Royal Smithfield Club; Royal Society of

Canada; Rules of the Supreme Court (Rep. of Ireland)

R.S.C.D.S. Royal Scottish Country Dance Society

rsch. research

R.S.C.J. L. *Virgines Religiosae Societatis Sacratissimi Cordis Jesus*, Nuns of the Most Sacred Heart of Jesus

R.S.C.M. Royal School of Church Music

R.S.C.N. Registered Sick Children's Nurse

R.S.D. recovery, salvage and disposal; returned stores department; rolling steel door; Royal Society of Dublin

R.S.D.L.P.(b.) Russian Social Democratic Labour Party (Bolsheviks)

R.S.E. Royal Society of Edinburgh

R.S.F. Royal Scots Fusiliers

R.S.F.S. Royal Scottish Forestry Society

R.S.F.S.R. Russian Soviet Federated Socialist Republic, largest of the republics forming the Union of Soviet Socialist Republics

R.S.G. regional seats of government; Royal Scots Greys (mil.)

R.S.G.B. Radio Society of Great Britain

R.S.G.S. Royal Scottish Geographical Society

R.S.H. Royal Society for the Promotion of Health

R.S.H.A. *Reichssicherheitshauptampt*, secret police of Nazi Germany

R.S.H.M. Religious of the Sacred Heart of Mary

RSI regional staff inspector

R.S.I. Research Studies Institute; Royal Sanitary Institute

R. Signals, R. Sigs. Royal Corps of Signals

RSJ rolled steel joist

R.S.L. Returned Services League of Australia; Royal Society, London, *usually* L omitted; Royal Society of Literature

R.S.L.A., also **R.O.S.L.A.** raising of school leaving age

RSM *s* San Marino (I.V.R.)

R.S.M. regimental sergeant major; regional sales manager; Royal School of Mines; Royal Society of Medicine; Royal Society of Musicians of Great Britain

R. & S.M. Royal and Select Masters

rsn. reason

R.S.N.A. Radiological Society of North America; Royal Society of Northern Antiquaries

R.S.N.Z. Royal Society of New Zealand

R.S.O. railway sorting office; railway

sub-office; range safety officer (mil.); recruiting staff officer; resident surgical officer; rural sub-office

R.S.P.A. Royal Society for the Prevention of Accidents, *also* RoSPA

R.S.P.B. Royal Society for the Protection of Birds

R.S.P.C.A. Royal Society for the Prevention of Cruelty to Animals

R.S.P.C.C. Royal Scottish Society for the Prevention of Cruelty to Children

R.S.P.E. Royal Society of Painter-Etchers and Engravers

R.S.P.P. Royal Society of Portrait Painters

rsq. rescue

RSR *s* Rhodesia, *formerly* Southern Rhodesia (I.V.R.)

RSROAA Roller Skating Rink Operators' Association of America

R.S.S. Royal Statistical Society

R.S.S. L. *Regiae Societatis Socius/Sodalis*, Fellow of the Royal Society

R.S.S.A.I.L.A. Returned Sailors, Soldiers and Airmen's Imperial League of Australia

R.S.S.I. Regional Science Research Institute (U.S.A.)

R.S.T. Rhodesian/Roan Selection Trust; Royal Society of Teachers

Rs, three reading, (w)riting and (a)rithmetic

R.S.T.M. & H. Royal Society of Tropical Medicine and Hygiene

rstr. restricted

RSU Road Safety Unit

R.S.U. Ragged School Union

R. Sussex Royal Sussex Regiment

R.S.V. Revised Standard Version (Bible)

R.S.V.P. random signal vibration protector; Fr. *répondez s'il vous plaît*, please reply

rsvr. reservoir

R.S.W. Royal Scottish Society of Painters in Water Colours

r.s.w.c. right side up with care

R. Sw. N. Royal Swedish Navy

R.S.W.S. Royal Scottish Water-Colour Society

RT *s* Suffolk, East (B.V.R.)

R/T radio telegraphy

rt. right

R.T. radio telegraphy/telephone/telephony; rated/reaction time; reading test; received text; recreational therapy; return ticket; rocket target; room temperature; round table/trip

R. & T. research and technology

RTA *Radiodiffusion et Télévision Algérienne*, Algerian radio and television

R.T.A. reciprocal trade agreements; Rhodesian Tobacco Association; Road Traffic Act; Rubber Trade Association

R.T.A.F. Royal Thai Air Force

RTAG Range Technical Advisory Group

r.t.b. return to base

R.T.B. Richard Thomas and Baldwins Limited

RTB/BRT *Radiodiffusion-Télévision Belge/Belgische Radio en Televisie* (Belg.)

rtc. ratchet

R.T.C. Royal Tank Corps, *now* Royal Tank Regiment

RTCA Radio Technical Commission for Aeronautics (U.S.A.)

RTCC real time computer complex (NASA)

R.T.C.E.G. Rubber and Thermoplastic Cables Export Group

rtd. returned

R.T.D. Religion through Drama

rtd. ht. retired hurt (cricket)

RTDS real time data system (computer)

rte. route

RTE. *Radio Telefís Eireann*, Irish Television

R.T.E.B. Radio Trades Examination Board

R. te G. *Rijksuniversiteit te Groningen*, State Univ. of Groningen (Neth.)

R.T.F. *Radiodiffusion-Télévision Française*, French TV network

RTG radiosotope thermoelectric generator

rtg. rating

Rt. Hon., Rt. Honble. Right Honourable

RTHPL Radio Times Hulton Picture Library

RTI *Radiodiffusion Télévision Ivoirienne*, Ivory Coast TV

R.T.I. Round Table International

R.T.I.T.B. Road Transport Industry Training Board

R. Tks. Royal Tank Regiment, *formerly* Royal Tank Corps

RTLA Road Transport Lighting Act

rtm registered trade mark

RTM rapid tuning magnetron; receiver-transmitter-modulator

rtn. retain; return

R.T.N. registered trade name; Royal Thai Navy

R.T.O. railway transport officer

R.T.P. *Radiotelevisão Portuguesa* S.A.R.L., Port. Television Co.

R.T.R. Royal Tank Regiment, *formerly* Royal Tank Corps

RTRA Road Traffic Regulation Act

R.T.R.A. Radio & Television Retailers' Association

308

Rt. Rev., Rt. Revd. Right Reverend

R.T.S. Religious Tract Society; reserve tug service; Royal Toxophilite Society

R.T.S.A. Retail Trading Standards Association

RTT *Radiodiffusion Télévision Tunisienne* (Tunisia)

RtT. radio-telegraphy

R.T.T.C. Road Time Trials Council (cycling)

RTU returned to unit (mil.)

R.T.V. re-entry test vehicle

Rt. W., Rt. Wpfl., Rt. Wpful. Right Worshipful

R.T.W. ready to wear; road tank wagon

rty. rarity

R.T.Y.C. Royal Thames Yacht Club

RTZ Rio Tinto Zinc Corporation Limited

Ru runic; *s* ruthenium (chem.)

RU *s* Bournemouth (B.V.R.); *s* Burundi (I.V.R.)

Ru. Rumania/Rumanian (*now generally* Romania/Romanian); Russia; Russian

R.U. Readers' Union; registered user; Rugby Union

R.U.A. Royal Ulster Academy of Painting, Sculpture and Architecture

R.U.A.S. Royal Ulster Agricultural Society

rub. rubber

Rube Reuben

R.U.C. Royal Ulster Constabulary

R.U.C.R. Royal Ulster Constabulary Reserve

rud. rudder

R.U.E. right upper entrance (theatre)

Rufe Rufus

Rug. Rugosa (roses)

rugger Rugby football

R.U.I. Royal University of Ireland

R.U.K.B.A., Rukba Royal United Kingdom Beneficent Association

RUM remote underwater manipulator

R.U.M. Royal University of Malta

R.U.P.P. road used as public path, usually green lanes, grass roads or old drove roads

R.U.R. *Rossum's Universal Robots,* play by Karel Capek; Royal Ulster Rifles

Rus., Russ. Russia; Russian

R.U.S.I. Royal United Service Institution

R.U.S.M. Royal United Service Museum

Rut., Rutd. Rutland

Ruth The Book of Ruth (Bible)

RV *s* Portsmouth (B.V.R.)

Rv. rendezvous

R.V. rateable value (fin.); research vessel; Revised Version (Bible); Rifle Volunteers (mil.)

R.V.A. Regular Veterans' Association of the United States

R. & V.A. Rating and Valuation Association

R.V.C. Rifle Volunteer Corps; Royal Veterinary College; Royal Victorian Chain

R.V.C.I. Royal Veterinary College of Ireland

RV(H)R Road Vehicles (Headlamps) Regulations

R.V.I.A. Royal Victoria Institute of Architects (Aust.)

RVL(Ex)R Road Vehicles Lighting (Standing Vehicles) (Exemption) Regulations

RVLR Road Vehicles Lighting Regulations

R.V.O. Royal Victorian Order

Rvp, RVP Reid vapour pressure

R.V.R. runway visual range

R. & V.R. *Rating and Valuation Reports*

R.V.S.V.P. Fr. *répondez vite, s'il vous plaît,* please reply quickly

R.V.U. research vessel unit

RW *s* Coventry (B.V.R.)

Rw. Rwanda

R.W. radiological warfare; rainwater; right of way: Right Worshipful/Worthy; Royal Warrant; runway

RWA Radiowriters' Association; Rwanda (I.V.R.)

R.W.A. Race Walking Association; Royal West of England Academy, *also* R.W.E.A.

R.W.A.F.F. Royal West African Frontier Force (mil.)

R. War. R. Royal Warwickshire Regiment

R.W.A.S. Royal Welsh Agricultural Society

R.W.D.G.M. Right Worshipful Deputy Grand Master (freem.)

R.W.F. Radio Wholesalers' Federation; Royal Welch Fusiliers

R.W.G.M. Right Worshipful Grand Master (freem.)

R.W.G.R. Right Worthy Grand Representative (freem.)

R.W.G.S. Right Worthy Grand Secretary (freem.)

R.W.G.T. Right Worthy Grand Templar/Treasurer (freem.)

R.W.G.W. Right Worthy Grand Warden (freem.)

R. Wilts. Yeo. Royal Wiltshire Yeomanry

R.W.J.G.W. Right Worthy Junior Grand Warden (freem.)

R.W.K. Queen's Own Royal West Kent Regiment

R.W.S. Member of the Royal Society of Painters in Water Colours; rainwater and soil

R.W.S.G.W. Right Worshipful Senior Grand Warden (freem.)

Rwy. railway

RX *s* Berkshire (B.V.R.); *s* Republic of Panama (I.C.A.M.); *s* Rye (B.F.P.)

Rx. rix-dollar, European coin; tens of rupees

RY *s* Leicester (B.V.R.); *s* Ramsey (B.F.P.)

Ry. railway; Ryukyu Islands (*also* Ryu.)

R.Y.A. Royal Yachting Association

R.Y.S. Royal Yacht Squadron

RZ *s* Antrim (B.V.R.)

r.z. return to zero

R.Z.Scot., R.Z.S.S. Royal Zoological Society of Scotland

R.Z.S.I. Royal Zoological Society of Ireland

S

s second of arc; second, unit of time interval; Dominant note in any key in Tonic Sol-fa, pron. soh; *s* snow (met.); stere; Fr. *sur*, on

s̄ *s* symmetrical (chem.)

's Dutch *des* (obsolete), of the (as 's Gravenhage, The Hague)

s/ Port. *sem*, without

S air raid shelter (WW2); *s* Edinburgh (B.V.R.); *s* scalar (math.); silver; *s* Skibbereen (Irish Rep. F.P.); slow, on clock/ watch regulator; strangeness (phys.); *s* sulphur (chem.); *s* Sweden (I.V.R.)

S111 BAC Super one-eleven (aircraft)

S L. *Sarnia*, Guernsey, in Brit. bot. records, also applied to Jersey and Alderney; L. *signa*, write, used in med. prescriptions to indicate directions to be placed on label of medicine

S/ *sol*, Peruvian currency

s. It. *sabato* (*also* sab.), Saturday; *Schilling* (Austrian currency); school; scruple; sea; seaman; section; see; semi; sermon; set; shilling, British currency until 1971 equiv. to five new pence; Fr. *siècle*, century; Ger. *siehe*, see; sign; signed; singular; It. *sinistra*, left; sire; sister; small; society; solo; son; *sou*, French currency; south; southern; spades; spherical; steel; stem; stock; stratus cloud (met.); substantive; succeeded; *sucre*, Ecuadorian currency; suit; sunny; surplus

s. L. *semi*, half; L. *sinister*, left; L. *solidus*, shilling; *soprano* (mus.)

S. Sabbath; sable; Saint; Fr. *saint*, Saint; It. *San, Santo*, Saint; Ger. *Sankt*, Saint; Port. *São*, Saint; Saturday; Saxon; Scotch; Scottish; scribe; secondary; secret; secretary; section, followed by number (tax.); Ger. *Seite*, page; Senate; Sp. *Señor*, Mr.; September; series; ship; signaller; It. *Signor*, Mr.; It. *Signora*, Mrs.; singular; socialist; society; solar; staff; statute (leg.); submarine; Ger. *Süd*, south; summer; sun; Sunday; Sweden

S. It. *Segno*, sign (mus.); L. *sepultus*, buried; L. *socius/sodalis*, Fellow

$ *s* dollar

∫ *s* integration (math.)

Sa. *s* samarium (chem.)

SA *s* Aberdeenshire (B.V.R.); *s* Swansea (B.F.P.)

Sa. sable; Saturday; Ger. *Summa*, total

s.a. safe arrival; see also; sex appeal; Ger. *siehe auch*, see also; small arms; soluble in alkaline; special agent; storage area; subject to approval; subsistence allowance

s.a. L. *secundum artem*, by skill (med.); L. *sine anno*, undated; L. *sub anno*, under the year

S.A. Salvation Army; *Samson Agonistes*; Saudi Arabia/Arabian; second attack (Lacrosse); Secretary of the Army (U.S.A.); semi-annual; services adviser; Shops Act (1950); small arms; *Sociedad Anónima*, Sp. limited company; *Société Anonyme*, Belgian/French limited liability; Society of Antiquaries/Authors; Soil Association; Fr. *Son Altesse*, Her/ His Highness; South Africa/African; South America / American; South Australia / Australian; *Sturm-Abteilung*, Nazi Ger. storm-troops; supply assistant

311

S.A. L. *Societas Adunatonis,* Society of the Atonement (Franciscans)

S.A.A. Shakespeare Association of America; small arms ammunition; South African Airways; Standards Association of Australia; surface-active agent

S.A.A.A. Scottish Amateur Athletic Association

SAAB *Svensk Aeroplan Aktiebolag,* Swed. Aeroplane Company

S.A.A.D. Small-Arms Ammunition Depot; Society for the Advancement of Anaesthesia in Dentistry

S.A.A.E.B. South African Atomic Energy Board

S.A.A.F. South African Air Force

SAAT Society of Architects and Allied Technicians

S.A.A.U. South African Agricultural Union

sab. Port. *sábado,* Saturday

Sab. Sabbath

S.A.B. Science/Scientific Advisory Board; Society of American Bacteriologists; *Sveriges Allmanna Biblioteksforening,* Swed. General Library Assn.

S.A.B. *Soprano, Alto, Bass* (mus.)

S.A.B.A. Scottish Amateur Boxing Association

Sabat. Sabbatical

SABC Scottish Association of Boys' Clubs

S.A.B.C. South African Broadcasting Corporation

S.A.B.E.N.A., SABENA *Société anonyme belge d'exploitation de la navigation aérienne,* Belg. World Air Lines

SABMIS seaborne anti-ballistic missile intercept system

sabo. sabotage

S.A.B.R.A. South African Bureau of Racial Affairs

S.A.B.S. South African Bureau of Standards

SAC Security and Administration Council, operates at state, district, township and village levels to ensure law and order and promote the central government's social and economic programmes (Burma)

s.a.c. qualified at a small arms technical long course

S.A.C. Scientific Advisory Council; Scottish Automobile Club; senior aircraftman; small arms club; Fr. *Société africaine de culture,* Soc. of African Culture; Society for Analytical Chemistry; south Atlantic coast; State Advisory Committee; State Athletic Commission (U.S.A.); Strategic Air Command (U.S.A.)

S.A.C.A. Steam Automobile Club of America; Supreme Allied Commander Atlantic

S.A.C.A.D. stress analysis and computer aided design (computer)

S.A.C.A.N.G.O. Southern Africa Committee on Air Navigation and Ground Operation

S. Acc. It. *Società Accomandita,* limited partnership

SACEUR, SACEUR Supreme Allied Commander Europe

S.A.C.I. South Atlantic Co-operative Investigations

SACLANT Supreme Allied Command Atlantic

SACOR *Sociedade Anónima Concessionária de Refinação de Petróleos em Portugal,* joint stock co. holding the concession to refine petrol in Portugal

Sacr. Sacramento (U.S.A.); Sacrist

S.A.C.S.E.A. Supreme Allied Command South-East Asia

S.A.C.S.I.R. South African Council for Scientific and Industrial Research

S.A.C.T.U. South African Congress of Trade Unions

SACVT Society of Air Cushion Vehicle Technicians (Can.)

S.A.D.F. South African Defence Forces

S.A.D.G. Fr. *Société des architectes diplômés par le gouvernement,* Soc. of Government-certified Architects

Sadie Sarah

SADIE scanning analog-to-digital input equipment (computer)

S. Ad. O. senior/station administrative officer

s.a.e. stamped addressed envelope

S.A.E. Society of American Etchers; Society of Automotive Engineers (U.S.A.); Society of British Automotive Engineers

saec. L. *saeculum,* century

S.A.F. Secretary of the Air Force (U.S.A.); Society of American Foresters; Strategic Air Force (U.S.A.)

S.A.F.A. South Africa Freedom Association

SAF black super abrasion furnace black, filler in rubber compounding

SAFCO Standing Advisory Committee on Fisheries of the Caribbean Organisation

SAFE South African Friends of England

s.a.f.e. stamped addressed foolscap envelope

S. Afr. South Africa/African

S. Afr. D. South African Dutch

S.A.F.U. Scottish Amateur Fencing Union

SAG Screen Actors' Guild

312

S.A.G.A. Sand and Gravel Association of Great Britain; Scandinavian Mink Association; Scout and Guide Activity; Society of American Graphic Artists

S.A.G.B. Spiritualist Association of Great Britain

SAGE semi-automatic ground environment

S.A.G.G.A. Scout and Guide Graduate Association

S.A.H. Society of American Historians; supreme allied headquarters

S.A.H.R. Society for Army Historical Research

Sai. Saigon

S.A.I. *Società Anomina Italiana*, Italian incorporated company; Fr. *Son Altesse Impériale*, Her/His Imperial Highness

S.A.I.A. South Australian Institute of Architects

S.A.I.F. South African Industrial Federation

S.A.I.M.R. South African Institute of Medical Research

S.A.I.R.R. South African Institute of Race Relations

SAJ *Suomen Ammattijärjestö*, Finnish Federation of Trade Unions

S.A.J.C. South Australian Jockey Club

SAK *Suomen Ammattiydistysten Keskusliitto*, Confederation of Finnish Trade Unions

Sal, Sallie, Sally Sarah

sal. salary; Sp. *salida*, departure

s.a.l. L. *secundum artis leges*, according to the rules of art

S.A.L.A. South African Library Association

S.A.L.J. South African Law Journal

Sall. Gaius Sallustius Crispus (86–34 B.C.), Roman historian

Salop Shropshire

S.A.L.P. South African Labour Party

S.A.L.R. *South African Law Reports*

SALT Strategic Arms Limitation Talks between U.S.A. and U.S.S.R.

salv. salvage

Salv. Salvador

Sam Samson; Samuel

SAM surface-to-air missile

sam. Fr. *samedi*, Saturday

Sam. Samaria; Samaritan (*also*, Samar.); Samoa; Ger. *Samstag*, Saturday; The First and Second Books of Samuel, *also* known as Books of the Kings (Bible)

S. Am., S. Amer. South America/American

S.A.M. School of Aerospace Medicine (USAF); Social Accounting Matrix; Society for the Advancement of Management (U.S.A.)

S.A.M.C. South African Medical Corps

SAME Society of American Military Engineers

S.A.M.H. Scottish Association for Mental Health

Sammie, Sammy, Saml. Samuel

SAMPE Society of Aerospace Materials and Process Engineers

S.A.M.S. South American Missionary Society

S.A.M.S.A. Silica and Moulding Sands Association

SAN styrene-acrylonitrile copolymer

san. sanitary

Sanat. sanatorium

S.A.N.B. *South African National Bibliography*

SANCAD Scottish Association for National Certificates and Diplomas

SANCOR South African National Committee for Oceanographic Research

San. D. Doctor of Sanitation

S.A.N.D.T. School of Applied Non Destructive Testing

Sandy Alexander

San Fran. San Francisco (U.S.A.)

s.a.n.r. subject to approval, no risk

S.A.N.R.O.C. South African Non-Racial Olympics Committee

sans sans serif or Sanserif, Fr. *sans*, without + serif, terminal fine cross-strokes of letters e.g. in this definition, and lacking in the following word SANSERIF

Sans. Sanskrit

S.A.N.S. South African Naval Service

S.A.N.T.A. South African National Tuberculosis Association

S.A.N.U. Sudanese African National Union

S.A.N.Z. Standards Association of New Zealand

S.A.O. Scottish Association of Opticians; senior/squadron accountant officer

S.A.O.S. Scottish Agricultural Organization Society

s. ap. apothecaries' scruple

s.a.p. soon as possible

S.A.P. South African Police

S.A.P.A. South African Publishers' Association

S.A.P.M. Scottish Association of Paint Manufacturers

Sap. No. saponification number

S.A.P.S. South African Price Schedule

SAR Sons of the American Revolution

Sar. Sarawak (*also* Saraw.); Sardinia; Sardinian

S.A.R. search and rescue centre; Fr. *Son Altesse Royale*, His Royal Highness; South African Railways/Republic; *South*

313

Australian Industrial Court Reports; standardized abnormality ratio

SARAH, S.A.R.A.H. search and rescue and homing

S.A.R.B.E. search and rescue beacon equipment

S.A.R.C.C.U.S. South African Regional Committee for the Conservation and Utilisation of the Soil

sarge. sergeant

S.A.R. & H. South African Railways and Harbours

S.A.R.L. *Sociedade Anónima de Responsabilidade Limitada*, Joint Stock limited liability co. (Port.); *Société à responsabilité limitée*, Limited Liability Co. (Belg./France)

Sarum. *Sarumensis*, of Salisbury, Eng. episcopal title, used in bishop's signature

S.a.s. *Società in accomandita semplice*, limited partnership (Italy)

S.A.S. Scandinavian Airlines System; L. *Societatis Antiquariorum Socius*, Fellow of the Soc. of Antiquaries (U.S.A.); Fr. *Son Altesse Sérénissime*, Her/His Serene Highness

S.A.S.C. small arms school corps

Sask. Saskatchewan (Can.)

S.A.S.L.O. South African Scientific Liaison Office

SASMIRA Silk and Artificial Silk Mills Research Association (India)

S.A.S.R. *South Australian State Reports*; Special Air Service Regiment

SAT scholastic aptitude test

sat. saturate

Sat. satellite; Saturday; Saturn

S. At. South Atlantic

S.A.T. ship's apparent time; Society for Acoustic Technology

S.A.T.A.F. Second Allied Tactical Air Force

S.A.T.B. *soprano, alto, tenor, bass* (mus.)

Satchmo satchel-mouth, Louis Armstrong (1900–71), Amer. jazz trumpeter

SATCO signal automatic air traffic control system

SATCOMA satellite communications agency

SATEX semi-automatic telegraph exchange

SATIF scientific and technical information facility (NASA)

satn. saturation

S.A.T.O. South American Travel Organization

S.A.T.R.A. Shoe and Allied Trades' Research Association

S.A.T.U. South African Typographical Union

S. Aus., S. Austral. South Australia/Australian

s.a.v. sale/stock at valuation

S.A.V.S. Scottish Anti-Vivisection Society

S.A.W. space at will (advert.)

S.A.W.A.S. South African Women's Auxiliary Services

sax. *saxophone* (mus.)

Sax. Saxon; Saxony

S.A.Y.E. save as you earn

S.A.Y.F.C. Scottish Association of Young Farmers' Clubs

Sb *s* L. *stibium*, antimony (chem.)

SB *s* Argyll (B.V.R.)

sb. substantive

s.b. single breasted

s.b., S.-B. small bore, rifles of calibre of .22″ or less; small business; smooth bore

S.B. sales book; Sam Browne, army officer's belt and strap named after its inventor, Sir Samuel Browne (1824–1901); savings bank; L. *Scientiae Baccalaureus*, Bachelor of Science; selection board; serving brother; short bill; sick bay; signal boatswain/book; simultaneous broadcast/broadcasting; special branch of police; spring back; Statute Book; stretcher bearer; sub branch

SBA School of Business Administration; Small Business Administration (U.S.A.)

S.B.A. sick-bay attendant

S.B.A.C. Society of British Aerospace Companies; Society of British Aircraft Constructors

S-Band 1,550–5,200 megahertz radio frequency band

S.B.B. *Schweizerische Bundesbahnen*, Swiss Federal Railways

S.B.B.N.F. Ship and Boat Builders' National Federation

S.B.C. School Broadcasting Council; signal books correct; Southern Baptist Convention

S.B.C.P.O. sick-bay chief petty officer

S.B.G.I. Society of British Gas Industries

S.B.H. Scottish Board of Health

SBII *Serikat Buruh Islam Indonesia*, Central Islamic Labour Union of Indonesia

S.B.M. single buoy mooring; Fr. *Société des Bains de Mer*, corporation owning the Monte Carlo Casino, main hotels and considerable real estate (Monaco)

S.B.N. standard book number

S.B.N.O. Senior British Naval Officer

S.B.N.S. Society of British Neurological Surgeons

S'board starboard (nav.)

314

S.B.O.T. Sacred Books of the Old Testament

S.B.P. Society of Biological Psychiatry (U.S.A.)

S.B.P.I.M. Society of British Printing Ink Manufacturers

S.B.R. Society for Biological Rhythm

sbre. Sp. *septiembre*, September

S.B.S.A. Standard Bank of South Africa

S.B. St. J. Serving Brother of the Order of Saint John of Jerusalem

S.B.V. sea bed vehicle

S. by W. south by west

Sc *s* scandium (chem.)

SC *s* Edinburgh (B.V.R.); *s* Scilly (B.F.P.); Security Council (U.N.O.); South Carolina (U.S.A.)

5SC *s* Glasgow (radio call-sign)

sc. scene; science; screw; scruple

sc., s.c., scil. L. *scilicet*, namely

sc., sculp., sculps. L. *sculpsit*, carved/engraved it

Sc. Scandinavia; Scandinavian; Science; Scotch; Scotland; Scots; Scottish; sculptor

s.c. self contained; single column; small capitals (typ.); steel casting

S.C. safe custody; sailing club; salvage corps; same case (leg.); school certificate; senior counsel; service certificate; session cases; shooting club; short course; signal corps; single column (advert.); skating/skiing/social/sports club; small craft; South Carolina (U.S.A.); southern command; special constable/constabulary; staff captain/college/corps; standing/statutory committee; Star of Courage (Can.); Suffolk and Cambridgeshire Regiment; supercalendered, paper which has been given smooth finish by being passed between heated rollers during manufacture; Supreme Court; swimming club

S.C. L. *Senatus Consultum*, decree of the Senate

S.C.A.A.A. Southern Counties Amateur Athletic Association

S.C.A.A.P. Special Commonwealth African Assistance Plan

SCADAR scatter detection and ranging

SCADS Sioux City Air Defense Sector (U.S.A.)

S.C.A.F. Supreme Commander of Allied Forces

SCAN schedule analysis; stock market computer answering network; Switched Circuit Automatic Network (U.S.A.)

Scan., Scand. Scandinavia; Scandinavian

scan. mag. L. *scandalum magnatum*, defamation of high personages

S.C.A.O. senior civil affairs officer

SCAP Supreme Command/Commander, Allied Powers

S.C.A.P.A. Society for Checking the Abuses of Public Advertising

s. caps. small capitals (typ.)

S.C.A.R. Scandinavian Council for Applied Research; Scientific Committee on Antarctic Research

S.C.A.T.S. Southern Counties Agricultural Trading Society Ltd.

Sc. B. L. *Scientiae Baccalaureus*, Bachelor of Science

S.C.B. Speedway Control Board (motor-cycling)

S.C.B.C. Somerset Cattle Breeding Centre

Sc. C. Scottish Command (mil.)

S.C.C. Sea Cadet Corps; Society of Church Craftsmen

S.C.C.A. Sports Car Club of America

S.C.C.A.P.E. Scottish Council for Commercial, Administrative and Professional Education

Scd. scheduled

Sc. D. L. *Scientiae Doctor*, Doctor of Science

S.C.D.A. Scottish Community Drama Association; Standing Conference of Drama Associations

SCE schedule compliance evaluation

Sce. scenario

S.C.E. Scottish Certificate of Education

S.C.E.G.S. Sydney Church of England Grammar School (Aust.)

S.C.F. satellite control facility (USAF); Save the Children Fund; senior chaplain to the forces

scg. scoring

S.C.G. Screen Cartoonists' Guild; Social Credit Group

Sc. Gael. Scottish Gaelic

S.C.G.B. Ski Club of Great Britain, formed 1903

S.C.G.R.L. signal corps general research laboratory

S.C.G.S.A. signal corps ground signal agency

S.C.G.S.S. signal corps ground signal service

SC gully gully-climb of Stob Coire nan Lochan in Glencoe (Scot.)

sch. scholar (*also*, schol.); scholarship (*also*, schol.); scholastic (*also*, schol.); school; schooner, *also*, schr.

sch., schol. L. *scholium*, note

Sch. schedule, followed by letter A to F (tax.); *Schillings*, Austrian currency

sched. schedule

315

schem. schematic

Scherz. It. *Scherzando*, playful, humorous (mus.)

Sc. Hist. Scottish History

schol. L. scholastic Latin

sci. science; scientific

s.c.i. single-column inch (advert.)

S.C.I. Fr. *Service Civil International*, Intern. Voluntary Service; Society of Chemical Industry

S.C.I.B.P. Special Committee for the International Biological Programme

sci-fi science fiction

scil. L. *scilicet*, namely

Sci. M. science master; — **Mist.** science mistress

S.C.J. L. *Societas Cordis Jesu*, Soc. of Priests of the Sacred Heart of Jesus

S.C.(J.) Sessions Cases (Judiciary Reports)

S.C.K. Servants of Christ the King

S.C.L. Scottish Central Library; Student of Civil Law

S.C.L.C. Southern Christian Leadership Conference

S.C.L.H. Standing Conference for Local History

S.C.L.I. Somerset and Cornwall Light Infantry

Sc. M. L. *Scientiae Magister*, Master of Science

S.C.M. L. *Sacra Caesarea Majestas*, Sacred Imperial Majesty; State Certified Midwife; Student Christian Movement; summary court-martial

S.C.M.A. Society of Cinema Managers of Great Britain and Ireland (Amalgamated)

SCMES Society of Consulting Marine Engineers & Ship Surveyors

SCNE Select Committee on National Expenditure

S.C.N.O. Senior Canadian Naval Officer

SCNQT Standing Conference for National Qualification and Title

S.C.N.V.Y.O. Standing Conference of National Voluntary Youth Organisations

SCOEG Standing Conference of Employers of Graduates

SCOFF Society for the Conquest of Flight Fear

S.C.O.L.A. Second Consortium of Local Authorities

S. Coll. staff college

S.C.O.L.M.A. Standing Conference on Library Materials on Africa

S. Coln. supply column

s. con. self contained

S.C.O.N.U.L. Standing Conference of National and University Libraries

S.C.O.R. Scientific Committee on Oceanic Research

Scot. Scotch; Scotland (*also*, Scotl.); Scotsman; Scottish

S.C.O.T.A.P.L.L. Standing Conference of Theological and Philosophical Libraries in London

SCOTUS Supreme Court of the United States

S.C.P. Social Credit Party (Can.); *Sporting Clube de Portugal*, Sporting Club of Portugal

S.C.P.A. Scottish Chick Producers' Association

S.C.P.R. Scottish Council of Physical Recreation

scr. scrip (fin.); scruple, unit of weight

S.C.R. senior common room; silicone controlled rectifier; Society for Cultural Relations with the U.S.S.R.

S.C.R.A.T.A. Steel Castings Research and Trade Association

S.C.R.C.C. Soil Conservation and Rivers Control Council (N.Z.)

S.C.R.E. Scottish Council for Research in Education

SCREAM Society for the Control and Registration of Estate Agents and Mortgage Brokers

Scrip., Script. scriptural; scripture

S.C.R.L. signal corps radar laboratory

Scrt. Sanscrit

Scrubs Wormwood Scrubs, one of H.M. Prisons (Lond.)

scrum scrummage (Rugby football)

S.C.S. Society of Civil Servants; space communications systems

S.C.S.A. Soil Conservation Society of America

S.C.S.C. semiconductor standardization sub-committee

S.C.S.S. Scottish Council of Social Service

Sc. & T. Science and Technology

S.C.T. Society of Commercial Teachers

SCTET(L) Standing Conference for Technician Engineers & Technicians (Limited)

S.C.T.R. Standing Conference on Telecommunications Research

S.C.U. Scottish Cricket/Cycling/Cyclists' Union

S.C.U.A. Suez Canal Users' Association

S.C.U.B.A. self contained underwater breathing apparatus·

sculp. sculptor; sculptress; sculptural; sculpture

S.C.V. It. *Stato della Città del Vaticano*, Vatican City State

S.C.V.A.N.Y.O. Standing Conference of Voluntary Youth Organisations

S.C.W.S. Scottish Co-operative Wholesale Society

S.C.Y.A. Scottish Christian Youth Assembly

s/d solid drawn

SD *s* Ayrshire (B.V.R.); *s* Sunderland (B.F.P.); *s* Swaziland (I.V.R.)

sd. said; sewed (books); sound

s.d. safe deposit; same date; second defence (lacrosse); semi-detached (*also, s.* det.); semi-diameter; semi-double; several dates; Ger. *siehe dies,* see this

s.d. L. *sine die,* without date

s. & d. song and dance

S.D. Diploma in Statistics; L. *Scientiae Doctor,* Doctor of Science; Secretary of Defense (U.S.A.); send direct; senior deacon; service dress; sight draft (fin.); signal department/division; special delivery/duty; staff duties; stage door; standard deviation (math.); standard displacement; State Department (U.S.A.); submarine detector; supply department/depot

S.D. L. *Senatus Decreto,* by decree of the senate

S.D.A. Scottish Dinghy Association; Seventh Day Adventist; source data automation

S. Dak., S.D. South Dakota (U.S.A.)

S.D.B.L. sight draft bill of lading

S.D.C. Society of Dyers & Colourists; Submersible Decompression Chamber

S.D.C.A. Society of Dyers and Colourists of Australia

S.D.F. Sudan Defence Force

S.D.G. L. *Soli Deo Gloria,* Glory to God Alone

SDHE spacecraft data handling equipment

SDI selective dissemination of information

sdl. saddle

S.D.L. special duties list

S.D.L.P. Social and Democratic Labour Party (N. Ireland)

S.D.M.A. Surgical Dressing Manufacturers' Association

S.D.M.J. September, December, March, June

S.D.N. Fr. *Société des Nations,* League of Nations

S.D.N.S. Scottish Daily Newspaper Society

S.D.O. senior dental/duty officer; signal distributing office; squadron dental officer; station duty officer

S. Doc. senate/state document

S. Dpo. stores depot

SDP social, domestic and pleasure (insce.)

SDR Small Development Requirement (U.S.A.)

S.D.R. special despatch rider

S.D.R., SDRs Special Drawing Rights, equivalent to US $ at par value Dec. 1946 (IMF)

SDS scientific data systems

S.D.S. Sisters of the Divine Saviour; Students for a Democratic Society (U.S.A.)

SDSS self-deploying space station

S.D.T. Society of Dairy Technology

S.D. & T. staff duties and training

S.D.T.U. Sign and Display Trades Union

SDU Social Democratic Union (Finland); Somali Democratic Union (Somalia)

S.D.U.K. Society for the Diffusion of Useful Knowledge

Se *s* selenium (chem.)

SE *s* Banffshire (B.V.R.); *s* Salcombe (B.F.P.); starch equivalent

s.e. single end / ended / engine / entry; special equipment; spherical equivalent; standard error; straight edge

S/E., S.E. stock exchange

S.E. sanitary engineering; Society of Engineers; Fr. *Son Excellence,* His Excellency; south-east; south-easterly; south-eastern; staff engineer

S.É. Fr. *Son Éminence,* His Eminence

SEA Subterranean Exploration Agency

S.E.A. Society for Education through Art; South East Asia; Southern Economic Association (U.S.A.)

S.E.A.A.C. South-East Asia Air Command

SEAC standards electronic automatic computer

S.E.A.C. South-Eastern Architects' Collaboration; South-Eastern Asia Command

SEACOM telephone cable, connecting Australia, New Guinea, Guam, Hong Kong, Malaysia and Singapore, opened 1967

Sea. H. Seaforth Highlanders (mil.)

SEAL sea-air-land (USN)

S.E.A.L. South-East Area Libraries

S.E.A.L.F. South-East Asia Land Forces

S.E.A.N. State Enrolled Assistant Nurse

SEARCH Systematized Excerpts, Abstracts, and Reviews of Chemical Headlines

SEATO, S.E.A.T.O., SEATO South-East Asia Treaty Organization, *also* South-East Asia Collective Defence Treaty Organisation, estab. 1955

S.E.B.   Southern Electricity Board
S.E.B.T.   South-Eastern Brick and Tile Federation
S.E. by E.   south-east by east
S.E. by S.   south-east by south
sec.   secant; It. *secolo*, century; second, angular measure unit; second, time unit (*also*, secd.); secondary; seconded; secretary (*also*, Sec., Secy., Sec'y.); section (*also*, sect.); sector (*also*, sect.); security
sec.   L. *secundum*, according to
S.E.C.   Securities and Exchange Commission (U.S.A.); simple electronic computer; Fr. *Société européenne de culture*, European Soc. of Culture; south-eastern command (mil.); State Electricity Commission
SECAM   Fr. *Sequential couleur à mémoire*, sequence by colour/memory television system
sec. art.   L. *secundum artem*, according to the art
SECFLT   Second Fleet, Atlantic (USN)
Sec. Gen., Sec-Gen.   Secretary-General
sec. leg.   L. *secundum legem*, according to law
Sec. Leg.   Secretary of the Legation
sec. nat.   L. *secundum naturam*, according to nature
SECOR   sequential collation of range satellite
S.E. & C.R.   South Eastern and Chatham Railway, *now* part of Southern Region, British Rail
sec. reg.   L. *secundum regulam*, according to rule
SED   *Sozialistische Einheitspartei Deutschlands*, Socialist Unity Party of Germany (E. Ger.)
sed.   sedative; sediment (*also*, sedt.)
S.E.D.   Scottish Education Department
SEDAR   submerged electrode detection and ranging
sedtn.   sedimentation
S.E.E.   senior electrical engineers; signals experimental establishment; Fr. *Société d'études et d'expansion*, Studies and Expansion Soc.
S.E.E.A.   Fr. *Société européenne d'énergie atomique*, European Atomic Energy Soc.
S.E.E.B.   South-Eastern Electricity Board, *also* Seeboard
S.E.e.O.   Fr. *sauf erreur et omission*, L. *salvis erroribus et omissis*, errors and omissions excepted
S.E.F.   Shipbuilding Employers' Federation
S.E.F.A.   Scottish Educational Film Association

S.E.F.E.L.   Fr. *Secrétariat européen des fabricants d'emballages métalliques légers*, European Secretariat for Manufacturers of Light Metallic Packings
S.E.F.T.   Society for Education in Film and Television
SEG   Solartron Electronic Group
seg.   segment; It. *segno*, sign; segregate; It. *seguente*, following
Seg.   It. *Segue*, follows, comes after (mus.)
S.E.G.   Society of Economic Geologists (U.S.A.); Society of Exploration Geophysicists; *Stock Exchange Gazette*
S.E.H.   Fr. *Société européenne d'hématologie*, European Soc. of Haematology
S.E.H.M.F.   South of England Hat Manufacturers' Association
S.E.I.F.   Port. *Secretaria de Estado da Informação e Turismo*, State Information and Tourist Board, *formerly* S.N.I.
S.E.I.F.S.A.   Steel and Engineering Industries' Federation of South Africa
S.E.I.S.   submarine escape immersion suit
Seismol.   seismology
sel.   select; selected; selection; Ger. *selig*, deceased
Sel., Selw.   Selwyn College,Cambridge, founded 1882
S.E.L.   Scouts' Esperanto League
Selk.   Selkirk (Scot.)
SELNEC, SELNEC   South-East Lancashire, North-East Cheshire
sem.   Fr. *il semble*, it seems; semicolon; seminary
Sem.   Semitic
Sem., Semp.   It. *Sempre*, always (mus.)
S.E.M.A.   Spray Equipment Manufacturers' Association
S.E.M.F.A.   Scottish Electrical Manufacturers' and Factors' Association
semi., semicol.   semicolon
sen   It. *seno*, sine (math.)
sen.   senate; senator; It. *senatore*, senator; senior
sen.   It. *senza*, without (mus.)
Sen.   Marcus Annaeus Seneca (*c* 55 B.C.–A.D. 41), Roman writer
S.E.N.   State Enrolled Nurse; — (M.) State Enrolled Nurse (Mental); — (M.S.) State Enrolled Nurse (Mentally Subnormal)
S. en C.   Fr. *Société en Commandite*, limited partnership
Sen. Cd.   senior commissioned
sen. clk.   senior clerk
Sen. Doc.   Senate Document
S. Eng. O.   senior engineering officer
Sen. M.   senior master
Sen. Mist.   senior mistress

S. en N.C. Fr. *Société en nom collectif*, joint stock co.

Sen. Opt. senior optime

senr. senior

sent. sentence

Sen. Tech. Weld. I. Senior Technician of the Welding Institute

Sen. Wt. O. senior warrant officer

S.E.O. senior equipment/executive/experimental/officer

s.e.o.o. Fr. *sauf erreurs ou omissions*, errors or omissions excepted

s.e.u.o. Sp. *salve error u ommision*, errors and omissions excepted

sep. separate; separation, *also*, sepn.

Sep. September (*also*, Sept.); Septuagint

S.E.P. *Saturday Evening Post*

S.E.P.C.O. Services Electronic Parts Co-ordinating Committee

sept. L. *septem*, seven

seq. sequel; sequence

seq., seqq. L. *sequens*, the following; L. *sequente*, and in what follows; L. *sequitur*, it follows

seq. luce L. *sequenti luce*, the following day

ser. serial; series; sermon

Serb. Serbia; Serbian

Serg., Sergt. sergeant

Serj., Serjt. Serjeant

S.E.R.L. Services Electronics Research Laboratory

SERLANT Service Forces, Atlantic (USN)

SERPAC Service Forces, Pacific (USN)

SERT spinning satellite for electric rocket test

ser. servant (*also*, servt.); service

Serv. Servia/Servian, earlier forms of Serbia/Serbian; service; services

S.E.S. Seafarers' Education Service; Solar Energy Society (U.S.A.); Standards Engineers' Society (U.S.A.); Studies and Expansion Society

S.E.S.A. Society for Experimental Stress Analysis (U.S.A.)

SESCO secure submarine communications

S.E.S.O. senior equipment staff officer

S.E.S.R. Fr. *Société européenne de sociologie rurale*, European Soc. for Rural Sociology

sess. session

SET Selective Employment Tax/Taxation

set. Port. *setembro*, September; settlement

set^e. Sp. *septiembre*, September

S.-et-L. Saône-et-Loire (France)

S.-et-M. Seine-et-Marne (France)

S.-et-O. Seine-et-Oise (France)

SETS solar energy thermionic conversion system (NASA)

sett. It. *settembre*, September

SEV *Soviet Ekonomicheskoy Vzaimopomoshchi*, Council for Mutual Economic Aid, known in West as COMECON (U.S.S.R.)

sev. sever; several (*also*, sevl.)

SEVFLT Seventh Fleet, Pacific (USN)

SEW *Sozialistische Einheitspartei West-Berlins*, West Berlin Socialist Unity Party

sew. sewage; sewer; sewerage

S.E.W. safety equipment worker

sex. sextet; sexual

Sexag. Sexagesima, eighth Sunday before Easter, second before Lent

sext. sextant

SF *s* Edinburgh (B.V.R.); *s* Finland (I.V.R.); *Sosialistisk Folkeparti*, Socialist People's Party (Nor.)

sf. It. *Sforzando*, note or chord so marked to be emphasized (mus.)

s.f. Fr. *sans frais*, without expense; signal frequency; sinking fund (fin.); surface feet/foot

s.f. L. *sub finem*, towards the end

s.-f., s.f., S.F. science fiction

S.F. San Francisco (U.S.A.); senior fellow; Sherwood Foresters (mil.); shipping federation; sinking fund, any amounts put aside to reduce total indebtedness, but particularly to reduce the national debt. First introduced 1717; Sinn Fein, We Ourselves, Irish political party formed (1905) to further self-determination; Society of Friends; special facilities/forces; standard frequency

S.F.A. Scientific Film Association; Scottish Football Association; *Société Française d'Astronautique*, French Astronautical Soc.; Soroptimist Federation of the Americas; Stourbridge Firebrick Association; sulphated fatty alcohol, class of detergents; Sweet Fanny Adams, *i.e.* nothing at all

S. & F.A. shipping and forwarding agents

SFB Ger. *Sender Freies Berlin*, Broadcasting Station of Free Berlin

SFBMS Small Farm Business Management Scheme

S.f.c. sergeant first class

S.F.C. Scottish Film Council; specific fuel consumption; Standing Federation Committee (West Indies)

SFEL standard facility equipment list (USAF)

s.f.f. Port. *se faz favor*, please

S.F.G. Ger. *Studien und Förderungsgesellschaft*, Studies and Expansion Soc.

sfgd. safeguard
S.F.I. Fr. *Société financière internationale*, Intern. Finance Corporation
SFL Sequenced Flashing Lights, high-intensity lights placed along the centre line of the approach lighting system and flashed in sequence toward the runway of an airport
S.fl. Surinam florin (currency)
S.F.L. Scottish Football League
S.F.M.A. School Furniture Manufacturers' Association
S.F.M.T.A. Scottish Federation of Meat Trades Associations
S.F.O. senior flag officer
S.F.O.F. space flight operations facility (NASA)
SFP supplementary fire party
Sfp. It. *Sforzato piano*, an emphasis followed immediately by *piano* (mus.)
S.F.P.E. Society of Fire Protection Engineers (U.S.A.)
SFR Sinking Fund rate of return
S.F.R.Y. Socialist Federal Republic of Yugoslavia
S.F.S. Society for Freedom in Science
S.F.S.A. Scottish Field Studies Association Limited
S.F.T.A. Society of Film and Television Arts
S.F.U. signals flying unit
Sfz. It. *Sforzando*, note or chord so marked to be emphasized (mus.)
SG *s* Edinburgh (B.V.R.)
Sg. surgeon
s.g. specific gravity; steel girder
S.G. Fr. *Sa Grâce*, Her/His Grace; Fr. *Sa Grandeur*, Her/His Highness; Scots Guards; seaman gunner; Society of Genealogists; Solicitor-General; specific grants; surgeon general
S.G. L. *Salutis Gratia*, for the sake of safety
S.G.A. Society of Graphic Artists/Arts
SGB Ger. *Schweizerischer Gewerkschaftsbund*, Swiss Fed. of Trade Unions
Sg. C. surgeon captain
Sg. Cr. surgeon commander
sgd. signed
S.G.D. Senior Grand Deacon
s.g.d.g. Fr. *sans garantie du gouvernement*, without government guarantee and generally applied to some patents
S.G.F. Scottish Grocers' Federation
S.G.H.W.R. steam generating heavy water reactor
sgl. single
Sg. L. Cr. surgeon lieutenant commander
SGLS space-to-ground link sub-system (NASA)

S.G.M. Scripture Gift Mission; sea gallantry medal
S.G.O. squadron gunnery officer
SGP *s* Singapore (I.V.R.); *Staatkundig Gereformeerde Partij*, Political Reformed Party, an extreme right-wing Calvinist party, the SGP bases its political and social outlook on its own interpretation of the Bible (Neth.)
Sg. R.A. surgeon rear-admiral
S.G. Rep. standing group representative
S.G.S. Stage Golfing Society
Sgt. sergeant; — **Maj.** sergeant major
S.G.T. Society of Glass Technology
S.G.U. Scottish Gliding/Golf Union
Sg. V.A. surgeon vice-admiral
S.G.W Senior Grand Warden (freem.)
SH *s* Berwickshire (B.V.R.); *s* Scarborough (B.F.P.); small head (numis.)
sh. shall; share (fin.); sheet; shilling; shower
Sh. Shipwright
s.h. second-hand; surgical hernia
S.H. Schleswig-Holstein; school house; scrum-half (Rugby football); staghounds
S.H.A. Scottish Hockey Association; sidereal hour angle
SHAC Shelter Housing Aid Centre
S.H.A.E.F. Supreme Headquarters, Allied Expeditionary Force
Shak., Shake. William Shakespeare (1564–1616), Eng. dramatist and poet
shandy shandygaff, ale and ginger beer mixed
shan't shall not
SHAPE, SHAPE Supreme Headquarters Allied Powers in Europe, *estab.* 1950, for the defence of the allied countries of Western Europe (NATO)
SHB *Svenska Handelsbanken*, largest Swedish bank
S.H.C.J. Society of the Holy Child Jesus
shd. should
S.H.D. Scottish Home Department; State Hydro-electric Department (N.Z.)
she'd she had/would
Shef., Sheff. Sheffield
she'll she shall/will
she's she has/is
Shet., Shetl. Shetland Islands
S.H.E.X. Sundays and Holidays excepted, meaning Sundays & Holidays will not count as laytime (shipping)
shf, SHF, s.h.f. superhigh frequency
S.H.F.F. Scottish House Furnishers' Federation
shipt. shipment
Sh. L. shipwright lieutenant

S.H.L.M. Society of Hospital Laundry Managers

S.H.M. Society of Housing Managers

S.H. & M.A. Scottish Horse and Motormen's Association

S.H.M.O. senior hospital medical officer

S.H.O. senior house officer

6-shooter revolver holding six cartridges

SHORAN short-range aid to navigation

SHOT Society for the History of Technology (U.S.A.)

show biz show business

s.h.p. shaft horsepower

SHPBG Small Horticultural Production Business Grant

S.H.P. single-flowered hardy perennial or hybrid perpetual rose

shpt. shipment

S.H.Q. station/supreme headquarters

shr. share (fin.)

shrap. shrapnel

Shrops. Shropshire; — **Yeo.** Shropshire Yeomanry

S.H.S. Shire Horse Society; *Srba, Hrvata i Slovenaca (Kraljevina),* Serb-Croat for Kingdom of the Serbs, Croats, and Slovenes, *popularly* Yugoslavia

S.H.S. L. *Societatis Historicae Socius,* Fellow of the Historical Soc.

S.H.T. single-flowered hybrid tea rose

shtg., shortg. shortage

s.h.v. L. *sub hac voce/hoc verbo,* under this word

SHW safety, health and welfare

Si *s* silicon (chem.)

SI substituted polysiloxane (silicone); Superintending Inspector of Factories; Fr. *Système Internationale d'Unités,* Standardised metric units

S.I. The Most Exalted Order of the Star of India; Sandwich Islands; *Século Ilustrado,* a weekly illustrated magazine owned by *O Século* daily newspaper (Port.); Seine-Inférieure (France); seriously ill (med.); Shetland Isles; Smithsonian Institute (U.S.A.); Society of Illustrators (U.S.A.); staff inspector; Staten Island, N.Y. (U.S.A.); Statutory Instrument, Government orders; Fr. *Système Internationale,* Intern. system of Measurement

SIA *Schweizerischer Ingenieur- und Architekten-Verein,* Member of the Swiss Institute of Architects and Engineers

S.I.A. Saskatchewan Institute of Agrologists (Can.); Fr. *Société internationale d'acupuncture,* Intern. Acupuncture Soc.; Society of Industrial Artists, *now* S.I.A.D.; Society of Investment Analysts; Soropti-

mist International Association; Structural Insulation Association

S.I.A.D. Society of Industrial Artists and Designers

S.I.A.P. Sp. *Sociedad Interamericana de Planificación,* Inter-American Planning Soc.

Sib Sibyl; Sybil

Sib., Sibr. Siberia; Siberian

S.I.B. Special Investigation Branch (Police)

S.I.B.C. Fr. *Société internationale de biologie clinique,* Intern. Soc. of Clinical Biology

Sib. Or. Sibylline Oracles

SIC Scientific Information Center (U.S.A.)

sic. L. *siccus,* dry

Sic. Sicilian; Sicily

S.I.C. Fr. *Société internationale de cardiologie,* Intern. Soc. of Cardiology; Fr. *Société internationale de chirurgie,* Intern. Soc. of Surgery; specific inductive capacity; standard industrial classification

S.I.C.A. Society of Industrial and Cost Accountants of Canada

S.I.C.O.T. Fr. *Société internationale de chirurgie orthopédique et de traumatologie,* Intern. Soc. of Orthopaedic Surgery and Traumatology

Sid Sidney; Sydney

S.I.D. sudden ionospheric disturbances

S.I.D. L. *Spiritus in Deo,* his spirit is with God

S.I.D.S. Fr. *Société internationale de défense sociale,* Intern. Soc. of Social Defence

S.I.E.C. Scottish Industrial Estates Corporation; Fr. *Société internationale pour l'enseignement commercial,* Intern. Soc. for Business Education

S.I.E.E. Student of the Institution of Electrical Engineers

S.I.E.S. Soils and Irrigation Extension Service (Aust.)

SIF selective identification feature

S.I.F.E. Society of Industrial Furnace Engineers

S.I.F.S. special instructors flying school

SIG signature of engraver present (numis.)

sig. signal; signature; signification; signifies; signor; signora; signore

sig. L. *signetur,* let it be labelled (med.)

SIGAC Scottish Industrial Groups Advisory Council

S.I.G.E.S.O. Sub-committee, Intelligence German Electronics Signals Organization

sigill. L. *sigillum,* seal

Sig. L. signal lieutenant
SIGMA Science in General Management
Sigmn. signalman
sign. signature
Sig.na It. *Signorina*, Miss
sig. n. pro. L. *signa nomine proprio*, label with the proper name (med.)
Sig. O. signal officer
S.I.H. Fr. *Société internationale d'hématologie*, Intern. Soc. of Haematology; Society for Italic Handwriting
S.I.I.A.E.C. Fr. *Secrétariat international des ingénieurs, des agronomes et des cadres économiques catholiques*, Intern. Secretariat of Catholic Technologists, Agriculturalists and Economists
S.I.I.C. Fr. *Secrétariat international des groupements professionels des industries chimiques des pays de la C.E.E.*, Intern. Secretariat of Professional Groups in the Chemical Industries of the E.E.C. Countries
Sil. Silesia
S.I.L. Fr. *Société internationale de la lèpre*, Intern. Leprosy Assn.
Silas Silvanus
SILWFC Sugar Industry Labour Welfare Fund Committee
Sim, Simmy Simeon; Simon
SIM scientific inventory management (computer)
sim. similar; similarly; simile
S.I.M. self-inflicted mutilation; sergeant instructor of musketry; Fr. *Société internationale de la Moselle*, Intern. Moselle Co.; Fr. *Société internationale de musicologie*, Intern. Musicological Soc.
S.I.M.A. Scientific Instrument Manufacturers' Association; Steel Industry Management Association
S.I.M.C. Fr. *Société internationale de médecine cybernétique*, Intern. Soc. of Cybernetic Medicine; Fr. *Société internationale pour la musique contemporaine*, Intern. Soc. for Contemporary Music
SIMCA *Société Industrielle de Mécanique et Carosserie Automobile*, Fr. car manufacturers
SIMEX state trading company (Syria)
S.I.M.H.A. Fr. *Société internationale de mycologie humaine et animale*, Intern. Soc. for Human and Animal Mycology
simp simpleton
S.I.M.P.L. Scientific, Industrial and Medical Photographic Laboratories
sin *s* sine (math.)
Sin' It. *Sino*, to, as far as, until, *e.g.* sin' al segno, to the sign (mus.)
sin. sinecure; It. *sinistra*, left
Sinf. It. *Sinfonia*, symphony, originally 'overture' (mus.)

S.-Infre. Seine-Inférieure (France)
sing. singular
sing. L. *singulorum*, of each (med.)
Sing. Singapore
sinh hyperbolic sine (math.)
Sinh. Sinhalese
S.I.N.S. ships inertial navigation system (USN)
SINTO Sheffield Interchange Organisation
S.I.O. Scripps Institution of Oceanography (U.S.A.); senior intelligence officer
S.I.P. Fr. *Société interaméricaine de psychologie*, Inter-American Soc. of Psychology
S.I.P.G. Fr. *Société internationale de pathologie géographique*, Intern. Soc. of Geographical Pathology
S.I.P.R.C. Society of Independent Public Relations Consultants
SIPRI Stockholm International Peace Research Institute, set up in 1966 by Swedish Govt. for research into problems of peace and conflict, with particular attention to the problems of arms control and disarmament
S.I.R. Member of the Institute of Industrial Realtors (U.S.A.); small income relief (tax.)
Sɪʀᴀ Scientific Instrument Research Association
SIS Secret Intelligence Service
sis. sister
SISS submarine integrated sonar system
S.I.S.S. Fr. *Société internationale de la science du sol*, Intern. Soc. of Soil Science
S.I.S.T.E.R. Special Institutions for Scientific and Technological Education and Research
SIT spontaneous ignition temperature
sit. sitting-room; situation
s.i.t. stopping/storing in transit
S.I.T. Singapore Improvement Trust; Society of Industrial/Instrument Technology
S.I.T.A. Students' International Travel Association
S.I.T.C. Standard International Trade Classification; — (R.) Standard Intern. Trade Classification (Revised)
SITPRO Simplification of International Trade Procedures
S.I.T.R.A. South India Textile Research Association
S.I.T.S. Fr. *Société internationale de transfusion sanguine*, Intern. Soc. of Blood Transfusion
sitt., sitter sitting-room

322

S.I.U. Fr. *Société internationale d'urologie*, Intern. Soc. of Urology
SI unit *Système International unit*, International System of Units
S.I.W. self-inflicted wound
SIXFLT Sixth Fleet, Atlantic (USN)
SJ *s* Bute (B.V.R.)
s.j. L. *sub judice*, under legal consideration
S.J. Society of Jesus, Jesuit Order; *Solicitors' Journal*
S.J.A.A. St. John Ambulance Association
S.J.A.B. St. John Ambulance Brigade
S.J.A.C. Society of Japanese Aircraft Constructors
S.J.C. Standing Joint Committee; Supreme Judicial Court (U.S.A.)
S.J.D. Doctor of Juristic Science; L. *Scientiae Juridicae Doctor*, Doctor of Juridical Science
$^s\!/\!_\chi{}^k$ *s* slight storm of drifting snow, generally high (met.)
S/k *s* heavy storm of drifting snow, generally high (met.)
SK *s* Caithness (B.V.R.)
sk. sack; sick; sketch
SKAMP station keeping and mobile platform, unmanned self-navigating sailing boat
S.K.C. Scottish Kennel Club
SKDL *Suomen Kansan Demokraattinen Liitto*, Finnish People's Democratic League
S. Ken. South Kensington (Lond.)
SKF *Svenska Kullagerfabriken*, Swedish ball-bearing factory
SKILL satellite kill
SKJ *Savez Komunista Jugoslavije*, League of Communists of Yugoslavia
S.K.K.C.A. Supreme Knight of the Knights of Columbus (U.S.A.)
Skm. Stockholm (Sweden)
SKP *Suomen Kommunistinen Puolue*, Finnish Communist Party (Finland)
s.k.p.o. slip one, knit one, pass slipped stitch over (knit.)
Skr. Sanskrit (*also*, Skrt., Skt.); skipper
S. Kr. Swedish Krona (currency)
S.K.R. South Korean Republic
s/l Port. *sobreloja*, mezzanine floor
SL *s* Clackmannanshire (B.V.R.)
2SL *s* Sheffield (radio call-sign)
sl. slightly; slip
Sl. Slovak; Slovakian
s.l. seditious libel; south latitude (*also*, S. lat.); support line
s.l. L. *secundum legem*, according to the law

S.l. L. *Sine loco*, no place of publication
S.L. salvage loss (insce.); Saône-et-Loire (France); scout leader; sea level; searchlight; second lieutenant; security list; serjeant-at-law; solicitor-at-law; southern league; squadron leader; sublieutenant; supplementary list
s.l.a. single line approach
S.L.A. Scottish Library Association; Showmen's League of America; Special Libraries Association (U.S.A.)
S.L.A.D.E. Society of Lithographic Artists, Designers, Engravers and Process Workers
S.L.A.E.T. Society of Licensed Aircraft Engineers and Technologists
SLAM supersonic low-altitude missile
s.l.a.n L. *sine loco, anno, vel nomine*, without place/year/name of printer
S. Lan. R. South Lancashire Regiment
SLATE small lightweight altitude transmission equipment
Slav. Slavic; Slavonian; Slavonic
SLBM submarine launched ballistic missile
s.l. & c. shipper's load and count
S.L.C. Scottish Leaving Certificate; Statute Law Committee; Surgeon Lieutenant Commander
SLCL Sierra Leone Council of Labour
S.L.C.R. *Scottish Land Court Reports*
sld. sailed; sealed; sold; solid
S. Ldr. squadron leader
S.L.E.A.T. Society of Laundry Engineers and Allied Trades
s.l.et a. L. *sine loco et anno*, without place and year of publication
S. level Scholarship level of the General Certificate of Education
SLF Scottish Landowners' Federation; Silcock & Lever Feeds Limited
s.l.f. straight line frequency
S.L.F. *Skandinaviska Lackteknikers Förbund*, Fed. of Scandinavian Paint and Varnish Technicians
SLFP Sri Lanka Freedom Party (Ceylon)
SLFSP Sri Lanka Freedom Socialist Party, a breakaway group from Sri Lanka Freedom Party (Ceylon)
S.L.G.B. Society of Local Government Barristers
S.L.I.M. South London Industrial Mission
S.L.L.A. Scottish Ladies Lacrosse Association
SLM ship-launched missile
s.l.m. It. *sul livello del mare*, above sea level
SLMC Scottish Ladies' Mountaineering Club

SLMR Motor Vehicles (Speed Limit on Motorways) Regulations, 1966

s.l.n.d. L. *sine loco nec data*, without indication of date/place of printing

S.L.O. senior liaison officer

SLOMAR space logistics maintenance and rescue

slp. slip

s.l.p. L. *sine legitime prole*, without lawful issue

S.L.P. Socialist Labour Party

SLPP Sierra Leone People's Party

S.L.R. *Scottish Land Reports*; self-loading rifle, not requiring manual reloading after initial charge; Statute Law Revision Act

S. L. Rev. *Scottish Law Review*

S.L.S. Stephenson Locomotive Society

S.L.S.C. surf life saving club

sl. st. slip stitch (crochet)

S.L.S.T. Sierra Leone Selection Trust

S. Lt. sub-lieutenant

S.L.T. *Scots Law Times*

S.L.T.A. Scottish Licensed Trade Association

S.L.T.C. Society of Leather Trades Chemists

S.L.T.E.A. Sheffield Lighter Trades Employers' Association

SLURP self levelling unit to remove pollution

SLV space/standard launch vehicle

sly. slowly; southerly

sm Ger. *Seemeile*, nautical mile

Sm *s* samarium (chem.)

SM *s* Dumfriesshire (B.V.R.); *s* Shoreham (B.F.P.); strategic missile

sm. small

s.m. short metre (mus.)

s. & m. sausages and mash

S.M. sales manager; Fr. *Sa Majesté*, His Majesty; *Scientiae Magister*, Master of Science; Ger. *Seine Majestät*, His Majesty; senior magistrate; sergeant-major; service module; shipment memorandum; silver medallist; Sisters of Mercy; Society of Miniaturists; soldier's medal; Sons of Malta; staff-major; stage manager; state militia; station master; It. *Stato Maggiore*, General Staff; stipendiary magistrate; It. *Sua Maestà*, Her/His Majesty; Sp. *Su Magestad*, His Majesty; surgeon-major

S.M. L. *Sanctae Memoriae*, of holy memory

S. & M. Bp. of Sodor and Man

S.M.A. Sheffield Metallurgical and Engineering Association; Society for Medieval Archaeology; Society of Marine Artists; Solder Makers' Association;

Superphosphate Manufacturers' Association

S.M.A.C. Standing Medical Advisory Committee

S.M.A.E. Society of Model Aeronautical Engineers

SMAJ Sugar Manufacturers' Association Jamaica

SMAMA Sacramento air materiel area

S.M.B. Fr. *Sa Majesté Britannique*, Her/His Britannic Majesty

S.M.B.A. Scottish Marine Biological Association

S.M.C. Fr. *Sa Majesté Catholique*, Her/His Catholic Majesty; Scottish Mountaineering Club

sm. caps. small capitals (typ.)

S.M.C.C.L. Society of Municipal and County Chief Librarians

S.M.C. (Disp.) Dispensing Certificate of the Worshipful Company of Spectacle Makers

S.M.D. submarine mine depot; superintendent of mine design

S.M.D. *Short Metre Double* (mus.)

S.M.D.A. Sewing Machine Dealers' Association Limited

Sm. date. small date (numis.)

SME *s* Surinam, Dutch Guiana (I.V.R.)

S.M.E. school of military engineering

S.M.E. L. *Sancta Mater Ecclesia*, Holy Mother Church

Smectymnuus pseudonym (formed upon first letters of their names) of Stephen Marshall, Edmund Calamy, Thomas Young, Matthew Newcomen and William Spurstow, joint authors in 1641 of an attack on episcopacy entitled *An Answer to a Booke*, by J. Hall, Bp. of Norwich

S.M.E.G. Spring Makers' Export Group

SMERSH Russ. *Smert Shpionam*, death to spies

S. Met. O. senior meteorological officer

S.M.F.U.A. Silk and Man-made Fibre Users' Association

S.M.G. sub-machine gun

SMH *s* St. Margaret's Hope (B.F.P.)

S.M.H.D. Higher Diploma in Ophthalmic Optics of the Worshipful Company of Spectacle Makers

S.M.I. Fr. *Sa Majesté Impériale*, Her/His Imperial Majesty

S.M.I.A. Sheet Metal Industries Association

Smith. Inst. Smithsonian Institution, Washington (U.S.A.)

S.M.J. Sisters of Mary and Joseph

smk. smoke

sml. simulate; simulation; simulator; small

S.M.L. Science Museum Library

S.M.L.E. short magazine Lee-Enfield (rifle)

S. M. Lond. Soc. L. *Societatis Medicae Londiniensis Socius*, Member of the London Medical Soc.

S.M.M. L. *Sancta Mater Maria*, Holy Mother Mary

S.M.M.B. Scottish Milk Marketing Board

S.M.M.T. Society of Motor Manufacturers and Traders

SMNO Singapore Malays National Organization

S.M.O. senior/squadron medical officer

smog smoke-laden fog

Smorz. It. *Smorzando*, dying away (mus.)

SMP *Suomen Maaseudun Puloue*, Finnish Rural Party

s.m.p. L. *sine mascula prole*, without male issue

S.M.P. School Mathematics Project; Society of Mural Painters

S.M.P.S. Society of Master Printers of Scotland

S.M.P.T.E. Society of Motion Pictures and Television Engineers (U.S.A.)

S.M.R. Fr. *Sa Majesté Royale*, Her/His Royal Majesty; standardized mortality ratio

S.M.R.A. Spring Manufacturers' Research Association

S.M.R.E. Safety in Mines Research Establishment

S.M.R.I. Sugar Milling Research Institute (S. Afr.)

SMS sequence milestone system; synchronous meteorological satellite

S.M.S. Secondary Modern School; Ger. *Seiner Majestät Schiff*, His Majesty's Ship

s.m.s.a. standard metropolitan statistical area

S.M.S.A. Senior Award of the Worshipful Company of Spectacle Makers

S.M.S.O. senior maintenance staff officer

S.M.T. Scottish Motor Traction Company; ship's mean time

S.M.T.A. Scottish Motor Trade Association

S.M.T.C. Fr. *Sa Majesté très Chrétienne*, His Most Christian Majesty

S.M.T.F. Scottish Milk Trade Federation

S.M.T.O. senior mechanical transport officer

S.M.T.S. Scottish Machinery Testing Station

SMU *Surinaamse Mijnwerkers Unie*, Surinam Mine Workers' Union

S.M.U.S.E. Socialist Movement for the United States of Europe

S.M.W. standard metal window

Sn *s* L. *stannum*, tin (chem.)

SN Belgian Airlines; *s* Dunbartonshire (B.V.R.); *s* North Shields (B.F.P.); *s* Senegal (I.V.R.)

S/N, S.N. shipping note

s.n. serial/series/service number

s.n. L. *secundum naturam*, according to nature; L. *sine nomine*, without name

S/N. signal to noise ratio

S.N. Secretary of the Navy (U.S.A.); sergeant navigator

SNAFU situation normal, all fouled up

SNAME Society of Naval Architects and Marine Engineers (U.S.A.)

SNAP Shelter Neighbourhood Action Project; systems for nuclear auxiliary power (NASA/USAF)

S.N.C.B. *Société nationale des chemins de fer belges*, Belgian National Railways

SNCC Student Non-Violent Coordinating Committee (U.S.A.)

S.N.C.F. *Société nationale des chemins de fer français*, French Nat. Railways

Snd. Sound

S.N.D.A. Sunday Newspaper Distributing Association

SNECMA, Snecma *Société Nationale d'Étude et de Construction de Moteurs d'Aviation*, French state-owned aeroengine company

SNF system noise figure

SNFA Standing Naval Force, Atlantic

S.N.F.U. Scottish National Farmers' Union

Sng. Singapore

s.n.g. Fr. *sans notre garantie*, without our guarantee

S.N.L. standard nomenclature list

S.N.L.R. services no longer required

S.N.M. Society of Nuclear Medicine (U.S.A.)

S.N.O. Scottish National Orchestra; senior naval/navigation officer

S.N.P. Scottish National Party

S.N.P.A. Scottish Newspaper Proprietors' Association

SNPO Space Nuclear Propulsion Office (NASA)

Snr. Port. *Senhor*, Mr

Sñr. Sp. *Señor*, Mr

S.N.R. Society for Nautical Research

Snra. Port. *Senhora*, Mrs

Sñra. Sp. *Señora*, Mrs

Snrta. Port. *Senhorita*, Miss

Sñrta. Sp. *Señorita*, Miss
S.N.S.C. Scottish National Ski Council, formed 1963
S.N.S.O. superintending naval stores officer
S.N.T.P.C. Scottish National Town Planning Council
SO *s* Moray (B.V.R.); *s* Sligo (Rep. of Ireland F.P.); Ger. *Sudosten*, south-east
S/O section officer; Substance of, term used in specifying weight of paper
So. South; Southern
So. *Sonata* (mus.)
s.o. seller's option; Ger. *siehe oben*, see above; strike out
S.O. Scottish Office, Section Officer (*also* S/O); senior/signals/staff/supply officer; sorting office; standing order; Stationery/statistical office; sub-office; It. *Sud Ovest*, South West; symphony orchestra
S.O.A. staff officer, administration
S.O.A.A. Solus Outdoor Advertising Association
S.O.A.D. staff officer, air defence
S.O.A.S. School of Oriental and African Studies, Univ. of Lond.
S.O.B. senate/state office building; silly old blighter; Society of Bookmen; son of a bitch
S.O.B.H.D. Scottish Official Board of Highland Dancing
SOBLIN self-organizing binary logical network (computer)
soc. social; socialist; society, *also*, socy.
Soc. It. *Società*, Company/Partnership; Socrates (469–399 B.C.), Gk. philosopher
S.O.C. Scottish Ornithologists' Club; slightly off colour
soccer association football
Soc. Dem. Social Democrat
S.O.C.E.M. Society of Objectors to Compulsory Egg Marketing
S.O.C.G.P.A. Seed, Oil Cake and General Produce Association
sociol. sociological; sociologist; sociology
Soc. Isl. Society Islands
S.O.C.M.A. Synthetic Organic Chemical Manufacturers' Association (U.S.A.)
Soc. N.C. Sp. *sociedad en nombre collectivo*, partnership with collective name
SOCONY Standard Oil Corporation of New York
soc. sci. social science/scientist
sod. sodium
SODAC Society of Dyers and Colourists
SODOMEI *Nihon Rodo Kumiai Sodomei*, Japan Fed. of Trade Unions

SODRE *Servicio Oficial de Difusion Radio-electrica,* government-owned radio and television network (Uru.)
S.O.E. special operations executive (WW2)
S.O.E.D. *Shorter Oxford English Dictionary*
SOFAR sound fixing and ranging (nav.)
SOFCS self-organizing flight control system
S. of M. School of Musketry (mil.)
S. of S. Secretary of State
S. of Sol. Song of Solomon (Bible)
S. of T. Sons of Temperance
S. of T.T. School of Technical Training
sog. Ger. *sogennant*, so-called
S.O.G.A.T. Society of Graphical and Allied Trades
sogg. It. *soggettivo*, subjective; It. *soggetto*, subject
SOHIO Standard Oil of Ohio
SOHYO *Nihon Rodo Kumiai Sohygikai*, General Council of Trade Unions of Japan
S.O.(I.) Staff Officer (Intelligence)
S.O.-in-C. signal officer-in-chief
SOK-group. *Suomen Osuuskauppojen Keskuskunta*, Finnish Co-operative Wholesale Soc.
SOKSI *Serekat Organasasi Karjawan Seluruh Indonesia*, Rep. of Indonesia, Trade Union
Sol, Solly Solomon
sol. soluble; solution, *also*, soln.
Sol. Solicitor (*also*, Solr.); — **Gen.** Solicitor-General; Solomon Islands
s.o.l. ship owner's liability (insce.)
Sol. J. *Solicitors' Journal*
SOLOMON simultaneous operation linked ordinal modular network
solv. solvent
soly. solubility
SOM Society of Occupational Medicine
Som., Soms. Somerset; Somersetshire
SOMA Society of Mental Awareness
S.O.M.E. senior ordnance mechanical engineer
somet. sometimes
Som. L.I. Somerset Light Infantry
Som. Sh. Somali shilling (currency)
SON Spear of the Nation, founded 1962 as military arm of African National Congress
Son. sonnets (Shake.)
SONAP *Sociedade Nacional de Petroleos*, Nat. Petrol Company (Port.)
SONAR sound navigation and ranging
SONOAN sonic noise analyser

S.O.(O.) Staff Officer (Operations)
SOP standard operating procedure
sop. *soprano* (mus.)
S.O.P. sleeping-out pass; staff officer of pensioners
soph. sophomore
Soph. Sophocles (496–406 B.C.), Gk. dramatist and poet
SOR specific operational requirement (USAF)
s.o.r. sale or return
S.O.R.D. submerged object recovery device
SORTI satellite orbital track and intercept
SOS intern. morse last signal distress/ 'save our souls'
Sos. *Sonatas* (mus.)
s.o.s. L. *si opus sit*, if necessary (med.)
S.O.S. secretary of state; senior officers' school; services of supply
S.O.S.B. L. *Congregatio Silvestrina Ordinis Sancti Benedicti*, Sylvestrine Congregation of the Order of Saint Benedict
S.O.S.C. Smithsonian Oceanographic Sorting Center (U.S.A.)
S.O.S.I.A.C. Singapore-Soviet Shipping Agency
S.O.S.S. shipboard oceanographic survey system
sost. It. *sostenuto*, sustained (mus.)
SOTIM sonic observation of the trajectory and impact of missiles
Sou. south; Southampton (*also*, Soton.); southern
sov. sovereign
Sov. Soviet
s.o.v. shut off valve
SP *Senterpartiet*, Centre Party formed 1920 *orig.* Agrarian Party (Norway); *s* Fife (B.V.R.)
sp. space; special; specie; species; specific; specimen; speed; spelling; spirit; sport; It. *sposa*, wife
sp. L. *sine prole*, without issue
Sp. Spain; Spaniard (*also*, Span.); Spanish (*also*, Span.); specialist; spring
s.p. self-propelled; short page signal publication; single phase (elec.); single pole; small paper; small pica (typ.); starting point/price; stop payment
s.p. *senza pedale*, without pedal (mus.); L. *sine prole*, without issue
S.p. special position (advert.)
S.P. Sp. *Santo Padre*, Holy Father; Port. *Sentidos pêsames*, deepest sympathy; service pistol (mil.); service police; shore patrol; Sisters of Providence; sparking plug; staff paymaster; stirrup pump; stop press; stretcher party; supply point
S.P. L. *Sanctissimus Pater*, Most Holy Father; L. *Summus Pontifex*, Supreme Pontiff, the Pope
SPA Singapore People's Alliance; Sugar Producers' Association (Guyana)
S.p.A. *Società per Azioni*, Italian joint stock co.
S.P.A. Society for Personnel Administration (U.S.A.); Society of Saint Peter the Apostle for Native Clergy; sundry persons' account
S.P.A.B. Society for the Protection of Ancient Buildings
Spam spiced ham, trademark for spiced pork products/tinned meat
S.P.A.N.A. Society for the Protection of Animals in North Africa
SPANDAR space and range radar (NASA)
SPAR member of the women's reserve of the U.S. Coast Guard, from motto *Semper Paratus*
S.P.A.R. seagoing platform for acoustic research (USN); super precision approach radar
S.P.A.S. L. *Societatis Philosophicae Americanae Socius*, Fellow of the American Philosophical Soc.
SPASUR space surveillance system (USN)
S.P.A.T.C. South Pacific Air Transport Council
SPC stored program control
S.P.C. Society for the Prevention of Crime; South Pacific Commission
S.P.C.A. Society for the Prevention of Cruelty to Animals, *now* R.S.P.C.A.
S.P.C.C. Society for the Prevention of Cruelty to Children, *now* N.S.P.C.C.
S.P.C.K. Society for Promoting Christian Knowledge
SPD *Sozialdemokratische Partei Deutschlands*, Social Democratic Party, founded in 19th cent. and re-estab. 1945 (W. Ger.)
s.p.d. subject to permission to deal (fin.)
S.P.D. South Polar Distance
S.P.D.C. spare parts distributing centre
S.P.E. Society for Pure English, founded 1913
SPEARS satellite photo-electronic analog rectification system
spec. special; specially; specific; specifically; specification; specimen; spectrum; speculation
SPEC. Society for Pollution and Environmental Control (Can.)
spec. appt. special appointment
spec. emp. specially employed
special. specialized
specif. specifically; specification

specs. specifications; spectacles
SPECTRE 'The Special Executive for Counter-Intelligence, Revenge and Extortion', terrorist organ. combated by James Bond in Ian Fleming's novels
SPEED signal processing in evacuated electronic devices
speedo. speedometer
Spett. It. *Spetabile*, dear sir
S.P.G. Society for the Propagation of the Gospel
S.P.G.A. Scottish Professional Golfers' Association
S.P.G.B. Socialist Party of Great Britain
sp. gr. specific gravity
S.P.H.E. Society of Packaging and Handling Engineers (U.S.A.)
sp. ht. specific heat
SPI selected period investment (fin.)
S.P.I. Fr. *Secrétariats professionnels internationaux*, Intern. Trade Secretariats; Society of the Plastics Industry (U.S.A.)
S.P.I.E. Fr. *Secrétariat professionnel international de l'enseignement*, Intern. Fed. of Free Teachers' Unions
S.P.I.L. Society for the Promotion and Improvement of Libraries (India)
Spirit. spiritualism; spiritualistic
Spirit. It. *Spiritoso*, in a spirited manner (mus.)
S.P.I.S. services packaging instruction sheet
S.P.I.W. special purposes individual weapon
s.p.l. L. *sine prole legitima*, without legitimate issue
S.P.L.S.M. single position letter sorting machine
s.p.m. L. *sine prole mascula*, without male issue
S.P.M. Saint-Pierre et Miquelon
S.P.M. short particular metre (mus.)
S.P.M.A. Sewage Plant Manufacturers' Association
S.P.M.U. Society of Professional Musicians in Ulster
S.P.N. stop press news
S.P.N.M. Society for the Promotion of New Music
S.P.N.R. Society for the Promotion of Nature Reserves
SPO special projects office (USN); system program office (USAF)
s.p.o. sausages potatoes and onions
S.P.O. senior press officer; Ger. *Socialistische Partei Österreichs*, Austrian Socialist Party; stoker petty officer
SPOC single point orbit calculator
S.P.O.E. Society of Post Office Engineers
sport. sporting

spot. spotlight
spots spotlights
spp. species
S.P.Q.R. small profits and quick returns
S.P.Q.R. L. *Senatus Populusque Romanus*, the Senate and Roman people
Spr. sapper; sprinkle
S.P.R. semi-permanent repellent; Society for Psychical Research
S.P.R.C. Society for the Prevention and Relief of Cancer
spre. Sp. *siempre*, always
S.P.R.I. Scott Polar Research Institute
SPRINT solid propellant rocket intercept missile
S.P.R.L. Fr. *Société de Personnes à Responsabilité Limitée*, private limited co.; Society for the Promotion of Religion and Learning
s.p.s. L. *sine prole supersite*, without surviving issue
S.P.S. Scottish Painters' Society; service propulsion system
S.P.S.E. Society of Photographic Scientists and Engineers (U.S.A.)
S.P.S.L. Society for the Protection of Science and Learning
S.P.S.O. senior personnel staff officer; senior principal scientific officer
S.P.S.P. St. Peter and St. Paul
sp. surf. specific surface
spt. seaport; support
sptg. sporting
S.P.T.L. Society of Public Teachers of Law
SPUR space power unit reactor; source program utility routines (computer)
Spurs Tottenham Hotspur Association Football Club
S.P.U.R.V. self-propelled underwater research vehicle
S.P.V.D. Society for the Prevention of Venereal Disease
sq. squadron (*also*, sqd., sqdn.); square
sq. L. *et sequentia*, and what follows; L. *sequens*, the following
S.Q. sick quarters; survival quotient
Sqdn. Ldr., Sqn. leader squadron leader
sq. ft. square feet/foot
sq. in. square inch
sq. m. square metre/mile
S.Q.M.S. staff quartermaster-sergeant
Sqn.Q.M.S. squadron quartermaster-sergeant
Sqn.S.M. squadron sergeant-major
Sq.O. squadron officer
sqq. L. *et sequentia*, and what follows
sq. rd. square rod

sq. yd. square yard
Sr *s* strontium (chem.)
SR *s* Angus (B.V.R.); Saudi rial (Saudi Arabian currency); *s* Stranraer (B.F.P.); study requirement (USAF); synthetic rubber
sr. senior; steradian
Sr. Señor; Sir; sister (religious)
s.r. self raising; shipping receipt; short rate
S.R. Schopper-Riegler, scale of freeness of pulp suspension in paper-making; Senate Resolution; service rifle; *Serviço da República*, the service of the Portuguese Rep.; Society of Radiographers; Southern Railway, prior to nationalization (British Rail); Southern Rhodesia, *now* Rhodesia; special/supplementary reserve; standard rate (tax.); *Sveriges Radio*, Swed. radio network
Sra. Sp. Señora, Mrs
S.R.A. Spring Research Association; Squash Rackets Association; surgeon rear-admiral
S.R.B.M. short range ballistic missile
S.R.B.P. synthetic resin-bonded paper
S.R.C. sample return container; Science Research Council; Swiss Red Cross
S.R.C. L. *Sacra Rituum Congregatio*, Sacred Congregation of Rites; It. *Santa Romana Chiesa*, Holy Roman Church
s.r.c.c., SR & CC strikes, riots, and civil commotions
S.R.D. service rum diluted; Society for the Relief of Distress
S.R.D.A. Scottish Retail Drapers Association
S.R.D.E. Signals Research and Development Establishment
S.R.E. scientific research and experiments department
S.R.E. L. *Sancta Romana Ecclesia*, Holy Roman Church
SRF black semi-reinforcing furnace black, filler in rubber compounding
S. Rg. sound-ranging
SRHE Society for Research into Higher Education
S.R.I. L. *Sacrum Romanum Imperium*, the Holy Roman Empire
SRILTA Stanford Research Institute Lead Time Analysis
srio. Sp. *secretario*, secretary
S.r.l. It. *Società a responsabilità limitata*, Limited Partnership
SRM short range missile; speed of relative movement
S.R.M.U. space research management unit
SRN hovercraft, from Saunders Roe, the 'N' being merely a project letter
S.R.N. State Registered Nurse

S.R.N.A. Shipbuilders and Repairers National Association
S.R. (N.S.W.) *State Reports*, New South Wales (Aust.)
S.R.O. squadron recreation officer; standing room only; statutory rules and orders (*also*, S.R. & O.); supplementary reserve of officers
S.R.P. supply refuelling point
S.R.Q. *State Reports*, Queensland (Aust.)
S.R.R. supplementary reserve regulations
S.R.R.A. Scottish Radio Retailers' Association
S.R.S. Soil Research Station
S.R.S. L. *Societatis Regiae Sodalis*, Fellow of the Royal Society
S.R.S.A. Scientific Research Society of America
Srta. Sp. Señorita, Miss
S.R.U. Scottish Rugby Union
S.R.U.B.L.U.K. Society for the Reinvigoration of Unremunerative Branch Lines in the United Kingdom
S.R.Y. Sherwood Rangers Yeomanry
SS *s* East Lothian (B.V.R.); *s* St. Ives (B.F.P.)
S/S same size, used on drawings to indicate that enlargement/reduction is not required; self shank (buttons); station to station
ss. L. *scilicet*, namely; L. *semis*, half (med.); L. *supra scriptum*, written above
s.s. screw steamer; simplified spelling; single strength; sword stick; sworn statement
s.s. It. *senza sordini*, without mutes (mus.)
s.S. Ger. *siehe Seite*, see page
SS. Saints
SS. L. *sanctissimus*, most holy
S/S. silk screen (typ.)
S.S. Royal Statistical Society; Sabbath school; L. *Sacra Scriptura*, Holy Scripture; It. *Santa Sede*, Holy See; Fr. *Sa Sainteté*, His Holiness; Ger. *Schutz-Staffel*, protective squadron, Black Guards, elite Nazi corps; science/secret service; secondary school; Secretary for Scotland; Secretary of State; Selden Society; senior sister; short sleeves; Sidney Sussex College, Cambridge, founded 1596; silver star; social security; special settlement; staff surgeon; stainless steel; standard size; steamship; It. *Strada Statale*, National Highway; Straits Settlements; Sunday school; supply and secretariat
S. & S. slings and springs (physiotherapy)
SSA Swaledale Sheepbreeders' Association

S.S.A. Scottish Schoolmasters' Association; Secretary of State for Air; Seismological Society of America; senior service accountant; senior statistical assistant; Social Security Administration (U.S.A.); Society for the Study of Addiction, to Alcohol and other Drugs; Society of Scottish Artists

SS.AA.II. Fr. *Ses Altesses Impériales*, Their Imperial Highnesses

SS.AA.RR. Fr. *Ses Altesses Royales*, Their Royal Highnesses

S.S.A.C. Scottish Sub-Aqua Club

S.S.A.F.A. Soldiers', Sailors' and Airmen's Families Association

S.S.A.G.O. Student Scout and Guide Organisation

s.s.b. single sideband

S.S.B. L. *Sacrae Scripturae Baccalaureus*, Bachelor of Sacred Scripture; Social Security Board (U.S.A.)

S.S.C. Scottish Ski-Club; Sculptors' Society of Canada; services' standardization sub-committee; Solicitor before the Supreme Courts (Scot.)

S.S.C. L. *Societas Sanctae Crucis*, Society of the Holy Cross

S. Sc. D. Doctor of Social Science

SS.D. L. *Sanctissimus Dominus*, Most Holy Lord, *i.e.* the Pope

S.S.D. L. *Sacrae Scripturae Doctor*, Doctor of Sacred Scripture

S.S.D.A. Self Service Development Association

S.S.E. Society of Saint Edmund; south-south-east

S.S.E.B. South of Scotland Electricity Board

SSEC Secondary School Examinations Council

SSEES School of Slavonic and East European Studies (Univ. of Lond.)

SSF seconds saybolt furol

S.S.F. single-seater fighter; Society of Saint Francis

S.S.F.A. Scottish Schools' Football Association; Scottish Steel Founders' Association

S.S.F.F. Solid Smokeless Fuels Federation

S.S.G.G. Ger. *Stock, Stein, Gras, Grein*, stick, stone, grass, groan

S/Sgt., S.Sgt. staff sergeant

SSHA Scottish Special Housing Association

S. Sh. A. Russ. *Soyedinennye Shtaty Ameriki*, United States of America

S.S.I. Fr. *Service social international*, Intern. Social Service; sites of scientific importance; Society of Scribes and Illuminators

S.S.I.S.I. Statistical and Social Inquiry Society of Ireland

S.S.J.E. Society of St. John the Evangelist

S.S.L. L. *Sacrae Scripturae Licentiatus*, Licentiate of Sacred Scripture

SSM single sideband modulation; surface-to-surface missile

S.S.M. Society of the Sacred Mission; squadron/staff sergeant-major

S.S.M.A. Stainless Steel Manufacturers' Association; State Servants and Allied Motoring Association

S.S.N. Fr. *Sociétaire de la Société Nationale des Beaux Arts*, Member of the Nat. Soc. of Fine Arts

S.S.O. senior scientific/supply officer; special service officer; squadron/staff signals officer; station staff officer

S. sord. It. *Senza sordini*, without mutes (mus.)

S.S.P. Pious Society of Saint Paul

S.S.P.C.A. Scottish Society for the Prevention of Cruelty to Animals

SS.PP. L. *Sancti Patres*, Holy Fathers

S.S.P.P. Society for the Study of Physiological Patterns

S.S.P.V. Scottish Society for the Prevention of Vivisection

S.S.Q. station sick quarters

S.S.R. Soviet Socialist Republic

S.S.R.A. Scottish Squash Rackets Association

S.S.R.B. Soil Survey Research Board

S.S.R.C. Social Science Research Council; Social Sciences Research Council (U.S.A.)

S.S.R.I. Social Science Research Institute (U.S.A.)

SSRNJ *Socijalistički Savez Radnog Naroda Jugoslavije*, Socialist Alliance of the Working People of Yugoslavia

SSS *s* South Shields (B.F.P.)

S.S.S. Secretary of State for Scotland; selective service system; single screw ship; System Safety Society (U.S.A.)

S.S.S. L. *Societas Sanctissimi Sacramenti*, Congregation of the Most Blessed Sacrament

S.S.S.C. soft-sized, super-calendered paper

SSSh security police (Albania)

S.S.S.I. sites of special scientific importance

S.S.S.R. *Soyuz Sovietskikh Sotsialisticheskikh Respublik*, Union of Soviet Socialist Republics

S.S.St.J. Serving Sister, Order of Saint John of Jerusalem

S.S.T. supersonic transport/travel

S.S.T.A. Scottish Secondary Teachers' Association

S.S.T.O. superintending sea transport officer

S.S.U. Sunday School Union

S.S.W. Secretary of State for War; south-south-west

S.S.W.A. Scottish Society of Women Artists

ST *s* Inverness-shire (B.V.R.); *s* Stockton (B.F.P.)

6 ST *s* Stoke on Trent (radio callsign)

S & T Salmon & Trout Association

st. stanza; state; statement; Ger. *statt*, instead of; statute; stem; steradian, unit of solid angle; stitch (knit.); stone (weight); street (*also*, St., Str.); strophe; stumped (cricket)

1st. cl. hon. first class honours (degree)

st. L. *stet*, let it remain (typ.)

St. Saint; Ger. *Sankt*, Saint; strait; Ger. *Stück*, piece; Ger. *Stunde*, hour, *also*, Std.

s.t. select time; short ton, 2,000 lb; static thrust; syncopated time

s.t. It. *senza tempo*, without time (mus.)

S.T. shipping ticket; shock troops; spring tide; standard/summer time; surtax; the *Sunday Times*

S. & T. supply and transport

sta. station; stationary

*Sta., St*ᵃ It., Port., Sp. santa, female saint

S.T.A. Sail Training Association; Science and Technology Agency (Jap.); Scottish Typographical Association; Seed Trade Association of the United Kingdom; Society of Typographic Arts; Swimming Teachers' Association

stab. stabilizer

stacc. It. *staccato*, detached (mus.)

S.T.A.C.O. Society of Telecommunications Administrative and Controlling Officers

Staffs. Staffordshire

stag. stagger

Stan Stanley

S.T.A.N.A.G. Standard NATO Agreement

stand. standard

St. And. St. Andrews (Scot.)

STAR *Scientific and Technical Aerospace Reports* (NASA); ship tended acoustic relay (USAF)

stat. statics; stationary; statistical; statistics; statuary; statute

stat. L. *statim*, immediately (med.)

S.T.A.T.E. simplified tactical approach and terminal equipment

Stat. Hall. Stationers' Hall (Lond.)

S.T.A.U.K. Seed Trade Association of the United Kingdom

S.T.B. L. *Sacrae Theologiae Baccalaureus*, Bachelor of Sacred Theology

stbd. starboard

stbt. steamboat

STC. satellite test center (U.S.A.); sensitivity-time control

S.T.C. Samuel Taylor Coleridge (1772–1834), Eng. poet and philosopher; senior training corps (mil.); *Short Title Catalogue* of Books Printed in England, Scotland and Ireland, and of English Books Printed Abroad, 1477–1640; Standard Telephones & Cables Ltd.; Sydney Turf Club (Aust.)

Stckhlm. Stockholm

S.T.C.S. Society of Technical Civil Servants

std. standard; started

S.T.D. L. *Sacrae Theologiae Doctor*, Doctor of Sacred Theology; salinity-temperature-depth sensor system; sea transport department; subscriber trunk dialling (telephone)

St. Diap. stopped diapason, relating to the organ (mus.)

Stdy. Saturday

Ste. Fr. *Sainte*, female saint

Sté. Fr. *Société*, company

S.T.E. Society of Telecommunications Engineers

S.T.E.C.C. Scottish Technical Education Consultative Council

STEG *Société Tunisienne d'Électricité et du Gaz*, Nationalized Electricity and Gas undertaking (Tunisia)

S.T.E.L.O. *Studenta Tutmonda Esperantista Ligo*, World League of Esperanto-Speaking Students

sten., stenog. stenographer; stenography

Sten gun. *S*heppard and *T*urpin (inventors) and *En*gland/or *en* of Bren, an inexpensive sub-machine gun (WW2)

Stent. It. *Stentando*, delaying (mus.)

STEP Stop the Eleven Plus (educ.)

ster. stereotype; sterling, *also*, sterl.

stereo. stereophonic; stereotype

Steve, Stevie Stephan; Stephen; Steven

St. Ex., St. Exch. Stock Exchange

stg. sterling

Stg. *String* (mus.)

StGB Ger. *Strafgesetzbuch*, Penal Code

stge. storage

Stgs. *Strings* (mus.)

S.T.G.W.U. Scottish Transport and General Workers' Union

Sth., Sthn. south; southern

S. Th. Scholar in/of Theology

S.T.I.D. scientific and technical information division (NASA)

STINGS stellar inertial guidance system

stip. stipend; stipendiary; stipulation

Stir. Stirling

s.t.i.r. surplus to immediate requirements

stk. stock

STL studio-to-transmitter link

S.T.L. L. *Sacrae Theologiae Licentiatus*, Licentiate of Sacred Theology; Standard Telecommunications Laboratories

STL-group *Suomen Tukkukauppiaiden Liitto*, Finnish Wholesalers' and Importers' Assn.

STLO scientific technical liaison office /officer

S.T.M. L. *Sacrae Theologiae Magister*, Master of Sacred Theology

S.T.M.S.A. Scottish Timber Merchants' and Sawmillers' Association

stn. stain; station

STO standing order

Sto. stoker

Stº. Port. *Santo*, Saint

S.T.O. sea transport officer; senior technical officer

S.T.O.L. short take-off and landing; **—/V.C.D.** short take-off and landing/ vertical climb and descent

S'ton. Southampton

S.T.O.P.P. Society of Teachers Opposed to Physical Punishment

S.T.O.R. ScrippsTuna Oceanographic Research (U.S.A.)

S. to S. ship to shore; station to station

S.T.P. L. *Sacrae Theologiae Professor*, Professor of Sacred Theology; scientific and technical potential; standard temperature and pressure

S.T.P.M.A. Scottish Theatrical Proprietors' and Managers' Association

S.T.P.T.C. Standard Tar Products Testing Committee

str. seater; steamer; straight; strait; strength; streptococcus; string; stringer; stroke (rowing); strong; structural; structure

str. *stringed*, instruments (mus.)

Str. Ger. *Strasse*, street

s.t.r. surplus to requirements

S.T.R. Society for Theater Research (U.S.A.)

STRAC strategic air command (U.S.A.); strategic army corps

Strad. Stradivarius violin

S.T.R.A.D. signal transmitting, receiving and distribution

STRADAP storm radar data processor

STRATAD strategic aerospace division (USAF)

strep. streptococcus

STRICOM U.S. Strike Command

String. It. *Stringendo*, getting gradually quicker (mus.)

STRIP standard taped routines for image processing (computer)

STROBE satellite tracking of balloons and emergencies

S.T.S. Scottish Text Society; Spring Trapmakers' Society

S.T.S.D. Society of Teachers of Speech and Drama

S.T.S.O. senior technical staff officer

st. st. stocking stitch (knit.)

S.T.T.A. Scottish Table Tennis Association

S. Tube steel tubing

S.T.U.C. Scottish Trades Union Congress

Stud. student; **— Inst. Gas E.** Student of the Institution of Gas Engineers; **— Inst. P.C.** Student of the Institute of Pnblic Cleansing; **— Inst. R.** Student of the Institute of Refrigeration; **— Weld. I.** Student of the Welding Institute

STUFF system to uncover facts fast

Stuka Ger. *Sturzkampf Flugzeug*, dive bomber

STV Sp. *Solidaridad de Trabajadores Vascos*, Solidarity of Basque Workers; standard test vehicle; subscription television

S.T.V. Scottish Television Limited; single transferable vote; standard tar viscometer

stvdr. stevedore

S.T.W.P. Society of Technical Writers and Publishers (U.S.A.)

stwy. stairway

SU *s* Kincardineshire (B.V.R.); sensation unit, auditory unit of loudness (psy.); *s* Southampton (B.F.P.); Soviet Air Lines; *s* Unit of Soviet Socialist Republics (I.V.R.)

Su. Sudan; Sudanese; Sunday

s.u. service unit; set up; Ger. *siehe unten*, see below

S.U. Soviet Union; strontium unit

S.U.A. Silver Users' Association (U.S.A.); State Universities Association (U.S.A.)

sub. subaltern; sub-editor; subject (*also*, subj.); subjunctive (*also*, subj.); submarine; subscription (*also*, subs.); subsidiary (*also*, subs.); subsistence (*also*, subs.); substantive (*also*, subst.); substitute (*also*, subs., subst.); suburb; suburban; subway

S.U.B.A.N. Scottish Union of Bakers and Allied Workers

subd. subdivision

subdéb subdébutante, young girl who has not made her début in society

sub.-ed. sub-editor

SUBIC submarine integrated control system

Sub. L., Sub.-Lt., Sub-Lieut. Sub-Lieutenant

SUBLANT Submarine Forces, Atlantic (USN)

subord. cl. subordinate clause

SUBPAC Submarine Forces, Pacific (USN)

SUBROC submarine rocket

subsec. subsection

subseq., subsq. subsequent; subsequently

substand. substandard

Sub. U. substitution unit

suc. succeed (*also*, succ.); success (*also*, succ.); successor (*also*, succ.); suction

Suc. Fr. *sucre*, sugar

S.U.C.E.E. Socialist Union of Central Eastern Europe

SUD *s* Sudan (I.V.R.); symbol unit designator (computer)

Sue, Susie, Susy Susan

Suet. Suetonius (*c* 70–*c* 140) Roman historian

suf., suff. suffix

suff. sufficient

Suff. Suffolk; Suffragan (*also*, Suffr.); — B. Suffragan Bishop

sug. suggest; suggestion

Suid. Suidas, name of a Gr. lexicon *c* A.D. 1000

S.U.I.T. Scottish and Universal Investment Trust

suiv. Fr. *suivant*, following

Sult. Sultan; Sultana

sum. summary

sum. L. *sumat*, let him take (med.); L. *sumendum*, let it be taken (med.)

S.U.M. surface-to-underwater missile

sums. summons

SUN symbolic unit number (computer)

Sun., Sund. Sunday

S.U.N.F.E.D. Special United Nations Fund for Economic Development

S.U.N.S. sonic underwater navigation system

SUP Socialist Unity Party (N.Z.)

sup., super. superficial; superfine; superior; superlative

sup. supine; supplement; supplementary; supply; supreme

sup. L. *supra*, above

Sup. Ct. superior/supreme court

Sup. Dpo. supply depot

Supdt., Supt. Superintendent

superf. It. *superficie*, area, surface

superl. superlative

sup. lint. L. *super linteum*, on lint (med.)

S.U.P.M. Society of Underwood Products Manufacturers

Sup. O. supply officer

supp., suppl. supplement; supplementary

Sup. P. supply point

supr. superior; supervisor; supreme

Supvr. supervisor

sur. surface; surplus

Sur. Surrey

SURANO surface radar and navigation operation

SURCAL surveillance calibration satellite

surf. a. surface area

surg. surgeon; surgery; surgical

Surg.-Comdr., Surg.-Cdr. surgeon-commander

Surg.-Gen. surgeon-general

Surg.-Lt. Comdr. surgeon-lieutenant commander

Surg.-Maj. surgeon-major

SURIC surface ship integrated control system

surr. surrender

Surr., Surro. Surrogate

Surr. A.C. Surrey Archaeological Collections

surv. survey; surveyor; survive

S.U.R.V. standard underwater research vessel

Surv.-Gen. surveyor-general

SUS saybolt universal second; Students Union Society

Sus., Suss. Sussex

S.U.S. Scottish Union of Students

susp. suspend; suspension

sus. per coll. L. *suspensio per collum*, hanging by the neck

Suss. A.C. Sussex Archaeological Collections

S.U.T. Society for Underwater Technology

Suth. Sutherland (Scot.)

SV *s* Kinross-shire (B.V.R.); side valve

S/V surrender value

s.v. L. *spiritus vini*, spirits of wine (med.); L. *sub verbo/sub voce*, under a specified word

S.V. sailing vessel; Sons of Veterans

S.V. L. *Sancta Virgo*, Holy Virgin; L. *Sanctitas Vestra*, Your Holiness

Sval. Svalbard (Spitzbergen)

S.V.C. Society of Vacuum Coaters (U.S.A.)

S.V.D. swine vesicular disease

S.V.F. Ger. *Schweizerische Vereinigung von Färbereifachleuten*, Swiss Dyers' Assn.

svg. saving
s. v. gall. L. *spiritus vini galici*, brandy (med.)
SVI Ger. *Vereinigung Schweizerischer Verkehrsingenieure*, Member of the Assn. of Swiss Traffic Engineers
S.V.M. Fr. *Service volontaire ménnonite*, Mennonite Voluntary Service
S.V.O. Scottish Variety Orchestra; superintending veterinary officer
s.v.p. Fr. *s'il vous plaît*, if you please
S.V.P. small vessels pool
s.v.r. L. *spiritus vini rectificatus*, rectified spirit of wine (med.)
S.V.S. Society for Visiting Scientists; *Sveriges Standardisering-kommission*, Swed. Standards Institute
s.v.t. L. *spiritus vini tenuior*, proof spirit of wine
S.V.T.L. services valve testing laboratory
SVTP sound, velocity, temperature, pressure
s.v.v. L. *sit venia verbo*, forgive the expression
Svy. survey
SW *s* Kircudbrightshire (B.V.R.); sandwich (training course)
sw. switch
s/w. sea water; seaworthy
Sw. Sweden (*also*, Swe., Swed.); Swedish (*also*, Swe., Swed.); Swiss
Sw. *Swell organ* (mus.)
s.w. salt/sea water; short wave; small women; specific weight
S.W. Senior Warden; South Wales; south - west; south - westerly; standard weight; static water
SWA *s* South-West Africa (I.V.R.)
S.W.A. South West Africa
SWACS space warning and control system
S.W.A.F.A.C. Southwest Atlantic Fisheries Advisory Commission
S.W.A.L.K. sealed with a loving kiss
SWANU South West Africa National Union
SWANUF South West Africa National United Front
SWAPO South West Africa People's Organization
S.W.B. short wheel base; South Wales Borderers (mil.)
swbd. switchboard
SWbW southwest by west
Swd. sewed
S.W.D.A. Scottish Wholesale Druggists' Association
S.W.E. Society of Women Engineers (U.S.A.)
S.W.E.B. South Wales/West Electricity Board

SWEPC South-West Economic Planning Council
S.W.E.T.M. Society of West End Theatre Managers
S.W.G. standard wire gauge, British Imperial
S.W.I.E. South Wales Institute of Engineers
SWIRL South Western Industrial Research Limited
Swissair Swiss Air Transport
Switz. Switzerland
S.W.L. safe working load, this is usually stamped on derricks of British vessels indicating safe working load allocated by govt., e.g. S.W.L. 12 tons
S.W.L.A. South Women's Lacrosse Association
S.W.M.A. Steel Wool Manufacturers' Association
S.W.M.F. South Wales Miners' Federation
SWO *Surinaamse Werknemers-Organisatie*, Surinam Workers' Organization
S.W.O. squadron wireless officer/operator; station warrant officer
S.W.O.A. Scottish Woodland Owners' Association
SWORD shallow water oceanographic research data system (U.S.A.)
SWP safe working pressure
S.W.P.A. south-west pacific area; Steel Work Plant Association
S.W.S. static water supply
S.W.T. School of Welding Technology
S.W.T.E.A. Scottish Woollen Trade Employers' Association
S.W.T.M.A. Scottish Woollen Trade Mark Association
S.W.W.J. Society of Women Writers and Journalists
SX *s* West Lothian (B.V.R.)
5SX *s* Swansea (radio call-sign)
Sx. Sussex
SXT sextant
SY *s* Midlothian (B.V.R.); *s* Seychelles (I.V.R.); *s* Stornoway (B.F.P.)
Sy. Seychelles; supply; Surrey; Syria
S.Y. steam yacht
S.Y.B. *Statesman's Year-Book*
Sy. Crs. sundry creditors
Syd. Sydney (Aust.); — **L.R.** *Sydney Law Review*
S. Yd. Scotland Yard
Syd. Soc. Lex. *The New Sydenham Society's Lexicon*
S.Y.H.A. Scottish Youth Hostels Association
syl., syll. syllable; syllabus
sym. symbol; symbolic; symmetrical; symmetry

sym., symph. *symphony* (mus.)
Symp. symposium
syn. synchronize; synonym; synonymous; synonymy; synthetic
SYNCOM synchronous communication satellite
synd. syndicate
synon. synonymous
synop. synopsis
syntan. synthetic tanning material

synth. synthetic
S.Y.P. Society of Young Publishers
Sy. P.O. supply petty officer
SYR *s* Syria (I.V.R.)
syr. syrup
Syr. Syria; Syriac (typ.); Syrian
syst. system; systematic
SZ *s* Down (B.V.R.)
sz. size

T

T

t *s* thickness; *s* thunder (met.); leading-note in Tonic Sol-fa, pron. Te; *s* meridian angle

't Dutch *het*, the, as van't Hoff; it, as in 'twas

T *s* Devon (B.V.R.); *s* surface tension (phys.); Telephone (cartog.); tera, 10^{12}; tesla, unit of magnetic flux density (T = Wb/m^2); *s* Thailand (I.V.R.); *s* time reversal (math.); *s* Tralee (Irish Rep. F.P.)

2, 4, 5-T 2, 4, 5-trichlorophenoxyacetic acid, herbicide used as defoliant

t. table; tabulated; tackle; taken; tare (com.); teaspoon; teaspoonful; teeth; tenor; tense; terminal; territorial; territory; that; time; Fr. *tome*, volume; ton; Fr. *tonneau*, ton; town; township; transit; transitive; troy; tun; turn

t. It. *tempo*, time (mus.); L. *tempore*, in the time of; It. *tenore*, tenor (mus.)

T. tanker; target; Tea (rose); teacher; Ger. *Teil*, part; telegraph; telegraphic; telephone; temperature (med.); temporary; terms (math.); Testament; thermometer; third of a page, type area (advert.); tiler; Titus; topical; torpedo; Sp *torre*, tower (cartog.); Fr. *tour*, tower (cartog.); transaction; translation; transport; transportation; transverse, baby's head facing sideways in labour; Treasury; Trinity; True, direction measured clockwise through 360° from direction of the true north and suffixed T. (nav.); Tuesday; Finn. *tulo*, arrival; Turkish; twist (knitting)

T. It. *tace*, be silent (mus.); It. *tasto*, key (of keyboard instruments), fingerboard (of stringed instruments) (mus.);

It. *tempo*, time (mus.); L. *Tempore*, in the time of; *tenor* (mus.); It. *tutti*, all (mus.)

Ta *s* tantalum (chem.)

TA *s* Devon (B.V.R.)

ta. tableau; tablet

t.a. target area; test accessory; third attack (lacrosse); time and attendance; transit authority (U.S.A.); travel allowance; true altitude

t.a. L. *testantibus actis*, as the acts show

T/A temporary assistant

T.A. table of allowances (tax.); teachers' assurance; telegraphic address; territorial army; tithe annuity; traffic agent/ auditor; training adviser; Translators' Association; turbulence amplifier; Typographical Association, *now* N.G.A.

T.A.A. Territorial Army Association; test of academic aptitude; Trans-Australia Airlines; Transportation Association of America

TAAF Fr. *Terres Australes et Antarctiques Françaises*, French Southern and Antarctic Territories

tab. table; tablet; tabulate; tabulation

T.A.B. Technical Assistance Board (U.N.O.); Total Abstinence Brotherhood; Triple vaccine to prevent typhoid, paratyphoid A and paratyphoid B (med.)

T.A.B.A. Timber Agents' and Brokers' Association of the United Kingdom

T.A.B.L. Tropical Atlantic Biological Laboratory (U.S.A.)

TABSO *Transport Aérien Civil Bulgare*, Bulgarian Nat. Airline, *now* BALKAN

TAC Tactical Air Command (USAF); Thai Airways Company; *Transportes Aéreos Continentais*, Continental Airways (Port.)

Tac. Publius Cornelius Tacitus (*c* A.D. 55–*c* 120) Roman historian

T.A.C. Tanganyika Agricultural Corporation; Technical Assistance Committee (U.N.O.); Television/Tobacco Advisory Committee; Trades Advisory Council; trapped air cushion

TACAN tactical air navigation

TACCAR time averaged clutter coherent airborne radar

tach. tachometer

T.A.C.L. Technical Advisory Committee on Electronics; Training for Action Centred Leadership

TACMAR tactical multi-function array radar

TACS tactical air control system

TACV tracked air cushion vehicle, such as hovertrain

Tad Thaddaeus; Theodore

ta'en taken

Taf. Ger. *Tafel*, a plate (typ.)

T.A.F. Tactical Air Force; time and frequency; toxoid-antitoxin floccules (med.)

T. & A.F.A. Territorial and Auxiliary Forces Association

TAFUBAR things are fouled up beyond all recognition (computer)

Tag. Tagalog

T.A.G. telegraphist air gunner; The Adjutant-General (U.S.A.)

Tai. Taiwan

tal. L. *talis*, such

Tal. *Talmud*, in turn an abbrev. of *Talmud Torah*, Study of the Torah, a collection of Jewish books containing traditions, laws, rules and institutions, by which, in addition to the Heb. Bible, the conduct of Jewry is regulated

TAL. traffic and accident loss (insce.)

T.A.L.I.C. Tyneside Association of Libraries for Industry and Commerce

Tal. qual. L. *Talis qualis*, average quality/just as they come

TALUS transportation and land use study

Tam Thomas (Scot.)

Tam. Tamil, Dravidian language spoken by 18m. in Ceylon and India

T.A.M. Tactical Air Missile; Television Audience Measurement Limited

tammy, tam Tam o' Shanter, Scottish bonnet, woollen knit, 'Kilmarnock' bonnet worn by the hero of Burns's poem

tan *s* tangent (math.)

Tang. Tanganyika; Tangier

tanh hyperbolic tangent

TANS terminal area navigation system

T.A.N.S. Territorial Army Nursing Service, *now* Q.A.R.A.N.C.

TANU Tanganyika African National Union (Tanzania)

Tan-Zam railway linking Dar es Salaam with Kipiri Mposhi on the Zambian border, begun in 1970

T.A.O. Technical Assistance Operations (U.N.O.)

TAOC Tactical Air Operations Center (U.S.A.)

TAP Total Action Against Poverty; *Transportes Aéreos Portugueses*, Portuguese Air Lines; Treasury additional paper (fin.); *Tunis Afrique Presse*, Tunisian press agency

T.A.P. Technical Assistance Program (U.S.A.)

Tapline Trans-Arabian Pipeline Company (Saudi Arabia)

TAPPI Technical Association of the Pulp & Paper Industry

tar sailor

TAR terrain avoidance radar; thrust-augmented rocket

tar. tariff; tarpaulin

T.A.R. Territorial Army Regulations

T.A.R.A. Technical Assistant, Royal Artillery; Territorial Army Rifle Association

TARAN test and replace as necessary

TARFU things are really fouled up (computer)

tarmac. Tar Macadam, road surfacing (John Loudon McAdam, 1756–1836)

T.A.R.O. Territorial Army Reserve of Officers

TAROM *Transporturi Aeriene Române*, state airline of Romania

T.A.R.S. Technical Assistance Recruitment Service (U.N.O.)

Tart. Tartaric

Tas., Tasm. Tasmania; Tasmanian

TAS. true air speed, the speed of a craft relative to the air around it (nav.)

T.A.S.I. Time Assignment Speech Interpolation

TASR terminal area surveillance radar

TASS *Telegrafnoje agentsvo Sovietskovo Sojuza*, telegraph agency of the Soviet Union

T.A.S.S. Transport Aircraft Servicing Specialist (R.A.F.)

Tas. Univ. L. Rev. *Tasmanian University Law Review*

TAT Thrust-Augmented Thor (NASA)

T.A.T. Transatlantic Telephone Cable

'tater a potato, *also* tattie (Scot.)

TATSA transportation aircraft test and support activity

T.A.U.N. Technical Assistance of the United Nations

taut. tautology

tav. tavern

T.-à-v. Fr. *Tout-à-vous*, wholly yours

Tave, Tavy Octavius

T. Aviv Tel Aviv

T.A.V.R., T. & A.V.R. Territorial and Army Volunteer Reserve

t.a.w. twice a week

tax., taxn. taxation

taxi taxi-cab

Tb *s* terbium (chem.)

TB *s* Lancashire (B.V.R.)

t.b. temporary buoy; terminal board; title block; trial balance; true bearing; tubercle bacillus

t. & b. top and bottom

T.B. torpedo boat/bomber; training battalion; treasury bill; tuberculosis

t.b.a. to be announced

T-bar T-shaped bar

T.B.C. Trinidad Broadcasting Company

TBCEP tri-beta-chloroethyl phosphate, flame retardant additive for urethane foams

t.b.d. to be determined

T.B.D. torpedo-boat destroyer

T.B.E. Fr. *Fédération européenne des fabricants de tuiles et de briques*, European Fed. of Tile and Brick Manufacturers

T-beam a reinforced concrete beam in which the upper slab or flange forms part of the floor and the projecting portion below provides the reinforcement

TBF Teachers Benevolent Fund, *formerly* Benevolent & Orphan Fund

T.B.G.A.S. *Transactions of the Bristol and Gloucestershire Archaeological Society*

t.b.l. through back of loops (knit.)

T.B.L. through bill of lading

T.B.M. tactical ballistic missile; temporary bench mark; terabit memory (computer)

T.B.M.A. Timber Building Manufacturers' Association of Great Britain

T-bolt bolt with head in the shape of short cross piece, used particularly in machine tool beds where head of bolt fits into slot in bed of machine

T-bone T-bone steak; T-shaped bone

tbone. *trombone* (mus.)

tbp true boiling point

TBS training battle simulation

tbs., tbsp. tablespoon; tablespoonful

t.b. & s. top, bottom and sides

Tc *s* technetium (chem.)

TC *s* Lancashire (B.V.R.)

tc . Fr. *tierce*, a third (mus.)

t.c. temperature control; terra cotta; till cancelled; time check; tropic tides; true course

T.C. Tank Corps (mil.); Tariff Commission (U.S.A.); Tax Cases; technical college; temporary clerk/constable; tennis/touring club; town clerk/council/councillor; training center/centre/college/corps; transport command; traveller's cheque; treble chance; Trinity College; Trusteeship Council (U.N.O.)

T.C. It. *Tre corde*, 3 strings, a direction in pianoforte mus. indicating that after use of left pedal (*una corda*) normal playing is to be resumed (mus.)

T.C.A. Television Consumer Audit; Textile Converters' Association (U.S.A.); Trans-Canada Air Lines, *now* Air Canada

T.C.A.A. Technical Communication Association of Australia

T.C.B. Thames Conservancy Board; title certificate book

TCC thermofor catalytic cracking; time compression coding; tracking and control center (U.S.A.)

T.C.C. Temporary Council Committee (NATO); Transport and Communications Commission (U.N.O.); Trinity College, Cambridge; Troop Carrier Command (U.S.A.)

TCCB Test and County Cricket Board

T.C.D. Trinity College, Dublin

T.C.F. temporary chaplain to the forces; time correction factor; *Touring Club de France*, French Touring Club; Twentieth Century Fund

T.C.F.B. Transcontinental Freight Bureau

Tchg. teaching

tchr. teacher

T.C.I. *Touring Club Italiano*, Italian Touring Club

T.C.J.C.C. Trades Councils' Joint Consultative Committee

TCL, Trik. trichloroethylene, substance used for degreasing harmful vapours

T.C.L. Trinity College of Music, London

T.C.M. Trinity College of Music, London

T.C.M.A. Telephone Cable Makers' Association; Tufted Carpet Manufacturers' Association

T.C.M.B. Tomato and Cucumber Marketing Board

TCO Swed. *Tjänstemännens Central-organisation*, Central Organization of Salaried Employees

T.C.O. test control officer; Trinity College, Oxford, founded 1554

TCP trichloro-phenyl-iodo-methylsalicyl (antiseptic); tricresyl phosphate, plasticizer for PVC

T.C.P. Technical Co-operation Programme between Aust., Can., U.K., U.S.A.; traffic-control post

T.C.P.A., T. & C.P.A. Town and Country Planning Association

TCR total controlled return

TCS target cost system

TCT total controlled tabulation

tctl. tactical

TCTO time compliance technical order (USAF)

T.C.W.A.S. *Transactions of the Cumberland and Westmorland Archaeological Society*

TD *s* Lancashire (B.V.R.)

td. tod, 28 lb. of wool; touch-down

t.d. tank destroyer; technical/test data; third defence (lacrosse); time delay/deposit; tractor-drawn

t.d. L. *ter in die*, three times a day (med.)

t. & d. taps and dies

T.D. tactical division; Teaching Diploma; Teachta Dála, deputy of the Dáil, the lower house of Irish Parliament; technical development; telegraph/telephone department; Territorial Decoration; Tilbury docks; torpedo depot; traffic director; Treasury Decisions/Department; True Democratic; typographic draughtsman

T.D.A. Textile Distributors' Association; Timber Development Association

T.D.B. Total Disability Benefit

T.D.C. top dead centre

T.D.D. Diploma in Tubercular/Tuberculous Diseases

TDDL time division data link

T.D.G. twist drill gauge

T.D.I. tolylene diisocyanate (chem.)

TDM telemetric data monitor; time division multiplex

TDM/PCM time-division multiplex using pulse-code-modulation

T.D.N. total digestible nutrients

TDP technical development plan; Transkei Democratic Party (S. Afr.)

t.d.r. Fr. *tous droits réservés*, all rights reserved

t.d.s. L. *ter die sumendum*, to be taken three times a day (med.)

Te *s* tellurium (chem.)

TE *s* Lancashire (B.V.R.)

t/e time-expired; twin-engined

t.e. task element; thermal efficiency; tinted/trailing edge; trial and error; turbine engine

T.E. Telecommunications engineering; *Telefis Eireann*, Television Ireland; topographical engineer; trade expenses

T. & E. test and evaluation

T.E.A.L. Tasman Empire Airways Limited

T.E.A.M. The European-Atlantic Movement; Top European Advertising Media

teatre. It. *teatrale*, theatrical

TEC Technician Education Council; ternary eutectic chloride, used for fire fighting in flammable metals (chem.)

tec. detective; technical college

tech., techn. technical; technically; technics; technique; technology

tech. technical; — **ed.** technical editor; — **rep.** technical representative; — **sgt.** technical sergeant; — **w.** technical writer

Tech.(CEI) Engineering Technician (Council of Engineering Institutions)

technol. technological;technologically; technology

Tech. Weld. I. Technician of the Welding Institute

tecn., tecnol. It. *tecnica*, technique; It. *tecnico*, technical; It. *tecnologia*, technology

Ted, Teddy Edward; Theodore

ted. It. *tedesco*, German

T.E.D. Territorial Efficiency Medal

TEDCo Targets for Economic Development Commission

T.E.E. Telecommunications Engineering Establishment; Torpedo Experimental Establishment; Trans-Europe Express

Teenie Christiana; Christina; Christine

T.E.F.L. teaching English as a foreign language

t.e.g. top edges gilt (book-binding)

Teh. Teheran (Iran)

TEI transearth insertion

T.E.J.A. *Tutmonda Esperantista Jurnalista Asocio*, World Association of Esperantist Journalists

T.E.J.O. *Tutmonda Esperantista Junulara Organizo*, World Esperantist Youth Organization

TEL tetra-ethyl lead, toxic petroleum additive; transporter-erector-launcher

tel., tele., teleg., telg. telegram; telegraph; telegraphic; telegraphist

tel. telephone

Tel. Bn. telegraph battalion

telecom., telecomms. telecommunications

Telef. Port. *telefone*, telephone

Teleg. Port. *telegramas*, cable address

teleph. telephone; telephony

telex teletype exchange

telly television

Tel. no. telephone number

tem., temp. temperature

T.E.M.A. Telecommunications Engineering and Manufacturing Association

339

temp. temperance; temperate; temperature; temporal; temporary

temp. It. *tempo*, time (mus.); L. *tempore*, in the time of

Temp. *The Tempest* (Shake.)

temp. dext. L. *tempori dextro*, to the right temple

temp. prim. It. *tempo primo*, the speed as at first (mus.)

temp. sinist. L. *tempori sinistro*, to the left temple

tempy. temporary

ten. tenant; tenement

ten. tenor (mus.); It. *tenuto*, sustained (mus.)

Ten. It. *tenente*, lieutenant; Tennessee, *also* Tenn. (U.S.A.)

tency. tenancy

T. Eng.(CEI) Technician Engineer (Council of Engineering Institutions)

TENOC Ten-year Oceanographic program (USN)

T.E.P. tetraethyl-pyrophosphate

ter., terr. terrace; territorial; territory

Ter. Terence, Publius Terentius Afer (*c* 195–159 B.C.), Roman poet

terat. teratology

TERCOM terrain contour matching

term. terminal; terminate; termination; terminology; termite

Terrier member of the territorial army

Terry Terence; Teresa; Theresa

ter. sim. L. *tere simul*, rub together

tert. tertiary

T.E.S. *Times Educational Supplement*

Tess, Tessa Esther; Hester; Teresa; Theresa

tess. It. *tessili*, textiles

test. testament; testator; testatrix; testimonial; testimony

testo. Sp. *testigo*, witness

T.-et.G. Tarn-et-Garonne (France)

T.E.T.O.C. Technical Education and Training for Overseas Countries

tet. tox. tetanus toxin

Teut. Teuton; Teutonic

T.E.W.T. tactical exercise without troops

Tex. Texan; Texas

text. textile

TEXTEL Trinidad and Tobago External Telecommunications Company

text. rec. L. *textus receptus*, the received text

TF *s* Lancashire (B.V.R.)

t.f. tabulating form; tax free; thin film; till forbidden; training film

T.F. task force; Territorial Force; Fr. *travail forcé*, penal servitude

t.f.a. total fatty acids

T.F.A. Textile/Tie Fabrics Association (U.S.A.)

T.F.A.I. *Territoire Français des Afars et des Issas*, Territory of the Afars and the Issas, French poss. in N.E. Africa

tfc. traffic

T.F.C.R.I. Tropical Fish Culture Research Institute

tfg. typefounding

TFL Tanganyika Federation of Labour

tfr. transfer

T.F.R. territorial force reserve

T.F.T.A. Textile Finishing Trades Association

T.F.U. telecommunications flying unit

TFX tactical fighter experimental

tg It. *tangente*, tangent, *also* tan.

T2g technician, second grade (U.S.A.)

TG *s* Glamorgan (B.V.R.); *s* Togo (I.V.R.)

T & G Transport and General Workers' Union, *alternative* T.G.W.U.

t.g. tail gear; thermogravimetry; type genus

t. & g. tongue and groove

T.G. Tate Gallery (Lond.); Theatre Guild (U.S.A.); Ger. *Theosophische Gesellschaft*, Theosophical Soc.; training group; Translators' Guild (Lond.)

t.g.b. tongued, grooved and beaded

T.G.M. torpedo gunner's mate

T.G.O. Timber Growers' Organization

T-Group training group (Institute of Personnel Management)

Tgt. target

T.G.V. *The Two Gentlemen of Verona* (Shake.)

T.G.W.U., T. & G.W.U. Transport and General Workers' Union, largest of Brit. unions

Th *s* thorium (chem.); Thursday

TH *s* Carmarthenshire (B.V.R.); Ger. *Technische Hochschule*, technical university/college; *s* Teignmouth (B.F.P.); toothed border (numis.); town hall (cartog.)

th. thermal

Th. Theatre; Theology; Thermal; Thomas; Thursday

T.H. Toynbee Hall; Transport/Trinity House

Th. A. Theological Association

T.H.A. Trade Hemstitchers' Association

Thad Thaddaeus

Thai. Thailand

thanat. thanatology

Th. B. *Theologiae Baccalaureus*, Bachelor of Theology

Th. D. *Theologiae Doctor*, Doctor of Theology

T.H.E. technical help to exporters, division of Brit. Standards Institute

theat. theatre; theatrical
Theo Theodore
Theo., theol. theologian; theological; theology
Theoc. Theocritus (b. *c* 310 B.C.), Greek poet
Theoph. Theophrastus (*c* 370–*c* 286 B.C.) Greek philosopher
theor. theorem; theoretical; theory
theos. theosophist; theosophy
therap. therapeutic
there's there is
therm., thermom. thermometer; thermometric
thermochem. thermochemistry
thermodyn. thermodynamics
THES *Times Higher Education Supplement*
thes. thesis
thesp. thespian
Thess. The Epistles to the Thessalonians (Bible); Thessaly (Greece)
they'd they had/would
they'll they will
they're they are
they've they have
T.H.G. *Technische Hochschule Graz*, Technical Univ. of Graz (Austria)
T.H.H.M. Trinity House High Water Mark
t.h.i. time handed in
T.H.I. temperature humidity index
Thk. thick
Th. L. Theological Licentiate
Th. M. *Theologiae Magister*, Master of Theology
tho' though
Tho., Thos. Thomas
thor. thorax
thoro' thorough
thoro. thoroughfare
thou. one-thousandth of an inch; thousand
thp thrust horsepower
thr. their; through; thrust
T.H.R.A. Tasmanian Historical Research Association
Three Rs reading, (w)riting and (a)rithmetic
thro' through
Thro' B/L through bill of lading
thrombo. thrombosis
throt. throttle
thru through
Thuc. Thucydides (*c* 464–*c* 401 B.C.), Greek historian
Thur. Thuringia (E. Ger.); Thuringian (E. Ger.); Thursday, *also* Thurs.
T.H.W. *Technische Hochschule Wien*, Technical Univ. Vienna (Austria)
T.H.W.M. Trinity High Water Mark

THY *Turk Hava Yollari*, Turkish Airlines
THz terahertz
Ti *s* titanium (chem.)
TI Tube Investments Limited
Ti. Tiberius; Tibet; Tibullus, Albius (*c* 54–19 B.C.), Roman poet
T/I. target identification/indicator
T.I. technical inspection; technical/ textile institute; temperature indication/ indicator; Texas Instruments (U.S.A.); textile industry
T.I.A. Tax Institute of America
Tib, Tibbie, Tibby Isabel; Isabella; Ishbel; Ishbelle
Tib. Tibet; Tibetan
t.i.b. trimmed in bunkers
T.I.B. tourist information bureau
T.I.C. Tyne Improvement Commission
TICCI Technical Information Centre for Chemical Industry (India)
TICTAC time compression tactical communications
t.i.d. L. *tres in die*, three times a day (med.)
T.I.D.U. Technical Information and Documents Unit
tier. Fr. *tierce*, a third (mus.)
t.i.f. telephone influence/interference factor
T.I.F.R. Tata Institute of Fundamental Research, Bombay (India)
T.I.G. the inspector general
T.I.H. Their Imperial Highnesses
T.I.I.A.L. The International Institute of Applied Linguistics
Tilda, Tilly Matilda
T.I.L.S. Technical Information and Library Service
TILT infra-red scoring device
Tim, Timmie, Timmy, Timo Timothy
Tim. The Epistles of Paul the Apostle to Timothy (Bible); *Timon of Athens* (Shake.)
t.i.m. time is money
timb. Fr. *timbales*, kettle-drums (mus.)
TIMM thermionic integrated micromodule
timp. It. *timpani*, kettle-drums (mus.)
T.I.M.S. The Institute of Management Sciences
Tina Christina; Christine
tinct. L. *tinctura*, tincture (med.)
TINRO Pacific Scientific Research Institute of Marine Fisheries and Oceanography (U.S.S.R.)
TINTUC Trinidad and Tobago National Trade Union Congress
T.I.O. Technical/Television/Troop/ Information Officer
tip 'to insure promptness' (gratuity)

TIP *Türkiye Işçi Partisi*, Turkish Labour Party

tip. It. *tipografia*, printers

Tip. Tipperary (Rep. of Ireland)

TIPS telemetry impact prediction system (USAF)

T.I.R. Fr. *Transport international des marchandises par la route*, Intern. transport of goods by road. Customs agreement covering 26 countries allowing T.I.R. lorries to avoid customs until reaching final destination

T.I.R.C. Tobacco Industry Research Committee

Tir. G.O. Fr. *Tirasse du Grande Orgue*, coupler of organ (mus.)

T-iron structural wrought iron/rolled steel of 'T' shaped section

TIROS television and infra-red observation satellite (U.S.A.)

Tir. P. Fr. *Tirasse du Positif*, coupler of organ (mus.)

Tir. R. Fr. *Tirasse du Récit*, coupler of organ (mus.)

'tis it is

Tis. tissue

T.I.S. technical information service

tit. title; titular

Tit. The Epistle of Paul to Titus (Bible)

Tit. A. *Titus Andronicus*, attrib. to Shake.

Tiv. Tivoli Music Hall (Lond.)

TJ *s* Lancashire (B.V.R.)

T.J. triple jump (athletics)

TK *s* Dorset (B.V.R.)

tk. tank; truck

t.k.o. technical knockout

TKP *Türkiye Komünist Partisi*, Turkish Communist Party, proscribed since 1925

tkr. tanker

tks. thanks

tkt. ticket

Tl *s* thallium (chem.)

TL *s* Lincolnshire, Kesteven (B.V.R.); Turkish lira (currency)

T/L telegraphist lieutenant

t.l. test/thrust link; time length/loan; title list; total load/loss

T.L. torpedo lieutenant; trade-last

t.l.b. temporary lighted buoy

TLC tender loving care

tld. tooled

T.L.E. Telecommunication Industry Standards Committee

T.L.G. Theatrical Ladies' Guild

T.L.H.S. *Transactions of the Leicestershire Archaeological Society*

T.L.I. translunar injection/insertion

t.l.o. total loss only, meaning only total loss claims will be met (insce.)

T.L.O. technical liaison officer

T.L.P. Tasmanian Labour Party (Aust.); Port. *Telefones de Lisboa e Pôrto*, Lisbon and Oporto Telephone Co.

tlr. tailor; trailer

T.L.R. *Tanganyika/Tasmania/Times/ Law Reports*

T.L.s. typed letter, signed

T.L.S. Territorial Long Service; *Times Literary Supplement*

TLT transportable link terminal

tltr. translator

TLV threshold limit value

T.L.W.M. Trinity House low water mark

Tm *s* thulium (chem.)

TM *s* Bedfordshire (B.V.R.); tactical missile; tone modulation

t.m. temperature meter; trade mark; trench mortar; true mean

T.M. technical manual/memorandum/ minutes/monograph; test manual; Their Majesties; traffic manager; trained man; training manual/memorandum; tropical medicine

T.M.A. Theatrical Managers' Association; Trans-Mediterranean Airways (Lebanon); Twine Manufacturers' Association

T.M.A. 1970 Taxes Management Act 1970

T.M.A.M.A. Textile Machinery and Accessory Manufacturers' Association

T.M.B. travelling medical board

tmbr. timber

TMC Transportation Materiel Command (U.S.A.)

T.M.C. Tyre Manufacturers' Conference

Tme. time

T'ment tournament

TMG. track made good, identical with track (nav.)

TMJ *Trade Marks Journal*

tmkpr. timekeeper

TML tetramethyl lead

T.M.L. three mile limit (shipping); transport managers licence

T.M.M.G. Teacher of Massage and Medical Gymnastics

T.M.O. telegraph money order

tmpry. temporary

tmr. timer

T.M.S. Tramway Museum Society

T.M.S.C. Tobacco Manufacturers' Standing Committee

TMT turbine motor train

T.M.V. tobacco mosaic virus; true mean value

Tn *s* thoron (chem.)

TN *s* Newcastle-upon-Tyne (B.V.R.); Tennessee (U.S.A.); *s* Troon (B.F.P.); *s* Tunisia (I.V.R.)

tn. ton; town; township; train
Tn. transportation
t.n. technical note; telephone number
T.N. true north; *Twelfth Night* (Shake.)
T.N.C. Theatres National Committee; total numerical control
T.N.D.F.C. *Transactions of the Newbury and District Field Club*
tng. training; turning
Tn. I.O.B. Technician of the Institute of Building
TNIP Transkei National Independence Party (S. Afr.)
T.N.M. tactical nuclear missile
TNP Fr. *Théâtre National Populaire*
T.N.P.G. The Nuclear Power Group
tnpk. turnpike
TNT trinitrotoluene, an explosive
TNX trinitroxylene (chem.)
TO *s* Nottingham (B.V.R.); technical order (USAF); *s* Truro (B.F.P.)
To. Togo
t.o. take off; time opening; tool order; traditional orthography; turn over
t.o. L. *tinctura opii*, tincture of opium
t. & o. taken and offered (betting)
T.O. technical officer; telegraphic order; telegraph/telephone office; telephone order; torpedo officer; trained operator; transport officer
TOA Theater Owners of America; total obligational authority
ToB Tour of Britain (cycling)
tob. tobacco; tobacconist
Tob. Tobit
T.O.B. take-off boat; temporary office building
Toby Tobias
TOC technical order compliance
Toc H Talbot House, movement to bring together into Christian fellowship people undertaking social service. Founded as Talbot House in 1915 at Poperinghe, Toc H comes from army signallers' designation T. H., Talbot House
T.O.D. The Open Door, originally started to help agoraphobics, now developed to include other phobias; time of delivery; trade and operations division
TOES tables of organization and equipment (U.S.A.); trade-off evaluation system
T.O.E.T. test of elementary training
T. of A. *Timon of Athens* (Shake.)
tog., togr. together
TOJ track on jamming
Tok. Tokyo (Jap.)
T.O.L. Tower of London
to. lt. towing light
Tom, Tommie, Tommy Thomas
Tom., Tomat. tomato

T.O.M. Fr. *Territoire d'Outre Mer*, overseas territory
TOMCAT theater of operations missile continuous-wave anti-tank weapon (U.S.A.)
Tommy gun Thompson submachine gun
TOMS tired old movies (Aust.)
tonn. tonnage
Tony Anthony; Tony medallion, Broadway (U.S.A.) equivalent of Oscar award
t.o.o. time of origin
TOP temporarily out of print, no reprint at present in hand
topog. topographer; topographical; topography
topol. topology
TOPS The Operational PERT System
Tor. Toronto (Can.)
t.o.r. time of receipt/reception
T.O.R. Third Order Regular of Saint Francis
tor. dep. torpedo depot
torn. tornado
Torp. torpedo
t.o.s. terms of service
T.O.S.D. Third Order of Saint Dominic
T.O.S.F. Third Order of Saint Francis
Toshiba Tokio Shibaura Electric (Jap.)
TOSHIKOTSU *Nihon Toshikotsu Rodo Kumiai Rengokai*, Jap. Fed. of Municipal Transportation Workers Unions
tot. total
t.o.t. time on/over target
tote totalizator
Tou. Toulon (France)
tour. tourism; tourist
tourn. tournament
TOVALOP Tanker Owners' Voluntary Agreement concerning Liability for Oil Pollution
TOW tube-launched optically tracked wire-guided anti-tank missile
T.O.W. tug-of-war
toxicol. toxicological; toxicologist; toxicology
TP *s* Portsmouth (B.V.R.); third party (insce.)
tp. township; troop
t.p. target/teaching practice; Fr. *timbre-poste*, postage-stamp; title page; toilet paper; to pay
T.P. tax payer; technical paper/pool/publications; teleprinter; test panel; translucent paper; Transvaal Province (S. Afr.); treaty port; true position
T.P. It. *Tempo Primo*, the speed as at

343

first (mus.); L. *Tempore Paschale*, at Easter

T.P.A. Technical Publications Association, *now* Institution of Technical Authors and Illustrators

T.P.C. The Peace Corps (U.S.A.)

t.p.d. tons per day

T.P.F. Toilet Preparations Federation

t.p.h. tons per hour

TPI terminal phase initiation

t.p.i. teeth/threads/tons/turns/per inch

T.P.I. tons per inch immersion; Town Planning Institute; transpolyisoprene, synthetic gutta percha; Tropical Products Institute

tpk. turnpike

t.p.m. tons per minute

T.P.M. triphenylmethane, basis of important class of dyes

TPO Tree Preservation Order

tpo. Sp. *tiempo*, time

T.P.O. travelling post office

Tpr. trooper

t.p.r. temperature, pulse, respiration

T.P.R.I. Tropical Pesticides Research Institute

TPS Teachers' Provident Society; toughened polystyrene

T.P.S. Fr. *Télégraphie par le soleil*, telegraphy by the sun

TPSL *Työväen Ja Pienviljelijain Sosialidemokraattinen Liitto*, Social Democratic League of Workers and Small Farmers, *also* known as 'Simonists' (Finland)

tpt. transport

tpt. *trumpet* (mus.)

tptr. *trumpeter* (mus.)

t.p.w. title page wanting

t.q. L. *tale quale*, as is

T.Q.C.A. Textile Quality Control Association (U.S.A.)

TQE technical quality evaluation (Polaris)

Tr *s* Terbium (chem.), *usually* Tb

TR *s* Southampton (B.V.R.); Telephone Rentals Limited; *s* Turkey (I.V.R.)

tr. trace; track; tragedy; train; transaction; transfer; transitive; translate; translation; translator; transport; transportation; transpose (typ.); transposition; treasurer; treble (crochet); troop; truck; trust; trustee

tr. L. *tinctura*, tincture (med.)

Tr. trainee

Tr. *Trill* (mus.); *Trumpet* (mus.); *Trumpeter* (mus.)

T/R. Transmitter-Receiver

T.R. target rifle; tariff reform; *Taxation Reports*; territorial reserve; test run; tons registered; tooth ringed; tracking radar; trust receipt

TRA Textile Refinishers Association

(U.S.A.); Travel Research Association (U.S.A.)

TRAAC transit research and altitude control satellite

trac. tracer; tractor

TRACALS traffic control and landing system

TRACE task reporting and current evaluation; taxiing and routing of aircraft co-ordinating equipment

trad. tradition; traditional; It. *traduttore*, translator; It. *traduzione*, translation; translation

T.R.A.D.A. Timber Research and Development Association

TRADEX target resolution and discrimination experiment

trag. tragedy; tragic; tragical

TRALANT fleet training command, Atlantic (USN)

tram. tramway car

TRAMPS temperature regulator and missile power supply

trans. transaction; transfer; transistorize; transitive; transitory; translate; translation; translator; transport; transportation; transpose; transposition; transverse

Trans. Transvaal (S. Afr.)

transf. transfer; transference

transl. translate; translation; translator

translit. transliterate; transliteration

TRANSMARK Transportation Systems and Market Research Ltd., British Rail associate

transp. transportation

trany. transparency

TRAPAC fleet training command, Pacific (USN)

trav. travel; traveller

Trav. Port. *Travessa*, lane

Trb. Tribune

Tr. & C. *Troilus and Cressida* (Shake.)

T.R.C. Tasmanian Racing Club (Aust.); Thames Rowing Club; tithe rent charge; Tobacco Research Council

TRCCC tracking radar central control console

Tr. Co. trust company

Tr. Coll. training college

Trd. Trinidad

TRDA Timber Research and Development Association

TRDTO tracking radar data take-off

Tre., Treas. Treasurer; Treasury

T.R.E. Telecommunications Research Establishment

TRECOM transportation research command

tree. trustee

Trem. It. *tremolando*, trembling

(mus.); *tremulant*, a mechanical device in an organ (mus.)

trem card transport emergency card, carried by chemical tank vehicle to provide identification of load carried and advice about action if accident occurs

TREND tropical environment data

trf. tariff; transfer

t.r.f. tuned radio frequency

Trg. training

Trg., Trge. *Triangle* (mus.)

T.R.H. Their Royal Highnesses

T.R.I. Tea Research Institute (Ceylon); Television Reporters International; Textile Research Institute (U.S.A.); total response index

trib. tribal; tributary

Trib. *Tribune* (newspaper)

trid. L. *triduum*, three days

Trid. Hawker-Siddeley Trident (aircraft)

T.R.I.E.A. Tea Research Institute of East Africa

trig. trigger

trig., trigon. trigonometric; trigonometry

Trig. trigonometrical

TRIGA trigger reactor

Trik trichloroethylene, substance used for degreasing harmful vapours

trike tricycle

trim. L. *trimestre*, quarter of a year

Trin. Trinidad; Trinity

Trin. H. Trinity Hall, Cambridge, founded 1350

Trip. tripos

tripl. triplicate

trit. triturate

Trix, Trixie, Trixy Beatrice

TRLB temporarily replaced by lighted buoy

TRLFSW tactical range landing force support weapon

Tr. L.R. *Trinidad Law Reports*

trml. terminal

t.r.n. technical research note

trng. training

T.R.O. temporary restraining order; Turkey red oil

trom., tromb. *trombone* (mus.)

Trombst. *trombonist* (mus.)

TROMEX Tropical Oceanographic and Meteorological Experiment (1971–1972)

Tromp. Fr. *Trompette*, trumpet (mus.)

trop. tropic; tropical

Trop. Can. Tropic of Cancer, $23\frac{1}{2}°$ N. Latitude

Trop. Cap. Tropic of Capricorn, $23\frac{1}{2}°$ S. Latitude

Trop. Med. tropical medicine

trp. troop

TRS tetrahedral research satellite

trs. transfer; transpose (typ.); trustees

T.R.S. Tobacco Research Station (N.Z.); Torry Research Station (Scot.)

trsd. transferred; transposed

trsp. transport

TRSR taxi and runway surveillance radar

TRSSGM tactical range surface-to-surface guided missile

TRSSM tactical range surface-to-surface missile

trt. turret

T.R.T.A. Traders' Road Transport Association

TRUB temporarily replaced by unlighted buoy

Trudy Gertrude

TRUMP target radiation measurement program (U.S.A.)

Truron. L. *Truronesis*, of Truro, Eng. episcopal title, in bishop's signature

try. truly

TS *s* Dundee (B.V.R.)

t.s. temperature switch; tensile strength; test summary; till sale; turbine steamship; twin screw; typescript; type specification

t. & s. toilet and shower

T.S. Television/Theosophical Society; tool steel; Training Ship; Treasury solicitor; tub-sized (paper)

T.S. It. *Tasto solo*, one key alone, a direction in figured-bass playing (mus.)

T. & S. transport and supply

T.S.A. Tasmanian State Archives; time series analysis

T.S.B. Trustee Savings Bank

T.S.B.A. Trustee Savings Banks Association

t.s.c. passed a territorial army course in staff duties

T.S.C. Tonic Sol-fa College

T.S.D.S. two-speed destroyer sweeper

t.s.f. Fr. *télégraphie sans fil*, wireless telegraphy

T.S.F. Port. *telefonia sem fios*, wireless; two-seater fighter

tsfr. transfer

T. & S.G. Television and Screen Writers' Guild

T. Sgt. top sergeant

T.S.H. Their Serene Highnesses

t.s.i. tons per square inch

T.S.O. town sub-office

TSOR tentative specific operational requirement

tsp. teaspoon; teaspoonful

T.S.R. tactical strike reconnaissance; torpedo-spotter-reconnaissance; Trans-Siberian Railway

tss. typescripts

345

T.S.S. time sharing system; turbine steamship; twin-screw ship/steamer/steamship

T.S.S.A. Transport Salaried Staffs' Association

tstr. tester

t.s.u. this side up

t.s.v.p. Fr. *tournez s'il vous plaît*, please turn over

TSX Telecommunications Satellite Experiment

TT *s* Devon (B.V.R.); *s* Tarbert (B.F.P.); time trial (cycling); *s* Trinidad and Tobago (I.V.R.)

t.t. tank technology/top

T.T. technical/testing training; teetotal; teetotaller; telegraphic transfer; tetanus toxoid; torpedo tube; tourist trophy; transit time; tuberculin-tested

T. & T. Trinidad and Tobago

T.T.A. Travel Trade Association

T.T.A.B. Trade Mark Trial and Appeal Board (U.S.A.)

T.T.C. technical training command

T.T.C.P. The Technical Co-operation Programme (Aust., Can., U.K. and U.S.A.)

T.T.C.R.A.D. Teachers' Training Course of the Royal Academy of Dancing

T.T.E. tropical testing establishment

T.T.F. Timber Trade Federation of the United Kingdom

TTFN ta-ta for now, expression used by Tommy Handley in BBC comedy programmes Itma (It's that man again)

TTFTU Trinidad and Tobago Federation of Trade Unions

T.T.J.C. Tyre Trade Joint Committee

TTL transistor-transistor logic

t.t.l. to take leave

TTM two-tone modulation

T.T.M.A. Truck Trailer Manufacturers' Association (U.S.A.); Tufted Textile Manufacturers' Association (U.S.A.)

Tto Toronto (Can.)

TTP tritolyl phosphate, plasticizer or PVC

T.T.S. teletypesetting

TTT team time trial (cycling)

T.T.T. Tyne Tees Television Limited

T.T.T.C. Technical Teachers Training College

TTY teletypewriter (computer)

Tu *s* thulium (chem.)

TU *s* Cheshire (B.V.R.); transmission unit (psy.)

TU104 Tupolev TU104; — **134** (aircraft)

Tu. tudor; Tuesday

T.U. Fr. *temps universel*, universal time; thermal/toxic unit; trade union

T.U.A.C. Trade Union Advisory Committee to Organisation for Economic Cooperation and Development

Tub. tubular (cycle racing tyre)

Tuberc. Tuberculosis

T.U.C. Trades Union Congress, a permanent association of Brit. trade unions, founded 1868

T.U.C.C. Transport Users' Consultative Committee/Council

T.U.C.G.C. Trades Union Congress General Council

T.U.C.S.A. Trades Union Council of South Africa

Tue., Tues. Tuesday

T.U.F. Tokyo University of Fisheries

T.U.F.E.C. Thailand-UNESCO Fundamental Education Centre

T.U.I.A.F.W. Trade Unions International of Agricultural and Forestry Workers

T.U.M. Trades Union Movement

tuppeny twopenny

turb. turbine

turboprop. turbine propelled

Turk. Turkey; Turkish

TÜRK-IS *Türkiye Isçi Sendikalari Konfederasyonu*, Turkish Confed. of Trade Unions—TCTU

turp., turps. turpentine

tus. L. *tussis*, cough (med.)

TUV Ger. *Vereinigung der Technischen Überwachungs-Vereine*, Electrical inspection organization, Austria

TV *s* Nottingham (B.V.R.); television, *also* T.V.

t.v. terminal velocity; test vehicle; true view

T.V.A. Fr. *taxe sur la valeur ajoutée*, tax value added, arranged to tax expenditure by way of fractional payments levied at each stage of production/distribution; Tennessee Valley Authority (U.S.A.)

T.V.C. Technical Valve Committee

tvl. travel

Tvl. Transvaal (S. Afr.)

T.V.R. temperature variation of resistance

TW *s* Essex (B.V.R.)

°Tw., °Twad. Twaddell degrees, specific gravity of liquids scale

t.w. tail wind

TWA time weighted average

T.W.A. Trans-World Airlines

T.W.A.R.O. Textile Workers' Asian Regional Organisation

'twas it was

T.W.C. Tail Waggers' Club

'tween between

Twel. N. *Twelfth Night* (Shake.)

'twere it were

T.W.I. training of supervisors within industry

'twill it will

T.W.I.M.C. to whom it may concern

'twixt betwixt

T.W.O. this week only

Two Gent. *Two Gentlemen of Verona* (Shake.)

'twould it would

twp. township

T.W.P.D. tactical and weapons policy division

T.W.S. timed wire service

tw.-sc. twin-screw

T.W.T. transonic wind tunnel; travelling-wave tube

T.W.U. Transport Workers' Union

T.W.U.A. Textile/Transport Workers' Union of America

T.W.W. Television Wales and West Limited, *now* ceased operations

twy. twenty

TX *s* Glamorgan (B.V.R.); Texas (U.S.A.)

tx. tax; taxation

TY *s* Northumberland (B.V.R.)

Ty. territory; truly

T.Y.C. Thames Yacht Club; two-year-old course (horse racing)

Tymp. It. *Tympani*, kettle-drums (mus.)

t.y.o. two-year-old (horse racing)

typ. type; typical; typing; typist

typ., typo., typog. typographer; typographic; typographical; typographically; typography

typh. typhoon

TYPOE Ten-Year Plan for Ocean Exploration (U.S.A.)

typw. typewriter; typewriting; typewritten

Tyr. Tyrone

Tyrol. Tyrolean, Tyrolese

TZ *s* Belfast (B.V.R.)

347

U

u *s* ugly/threatening sky/weather (met.); *s* unified atomic mass (phys.) *s* viscosity

U *s* Leeds (B.V.R.); *s* union (math.); uranium (chem.); *s* Uruguay (I.V.R.)

u. Ger. *und*, and; unit; Ger. *unter*, lower; up; upper; utility

U. Dan. *ud*, out; Ger. *Uhr*, clock, o'clock; Dutch *uit*, out; Finn. *ulos*, out; uncle; union; unionist; unite; universal (film); university; urinal; Utah (U.S.A.); Swed. *ute*, arrival; you, as in I.O.U.

UA *s* Leeds (B.V.R.)

U/a. underwriting account (insce.)

u.a. under age; Ger. *unter anderem*, among other things

u.a. L. *usque ad*, as far as

U.A. Ulster Association; United Artists Corporation

UAA United Arab Airlines; University Aviation Association (U.S.A.)

U.A.B. Unemployment Assistance Board; Universities Appointments Board

U.A.B.S. Union of American Biological Societies

U.A.C. Ulster Automobile Club; United Africa Company, *also* U.A.Co.

U.A.C.E.E. Fr. *Union de l'artisanat de la C.E.E.*, Union of Master-Craftsmen of the E.E.C.

U.A.D.W. Universal Alliance of Diamond Workers

U.A.E. United Arab Emirates formed 1971, *formerly* Trucial States of the Persian Gulf

U.A.I. Fr. *Union académique internationale*, Intern. Union of Academies; Fr. *Union astronomique internationale*, Intern. Astronomical Union; Fr. *Union des associations internationales*, Union of Intern. Assns.

U.A.L. United Air Lines

u.a.m. Ger. *und andres mehr*, and so forth

U.A.M. underwater-to-air missile; Fr. *Union africaine et malgache*, African and Malagasy Union

U.A.M.P.T. Fr. *Union africaine et malgache des postes et télécommunications*, African and Malagasy Postal and Telecommunications Union

U.A.N.A. Sp. *Unión Amateur de Natación de Las Americas*, Amateur Swimming Union of the Americas

U.A.O.D. United Ancient Order of Druids

U.A.O.S. Ulster Agricultural Organisation Society

U.A.P. United Australia Party

U.A.R. United Arab Republic, *now* Arab Republic of Egypt

u.a.s. upper airspace

U.A.S. university air squadron

U.A.T.I. Fr. *Union des associations techniques internationales*, Union of Intern. Engineering Organisations

U.A.T.P. Universal Air Travel Plan

U.A.U. Universities Athletic Union

U.A.W. United Auto, Aircraft and Agricultural Implements Workers (U.S.A.); United Automobile Workers (U.S.A.)

u.A.w.g. Ger. *um Antwort wird gebeten*, an answer is requested

UB *s* Leeds (B.V.R.)

348

U.B. Union of Burma; United Brethren; Upper Bench (leg.)

UBC University of British Columbia (Can.)

übers. Ger. *übersetzt*, translated

U.B.F. Union of British Fascists

UBITRON undulating beam interaction electron tube

U.B.L.S. University of Botswana, Lesotho and Swaziland

U.-boat Ger. *Unterseeboot*, submarine

UBP United Bermuda Party

U.B.R. University Boat Race, initials carved on side of Putney bridge indicating starting point of annual race between Cambridge and Oxford

U.B.S. United Bible Societies

UC *s* London (B.V.R.)

u.c. upper case (typ.)

U.C. University College; upcast shaft; Upper Canada; urban council

U.C. It. *Una corda*, on one string, use soft pedal (pianoforte) (mus.); L. *Urbe Condita*, the city being built

U.C.A. United Chemists' Association

U.C.A.E. Universities' Council for Adult Education

UCATT Union of Construction, Allied Trades and Technicians

u.c.b. unless caused by

U.C.B. Unemployment Compensation Board (U.S.A.)

UCC University Computing Company

U.C.C. Universal Copyright Convention

U.C.C.A. Universities Central Council on Admissions estab. 1961 by U.K. universities to solve some problems arising from increased pressure of applicants for admission

U.C.C.C. uniform consumer credit code (U.S.A.)

U.C.C.D. United Christian Council for Democracy

U.C.D. University College, Dublin; upper critical depth (ocean.)

U.C.D.E.C. Fr. *Union chrétienne democrate d'Europe centrale*, Christian Democratic Union of Central Europe

U.C.H. University College Hospital

U.C.H.D. usual childhood diseases

U.C.I. Fr. *Union cycliste internationale*, Cyclists' Union

U.C.I.S.S. Fr. *Union catholique internationale de service social*, Catholic Intern. Union for Social Service

UCIW Union of Commercial and Industrial Workers (Trinidad)

U.C.J.G. Fr. *Alliance universelle des unions chrétiennes de jeunes gens*, World Alliance of Young Men's Christian Assns.

UCL upper control limit

u.c.l. upper cylinder lubricant (eng.)

U.C.L. University College, London

U.C.L.A. University of California at Los Angeles

UCM University Christian Movement

U.C.M.D.S. Unilever Companies Management Development Scheme

UCMJ uniform code of military justice (U.S.A.)

U.C.N.W. University College of North Wales

U.C.P. United Country Party (Aust.)

U.C.P.T.E. Fr. *Union pour la coordination de la production et du transport de l'électricité*, Union for Co-ordinating Production and Distribution of Electricity

U.C.S. University College School (Lond.); Upper Clyde Shipbuilders

U.C.S.W. University College of South Wales

U.C.T.A. United Commercial Travellers' Association of Great Britain and Ireland

U.C.W. University College of Wales

U.C.W.R.E. Under-Water Counter-Measures and Weapons Research Establishment

UD *s* Oxfordshire (B.V.R.)

u.d. L. *ut dictum*, as directed

U.D. United Dairies

UDC Uganda Development Corporation; Urban Development Corporation (U.S.A.)

u.d.c. upper dead centre

U.D.C. Union of Democratic Control; universal decimal classification; urban district council

U.D.C.A. Urban District Councils' Association

U.D.E. Under-Water Development Establishment

UDEAC. Fr. *Union douanière et économique de l'Afrique centrale*, Central African Customs and Economic Union

UDEAO. Fr. *Union douanière des états d'Afrique occidentale*, Customs Union of West African States

UDECEVER Fr. *Union européenne des détaillants en céramique et verrerie*, European Union of Ceramic and Glassware Retailers

U.D.E.L. Fr. *Union des Editeurs de Littérature*, Union of Publishers of Literature

u.d.f. Ger. *und die folgende*, and the following

U.D.F. Ulster Defence Force; Union Defence Force (S. Afr.)

udg. Dan. *udgave*, edition

u. dgl. Ger. *und dergleichen*, and the like

349

U.d'H. *Université d'Haiti,* Univ. of Haiti

u.d.i., UDI unilateral declaration of independence

U.D.I. It. *Unione Donne Italiane,* Italian Women's Association

U. di B. *Università di Bologna,* Univ. of Bologna (Italy)

U. di F. *Università di Firenze,* Univ. of Florence (Italy)

U. di M. *Università di Milano,* Univ. of Milan (Italy)

U. di N. *Università di Napoli,* Univ. of Naples (Italy)

u.d.M. Ger. *unter dem Meeresspiegel,* below sea level

UDMH unsymmetrical dimenthyl hydrazine

UDN ulcerated dermal necrosis, fish disease; *Union Démocratique Nigérienne,* Niger Democratic Union, *now* Sawaba Party

U. do B. *Universidade do Brasil/Brasilia,* Univ. of Brasil/Brasilia

UDP United Democratic Party (Lesotho)

UDR *Union des Démocrates pour la Vème République,* Union of Democrats for the Fifth Republic (France)

U.D.S. United Drapery Stores

UDT underwater demolition team (USN)

U.D.T. United Dominions Trust

UE *s* Warwickshire (B.V.R.)

ue. unexpired

u.E. Ger. *unseres Erachtens,* in our opinion

U.E. university extension; upper entrance

U.E.A. Fr. *Union européenne de l'ameublement,* European Furniture Fed.; Universal Esperanto Association

U.E.B. *Union Économique Benelux,* Benelux Economic Union

U.E.C. Fr. *Union européenne de la carrosserie,* European Union of Coachbuilders; Fr. *Union européenne des experts comptables économiques et financiers,* European Union of Accountants

U.E.C.B. Fr. *Union européenne des commerces du bétail,* European Cattle Trade Union

U.E.C.L. Fr. *Union européenne des constructeurs de logements, secteur privé,* European Union of Independent Building Contractors

u.e.f. universal extra fine (screw)

U.E.F. Fr. *Union européenne des fédéralistes,* European Union of Federalists; Fr. *Union européenne féminine,* European Union of Women

U.E.F.A. Union of European Football Associations

U.E.I. Union of Educational Institutions

U.E.I.C. United East India Company

UEL Unilever Export Limited

U.E.L. United Empire Loyalists

U.E.M.S. Fr. *Union européenne de médecine sociale,* European Assn. of Social Medicine; Fr. *Union européenne des médecins spécialistes,* European Union of Medical Specialists

U.E.N.C.P.B. Fr. *Union européenne des négociants en cuirs et peaux bruts,* European Union of Hide and Skin Merchants

U.E.O. Fr. *Union de l'Europe occidentale,* Western European Union; unit education/educational officer

U.E.P. Fr. *Union européenne de paiements,* European Payments Union; Fr. *Union européenne de pédo-psychiatres,* European Union for Child Psychiatry

UER unsatisfactory equipment report

U.E.R. Fr. *Union européenne de radiodiffusion,* European Broadcasting Union; university entrance requirements

UETA universal engineer tractor, armored (U.S.A.)

UETRT universal engineer tractor, rubber-tired (U.S.A.)

U.E.W. United Electrical, Radio, and Machine Workers of America

u/f urea-formaldehyde resin

UF *s* Brighton (B.V.R.); United Force Party (Guyana)

U.F. United Free Church of Scotland; utilisation factor (lighting)

U.F.A. Ger. *Universal-Film-Aktiengesellschaft,* Universal Film Company

U factor *s* measure of insulating power

U.F.A.W. Universities Federation for Animal Welfare

U.F.C. United Free Church (Scot.); United Fruit Company

U.F.C.E. Fr. *Union fédéraliste des communautés ethniques européennes,* Federal Union of European Nationalities

U.F.E. Fr. *Union des groupements professionnels de l'industrie de la féculerie de pommes de terre de la C.E.E.,* Union of Specialist Groups of the Potato-Starch Industry of the E.E.C.

U.F.E.R. Fr. *Mouvement international pour l'union fraternelle entre les races et les peuples,* Intern. Movement for Fraternal Union among Races and Peoples

uff. It. *ufficiale,* official

U.F.I. Fr. *Union des foires internationales,* Union of Intern. Fairs

U.F.L.C. Fr. *Union internationale des*

femmes libérales chrétiennes, Intern. Union of Liberal Christian Women

U.F.M.A.T. Fr. *Union des fédérations nationales des négociants en matériaux de construction de la C.E.E.*, Union of Nat. Feds. of Building Merchants in the E.E.C.

u.f.o., UFO unidentified flying object

UFORA Unidentified Flying Objects Research Association

u.f.p. unemployed full pay

U.F.P.A. University Film Producers' Association

UFT United Federation of Teachers

U.F.U. Ulster Farmers' Union

U.F.W. United Furniture Workers

UG *s* Leeds (B.V.R.)

u/g. underground

Ug., Ugan. Uganda; Ugandan

U.G.C. University Grants Committee

U.G.G.I. Fr. *Union géodésique et géophysique internationale*, Intern. Union of Geodesy and Geophysics

U.G.I. Fr. *Union géographique internationale*, Intern. Geographical Union

U.G.L.E. United Grand Lodge of England

U.G.M. Union of Graduates in Music

U.G.S. United Girls' School Settlement

U.G.S.M. United Girls' School Mission

U.G.S.S.S. Union of Girls' Schools for Social Service

UGT Sp. *Unión General de Trabajadores de España, en-el-Exilio*, General Union of Spanish Workers, in Exile; urgent (telegram)

UGTT Fr. *Union Générale Tunisienne du Travail*, General Fed. of Tunisian Workers

U.G.W. United Garment Workers

UH *s* Cardiff (B.V.R.)

U.H. upper half; utility helicopter

U.H.A. Union House of Assembly (S. Afr.)

U.H.A.A. United Horological Association of America

U.H.C.C. Upper House of the Convocation of Canterbury

U.H.C.Y. Upper House of the Convocation of York

u.h.f. ultra high frequency

u.h.t. ultra high temperature

u.h.v. ultra high vacuum/voltage

u/i. under instruction; unit of issue

u.i. ultrasonic industry; unemployment insurance

u.i., ut. inf. L. *ut infra*, as below

U.I.A. Fr. *Union internationale des architectes*, Intern. Union of Architects; Fr. *Union internationale des avocats*, Intern. Assn. of Lawyers; Fr. *Union*

internationale des travailleurs des industries alimentaires et connexes, Intern. Union of Food and Allied Workers Assns.; Union of International Associations

U.I.A.A. Fr. *Union internationale des associations d'alpinisme*, Intern. Union of Alpine Assns.; Fr. *Union internationale des associations d'annonceurs*, Intern. Union of Advertisers' Assns.

U.I.A.C.M. Fr. *Union internationale des automobile-clubs médicaux*, Intern. Union of Assns. of Doctor-Motorists

U.I.A.P.M.E. Fr. *Union internationale de l'artisanat et des petites et moyennes entreprises*, Intern. Assn. of Crafts and Small and Medium-Sized Enterprises

U.I.A.T. Fr. *Union internationale des syndicats des industries de l'alimentation et des tabacs*, Intern. Union of Food, Drink and Tobacco Workers' Assns.

U.I.B. Fr. *Union internationale des maîtres boulangers*, Intern. Union of Master Bakers

U.I.B.W.M. Trade Unions International of Workers of Building Wood and the Building Materials Industries

U.I.C. Fr. *Union internationale des chemins de fer*, Intern. Union of Railways

U.I.C.C. Fr. *Union internationale contre le cancer*, Intern. Union against Cancer

U.I.C.G.F. Fr. *Union internationale du commerce en gros de la fleur*, Intern. Union for the Wholesale Flower Trade

U.I.C.M. Fr. *Union internationale catholique des classes moyennes*, Intern. Catholic Union of the Middle Classes

U.I.C.N. Fr. *Union internationale pour la conservation de la nature et de ses resources*, Intern. Union for Conservation of Nature and Natural Resources

U.I.C.P.A. Fr. *Union internationale de chimie pure et appliquée*, Intern. Union of Pure and Applied Chemistry

U.I.C.T. Fr. *Union internationale contre la tuberculose*, Intern. Union against Tuberculosis

U.I.D.A. Fr. *Union internationale des organisations de détaillants de la branche alimentaire*, Intern. Fed. of Grocers' Assns.

U.I.E. Fr. *Union internationale d'électrothermie*, Intern. Union for Electroheat; Fr. *Union internationale des étudiants*, Intern. Union of Students

U.I.E.C. Fr. *Union internationale de l'exploitation cinématographique*, Intern. Union of Cinematograph Exhibitors

U.I.E.I.S. Fr. *Union internationale pour l'étude des insectes sociaux*, Intern. Union for the Study of Social Insects

U.I.E.O. Union of International Engineering Organisations

U.I.E.P. Fr. *Union internationale des entrepreneurs de peinture*, Intern. Union of Housepainting Contractors

U.I.E.S. Fr. *Union internationale pour l'éducation sanitaire*, Intern. Union for Health Education

U.I.F.I. Fr. *Union internationale des fabricants d'imperméables*, Intern. Rainwear Council

U.I.H.L. Fr. *Union internationale de l'humanisme laïque*, Intern. Humanist and Ethical Union

U.I.H.P.S. Fr. *Union internationale d'histoire et de philosophie des sciences*, Intern. Union of the History and Philosophy of Science

U.I.I.G. Fr. *Union internationale de l'industrie du gaz*, Intern. Gas Union

U.I.J.S. Fr. *Union internationale de la jeunesse socialiste*, Intern. Union of Socialist Youth

U.I.L. It. *Unione Italiana del Lavoro*, Italian Fed. of Trade Unions

U.I.L.E. Fr. *Union internationale pour la liberté d'enseignement*, Intern. Union for the Freedom of Education

U.I.M. Fr. *Union internationale motonautique*, Intern. Union for Motorboating

U.I.M.C. Fr. *Union internationale des services médicaux des chemins de fer*, Intern. Union of Railway Medical Services

U.I.M.P. Fr. *Union internationale pour la protection de la moralité publique*, Intern. Union for Protecting Public Morality

U.I.N.F. Fr. *Union internationale de la navigation fluviale*, Intern. Union for Inland Navigation

U.I.N.L. Fr. *Union internationale du notariat latin*, Intern. Union of Latin Notaries

U.I.O. Fr. *Union internationale des orientalistes*, Intern. Union of Orientalists

U.I.O.F. Fr. *Union internationale des organismes familiaux*, Intern. Union of Family Organisations

U.I.O.O.T. Fr. *Union internationale des organismes officiels de tourisme*, Intern. Union of Official Travel Organisations

U.I.O.T. It. *Unione Internazionale Organizzatori Turismo*, Touring Organizers' Intern. Assn.

U.I.P. Fr. *Union internationale d'associations de propriétaires de wagons de particuliers*, Intern. Union of Private Railway Truck Owners' Assns.; Fr. *Union internationale de patinage*, Intern. Skating Union; Fr. *Union internationale de physique pure et appliquée*, Intern.

Union of Pure and Applied Physics; Fr. *Union internationale des publicitaires*, Intern. Union of Practitioners in Advertising; Fr. *Union interparlementaire*, Inter-Parliamentary Union

U.I.P.C. Fr. *Union internationale de la presse catholique*, Intern. Catholic Press Union

U.I.P.C.G. Fr. *Union internationale de la pâtisserie, confiserie, glacerie*, Intern. Union of Bakers and Confectioners

U.I.P.E. Fr. *Union internationale de protection de l'enfance*, Intern. Union for Child Welfare

U.I.P.F.B. Fr. *Union internationale de la propriété foncière bâtie*, Intern. Union of Landed Property Owners

U.I.P.M. Fr. *Union internationale de la presse médicale*, Intern. Union of the Medical Press; Fr. *Union internationale de pentathlon moderne*, Intern. Modern Pentathlon Union

U.I.P.M.B. Fr. *Union internationale de pentathlon moderne et biathlon*, supreme international authority for Biathlon, cross-country skiing with shooting

U.I.P.P.I. Fr. *Union internationale pour la protection de la propriété industrielle*, Intern. Union for the Protection of Industrial Property

U.I.P.V.T. Fr. *Union internationale contre le péril vénérien et les tréponématoses*, Intern. Union against Venereal Diseases and Treponematoses

U.I.R.D. Fr. *Union internationale de la résistance et de la déportation*, Intern. Union of Resistance and Deportee Movements

UIS Union of Insurance Staffs

U.I.S. Fr. *Union internationale de secours*, Intern. Relief Union

U.I.S.A.E. Fr. *Union internationale des sciences anthropologiques et ethnologiques*, Intern. Union of Anthropological and Ethnological Sciences

U.I.S.B. Fr. *Union internationale des sciences biologiques*, Intern. Union of Biological Sciences

U.I.S.E. Fr. *Union internationale de secours aux enfants*, Intern. Union for Child Welfare

U.I.S.M. Fr. *Union internationale des syndicats des mineurs*, Miners' Trade Unions Intern.

U.I.S.M.M. Fr. *Union internationale des syndicats des industries métallurgiques et mécaniques*, Trade Unions Intern. of Metal and Engineering Industries

U.I.S.N. Fr. *Union internationale des sciences de la nutrition*, Intern. Union of Nutritional Sciences

U.I.S.P.P. Fr. *Union internationale*

des sciences préhistoriques et protohistori-
ques, Intern. Union of Prehistoric and
Protohistoric Sciences

U.I.S.T.A.F. Fr. *Union internationale
des syndicats des travailleurs agricoles et
forestiers,* Trade Unions Intern. of Agricultural and Forestry Workers

U.I.S.T.C. Fr. *Union internationale
des syndicats des travailleurs du commerce,* Trade Unions Intern. of Workers
in Commerce

uit. Dutch *uitgaaf,* publication

U.I.T. F. *Union internationale des
télécommunications,* Intern. Telecommunications Union

U.I.T.A. Sp. *Unión Internacional de
Asociaciones de Trabajadores de Alimentos
y Ramos Afines,* Intern. Union of Food
and Allied Workers' Assns.

U.I.T.A.M. Fr. *Union internationale de
mécanique théorique et appliquée,* Intern.
Union of Theoretical and Applied Mechanics

U.I.T.B.B. Fr. *Union internationale
des syndicats des travailleurs du bâtiment,
du bois et des matériaux de construction,*
Trade Unions Intern. of Workers of the
Building Wood and Building Materials
Industries

U.I.T.P. Fr. *Union internationale des
transports publics,* Intern. Union of Public
Transport

U.I.U.S.D. Fr. *Union internationale
universitaire socialiste et démocratique,*
Intern. Union of Social Democratic
Teachers

U.I.V. Fr. *Union internationale des
villes et pouvoirs locaux,* Intern. Union of
Local Authorities

UJ *s* Salop (B.V.R.)

U.J. Union Jack, *correctly* Union
Flag, from 1606 combined crosses of St.
George (red cross in white field) and St.
Andrew (white saltire in blue field).
James I ordered this to be borne on jack-
staff of warships, whence erroneous name
U.J. In 1801 was added cross of St.
Patrick (red saltire in white field), and
the flag thus formed is the national flag
of U.K.

U.J.C. Union Jack Club, Waterloo
Road (Lond.), opened 1907 as residential
club for all service men below commissioned rank on leave in or passing through
Lond.

U.J.D. L. *Utriusque Juris Doctor,*
Doctor of Civil and Canon Law

UK *s* Wolverhampton (B.V.R.)

U.K. United Kingdom consisting of
England, Wales, Scotland, the Isle of
Man, the Channel Is. and 6 of the 9
counties of Ulster

U.K.A. Ulster King of Arms; United
Kingdom Alliance

U.K.(A) United Kingdom Allcomers
(athletics)

UKAC United Kingdom Automation
Council

U.K.A.E.A. United Kingdom Atomic
Energy Authority

UKAPE United Kingdom Association
of Professional Engineers

UKBG United Kingdom Bartenders'
Guild

U.K.C.A.T.R. United Kingdom Civil
Aviation Telecommunications Representative

U.K.C.B.D.A. United Kingdom Carbon Block Distributors' Association

U.K.C.S.B.S. United Kingdom Civil
Service Benefit Society

U.K.C.T.A. United Kingdom Commercial Travellers' Association

U.K.D.A. United Kingdom Dairy Association

uke. ukulele

U.K.G.P.A. United Kingdom Gly-
cerine Producers' Association

U.K.J.G.A. United Kingdom Jute
Goods Association

U.K.(N.) United Kingdom National
(athletics)

UKOP United Kingdom Oil Pipelines

U.K.P.A. United Kingdom Pilots' Association

Ukr. Ukraine; Ukrainian

UKSATA United Kingdom South
Africa Trade Association

U.K.S.M. United Kingdom Scientific
Mission

U.K.S.M.A. United Kingdom Sugar
Merchants' Association

UKW Ger. *Ultrakurzwelle,* ultra-short
wave/very high frequency

UL *s* London (B.V.R.) *s* Ullapool
(B.F.P.)

u.l. upper left/limit

U.L. universal league; university library; upper limb

U.L.A. Ulster Launderers' Association

ULAD Unilever Limited Accounts
Department

U.L.A.J.E. Sp. *Unión Latino Améri-
cana de Juventudes Evangélicas,* Union
of Latin-American Evangelical Youth

U.L.A.P.C. Sp. *Unión Latino Améri-
cana de Prensa Católica,* Latin-American
Catholic Press Union

U.L.A.S.T. Sp. *Unión Latino Améri-
cana de Sociedades de Tisiologia,* Latin-
American Union of Socs. of Phthisiology

ULC United Labour Congress (Nigeria)

u.l.c. upper left centre
u. & l.c. upper and lower case (typ.)
ULCI Union of Lancashire & Cheshire Institutes
u.l.f. ultra low frequency; upper limiting frequency
U.L.I. Fr. *Union pour la langue internationale Ido*, Union for the Intern. Language Ido
ULICS University of London Institute of Computer Science
ULLV unmanned lunar logistics vehicle
u.l.m. ultrasonic light modulator; universal logic module
ULMS undersea long-range missile system
U.L.P. University of London Press
U.L.R. *Uganda Law Reports*
u.l.s. unsecured loan stock (fin.)
ult. L. *ultimo*, last month
U.L.T. United Lodge of Theosophists
ult. praes. L. *ultimum praescriptum*, last prescribed
u.l.v. ultra low volume
üM Ger. *über dem Meeresspiegel*, above sea level
UM *s* Leeds (B.V.R.)
um. unmarried
u.m. under-mentioned
U.M.A. Ultrasonic Manufacturers' Association (U.S.A.)
U.M.B. Fr. *Union mondiale de billard*, World Billiards Union
umbl. umbilical
Umbr. Umbria; Umbrian
U.M.C. Upper Mantle Committee
U.M.C.A. Universities Mission to Central Africa
U.M.E.C. Fr. *Union mondiale des enseignants catholiques*, World Union of Catholic Teachers
U.M.E.J. Fr. *Union mondiale des étudiants juifs*, World Union of Jewish Students
U.M.F.C. United Methodist Free Churches
UMFIA Fr. *Union médicale latine*, Latin Medical Union
umgearb. Ger. *umgearbeitete*, revised
U.M.H.P. Fr. *Union mondiale des sociétés d'histoire pharmaceutique*, World Organisation of Socs. of Pharmaceutical History
U/min. Ger. *Umdrehungen in der Minute*, revolutions per minute
U.M.I.S.T. University of Manchester Institute of Science and Technology
U.M.N.O. United Malays National Organisation
U.M.O.F.C. Fr. *Union mondiale des organisations féminines catholiques*, World

Union of Catholic Women's Organisations
U.M.O.S.B.E.S.L. Fr. *Union mondiale des organisations syndicales sur base économique et sociale libérale*, World Union of Liberal Trade Union Organisations
U.M.O.S.E.A. Fr. *Union mondiale des organismes pour la sauvegarde de l'enfance et de l'adolescence*, World Union of Organisations for the Safeguard of Youth
ump. umpire
U.M.S. Unfederated Malay States
UMT Fr. *Union Marocaine du Travail*, Moroccan Labour Union; universal military training
UMTA Urban Mass Transportation Administration (U.S.A.)
UMTS universal military training service/system
UMW United Mine Workers
U.M.W.A. United Mine Workers of America
UN *s* Denbighshire (B.V.R.); *Unificación Nacional*, National Unification (Costa Rica)
un. unified; union; united; unsatisfactory
U.N. United Nations, *estab.* 24 Oct. 1945
U.N.A. United Nations Association
U.N.A.A. United Nations Association of Australia
unab. unabridged
U.N.A.C.C. United Nations Administrative Committee and Co-ordination
unaccomp. unaccompanied
UNACIL United Africa Commercial and Industrial Limited
UNACOM universal army communication system
UNAMACE universal automatic map compilation equipment
un-Amer. un-American
unan. unanimous
U.N.A.R.C.O. United Nations Narcotics Commission
unasgd. unassigned
U.N.A.T. It. *Unione Nazionale Artisti Teatrali*, Theatre Actors' Nat. Assn.
unatt. unattached
U.N.A.U.S. United Nations Association of the United States
unauthd. unauthorized
UNB universal navigation beacon
unb., unbd. unbound
U.N.B. United Nations Bookshop
UNC uncirculated (numis.); *Union Nationale Camerounaise*, Cameroun Nat. Union (Cameroun)
unc. uncertain
Unc. uncle
U.N.C. United Nations Command

UNCAST United Nations Conference on the Applications of Science and Technology

U.N.C.C. United Nations Cartographic Commission

U.N.C.C.P. United Nations Conciliation Commission for Palestine

U.N.C.I.O. United Nations Conference on International Organisation

U.N.C.I.P. United Nations Commission on India and Pakistan

uncir. uncirculated

unclas., unclass. unclassified

U.N.C.L.E. United Network Command for Law Enforcement (television)

U.N.C.O. United Nations Civilian Operations Mission (Congo Republic)

U.N.C.O.K. United Nations Commission on Korea

uncond. unconditioned

uncor. uncorrected

U.N.C.P. United Nations Conference of Plenipotentiaries

unct. L. *unctus*, smeared

U.N.C.T.A.D. United Nations Conference on Trade and Development

U.N.C.U.R.K. United Nations Commission for Unification and Rehabilitation of Korea

UND *Union Nationale et Démocratique*, Nat. and Democratic Union (Monaco)

U.N.D.A. Fr. *Association catholique internationale pour la radiodiffusion et la télévision*, Intern. Catholic Assn. for Radio and Television

undergrad. undergraduate

undies underclothes

U.N.D.P. United Nations Development Programme

undsgd. undersigned

undtkr. undertaker

U.N.E.C. United Nations Education Conference

U.N.E.C.A. United Nations Economic Commission for Asia

UNECOLAIT Fr. *Union européenne du commerce laitier*, European Milk Trade Union

U.N.E.D.A. United Nations Economic Development Administration

U.N.E.F. United Nations Emergency Force

UNEK *Union Nationale des Étudiants Kamerunais*, Nat. Union of Cameroun Students (Cameroun)

U.N.E.S.C.O. United Nations Educational, Scientific and Cultural Organization

U.N.E.S.E.M. Fr. *Union européenne des sources d'eaux minérales naturelles du Marché Commun*, European Union of Natural Mineral Water Sources of the Common Market

U.N.E.T.A.S. United Nations Emergency Technical Aid Service

unexpl. unexplained; unexploded; unexplored

U.N.F.A.O. United Nations Food and Agricultural Organization

U.N.F.B. United Nations Film Board

U.N.F.C. United Nations Food Conference

U.N.F.I.C.Y.P. United Nations Peace-Keeping Force in Cyprus

UNFP *Union Nationale des Forces Populaires*, Nat. Union of Popular Forces (Morocco)

ung. Ger. *ungarisch*, Hungarian

ung. L. *unguentum*, ointment (med.)

U.N.G.A. United Nations General Assembly

ung. H.A.D. L. *unguentum Hydrargyri Ammoniati dilutum*, ammoniated mercury ointment (med.)

U.N.H.C.R. United Nations High Commissioner for Refugees

U.N.H.Q. United Nations Headquarters

U.N.I. *Ente Nazionale Italiano di Unificazione*, Italian Standards Assn.

UNIATEC Fr. *Union internationale des associations techniques cinématographiques*, Intern. Union of Motion Picture Engineering Societies

U.N.I.C. United Nations Information Centre

UNICA Fr. *Union internationale du cinéma d'amateurs*, Intern. Union of Amateur Cinema

U.N.I.C.E. Fr. *Union des industries de la communauté européenne*, Union of Industries of the European Community

U.N.I.C.E.F. United Nations International Children's Emergency Fund, *estab.* 1946 to assist governments to meet long-term needs of maternal and child welfare

UNICHAL Fr. *Union internationale des distributeurs de chaleur*, Intern. Union of Heating Distributors

UNICOM universal integrated communication system

U.N.I.D.O. United Nations Industrial Development Organization

UNIDROIT Fr. *Institut international pour l'unification du droit privé*, Intern. Institute for the Unification of Private Law

unif. uniform

UNIMA Fr. *Union internationale de grands magasins*, Intern. Union of Department Stores

U.N.I.O. United Nations Information Organization

UNIP United National Independence Party (Zambia)

UNIPEDE Fr. *Union internationale des producteurs et distributeurs d'énergie électrique*, Intern. Union of Producers and Distributors of Electrical Energy

unis. It. *unisoni*, unison

Unis.   *Unison* (mus.)

U.N.I.S.   United Nations International School

U.N.I.S.C.A.T.   United Nations Expert Committee on the Application of Science and Technology

UNISIST   Universal System for Information in Science and Technology

Unit.   Unitarian; Unitarianism

U.N.I.T.A.R.   United Nations Institute for Training and Research

univ.   universal; universalist; university

Univ.   University College, Oxford, founded 1249

UNIVAC   universal automatic computer

Univ. Q.L.J.   *University of Queensland Law Journal*

U.N.J.S.P.B.   United Nations Joint Staff Pension Board

Unk.   uncle

unkn.   unknown

U.N.K.R.A.   United Nations Korea Reconstruction/Relief Agency

U.N.L.C.   United Nations Liaison Committee

unm.   unmarried

U.N.M.C.   United Nations Mediterranean Commission

U.N.M.O.G.I.P.   United Nations Military Observer Group in India and Pakistan

UNO   *Union Nacional Odrŭsta*, Odría Nat. Union (Peru)

U.N.O.   United Nations Organization

UNOH   Fr. *Union National des Ouvriers de Haïti, en exil*, Nat. Union of Haitian Workers in exile

unop.   unopposed

UNP   United National Party (Ceylon)

unp., unpd.   unpaged; unpaid

U.N.P.A.   United Nations Postal Administration

U.N.P.C.   United Nations Palestine Commission

U.N.P.C.C.   United Nations Conciliation Commission for Palestine

unpd.   unpaid

U.N.P.O.C.   United Nations Peace Observation Commission

unpub.   unpublished

U.N.R.E.F.   United Nations Refugee Emergency Fund

U.N.R.I.S.D.   United Nations Research Institute for Social Development

U.N.R.P.R.   United Nations Relief for Palestine Refugees

U.N.R.R.A.   United Nations Relief and Rehabilitation Administration

U.N.R.W.A.   United Nations Relief and Works Agency for Palestinian Refugees

U.N.R.W.A.P.R.N.E.   United Nations Relief and Works Agency for Palestine Refugees in the Near East

UNSA   University of Nottingham School of Agriculture

unsat.   unsatisfactory; unsaturated

U.N.S.C.   United Nations Security Council; United Nations Social Commission

U.N.S.C.C.   United Nations Standards Co-ordinating Committee

U.N.S.C.C.U.R.   United Nations Scientific Conference on the Conservation and Utilization of Resources

U.N.S.C.E.A.R.   United Nations Scientific Committee on the Effects of Atomic Radiation

U.N.S.C.O.B.   United Nations Special Committee on the Balkans

U.N.S.C.O.P.   United Nations Special Committee on Palestine

U.N.S.F.   United Nations Special Fund for Economic Development

U.N.S.G.   United Nations Secretary General

U.N.S.R.   United Nations Space Registry

UNSTHV   Fr. *Union Nationale des Syndicats des Travailleurs de la Haute Volta*, Nat. Federation of Workers' Unions of the Upper Volta

U.N.S.W.   University of New South Wales (Aust.)

UNT   *Union Nationale Tchadienne*, Chadian Nat. Union (Chad)

U.N.T.A.   United Nations Technical Assistance

U.N.T.A.A.   United Nations Technical Assistance Administration

U.N.T.A.B.   United Nations Technical Assistance Board

U.N.T.A.M.   United Nations Technical Assistance Mission

U.N.T.C.   United Nations Trusteeship Council

U.N.T.C.O.K.   United Nations Temporary Commission on Korea

U.N.T.E.A.   United Nations Temporary Executive Authority West New Guinea

U.N.T.S.O.   United Nations Truce Supervision Organization in the Middle East

UNTT   National Union of Togolese Workers

U.N.T.T.   United Nations Trust Territory

UNU Uganda National Union (Uganda)

U.N.W.C.C. United Nations War Crimes Commission

U.N.Y.O.M. United Nations Yemen Observation Mission

UO *s* Devon (B.V.R.)

u.o. Ger. *und ofters*, and often

u. & o. use and occupancy

u.o.c. ultimate operating capability

U.O.D. ultimate oxygen demand (water conservation)

U. of A. University of Alaska

U. of N.C. University of North Carolina

U. of S. University of Saskatchewan

U.O.F.S. University of the Orange Free State (S. Afr.)

U. of T. University of Toronto (Can.)

UOV Fr. *Union Ouvrière du Viet-Nam*, Viet-Nam Labour Union

UP *s* Durham (B.V.R.); United Party (Gambia); United Party (S. Afr.); unsaturated polyester

up. upper

u.p. under proof (spirits)

U.P. Ulster Parliament; Union Pacific; United Party (Ghana); United Presbyterian; United/University Press; University of Paris/Pennsylvania/Pittsburgh; Uttar Pradesh, *formerly* United Provinces (India)

UPA *Unión para Avanzar*, Union for Progress (Ven.)

U.P.A. Fr. *Union postale arabe*, Arab Postal Union; United Patternmakers' Association

U.P.A.D.I. Sp. *Unión Panamericana de Asociaciones de Ingenieros*, Pan-American Federation of Engineering Societies

U.P.A.E. Fr. *Union postale des Amériques et de l'Espagne*, Postal Union of the Americas and Spain

UPC Uganda People's Congress; *Union des Populations Camerounaises*, Cameroun People's Union

U.P.C. UNESCO Publications Centre; United Presbyterian Church; Universal Postal Convention

UPD united port district; urban planning directorate

Upd. unpaid

uphd. uphold (leg.)

uphol. upholsterer; upholstery

U.P.I. United Press International (U.S.A.)

U.P.I.G.O. Fr. *Union professionnelle internationale des gynécologues et obstétriciens*, Intern. Union of Professional Gynaecologists and Obstetricians

U.P.O.A. Ulster Public Officers' Association

UPOV Fr. *L'Union Internationale pour la Protection des Obtentions Végétales*, Intern. Union for the Protection of New Plant Varieties

U.P.O.W. Union of Post Office Workers

UPP United Peasant Party, *Zjednoczone Stronnictwo Ludowe* (Poland)

upp., uppl. Swed. *upplaga*, edition

U.P.R. Union Pacific Railroad

UPRONA National Party for the Unity and Progress of Burundi, *Parti de l'Unité et du Progrès National du Burundi* (Burundi)

UPS *Union Progressiste Sénégalaise*, Senegalese Progressive Union (Senegal)

u.p.s. uninterrupted power supply

U.P.S. United Publishers' Services

U.P.T.C. Fr. *Union panafricaine des travailleurs croyants*, Pan-African Workers Congress

Up. tr. up train

U.P.U. Universal Postal Union, *estab.* 1875 to unite members in a single postal territory

U.P.W. Union of Post Office Workers

Ur uranium (chem.)

UR *s* Hertfordshire (B.V.R.)

ur. urine (med.)

Ur. Urdu, Indian language; Uruguay; Uruguayan

U.R. unconditioned response; uniform regulations; unsatisfactory report; up/ upper right (theatre); urban renewal

URA University Research Associates (U.S.A.); Urban Renewal Administration (U.S.A.)

Uran. Uranus

urb. urban

U.R.B.M. ultimate range ballistic missile

URD *Union pour le Renouveau du Dahomey* (Dahomey); *Unión Republicana Democrática*, Democratic Republican Union (Ven.)

Urd. Urdu, Indian language

U.R.F. Fr. *Union des services routiers des chemins de fer européens*, Union of European Railways Road Services

urg. urgent

U.R.I. Fr. *Université radiophonique et télévisuelle internationale*, Intern. Radio-Television Univ.; upper respiratory infection (med.)

URL Unilever Research Laboratory

Urol. urology

U.R.P.E. Fr. *Union des résistants pour une Europe unie*, Union of Resistance Veterans for a United Europe

U.R.S.I. Fr. *Union Radio Scientifique*

357

Internationale, Intern. Scientific Radio Union

urspr. Ger. *ursprunglich*, original

U.R.S.S. Port. *União das Repúblicas Socialistas Soviéticas*, Union of Soviet Socialist Republics; Fr. *Union des Républiques Socialistes Soviétiques*, Union of Socialist Soviet Republics

U.R.T. infection upper respiratory tract infection, cold/influenza

U.R.T.U. United Road Transport Union

Uru. Uruguay; Uruguayan

u/s unserviceable

US *s* Glasgow (B.V.R.)

u.s. It. *ultimo scorso*, last month

u.s. L. *ut supra*, as above

U.S. It. *Ufficio Stampa*, Press Agency; Uncle Sam (U.S.A.); under secretary; uniform system of lens aperture (photo.); United Service; United States

USA United States of America (I.V.R.); United Swaziland Association

U.S.A. Union of South Africa; United States Army; United States of America

U.S.A.A.C. United States Army Air Corps, *now* U.S.A.A.F.

USAACDA United States Army Aviation Combat Developments Agency

USAADEA United States Army Air Defense Engineering Agency

USAAFO United States Army Avionics Field Office

USAAVNC United States Army Aviation Center

USAAVNS United States Army Aviation School

USABAAR United States Army Board for Aviation Accident Research

U.S.A.C. United States Air Corps; United States Auto Club

USACAC United States Army Continental Army Command

USACDC United States Army Combat Development Command

USAEC United States Army Electronics Command

U.S.A.E.C. United States Atomic Energy Commission

USAEMA United States Army Electronics Materiel Agency

USAEMSA United States Army Electronics Materiel Support Agency

USAERDL United States Army Electronics Research and Development Laboratory

USAF United States Air Force

USAFA United States Air Force Academy

USAFE United States Air Forces in Europe

U.S.A.F.I. United States Armed Forces Institute

U.S.A.I.D. United States Agency for International Development

USAIRE United States of America Aerospace Industries Representatives in Europe

USAMC United States Army Material / Missile / Mobility / Munitions Command

U.S.A.Med.S. United States Army Medical Service

USAR United States Army Reserve

USARADCOM United States Army Air Defense Command

USAREUR United States Army, Europe

USASA United States Army Security Agency

USASADEA United States Army Signal Air Defense Engineering Agency

USASAFO United States Army Signal Avionics Field Office

USASCC United States Army Strategic Communications Command

USASI United States of America Standards Institute, *now* American National Standards Institute

USASigC United States Army Signal Corps

USASMC United States Army Supply and Maintenance Command

USASMSA United States Army Signal Materiel Support Agency

USASRDL United States Army Signal Research and Development Laboratory

USASSA United States Army Signal Supply Agency

U.S.A.T. United States Army Transport

USATEC United States Army Test and Evaluation Command

USAWC United States Army Weapons Command

U.S.B.C. United States Bureau of the Census

U.S.B.M. United States Bureau of Mines

U.S.C. United Services Club; United States Code/Congress; United States of Colombia; up stage centre (theatre)

U.S.C.A. United States Code Annotated

U.S.C.C. United States Circuit Court

U.S.C.C.A. United States Circuit Court of Appeals

U.S.C.C.P.A. United States Court of Customs and Patent Appeals

U.S.C.G. United States Coast Guard

USCGA United States Coast Guard Academy

USCGAD United States Coast Guard Air Detachment

USCGAS United States Coast Guard Air Station

USCGC United States Coast Guard Cutter

USCGR United States Coast Guard Reserve

U.S.C.G.S. United States Coast and Geodetic Survey

U.S.C.L. United Society for Christian Literature

U.S.Corps United Services Corps

U.S.C.S.C. United States Civil Service Commission

U.S.C.Supp. United States Code Supplement

U.S.C.V. Fr. *Union Scientifique Continentale du Verre*, European Union for the Scientific Study of Glass

U.S.D.A. United States Department of Agriculture

U.S.D.A.W. Union of Shop, Distributive and Allied Workers

U.S.D.H.E. & W. United States Department of Health, Education and Welfare

U/sec. under secretary

USES United States Employment Service

usf. Ger. *und so fort*, and so on

U.S.F. United States Forces

U.S.F.W.S. United States Fish and Wildlife Service

U.S.G. United States gallon; United States Government; United States Standard Gauge

USGA United States Golf Association

U.S.H.L. United States Hygienic Laboratory

U.S.I. United Schools International; United Service Institution; United States Industries

U.S.I.A. United States Information Agency

U.S.I.S. United States Information Service

U.S.L. United States Legation; United States Lines

U.S.L.T.A. United States Lawn Tennis Association

U.S.M. ultrasonic machining; underwater-to-surface missile; United States Mail/Marines/Mint

U.S.M.A. Underfeed Stoker Makers' Association; United States Military Academy

U.S.M.C. United States Marine Corps; United States Maritime Commission

U.S.M.H. United States Marine Hospital

U.S.M.S. United States Maritime Service

U.S.N., USN United States Navy

U.S.N.A. United States Naval Academy

USNC United States National Committee

U.S.N.G. United States National Guard

U.S.N.H. United States north of Cape Hatteras, sometimes known as Northern Range/Range Ports (ship.)

U.S.N.H.O. United States Navy Hydrographic Office

USNI United States Naval Institute

U.S.N.R. United States Naval Reserve

U.S.N.S. United States Navy Ship

USNUSL United States Navy Underwater Sound Laboratory

U.S.O. United Service Organization, founded 1941 to provide recreation and entertainment for members of the U.S. armed forces

U.S.P. unbleached sulphite pulp (papermaking); United States Patent (*also*, U.S. Pat.); United States Pharmacopoeia, *also* U.S.Phar., U.S.Pharm.

USPC Ulster Society for the Preservation of the Countryside

U.S.P.G. United Society for the Propagation of the Gospel

U.S.P.H.S. United States Public Health Service

U.S.P.O. United States Post Office

U.S.R. United States Reserves; Usher of the Scarlet Rod, an officer of the Most Honourable Order of the Bath

USRA Universities Space Research Association (U.S.A.)

USS Fr. *Union Syndicale Suisse*, Swiss Federation of Trade Unions; United States Steel

U.S.S. Under Secretary of State; United States Senate/Ship/Standard Thread/Steamer

U.S.S.A.F. United States Strategic Air Force

U.S.-S.A.L.E.P. United States-South Africa Leader Exchange Programme

U.S.S.C. United States Supreme Court

U.S.S.R. Union of Soviet Socialist Republics, comprising the Russian Soviet Federated Socialist Republic, and the Armenian, Azerbaijan, Estonian, Finno-Karelian, Georgian, Kazakh, Kirghiz, Latvian, Lithuanian, Moldavian, Tadzhik, Turkmen, Ukrainian, Uzbek, and White Russian Soviet Socialist Republics

U.S.S.S. United States Steamship

ust undersea technology

ust. L. *ustus*, burnt

U.S.T.C. United States Tariff Commission

U.S.T.S. United States Travel Service

usu. usual; usually

usurp. L. *usurpandus*, to be used

U.S.V. United States Volunteers

U.S.V.B. United States Veterans' Bureau

U.S.V.H. United States Veterans' Hospital

u.s.w. ultra short wave; underwater sea warfare; Ger. *und so weiter*, and so forth/on

U.S.W.B. United States Weather Bureau

U.S.W.D. undersurface warfare division

U.S.W.I. United States West Indies

U.S.W.P. Ultra Short Wave Propagation Panel

U.S.W.V. United Spanish War Veterans

UT *s* Leicestershire (B.V.R.); *Unité Togolaise*, Togolese Unity (Togo); Utah (U.S.A.)

ut. utility

Ut. Utah (U.S.A.)

u.t. universal trainer; untrained; urinary tract; user test

U.T. Union Territory, India; unit trust; universal time; Utah Territory (U.S.A.)

U.T.A. Ulster Transport Authority

UTC Sp. *Unión de Trabajadores de Colombia*, Union of Colombian Workers

U.T.C. University Training Corps

U.T.C.P.T. Fr. *Union internationale des organismes touristiques et culturels des postes et des télécommunications*, Intern. Union of Tourist and Cultural Assns. in the Postal and Telecommunications Service

Utd. united

U.T.D.A. Ulster Tourist Development Association

ut dict. L. *ut dictum*, as directed

utend. L. *utendus*, to be used (med.)

utend. mor. sol. L. *utendus more solito*, to be used in the usual manner (med.)

utg. Nor. *utgave*, edition

ut inf. L. *ut infra*, as below

UTM Fr. *Union des Travailleurs de Mauritanie*, Union of Workers of Mauritania

U.T.O. United Town Organisation

U.T.P.P. United Thai People's Party, *Sahaprachathai*

u.t.s. ultimate tensile strength; underwater telephone system

ut sup. L. *ut supra*, as above

UTUC Uganda Trades' Union Congress

U2 high altitude photographic aircraft

UU *s* London (B.V.R.)

u.U. Ger. *unter Umständen*, circumstances permitting

U.U. Ulster Unionist

u.u.v. Ger. *unter üblichen vorbehalt*, errors and omissions excepted

UV *s* London (B.V.R.)

u.v., UV, U-V. ultra-violet

U.V. Upper Volta

UVAS ultra-violet astronomical satellite

UVASER ultra-violet amplification by stimulated emission of radiation

U.V.Co. United Veterans' Council (U.S.A.)

UVF Ulster Volunteer Force

U.V.L. ultra-violet light

UW *s* London (B.V.R.)

U/W underwriter

U.W. under water; *Universität Wien*, Univ. of Vienna (Austria); unladen weight

U.W. Ger. *Unterwerk*, choir organ (mus.)

U.W.A. University of Western Australia

U.W.C.E. Under-Water Weapons and Counter-Measures Establishment

u.-wear underwear

U.W.H.C. Ulster Women's Hockey Union

UWI University of the West Indies

UWIST University of Wales Institute of Science and Technology

UX *s* Salop (B.V.R.)

ux. L. *uxor*, wife

UXB unexploded bomb

UY *s* Worcestershire (B.V.R.)

U.Y. Universal Youth

UZ *s* Belfast (B.V.R.)

Uz. Uzbek; Uzbekistan; Uzbekistani

U.Z. University of Zürich (Switz.)

U.Z.R.A. United Zionist Revizionist of America

V

v *s* unusual visibility (met.)

v/ Port. *vosso*, yours

V five (Roman); *s* Lanarkshire (B.V.R.); *s* potential energy (math.); *s* vanadium (chem.); *s* Vatican City (I.V.R.); *s* velocity (phys.)

Ṽ *s* versicle

v. vacuum; vagrant; vale; valley; valve; vector (math.); vein; ventilator; ventral; verb; verbal; verse; version; verticle; very; vicar; vicarage; vice, in titles; village; virus; viscosity; visibility; vision (med.); vocative; voice; volcano; voltage; voltmeter; volume; volunteer; Ger. *von*, of (used in personal names); from, by; Fr. *votre*, your; vowel

v. L. *vel*, or; L. *verso*, left-hand page of open book, usually bearing an even number, also *vo* (typ.); L. *versus*, against; L. *via*, by way of; L. *vice*, in place of; L. *vide*, see

V. Venerable; *Venstre*, Liberal Party, formed 1884 (Nor.); Ger. *Vergeltungswaffe*, reprisal weapon; version; very, in titles; vespers; It. *Via*, Street; vice, in titles; Victoria; victory; Viscount; Viscountess; volt (unit of electric potential); Ger. *Volt*, volt; Ger. *Volumen*, volume; volunteer

V.1. *s Vergeltungswaffe* (weapon of vengeance), Mark I, flying bomb used WW2; — **2.** rocket bomb Mark II

V. violin (mus.); It. *Voce*, voice (mus.); It. *Volti*, turn over (mus.)

V² It. *Violino secondo*, second violin (mus.)

VA *s* Lanarkshire (B.V.R.); Virginia (*also* Va.); *s* voltaic alternative

V/A voucher attached

Va. *viola* (mus.)

v.a. value analysis; verb active; vinyl acetate; volt ampère (elec.)

v.a. L. *vixit . . . annos*, lived . . . years

V.A. Royal Order of Victoria and Albert, order for ladies instituted in 1862, no conferments since 1902; *Venus and Adonis* (Shake.); Veterans' Administration (U.S.A.); Vicar Apostolic; Vice-Admiral (*also* V.-Adm.); Vickers Armstrong Limited; Voice of America; volunteer artillery; Volunteers of America; Fr. *Votre Altesse*, Your Highness; It. *Vuestra Altezo*, Your Highness

V. and A., V. & A. Victoria and Albert Museum (Lond.)

VAA Vaccination Assistance Act

V-AA Vietnamese-American Association

VAB vertical assembly building, used to assemble spacecraft at Cape Kennedy (NASA)

Vab. Van Allen belt (astr.)

V.A.B.F. Variety Artistes' Benevolent Fund

VABM vertical angle bench mark

VAC Vector analogue computer

vac. vacancy; vacant; vacation; vacuum; volts alternating current

vacc., vacci. vaccination; vaccine

vac. dist. vacuum-distilled

Vacemp Vacation Employment Agency

vac. pmp. vacuum pump

V.A.D. Voluntary Aid Detachment, formed 1909 to give nursing and other help in wartime, from 1914 work organized by the British Red Cross Society

V.A.E. Fr. *Votre Altesse Électorale*, Your Electoral Highness

V.A.F. Variety Artistes' Federation

vag. vagabond; vagina; vagrancy; vagrant

V.A.H. Veterans' Administration Hospital (U.S.A.)

v.a. & i. verb active and intransitive

VAK 191B experimental V/Stol fighter aircraft

Val Valentine; Valerie

val. valley; valuation (*also* valn.); value; valvular

V.A.L.A. National Viewers' and Listeners' Association

valid. validate; validation

Valpo. Valparaiso

VAMP variable anamorphic motion picture; visual acoustic magnetic pressure; visual approach for management planning

vamp. vampire

van. advantage (lawn tennis); vanguard; vanilla

Vanc. Vancouver (Can.)

VANDPF Vietnam Alliance of National, Democratic and Popular Forces

Vang. Vickers-Armstrongs Vanguard (aircraft)

Vapi visual approach path indicator

vapor. vaporization

vap. prf. vapour proof

var. variable; variant (math.); variation; It. *variazione*, variation; variety; various

V.A.R. visual-aural radio range; volunteer air reserve; Fr. *Votre Altesse Royale*, Your Royal Highness

varactor. variable capacitor

var. cond. variable condenser

var. dial. various dialects

var. ed. & tr. various editions and translations

VAR 1 Variety 1, no groove between crown/shield (numis.); — **11,** groove exists between crown/shield (numis.)

VARIG-S.A. Port., *Empresa de Viação Aérea Rio Grandense*, Brazilian airline

varistor variable resistor

var. lect. L. *varia lectio*, a variant reading

varn. varnish

Varn. Variation, direction of magnetic meridian measured in degrees east or west from true north (nav.)

vas. vasectomy

vasc. vascular

V.A.S.C.A. Electronic Valve and Semiconductor Manufacturers' Association

Vasi visual approach slope indicator

varsity university

vas vit. L. *vas vitreum*, glass vessel

VAT value-added tax

Vat. Vatican; — **Lib.** Vatican Library

V.A.T.C. Victoria Amateur Turf Club

VATE versatile automatic test equipment

vaud. vaudeville

v. aux. verb auxiliary

VB *s* London (B.V.R.)

vb. verb; verbal

v.b. vehicle borne; vertical bomb

V.B. volunteer battalion

°V.B. Vee Bee Consistometer degrees, scale of 'workability' of cement/concrete mixes

— vbl. verbal; — **a.** verbal adjective; — **n.** verbal noun; — **sb.** verbal substantive

V-bomb missile type long range bomb, used by Ger. in WW2, see V.1., V.2.

V.B.R.A. Vehicle Builders' and Repairers' Association

VC *s* acuity of colour vision; *s* Coventry (B.V.R.)

VC10 Vickers-Armstrongs VC10 (aircraft)

Vc., Vcl., Vcllo. violoncello (mus.)

v.c. valuation clause; vehicular communication; venereal case; vinyl chloride; visual communication

v.c. L. *verbi causa,* for example; L. *visum cultum,* seen cultivated (bot.)

v.C. Dutch *voor Christus,* before Christ (B.C.)

V.C. Vatican City; velo club (cycling); veterinary corps (U.S.A.); vice-chairman/-chamberlain/-chancellor/-consul; Victoria Cross, a bronze Maltese cross inscribed *For Valour,* with crimson ribbon, instituted 1856 for conspicuous bravery in war. Each holder receives a tax-free annuity of £100; Vietcong

V.C., v.cl. L. *Vir Clarissimus,* most famous man, title of Roman senators and (after Constantine) of many other dignitaries

VCA vinylene carbonate (chem.); virtual crystal approximation; Volunteer Civic Association (U.S.A.)

V.C.A.S. Vice-Chief of Air Staff

V.C.C. valve control co-ordinator; Veteran Car Club of Great Britain; vice-chancellors' committee

V.C.C.S. voltage controlled current source (elect.)

Vce. Venice (Italy)

v. cel. L. *vir celeberrimus,* most celebrated man

V.C.G. vertical centre of gravity; vice-consul general

VCH vinyl cyclohexene (chem.)

vch. vehicle
V.C.H. Victoria County History
v. Chr. Ger. *vor Christus, vor Christo/ vor Christi Geburt*, before Christ (B.C.)
V.C.I. volatile corrosion inhibitor
V.C.I.G.S. Vice-Chief of the Imperial General Staff
vcm. vacuum
V.C.M.O. voluntary county markets organizer (W.I.)
V.C.N.S. Vice-Chief of the Naval Staff
venty. vicinity
V.C.O. voltage controlled oscillator; voluntary county organizer (W.I.)
Vcr. Vancouver (Can.)
vcs. voices
V.C.X.O. voltage controlled crystal oscillator
V. Cz. Vera Cruz (Mex.)
Vd *s* vanadium (chem.)
VD *s* Lanarkshire (B.V.R.)
vd. void
Vd. Vaud (Switz.)
v.d. vapour density; various dates; verbal discrimination
V.D. Royal Naval Volunteer Reserve Decoration, *now* V.R.D.; venereal disease
Vda. Sp. *Vinda*, widow
V. day victory day
V.D.B. *Verband Deutscher Biologen*, (W.) Ger. Assn. of Biologists
vdc volts direct current (elec.)
V.D.E. *Verband Deutscher Elektrotechniker*, (W.) Ger. Assn. of Electrical Engineers
v. def. verb defective
V. De. H., VDEH *Verein Deutscher Eisenhuttenleute*, (W.) Ger. Iron and Steel Research Assn.
v. dep. verb deponent
V.D.G. *Verein Deutscher Giessereifachleute*, (W.) Ger. Assn. of Foundry and Casting Operations
V.D.H. valvular disease of heart
V.D.I. vegetation drought index; *Verein Deutscher Ingenieure*, (W.) Ger. Assn. of Engineers
V.D.L. Van Diemen's Land, Tasmania (Aust.)
V.D.M. L. *Verbi Dei Minister*, Minister/Preacher of the Word of God (U.S.A.)
V.D.M.A. *Verein Deutscher Maschinenbau Anstalten*, (W.) Ger. Mechanical Engineering Assn.
V.D.M.I.E. L. *Verbum Domini Manet in Eternum*, The word of the Lord endureth for ever
V.D.Q.S. Fr. *Vins délimités de qua ité supérieure*, high quality wines covered by special regulations enforced by French Ministry of Agriculture

V.D.R. variable diameter rotor
V.D.R.L. venereal disease research laboratory
VDS variable-depth sonar
V.D.S.I. *Verein Deutscher Sicherheits Ingenieure*, (W.) Ger. Assn. of Safety Engineers
v.d.t. variable density wind tunnel; video tape terminal
VDU visual display unit
've have
VE *s* Cambridgeshire (B.V.R.)
ve., v^e Fr. *veuve*, widow
V.E. valve engineer/engineering; vocational education; It. *Vostra Eccellenza*, Your Excellency; Fr. *Votre Éminence*, Your Eminence; Sp. *Veustra Excelencia*, Your Excellency
V.E.A. Valve Engineering Association; Vehicles (Excise) Act, 1962
VEB Ger. *Volkseigener Betrieb*, People's Concern
veb. variable elevation beam
vec. vector
ved. It. *vedova*, widow
V.E. day Victory in Europe, 8 May 1945, German surrender in Europe, WW2
V.E.D.C. Vitreous Enamel Development Council
veg. vegetable; vegetarian; vegetation
vegtan. vegetable tanning material, mimosa, quebracho, valonea, chestnut, redunca (tanning)
veh. vehicle; vehicular
vel. vellum (bookbinding); velocity; velvet
ven. Fr. *vendredi*, Friday; veneer; It. *venerdi*, Friday; venereal; venery; venison; venom; venomous; ventral; ventricle
Ven. Venerable, Archdeacons' title; Venetian (*also* Venet.); Venezuela (*also* Venez.); Venezuelan (*also* Venez.); Venice; Venus
V.E.N.I.S.S. Visual Education National Information Service for Schools
vent. ventilate; ventilation; ventriloquist
ver. verification; verify; vermilion (*also* verm.); It. *versamento*, payment; verse; version, *also* vers.
Ver. Ger. *Verein*, Association/Company
V.E.R.A. versatile experimental reactor assembly; vision electronic recording apparatus
veränd. Ger. *verändert*, revised
verb. Ger. *verbessert*, improved or revised
verb. et lit. L. *verbatim et literatim*, word for word, exact copy (leg.)
verb. sap., verb. sat. L. *verbum satis sapienti*, a word to the wise is enough

verdt. verdict (leg.)
Verf. Ger. *Verfasser*, author
Vergl. Ger. *Vergleische*, compare
Verl. Ger. *Verlag*, publisher
verm. Ger. *vermehrte*, enlarged; vermiculite
Verm. Vermont (U.S.A.)
vern. vernacular
verso reverso, left-hand page of open book
Ver. St. Ger. *Vereinigte Staaten*, United States of America
vert. vertebra; vertical; vertigo
Very Rev., Very Revd. Very Reverend, title of Dean (Anglican) and Moderator (Church of Scot.)
ves. vessel; vestry
ves. L. *vesica*, bladder; L. *vesicula*, blister; L. *vespere*, in the evening (med.), also *vesp.*
V.E.S.P.E.R. Voluntary Enterprises and Services and Part-Time Employment for the Retired
vet. veteran; veterinarian; veterinary (*also* veter.); veterinary surgeon
Vet. Admin. veterans' administration (U.S.A.)
Vet. M. B. Bachelor of Veterinary Medicine
Vet. Sci. Veterinary Science
Vet. Surg. Veterinary Surgeon
V. Ex.ᵃ Port. *Vossa Excelência*, Your Excellency
VF *s* Norfolk (B.V.R.)
v.f. very fair/fine
V.F. Vicar Forane; video/voice frequency; visual field
v.-f. band voice-frequency band
V.F.C. voltage-to-frequency converter
V.F.F. black very fine furnace black, filler in rubber compounding
V.F.O. variable-frequency oscillator
V.F.O.A.R. Vandenberg Field Office of Aerospace Research (USAF)
V.F.P. variable factor programming (computer)
V.f.R. Ger. *Verein für Raumschiffahrt*, Society for Space Travel
V.F.R. Visual Flight/Flying Rules
VFU Vertical Format Unit (computer)
VFW-614 feeder short-haul airliner
V.F.W. Veterans of Foreign Wars (U.S.A.), organized 1899 to look after the interests of ex-servicemen and their dependants
vfy. verify
VG *s* Norwich (B.V.R.)
vg. Sp. *verbigracia*, for example; Sp. *Virgen*, Virgin
Vg. Virgin

v.g. L. *verbi gratia*, for the sake of example
V.G. Fr. *Vaisseau de Guerre*, warship; velocity gravity; very good; Vicar-General; Vice Grand (freem.); vinylene glycol; Fr. *Votre Grâce*, Your Grace
V.G.A.A. Vegetable Growers' Association of America
v.g.c. very good condition; viscosity gravity constant
vgl. Dutch *vergelijken*, compare; Ger. *vergleiche*, compare
VGPI visual glide path indicator
VH *s* Australia (I.C.A.M.); *s* Huddersfield (B.V.R.)
v.h. very high
v.H. Ger. *vom Hundert*, per cent
v.h.b. very heavy bombardment
v.h.c. very highly commended
VHF very high fidelity/frequency
VHF/UHF very high and ultra high frequency
V.H.O. very high output
v.i. verb intransitive
v.i. L. *vide infra*, see below
V.I. Vancouver Island (Can.); *Veiligheidsinstitut*, Netherlands Safety Institute; vertical interval (cartog.); Virgin Islands; viscosity index; volume indicator
viad. viaduct
vias voice interference analysis system
VIASA *Venezolana Internacional de Aviácion, S.A.*, Venezuelan airline
VIB vertical integration building
vib. vibrate; vibration
Vic. Victor; Victoria
vic. vicar; vicarage; vicinity; victory
Vic., Vict. Victoria (Aust.)
Vic. Ap., Vic. Apos. Vicar Apostolic (R.C.)
Vic. Gen. Vicar General
Vic. Hist. *Victoria History of the Counties of England*
Vicki, Vicky Victoria
V.I. Corp. Virgin Islands Corporation
VID Volunteers for International Development
vid. L. *vide*, see; L. *vidua*, widow
Vien. Vienna (Austria)
vig., vign. vignette
v.i.i. viscosity index improver
vil., vill. village
V.i.m. Vertical improved mail; — s. Vertical improved mail service
v. imp. verb impersonal
v. imper. verb imperative
Vin, Vince, Vinny Vincent
vin. vinegar
VINB Virgin Islands National Bank
vind. vindicate; vindication
vini. viniculture
V.I.O. veterinary investigation officer;

voluntary island organizer, W.I. in Channel Is., Isle of Man

Viol. It. *Violino*, violin (mus.)

V.I.P. value improvement project; variable/versatile information processing (USN); very important person; *Vias Internacionales de Panamá*, Panamanian airlines visual image processor

VIPRE visual precision

vir. L. *viridis*, green

Vir., Virg. Virgil; Virgo

V.I.R. L. *Victoria Imperatrix Regina*, Victoria Empress and Queen

v. irr. verb irregular

vis. viscosity (*also* visc.); visibility; visible; visual

Vis., Visc., Visct. viscount, one who acts as deputy to a count/earl. It became a title of nobility in 15th cent.; viscountess; viscounty

V.I.S. Veterinary Investigation Service

Visc. Vickers-Armstrongs Viscount (aircraft)

VISTA viewing instantly security transactions automatically; Volunteers in Service to America, organ. sponsored by U.S. Office of Economic Opportunity, being volunteers devoted to educating and teaching the poorer citizens (U.S.A.)

VIT vertical interval test

vit. vitreous

VITA Volunteers for International Technical Assistance

VITAL variably initialized translator for algorithmic languages

viti. viticulture

vit. ov. sol. L. *vitello ovi solutus*, dissolved in yolk of egg (phar.)

vitr. L. *vitreum*, glass

vit. stat. vital statistics

Viv Vivian; Vivien

viv. It. *vivace*, lively, animated (mus.)

Vivette Genevieve

vivi. vivisection

vix. L. *vixit*, he/she lived

viz. L. *videlicet*, namely

VJ *s* Herefordshire (B.V.R.)

v.J. Ger. *vorigen Jahres*, of last year

V.J. day 15 Aug. 1945, Japanese surrender in Asia, WW2 (2 Sept. 1945 in U.S.A.)

VK *s* Newcastle upon Tyne (B.V.R.)

v.k. vertical keel; volume kill

VL *s* Lincoln (B.V.R.)

Vl. It. *Violino*, violin (mus.)

v.l. L. *varia lectio*, a variant reading

V.L. vice-lieutenant; vulgar latin

vla. viola (mus.)

Vlad Vladimir

Vlad. Vladivostock

v.-l.b. vertical-lift bridge

VLCC very large crude carrier, oil

tanker; voluntary leaders' certificate course, boys' clubs

v.le It. *viale*, boulevard

v.l.f. very low frequency

vln. violin (mus.)

V.L.N. very low nitrogen

V.L.R. very-long-range (aircraft); *Victorian Law Reports* (Aust.)

vltg. voltage (elec.)

vlv. valve; valvular

V/m *s* unit of electric field strength

VM *s* Manchester (B.V.R.)

v/m. volts per meter/mile

v.m. Dutch *voormiddag*, forenoon; Ger. *vormittags*, forenoon, also *vorm.*

v.M. Ger. *vorigen Monats*, last month

V.m. Sp. *Vuestra merced*, Your Worship

V.M. velocity modulation; Veteran Motorists, the Company of; victory medal; Viet Minh; volatile matter; Fr. *Votre Majesté*, Your Majesty

V. & M., V.M. Virgin and Martyr

V.M.A. Valve Manufacturers' Association (U.S.A.)

vmap video map equipment

V.M.C. visual meteorological conditions

VMCCA Veteran Motor Car Club of America

V.M.D. vertical magnetic dipole; *Veterinariae Medicinae Doctor*, Doctor of Veterinary Medicine

V.M.H. Victoria Medal of Honour (hort.)

v. & m.m. vandalism and malicious mischief

v.m.t. very many thanks

VN *s* Viet-Nam (I.V.R.); *s* Yorkshire (B.V.R.)

v.n. verb neuter

V.N. Vietnam; Vietnamese

Vna. Vienna

V-neck V-shaped neck

Vni. It. *Violini*, violins (mus.)

VNIRO *Vsesoyuznȳi Nauchno-issledovatel'skii Institut Morskogo Rȳbnogo Khozyaistva i Okeanografii*, All-Union Scientific Research Institute of Marine Fisheries and Oceanography (U.S.S.R.)

V.N.M. Victoria National Museum (Can.)

Vno. It. *Violino*, violin (mus.)

VNRC Vegetarian Nutritional Research Centre

VO *s* Nottinghamshire (B.V.R.)

vo. verso, left-hand page

v.o Port. *verso*, reverse side

v/o. Port. *vossa ordem*, your order

v.o. Ger. *von oben*, from the top

V.O. valuation officer; verbal order; very old; veterinary officer; Victorian

Order, Royal, founded 1868; Voice over, denoting commentary spoken off-screen (broadcasting)

V.O.A. *Vereeniging Ontwikkeling Arbeidstechniek*, Work Study Assn. (Neth.); Voice of America (broadcasting)

VoBo Sp. *visto bueno*, approved

voc. vocal; vocalist; vocation; vocative

V.O.C. vehicle observer corps

vocab. vocabulary

Você Port. *Vossa mercê*, You, familiar form used to address equals or social inferiors

V.O.C.O.S.S. Voluntary Organisations Co-operating in Overseas Social Service

voctl. vocational

VOD velocity of detonation

VODAT voice-operated device for automatic transmission

Voit. Fr. *Voiture*, wagon or truck

vol. volatile; volume; voluntary; volunteer

vol. ash volcanic ash

volc. volcanic; volcano

volum. volumetric

volvend. L. *volvendus*, to be rolled

voly. voluntary

8va It. *ottava*, octave

VONA Vehicle of the New Age, computer controlled, short distance, rapid transport shuttle

V1 It. *Violino primo*, first violin (mus.)

V.O.P. very oldest procurable

VOR very high frequency navigational facility

vorm. Ger. *vormals*, formerly

Vors. Ger. *Vorsitzender*, chairman

VOT Soviet Intelligence Forces Foreign Operational Centre

VOTEM voice-operated typewriter employing morse

vou. voucher

V.O.W. Voice of Women

vox pop. L. *vox populi*, voice of the people

voy. Fr. *voyez*, see

VP *s* Birmingham (B.V.R.); *s* British Colonies and Protectorates (I.C.A.M.)

v.p. vanishing point; vapour pressure; variable pitch; various pagings

V.P. Vice-President/-Principal; victory points

V.P.A. Village Produce Association

v.p.d. variations/vehicles per day

V.P.F.A.S. Vice-President of the Faculty of Architects and Surveyors

V.P.G.S. Vice-President of the Geological Society

v. ph. vertical photography

v.p.h. variation/vehicles per hour

V.-P. Hor. Inst. Vice-President of the Horological Institute

V.P.L.S. Vice-President of the Linnaean Society

v.p.m. vehicles per mile; vendor part modification; volts per mil

v.p.n. vendor part number

Vpo. Valparaiso

V.P.O. Vienna Philharmonic Orchestra

V. Pres. Vice-President

V.P.R.G.S. Vice-President of the Royal Geographical Society

V.P.R.I. Vice-President of the Royal Institute (of Painters in Water-Colours)

V.P.R.S. Vice-President of the Royal Society

v.p.s. vibrations per second; volume pressure setting

V.P.S.A. Vice-President of the Society of Antiquaries

V.P.Z.S. Vice-President of the Zoological Society

VQ *s* British Colonies and Protectorates (I.C.A.M.)

V.Q.M.G. vice-quartermaster-general

VR *s* British Colonies and Protectorates (I.C.A.M.); *s* Manchester (B.V.R.); *Vanguardia Revolucionaria*, Revolutionary Vanguard (Peru); vertical retort, plant for pyrometallurgical smelting of zinc

v.r. variant/various reading; It. *vedi retro*, please turn over; verb reflexive; voltage regulator (elec.); vulcanized rubber

V.R. *Valtionrautatiet*, Finnish State Railways; variety reduction; Vicar Rural; Victoria Reports; volunteer reserve

V.R. L. *Victoria Regina*, Queen Victoria

V.R.A. Vocational Rehabilitation Administration (U.S.A.)

V.R.C. Vehicle Research Corporation; Victoria Racing Club, Melbourne (Aust.); Volunteer Rifle Corps

V.R.D. Royal Naval Volunteer Reserve Decoration

v. refl. verb reflexive

V.R. et I., V.R.I L. *Victoria Regina et Imperatrix*, Victoria Queen and Empress

V. Rev., Vy. Rev. Very Reverend

VRG Varig, Brazilian Airlines, *formerly* PANNAIR

vrg. veering

Vri. Dutch *Vrijdag*, Friday

v.r.i. visual rule instrument landing (aircraft)

V.R.P. Volta River Project

V.R.P. L. *Vestra Reverendissima Paternitas*, Your Most Reverend Paternity

Vry. Viceroy

VS *s* Greenock (B.V.R.); Ger. *Verband Deutscher Schriftsteller*, German Writers' Association

vs., Vs. It. *vostro*, your, yours

vs. L. *versus*, against

vs. L. *vide supra*, see above; L. *volta subito*, turn over quickly

Vs. venesection

v.s. variable speed; It. *vedi sopra*, see above; Fr. *vieux style*, old style

V.S. Venerable Sage (freem.); veterinary surgeon; Virgil Society; It. *Vostra Santità*, Your Holiness

V.S. It. *Volti subito*, turn over quickly (mus.)

V.S^as^ Port. *Vossas Senhorias*, your goodselves

Vs. B. L. *venaesectio brachii*, bleeding in the arm

vsby. visibility

V.S.C. Volunteer Staff Corps

V.S.C.C. Vintage Sports Car Club

VSD vendor's shipping document

v.s.f.f. Port. *volte, se faz favor*, please turn over

VSI. vertical speed indicator (nav.)

V-sign *s* first and middle fingers forming V for victory

V.S.L. venture scout leader

VSM vestigial sideband modulation

VSMF visual search microfilm file

vsn. vision

V.S.O. very superior old; Vienna State Opera; Voluntary Service Overseas

V.S.O.P. very special old pale (Cognac)

V.S.Q. very special quality

V.S.R. very short range; very special reserve

Vst. *Violinist* (mus.)

V/Stol, V/S.T.O.L. vertical and short take-off and landing (aviation)

vsw. vitrified stoneware

V.S.W.R. voltage standing wave ratio (elec.)

VT *s* India (I.C.A.M.); *s* Stoke-on-Trent (B.V.R.); Vermont, *also* Vt. (U.S.A.)

v.t. vacuum technology; variable time/transmission; verb transitive

v. & t. volume and tension (med.)

v.T. Ger. *vom Tausend*, per thousand

V.T. It. *Vecchio Testamento*, Old Testament (Bible)

v^ta^. Sp. *vuelta*, turn

V.T.C. volunteer training corps; voting trust certificate

Vte. Fr. *Vicomte*, Viscount

Vtesse. Fr. *Vicomtesse*, Viscountess

VT fuze variable time fuse (mil.)

vtg. voting

VTL variable threshold logic (computer)

vto. Sp. *vuelto*, change (fin.)

V.T.O. vertical take-off

V.T.O.H.L. vertical take-off and horizontal landing (aircraft)

V.T.O.L. vertical take-off and landing (aircraft)

V.T.O.V.L. vertical take-off vertical landing (aircraft)

V.T.R. video-tape recording, of picture and sound of T.V. programme on magnetic tape

V.T.T.A. Veteran's Time Trial Association (cycling)

VTU volunteer reserve training unit, US Coast Guard

vtvm vacuum tube volt meter

VU *s* Manchester (B.V.R.)

v.u. volume unit; Ger. *von unten*, from the bottom

vul., vulg. vulgar

Vulg. Vulgate, Latin translation of the Bible

v.u.p. very unimportant person

v/v volume/volume; volume per volume

VV *s* Northampton (B.V.R.)

vv. verbs; verses

vv. *violins* (mus.)

v.v. L. *vice versa*, interchanged; L. *viva voce*, spoken aloud

VVD *Volkspartij voor Vrijheid en Democratie*, Liberal Party (Neth.)

vv. ll. L. *variae lectiones*, variant readings

V.V.O. very very old

v.v.v. L. *veni, vidi, vici*, I came, I saw, I conquered, words displayed (probably on a picture) at Caesar's Pontic triumph, 46 B.C., and not, as commonly supposed, a laconic dispatch to the Senate after Zela

VW *s* Essex (B.V.R.); Volkswagen, People's Car manuf. in Ger. (*also*, Volks.)

V.W. Very Worshipful

V.W.G. vibrating wire gauge

V.W.H. Vale of the White Horse

V.W.P.I. Vacuum Wood Preservers' Institute (U.S.A.)

VX *s* Essex (B.V.R.)

Vx. vertex, topmost point

VY *s* York (B.V.R.)

vy. very

v.y. various years (bibliog.)

V.Y. victualling yard

VZ *s* Tyrone (B.V.R.)

W

W It. *Evviva!*, Long Live! Up with; *s* gross weight; *s* prefix to call letters of some radio and television stations (U.S.A.); *s* Sheffield (B.V.R.); *s* very wide; *s* Waterford (Rep. of Ireland F.P.); *s* watt, unit of power (W = J/s); *s* wolfram, tungsten (chem.); *s* work (phys.)

w. waist; wall; war; warm; waste; water; watt (elec.); weather; week; weight; west; western; wet; *s* wet dew (met.); white; wicket (cricket); wide (cricket); width; wife; win; wind; wire; with; woman (size); won; wooden (ship.); word; work; wrong

W. Wales; warden; Dutch, Ger. *Warm*, warm; Waterloo (mil.); Wednesday; Welch; Welsh; Wesleyan; West; Dutch, Ger. *West*, west; westerly; Western postal district (Lond.); widow; widower; William

WA *s* Sheffield (B.V.R.); *s* Whitehaven (B.F.P.)

5WA *s* Cardiff (radio call-sign)

WA., Wa. Washington, state and city (U.S.A.)

W.A. Watchmen's Association (U.S.A.); Welfare Administration (U.S.A.); West Africa/African; West/Western Australia; Western Approaches (to Britain); Westminster Abbey; wing attack (netball); Wire Association (U.S.A.); *World Almanac and Book of Facts* (U.S.A.)

W. & A. Wight and Arnott (bot.)

W.A.A. War Assets Administration (U.S.A.); Wardens' Association of America; Western Amateur Astronomers; Women's Auxiliary Association

W.A.A.A. Women's Amateur Athletic Association

W.A.A.A.F. Women's Auxiliary Australian Air Force, *now* W.R.A.A.F.

W.A.A.C. War Artists' Advisory Committee; Women's Army Auxiliary Corps, *now* W.R.A.C.

WAADS Washington Air Defense Sector (U.S.A.)

W.A.A.E. World Association for Adult Education

W.A.A.F. Women's Auxiliary Air Force, *now* W.R.A.F.

W.A.A.S. Women's Auxiliary Army Service; World Academy of Art and Science

W.A.B. Wage Adjustment Board (U.S.A.); Wire Advisory Board (U.S.A.)

W.A.B.A. Welsh Amateur Basketball Association

W.A.C. Wake Analysis and Control; Women's Advisory Committee (B.S.I.); Women's Army Corps, *also* Wac. (U.S.A.); World Aeronautical Chart

W.A.C.A. *West Africa Court of Appeal Reports*

W.A.C.B. World Association for Christian Broadcasting

WACCC Worldwide Air Cargo Commodity Classification (I.A.T.A.)

W.A.C.I. Women's Army Corps of India

W.A.C.R.I. West African Cocoa Research Institute

W.A.C.S.M. Women's Army Corps Service Medal

Wad., Wadh. Wadham College, Oxford, founded 1612

368

WADC Wright Air Development Center (U.S.A.)

WADD Wright Air Development Division (U.S.A.)

WADEX, Wadex word and author index

WADF Western Air Defense (U.S.A.)

WADS wide area data service

w.a.e. when actually employed

W.A.E.C. War Agricultural Executive Committee

W.A.F. West African Forces; with all faults (*also* w.i.f.); Women in the Air Force (U.S.A.)

W.A.F.C. West African Fisheries Commission (FAO)

W.A.F.F. West African Frontier Force

WAFFLE wide angle fixed field locating equipment

W. Afr. West Africa/African; — **R.** West African Regiment

W.A.F.S. Women's Auxiliary Ferrying Squadron (U.S.A.); Women's Auxiliary Fire Service

WAG *s* Gambia (I.V.R.); Writers' Action Group

W.A.G.B.I. Wildfowlers' Association of Great Britain & Ireland

W.A.G.G.G.S. World Association of Girl Guides and Girl Scouts

W.A.G.R. Western Australian Government Railways; Windscale advanced gas-cooled reactor

W.A.I.F. World Adoption International Fund

W.A.I.S. Wechsler's adult intelligence scale (psy.)

W.A.I.T.R. West African Institute for Trypanosomiasis Research

Wal Wallace; Walter

WAL *s* Sierra Leone (I.V.R.); Western Airlines; Westland Aircraft Limited

Wal., Wall. Walloon, Romance dialect spoken in provinces of Liège, Luxembourg, Namur, Hainaut and part of Brabant

W.A.L.A. West African Library Association

WALIC Wiltshire Association of Libraries of Industry and Commerce

Wall. London Wall; *Wallace, US Supreme Court Reports*

Wally Wallace; Walter

W.A.L.R. *Western Australia Law Reports*

Walt Walter

W.A.M. wife and mother; *Wiltshire Archaeological Magazine*; words a minute; work analysis and measurement; Working Association of Mothers

W.A.M.R.A.C. World Association of Methodist Radio Amateurs and Clubs

W.A.M.R.U. West African Maize Research Unit

WAN *s* Nigeria (I.V.R.)

Wand. Wanderers (football)

WANDPETLS Wandsworth Public Educational and Technical Library Services

W.A.N.S. Women's Australian National Service

W.A.O.S. Welsh Agricultural Organization Society

WAP work assignment plan/procedure

W.A.P.C. Women's Auxiliary Police Corps

W.A.P.D.A. Water and Power Development Authority (Pak.)

W.A.P.O.R. World Association for Public Opinion Research

W.A.P.T. Wild Animal Propagation Trust

war. warrant

War. Warsaw; Warwickshire, *also* Warw., Warwicks.

W.A.R. West Africa Regiment

W.A.R.C. Western Air Rescue Center (U.S.A.); World Administrative Radio Conference, held in 1967 to allocate frequencies

W.A.R.I. Waite Agricultural Research Institute (Aust.)

warn. warning

warr. warranty

W.A.R.R.S. West African Rice Research Station

W.A.S.A. Welsh Amateur Swimming Association

Wash. Washington, state and city (U.S.A.); Washingtonian

Wash. Pst. *Washington Post* (U.S.A.)

wasn't was not

W.A.S.P. White Anglo-Saxon Protestant (U.S.A.); Women Auxiliary Service Pilots (U.S.A.)

Wass. Wassermann test of blood originated by August von Wassermann (1866–1925), Ger. bacteriologist and immunologist, for detection of syphilis

W.A.S.T. Western Australia Standard Time

W.A.S.U. West African Students' Union

Wat, Wattie, Watty Walter

Wat. Waterford

W.A.T. weight, altitude and temperature; word association test (psy.)

W.A.T.A. World Association of Travel Agencies

W.A.T.C. West Australian Turf Club

WATS Wide Area Telephone Service

W. Aus., W. Aust. Western Australia

W. Aust. Cur. West Australian Current

W.A.V.E.S. Women Accepted for Volunteer Emergency Service (U.S.A.)

Wavy Navy Royal Naval Volunteer Reserve, WW2 slang, from wavy braid rank bands

W.A.W.F. World Association of World Federalists

W.A.Y. World Assembly of Youth

W.A.Y.C. Welsh Association of Youth Clubs

Wb weber, unit of magnetic flux

WB s Sheffield (B.V.R.); weekly benefits (insce.)

w.b. wage board; waste/water ballast; wave band; west bound; wheel base; wool back

W/B., w.b., W.B. way bill

W.B. warehouse book (*also* W/B); Warner Brothers Pictures Incorporated; washable base; water board; weather bureau; wet bulb; World Bank for Reconstruction and Development (U.N.); World Brotherhood

W.B.A. West Bromwich Albion Football Club; World Boxing Association of America

WBAFC Weather Bureau Area Forecast Center (U.S.A.)

WBAN Weather Bureau, Air Force and Navy (U.S.A.)

W.B.B.G. Ger. *Weltbund der Bibelgesellschaften*, United Bible Socs.

W.B.C. white blood cell/corpuscle/count; World Boxing Council

WBGT wet bulb globe temperature/thermometer

W.B.H. Welsh Board of Health

w.b.i. will be issued

WBIT Wechsler-Bellevue intelligence test (psy.)

Wbl. Ger. *Wochenblatt*, weekly publication

WBMA Wirebound Box Manufacturers' Association (U.S.A.)

W.b.N. west by north

w.b.p. weather and boil proof

w.b.s. walking beam suspension; without benefit of salvage (insce.); work breakdown structure

W.b.S. west by south

W.B.T. wet bulb temperature

W. By. Walvis Bay

WC s Essex (B.V.R.)

W/C wing commander, *also* W. Cdr., W. Comm.

w.c. walking club; watch committee; water closet/cock; wheel chair; without charge

W.C. war cabinet/communications/council/credits; Wesleyan chapel; Western Central, postal district (Lond.); Western

Command; Whitley Council; working capital; workmen's circle/compensation

W.C.A. west coast of Africa; Wholesale Confectioners' Alliance; Women's Christian/Citizens' Association; Workmen's Compensation Act; World Calendar Association

W.C.A.T. Welsh College of Advanced Technology

W.C.C. War Crimes Commission; White Citizens' Council (U.S.A.); World Council of Churches

W.C.C.E.S.S.A. World Council of Christian Education and Sunday School Association

W.C.E.U. World's Christian Endeavour Union

W.C.F. World Congress of Faiths

W.C.M.A. Wiping Cloth Manufacturers' Association

W.C.O.T.P. World Confederation of Organisations of the Teaching Profession

WCP World Council of Peace

W.C.P.T. World Confederation for Physical Therapy

W.C.R.A. Weather Control Research Association (U.S.A.); Women's Cycle Racing Association

W.C.R. (N.S.W.) *Workers' Compensation Reports*, New South Wales (Aust.)

WCT World Championship Tennis

W.C.T.U. Women's Christian Temperance Union

W.C.W.B. World Council for the Welfare of the Blind

WD s Dominica, Windward Islands (I.V.R.); s Warwickshire (B.V.R.); s Wexford (Rep. of Ireland F.P.)

wd. ward; warranted; weed; wood; word; would; wound

w/d. well developed

W/D. wind direction

W.D. war/water department; wife's divorce (leg.); wing defence (netball); works department

W.D.A. writing down allowance (tax.)

W.D.C. War Damage Commission/Contribution; Women's Diocesan Association; World Data Centre, centre 'A' is in Washington, 'B' in Moscow

w.d.f. wood door and frame

wdg. winding

W.D.M. weapon delivery model

WDPC Western Data Processing Center (U.S.A.)

Wdr. wardmaster; — L. wardmaster lieutenant

wd. sc. wood screw

wdt. width

W.D.V. written down value (tax.)

WE s Sheffield (B.V.R.)

We., Wed., Wednes. Wednesday

w.e. watch error; week end; white edge

W.E. War Establishment

wea. weapon; weather

W.E.A. Royal West of England Academy; Workers' Educational Association founded by Albert Mansbridge, 1903; World Expeditionary Association

WEAAC Western European Airports Association Conference

WEARCON weather observation and forecasting control system

weat. weathertight

WECOM weapons command (U.S.A.)

we'd we had; we should; we would

Wed. Dutch *Weduwe*, widow

W.E.D.A. Wholesale Engineering Distributors' Association

Wedy. Wednesday

w.e.f. war emergency formula; with effect from

W.E. & F.A. Welsh Engineers' and Founders' Association

W.E.F.C. West European Fisheries Conference

w.e.f.t. wings, engine, fuselage, tail

w.e.g. war emergency grant

W.E.I.A. wife's earned income allowance (tax.)

W.E.I.R. wife's earned income relief (tax.)

Wel. Welsh

Wel. Adm. welfare administration

Wel. Can. Welland Canal

weld. welding

Wel. Dept. welfare department

we'll we shall; we will

Well. Wellington

wellies Wellington boots

W.E.M.A. Western Electronics Manufacturers' Association (U.S.A.); Winding Engine Manufacturers' Association

WEP water extended polyester

we're we are

weren't were not

Wes. Wesleyan

W.E.S. war equipment scale; waterways experiment station; Women's Engineering Society; World Economic Survey

WESCON Western Electronics Show and Convention

WESO Weapons Engineering Standardization Office (USN)

West. western

Westm. Westmeath; Westminster (*also* Westmr.); Westmorland, *also* Westmd.

Wes. Univ. Wesleyan University

W.E.T.U.C. Workers' Educational Trade Union Committee

W.E.U. Western European Union

we've we have

Wex., Wexf. Wexford

WEZ Ger. *Westeuropäische Zeit*, Western European time (Greenwich time)

WF *s* Yorkshire (B.V.R.)

w.f. wrong fount (typ.)

W.F. Wells Fargo and Company (U.S.A.); White Fathers; wing forward

W.F.A. White Fish Authority; Women's Football Association; World Friendship Association

w factor will factor (psy.)

W.F.A.L.W. Ger. *Weltbund Freiheitlicher Arbeitnehmerverbände auf Liberaler Wirtschaftsgrundlage*, World Union of Liberal Trade Union Organisations

W.F.B. World Fellowship of Buddhists

W.F.B.M.A. Woven Fabric Belting Manufacturers' Association

W.F.C.Y.W.G. World Federation of Catholic Young Women and Girls

w.fd., w.fwd., wl.fwd. wool forward (knit.)

W.F.D. World Federation of the Deaf

W.F.D.A. Wholesale Floorcovering/Footwear Distributors' Association

W.F.D.Y. World Federation of Democratic Youth

w.f.e. with food element

WFEO World Federation of Engineering Organizations

W.F.F. World Friendship Federation

W.F.G.A. Women's Farm and Garden Association

wfl. worshipful

W.F.L. Women's Freedom League

W.F.M.H. World Federation for Mental Health

W.F.M.W. World Federation of Methodist Women

W.F.N. World Federation of Neurology

W.F.O.T. World Federation of Occupational Therapists

W.F.P. World Food Programme (FAO)

W.F.P.A. World Federation for the Protection of Animals

W. Fris. West Frisian

W.F.S.A. World Federation of Societies of Anaesthesiologists

W.F.S.W. World Federation of Scientific Workers

W.F.T.U. World Federation of Trade Unions

W.F.U.N.A. World Federation of United Nations Associations

W.F.W. Ger. *Weltföderation der Wissenschaftler*, World Fed. of Scientific Workers

WG *s* Grenada, Windward Islands (I.V.R.); *s* Stirlingshire (B.V.R.)

wg. weighing; wing

w.g. water gauge; weight guaranteed; wire gauge

W.G. Welsh Guards; West German/Germanic; W.G. Grace (1848–1915), Eng. cricketer and doctor; *The Westminster Gazette*

W.G.A. Writers' Guild of America

W.G.B. Ger. *Weltgewerkschaftsbund*, World Fed. of Trade Unions

W.G.C. Welwyn Garden City; worthy grand chaplain (freem.); worthy grand conductor

Wg.-Comdr. wing-commander

W. Ger. West German/Germanic, *also* W. Gmc.

W.G.F. Women's Gas Federation

W.G.G. worthy grand guardian/guide (freem.)

W.G.H. Warren G. Harding, pres. of U.S.A. 1921–3; worthy grand herald

W.G.I. World Geophysical Interval

w. gl. wired glass

W.G.M. worthy grand master

WGPMS warehouse gross performance measurement system

W. Grnld. Cur. West Greenland Current

W.G.S. worthy grand sentinel (freem.)

W.G.U. Welsh Golfing Union

w/h with holding

WH s Bolton (B.V.R.); s Weymouth (B.F.P.)

wh. wharf; which; whispered; white

Wh. Watt hour (elec.)

WH. wheelers (cycling)

W.H. water heater; White House; wing half

W.H.A. Welsh Hockey Association; World Health Assembly (W.H.O.)

W'hampton Wolverhampton

whate'er whatever

what's what has; what is

whatsoe'er whatsoever

whd. warhead

whene'er whenever

where'er wherever

wheresoe'er wheresoever

Wh. Ex. Whitworth Exhibitioner

whf. wharf

whfg. wharfage

whfr. wharfinger

W.H.H. William H. Harrison, pres. of U.S.A. 1841

W.H.H.A. White House Historical Association

Whi. Whitehall (Lond.)

whis. whistle

Whitaker *Whitaker's Almanack*

W.H.M.A. Women's Home Missionary Association

whmstr. weighmaster

W.H.O., WHO White House Office;

World Health Organisation, specialized agency of UNO *estab.* 1948 to raise health standards

who'd who had

W.H.O.I. Woods Hole Oceanographic Institution (U.S.A.)

who'll who shall; who will

who's who is

w.h.p. water horse power

wh. pl. whole plate (jewellery)

whr. watt hour (elec.); whether

WHRA World Health Research Centre

W.H.R.A. Welwyn Hall Research Association

whs., whse. warehouse

whsl., whsle. wholesale

whsmn. warehouse man

whsng. warehousing

whs. rec. warehouse receipt

w.h.y. what have you?

WI s Waterford (Rep. of Ireland V.R.); s Wisbech (B.F.P.); Wisconsin

w.i. when issued (fin.); wrought iron

w. & i. weighing and inspection

W.I. West India/Indian/Indies; Windward Islands; Women's Institute, *also* W. Inst.

w.i.a. wounded in action

W.I.B. *Werkgroep Instrument Beoordeling*, Working Group on Instrument Behaviour (Neth.); Ger. *Wissenschaftliche Internationale Bibliographie*, International Scientific Bibliography

WIC West India Committee

Wich. Wichuraiana (rose)

Wick. Wicklow

wid. widow; widower

W.I.D. West India Docks (Lond.)

W.I.D.F. Women's International Democratic Federation

W.I.F. West Indies Federation

Wig. Wigtown (Scot.)

Wigorn. L. *Wigorniensis*, of Worcester, Eng. episcopal title, in bishop's signature

w.i.h. went in hole

Wil Wilber; Wilbur; Wilfred, *also* Wilf

WILCO will comply

Will Wilfred; Willard; William; Willis

Willa, Wilma Wilhelmina

Willie, Willy William

W.I.L.P.F. Women's International League for Peace and Freedom

Wilts. Wiltshire

Wilts. R. Wiltshire Regiment

Wimb. Wimborne (Dorset)

win'ard windward

Winch. Winchester

W. Ind. West Indies

Wind. I. Windward Islands

WINE Webb Institute of Naval Engineering (U.S.A.)

Wing Cdr. wing commander

Winn. Winnipeg (Can.)

Winnie Winifred

W.I.N.S. Women's Industrial and National Service Corps

Winton. L. *Wintoniensis*, of Winchester, Eng. episcopal title, in signature of bishop, who is also Prelate of the Order of the Garter

Wint. T. *The Winter's Tale* (Shake.)

w.i.p. work in process/progress

W.I.P.O. World Intellectual Property Organization, *successor* to B.I.R.P.I.

W.I.R. *West Indian Reports*; West India Regiment

W.I.R.A., Wira Wool Industries Research Association

WIRDS weather information reporting and display system

Wis., Wisc. Wisconsin

WISA West Indies Students'/Sugar Association

W.I.S.C. Wechsler's Intelligence Scale for Children (psy.); West Indian Standing Conference

WISCo West Indies Sugar Company

Wisd. Wisdom, Book of (Apocrypha; R.C. canonical)

WISP wide range imaging spectrometer

wit witness

W.I.T.B. Wool, Jute and Flax Industry Training Board, *also* WJFITB

withdrl. withdrawal

witht. without

WITS Westinghouse interactive time-sharing system

Wits. Witwatersrand

W.I.V.A.B. Women's Inter-Varsity Athletic Board

Wiz. wizard

W.I.Z.O. Women's International Zionist Organisation

WJ *s* Sheffield (B.V.R.)

W.J.C. World Jewish Congress

W.J.C.B. World Jersey Cattle Bureau

WJCC Western Joint Computer Conference (U.S.A.)

W.J.E.C. Welsh Joint Education Committee

w.j.s. wife's judicial separation (leg.)

Wk Walk (street directory)

WK *s* Coventry (B.V.R.); *s* Wick (B.F.P.)

wk. weak; week; work; wreck

w.k. warehouse keeper; well-known

wkds. week days

wkg. working

wkly. weekly

wkr. worker; wrecker

wks. works; workshop

wkt. wicket (cricket)

wk. vb. weak verb

WL *s* Oxford (B.V.R.); *s* St. Lucia, Windward Islands (I.V.R.)

Wl. wool

W.L. Fr. *Wagon-lit*, sleeping car; Waiting List; Water Line; wave-length (*also* W/L); West Lothian, *also* W. Loth. (Scot.); Women's Liberation (movement)

W. & L. Washington and Lee University (U.S.A.)

W.L.A. Women's Land Army

W.L.B. War Labor Board (U.S.A.)

wl. coef. waterline coefficient

wld. would

W.L.D. war load displacement

Wld. Ch. World Championship

wldr. welder

W.L.F. Women's Liberal Federation

wl. fwd. wool forward (knit.)

W.L.G.S. Women's Local Government Society

W.L.H.B. Women's League of Health and Beauty, founded 1930 by Mrs. Bagot Stack

W.L.L.A. Welsh Ladies' Lacrosse Association

Wln. Wellington (N.Z.)

W. lon., W. long. west longitude

W'loo Waterloo

W.L.P.S.A. Wild Life Preservation Society of Australia

Wlr. Walter

W.L.R. *Weekly Law Reports*

W.L.R.I. World Life Research Institute

W.L.T.B.U. Watermen, Lightermen, Tugmen and Bargemen's Union

W.L.U. World Liberal Union

W.L.U.S. World Land Use Survey

wly. westerly

wlz. waltz

WM *s* Southport (B.V.R.); war memorial

Wm. William

W.M. watt/wave meter; white metal; wire mesh; Worshipful Master (freem.)

W. & M. King William and Queen Mary

W.M.A. Webbing Manufacturers' Association; Workers' Music Association; World Medical Association

WMAA Whitney Museum of American Art

WMATC Washington Metropolitan Area Transit Commission (U.S.A.)

W.M.C. War Manpower Commission; Ways and Means Committee; World Methodist Council; Working Men's Club/College

373

W.M.C.I.U. Working Men's Club and Institute Union Limited

Wmd. Willemstad (Neth. Antilles)

w. midl. west midland

W/m°K watt per metre degree Kelvin, unit of thermal conductivity

W/m²°K unit of heat transfer coefficient

wmk. watermark

W.M.M. World Movement of Mothers

W.M.M.A. Woodworking Machinery Manufacturers' Association

W.M.O. World Meteorological Organization, founded in 1951 to succeed the I.M.O. which was founded in 1878 for voluntary exchange of vital weather data

W.M.O.A.S. Women's Migration and Overseas Appointments Society

W.M.P. with much pleasure

W.M.S. Wesleyan Missionary Society; World Magnetic Survey

W.M.T.C. Women's Mechanized Transport Corps

WN s Swansea (B.V.R.); s Wigtown (B.F.P.)

Wn. Washington (U.S.A.); Wisconsin (U.S.A.)

WNCCC Women's National Cancer Control Campaign

w.n.d.p. with no down payment

W.N.E. Welsh National Eisteddfod

W.N.L. within normal limits

W.N.L.F. Women's National Liberal Federation

W.N. (N.S.W.) *Weekly Notes*, New South Wales (Aust.)

W.N.P. Welsh Nationalist Party

WNRE Whiteshell Nuclear Research Establishment (Can.)

WNSB White Nile Scheme Board, cotton production (Sudan)

W.N.W. west-north-west

WO s Monmouthshire (B.V.R.); s Workington (B.F.P.)

wo. Ger. *wie oben*, as mentioned earlier

w/o. without

W.O. walk-over, no competition; War Office; warrant officer; welfare officer (*also*, W/offr.); wireless operator; written order

W.O.A. Wharf Owners' Association

w.o.b. washed overboard

w.o.c. without compensation

W.O.C.C.I. War Office Central Card Index

WOCG weather outline contour generator

W.O.C.L. War Office Casualty List

WODA World Dredging Association

WODCON World Dredging Conference

Woe. Dutch *Woensdag*, Wednesday

w.o.e. without equipment

'wog golliwog

w.o.g. water, oil or gas; with other goods

w.o.l. wharf-owner's liability

W.O.L. War Office Letter; wedge-opening loaded/loading

Wolfs. Wolfson College, Oxford, founded 1965

Wolves Wolverhampton Wanderers football club

Wom. Woomera, tracking station (Aust.)

W.O.M. Wireless Operator Mechanic

WOMAN World Organization for Mothers of All Nations

Women's Lib Women's Liberation (movement)

w.o.n. wool on needle (knit.)

won't will not

WOO western operations office (NASA)

W.O.O. Warrant Ordnance Officer (naval); World Oceanographic Organisation

w.o.o.o.l. words out of ordinary language

w.o.p. with other property; without personnel

w.o.p.e. without personnel or equipment

Wor. Worshipful

W.O.R. without our responsibility

WORC Washington Operations Research Council (U.S.A.)

Worc. Worcester College, Oxford, founded 1714

Worc. R. Worcestershire Regiment

WORCRA process for smelting iron, copper, tin and nickel based on counter-current flows of metal and slag, inventor Dr. H. K. *Worner* and co. *CRA*

Worcs. Worcestershire

Words., Wordsw. William Wordsworth (1770–1850), Eng. poet

workh. workhouse

WORSE word selection

W.O.S. Western Orchestral Society Limited

wosac worldwide synchronization of atomic clocks

W.O.S.B. War Office selection board

WOSD weapons operational systems development

w.o.t. wide open throttle

Wotag Women's Taxation Action Group

wouldn't would not

W.O.W. waiting on weather; women ordnance workers; Woodmen of the World (U.S.A.)

WP *s* Worcestershire (B.V.R.)

Wp. Worship; Worshipful

w.p. waste paper/pipe; weather permitting; will proceed; working paper/party/point/pressure

W.P. Western Province (S.A.); West Point; White Paper; Without prejudice, *also* w/p. (insce.); Worthy Patriarch (freem.); Worthy President

W.P.A. Water Polo Association; Western Providence Association; Wire Products Association; with particular average (insce.); Works Progress/Projects Administration (U.S.A.), begun in 1935 to provide work for needy unemployed; World Parliament Association; World Presbyterian Alliance

w.p.b. waste paper basket

W.P.B. War Production Board, WW2

W.P.B.S. Welsh Plant Breeding Station

W.P.C. war pension(s) committee; woman police constable; word plastic combination/composite; World Petroleum Congress; World Power Conference, *now* World Energy Conference

W.P.C.A. Water Pollution Control Administration (U.S.A.)

W.P.C.F. Water Pollution Control Federation (U.S.A.)

W.P.E. white porcelain enamel

W.P.F. World Prohibition Federation

W.P.F.C. West Pacific Fisheries Commission

Wpfl. Worshipful

W.P.F.L. West Pakistan Federation of Labour

wpg. water proofing

W.P.H.C. Western Pacific High Commission

W.P.I. World Press Institute

W.P.I.D.C. West Pakistan Industrial Development Corporation

wpl warning point level

W.P.L.A. West Pakistan Library Association

w.p.m. words per minute

wpn. weapon

W.P.N. *World's Press News*

W.P.O. Ger. *Wiener Philharmonische Orchester*, Vienna Philharmonic Orchestra; World Ploughing Organisation

W.P.R.A. Wallpaper and Paint Retailers' Association of Great Britain; Waste Paper Recovery Association

W.P.R.L. Water Pollution Research Laboratory

w.p.s. with prior service

W.P.S.A., W.P.Sc.A. World's Poultry Science Association

WR *s* Yorkshire, WR (B.V.R.)

Wr. Walter

w.r. war risk; water repellent

W.R. ward room; war reserve; Wassermann Reaction; Western Region (rail.); West Riding, Yorks

W.R. L. *Willelmus Rex*, King William

W.R.A. Water Research Association; Wisley Rose Award (hort.)

W.R.A.A.C. Women's Royal Australian Army Corps

W.R.A.A.F. Women's Royal Australian Air Force

W.R.A.C. Women's Royal Army Corps, *formerly* W.A.A.C.

W.R.A.F. Women's Royal Air Force, *formerly* W.A.A.F.

WRAMA Warner Robbins Air Materiel Area

wrang. wrangler

W.R.A.N.S. Women's Royal Australian Naval Service

WRAP weapons readiness analysis program (U.S.A.)

W.R.C. water-retention coefficient; Welding Research Council (U.S.A.)

W.R.C.R. wife's (suit for) restitution of conjugal rights (leg.)

W.R.E. Weapons Research Establishment (Aust.)

w. ref. with reference (to)

w. reg. with regard (to)

W.R.I. War Resisters International; war risks insurance; Women's Rural Institute

w.r.n. wool round needle (knit.)

W.R.N.L.R. *Western Region of Nigeria Law Reports*

W.R.N.R. Women's Royal Naval Reserve

W.R.N.S. Women's Royal Naval Service, *known as* Wrens

wrnt. warrant

w.r.o. war risks only (insce.)

W.R.O. Weed Research Organization (A.R.C.)

W.R.R.A. Women's Road Records Association (cycling)

WRSIC Water Resources Scientific Information Center (U.S.A.)

wrt. wrought (iron)

W.R.U. Welsh Rugby Union; Wesleyan Reform Union

W.R.V.S. Women's Royal Voluntary Service

W.R.Y. World Refugee Year

WS *s* Edinburgh (B.V.R.); *s* Western Samoa (I.V.R.)

w. & s. whisky and soda

W.S. Wallops Station (NASA); war scale/substantive; *Washington Star* (U.S.A.); water soluble; weapon system; West Saxon; Writer to the Signet, attorney (Scot.)

W.S.A. war shipping administration; Weed Society of America
W.S.A.C. West of Scotland Agricultural College
W. Sam. Western Samoa
W.S.C.F. World Student Christian Federation
w.s.d. working stress design
W.S.E. Washington/Western Society of Engineers (U.S.A.); west-south-east
WSEC Washington State Electronics Council (U.S.A.)
WSED weapons systems evaluation division
WSEG weapons systems evaluation group
WSI Writers and Scholars International
WSJ *Wall St Journal* (U.S.A.)
WSL Warren Spring Laboratory
W.S.M. Women's Suffrage Movement
WSMR White Sands Missile Range (US Army)
W.S.O.C. Wider Share Ownership Council
w.s.p. water supply point
WSPACS weapon system programming and control system
W.S.P.U. Women's Social and Political Union
W.S.S.A. Welsh Secondary Schools Association
W.S.W. west-south-west
WT *s* Westport (Irish Rep. F.P.); *s* Yorkshire, WR (B.V.R.)
W/T wireless telegraphy
wt. warrant; weight; without
w.t. watertight
W.T. *The Winter's Tale* (Shake.); warrant telegraphist (naval); war transport; watch time; wireless technology/telegraphy/telephony; withholding tax
W. & T. wear and tear (tax.)
W.T.A. World Transport Agency
W.T.A.A. World Trade Alliance Association
W.T.A.U. Women's Total Abstinence Union
Wtb. Ger. *Wörterbuch*, dictionary
W.T.B.A. Water-Tube Boilermakers' Association
W.T.C. Women's Timber Corps
wtd watertight door
W.T.D. war trade department; wool textile delegation
Wtf. Water ford
W.T.G. Ger. *Welt-Tierärztegesellschaft*, World Veterinary Assn.
wthr. weather
WTIS World Trade Information Service
W.T.M.H. watertight manhole

W.T.O. Warsaw Treaty Organization
W.T.P. weapons testing program (U.S.A.); World Tape Pals
wtr. winter; writer
W.T.R. Western test range (U.S.A.)
W.T.R.C. Wool Textile Research Council
W.T.S. Women's Transport Service
W.T.T.A. Wholesale Tobacco Trade Association of Great Britain and Northern Ireland
W.T.U.C. World Trade Union Conference
WU *s* Yorkshire, WR (B.V.R.)
W.U. Western Union
W.U.A. Western Underwriters' Association (U.S.A.)
W.U.C.T. World Union of Catholic Teachers
W.U.C.W.O. World Union of Catholic Women's Organisations
W.U.F. World Underwater Federation; World Union of Freethinkers
W.U.J.S. World Union of Jewish Students
W.U.L.T.U.O. World Union of Liberal Trade Union Organisations
W.U.P.J. World Union for Progressive Judaism
W.U.R. World University Round Table
W.U.S. World University Service
W.U.S.L. Women's United Service League
w/v weigh in volume; weight/volume
WV *s* St. Vincent, Windward Islands (I.V.R.); *s* Wiltshire (B.V.R.)
w.v. water valve
W. Va. West Virginia, *also* WV (U.S.A.)
W.V.A. World Veterinary Association
wvd. waived
W.V.D. Dutch. *Wereldverbond van Diamant bewerkers*, Universal Alliance of Diamond Workers
W.V.F. World Veterans' Federation
W.V.P.A. World Veterinary Poultry Association
W.V.S. Women's Voluntary Services, *now* W.R.V.S.
wvt water vapour transfer/transmission
wvtr water vapour transmission rate
w/w weight for weight; weight/weight
WW *s* Yorkshire, WR (B.V.R.)
WW1 world war one, 1914–18; — **2** world war two, 1939–45
Ww., Wwe. Ger. *Witwe*, widow
W.W. Warehouse Warrant (*also* W/W); warrant writer; *Who's Who*; world wide

W.W.C.P. Walking Wounded Collecting Post

W.W.C.T.U. World's Women's Christian Temperance Union

W.W.D.C. World War Debt Commission

W. Wdr. warrant wardmaster

W.W.D.S.H.E.X. Weather Working Days Sundays & Holidays Excluded

W.W.F. World Wildlife Fund

W.W.L.A. West Women's Lacrosse Association

W.W.O. wing warrant officer

W.W.R. *Western Weekly Reports*

W. W. Raised engraver's initials raised on truncation (numis.)

WWSSN world wide standard seismograph network

W.W.S.U. World Water Ski Union

ww tyres white wall tyres

W.W.W. *Who Was Who*; world weather watch (WMO)

W.W.Y. Queen's Own Warwickshire and Worcestershire Yeomanry

WX *s* Yorkshire, WR (B.V.R.)

W.X. women's extra (size)

wxy. warning

WY *s* Whitby (B.F.P.); *s* Yorkshire, WR (B.V.R.)

Wycl., Wy. Wycliffe

Wyo., WY Wyoming

W.Y.R. West Yorkshire Regiment

WZ *s* Belfast (B.V.R.)

W.Z. Ger. *Weltzeit*, universal time

W.Z.O. World Zionist Organization

X

x   *s* mechanical defect; ten (Roman)
x   *s* multiplication (math.); *s* unknown
quantity (math.)
X   *s* Christ/Christian from Gk *X* chi;
s on a map/diagram to mark the location/
position of a point; *s* beer strength; *s* cross,
St Andrew's; *s* Cross (King's X, etc.);
s films to which persons under 16 years
are not admitted; *s* his/her mark; *s* hoar-
frost (met.); *s* a kiss; *s* Northumberland
(B.V.R.); *s* reactance; ten (Roman);
s xylonite
x.   ex. (com.); extra
X.   *s* experiment; explosive; extension
XA   *s* Mexico (I.C.A.M.)
x.a.   ex all (fin.)
XACT   X (unnamed computer) automatic code translation
xan.   xanthic; xanthene
Xan.   Xanthus, anct. city of Lycia
x. arm   cross arm
X-axis   horizontal axis
XB   *s* Mexico (I.C.A.M.)
Xber.   December
Xbre., xbre.   Fr. *décembre*, December
XBT   expendable bathythermograph
xbt.   exhibit
XC   *s* Mexico (I.C.A.M.); ninety
(Roman)
x.c.   ex capitalization (fin.); ex (i.e.
without) coupon (fin.)
XCIX   ninety-nine (Roman)
x.c.l.   excess current liabilities
xcp., x.cp., x/cp.   ex coupon
xcpt.   except
x. cut   cross cut
x.cy.   cross country

x.d., x/d, X.D., x.div.   ex dividend, not
including right to dividend
x.'d.   executed
x'd. out   crossed out, word or lines
obliterated by typing xxx
x.dr.   ex drawings (fin.)
Xdr.   crusader
Xe   *s* xenon (chem.)
X.E.   experimental engine
Xen.   Xenophon (*c* 430–*c* 356 B.C.),
Greek historian
Xer.   Xerox reproduction
x.f.   *s* extra fine
xfa.   cross fired acceleration
xfer.   transfer
xfmr., x former   transformer
XG   *s* Middlesbrough (B.V.R.)
xg.   crossing
xgam.   experimental guided air missile
XH   *s* Honduras (I.C.A.M.); *s* London
(B.V.R.); *s* experimental helicopter (naval)
x-height   term used to describe the
average depth of lower case letters in a
fount of type, if projecting stems, ascen-
ders of letters, and the tails, descenders of
letters, are disregarded (typ.)
XHMO   extended huckel molecular
orbit
xhst.   exhaust
x.hvy.   extra heavy
XI   *s* Belfast (B.V.R.)
x.i.   ex (without) interest (fin.)
XJ   *s* Manchester (B.V.R.)
XK   *s* London (B.V.R.)
XL   extra large; forty (Roman); *s*
London (B.V.R.)
xl. & ul.   exclusive of loading and un-
loading

xlnt., x/nt. excellent
xlwb, x/wb. extra long wheelbase
XM *s* London (B.V.R.)
Xm. Christmas
X.M. experimental missile
Xmas. Christmas
xmfr. transformer
xmit. transmit
xmsn. transmission
xmtr. transmitter
XN *s* London (B.V.R.) •
Xn. Christian
x.n. ex new, without right to new shares (fin.)
X.-note US $10 note
Xnty. Christianity
XO *s* London (B.V.R.)
x.o. examination executive officer
X-O test test for investigation of emotional attitudes in which the subject is required to cross out certain words and, repeating the test, circle one word in each line (psy.)
x. out cross out, delete
XP *s* London (B.V.R.); monogram used to represent Christ/Christianity, composed of chi and rho, the first two letters of Greek word for Christ
x.p. express paid
xpl. explosive
xplt. exploit
xpn. expansion
Xpo. Sp. *Christo*, Christ
x.p.p. Fr. *exprès payé lettre*, express paid letter
x.p.t. Fr. *exprès payé télégraphe*, express paid telegraph
Xpt. Sp. *Christobal*, Christopher
x.q. cross question
XR *s* London (B.V.R.)
x.r. ex rights (fin.)

Xr. Christopher; examiner
X.R. External Relations Service (U.N.E.S.C.O.)
X.rds., x. roads cross roads
x. ref. cross reference
x.rts. without rights (fin.)
XS *s* Paisley (B.V.R.)
xs. expenses
XT *s* China, Nationalist (I.C.A.M.); *s* London (B.V.R.)
Xt. Christ
xtal. crystal
Xth. tenth
Xtian. Christian
xtra extra
xtran. experimental language (computer)
xtry. extraordinary
Xty. Christianity
XU *s* London (B.V.R.)
XUV extreme ultra violet
XV *s* London (B.V.R.)
XW *s* London (B.V.R.)
x.w. ex warrants (fin.)
XX *s* ale of double strength; *s* London (B.V.R.); *s* retree (paper); twenty (Roman)
5XX *s* Chelmsford (radio call-sign)
XX.-note US $20 note
xxri 1881 error in date, correct is xxxi (numis.)
XXX *s* ale of triple strength; *s* broken or outsides (paper); thirty (Roman)
XXXX *s* quadruple strength of ale
XXXXX *s* quintuple strength of ale
XY *s* Burma (I.C.A.M.); *s* London (B.V.R.)
Xy. xylography, word engraving
xylo. *xylophone* (mus.)
XZ *s* Armagh (B.V.R.); *s* Burma (I.C.A.M.)

Y

y   s admittance (elec.); s altitude; s dry air (met.); s lateral axis; s ordinate

y   s second unknown quantity (math.)

Y   s hypercharge; s Somerset (B.V.R.); s Youghal (Rep. of Ireland F.P.); Youth Hostel on early 1-in. O.S. map; s yttrium (chem.)

y.   yacht; yard; year; yellow; young; youngest

Y.   Yen, Japanese currency (*also* ￥); shortened form of abbrev. Y.M.C.A., Y.M.H.A., Y.W.C.A., Y.W.H.A.; Yugoslavia

YA   s Afghanistan (I.C.A.M.); s Somerset (B.V.R.)

Y/A, Y.A.   York Antwerp rules (insce.)

Y.A.   young adults, teenagers

YAG   yttrium aluminium garret (simulated diamond)

Y.A.J.   *Yorkshire Archaeological Journal*

Y.A.L.   Young Australia League

Yale L.J., Y.L.J.   *Yale Law Journal*

'yard   shipyard

Y-ARD   Yarrow-Admiralty research department

Y.A.S.   Yorkshire Agricultural Society

Y.A.S.S.R.   Yakut Autonomous Soviet Socialist Republic

Y-axis   s vertical axis

Yb   s ytterbium (chem.)

YB   s Somerset (B.V.R.)

Y.B.   year-book

YC   s Somerset (B.V.R.)

Y.C.   yacht club; Yale College (U.S.A.); Young Conservative; youth club

Y.C.A.   Youth Camping Association

Y.C.F.E.   Yorkshire Council for Further Education

Y.C.L.   Youth Communist League

Y.C.S.   International Young Catholic Students

yct.   yacht

Y.C. & U.O.   Young Conservative and Unionist Organisation

y.c.w.   you can't win

Y.C.W.   International Young Christian Workers

YD   s Somerset (B.V.R.)

yd.   yard

Y.D.   Yugoslav dinar (currency)

Y. & D.   yards and docks (USN)

y'day., yday.   yesterday

ydg.   yarding

ydi   yard drain inlet

ye, yᵉ   you, O.E. for thou

YE   s London (B.V.R.); s Yemen (I.C.A.M.)

y.e.   yellow edge

Y.E.A.   Yale Engineering Association (U.S.A.)

yearb.   year-book

YEB   Yorkshire Electricity Board (trade mark)

yel.   yellow

Yel. N.P.   Yellowstone National Park (U.S.A.)

Yem.   Yemen; Yemenite

yeo., yeomn.   yeoman; yeomanry

Y.E.O.   Youth Employment Officer

Y.E.S.   Youth Employment Service

yesty.   yesterday

Y.E.W.T.I.C.   Yorkshire, East and West Ridings, Technical Information Centre

YF *s* London (B.V.R.)
Y.F.C. Young Farmers' Club
Y.F.C.U. Young Farmers' Clubs of Ulster
y. fwd. yarn forward (knit.)
YG *s* Yorkshire, WR (B.V.R.)
Y.G.S. Yorkshire Grassland Society
Y-gun gun with two firing-arms for discharging depth-bombs
YH *s* London (B.V.R.); *s* Yarmouth (B.F.P.); Young head, Victoria (numis.)
Y.H. youth hostel
Y.H.A. Youth Hostels Association
Y.H.A.N.I. Youth Hostel Association of Northern Ireland
YHWH, YHVH, JHWH, JHVH Hebrew Tetragrammaton representing name of God
YI *s* Dublin (B.V.R.); *s* Iraq (I.C.A.M.)
Yi., Yid. Yiddish
YIG yttrium iron garret
Yippie Member of the Youth International Party
YJ *s* Dundee (B.V.R.)
Y.-joint Y-shaped joint
YK *s* London (B.V.R.); *s* Syria (I.C.A.M.)
Yks. Yorkshire
YL *s* London (B.V.R.)
y.l. yield limit
Y.L.C.G.S. Yorkshire Launderers' and Cleaners' Golfing Society
Y.L.I. Yorkshire Light Infantry
Y. and L.R., Y. & L.R. York and Lancaster Regiment
YM *s* London (B.V.R.)
Y.M.B.A. Yacht and Motor Boat Association
Y.M.C.A. Young Men's Christian Association
Y.M. Cath. A. Young Men's Catholic Association
Y.M.C.U. Young Men's Christian Union
Y.M.F.S. Young Men's Friendly Society
Y.M.H.A. Young Men's Hebrew Association
Y.M.P.A. Young Master Printers' Alliance
YN *s* London (B.V.R.)
Y.N.P. Yellowstone National Park (U.S.A.)
yo yarn over (knit.)
YO *s* London (B.V.R.)
y.o. year old
2-Y-O two-year-old (horse racing)
y.o.b. year of birth
YOC Young Ornithologists' Club, junior section of Royal Society for the Protection of Birds

y.o.d. year of death
YOM yellow oxide of mercury
y.o.m. year of marriage
Yorks. Yorkshire
you'd you had; you would
you'll you shall; you will
you're you are
you've you have
YP *s* London (B.V.R.)
y.p. year's purchase (fin.); yellow peril; yield point, p.s.i.; young people/person
Y.P.A. Young Pioneers of America
YPF Sp. *Yacimientos Petroliferos Fiscales*, Argentina
Y.P.S.C.E. Young People's Society for Christian Endeavour
Y.P.S.L. Young People's Socialist League (U.S.A.)
YR *s* London (B.V.R.); *s* Romania (I.C.A.M.)
yr. year; younger; your
Y.R.A. Yacht Racing Association
Yr. B. year book
yrly. yearly
yrs. yours; — ty. yours truly
Y. Rs. Young Republicans (U.S.A.)
YS *s* El Salvador (I.C.A.M.); *s* Glasgow (B.V.R.); Young Socialists
Ys. Yugoslavia; Yugoslavian
y.s. yard super; yard superintendent; yield strength; young soldier
YS11 Namco YS11 (aircraft)
Y.S.A. Young Socialist Alliance (U.S.A.)
ysh. yellowish
yst. youngest
Y.S.T. Yukon standard time
Yt yttrium (chem.)
YT *s* London (B.V.R.)
Y.T. Yukon Territory (Can.)
y.t.b. yarn to back (knit.)
y.t.f. yarn to front (knit.)
YTP *Yeni Türkiye Partisi*, New Turkey Party, founded 1961, and advocates planned economy and state-supported private enterprise
YU *s* London (B.V.R.); *s* Yugoslavia (I.C.A.M. and I.V.R.)
Y.U. Yale University (U.S.A.)
Yugo. Yugoslavia
Yuk. Yukon
Y.U.L. Yale University Library
Y.U.P. Yale University Press
YV *s* London (B.V.R.); *s* Venezuela (I.C.A.M. and I.V.R.)
Yv. Yvette; Yvonne
Y.V.F. Young Volunteer Force
YW *s* London (B.V.R.)
Y.W.C.A. Young Women's Christian Association

Y.W.C.T.U. Young Women's Christian Temperance Union

Y.W.F. Young World Federalists

Y.W.H.A. Young Women's Hebrew Association

Y.W.S. Young Wales Society

YX *s* London (B.V.R.)

YY *s* London (B.V.R.)

Y.Y. pseudonym and signature of Robert Lynd (1879–1949), Brit. essayist, in contributions to *New Statesman*

YZ *s* Londonderry (B.V.R.)

Z

z   s dust haze (met.)
z   third unknown quantity (math.)
Z   s atomic number; s Dublin (B.V.R.);
s impedance (elec.); s radius of circle of
least confusion
z.   zenith; zenith distance; zero;
zone
Z.   Ger. *Zeile*, line; Ger. *Zeit*, time;
zero; Zion; Zionist; Ger. *Zoll*, customs;
Ger. *Zuckung*, contraction; Dutch *zuid*,
south
ZA   s Albania (I.C.A.M.); s Dublin
(B.V.R.); s South Africa (I.V.R.)
za.   Ger. *zirka*, approximately
Z.A.   Fr. *Zéro absolu*, absolute zero;
Zuid Africa, South Africa
zab.   It. *zabaglione*, egg-yolk and wine-
based dessert dish
ZAC   zinc ammonium chloride
Zach, Zack   Zachariah
Zach.   Zachary
Z.A.D.C.A.   Zinc Alloy Die Casters'
Association
Z.A.E.D.   *Zentralstelle für Atomkern-
energie Dokumentation*, Atomic Energy
Documentation Centre (Germany)
zag.   Sp. *zagnán*, alley way
Zag.   Zagreb, Yugoslavia
Zam.   Zambia
Zan., Zanz.   Zanzibar
ZANU   Zimbabwe African National
Union, illegal opposition party not recog-
nized officially by Zambia but allowed to
operate from there (Rhodesia)
ZAP   Zero anti-aircraft potential
ZAPU   Zimbabwe African People's
Union, illegal opposition party based in
Zambia, which officially recognizes it as

the representative of Rhodesia's black
Africans
Zat.   Dutch *Zaterdag*, Saturday
ZB   s Cork (B.V.R.)
z.B.   Ger. *zum Beispiel*, for instance
Z.B.   Zen Buddhist; zero beat
Zbl.   Ger. *Zentralblatt*, central publi-
cation
ZC   s Dublin (B.V.R.)
Z.C.   Zionist Congress; Zirconium
Corporation of America
ZCBC   Consumer Buying Corporation
of Zambia
Z.C.L.   It. *Zona di Commercio Libero*,
Free Trade Area
Z.C.M.I.   Zion's Co-operative Mercan-
tile Institution, Mormon Church Stores,
Utah (U.S.A.)
ZD   s Dublin (B.V.R.)
z.d.   zener diode; zenith description/
distance; zero defect
Z.D.A.   Zinc Development Associa-
tion
ZE   s Dublin (B.V.R.)
Z.E.B.R.A.   zero energy breeder re-
actor assembly
zebrass   *zebra+ass*
Zech.   Zechariah
Zeep   zero energy experimental pile
Zeke   Ezekiel
Zelda   Griselda
zen.   zenith
ZEN EIEN *Zenkoku Eiga Engeki Rodo
Kumiai*, Nat. Movie and Theater Workers'
Union (Jap.)
ZENITH   zero energy nitrogen heated
thermal reactor
ZENKO *Zen Nihon Kinzoku Kozan*

Rodo Kumiai Rengokai, All-Japan Fed. of Metal Miners' Unions
ZENRO *Zen Nihon Rodo Kumiai Kaigi,* All-Japan Trade Union Congress
ZENSEN DOMEI *Zenkoku Sen-i Sangyo Rodo Kumiai Domei,* National Fed. of Textile Industry Workers' Unions (Jap.)
ZENTEI *Zen Teishin Rodo Kumiai,* Jap. Postal Workers' Union
Zeph. Zephaniah (Bible)
Zepp. zeppelin
zero-g zero gravity, weightlessness
Z.E.T.A. zero energy thermonuclear apparatus/assembly
Z.E.T.R. zero energy thermal reactor
Z.F. zero frequency; zone of fire
Z.F.G.B.I. Zionist Federation of Great Britain and Ireland
ZFMA Zip Fastener Manufacturers' Association
Z.F.V. Ger. *Deutsche Zentrale für Fremdenverkehr,* German Central Tourist Assn.
Zg. Zug (Switz.)
Z.G. Zoological Gardens
ZGS zero gradient synchrotron
Z.-gun type of anti-aircraft rocket gun, 1944
ZH *s* Dublin (B.V.R.)
z.H. Ger. *zu Händen,* attention of, care of
Z.H. Fr. *Zone d'Habitation,* residential area
Z. Hr. zero hour
ZI *s* Dublin (B.V.R.)
Z.I. Fr. *Zone Industrielle,* industrial area; Fr. *Zone interdite,* prohibited zone
Z.I.P. Zoning Improvement Plan
zip code zone improvement program code, system designed to speed sorting and delivery of mail by assigning a five-digit code to each delivery area (U.S.A.)
ZJ *s* Dublin (B.V.R.)
ZK *s* Cork (B.V.R.); *s* New Zealand (I.C.A.M.)
zl *s* freezing drizzle (met.)
ZL *s* Dublin (B.V.R.); *s* New Zealand (I.C.A.M.)
Zl. *złoty,* Polish currency
ZM *s* Galway (B.V.R.); *s* New Zealand (I.C.A.M.)
Z-man army reservist (U.S.A.)
ZMAR zeus multifunction array radar
ZMRI Zinc Metals Research Institute (U.S.A.)
Zn *s* zinc (chem.)
ZN *s* Meath (B.V.R.)
ZO *s* Dublin (B.V.R.)

Z.O. Zionist Organization; F. *zone occupée,* occupied zone
Z.O.A. Zionist Organization of America
zóc. Sp. *zócalo,* public square
Zod. zodiac
Z. of I. zone of interior
Zoo. zoological gardens
zoochem. zoochemistry
zoogeog. zoogeography
zool. zoological; zoologist; zoology
zooph. zoophytology
zounds God's wounds
ZP *s* Donegal (B.V.R.); *s* Paraguay (I.C.A.M.)
Z. & P. Fr. Zanzibar and Pemba
ZPA zeus program analysis
Z.P.D.A. Zinc Pigment Development Association
ZPEN zeus project engineer network
ZPG zero population growth
ZPO zeus project office
ZPT zero power test
Zr *s* zirconium (chem.)
ZR *s* freezing rain (met.); *s* Wexford (B.V.R.)
Z.R. Fr. *Zone de Rénovation Urbaine,* urban redevelopment area
ZS *s* S. Africa (I.C.A.M.)
Zs. Ger. *Zeitschrift,* periodical, *also Ztschr.*
Z.S. Zoological Society
Z.S.F. zero skip frequency
Z.S.I. Zoological Society of Ireland
Z.S.T. zone standard strength/time
ZT *s* Cork (B.V.R.); *s* S. Africa (I.C.A.M.)
z.T. Ger. *zum Teil,* partly
Z.T. zone time; Fr. *zone torride,* torrid zone
Ztg. Ger. *Zeitung,* newspaper
Ztr. Ger. *Zentner,* hundredweight
ZU *s* Dublin (B.V.R.); *s* S. Africa (I.C.A.M.)
Zulu. Zululand
Zur. Zürich
zus. Ger. *zusammen,* together
Zv. Ger. *Zollverein,* Customs Union
ZW *s* Kildare (B.V.R.)
zw. Ger. *zwischen,* between
ZX *s* Kerry (B.V.R.)
ZY *s* Louth (B.V.R.)
2ZY *s* Manchester (radio call-sign)
Zyr. Zyrian
ZZ *s* Dublin, for vehicles temporarily imported from abroad (B.V.R.)
Zz. L. *zingiber,* ginger
z.z. zig zag
z.Z. Ger. *zur Zeit,* at present